Fundamental Concepts of Language Teaching

Fundamental Concepts of Language Teaching

H. H. Stern

Oxford University Press

Oxford University Press
Walton Street, Oxford OX2 6DP

Oxford   New York   Toronto
Delhi   Bombay   Calcutta   Madras   Karachi
Petaling Jaya   Singapore   Hong Kong   Tokyo
Nairobi   Dar es Salaam   Cape Town
Melbourne   Auckland

and associated companies in
Berlin   Ibadan

OXFORD and OXFORD ENGLISH are trade marks
of Oxford University Press

ISBN 0 19 437065 8

© H. H. Stern 1983

First Published 1983
Seventh impression 1991

Set in Linotron Sabon by Tradespools Ltd., Frome
Printed in Hong Kong

To Rhoda

Contents

Acknowledgements

Acknowlegements are made to the following publishers from whose texts the extracts and papers below have been taken:

Newbury House, for figures 3.1–3.4, published in *On the Scope of Applied Linguistics* by R.B. Kaplan, 1980; figure 3.5, from 'Interaction model of language learning, language teaching and language policy' by W.F. Mackey, first published in *Foreign Language Learning* by L.A. Jakobovits, 1970; figure 5.1, published in *25 Centuries of Language Teaching* by L. Kelly, 1969; an extract published in *Sociology of Language* by J. Fishman, 1972; questions and answers from an article 'Acquisition of syntax in a second language' by E. Hatch, published in *Understanding Second and Foreign Language Learning: Issues and Approaches* edited by J.C. Richards, 1978, and semantic differential examples from *Attitudes and Motivation and Second Language Learning* by R.C. Gardner and W.E. Lambert, 1972.

The Ontario Institute for Studies in Education, for figure 3.6 from 'Theoretical model of the language learning/teaching process', first published in *Working Papers on Bilingualism*, No. 11, August 1976. The Council of Europe, for an extract from 'The analysis of language needs: illusion – pretext – necessity' by R. Richterich, published in *A European Unit/Credit System for Modern Language Learning by Adults*, 1978.

The International Phonetic Association, for six articles translated by H.H. Stern, from *Chrestomathie française: morceaux choisis de prose et de poésie avec prononciation figurée à l'usage des étrangers*, edited by J. Passy and A. Rambeau, 1897.

Penguin Books Limited, for figure 9.1, published in *Introducing Applied Linguistics* by S. Pit Corder, 1973 and figures 11.3 and 11.4, published in *Language and Social Behaviour* by W.P. Robinson, 1972. Routledge and Kegan Paul (London) for an extract published in *The Meaning of Meaning* by C.K. Ogden and I.A. Richards, 1923.

Teachers of English to Speakers of Other Languages, for an extract from 'The second language: an anthropological view' by U. Hannerz, published in *TESOL Quarterly*, 7, 1973.

The Center for Applied Linguistics, for figure 11.5 and an extract from 'An outline of linguistic typology for describing multilingualism' by W.A. Stewart, published in *Study of the Role of Second Languages in Asia, Africa, and Latin America* edited by F.A. Rice, 1962.

John Wiley & Sons Inc., for an extract from *Language Problems of Developing Nations*, edited by J. Fishman, C.A. Ferguson and J. Das Gupta, 1968. Encyclopaedia Britannica Inc., (Chicago), for a description of Nostrand's 'emergent model' adapted from 'Analysis and teaching of the cross-cultural context' by H.N. Seelye, published in *Britannica Review of Foreign Language Education*, Vol 1; and from 'Empathy for second culture: motivations and techniques', published in *Responding to New Realities*, ACTFL Review of Foreign Language Education, Vol. 5, 1974. Reprinted by permission of the National Textbook Company. The American Council on the Teaching of Foreign Languages, for figure 13.1 from 'A typology of bilingual education' by W.F. Mackey, published in *Foreign Language Annals*, 3, 1970.

University of New Mexico, for figure 13.2 published in *A Model for the Description, Analysis and Perhaps Evaluation of Bilingual Education* (Navajo Reading Study Progress Report No. 23) by B. Spolsky, J.B. Green and J. Read, 1974.

Indiana University Press, for figures 14.2 and 14.3 published in *Psycholinguistics: A Survey of Theory and Research Problems* by C.E. Osgood and T.A. Sebeok, 1965. Northeast Conference on the Teaching of Foreign Languages Inc., for an extract from Noam Chomsky's address 'Linguistic theory' published in *Language Teaching: Broader Contexts* edited by R.G. Mead Jr. 1966.

NABE Journal, for figure 16.2 from 'The entry and exit fallacy in bilingual education' by J. Cummins, Spring 1980. Reprinted by permission of the editor. The University of Wisconsin Press, for an extract from 'Adults versus children in second-language learning: psychological considerations' by D.P. Ausubel, published in *Modern Language Journal* 48, 1964.

Research Bulletin No.276, for figure 17.2 from 'Aspects of the motivation to learn French', published in *Motivation and Second Language Acquisition* by R.C. Gardner, 1973. Reprinted by permission of the author.

Ontario Modern Language Teacher's Association, for an extract from *Learning a Sixth Language: An Adult Learner's Daily Diary* by W.M. Rivers, first published in *Canadian Modern Language Review*, Vol. 36, No.1, October 1979. Reprinted by permission of the Editor, A.S. Mollica.

Prentice-Hall Inc., for an extract, published in *Theories of Learning* by E.R. Hilgard and G.H. Bower, 1975.

Language Learning, Vol.28, No.1, for figure 18.2, from 'A theoretical model of second language learning' by E. Bialystock, 1978. Reprinted by permission of the Editor.

Little, Brown & Co., for an extract published in *Educational Philosophy and Theory: An Introduction* by C.M. Beck, 1974. Reprinted by permission of the author.

McGraw-Hill Book Company, for an extract from 'The contributions of psychological theory and educational research to the teaching of foreign languages' by J.B. Carroll, published in *Trends in Language Teaching* edited by A. Valdman, 1966 and for figure 22.3 from *Handbook on Formative and Summative Evaluation of Student Learning* by B. Bloom, J.Y. Hastings and G. Madaus, 1971.

Julius Groos Verlag for figure 21.3 from 'Instructional strategies: their psychological and linguistic bases', first published in IRAL VIII, 1, 1970. Holt, Rinehart and Winston, CBS College Publishing, for figure 22.1, published in *The Study of Teaching* by M.J. Dunkin and B.J. Biddle, 1974.

Introduction

It might as well be admitted right at the outset: this is a book about *theory* of language teaching. This 'confession' may immediately put off some readers who have no truck with 'ivory tower' theoreticians, and who may therefore feel disinclined to read any further. But taking a chance on it, I hope that, in the chapters that follow, those who have this deep antipathy to anything 'theoretical' can be convinced that 'good teaching practice is based on good theoretical understanding. *There is indeed nothing so practical as a good theory*' (Wardhaugh 1969:116).

This book is therefore addressed to anyone who has a serious interest in language teaching and who is prepared to give some time and thought to an understanding of what lies behind the practices of the classroom. The readers I have particularly in mind are the many thoughtful and responsible practitioners or student teachers who seek orientation or professional development. It may also be of interest to others who, in one way or another, are concerned with these questions: administrators, policy makers, teacher trainers, textbook writers, researchers, and students of applied linguistics, language pedagogy, and education generally.

The reader is invited to take part in an *exploration of second or foreign language teaching and learning*. We set out from the assumption that languages are difficult to learn and no less difficult to teach. Over the past one hundred years or so, and indeed for centuries before that, as Kelly (1969) has shown in his fascinating *Twenty-Five Centuries of Language Teaching*, a great deal of theorizing, experimentation, innovation, debate, and controversy has occurred in the hope of improving practice and of making language teaching more manageable, more effective, and more interesting. Teachers have for decades been told to follow this method or that. In recent times they have been urged to become scientific and to rely on the language sciences and on research. Then, again, they have been admonished to be self-reliant and not to depend on the dictates of 'pseudo-science'.

For the thoughtful practitioner and the student of language teaching it is extremely hard to pick his way through the mass of accumulated information, opinion, and conflicting advice, to make sense of the vast literature, and to distinguish between solid truth and ephemeral fads or plain misinformation. Above all, it is hard for him[1] to decide what of all this contributes to any improvement in language learning.

This book makes no attempt to proclaim yet another ready-made solution. Our main purpose is to help readers to help themselves. Theorists and practitioners alike want to improve language learning, and they must decide for themselves what to do about it. The question is whether the decisions made individually or collectively are well thought out, informed, based on sound theoretical foundations, and are as effective as they can be expected to be, or whether they are patently naive, uninformed, ill-founded, and inconsistent.

This guide is meant to help readers in their quest, to sharpen their professional judgement, not to make judgements for them. It is an invitation to think about language teaching, to find out what is known, and to distinguish the known from the unknown or doubtful. Since language teaching is a complex affair, our exploration is not a simple one. If we are impatient and look for a quick answer, we will not get very far.

This book, which offers a framework for analysing language teaching issues and problems, is *not* specific to any particular language or to any particular group of language learners or teachers, nor to a particular country, educational system, or level of education. It is intended to be applicable to language teaching *in general* under the many varied circumstances under which it occurs anywhere in the world today.

Accordingly we will bear in mind a great variety of situations which are sometimes identified under such labels as: foreign language learning, second language learning, minority and majority language learning, bilingual education, third language learning, multiple language acquisition, acquisition of bilingual proficiency. *In short, the focus of the book is the learning of languages other than the mother tongue.*

Although this book, then, does not deal with mother tongue education, we need not draw a sharp line of demarcation between mother tongue and second language teaching. On the contrary, in many instances this line is so thin that it is practically indistinguishable. We support the principle of transcending the division between native and non-native language education and share the belief in a more unified view.[2] Much of what is addressed in the following pages to foreign language teachers has some application to native language education, and it is hoped that mother tongue educators can use this text as a basis for a common viewpoint. Nevertheless, in fairness to readers it must be made clear that our main concern is the learning of other languages and bilingual proficiency, not language arts in mother tongue education.

A limitation in another direction should also be pointed out. While this book aims to be 'practical' in a broad sense and, we hope, is not 'theoretical' in a pejorative sense, the *practice* of language teaching as such is not the main subject of this volume. This means that those readers—particularly new teachers or student teachers—who seek information on class management and various teaching techniques would probably not find in these pages the kind of guidance they are looking for. There are a number of excellent practical guides on the market which are designed to fulfil this function.[3]

How, then, do we proceed? We begin our enquiry (Part 1) by clearing the ground through a discussion of a few commonly used terms in language teaching. We also examine the relations between theory and practice and the role of research, and establish a conceptual framework for our study. In Part 2 we will attempt to obtain the necessary historical orientation, particularly as it relates to recent and current developments. The remaining four parts of the book focus each on a key concept in language teaching: language (Part 3), society (Part 4), learning (Part 5), and teaching (Part 6). These concepts are discussed in relation to one or several disciplines: linguistics (Part 3), anthropology, sociology and sociolinguistics (Part 4), psychology and psycholinguistics (Part 5), and educational theory (Part 6). The disciplines are first looked at independently as studies in their own right, although always from a language teacher's perspective. They are then considered in relation to language teaching and with particular reference to the key concept in question. In each part readers are urged to think about their personal views and to reflect on their experience as language learners and language users, no less than as language teachers. Our expectation is that by relating our experience to the history of language teaching and various disciplines and research, we gain an understanding of the interaction between the language sciences, research, and language teaching practice, past and present.

Doing this systematically, it is hoped that we will end up by understanding language teaching better and by making sense of the multifarious influences that impinge upon us in our professional role. In other words, the 'exploration' about which we spoke at the beginning should give us a mental 'map' of language pedagogy and enable us to locate our own position on it. Ideally, we would wish that through this exercise we arrive at an informed, professionally sophisticated, and balanced 'theory' of language teaching which is personally valid for ourselves as a guide to action. If we reach that goal it should have an effect on the way we work with our students, deal with curriculum questions and, more generally, the way we examine issues, make judgements, and take decisions in our professional capacity. Our ultimate hope is of course that the suggested approach would in the long run help in overcoming some of the century-old frustrations and failures and contribute to the improvement and greater effectiveness of language teaching that we all strive to achieve.

This book has taken a long time to write and an even longer time to grow. Its view of language teaching has developed over far more years than I care to admit, out of a life-time of language learning, language teaching, language teacher training, and many years of language research and academic work with experienced teachers and advanced students in applied linguistics both in Britain and Canada.

Too many people, with or without their knowledge, have had a hand in this book that I could individually name them and adequately thank them. Their influence will be evident in the text itself, and the bibliography at the end of the book is perhaps the best list of credits to those friends, colleagues, and other writers to whom I feel indebted. Canada with its extraordinarily varied approach to language issues, the openness of Ontario language educators, and the privilege of frequent collaboration with them have created a very favourable ambience and a constant stimulus to thinking about the topics discussed in these pages.

The book, which was written during the major part of a period of service in the Modern Language Centre (MLC) of the Ontario Institute for Studies in Education (OISE) in Toronto, Canada, has been shaped in its present form out of a dozen years or so of close association with a group of capable and enthusiastic colleagues, as well as with a variety of interesting and highly motivated students in the Modern Language Centre; and this has meant a great deal to me. In this Introduction I can only name a few of those who in one way or another had something directly to do with the preparation of the manuscript. I want to thank Alice Weinrib, the Librarian of the Modern Language Centre, for being ever ready with bibliographical information, Marjorie B. Wesche and Birgit Harley for perceptive reading and comments on early chapters and for co-operation on a joint paper which provided a condensed pre-run to part of the argument of this book (Stern, Wesche, and Harley 1978), and Jim Cummins for permission to make use of a paper on language learning which we wrote jointly and which has formed the basis for Part 5 (Stern and Cummins 1981). I am very grateful to Patrick Allen for reading and commenting on the manuscript in its final form and to Ellen Jeske, who transcribed the entire manuscript, for undertaking this arduous task with patience and professional skill. I also thank Oxford University Press for their forbearance, encouragement, and goodwill without which this project would not have been completed. Apparently I am not the most dilatory author. Somewhere in the history of the Press a writer kept them waiting for seventy years. I was determined not to beat that record. Lastly a long-term project like this makes inroads on one's home life and demands a certain sacrifice. For her unfailing support, balance, and timely shots of realism I dedicate this book to my wife.

Notes

1 He/she? Him/her? While I accept the principle of 'non-sexist language' in scholarly writing commonly recommended in recent years, I
have tried not to make too much of an issue of it in this book and
have used masculine forms 'he/his/him', etc. whenever they seemed
natural and stylistically convenient on the argument that they can be
understood as unmarked for sex unless otherwise indicated by the
context.

2 A strong plea for treating native and non-native language education
in an integrated fashion has been repeatedly made in recent years, for
example, by Roulet (1980) who writes:

> 'Pour faire progresser les pédagogies de langue maternelle et de
> langues secondes, il est nécessaire de considérer l'étude de la langue
> maternelle et l'apprentissage des langues secondes à l'école comme
> un processus intégré' (op. cit.:27).

See also Hawkins (1981) who speaks of a new 'trivium of mother
tongue/"language"/foreign language' (op. cit.:57).

3 Some mention should be made, above all, of Rivers' *Teaching
Foreign-Language Skills* which is a broad-ranging practical guide
with a strongly theoretical orientation. First published in 1968, it has
been widely read for well over a decade; it appeared in a new and
expanded edition in 1981. Rivers has also initiated a number of
language-specific practical guides in French (Rivers 1975), English
(Rivers and Temperley 1978), German (Rivers, Dell'Orto, and
Dell'Orto 1975) and Spanish (Rivers, Azevedo, Heflin, and Hyman-
Opler 1976). Other well known practical guides include: Finocchiaro
and Bonomo (1973), Hornsey (1975), Chastain (1976), Paulston and
Bruder (1976), Allen and Valette (1977), Grittner (1977), and AMA
(1979). For an analysis of some of these works see Chapter 21.

PART ONE
Clearing the ground

1   Talking about language teaching

In language teaching we use such terms as 'second language', 'foreign language', 'bilingualism', 'language learning', and 'language acquisition'. One would assume that as a language-conscious profession we had our own house in good order and would use terms which are neatly defined and totally unambiguous. But far from it. The ironic fact is that the terminology we need in language pedagogy is often ambiguous and sometimes downright confusing. We must from the outset be alert to this source of possible misunderstanding and try to minimize it by explaining the terms we use. We can at this point only illustrate the problem of terminology by discussing terms which are of critical importance throughout this book: 'second' or 'foreign language', 'bilingualism', 'teaching', and 'learning'.

Second language

We start from the common-sense distinction between 'mother tongue' or 'native language' and 'second language' or 'foreign language'. At a more technical level we also find for the first two the terms 'primary language' and 'L1' and for the second two 'secondary language' and 'L2'. We can tabulate the two sets of terms as follows:

L1	L2
first language	second language
native language	non-native language
mother tongue	foreign language
primary language	secondary language
stronger language	weaker language

These two sets of terms—like such words as 'left' and 'right', 'I/we' and 'you', or 'at home' and 'abroad'—are always relative to a person or a group of persons. They indicate a *subjective relationship* between a language and an individual or a group. We can never assign any particular language, for example, French, English, Arabic, or Japanese, in any absolute way to one or the other set of terms.[1]

There is a third set of terms which describes language objectively, i.e., without reference to the relationship of individuals to that language.

This set refers to the geographical distribution, social function, political status, origin, type or importance of the language, and so on; for example,

> language of wider communication
> standard language
> regional language
> national language
> official language
> modern language
> classical language.

Some terms fall into more than one category. For example, 'foreign language' can be subjectively 'a language which is not my L1', or objectively 'a language which has no legal status within the national boundaries'. There is simply a semantic confusion between the first two sets of terms and the third in the following instance in which a certain French Canadian said

1 I object to you speaking of 'learning French as a second language' in Canada; French is as much a first language as English.

It is indeed perfectly true to say that for most French Canadians French is the 'first language', 'L1', or 'mother tongue'. For them, English is a 'second language' or 'L2'. But for English native speakers in Canada French is a 'second language' or 'L2'. In this example, the confusion has been created by equating 'first' with 'national', 'historically first' or 'important', and 'second' with 'less important' or 'inferior', and thus mixing up the third set of objective terms which attributes a position, value or status to a language with the first two sets of subjective terms which relate individuals and their use of languages. In this book talking about learning a second language implies no value judgement about the language itself.

However, even within the first two sets of terms confusion arises because in common parlance certain distinctions are not always clearly made: i.e., the distinction between the way language X or Y was acquired by an individual, or the level of proficiency an individual has attained in that language.

Thus, the L1 terms are used to indicate, first of all, that a person has acquired the language in infancy and early childhood (hence 'first' or 'native') and generally within the family (hence 'mother tongue'). For example,

2 English is my mother tongue.

3 I am a native speaker of French.

4 His first language was Hungarian.

all suggest this particular way of acquiring a language at this particular time in life.

Secondly, the L1 terms signal a characteristic level of proficiency in the language. They suggest an intuitive, 'native-like', 'full', or 'perfect' command of the language. The speakers in (2) or (3) and the person spoken about in (4) can identify themselves as 'speakers of' English, French, or Hungarian. We would normally assume that the English speaker in (2), the French speaker in (3), and the Hungarian in (4) have this full command of the language which they acquired in their early years, because in many cases the two uses of the terms coincide. But this is not always so and the use of the same term for the personally felt level of proficiency (feeling 'at home' in the language) and the manner of acquisition can be misleading. The Hungarian in (4), for example, might have elaborated his position as follows:

5 My native language was Hungarian, but I now use English as my first language.

Under certain circumstances he might even have said:

6 Hungarian was my first language, but it is now rather rusty.

7 Hungarian was my first language, but I have completely forgotten it.

We must therefore distinguish between L1 as 'language acquired first in early childhood' and L1 as 'language of dominant or preferred use'. The context usually makes the distinction clear provided one is aware of the ambiguity. Thus, there would be no confusion if the speaker in (5), (6), or (7) said:

8 Hungarian was my first language when I was small, but English is my first language now.

But if someone asked him

9 What is your first language?

it would be legitimate for him to seek clarification of the ambiguity:

10 Do you mean my native language, or the language I regard as my primary language now?

Consequently, it would be best to reserve the term 'native language' for the language of early-childhood acquisition and 'primary language' for the language of dominant or preferred use when this distinction has to be made, with the terms 'first language' or 'L1' to cover both uses, allowing the context to make clear the distinction.

The concept of L2 ('non-native language', 'second language', 'foreign language') implies the prior availability to the individual of an L1, in other words some form of bilingualism. Again, the use of the L2 set of terms has a dual function: it indicates something about the acquisition of the language and something about the nature of the command.

11 We're learning French in school.

12 I'm trying to learn Singhalese.

13 Our Danish 'au pair' girl has been sent by her parents to England to learn English in our family. She has no lessons.

Whether the learning is formalized in any way, for example, through a language course in school (11), through private study (12), or is left informal (13), in all three cases the language is learnt as a 'second language' or 'foreign language'; that is to say, it implies that French (11), Singhalese (12), or English (13) are learnt by these individuals *after* they have already acquired an L1.

Secondly, the L2 terms may indicate a lower level of proficiency in the language in comparison with the primary language. The language is the individual's 'weaker' or 'secondary' language. It feels 'less familiar', 'new', or 'strange'.

14 I am French, I can *understand* English but I can *speak* only a little English.

15 He's Polish. He learnt English in school. Now, he lectures in English and writes books in English.

In (14) English has undoubtedly been learnt as a second or foreign language *after* French. French is this person's native and primary language: English is a weaker, secondary one. In the case of (15) we cannot be sure about the level of proficiency in the native language. It is possible that this native speaker of Polish uses Polish as his primary language, but he has acquired a very high level of proficiency in English so that he can lecture and write books in this (chronologically) second language. It cannot be said on the basis of the information in (15) whether, in comparison to Polish, English remains (subjectively) a secondary, less preferred language. It is conceivable that this native speaker of Polish has settled in an English-speaking country and that his command of Polish has deteriorated to the extent that English has moved up and is the stronger or primary language, and Polish, although his native language, has become a secondary language.

To sum up, the term 'second language' has two meanings. First, it refers to the chronology of language learning. A second language is any language acquired (or to be acquired) later than the native language. This definition deliberately leaves open how much later second languages are acquired. At one extreme the second language learning process takes place at an early age when the native language command is still rudimentary. At the other, it may take place in adult life when the

L1 acquisition process is virtually completed or slowed down. Or, it may take place at any stage between these two extremes. The present book is concerned with all such second language learning.

Secondly, the term 'second language' is used to refer to the level of language command in comparison with a primary or dominant language. In this second sense, 'second language' indicates a lower level of actual or believed proficiency. Hence 'second' means also 'weaker' or 'secondary'. As in many cases the two uses coincide, that is to say, proficiency in a language acquired later than the L1 is frequently lower than that in the L1, the term 'second language' or L2 is used to cover both meanings. If the lower proficiency level is to be referred to specifically, the terms 'weaker' or 'secondary' can be used for clarification.

The distinction between L1 and L2
In distinguishing the two sets of terms under L1 and L2 we have adopted the commonsense point of view that this distinction can in practice easily and regularly be made. In many instances, especially in European countries, it is indeed often quite self-evident. For example, many parts of Great Britain, France, or Germany have homogeneously English-speaking, French-speaking, or German-speaking populations respectively, for whom English, French, and German are native languages and languages of dominant and preferred use; in short, the first language in both senses can clearly be identified. If in their different school systems English, French, or German are taught as second or foreign languages, the distinction of L1 and L2 presents no problem. But in many language situations the relative position of the languages is not as simple. The languages of the home, neighbourhood, school, region, or nation may form intricate patterns of bilingualism and multilingualism. The language experiences of an individual in these situations make the boundaries between L1 and L2 learning far less definite. For example, many European countries have accepted migrant workers from abroad. In Germany, *Gastarbeiter* (migrant workers) have come from Spain, Italy, or Turkey. For their children German may be a second language. In Great Britain large numbers of immigrants from the Indian subcontinent use English as a second language. In a country of immigration like Canada, a teacher of English or French as L1 may find in his class pupils for whom English or French is an L2. On the other hand, a teacher of German as L2 may find in his German L2 class children whose parents are German-speaking immigrants, and who, through language experience in the home, have a native-like, yet inadequate, command of German. In many countries of Africa and Asia local dialects or languages are interwoven with regional languages and one or two languages of wider communication, such as English, French, Swahili, or Hindi. In these situations the L1/L2 distinction is by no means easy to

make. For this reason it is advisable to consider L1 and L2 jointly under the common concept of bilingualism.[2]

Second language learning and bilingualism

'Sources of continual confusion in the literature on bilingualism are the words "bilingual" and "bilingualism" themselves' (Macnamara 1966: 11). This is not the place to open up the whole question of bilingualism. We merely want to clarify in what way the terms 'bilingual' or 'bilingualism' can be helpful to the discussion on the concept of 'second language learning'.

Once again, we must make a distinction which is similar to the one we have made previously in talking about first and second language, i.e., a distinction between the 'objective' and the 'subjective' use of the terms.

When we say

16 Canada is a bilingual country.

we are making a statement about the objective or legal status of two languages (English and French) in that country. It does not necessarily mean that any and every individual in that country is 'bilingual', i.e., is proficient in both languages. It may mean no more than that some people in Canada are native speakers of one language and other people are native speakers of the other language.

The second use of the term, namely that of personal bilingualism, which relates languages to individuals is the one that corresponds to the subjective set of L1/L2 terms. For example, the statement

17 I'm bilingual in French and English.

—like the L1 and L2 expressions previously discussed—implies notions of (a) manner of language acquisition, and (b) level of proficiency in the two languages.

With regard to (a) it suggests a simultaneous language learning process in two languages which is analogous to first or native language acquisition in one language. In a typical case both languages are spoken in the immediate environment of the child, for example, one parent is English and the other French, so that the two languages are absorbed in the same way as one language is in a single-language family. Bilingualism in this sense is simultaneous first-language acquisition in two languages, and for short referred to as 'early-childhood bilingualism'.

(b) With reference to the level of command, the statement in (17) suggests a certain level of proficiency. Being bilingual is usually understood to mean that two languages are available to the bilingual on a par; it implies a high level of proficiency in two languages.

In more technical discussions the use of the concept of bilingualism in this respect has changed. Bilingualism interpreted as L1 proficiency in two languages has given way to a broader and more flexible definition. The reason for this is that perfect, full, or equal command in two languages (equilingualism, ambilingualism, balanced bilingualism), assumed in the interpretation of (17), is extremely rare. The command of both languages is hardly ever balanced; it displays a certain 'dominance configuration' (Fishman 1966:126), depending on such factors as a preference in one or the other language for receptive or productive use, written or spoken language, different degrees of formality, and for particular domains of verbal use. If, then, we recognize a whole gamut of differences in the command of two languages, it becomes impossible to draw a line of clear demarcation between 'knowing a second language' and 'being bilingual'. Consequently, 'bilingualism' has tended to be more broadly defined so that any proficiency level in more than one language can be referred to as bilingualism.[3] According to this point of view, the following statements

18 He has a smattering of French.

19 He speaks French fluently.

20 I feel equally at home in French or English; it does not make any difference to me which I use.

are all instances of bilingualism. In (18) or (19) there may be a considerable imbalance between the command of the two languages, whereas in (20) the proficiency in English and French approaches the popular notion of bilingualism. The consequence of this broad definition is that proficiency in each of the two languages must be accurately defined in order to understand what bilingualism means in a given instance. Where bilingualism is demanded as a desirable objective, for example, in a job specification, it has to be stated precisely what kind or level of proficiency in each of the two languages is to be regarded as appropriate in order to meet the specification. Thanks to this broad definition, the various forms of interplay between first and second language, described in the previous pages and illustrated by examples (4) to (15), can now also be treated as instances of bilingualism.

We conclude that, as all second language learning by definition implies the previous presence of a first language, it necessarily leads to bilingualism in the broad sense of this term.

Second versus foreign language

In the past, the term '*foreign* language' was most widely used in contrast to 'native language'. In recent decades the other term '*second* language' has been increasingly applied for all types of non-native language learning. Mostly the two are used synonymously, but in certain cases a conceptual distinction is expressed in the use of 'second' or 'foreign'.

Thus, the acronym TESL, 'Teaching of English as a Second Language' is distinguished from TEFL, 'Teaching of English as a Foreign Language'. TESL refers, for example, to the teaching of English in the U.S.A. to immigrants who are speakers of other languages.

In contrasting 'second' and 'foreign' language there is today consensus that a necessary distinction is to be made between a non-native language learnt and used *within* one country to which the term 'second language' has been applied, and a non-native language learnt and used with reference to a speech community *outside* national or territorial boundaries to which the term 'foreign language' is commonly given. A 'second language' usually has official status or a recognized function within a country which a foreign language has not.

These two different situations frequently have important consequences to which attention has been drawn in the literature (for example, Marckwardt 1963; Stern 1969a; Hartmann and Stork 1972; Quirk *et al.* 1972; Christophersen 1973; Harrison *et al.* 1975; Paulston 1974). The purposes of second language learning are often different from foreign language learning. Since the second language is frequently the official language or one of two or more recognized languages, it is needed 'for full participation in the political and economic life of the nation' (Paulston 1974:12–13); or it may be the language needed for education (Marckwardt 1963). Foreign language learning is often undertaken with a variety of different purposes in mind, for example, travel abroad, communication with native speakers, reading of a foreign literature, or reading of foreign scientific and technical works. A second language, because it is used within the country, is usually learnt with much more environmental support than a foreign language whose speech community may be thousands of miles away. A foreign language usually requires more formal instruction and other measures compensating for the lack of environmental support. By contrast, a second language is often learnt informally ('picked up') because of its widespread use within the environment.

However, none of the consequences that have been indicated as characteristic of foreign versus second language are inherent in the conceptual distinction between an L2 with status within a country, a second language, or an L2 spoken by a community outside territorial boundaries, a foreign language.

While the distinction between 'second' and 'foreign' has a certain justification, it is perhaps less important than it has sometimes been made out to be. Indeed, it may be misleading. The distinction became popular after World War II in international organizations, such as UNESCO, in order to meet nationalist susceptibilities in discussions on language questions. But the objection to calling a national language a foreign language is making precisely the confusion between the subjective and objective sets of terms that we have previously warned against.

'Foreign' in 'foreign language' can express a relationship between person and language, i.e., the language is 'new' or 'foreign' to an individual; it does not necessarily express the legal status of a language, regardless of persons, i.e., a foreign language as a 'non-national' language, a language which has no legal status within the nation. If we regard 'foreign language' merely as a variant of the L2 set of terms, it is no more absurd to say that for an immigrant into an English-speaking country English is a 'foreign language' as it is to say that English is a 'second language'. Conceptually, therefore, this distinction is to be employed with reservations. However, in conformity with established practice we will respect it whenever it is important to do so.

International/intranational
Another pair of concepts, distinct from the differences between second and foreign language, has in recent years been advocated by members of the East–West Center in Hawaii: *intranational* and *international* languages (Smith 1981). Thus, English falls into this category. Countries like Britain or America cannot claim proprietary rights and determine standards of what should be or should not be 'correct' English. The concepts referred to by the distinction international/intranational have not been previously unknown; for example, a typology by Stewart of languages in multilingual societies (1968) has subsumed both these functions under the term 'languages of wider communication'.[4] But the main characteristics of these two concepts have not been previously specifically formulated, nor had their implications between fully worked out. Second or foreign language learning both imply a specified speech community or communities as a territorial reference or contact group. International language and intranational language lack this characteristic. Thus, English in France is a foreign language and is normally learnt as such with reference to Britain and the U.S.A. Likewise, English for Francophones in Canada is learnt as a second language with a clear reference group in the Anglophone communities in North America. On the other hand, when English is used in India no such territorial linguistic reference group exists within India. For this situation, learning and using English for wider communication within a country, particularly for educational, commercial, and political purposes, English can be referred to as an *intranational language*. Equally, in Nigeria or Zambia, English, which has the status of an official language but has no specified reference group, is learnt as a means of internal or intranational communication. French in Ivory Coast has the same intranational function. If English is learnt in many countries across the world, this is not only with reference to specified English-speaking territories, but as a means of *international communication across national boundaries* among speakers of other languages. For this role the term *international* language has been proposed.

These distinctions can be tabulated as follows:

	Presence of a specified linguistic and cultural reference group	Absence of a specified linguistic or cultural reference group
Use of L2 within country	*Second language* learning	*Intranational language* learning
Use of L2 outside country	*Foreign language* learning	*International language* learning

Figure 1.1   Distinction between four second language situations

This fourfold division is clear enough but some confusion may still arise because all the four uses referred to in the diagram are subsumed generically under the L2 terms on p. 9, and are commonly treated as instances of second language learning (broadly interpreted). Sometimes, however, second language learning is used in the specific sense in contrast to foreign language learning as referred to in the diagram.

In general, then, we employ the term 'second language' for all forms of L2 teaching and learning, and sometimes for stylistic variation combine the words 'teaching' or 'learning' with 'L2', 'foreign language', or simply 'language' or 'languages'. We will draw special attention to the more technical distinction between 'second' and 'foreign', 'intranational' and 'international' when these distinctions have to be made in a given context.

Teaching and learning

Another set of terms which requires comment is 'teaching' and 'learning'.[5]

Language learning

The concept of learning, as it is understood today, has been greatly influenced by the psychological study of the learning process, and as a result it is much more widely interpreted than has been customary in popular uses of the term. The psychological concept of learning goes far beyond learning directly from a teacher or learning through study or practice. It includes not only the learning of skills (for example, swimming or sewing) or the acquisition of knowledge. It refers also to learning to learn and learning to think; the modification of attitudes; the acquisition of interests, social values, or social roles; and even changes in personality.

Language learning, in keeping with this broad interpretation, is also very widely conceived. It includes all kinds of language learning for which no formal provision is made through teaching. First of all, there is the vast area of first-language acquisition to be discussed shortly. Secondly, an individual in his lifetime, without any specific tuition, acquires new terms, meanings, jargons, slangs, codes, or 'registers'; he may learn new patterns of intonation, new gestures, or postures; he may acquire a new dialect; in many multilingual settings, he may learn to function in more than one language. Much, and perhaps even most, of such language learning goes on without any 'teaching', and some of it outside the conscious awareness of the learner. It has been observed that much second language learning 'takes place ... by relatively informal, unplanned imitation and use in actual communication situations' (Ferguson 1962:6).

We cannot afford to ignore all such 'natural', 'undirected', or 'informal' language learning. Indeed since the early seventies natural language learning has been the central subject of language learning research. But it must be stressed that our main concern in this book is learning which has been induced or influenced by some form of deliberately planned social intervention, in other words, learning in response to teaching.

Learning and acquisition

Several years ago it became customary to talk about language *acquisition* in preference to *learning*, especially with reference to a first language. The reason for this was that the process of language 'acquisition' in the child was viewed by some theorists as a biological process of growth and maturation rather than as one of social learning (through experience, environmental influence) or deliberate teaching. The theorists, advocating this viewpoint, did not wish to prejudge whether it was a *learning* process or not; hence the choice of the neutral term 'acquisition'. In our view, this terminological distinction is questionable. Psychologists are accustomed to using such terms as 'growth', 'development', and 'learning' in order to describe the interplay between genetic or biological factors and environmental or experiential influences. Thus, in studies of child development it is quite customary to talk about '*learning* to walk' or 'the *development* of walking', realizing that the crux of the problem lies in defining the relationship between biophysical and neural growth and the role of social experience. This is in no way different from the problem that presents itself in '*learning* to talk', 'language *development*' or 'language *acquisition*'. Consequently, we regard the use of the term 'language *acquisition*' as of no theoretical significance and treat it as a purely stylistic alternative to 'language learning'. One weakness of the word 'acquisition' in combination with 'language' is that it is associated with the notion of permanent possession. The language development of an individual, however, is subject to continuing modifications, and the notion of finality or permanency that might be evoked by the term 'acquisition' of language could be quite misleading.

From around 1975 the term 'language *acquisition*' has been given a special meaning and contrasted with language *learning* by the American applied linguist Krashen (1978, 1981). Krashen uses the term 'acquisition' to describe second language learning which is analogous to the way in which a child acquires his first language, that is 'naturally', without focus on linguistic form, and 'learning' as conscious language development particularly in formal school-like settings. Krashen's acquisition/learning distinction has become very popular in discussions on second language learning as a way of describing the intuitively known ways of language growth. A disadvantage of Krashen's terminology is that it runs counter to the terms used in psychology which, as we have noted, comprise Krashen's 'acquisition' and 'learning' as different ways of learning (more or less conscious). The distinction which Krashen has made is valuable, but the restriction it implies for the use of the term 'learning', namely as deliberate school-like learning, is a disadvantage. But we must be aware of the wider and the narrower use of the term 'learning' in current discussions on language 'learning' or 'acquisition'.[6]

To sum up our position on the concept of 'learning', we subsume under the concept of 'language learning' first or second language 'acquisition' or 'learning', the development of bilingualism, and the learning of linguistic variations within a language. Some learning is stimulated by teaching, but much of it may be independent of any teaching.

Language teaching

Individuals growing and living in given societies require, to varying degrees, new languages (second languages) after they have learnt their first language. The various reasons which prompt such second language learning are familiar enough and need not be gone into here. The principal question is what provision must be made by society to help these individuals to learn the second languages needed. The answer to this question is what is meant by language *teaching*.

If it is claimed that language teaching is unnecessary or that no effective provision can ever be made to induce language learning, then this could be an argument for the abandonment of all language teaching. In that case we must be prepared to leave language learning alone and treat it as an unplanned social process; and there would be no point in continuing this discussion. It is obvious that the present book does not subscribe to the thesis of the absolute and inevitable uselessness of language teaching, otherwise it would not have been written.

Language teaching can be defined as *the activities which are intended to bring about language learning.* The different aspects of language teaching are the main substance of this book. All that need be pointed out here is that 'language teaching' is more widely interpreted than 'instructing a language class'. Formal instruction or methods of training are included; but so is individualized instruction, self-study, computer-assisted instruction, and the use of media, such as radio or television. Likewise, the supporting activities, such as the preparation of teaching materials, teaching grammars, or dictionaries, or the training of teachers, as well as making the necessary administrative provision inside or outside an educational system—they all fall under the concept of teaching. Sometimes it is argued that informal methods of 'deschooling' (Illich 1971), using the language in unplanned situations, 'teach' languages more effectively than formal classroom instruction. Even in these cases, although a teacher is not much in evidence, we are still within the range of what legitimately can be described as teaching, as long as such informal approaches are planned for the purpose of language learning.

Since language teaching is defined as 'activities intended to bring about language learning', a theory of language teaching always implies concepts of language learning. In a given theory the concepts of learner and learning may not be made explicit, or they may be misguided, too rigid, too limited, too demanding; or they may fail in other ways to do justice to the learner or the learning process. But it is hardly possible to visualize a language teaching theory which is not also a theory of language learning. A good language teaching theory would meet the conditions and needs of learners in the best possible ways. It is the failure of language teaching in this respect that is often criticized and that has led to the demand for a greater concern for understanding the learner. This concern is justified. But it is an overstatement if, out of this concern, it is argued that we need only a theory of language *learning* and no theory of language *teaching.*[7]

To sum up, we interpret language teaching widely so as to include all activities intended to bring about language learning. Having made this clear, it would be pedantic always to speak of 'teaching and learning'. Therefore, if subsequently we only mention the one, it is useful to remember that in the right context the other is understood.

Other ambiguities

Many other terms used in language pedagogy are ambiguous. In the course of subsequent chapters we hope to clarify them as the need arises.[8]

Notes

1 The 'L1'/'L2' distinction was introduced by Catford in 1959. 'One may, for convenience, use the abbreviation "L1" for primary language, and "L2" for secondary language. L1 is usually, but not always, the language first acquired in childhood: it is the language of its speaker's intimate everyday life: it is also to a large extent the language of counting and other forms of self-stimulation, or "thinking in words". Most people—that is all except perhaps ambilinguals—have only one L1, but they may have a number of L2s, each perhaps being reserved for one particular purpose, as, for instance, reading scientific papers, enjoying a Mediterranean holiday, reading the Scriptures.' (Catford 1959:137–8) The L1/L2 distinction became popular, particularly in Britain, in the sixties (Halliday, McIntosh, and Strevens 1964:77–9). It has maintained itself and is now quite widely used in professional parlance in the English-speaking world.

2 The intricate patterns of languages in home, neighbourhood, school, region, and nation have been systematically described by Mackey (1970). See Chapter 13:272.

3 'Bilingualism is recognized wherever a native speaker of one language makes use of a second language, however partially or imperfectly.' (Halliday, McIntosh, and Strevens 1964:77)

4 Stewart's typology which first appeared in a small but seminal study of the Center for Applied Linguistics in Washington on the role of second languages in developing areas of the world (Rice 1962) is discussed in detail in Chapter 11:232–4.

5 For a helpful discussion on fundamental educational concepts, including 'teaching' and 'learning', see Hirst and Peters (1970). See also Chapter 19.

6 The question of learning and acquisition is more fully discussed in the chapters on psycholinguistics and learning in Part 5.

7 The concept of teaching in a language teaching theory is discussed in detail in Part 6.

8 Here is a short list of a few such ambiguous terms. The reader might like to try his hand at explaining them: method, methodology, methodics; language teaching method, approach, style, theory, strategy, technique, procedure; applied linguistics, educational linguistics, language pedagogy, language didactics; audiovisual method, audiolingual method; traditional method, direct method, modern method; course, method, programme, curriculum, syllabus. See also Chapter 19:421–2 and Chapter 20, Note 1.

2   Theory and practice

Why theorize?

Language teachers can be said to regard themselves as practical people and not as theorists. Some might even say they are opposed to 'theory', expressing their opposition in such remarks as 'It's all very well in theory but it won't work in practice', or 'The theoreticians tell us not to ·translate (*or* not to explain grammar rules, *or* not to show the printed word); but as a classroom practitioner I know it won't work'. Theory in this sense is an unattainable ideal or a set of postulates which are not applicable in the harsh world of reality.

Writers on language pedagogy have been aware of the discrepancy between theory and practice. Their efforts at healing the rift are reflected in such titles as that of Chastain's book *Developing Second-Language Skills: Theory to Practice* (1976).[1] Theory in recent writings is generally understood as the contribution to language teaching of the most important supporting disciplines, linguistics and psychology, and theory is, therefore, frequently equated with linguistic theory and psychological or learning theory. One of the main problems which writers on language pedagogy have tried to contend with have been the continuous changes in the language sciences themselves. Far from unifying theory and practice, these changes made it evident that there is a gulf.[2] Our treatment of language teaching theory must also come to grips with this problem. All the parts of this book dealing with the fundamental concepts, i.e., Parts 3–6, in one way or another are concerned with this issue. But important as the disciplines are in the development of a language teaching theory they constitute only a part of 'theory' in the sense in which it is understood in this book. 'Theory' is here simply *the thought underlying language teaching.*

The term 'theory', therefore, does not apply only to those statements that are formally described by authors as a 'theory', for example, 'linguistic theory', 'learning theory', 'audiolingual theory', or 'cognitive theory'.

Theory is implicit in the practice of language teaching. It reveals itself in the assumptions underlying practice, in the planning of a course of study, in the routines of the classroom, in value judgements about language teaching, and in the decisions that the language teacher has to make day by day. A language teacher can express his theoretical conviction through classroom activities as much as (or, indeed, better than) through the opinions he voices in discussions at professional meetings.

There are certain situations in which theory becomes particularly evident: in language teacher training, in advising or supervising language teachers, in curriculum planning, in the writing of textbooks, in the choice of a programme, or in justifying expenditure on equipment. In such situations we have to express our views on language teaching, to make choices, to take up a position, and often to defend it against opposing points of view. In short, theory manifests itself particularly clearly in debate and in policy decisions.

In the broad sense in which theory is understood here much theorizing goes on all the time, and by no means only at the subliminal level of an implicit theory. The keen interest aroused by conferences and discussions on professional problems indicates that there is no shortage of opinions and ideas. Even the general public—especially where language questions are politically sensitive—is often drawn into the language teaching debate. If we think also of the writings in professional reviews and teachers' magazines and the extensive literature on language teaching we may conclude that a demand for *more* theorizing is hardly necessary because there is so much of it already.

However, much of this theorizing has not been very productive. Witness the perennial complaints about the unsatisfactory state of language teaching, about its ineffectiveness, about the waste of money and energy on something that does not produce commensurate results. The need for constructive theorizing is revealed by the restlessness in the language teaching profession, the vain search for a panacea, the impatience with language instruction among parent groups, and the disappointment and resentment expressed by unsuccessful learners. The rapid turnover of ideas on language teaching, the long history of the method battles, the so-called discoveries and 'breakthroughs' and the subsequent disenchantment, all form a sad but telling cavalcade of theorizing through the ages. Understandably, experienced language teachers have become sceptical of 'new' theories, method reforms, and other innovations.

Even the intellectual contributions of linguistics, psychology, and sociology offer no protection against poor theorizing. On the contrary, scientific information can be distorted in its application or lead to confusion, contributing little more than scientific patter and an impressive-sounding new jargon.[3] The change of terms may sometimes indicate a genuine shift in thought or emphasis; but to the practitioner it often means no more than a switching of labels, of little significance to his teaching, and contributing few new insights to the problems he faces.[4]

The unsatisfactory state of language teaching theory has repeatedly been pointed out in the literature. As long ago as 1964 the American psychologist J. B. Carroll, in an address at a major international conference on modern language teaching in Berlin, made the point: '... what is needed even more than research is a profound rethinking of current theories of foreign language teaching in the light of contemporary advances in psychological and psycholinguistic theory' (Carroll 1966:105).

On another occasion, a few years later, he remarked on the 'bewildering interplay of diverse opinion and controversy' and concluded: 'Our field has been afflicted, I think, with many false dichotomies, irrelevant oppositions, weak conceptualizations, and neglect of the really critical issues and variables' (Carroll 1971:101–103).[5]

Since then, there has been a great deal of activity so that more recently Brown (1980) expressed the current view on theory in these terms: 'A full theory of second language acquisition has yet to be constructed, though a good deal of research, particularly in the past decade, has begun to dictate the general framework of a theory. We are in the process of theory building at the present time, but are much in need of further observation and feedback in order to press toward the goal of a viable, integrated theory of second language acquisition' (op. cit.: 229).

The meaning of theory

If, then, we wish to discover or develop good theories of language teaching we should begin by asking ourselves what a good theory is like, and by trying to develop criteria which can serve as a guide for establishing one. In this way we can reassure ourselves that it makes sense in a discussion on language pedagogy and is not just a pretentious cloak, or a 'courtesy title' (O'Connor 1957:110).

The concept of 'theory' is of course regularly employed in the physical sciences, for example, the theory of relativity and the wave theory of light. In the human sciences, too, it is customary to speak of theories. Learning theory or theory of personality are examples from the field of psychology. Other uses include theory of art, theory of music, linguistic theory, or educational theory. The word 'theory' is used in three fairly distinct but related senses, all of which are applicable to our discussion.[6]

When we speak of theory of art, or educational theory, the term 'theory' is used in the first and widest sense (T1). It refers to the systematic study of the thought related to a topic or activity, for example, art, music, or education. A theory views a topic or certain practical activities as something coherent and unified, but divisible into parts. A theory offers a system of thought, a method of analysis and synthesis, or a conceptual framework in which to place different observations, phenomena, or activities. It is in this widest sense that we can also speak of 'theory of second language teaching'.

In this broad sense, 'theory of second language teaching' agrees with the use of the term 'theory' adopted by educational philosophers in discussions on educational theory (for example, O'Connor 1957; Hirst 1966; Reid 1965; Kneller 1971). Kneller (1971), for example, distinguishes 'scientific theories' from the use of the term 'theory' as 'a general synonym for systematic thinking or a set of coherent thoughts' (op. cit.:41). An even wider definition is suggested by Reid (1965) who calls educational theory 'a large bag, a rag-bag if you like, containing all reflection and all talk about education', including 'all discussion about the curriculum and content of education, of good and bad teaching, teaching methods, ... and psychological, sociological, and philosophical questions that underlie these' (op. cit.:19). It has certain advantages to set out from such a very broad definition, so that the systematic and coherent development of thought can be regarded as a characteristic of a *good* theory.

Second, under 'theory', understood in this very broad and generic sense (T1), it is possible to subsume different schools of thought or 'theories' (T2s), each with their own assumptions, postulates, principles, models, and concepts. What are often loosely referred to as language teaching 'methods', 'approaches', 'philosophies', or 'schools of thought', such as the grammar-translation method, the direct method, the audiolingual approach, or the cognitive theory, are examples of different theories in this second sense. The subject of this book is theory of second language teaching in the first sense of the word (T1); but we cannot fail to recognize the existence of different theories of language teaching and learning, based on different linguistic and psychological assumptions, often emphasizing different objectives, and relying on different procedures (T2s).[7]

Lastly, in the natural and human sciences the concept of theory is employed in a more rigorous third sense (T3) as 'a hypothesis or set of hypotheses that have been verified by observation or experiment' (Kneller 1964/1971:41) or as 'a logically connected set of hypotheses whose main function is to explain their subject matter' (O'Connor 1957:92). The theory of evolution or the electromagnetic theory of light are examples. In psychology, theories of personality and theories of learning strive to meet the criteria of 'theories of science', as Hirst (1966) has called them. Scientific theories (T3) originating in linguistics and psychology have played a role in the development of language teaching theories (T2) thus contributing to language teaching theory in the widest sense (T1). This book on theory of second language teaching in this broad sense (T1), must include discussions of theories related to various aspects of language teaching and learning in the more restricted second and third sense (T2s and T3s).

Criteria

Faced with different theories in all three senses in language pedagogy, how can we distinguish between good and bad ones? One of the major criticisms of current thought lies precisely in the inadequacy of theoretical formulations, the 'false dichotomies', the 'irrelevant oppositions', the 'weak conceptualizations, and the 'neglect of the really critical issues and variables' (Carroll 1971). What qualities should theory development cultivate in order to meet these serious criticisms? If we relate the treatment of the concept of theory in the literature to current discussions on language teaching, we can identify the following criteria as particularly relevant to theory development in language teaching.[8]

Usefulness and applicability
This is perhaps the most important criterion. Since a theory of second language teaching (T1 or T2) is primarily a theory of practical activities it should be useful, effective, or applicable. It proves its usefulness, above all, by making sense of planning, decision making, and practice. It should help decision making both on the broader policy level and at the level of classroom activities. A language teaching theory which is not relevant to practice, which does not give meaning to it, or 'does not work in practice' is a weak theory and therefore bound to be suspect.[9] The crucial test of a language teaching theory is its effect on language learning.

Explicitness
A theory should state and define its principal assumptions. No language teacher—however strenuously he may deny his interest in theory—can teach a language without a theory of language teaching, even if it is only implicit in value judgements, decisions, and actions, or in the organizational pattern within which he operates. However, it is an important function of theory formation to advance from a naive and unreflecting 'realism' to a more conscious understanding of the assumptions, principles, and concepts underlying one's actions.[10] According to this criterion, the implicit 'theory' of an unreflecting teacher who fails to recognize the assumptions with which he operates is to that extent a weak theory. Books on language pedagogy are valuable in creating theoretical awareness.[11] Without explicitness no critical discussion, hence no advance in thought would be possible. It is therefore another important criterion.

Coherence and consistency

The fact that a theory (particularly a T1 or a T2) systematizes a multiplicity of events suggests that a third most important quality of a good theory is that it should reveal order, a pattern, or *Gestalt*, and establish in our minds an awareness of relationships which, without it, might not be recognized. A theory can be represented by a 'model' or figure which visually symbolizes the pattern.[12]

Related to the quality of coherence is the demand for consistency. A theory should be an ordered statement applicable to the total range of phenomena it claims to take into consideration. All parts should fit together in a manner which can be explained. It is this ordering of the data or ideas and the logical relationship between them that is likely to distinguish a good theory from a poor one. As long as a theory is merely a 'rag-bag', as Reid called it, it is weak to the extent that no attempt is made to establish order and systematization of the items and to eliminate inconsistencies. A theory of language teaching should help to make sense of the language learning activities that occur at different stages and in different branches of an educational system. Inconsistencies—due to tradition or chance—are common in language teaching. Thus, a teacher of language A may subscribe to one school of thought, whereas the teacher of language B follows another. Not that languages A or B inherently demand different approaches; these are often purely chance differences of background, training, or previous experience of teachers X or Y, or traditional differences between the accepted conventions of teaching language A or language B. For example, intensive study of literary passages (so-called 'explication de texte', 'analyse de texte', or 'lecture expliquée') as a method of language learning and literary analysis is often used by teachers of French, following a pedagogical tradition commonly employed in France in the teaching of French as a mother tongue in schools and universities. If such a technique has value in the teaching of French as a second language, it should be generalizable to other languages. If it is of doubtful value to the learning of other languages, should its value to the teaching of French not also be regarded as questionable?

A language department in a university, a language programme in a school, and a language course for adults on television do not serve identical purposes and are not directed to the same audience; therefore differences between them are to be expected. But it should be possible to account for these differences on the basis of principles, made explicit by an overall theory. Even within a single language programme at different levels of instruction there are often differences in approach between teaching beginners, intermediate, and advanced learners. These are often much more the result of tradition than of systematic curriculum development. Good theory would point out such inconsistencies, and help in separating the useful from the accidental or seek to remove the inconsistencies.[13]

Consistency in a language teaching theory, however, does not necessarily mean the exclusive application of a particular pedagogic, linguistic, or psychological theory (T2 or T3). For example, many language teachers consider themselves to be eclectics. That is, they do not subscribe to a distinct language teaching approach nor do they base their philosophy on a named psychological or linguistic theory. But there is all the difference between an eclectic choice among different schools of thought and an eclecticism which is merely 'an excuse for irresponsible ad-hocery' (Widdowson 1979:243).

The criterion of consistency demands that language teaching theory (T1 or T2) should endeavour to indicate the principle according to which sometimes one and sometimes another psychological, pedagogic, or linguistic theory is applicable. Otherwise a language teaching theory *is* only a rag-bag.

Comprehensiveness

This characteristic is not necessarily a virtue of all theories, because some theories, in the sense of T2 or T3, legitimately focus on special aspects. But since the theory of language teaching we are mainly concerned with is general (a T1) it should be as comprehensive as possible and should provide a framework within which special theories can have their place. The property of comprehensiveness, then, is not absolute, since the limits to the area treated by any given theory are a matter of practical decision. By invoking this criterion, we merely indicate that the area delimited should have some natural justification, so that all relevant phenomena that a given theory purports to embrace are given consideration.

Explanatory power and verifiability

This criterion is less applicable to a language teaching theory as a T1 than to some of its underlying scientific theories. The value of a scientific theory (T3) normally lies in its explanatory power, its capacity to predict, and in the direction it gives to empirical research. Since it normally derives from an existing body of knowledge and information, or from observed anomalies, difficulties or problems, a good theory is useful in identifying areas of knowledge to build upon and areas of ignorance still awaiting investigation or confirmation. In short, a good theory stimulates research.

Theory and research support each other. Research only makes sense if it can be related to an existing body of knowledge, or to questions and hypotheses which themselves form part of an ordered system of thought and enquiry.[14]

An illustration of the need to verify theoretical statements by empirical research is offered by a discussion in the sixties of one of the most influential books on language teaching of that period, *Language and Language Learning* by Brooks (1960/1964). It was an eloquent plea for the audiolingual approach. Brooks based his theory (a T2) of second language teaching on the model of the acquisition of two languages in early childhood. He adopted a theory of bilingualism which distinguishes between 'co-ordinate' and 'compound' bilingualism and suggested that the learning of a second language should establish in the learner a completely separate or 'co-ordinate' language system without reference to the mother tongue so as to recreate in the learner the conditions of a bilingual person who had learnt his two languages in the manner of native language acquisition in early childhood. Furthermore, Brooks advocated the separate introduction of the graphic skills (reading and writing) *after* the audiolingual skills on the ground that this procedure reflects the acquisition of the mother tongue. He also wanted the learning of a second language to be based on a stimulus-response-reinforcement model in which conscious direction and understanding of language rules were minimized. Brooks (1966:359) recognized that his theory was 'largely an act of faith; research to prove the validity of its basic principles is scanty'. As early as 1964 Bazan critically examined these principles in detail and was able to show that they constituted 'assumptions without proof' and were open to serious question (Bazan 1964). In other words, language teaching theory must not merely lead from claim to counterclaim. The theoretical discussion should eventually lead to the search for evidence, or, as Bazan expressed it, 'I should like to make a plea for analysis, research, experimentation, and evaluation as we seek to evolve a better methodology' (op. cit.:337). In short, if a language teaching theory (T2) claims to be based on a particular scientific theory (T3) it should be backed by empirical evidence or research.

During the past decade it has been increasingly recognized that language teaching must be supported by theories and hypotheses which are verified by research. Speculation of course has its place; but by itself it is not enough. Thought must eventually be put to the test. As we shall see in later chapters, the failure to account for the learning difficulties of second language learners in a convincing way has stimulated a great deal of theorizing on second language learning, and has led to productive research.

Simplicity and clarity
A common misconception is that a theory is inevitably a complex and incomprehensible statement. In fact, a good theory aims at being simple, economical, or parsimonious and is expressed in as clear and straight-

forward a language as possible. Simplicity must of course not be bought at the price of overgeneralization and over-simplification. It can be said with some justification that many language teaching theories have tended to minimize the complexity of language and the intricacies of the language learning process. Thus, a stimulus-response theory of second language learning can certainly be regarded as very parsimonious. It employs the same model for first and second language learning and indeed for all learned behaviour. However attractive this simplicity may be, the theory is open to criticism if it cannot account for many important aspects of language acquisition and language use.

Social consequences of theory development

A good theory enables us to view language teaching in a much better perspective and to recognize its relationship to other kindred activities. The wider context for language teaching theory is education, social policy, national and international politics, and scholarship in related disciplines (linguistics, psychology, sociology, and the humanities). Theory development thus should make language teaching more mean-ingful and intellectually more satisfying. As a result of theorizing, the practitioner—far from feeling caught up in scholastic battles or misled by the trappings of scholarship—should gain a sense of greater professional assurance and develop a fellow feeling with practitioners in related fields.

Good theory formation in language teaching should also be of value to the public, to politicians and administrators, and to language learners. At the present time the language policy of school systems often comes under political attack as a result of ignorance and misinforma-tion. The conceptions held by parents, politicians, and learners them-selves of what is involved in language teaching and learning may differ substantially from the views held by language teachers. The nature of the language learning process is frequently misunderstood. Advertise-ments of certain commercial language schools mislead when they suggest that a brief spell of language learning is quite sufficient to attain a high level of fluency. Equally misleading, the light-hearted use of the term 'bilingualism' to describe the objective of language teaching can arouse exaggerated expectations if it is not understood that the modern definition of bilingualism does not necessarily mean 'full' and 'equal' command of two languages. The diffusion of sound theories and the rejection of unsubstantiated and inadequate claims can have a salutary effect on language policy in education and society. From the point of view of the learner, too, good theorizing has advantages. It can help him to get a better understanding of the tasks involved in language learning.

Summary and concluding remarks

This chapter has tried to explain in what way it makes sense to talk about '*theory* of language teaching'; further, to make a case for good theory development; and, finally, to suggest some criteria characterizing a good language teaching theory: usefulness and applicability; explicitness; coherence and consistency; comprehensiveness; explanatory power and verifiability; simplicity and clarity.

Modifying a definition of theory by Nagel (1961:131) we can summarize by saying that *a good language teaching theory will strive to provide a conceptual framework devised for identifying all factors relevant in the teaching of languages and the relationships between them and for giving effective direction to the practice of language teaching, supported by the necessary research and enquiry.*[15]

Good theory development is an ongoing process. It is not something that can be done once and for all. All we can expect is that the criteria we have discussed provide guidelines to clearer and more productive thinking.

Notes

1 See also the final chapter 'From Theory to Practice' in Brown (1980).
2 This issue has been discussed in detail in a paper by Stern, Wesche, and Harley in a book which had as its main theme the relationship between theory and research in various disciplines and educational practice (Suppes 1978).
3 Lamendella (1969) called it the 'verbal overlay'.
4 It is illuminating to trace the ups and downs of such terms as 'language rules' or 'habit'. Many years ago, it was taken for granted that a language learner must learn language rules. Opinion then turned against the principle of rule learning. Rules became old-fashioned to the point that it was hardly respectable to talk about 'grammar rules'. Instead, it became acceptable to teach 'structures' or 'patterns' which students were helped to acquire as 'habits' by 'stimulus-response' techniques. Around 1970, the notions of 'habit', 'language pattern', 'language structures', and 'stimulus-response' became suspect. 'Rules', on the other hand, were no longer taboo. Carroll (1971:103–104), in turn, defended the use of 'habit' as much more fundamental, psychologically, than 'rule'. With reference to the same point Anthony and Norris (1969:1) write: 'Language teaching methods come and go, ebb and flow. Some achieve wide popularity, then decline. Why the swing from oral learning to rule learning, back to oral learning, and yet again to rules?' For a more recent treatment of the same issue see Seliger (1979).

5 Around the same time other writers were equally vocal about the unsatisfactory state of language teaching theory. For example, Mackey in the introduction to *Language Teaching Analysis* (1965:ix), recognized the need for coming to grips with 'the claims and counterclaims of conflicting schools', and for delimiting 'some of the century-old controversies in language teaching'. Mackey goes on (op. cit.:138–9) to characterize this state of affairs even more forcibly: 'While sciences have advanced by approximations in which each new stage results from an improvement, not a rejection, of what has gone before, language-teaching methods have followed the pendulum of fashion from one extreme to the other. So that, after centuries of language teaching, no systematic reference to this body of knowledge exists. The quality of the work is so poor as to discredit the entire field of language method, putting the charlatans and the scholars in the same boat. As a result, much of the field of language method has become a matter of opinion rather than of fact. It is not surprising that feelings run high in these matters, and that the very word "method" means so little and so much. The reason for this is not hard to find. It lies in the state and organization of our knowledge of language and language learning. It lies in wilful ignorance of what has been done and said and thought in the past'. Likewise, Halliday, McIntosh, and Strevens noted 'that there is not in operation, except in the vaguest sense, any generally current and accepted body of theory, or system of practice. Instead we have numerous different kinds of approach, varying greatly in degree of sophistication, . . .' (1964:ix).

6 The concept of theory is discussed in works on the philosophy of science (for example, Conant 1947; Nagel 1961). See also Snow's discussion (1973) of theory construction in research on teaching in the *Second Handbook of Research on Teaching* (Travers 1973).

7 Most books on language pedagogy can be regarded as theories of second language teaching in this second sense. They normally direct the reader to certain ways of teaching and often try to explain to him on what grounds a particular approach has been recommended.

8 Of particular value has been Hall and Lindzey's treatment of the concept of theory as an introduction to their exposition of several theories of personality (Hall and Lindzey 1957/1970, in particular: 9–17). Faced with the problem of assessing the merits of a number of different theories of personality they developed a set of criteria to use in evaluating them. While Hall and Lindzey's criteria are not directly applicable to language teaching theory, we have followed their example in this chapter by evolving a number of criteria. The reader may be interested in comparing our criteria with a fuller list prepared by Snow in the discussion referred to in 6 above (Snow 1973:104–106).

9 This criterion is so aptly expressed by Wardhaugh in the comment quoted in the Introduction, '*There is indeed nothing so practical as a good theory.*' Brown (1980:230) writes: 'But theories do not become good theories unless they are tested in practice, and theories are of little use to anyone without pragmatic applications. For the teacher of a foreign language, a theory of second language acquisition becomes valuable in so far as that theory has applications, or at least implications for certain practices in the classroom.'

10 Hall and Lindzey (1957/1970) described the status of personality theory in terms of degrees of explicitness and sophistication of the theoretical formulation. Their observations are applicable to language teaching theories: 'Poor though personality theories may be when compared to the ideal, they still represent a considerable step forward when compared to the thinking of the naive realist who is convinced that he is embracing or viewing reality in the only way in which it can be viewed. Even though personality theories do not possess the degree of explicitness which one might wish, their mere existence makes it possible to work toward this goal in a systematic manner' (1970:17).

11 Brown makes this point very strongly in his *Principles* (1980).

12 Models to represent language teaching, as we shall see in Chapter 3, have been developed by several theorists.

13 Contradictory research findings sometimes point to questions concerning a theory. For example, immersion as an approach to language learning was found to be successful in Canada, and it was argued that this was largely due to the fact that in an immersion class the language learner is immediately exposed to language use. However in the U.S.A. when Chicano immigrants were 'immersed' into English-speaking schools, this was found to be far less successful. These conflicting findings have given rise to discussion and research, in order to discover the cause of this inconsistency and, if possible, to deal with it as a practical social problem and as a theoretical issue concerning the conditions of successful language learning (for example, Cohen 1975; Paulston 1975). See also Chapter 13:271.

14 The complementary relationship between theory and research will be further developed in Chapter 4.

15 Nagel (1961:131) in a section on the instrumentalist view of theories summarizes the definition of theories according to this viewpoint as 'conceptual frameworks deliberately devised for effectively directing experimental inquiry, and for exhibiting connections between matters of observation that would otherwise be regarded as unrelated'.

3 Towards a conceptual framework

In order to discuss language teaching coherently we need a conceptual framework, a T1 in terms of the last chapter, as a map to guide our exploration. Such a map, at this stage of the enquiry, must be regarded as tentative and open to revision as we proceed.

Some schemes and models

To begin with, let us consider a few of the attempts that have already been made elsewhere with a similar purpose in mind. There has been a growing awareness over the last three or four decades of the enormous complexity of language teaching, leading to the conviction that if language teaching is to be a truly professional enterprise it must deal with the various aspects involved in a scholarly and scientific manner and establish a sound theoretical framework. From around 1940 to 1960 it looked as if a well-reasoned application of linguistics and psychology could provide the best basis for solving the problems of language teaching. But radical changes in both disciplines which took place between 1960 and 1970 dampened these hopes. The interaction between teaching languages as a practical activity and the theoretical developments in language sciences was recognized as less simple and straightforward than it had appeared in the earlier period. A number of scholars came to the conclusion that *applied linguistics* as a mediating discipline between theoretical developments in the language sciences and the practice of language teaching could perhaps smooth the way for a more effective participation of the language sciences in language teaching. A few influential books of the period 1964 to the mid-seventies expressed this viewpoint, for example, Halliday, McIntosh, and Strevens (1964), Mackey (1965), Corder (1973), and the Edinburgh Course in Applied Linguistics (Allen and Corder 1973–1977). At the same time this group of scholars, in particular Corder, warned that the role of applied linguistics although important in specific areas was limited.[1] Other factors besides the language sciences had to be taken into consideration in understanding language teaching, such as social, political, and economic realities. A lengthy discussion on the scope of applied linguistics which took place in the U.S.A. in connection with the foundation of the American Association of Applied Linguistics between

1973 and 1978 (Kaplan 1980) made it clear that these issues had not been resolved by the end of the last decade.

This prolonged debate has crystallized around a few questions: (1) Which of the language sciences can be said to have bearing on language teaching, and what is the most effective relationship to be established between them and language teaching practice? (2) What other factors besides the language sciences play a significant part in language teaching theory?

Various schemes or models have been proposed. They tried to deal with these questions and to establish a conceptual framework which would put the major factors to be considered into some ordered relationship to each other.

Language sciences and language teaching practice

Campbell

The relation between the language sciences and language teaching has emerged as one of the key issues in the development of a language teaching theory. A simple and clear presentation of these relationships by Campbell, an American applied linguist, would probably receive widespread support among scholars. In Campbell's view (1980:7) applied linguistics is the mediator between the practitioner and the theorist:

Figure 3.1   Campbell's model of the relationship between theory and practice I

But for second language pedagogy a relationship to linguistics alone is insufficient and therefore Campbell (op. cit.:8) suggests an expanded version of this model which again would hardly be called into question by any applied linguist today, although there might be differences of opinion as to which disciplines to include in the list:

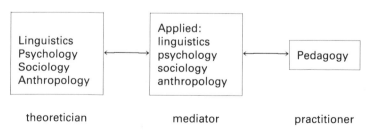

Figure 3.2   Campbell's model of the relationship between theory and practice II

Spolsky

A closely argued and detailed case for the contribution of certain disciplines is made in a model developed by Spolsky (1978).[2] Rather like Campbell and others have done, Spolsky (1980:72), with the help of two diagrams, first shows that linguistics alone is inadequate as a basis for language teaching, and that even linguistics and psychology are not sufficient. In a third and final figure he outlines what in his view represents a more adequate conceptual framework:

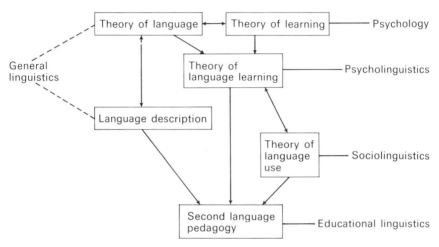

Figure 3.3   Spolsky's educational linguistics model

According to this representation language teaching ('second language pedagogy') has three main sources: (1) language description, (2) a theory of language learning, and (3) a theory of language use. A theory of language learning in turn must ultimately derive from a theory of language and a theory of learning. Language description must also be founded in a theory of language. The disciplines that provide the necessary theoretical foundations and the data underlying language teaching are *psychology* for the theory of learning, *psycholinguistics* for the theory of language learning, *general linguistics* for a theory of language and language descriptions, and *sociolinguistics* for a theory of language use in society. These four disciplines come together in dealing with the problem of language education and thus constitute a problem-oriented discipline which Spolsky calls *educational linguistics*, and which others have called *applied linguistics*. According to Spolsky, applied linguistics can adopt a similar approach to the one outlined by him for second language pedagogy in other applied fields such as translation, lexicography, and language planning. Educational linguistics is therefore a more clearly named specialization within applied linguistics. Naturally, educational linguistics is not only relevant to

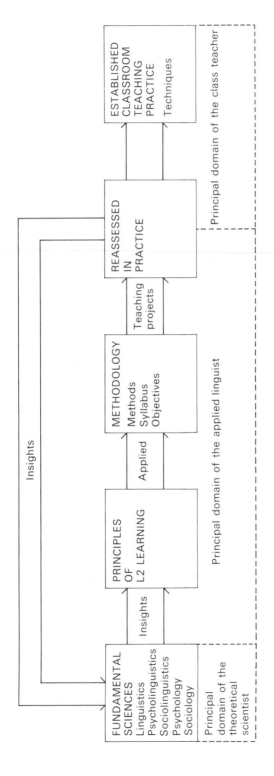

Figure 3.4   Ingram's model for the development of language teaching practice

second language pedagogy but has relevance to other questions of language education, such as first language teaching, reading instruction, or speech education. What Spolsky's model makes particularly clear are the main components of a language teaching theory, and the specific role that each discipline performs in relation to these components. We should note that in the Campbell and Spolsky models double-headed arrows indicate interactive processes. Spolsky's model by its own admission 'leaves out the practicalities and pressures of the world in which language education takes place' (Spolsky 1980:72). Moreover, the methodology of language teaching and other matters constituting the substance of pedagogy are also outside the purview of this model.

Ingram
A third model illustrates some of these missing features. Ingram (1980:42) once again offers a similar list of disciplines and allocates the tasks of theoretician, applied linguist, and practitioner in much the same way as Campbell does. This model shows in greater detail the functions of the applied linguist and the relative distribution of tasks among applied linguist and class teacher. Feedback from practice is acknowledged. However, we might be inclined to question the limited role that is allocated to the practitioner in comparison to the applied linguist, and the notion that methodology and practice are ultimately and exclusively derived from theoretical sciences is also open to question. In all three presentations in spite of the built-in feedback and interaction symbolism, the theoretician—mediator—practitioner relationship is viewed largely as unidirectional leading from the language sciences to practice rather than in the opposite direction.

Models representing other factors

To see how the other factors, which Corder and Spolsky have already mentioned, have been built into some models we consider one by Mackey and another by Strevens.

Mackey
In the foreword to *Foreign Language Learning: A Psycho-Linguistic Analysis of the Issues*, by Jakobovits (1970:xii), Mackey has developed an 'interaction model' which places language learning into its sociopolitical context. (Figure 3.5)

Mackey identifies five major variables: M (methods and materials, for example, textbook, tapes, and films), T (what the teacher does), I (instruction: what the learner gets), S (sociolinguistic and sociocultural influences of the environment), and L (what the learner does). Mackey's conceptual framework indicates how the teaching variables (the MTI triangle in the diagram) as well as the learning variables (the ISL triangle) are dependent upon political, social, and educational factors which dominate the upper part of the model. Mackey does not symbolize the role of the underlying disciplines in relation to the factors identified in the diagram. But the accompanying text makes it evident that their presence and importance is assumed. Mackey describes the model as an interdisciplinary framework involving 'such sciences as psychology, sociology, anthropology, law, education, government, linguistics, and other ancillary disciplines and technologies such as

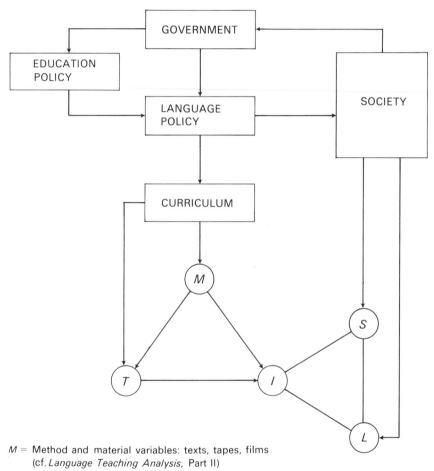

M = Method and material variables: texts, tapes, films
    (cf. *Language Teaching Analysis*, Part II)

T = Teacher variables: what the teacher does.
    (cf. *Language Teaching Analysis*, Part III)

I = Instruction variables: what the learner gets (cf. Jakobovits)

S = Sociocultural variables: what the environment does (cf. Jakobovits)

L = Learner variables: what the learner does (cf. Jakobovits)

Figure 3.5 Mackey's interaction model of language learning, teaching, and policy

computer science and psychoacoustics ...' (1970a:x). He believes that the different components of the framework or aspects of them deserve to be treated separately and in depth. In his own major work, *Language Teaching Analysis* (1965), the treatment was 'intentionally limited to the variables found in the activity of language teaching', i.e., the MTI variables in the model, 'as distinguished from those involved in language learning ...' (1970a:x), i.e., the ISL variables, which are the subject of the book by Jakobovits. In other words, Mackey adopts a broad theoretical perspective upon a multiplicity of factors which are relevant in language teaching, and at the same time advocates the detailed study of specific aspects which can be related to an overall design.

Strevens

A theoretical model of the language learning/teaching process (Figure 3.6), developed by Strevens (1976, 1977), has a somewhat different focus from the previous ones. Its intention is to combine in a single design all the essential features that make up language teaching and any learning resulting from such teaching.[3] Unlike Campbell's, Spolsky's, or Ingram's models, it is not principally concerned with the flow of ideas from the linguistic sciences to language teaching. Similar to Mackey's model, it includes policy and governmental agencies in its formulations, and like Ingram and Mackey, Strevens details the teaching process. It is in fact a flow chart of the teaching-learning process.

Strevens' model consists of twelve elements. The rationale is that someone initiates the language teaching operation (elements 1, 2, and 3). The next six elements (4–9) describe the implementation of the teaching intention, and the final three elements (10, 11, and 12) account for the learning outcome. The three initiating elements are (1) public will which manifests itself in the intention to make social provision for language teaching, (2) the financial and administrative apparatus needed to carry out this decision, and (3) the professional disciplines which constitute the intellectual resources for language teaching. Under the third element Strevens refers to education, linguistics, psychology, and social theory, as well as to psycholinguistics and sociolinguistics with applied linguistics as an interdisciplinary common denominator. In element (3), therefore, Strevens includes the main features of the Spolsky and Campbell schemes.

The language teaching intention can take various concrete forms, comprised under element 4 as 'LL/LT types', varied according to pupil age (child-adolescent-adult), aim (general education or special purpose), learner involvement (volunteer or non-volunteer), and a few other factors. The implementation includes teacher training (element 5), and methods and materials (elements 6–9), which correspond to Mackey's M (methods and materials), T (teacher variable), and I (instruction variables). Element 10 allows for a number of factors that influence the

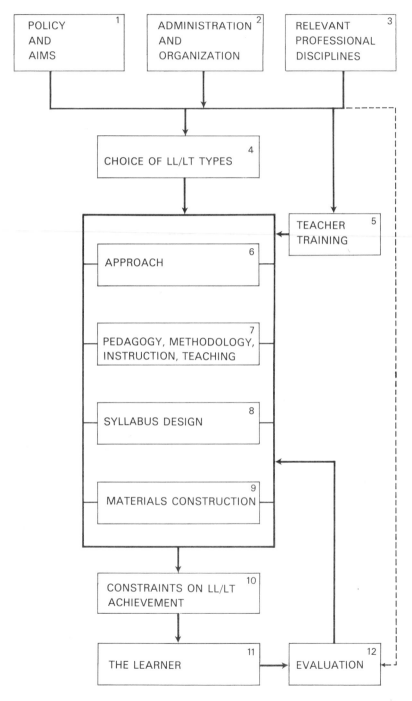

Figure 3.6 Strevens' model of the language learning/language teaching process

learning outcome, such as the time available for language learning, the quality of teaching, and some practical constraints, such as noise, overcrowding, or fatigue. Element 11 focuses on learner characteristics (ability, personality, and so on) which affect learning. Element 12 represents the assessment of the learning outcome and allows for feedback to the teaching process elements so that they can benefit from the evaluation of learning.

This model brings together in a single design aspects of teaching and learning which during the past decades have been recognized as important but have rarely been considered under one scheme.[4]

Comment
The different models we have described have a great deal in common. They suggest that there is a consensus about factors and issues that should be taken into account in developing a language teaching theory. All recognize the interaction of a multiplicity of factors; all are interdisciplinary. They all outline a kind of 'metatheory', i.e., a T1, which is neutral or objective on the major controversies in language pedagogy, presenting simply a framework for enquiry or action. The examples we have studied each lay emphasis on somewhat different but complementary features. Mackey and Strevens include and emphasize social and political factors, Campbell and Spolsky the relations of pedagogy to the major disciplines, Mackey, Ingram, and Strevens the teaching-learning process.

There is no single 'ideal' model. Language teaching can be interpreted in many different ways depending on the purpose for which the model has been developed. Thus, Campbell's and Spolsky's models arose out of the debate over the theory-practice relationship and the status of applied or educational linguistics in relation to certain parent disciplines. Mackey's model was intended as a map of major areas of investigation. Strevens' model was proposed to provide the language teaching profession with a general instrument of analysis.

A general model for second language teaching theory[5]

The model we propose (Figure 3.7) for our own study incorporates aspects of the models we have described. Nevertheless, we have not adopted any of them because none of them provide an entirely satisfactory framework for our purposes.

Purpose of the model
In proposing yet another model we have several purposes in mind:

1 It should serve, above all, as an aid to teachers to develop their own 'theory' or philosophy (a T2) in answer to these questions: 'Where do

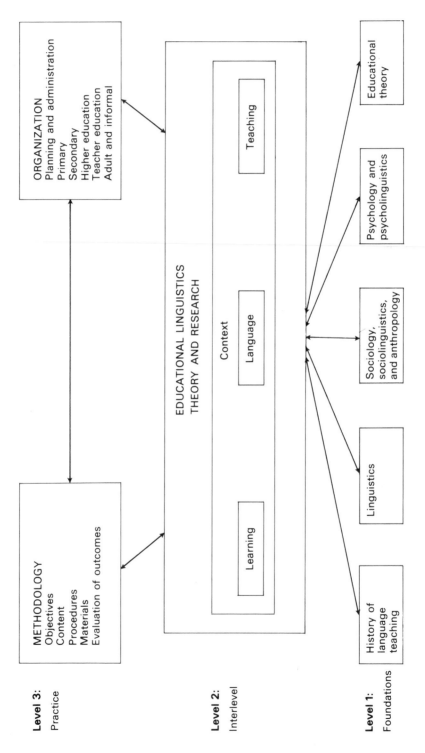

Figure 3.7 A general model for second language teaching

you stand on basic issues?' 'How do you see your own teaching?' 'What is your view of language and language learning?' 'What needs to be done to teach language X or Y?' and so on.

2 It should help a teacher in analysing, interpreting, and evaluating commonly held theories, views or philosophies on the teaching of languages (T2s), for example, in language teaching guides, in review articles on language teaching, or in policy statements.

3 It should assist a teacher in analysing a given teaching/learning situation so that he can cope with it more effectively. The situations in question might be the teaching of language X or Y in a particular school or university, or it might be the teaching of languages in general in an entire educational system.

Like Strevens and Mackey we believe that the model must be comprehensive enough to serve as a unifying and at the same time analytical instrument for all imaginable situations of language teaching. In agreement with Campbell and Spolsky we regard the relationship of theory to practice, and a definition of the role of the underlying disciplines to the practice of language teaching as crucial for a conceptual framework. Lastly, in keeping with Mackey, the model should not only be a practitioner's guide, it should serve as a research map.

In short, the object of the model is (1) to serve as a conceptual framework for theory development, (2) to provide categories and criteria for the interpretation and evaluation of existing theories, (3) to provide essential conceptualizations for planning and practice, and (4) to give directions to research.

Characteristics of the model

The present model—like the other examples we have considered—is intended to be a T1, a 'metatheory' or *general conceptual framework for language teaching*. Within this model it should be possible to identify, develop, or evaluate more specific theories in the second sense (i.e., T2s: different schools of thought or approaches) as well as theories in the third sense, 'theories of science', on particular aspects of language and language learning.

The model is general in that it attempts to offer a basis for an unbiased examination of relevant factors in language pedagogy, including controversial aspects. It does not *a priori* prescribe language teaching objectives, recommend or condemn particular methods of teaching, advocate a specific organizational pattern, or adopt a particular point of view on current theoretical controversies. But this does not mean that, working within this framework, we should always withhold all judgements. On the contrary, it is hoped that, on the basis of this analytical and detached approach, we will arrive at certain criteria which will make it possible to make more informed judgements, to define more clearly areas of knowledge and ignorance, to make better policy decisions, and to guide practice more effectively.

1. Comprehensiveness

Perhaps even more widely than the Strevens model our scheme is intended to represent all second language teaching and learning situations: not only foreign language learning in schools, universities, and other institutions in developed or developing countries, for example, French in schools or universities in Britain and the U.S.A., or English in France or Argentina, but also second language learning of language minorities, such as migrant workers or immigrants, or language learning in multiple language situations across the world, such as learning English in Zambia and Nigeria, or Hindi and English in India. The language learner is not necessarily a 'pupil' or 'student' in the specific sense, a learner at school or college. He may be an immigrant trying to master the language of his new country, a traveller on a visit abroad, a scientist who wants to read the scientific literature of another nation, a young school child whose native language is not the language of instruction, or simply a learner of any age 'picking up' the language in the 'field'.

2. Principle of interaction

Major relationships and the interdependence of the components are, as in the other models, symbolized by bidirectional arrows ↔. Not all relevant features and relationships are indicated in this diagram. The principle however is clear: the design expresses a demand for coherence and consistency of thought throughout the scheme and an awareness of interrelationships between the various components of the model. This principle is intended to counteract the compartmentalization and inconsistencies which have been common in language teaching thought and practice.

The same principle can also be interpreted as complementary co-operation among individuals fulfilling different roles in the total scheme as Campbell's model indicated (Figures 3.1 and 3.2). These different roles are suggested by the division of the diagram into levels. At level 1 we visualize specialists in the relevant disciplines, linguist, psychologist, historian, and so on—theoreticians in Campbell's diagram, at level 2 the language teaching theorist, the research worker, or applied linguist—the mediators in Campbell's terms, and at level 3 the practitioners, teachers, testers, administrators, and curriculum workers.

This division into levels represents differences in functions, but not necessarily a separation in terms of persons. A language teacher can be a researcher or theorist in language pedagogy at level 2, or have expertise in one of the fundamental disciplines, for example, in linguistics, psychology, or one of the humanities at level 1. A scholar in one of the disciplines, in turn, can act as an applied linguist and as a language teacher.[6]

The principle of interaction further implies that the initiative in theory development does not flow only from the disciplines upwards but may come from any of the positions indicated. The teacher is therefore not viewed as a passive recipient in the development of theory. The practice of language teaching and learning, a teacher's or learner's intuitions and experiences can contribute ideas, information, problems, and questions to theory development of language pedagogy and to the basic disciplines.[7] In other words, 'it is theoretically productive to get our ideas from applied work'.[8]

3. Multifactor view

Like some of the other models we have discussed (for example, Mackey and Strevens), this one, too, adopts a *multifactor view* of language teaching counteracting the notion that any single factor, for example, the teacher, the method, the materials, a new concept (such as individualization), or a technological device, can by itself offer a general solution to most language learning problems. It is not suggested that in all circumstances all factors are equally important. But because of the inherent complexity of language and language learning, in practice or research a multiple approach is likely to be more productive than a single-factor one. The model can therefore be read as an invitation, or a reminder, to take into account a number of factors and their interaction in the analysis of problems as well as in research or planning.

4. Multidisciplinary approach

Like most of the other models our scheme assumes that the scholarship underlying language teaching is *multidisciplinary*. The examination of the various models has indicated that this view is widespread now. It stands in marked contrast to earlier conceptions in which language teaching was founded entirely on the study of *belles lettres* or on linguistics alone. Apart from Spolsky's analysis, there has, however, been surprisingly little discussion on which disciplines are essential and which are peripheral, and what different disciplines contribute to pedagogy. Most models include linguistics, psychology, and sociology, or variants of these. Others go beyond that. Our own choice, which will be briefly explained below, is the main theme of this book.

The overall design of this model is similar to Spolsky's and Campbell's rather than to Mackey's or Strevens'. That is, the central issue for this book is the flow of thought from theoretical disciplines to practice and from practice to theory. The teaching process, as described by Strevens, appears in our formulation in a similar form at levels 2 and 3 as an interpretation of teaching.[9] The diagram of the conceptual framework can be read as representing levels of abstraction with level 1 as the most abstract and level 3 as the most concrete of the representations of language teaching theory.

Description of the model

The point of view represented by the model is that in language teaching we have to operate with four key concepts: language, learning, teaching, and context.

Any particular language teaching theory, that is a T2, whether it is a formulated expression of thought (for example, a 'method' or 'approach') or an unformulated theory or set of principles implicit in the organization or activities of language teaching practice can be regarded as an expression of these four key concepts. By asking a few questions about them we can begin to formulate, probe, interpret, or evaluate a language teaching theory.

1 Language teaching requires a concept of the nature of *language*. Implicitly or explicitly the teacher works with a theory of language. Therefore, one of the central questions to ask of a language teaching theory is: What is the view of language in this language teaching theory? The main disciplines that can be drawn upon to deal with this question are linguistics, psycholinguistics, sociolinguistics, and the study of particular languages.

2 Language teaching demands a view of the *learner* and of the nature of *language learning*. The fundamental questions are: What language learner does this theory envisage, and how does it view language learning? The disciplines which most directly relate to this question are psychology, particularly educational psychology, and psycholinguistics for language learning and language use.

3 Language teaching implies a view of the *language teacher* and *language teaching*. The question to ask is: How does the theory interpret teaching? What role and function does it assign to the teacher? How can teaching be described or analysed? The discipline that most directly relates to this concept is the study of education.

4 Finally, language teaching occurs in a given *context*. The interpretation of context is an essential part of a theory. Language, learning, and teaching must always be viewed in a context, setting, or background. Accordingly, there are three sets of questions:
(a) *The language context.* The learner's first language and the target language manifest themselves in certain social, cultural, and political contexts which have bearing on language learning. In developing a language teaching theory a question to ask is: What is the place of languages and language learning in this society? What is the

sociolinguistic context in which languages X or Y are to be taught? The social sciences—sociology, sociolinguistics, social psychology, and cultural anthropology—enable us to study these questions.

(b) The educational setting. Here the question is: What is the place of languages in the educational setting, and how is second language teaching fitted into the specific educational context? These questions require an educational analysis, backed by the sociological or sociolinguistic analysis under (a).

(c) The language teaching background. Context can also be interpreted in a third way which is highly relevant but seems to have been rather overlooked in the models we have previously examined. That is the historical and contemporary setting of language teaching itself. Language teaching has evolved against a background of existing and past developments in language pedagogy. They lead to such questions as: What are the historical antecedents of the theory, and what is its place in the historical development of language teaching? The history of language teaching, educational theory, and the interpretation of the current 'state of the art' are the studies underlying any analysis in response to these questions.

Our contention is that by asking these questions and by attempting to answer them we can develop, refine, probe, and evaluate language teaching theories (T2s). In this way we can sharpen our judgement and give our professional activities those qualities that we identified in Chapter 2 as characteristics of a good theory. Ultimately, one would hope, as was suggested in the Introduction this would have a significant bearing on the quality of language teaching itself.

Naturally, one can deal with these questions in different ways. One way would be to look for common-sense answers on the basis of our own experience. This is an obvious starting point. Undoubtedly, thinking about practice is at any time an indispensable part of theorizing. In the following chapters we deal with these questions systematically in the light of the disciplines or studies that have bearing on these concepts. The model is intended as a visual aid to the sequence of the argument.

Accordingly on level 1, the studies to be considered as foundations for theory development are: (1) the history of language teaching; (2) linguistics; (3) sociology, sociolinguistics, and anthropology; (4) psychology and psycholinguistics; and (5) educational theory.

In this respect, then, our conceptual framework is similar to the ones we have examined, particularly to Spolsky's. However, we place more emphasis on language pedagogy and educational thought than is perhaps evident in some of the others.

At level 2, like Campbell, Spolsky, and others, we regard it as imperative to assume a mediating interdisciplinary level between the disciplines at level 1 and the practice of language education at level 3. Spolsky's term 'educational linguistics' has been adopted to describe this mediating discipline and interdisciplinary synthesis of the contributions of level 1 studies. The four concepts referred to at that level constitute the key abstractions of educational linguistics. As a study involving theory and research, educational linguistics can be geared to language education in general or to specific topics within language education. While the present study confines itself to *second* language education, similar studies on other aspects of language education can be envisaged.

Level 3, which represents the level of practice, is divided into methodology and organization.[10] Under *methodology* are subsumed objectives, content, procedures (strategies and techniques), materials, and evaluation. Under *organization* we analyse the institutional arrangements made for language teaching: governmental planning and administration, the different stages of an educational system within which language teaching normally takes place, such as primary, secondary, and higher education, as well as the education of adults and of language teachers. Language teaching theory manifests itself through both categories. Methodology is relevant at the different stages of organization.[11]

Conclusion

As was pointed out at the beginning of this chapter, as a map or guide this model must be regarded as a tentative statement of a conceptual framework of a language teaching theory (T1). Whether it is useful as such can only be decided by looking at the different components and relationships in more detail. This book focuses mainly on levels 1 and 2 of the model. Level 3, Methodology and Organization, will of course be constantly in our minds as we discuss levels 1 and 2; but the systematic treatment of level 3 will be the subject of another study.

Before entering on the discussion of the fundamental concepts and their underlying disciplines, there is one more general issue in the development of a language teaching theory that needs to be considered in some detail: the role of research which is the subject of the next chapter.

Notes

1 For example, 'Some of the decisions ... will be based on principles which do not derive from the knowledge gained by the scientific study of language; those, for example, which are based on political, economic or educational policy and those which are matters of general pedagogy and teaching methodology' (Corder 1975:2–3).

2 Spolsky developed his model in a preliminary form in a paper at a Georgetown Round Table in 1970. In 1973 he presented it in an introductory essay (Spolsky 1973a) to a work of which he was the editor on current trends in educational linguistics (Spolsky 1973); this book has not yet been published. Meanwhile this paper appeared in an expanded version as Chapter 1 of *Educational Linguistics: An Introduction* (Spolsky 1978), and was reproduced in a revised form in Kaplan (1980).

3 This model, devised by Strevens in 1974 during a period spent at the Culture Learning Institute of the East–West Center, Honolulu, Hawaii, was first published in *Working Papers on Bilingualism* (Strevens 1976) and reprinted in 1977 in *New Orientations in the Teaching of English* (Strevens 1977).

4 The Strevens model has certain similarities with the well-known 'model for the study of classroom teaching' developed by Dunkin and Biddle (1974), which distinguishes presage and context variables (roughly equivalent to elements 1, 2, 3, and 10), process variables (like Strevens' elements 4–9), and product variables (Strevens' elements 11 and 12). As will be seen in Part 6 we will relate our interpretation of language teaching to Dunkin and Biddle's model.

5 This model was presented in 1971 at a meeting of the Canadian Society for the Study of Education, Memorial University, St John's, Newfoundland, and in the same year discussed in detail at the International Curriculum Seminar, organized by Bloom at Gränna in Sweden (Stern 1971). It was elaborated for the Third International Congress of Applied Linguistics, held in Copenhagen in 1972, and published in the *Proceedings* (Stern 1974) under the title 'Directions in Language Teaching Theory and Research', and in a shorter version as 'Retreat from Dogmatism: Toward a Better Theory of Language Teaching' (Stern 1974a). The present model is somewhat different from the earlier version. Retrospectively, I believe the earlier version has certain inconsistencies in that it is partly a flow chart of teaching and learning (in the Strevens manner) and partly a flow chart of *thought about* teaching and learning (in the Spolsky manner). The present model has attempted to remove this inconsistency.

6 A historical example would be the Danish scholar Otto Jespersen who was a linguistic scholar, a language teaching theorist—he had written the most widely read book on language teaching of his time (Jespersen 1904)—and a practising teacher of English as a foreign language. Other examples are provided by Henry Sweet and Harold Palmer.

7 The feedback in Ingram's diagram (Figure 3.4) reflects a similar viewpoint.

8 This remark by the Cambridge psychologist Donald Broadbent was quoted by Rutherford in the *Abstracts* (p. 168) for the Third International AILA Congress in Copenhagen in August 1972. The interaction processes between theory and practice are further developed in several chapters below.

9 See Part 6.

10 The *practice level* can be called the study of language education, language pedagogy or, in a term that had been introduced by Mackey, language didactics, comprising methodology and organization. In using the term language pedagogy—ignoring the etymological origin of pedagogy—I include pedagogy for adults, and therefore do not distinguish it from 'andragogy', as some recent writers have done. (There are many considerations that go into pedagogical decisions, the adult-child distinction is not the only one.) The relationship between educational linguistics and language pedagogy is further elaborated in the Conclusion.

11 The methodology category in this model corresponds to the MTI triangle in Mackey's analysis and elements 6–9 in Strevens' diagram. The *organization* component which, to a certain extent, is represented by elements 2, 4, and 5 in Strevens' model, is not treated in the other models, although, in most educational systems, the institutional arrangements for languages are an important and controversial topic of decision making.

4 Research

Attitudes to research

The idea of a research approach to questions of language teaching is certainly no longer so unfamiliar as it was a few decades ago. Nevertheless, many language teachers even today are as sceptical about research on language teaching as about language teaching theory. The idea of literary research and philological scholarship in foreign languages is acceptable to most, but the teaching of a language is often regarded more as a matter of practical intuition, inventiveness, and sensitivity than as a suitable subject for research.

Practitioners are irritated when the results of research seem inconclusive or remote from the realities of the classroom (Carroll 1969:59; Clark 1971:3), and they may shrug off research as 'useless ivory tower activities' or dismiss it as 'playing at science'. Even some scholars, while themselves involved in research, have expressed themselves quite scathingly about certain kinds of research studies. For example, Richterich, a Swiss scholar who was a leading participant in the seminal Council of Europe Modern Languages Project for adults, had this to say about a research approach:

'Some people, for instance, must use the scientific illusion, which they pass on to others, that it is useless and wrong to try to change anything without first having carried out, with all the necessary scientific rigour, a number of fundamental and definitive studies on the motivations and needs of adults or of certain groups of adults learning a modern language. A complex, cumbersome structure is thus set up to carry out long-term studies which, once finished, are usually out of date because all sorts of events (new theories; new experiments; new facts; social, economic, or political evolution or revolution) constantly alter the hypotheses, situations, and conditions of analysis'. (Richterich 1978:5)

In contrast to these negative views, one may occasionally find among some language educators an excessive belief in the value and importance of research. Without critically examining the intrinsic merit of a study or its relevance to a given situation, anything with the 'research' label is accepted as gospel truth. Such indiscriminate confidence in research may express itself through demands to the research worker for quick, complete, and incontrovertible answers to very complex questions. The tentative, approximative, and cumulative nature of research findings is often overlooked.

This chapter does not invite the uncritical acceptance of research *per se*, but rather advocates the recognition of a research approach as an essential component of effective language teaching and a necessary counterpart to language teaching theory.

Historical perspective

The beginnings of a research approach which date back to the end of the nineteenth century are bound up with the development of the language sciences and the scientific movement in education.[1] But it is only from about 1950 that language teaching became the subject of a more consistent and deliberate research effort.

In 1948 Agard and Dunkel at the University of Chicago boldly undertook a first major experimental study in which they attempted to compare 'new-type' and traditional methods of language teaching.[2] In connection with this study Dunkel (1948) also gathered in one volume all the studies he could find which shed light on language learning. In the same year a first journal with a strong research orientation *Language Learning* was launched by the English Language Institute at the University of Michigan in Ann Arbor, an institution which in the previous decade under its director, Charles Fries, had done more than anyone else to give language pedagogy a basis in linguistic research. A few years later Carroll (1953:168), who had become attracted to language research around that time, complained that, in spite of an enormous literature on language teaching, 'We are little better off in our knowledge of the problem than we were, say, thirty years ago.' Some years later the present writer characterized the situation on language teaching research in Britain as follows:

> In modern language teaching there is a shortage of research and no real research tradition. A review of articles published in *Modern Languages* over the past fifteen years suggests that only a handful of papers which report research results have been published.
> Most writing on the teaching of languages is at the level of reporting personal experiences, expressing opinions, or inviting discussion. Many articles give the impression that their authors do not even obey one of the simplest rules of scholarly work, i.e. to find out what others have previously said or thought on the same subject.
> The position in Britain may be summarized as follows: there is plenty of experience in language teaching, a fair amount of discussion, some individual experimentation, but there is very little systematic research, such as may be found in other areas of educational activity, for

example, in primary school reading. The serious studies that have been produced are widely scattered; some of them are difficult to find among theses in university libraries.[3]

The picture changed radically in the sixties. The interest in research increased enormously, and it was not until then that research began to impinge in any truly significant way on policy issues and the method debate in second language education. During these years Carroll was foremost in creating among language educators an awareness of the value of research and of the quality of good research. His own studies on language aptitude and aptitude testing, and the research reviews he prepared during this period were influential in this respect.[4] The work of another psychologist, Lambert, and his team at McGill University in Montreal, complemented Carroll's work through studies on attitudes to second language learning and on bilingualism.[5] The need for research was repeatedly expressed in the sixties.[6] It was the major theme of an influential international conference on language teaching which was held in Berlin in 1964 (Müller 1965).

In the fifties and sixties, language centres with a strong research orientation were established in several countries. In France after World War II the concern over the declining role of French as a world language led, in 1951, to the setting up of a government commission and a special research unit, the Centre d'Etude du Français Élémentaire, under the direction of a distinguished linguist, Georges Gougenheim. The development of a basic French, *français élémentaire*, or as it became known later, *français fondamental*, which was the task of this research unit, set an example of simple and practical empirical language research with a specific purpose, the teaching of French to beginners and the production of suitable teaching materials (Gougenheim *et al.* 1964). The work of this centre, which was renamed in 1959 the *Centre de Recherche et d'Etude pour la Diffusion du Français* (CREDIF), became widely known not only for its definition of the vocabulary and grammar of *français fondamental*, but also for pioneering a novel approach to audiovisual teaching on the basis of *français fondamental*. The work of the CREDIF has had a major influence on language teaching in the fifties, sixties, and seventies.

A language centre in a different context, the Center for Applied Linguistics (CAL), in Washington, D.C., which was founded in 1959, has for more than twenty years been an important centre of research activity and information in the U.S.A.[7] In Britain, in addition to a number of university centres in applied linguistics, a Centre for Information on Language Teaching and Research was established in 1966.[8] In Canada, the International Centre for Research on Bilingualism was founded in 1967 in Quebec, and in 1968 the Modern Language Centre of the Ontario Institute for Studies in Education (OISE) was set up in Toronto.[9]

The importance attributed to research in the sixties was demonstrated, above all, by the research approach that was applied to controversies and critical issues in language pedagogy. When in the late fifties the new audiolingual method and the language laboratory aroused widespread interest in many countries, these innovations prompted attempts to resolve controversies about their merits by methods of empirical enquiry. Several major investigations were carried out in the U.S.A., among others, studies by Scherer and Wertheimer (1964) and Chastain and Woerdehoff (1968; Chastain 1969), as well as the Pennsylvania Project (Smith 1970), and in Sweden the GUME Project (Levin 1972).[10] All these studies were intended to resolve the great debate on the audiolingual ('functional skills', or 'New Key') method and the traditional ('grammar-translation' or 'cognitive') method. Another group of studies went into the allied question of the pros and cons of the language laboratory.[11]

A third area of investigation which came to the fore around 1960 was the question of language teaching for younger children. On this topic UNESCO took the initiative and through two expert meetings at the UNESCO Institute for Education in Hamburg in 1962 and 1966 attempted to stimulate comparative research in different countries (Stern 1967, 1969). One major investigation on this very controversial question was carried out in Britain over a ten-year period (1964–74) through the co-operation of the Department of Education and Science of England and Wales, the National Foundation for Educational Research, the Nuffield Foundation, and later the Schools Council (Burstall *et al.* 1974).[12]

Another area of pedagogical experimentation and research was explored in Canada from the mid-sixties, a research effort that has maintained itself for well over a decade: the effectiveness of 'immersion' or 'home-school language switch' as an approach to language learning.[13] Finally, an ambitious international research project which surveyed and evaluated the teaching of English as a foreign language in ten countries and French in eight was launched in 1965 by the International Association for the Evaluation of Educational Achievement (IEA). These two studies surveyed the achievement in English or French as foreign languages in the schools in these different countries and related the findings to the language teaching situation and other background factors in the countries concerned (Carroll 1975; Lewis and Massad 1975; see also Chapter 19:432–4).

Except for the research on immersion, most of the enquiries have not always produced the clear-cut findings that had perhaps been expected from them when they were initiated. In many cases they did not completely satisfy the participants in these controversies, and in some instances, for example, the British study, the Pennsylvania Project, the

GUME Project in Sweden, and the studies on the language laboratory in fact added further fuel to the fire of controversy.[14]

The growing disillusionment about research on pedagogy led investigators, particularly in North America, to the conviction that the more fundamental issues of the nature of language learning should be studied by research methods, and a veritable explosion of studies on second language learning dominated research in the seventies. However, most of this highly productive work emphasized 'free' or 'undirected' language learning, contributing relatively little to the questions about more effective approaches to language teaching. In the meantime, several innovations were introduced in language pedagogy; yet few of these were supported by research.[15]

Understanding the role of research

Research has been part of the language teaching scene for long enough to enable us to make some general observations about the nature of research and the contribution of research to language pedagogy. Strangely enough, very little has been written *about* research on language teaching *per se*, perhaps because among many practitioners it is still regarded as a somewhat peripheral aspect of language teaching. Consequently language teaching research lacks direction. There has been little discussion about research emphases, nor has a distinct research methodology established itself as yet.[16]

The case for a research approach

Research can be justified on several arguments:

1 Second language teaching—like any other educational enterprise—represents an investment in human and financial resources. It engages large numbers of people full-time and for many it is a life-time career. It occupies many man-hours of student time. Considerable investment is required for facilities, technical equipment, and teacher education, and for the production of instructional materials, such as grammars, textbooks, dictionaries, and audiovisual aids.

   Planning, decision-making, practice, and innovation in this area should, therefore, not exclusively rely on tradition, opinion, or trial-and-error but should be able to draw on rational enquiry, systematic investigation, and, if possible, controlled experiment.

2 In demanding research, we openly admit lack of knowledge in certain areas of language teaching. We do not mean to say that we know absolutely nothing. On the contrary, language pedagogy has accumulated a fund of knowledge. An important task of research is to find

out what is known and to document it, and in this way, to give access to the large body of information which already exists (Clark 1971:4). At the same time research can dispel misinformation and point to those areas where knowledge is inadequate. It can indicate the kinds of investigation that are needed to fill these gaps.

3 A further implication of a research approach is that we do not expect language teaching to improve suddenly or miraculously as a result of an invention or some other breakthrough. Nor do we assume that there is somewhere in the world a great teacher, expert, or guru who has all the answers. Instead we believe that any improvement in language teaching is likely to come about by planned co-operation in which fact-finding, hypothesis testing, experimentation, and the cumulative effect of many painstaking studies will in the long run be more productive than vehement argumentation or the wholesale acceptance of untested global solutions.

4 The individual teacher's intuition and ingenuity, which have always contributed a great deal to the advancement of language pedagogy, continue to be important. Research is not an alternative to experience and invention. But our practical experience should be able to stand up to critical enquiry and to empirical tests.

5 The demand for research further implies that a continual examination of current practice should be made as a form of 'quality control'. Language teaching, like other educational activities, has a tendency to become institutionalized. Traditions have developed over more than a century; methods, content, age levels, and sequences of instruction have remained relatively unchanged. So-called 'new' methods, 'new' courses, and 'totally different' approaches often turn out to be only mild variations on traditionally established offerings. Is the stubbornness of language teaching traditions due to the inevitabilities imposed by the nature of language or language learning, or is it the consequence of a lack of a critical attitude? We should be prepared to scrutinize our established practices. Research represents this questioning element in the educational process.

6 As has been stressed in the two preceding chapters, research complements theory. Not only does it inject a questioning attitude to theoretical speculations; it also offers techniques of validation and verification, and in turn provides a stimulus to fresh theorizing.

7 Language teaching—perhaps more than many other educational activities—has been the victim of swings of fashion and opinion and has often aroused partisanship for particular viewpoints. Every now and then inventors of new methods or promoters of new ideas claim to have found decisive solutions to the problems of language teaching. Such claims cannot be dismissed out of hand. But unless they are verified by the best possible methods of empirical research, we will waste our energies again and again in futile controversy.

8 Lastly, by helping in developing a more objective outlook upon practice research can assist language pedagogy to grow in status as a 'well-conceived, rationally supported, and thoroughly professional endeavour' (Clark 1971:4).

Defining the research component

So far we have talked about research without specifically stating what we mean by it and what its scope should be. We begin by defining research quite broadly as *the systematic study of questions or problems related to language teaching and learning.* Such a definition is in keeping with a description of educational research as 'a systematic attempt to gain a better understanding of the educational process, generally with a view to improving its efficiency' (Entwistle 1973:14).[17]

Scope
A broad definition is called for to emphasize the pervasiveness of the research approach. In the past, the research component was often too narrowly interpreted. In the sixties it was mainly understood to be research on teaching methods, and in the seventies research on second language acquisition in a natural environment. These studies have been valuable, but if language teaching research is too limited in scope it can distort our interpretation of language teaching by neglecting other equally important aspects of the total enterprise which also need to be studied.

In principle, the range of topics, questions, or problems which could form the subject of research, can be defined by the general model described in Chapter 3 (Figure 3.7). Research relates to any of the disciplines indicated there. It can address itself to the central concepts— language, learning, teaching, or the context—singly or in relation to each other, or it can operate at the level of language pedagogy and deal with questions of methodology or policy issues in the organization of language teaching. In many instances, research will be interdisciplinary and involve all three levels of the model.

For example, the question of teaching languages to younger children is primarily a policy issue (at level 3). But a study such as the NFER research on French in British primary education (Burstall *et al.* 1974) involves fundamental issues of language learning in relation to age and maturity (at level 2). At level 1 it links up with questions of neurological, biological, and psychological development in children. We must also take into account political and sociolinguistic factors in the different contexts in which such teaching occurs, as well as questions of educational treatment.

The broad areas of language teaching research can be summarized as:

1 the language learner and language learning processes;
2 the language teacher and teaching;
3 the environmental contexts of language teaching and learning;
4 the methodology and organization of language teaching;
5 language in general and the languages and related cultures and societies;
6 historical studies of language teaching.

The fact that the scope of research is so wide does not mean that every researcher, let alone the reader, or even every institution involved in language research would necessarily cover the entire range of disciplines, levels, or topics. On the contrary, it is much more economical and productive if scholars and institutions specialize and let their research activities complement each other.[18] From another point of view, the scope of research can be regarded as more or less fundamental or as more or less applied. Studies at levels 1 and 2 are by definition more fundamental. Thus, enquiries on the nature of language learning of the kind carried out in the seventies are not specific to any particular educational system. Some of the questions that have been investigated by this research, for example, whether second language learning goes through similar stages as first language acquisition, deal with universal issues and findings can be regarded as widely applicable. On the other hand, the British research on French in British primary schools or the Canadian research on immersion-type language programmes are more applied in that they are undertaken in response to policy issues in the organization of second language teaching in a particular system. Although their immediate relevance is to the educational setting in which they were carried out, they frequently have wider applications and implications for other educational systems.[19]

At the pedagogical level it is useful *not* to make too sharp a distinction between practice and research, and development and research. A research approach can be closely interwoven with such pedagogical activities as the development of new materials. This was recognized in the mid-sixties by Mackey (1965) who proposed a scheme for the systematic analysis of teaching materials, and by the Nuffield Foundation in Britain which included in the development of new materials research on content and the evaluation of the use of the materials in a trial stage (Spicer 1969). Some of these research procedures were refined and systematically applied in the seventies in a project under the writer's direction which deliberately combined research with materials development (Stern *et al.* 1980). The importance of empirical research methods in materials development is, however, not yet widely recognized.[20]

Mention should also be made of the evaluation of established or new language courses and programmes which is increasingly undertaken by systematic research methods. In short the research component can be regarded as an essential part of the total language teaching enterprise in all its phases.

Research as systematic enquiry

What distinguishes research from casual enquiry or haphazard trial-and-error procedures is that it is a *systematic* process of finding out. But there is no absolute demarcation between common-sense enquiry and research. Thus, in one instance, when a French (second language) teacher (Merkley 1977) observed in classroom conversations with his pupils that he was frequently lost for French expressions for common objects, ideas, and activities which formed part of his pupils' everyday experience, he decided to compile a glossary of such lexical items that were not in his repertoire by collecting them from magazines, newspapers, and other sources and by classifying them according to topics. No doubt this project can be described as systematic and therefore as research. But research can vary in the degree of sophistication with which such a study might be undertaken. The study in question was an example of an enquiry into French lexicography. Did the investigator employ methods of lexicographical or field research? Did he find out whether such a glossary had not already been compiled elsewhere? By what procedures did he identify the topics on which to make a lexical search? Did he verify whether the expressions he found in magazines and newspapers are used by native speakers in conversation and are not simply advertising jargon? How did he report his findings? These questions suggest criteria which would make a study more or less systematic.[21]

An enquiry can be called systematic (a) if it has an explicit rationale, (b) if it has a theoretical basis, (c) if it is carried out with a deliberately chosen methodology, and (d) if its findings and interpretation of the findings are kept apart.

(a) *Reasons for a study.* As we saw in the historical review (pp. 54–7), research is not started out of the blue. Individual studies fit into a research context. They are prompted by fundamental questions or practical needs. Thus the research on teaching methods in the sixties responded to the theoretically interesting and practically important question of whether the new audiolingual method would lead to substantially better results than the traditional method. This was the research context of the Scherer-Wertheimer study which was undertaken 'to draw some definite scientific conclusions about the relative merits of the two methods' (Scherer and Wertheimer 1964:12). It built up on three previous studies which the authors thought were inconclusive.

A few years later the Pennsylvania Project (Smith 1970), pursuing a similar objective, again built upon previous investigations including the Scherer-Wertheimer study. Against the same background approximately sixteen other investigations were undertaken during the sixties. The inconclusiveness that was never completely overcome by the studies that compared global methods, prompted the Swedish investigators of the GUME Project to concentrate on the examination of more specific aspects. It also led other investigators to turn away from the study of teaching method to the investigation with a focus on learning.[22] In short, the reasons for a research study can be explicitly stated. Research is not prompted by idle, whimsical, or unspecified curiosity. The 'review of the literature' which usually introduces a research report is therefore not a research ritual. It provides necessary information on the background against which a new investigation makes sense. It is also a guarantee that the investigator is taking up a research theme where others have left off and that he does not, in ignorance of previous research, merely go over familiar ground.

Since research takes place in a context of enquiry it is almost inevitably *co-operative*. That is, the individual researcher can relate his own work to the work of other researchers working on the same or related problems. An individual study usually forms part of a network of studies. Ideally also research operates *cumulatively*. The method research of the sixties clearly illustrates this process of development from one study to another.[23] In this connection the creation, since the sixties, of various language information centres combined with reviews, abstracts, and surveys of research, has been an enormous service to investigators and the language teaching profession generally. The opportunities for documentation are now vastly improved.[24]

(b) *Theory and research*. A research must, secondly, be backed by theory in the three senses of Chapter 2 (T1, T2, and T3). First of all, a study makes more sense if it can be placed into a conceptual framework of the kind we discussed in the last chapter. From this point of view it is useful to have a 'map' of a T1 such as Mackey's (Figure 3.5), Strevens' (Figure 3.6), or the model in this book (Figure 3.7) in order to put different studies into a rational relationship to each other.

The method research of the sixties illustrates the confrontation of T2s, i.e., different schools of thought, as a basis for research. For studies of this kind the distinctiveness of these contrasting theories is crucial. If it can be shown that the distinction between the T2s is spurious the entire research effort can be called into question. Critical examination of the theories used in formulating research questions is, therefore, an important prerequisite to the execution of any worthwhile study.

An interesting characteristic of research on language learning in the seventies has been that it has generated challenging scientific concepts, models, and predictions, in other words, theories in the T3 sense, such as the concept of 'interlanguage', the 'monitor theory', and the 'acculturation theory', or the distinction between learning and acquisition. These theories will be discussed in Part 5. It is sufficient to point out here that the development of the constructs and theories has been productive in that they have stimulated thought and discussion, and the research on learning has given us a more differentiated understanding of language learning even if it has not answered all our most urgent questions. It is obviously the quality of the theorizing that determines the quality of the research. The most sophisticated research design or elaborate statistical procedures cannot compensate for inadequate underlying thought, theories, or concepts.

(c) *Research methodology.* Research is, thirdly, characterized by the fact that it employs explicitly stated methods of enquiry and is able to justify them. Broadly speaking, language teaching research, in the first instance, is educational research, and the principles and procedures of research in education and the behavioural sciences are applicable. These have been well set out in several works, for example, Entwistle (1973), Travers (1978), and Mason and Bramble (1978). In the second place, language teaching research has certain specific characteristics which make it different from other educational research because its subject matter is language. Hence the research procedures of the language sciences are applicable. It is this interdisciplinary combination of language research with educational and behavioural research that gives language teaching research its unique characteristics and peculiar difficulties. Although the research design and the techniques of data gathering and data analysis are essentially the same as research in other behavioural sciences, in practice this is often deceptive, because the fact that we are dealing with language and language learning may make it difficult or inappropriate to apply familiar procedures. For example, if a study requires classroom observation, the investigator can obviously draw on the experience in classroom observation that is available in educational research; but the categories that have been developed may have to be rethought to meet the conditions of the language class.

One of the crucial contributions of research to language teaching theory has been that it has introduced *empirical procedures* into the study of language education. Research is 'empirical' when it employs observation, description, and experiments as research techniques. We have already noted that language teaching theory has had a strong preference for speculation, the expression of personal opinion, the explanation of practical experience, and participation in controversy— all perfectly legitimate ways of finding directions provided they are balanced by systematic empirical procedures. But in language teaching theory we have tended to neglect the collection of empirical data. The research approach during the past twenty-five years has counteracted this neglect to a certain extent, and the association of language teaching theory with educational, behavioural, and linguistic research has introduced into language pedagogy greater awareness of empirical approaches, although advances in this direction have been patchy. In the early sixties, for example, UNESCO through its studies of languages for younger children strongly urged that the pioneering efforts should be supported by empirical investigations in different countries, but only a few countries took up this lead. The introduction of the language laboratory was undertaken with virtually no systematic research except on its engineering aspects. The teaching methodology was developed *ad hoc*, and what research was done was after the event.

Yet in language pedagogy even today it has not yet been adequately recognized that empirical procedures have a role to play in every aspect or at every level of our theoretical framework. Descriptive research is particularly needed to document, on an ongoing basis, the state of particular languages we teach, *l'état de langue*. The *français élémentaire* or *français fondamental* of the fifties was one such study. Similar investigations were initiated in other languages only to a limited extent.[25] Next to nothing has been done to describe cultural aspects of languages commonly taught (see Chapter 12).

A descriptive approach has its place in learner studies and in the study of teaching. Error analysis, as a technique of studying the patterns of difficulty in learning a second language, has been widely used in the seventies (for example, Richards 1974; Corder 1981).

A descriptive approach to the study of teaching would include surveys of language teaching and learning and observational studies of teaching in classroom settings. The IEA studies on English and French as foreign languages in different countries, mentioned on p. 56, are examples of surveys of achievement in English and French, and of teaching conditions and other background factors in these countries. However, factual data, based on systematic empirical investigations on teaching, are often very hard to come by. For example, during the seventies language educators, particularly in the U.S.A., were attracted to individualization of instruction and to several new teaching methods, such as, the Silent Way, Suggestopaedia, and Community Language Learning. While it is relatively easy to find partisan statements urging readers to adopt these new approaches, it is much more difficult, if not impossible, to obtain accurate accounts, based on observation or descriptive analysis, of how these innovative approaches operate in practice, let alone studies that use empirical methods to evaluate their effectiveness.

The term 'experimental' is applied to the research procedures that have been used in such studies as the Scherer-Wertheimer enquiry or the Pennsylvania Project in which relevant variables are to a certain extent controlled and manipulated by the investigator. In these investigations one group of students, the experimental group, exposed to an 'experimental', i.e., usually an innovative approach (for example, the audiolingual method, language laboratory teaching, immersion, the suggestopaedic method, etc.), is compared to an equivalent group of students, the control group, which is taught by another approach (the traditional approach, non-laboratory teaching, non-immersion, etc.). Group comparison as a research approach has been widely used in language teaching investigations, and in most instances to good effect. Sometimes, however, the variables to be compared are difficult to control and this is one reason why the findings of certain experimental studies, like the Pennsylvania Project, were criticized. The other reason, i.e., that some people simply did not like the results, will be discussed below. But sometimes this group comparison approach has also been overused at the expense of other empirical techniques which could have been used to better effect.[26]

Other 'laboratory-type' experimental techniques have been used very effectively in some language learning studies. For example, like Piaget, who undertook studies on intellectual growth in children through small-scale experiments and conversations with the children about the experiments, an American investigator, Hosenfeld (for example, 1979), set conventional language teaching tasks to individual students and asked them to 'think aloud' how they performed these exercises and to discuss with the experimenter what they had learnt from them. In this way she gained information about their language learning which is hidden from sight in the routines of class teaching.[27]

(d) *Findings and interpretations.* What finally differentiates research as a 'systematic study' from every-day 'finding out' is that the investigator has to present findings in an objective, concise, and unambiguous form, and separate results from interpretation. This characteristic of a research approach is particularly important because of the tendency towards excessive partisanship and a lack of objectivity in language pedagogy. Research since the sixties has boldly been carried out in controversial areas: languages for younger children, the method debate, the rise of the language laboratory, and language immersion. In many instances the findings have been badly received by the teaching profession, and in some instances 'political' considerations have influenced the reception of the research. For example, the findings of the Pennsylvania Project were attacked because they did not show a clear superiority of the innovative audiolingual approach or of the language laboratory. The British Primary French Project upset advocates of primary French because it did not demonstrate an overwhelmingly superior performance in the second language of children who had started early, and because the investigators expressed scepticism about the merits of an early start. In Canada, the immersion research was accused of bias in favour of immersion because it demonstrated the superiority in achievement of the immersion group. In all these instances research by its attempts to be objective had introduced an important element of realism into the policy debates. At the same time it has given the opportunity to make a distinction between research findings and their interpretation and policy implications. As one research report on immersion reminded readers:

'In short, research cannot provide the whole answer to the concerns of administrators. It can indicate the success of immersion and point out the problems or difficulties involved. It cannot, and should not, say whether bilingualism is worth having and what place it can be accorded in the system. This is a value judgement the policy-maker must make' (Stern *et al.* 1976:17–18).

Continuity and interpretation of research

Research problems that demand investigation in language education are rarely of a kind that a single investigation can resolve them in a conclusive way. It is often the cumulative and complementary effect of several studies carried out by different investigators or over several years by the same research group that can be most effective. Two of the most interesting research endeavours in the seventies from this point of view have been the Council of Europe Modern Languages Project and Canadian French immersion experiments. The Council of Europe Project as a language curriculum development project began in 1971 and has continued into the eighties involving the co-operation of scholars in several countries (for example, Trim 1980, Trim *et al.* 1980). Its publications have led to attempts to apply the findings in curriculum development. This vast project is likely to lead to further studies and to exercise its influence slowly and in diverse ways in language curricula everywhere. (Council of Europe 1981) The French immersion research in Canada which began in 1965 and is also still continuing at the time of writing illustrates well the possibility and usefulness of research in a single problem area over a period of time, in this instance an 'immersion' approach to second language learning. While some questions which were raised at the beginning could be dropped after a few years because they had been answered (for example, whether immersion is substantially more effective than the conventional language class), other questions cropped up at later stages of the immersion experience, for example, can the plateau in language proficiency that children seem to reach in an immersion programme after about three or four years be avoided or overcome, and if so, how? Or is 'late immersion' as effective as 'early immersion'? By servicing the immersion programmes on a continuing basis research and policy became integrated and a useful give-and-take between researcher and practitioner has evolved.[28] Contrast this development with studies in language teaching methods which, although often quite prolonged (for example, the Pennsylvania Project, the NFER Primary French Project) were designed as one-shot affairs giving definitive results to be accepted by the practitioners and policy-makers in a take-it-or-leave-it fashion. These major single investigations led to much controversy and did not, as had been expected of them, clinch the controversial issue to the satisfaction of the practitioners.

Research and the practitioner

It is often said that the results of research should be made more readily available to the practitioner than they usually are so that research can make an impact on practice. There is an element of truth in that. Studies that are locked up in a research report and not made accessible to practitioners or the general public can be very wasteful, and consequently researchers have rightly been urged to include 'dissemination' as an important final phase into their investigations.

However, the practitioner should think of himself involved in research not only as the *recipient* of the findings of a study relatively remote from his sphere of activity. Nothing is more unproductive than the cliché of the researcher as someone in an 'ivory tower'. The practitioner is best thought of as a *participant* in research. In the first instance, the tasks and the problems he faces and the questions he raises as they present themselves in the language class are those that should eventually be the subject of investigation. In many cases, as we have seen in the example of the vocabulary study by a single teacher, the practitioner will himself undertake the necessary enquiries.

Secondly, in other situations, the practitioner and the researcher will co-operate in an enquiry. Finally, what is more important for the practitioner than 'applying' research is to develop a research approach or a research attitude. While in his daily activities the practitioner— teacher or administrator—will proceed by intuitive judgement, hunches, and a flair for a situation, from time to time it is rewarding to stand back and to adopt a research mode of thought and action, to enquire, to examine, to diagnose, and to analyse. In our view it is the interaction between research and practice that can make both more productive.[29]

Conclusion

Within the short history of theory and research in relation to language teaching we must recognize that research is not the answer to all the problems of language teaching. Sometimes it has been argued that practical teacher training, materials development, and classroom work are more important than research. But these are not true alternatives. Research and theory can be viewed as necessary components of a well planned language teaching operation, not as substitutes for any of the other components.

Research represents an element of disciplined study and sustained enquiry. It provides documentation and evidence. It balances the commitment and global approach to teaching and the necessary value judgements of policy-making with an essential measure of information, conceptualization, and analysis, and an attitude of critical detachment and caution.

Notes

1 These earlier developments are referred to in Part 2.

2 The many difficulties (for example, lack of rigorous research design, and absence of suitable tests) that these investigators had to overcome have been described by Carroll (1961:9–11) who commented: 'The Agard-Dunkel study should be regarded as a comparative survey study rather than as a true experiment.'

3 From an unpublished report to the National Foundation for Educational Research for a *Map of Educational Research* (Thouless 1969). See also Carroll 1960.

4 Carroll undertook his own studies on aptitude testing in the fifties and prepared his well known Modern Language Aptitude Test in co-operation with Stanley Sapon (Carroll and Sapon 1959; see also Carroll 1981:90). Many language teachers in the sixties read Carroll's research reviews which in a concise and comprehensive way surveyed the field of research. See, in particular Carroll 1961/ 1963, 1966a, and 1969a. In connection with the UNESCO-sponsored project on language teaching to younger children, he identified problems of research (1967) and wrote a detailed research guide (1969b).

5 Under the guidance of W. E. Lambert, the psychology department at McGill University produced a number of scholars who, during the sixties, influenced language pedagogy through their studies and writings, for example, Robert Gardner, Leon Jakobovits, and Richard Tucker.

6 For example, by Bell 1960; Strevens 1963; Mackey 1965; Stern 1970.

7 For information on the Center for Applied Linguistics (CAL) see its Bulletin, *The Linguistic Reporter*, in particular Vol. 21 No. 7, 1979, which celebrates the twentieth anniversary of CAL and reviews its past and new directions. CAL also houses the ERIC Clearinghouse on Languages and Linguistics which provides a unique documentation service. Noteworthy among several American university centres of research is the School of Languages and Linguistics of

Georgetown University, Washington, D.C., which, since 1950, has organized annually a round table meeting on linguistics and language studies at which scholars discuss particular questions for two or three days. The reports on these meetings which have been published regularly since the Second Round Table in 1950 by Georgetown University Press are a valuable source of information on research preoccupations (for example, De Francis 1951 and Alatis 1980).

8 A Committee on Research and Development in Modern Languages was set up in Britain under government auspices in 1964. This committee ceased to exist in 1970. Two years later it was replaced by a National Council for Modern Languages which was created to encourage and co-ordinate research and development. Several British university centres have also been active in research in this area, for example, Edinburgh, Essex, Lancaster, and Reading, and in 1978 a National Congress on Languages in Education was created (Perren 1979 and 1979a).

9 While the ICRB was created to study bilingualism and language contact in all its aspects (Mackey 1978), the Modern Language Centre has focused specifically on second language learning and teaching, and on bilingual education (Stern 1970). Yalden (1976) has reviewed the information resources available in Canada and internationally to teachers and researchers.

10 Scherer and Wertheimer (1964) and Chastain and Woerdehoff (1968) were college-level comparisons of the two methods. The Pennsylvania Foreign Language Project (Smith 1970) was carried out in Pennsylvania from 1965 to 1968 in fifty-eight high schools with the purpose of studying alternative teaching strategies and the use of different types of language laboratories. The GUME Project (Levin 1972) which was a co-operative research effort of the Department of Educational Research of the School of Education in Gothenburg and the English Department of the University of Gothenburg consisted of several separate studies, partly at the school level and partly in adult education.

11 In 1963 the Keating Report caused a furore. For a critical review of many studies on the language laboratory see Forrester 1975.

12 In addition to the reports on the UNESCO initiative in 1962 and 1966 (Stern 1967, 1969) and the report on the British study (Burstall *et al.* 1974), see an overview from the perspective of the seventies by Stern and Weinrib (1977). See also Chapter 17:364–5.

13 The first basic studies were carried out at McGill and, in addition to journal articles, were summarized in a book by Lambert and Tucker (1972). The studies undertaken in Ontario and in the rest of Canada were periodically reported in the *Canadian Modern Language Review* (for example, Harley 1976) and, among others, in reports of

the Bilingual Education Project in the OISE Modern Language Centre. For references to the various studies and a review of the experience towards the end of the seventies see Swain 1978; Stern 1978, 1978a; and Swain and Lapkin 1981. See also Bibeau 1982. For the age issue in immersion see Chapter 17:364.

14 For example, the GUME Project gave rise to violent controversy in which the Project met the opposition of the Swedish Board of Education (Ellegard and Lindell 1970). The Pennsylvania Project was attacked for its findings and criticized for its research methodology. The appendixes to Smith (1970) contain a report on a discussion conference, an evaluation by Valette, and a reply to critics by Smith. The October 1969 issue of the *Modern Language Journal* contains a symposium on the Pennsylvania Project with contributions by Clark, Valette, Hocking, Otto, Roeming, and others. *Foreign Language Annals*, December 1969, has a full discussion of the Pennsylvania Project by Carroll and Wiley. For a bibliography on the Pennsylvania Project, see *Foreign Language Annals*, Vol. 3, 2, 1969:180–1. See also Ingram (1975:281–4). For reactions to the British primary French research, see references in Stern and Weinrib (1977), Hawkins (1981:180–190), and Stern 1982.

15 For a detailed discussion of language learning research and references, see Part 5.

16 Apart from Carroll's reviews of research written in the sixties, which contain observations about theoretical bases and rigour in research design, and the research guide he composed for the UNESCO project on languages for younger children (Carroll 1969b), there are only a few monographs on language teaching research methodology, for example, Clark 1971, Titone 1974, Allen and Davies 1977, and Hatch and Farhady 1982. The relations between research and practice have been discussed by Tarone *et al.* (1976), Stern (1978b), and Stern, Wesche, and Harley (1978). In Germany, a group of researchers reviewed the state of research in 1977 (Koordinierungsgremium 1977).

17 In a sophisticated essay on the philosopher's contribution to educational research, Peters and White (1973) distinguish between a narrow view which confines research to the attempt to test empirical hypotheses, and an excessively wide view in which every search is 'research'. They suggest that research should refer to 'systematic and sustained enquiry carried out by people well versed in some form of thinking in order to answer some specific type of question' (op. cit.:94). We also favour such a relatively wide definition.

18 For example, in an evaluation study on the effect on language learning and social attitudes of student exchange programmes between French-speaking and English-speaking children in Canada (Hanna *et al.* 1980) the research required skills which derive from

educational studies, psychology, sociology, and educational linguistics, quite apart from French, English, and statistics and familiarity with the school system in question. In order to meet the demands of this project, the co-operation of a team of researchers was needed.

19 For example, the British research on French in the primary school was immediately recognized as relevant in North America. Canadian immersion research has been of interest, among others, to educators in the U.S.A. and Wales

20 It might require, for example, research on language (Chapter 9) or aspects of culture (Chapter 12) or systematic evaluation.

21 In this instance, Merkley, the author of the glossary, was fully aware of the limitations of his research approach and made this clear in a postscript.

22 There were other reasons besides the reaction against studies on teaching methods for the shift of interest to an empirical approach to language learning, but these will be explained later. See Chapter 15.

23 The inconclusiveness of these studies does not mean that research is a waste of time. The studies gradually revealed that the 'methods' are not clearly defined entities that can be juxtaposed and compared. It would be a waste of time if that important lesson had not now been learnt. See Chapter 21.

24 Examples of the information resources are, among others, the following two journals: *Language Teaching: The International Abstracting Journal for Language Teachers and Applied Linguists* (formerly: *Language Teaching and Linguistics: Abstracts*), and *Language and Language Behavior Abstracts*. Research survey articles are published in Kinsella (1978). Increasing use is made of the information services provided by the Center for Applied Linguistics in Washington, the Centre for Information on Language Teaching in London, and the Modern Language Centre in Toronto.

25 One example of a major ongoing project of descriptive language research is the English language survey which led to the production of the *Grammar of Contemporary English* (Quirk *et al.* 1972). The issue of descriptive and contrastive language study is treated more fully in Chapter 9.

26 This overuse can be illustrated by the comment that was made on a major research effort in Canada, the so-called Ottawa–Carleton Project, in which several research teams compared three different approaches to the teaching of French in the schools of Canada's capital, Ottawa, and used this research technique almost exclusively: 'No one questions the necessity of measuring achievement and evaluating school programmes ... Indeed the Ottawa–Carleton project represents one of the most thorough and extensive efforts to measure student performance ever seen among projects of its kind. But, because of the size of the task, *other research techniques* such as

classroom observation, and the sampling of teachers' views by interviews, received less emphasis than they might have done. The differences between the programmes and the variations within programmes were largely taken at their face value. Little was done to describe the conditions under which these programmes were delivered. Nor were the interesting findings from teacher questionnaires and classroom observations related to the achievements and attitudes of the students ... The research would have had increased value if much more attention had been paid to what went on in the classroom and in the school environment' (Stern *et al.* 1976:32).

27 See also Chapter 14, Note 1 for references to other studies using the insights of language learners as a research technique. Other ingenious experimental techniques have been used in a series of studies by Bialystok in Toronto referred to in Chapter 18.

28 Some of the issues arising in such a prolonged and well developed co-operation between researchers and administrators/practitioners have been discussed in two publications on the French language projects in Ontario, referred to in Note 26: Stern, Swain, and McLean 1976 and Stern *et al.* 1976a. See also Stern 1978. Ten years of immersion research has been reviewed by Swain and Lapkin (1981).

29 Modes of interaction are discussed in greater detail by Stern, Wesche, and Harley (1978). See also the Conclusion, especially Note 4.

PART TWO

Historical perspectives

5   Approaches and studies

Historical awareness as a first step

A good way to start developing a language teaching theory is to look at ourselves and to explore to what extent our second language teaching has been influenced by our own language learning and language teaching experiences. The kind of background events that can be expected to influence our way of teaching, hence our language teaching theory, are likely to include some or all of the following:

1 our informal childhood language learning (first and second language) at home;
2 the way we were taught languages at school and how we responded to such teaching;
3 other formal or informal second language learning experiences as an adult;
4 what people in our milieu think and say about languages, language learning, and speakers of other languages;
5 language training at university or college, or other language-related activities in higher education;
6 any formal language teacher training we may have had;
7 our past and present language teaching experience;
8 discussions with other language teachers, professional conferences, inservice training, meetings of language teachers' associations;
9 reading on language pedagogy including books or articles in professional or popular reviews.

With the help of a checklist of this kind we can reconstruct our personal history as language teachers and estimate what particular ideas, experiences, or practices have shaped our past and present thoughts on second language teaching. We can also introspect where these influences might have come from. Are we teaching the way we were taught? Or are we reacting in our own teaching *against* experiences we have had? What changes over time in our own language teaching philosophy can we detect and what has prompted these changes? What appear to be the dominant influences in our own theory?

Beyond this personal and autobiographical approach, it is rewarding to enquire into the historical development of language teaching in the school, college, or community in which we teach. Ultimately, we will come to the point where we can place our own personal position in relation to where we are as a profession in our own country or internationally and attempt to understand current developments in relation to the history of language pedagogy.

Through studying the history of language teaching we can gain perspective on present-day thought and trends and find directions for future growth. Knowing the historical context is helpful to an understanding of language teaching theories. For example, a book or an article on language pedagogy makes much more sense to us if we have the necessary background knowledge. Thus, one of the most influential books on pedagogy in recent years has been Rivers' *Teaching Foreign Language Skills*, first published in 1968. While this work can give help to teachers on questions of language methodology which would be applicable at any time, its main emphasis can be better understood in the context of discussions on language teaching which occurred when this book was written in the mid-sixties. Against the background of contemporary doubts about the prevailing audiolingual theory and Rivers' own earlier critical assessment of this theory (Rivers 1964; see also Chapter 15), this book's main message came across as a strong endorsement of the audiolingual theory, although tempered and modified by a 'cognitive' approach which was beginning to assert itself at that time. The same book was published in a new edition in 1981. While the format of the earlier edition and much of its content have been maintained, the new edition of this standard work reflects new research as well as changes of thought and of professional opinion: 'much water has flowed under the bridge since the sixties' (Rivers 1981:xiii; see also Chapter 21:477–82).

The intention of this chapter, then, is to introduce a historical perspective into our approach to language teaching theory. In addition to thinking about our own personal history, as was suggested above, we will do this in three ways: orienting ourselves in the literature on the history of language pedagogy; exploring an historical document as an example of a first-hand study; and, in Chapter 6, reviewing recent and current trends of development.

Historiography of language teaching

Paucity of studies

What do we expect from a historical study of second language teaching? To say the least, it would establish a descriptive record of the development of language pedagogy in the past. In this way a store of ideas, experiences, and practices would be accumulated which might otherwise be lost and would have to be laboriously rediscovered in succeeding generations. Unfortunately the current state of historical documentation is far from satisfactory. Language teaching theory has a short memory. Perhaps because of our involvement in current problems and polemics, we have tended to ignore the past or to distort its lessons, and to re-enact old battles over and over again.[1] Accessible and reliable information is lacking even on quite recent and important trends of development, such as the history of the direct method, the origins of *français fondamental*, the American language teaching experience during World War II, or audiolingualism in the early sixties.[2]

Yet, the need for an historical perspective has always been strongly felt, and a number of historical studies have been made. Two major groups can be distinguished: general surveys and studies of particular aspects.

General historical surveys

It is probably because of the wish to give perspective that so many of the writings on language teaching begin with an historical introduction to current developments, for example, Pinloche (1913), Closset (1949), Mallinson (1953), Lado (1964), Grittner (1977), Chastain (1976), and Diller (1978). But because books of this kind are mainly concerned with modern thought, the historical antecedents are often no more than a backdrop to set off with bold strokes those aspects the writer wishes to emphasize, and the historical treatment is necessarily brief and often reveals a definite bias.

Composing a short historical introduction is quite a difficult task for writers, because, to-date, there are no comprehensive and authoritative general histories of language teaching to draw upon; nor have studies of special aspects been carried out in sufficient number, scope, and depth to allow the piecing together of a fully satisfactory general history of language teaching and learning. We have to rely on whatever sources happen to exist.

The critical reader of a historical account expects (but rarely finds) a clear indication of the research on which the account is based and a discussion of the reasons for the selection of the events, books, or names in the report. He would also like to know whether primary or secondary sources have been employed. Suspicions regarding the soundness of some common historical introductions are aroused by the extraordinary similarity between them. The same historical characters occur; the same quotations are cited; and even the same small factual error recurs in several of these brief histories of language teaching![3]

An historical survey should (but rarely does) distinguish between the history of *ideas* on language teaching and the development of *practice*, because evidence from polemical or theoretical writings cannot be treated as the same as evidence from language teaching manuals. Thus, a widely used teaching grammar, such as Duwes' French grammar in sixteenth-century England or the textbooks by Ploetz in nineteenth-century Germany, can give clues to current practice, whereas the reflections of a philosopher (for example, Montaigne or Locke) on how to learn a language provide evidence for the parameters of thought but do not *necessarily* describe common practice in a given period. Of course, the views of philosophers or reformers are sometimes expressions of a reaction to contemporary practices. Their criticism may indeed offer clues to common practice, but the possible bias of the writer must be borne in mind.[4] Gouin, for example, whose ideas became influential towards the end of the nineteenth century, introduces his own proposals for a language teaching reform with a vivid autobiographical account of how he struggled with the German language with the help of various contemporary methods of language teaching; he cites Ollendorf, Jacotot, Robertson, and Ploetz. These descriptions indicate how one writer felt about certain methods of teaching in vogue a century ago, and his story tells us a great deal about the contemporary language teaching scene. However, before treating Gouin's account as a definitive statement on the practices and viewpoints of his age, the historian would have to seek confirmation from other sources. Furthermore, in treating Gouin as a source on nineteenth-century language teaching, he would have to consider the extent to which Gouin's description is applicable only to one country, his native France, to Germany where he went to learn German, or to both, or whether it refers to the whole of Europe or the entire Western world.

The historian of language teaching must also exercise critical caution in citing evidence from historical writings in support of modern viewpoints. For example, Comenius, the seventeenth-century educator, whose modernity of outlook on language teaching has impressed many writers, is often quoted on the controversy concerning language rules versus practice without rules. Comenius is cited in support of the view that practice is all-important and that grammar rules are unnecessary. Indeed Comenius wrote: 'All languages are easier to learn by practice than from rules.' But we must not gloss over the fact that this proposition, which so neatly and dramatically underlines a particular modern viewpoint, is less conveniently followed by another less frequently quoted statement: 'But rules assist and strengthen the knowledge derived from practice.'[5]

These cautions should be kept in mind as we discuss a few of the noteworthy historical surveys available: (1) two examples of a chronological approach, and (2) a thematic treatment.

1. *General chronological treatment*
The most common approach to language teaching history has been to describe the development chronologically from antiquity to the present. Thus, in *Language Teaching Analysis*, Mackey (1965:141–151) describes in a few telling pages the main periods of the evolution of

language teaching from ancient Greece and Rome through the Middle Ages and the following centuries down to modern times. Titone's small book (1968)—apart from two brief sketches of language teaching in antiquity—begins with the Renaissance. Covering approximately the same ground as Mackey, but in more detail and with ample quotations from sources, Titone writes first about some of the major European teachers and writers between the Renaissance and the nineteenth century who have had something to say on language learning, such as Ascham, Ratke, Montaigne, Comenius, Locke, down to Hamilton and Jacotot at the end of the eighteenth century. However, his main attention is directed to the principal figures of the nineteenth and first half of the twentieth century, the fathers of the 'traditional' or 'grammar-translation' approach, and to such reformers as Gouin, Viëtor, and Ripman. To three great figures of the recent past, Sweet, Jespersen, and Palmer, he devotes a chapter each, and his study is completed by an account of more general trends before World War II, brief sketches of contemporary trends (i.e., 1967) in several countries, and a classification of recent methods.

Mackey and Titone view the historical development in a similar way. Tracing it back to antiquity, they recognize that thought on language teaching in Europe first crystallized round Latin as the principal medium of instruction, scholarship, and communication. Latin was taught 'to enable clerics to speak, read and write in their second language', (Mackey 1965:141). From the sixteenth century, as that role was increasingly assumed by the vernacular languages of Europe, these languages began also to be studied as foreign languages. At first they were learnt informally and in a practical way by those who needed them for social purposes, while the teaching of the Latin language, which over the following centuries gradually lost its unique position as the language of scholarship, became more and more stultified in narrow formalism. As the modern languages in turn became school subjects the formalism of Latin teaching was transferred also to them. Both Mackey and Titone recognize in the development of language teaching a long-standing conflict between two principles which have been characterized by Rivers (1981:25–27) as a conflict between 'formalism' and 'activism'. Again and again the one or the other trend appears to assert itself. The history of language teaching, as viewed by Mackey and Titone, has witnessed the work of 'activist' reformers, for example, between the sixteenth and the nineteenth century, Montaigne, Comenius, Locke, Basedow, Hamilton, Jacotot, Gouin, or Viëtor, and the formalistic trend represented, in particular during the late eighteenth and the nineteenth century, by Meidinger, Seidenstücker, Ahn, Ollendorf, and Ploetz. Language teaching method first swings from the active oral use of Latin in Ancient and Medieval times to the learning by rule of the Renaissance grammars, back to oral activity with Comenius, back to grammar rules with Ploetz, and back again to the primacy of speech in the direct method (Mackey 1965:151).

In short, both Mackey and Titone emphasize the conflict in teaching methods as the key principle in interpreting the history of language teaching.[6] In Mackey's account the to and fro is reported with less partisanship than in Titone who lays particular emphasis upon examples in history which roughly anticipate some of the 'activist' principles of modern audiolingualism (appeals to experience, induction, practice, etc.). In Titone's book the 'formal approach' is condemned from the outset as a 'deviation in teaching method that came about at, or shortly before, the beginning of the nineteenth century' (op. cit.:2) whose failings he attributes to lack of psychological and linguistic knowledge and to the inertia on the part of language teachers. In spite of this difference in bias, both accounts present a vivid panorama of historical trends and introduce the reader to some of the great names and important writings of the past. In our view, however, the explanation of the historical development in terms of a conflict of two broad principles appears as an oversimplification.[7]

2. Thematic surveys

A different approach to a historical perspective, developed by Kelly (1969) in a survey of the past 2,500 years of language teaching, has three distinguishing features. First, this impressive study is based on an examination of some 1,200 primary sources from antiquity to the modern era. Second, Kelly has not followed the customary chronological treatment of language teaching history but instead traces the origin and development of different themes or aspects. He has thus widened the scope of historical studies. In place of the preoccupation of most previous writers with the development of teaching method, he has extended the historical approach to a large number of other features in language pedagogy. Third, the features he has examined have been systematically chosen. Basing himself on the conceptual framework of Mackey (1965), he has explored the historical antecedents or equivalents of Mackey's scheme.

Kelly shows that many present-day practices and ideas have historical parallels. For example, pattern drill has forerunners in substitution tables in the teaching grammars of the sixteenth and seventeenth century. Dialogue, a popular form of text presentation in recent decades, was 'in constant use in the language classroom right through the history of language teaching' (Kelly 1969:120). Kelly has traced many other features from earlier times to the present, for example, the role of translation, composition, and reading as well as the teaching of grammar, vocabulary, and pronunciation. He has also investigated changes in the objectives of language teaching, the choice of languages, the role of the teacher and the influence of linguistic and psychological ideas on language and language learning.

Furthermore, on the basis of this thematic survey, Kelly (1969:394) has been able to derive a more differentiated picture of the chronological development than has hitherto been available, which he has summarized in Figure 5.1 overleaf.

In his view, 'The total corpus of ideas accessible to language teachers has not changed basically in 2,000 years. What have been in constant change are the ways of building methods from them, and the part of the corpus that is accepted varies from generation to generation, as does the form in which the ideas present themselves' (Kelly 1969:363). According to the conception expressed in Figure 5.1, language teaching in European civilization can be approximately divided into five periods: the Classical Period, the Middle Ages, Renaissance, the Age of Reason, and the Modern Period. The perspectives of language instruction have changed along with the role of languages in society and changes in the intellectual climate expressed by contemporary scholarship, which Kelly calls the 'parent sciences', and 'the critical sciences'.[8] Language teaching is principally an art which through the ages has pursued three major objectives: social (language as a form of communication), artistic-literary (language as a vehicle for artistic creation and appreciation), and philosophical (linguistic analysis). These broad aims have, in different periods in history, been emphasized to varying degrees. Another important variable in the development has been the distinction between classical languages and the European vernaculars. 'In classical Rome, Greek filled the functions of both classical and modern languages, being taught for a range of purposes from social chitchat to transmission of literary and philosophical thought' (op. cit.:397); but in more recent times the interplay between classical and modern languages has been an important factor in the development of second language teaching.

Kelly sees strong parallels between language teaching in the Classical Period, the Renaissance, and the Modern Age, and another parallel between the Middle Ages and the Age of Reason. In the former, social objectives were dominant, as shown for example in the Modern Age, in the strong emphasis on communication, whereas in the latter 'the balance had shifted towards written and analytical skills' (op. cit.:398). In accordance with these differing objectives, methods of teaching have varied between informal and formal. In other words, the long-standing conflict in methods between 'activism' and 'formalism', observed by Mackey, Titone, and Rivers, is interpreted by Kelly as a function of the social role of the languages taught and the objectives pursued in teaching them.

ERA	PARENT SCIENCES	AIMS — Lit. (CL / ML)	AIMS — Scholarly (CL / ML)	AIMS — Social (CL / ML)	ART — METHODS Informal	ART — METHODS Formal	CRITICAL SCIENCES
Classical	Logic, Grammar, Rhetoric, Philosophy, Theology	Gr X; CL X / ML X	Gr X; CL X / ML X	Gr X; CL X / ML X	Introduction at home & in society	Literary & Rhetorical schooling	Parent sciences with normative bias – observations erected into rules to govern activities drawn from them.
Middle Ages		CL X	CL X	CL Y		Teaching by book – social uses of Latin secondary – contemporary languages taught for literary purposes.	
12th–15th centuries		ML X	ML X				
Renaissance	Education, Grammar, Rhetoric	CL X / ML X	CL X / ML X	CL Y / ML X	Methods in ML mainly oral – example followed by some Classics teachers	Methods in CL follow medieval pattern – ML enter translation teaching for literary purposes	
17th, 18th & 19th centuries	Grammar, Philosophy, Education, Rhetoric	CL Y	CL X / ML X			Logical orientation of grammar – social purposes of language subordinate – grammar-translation evolves	
19th & early 20th	Linguistics, Psychology, Education, Anatomy		CL X / ML Y	CL X	Natural & Direct methods, etc. predominate – experimentation in Direct and 'structural' methods for Latin	Classical languages continue 19th-century practice – many modern-language teachers do likewise.	Experimental Psychology. Language Didactics. Methods Analysis.

X Main aim
Y Most important subsidiary aim

CL Classical Languages
ML Modern Languages
Gr Greek
Lit. Literature

Figure 5.1 Kelly's schema of the evolution of second language teaching

While there is hardly any aspect imaginable on which Kelly's wide-ranging study does not provide fascinating source material and thoughtful discussion his claim that his study is based on Mackey's scheme, has not been fully sustained. The reader has to guess whether deviations from Mackey are purely a matter of presentation, or whether they indicate that the historical events impose a framework which only partially coincides with Mackey's.

While *all* aspects under review appear to suggest historical precedents of some kind, it is obvious from Kelly's account that there are some on which the historical search is far less rewarding. Moreover, in some instances the history goes back the whole length of the historical scale of the study while for other features history begins only a few decades ago. These observations raise questions: What in fact does a history of any aspect or theme mean? Does it indicate that, given the need for language learning, different ages and different language learning settings inevitably face identical problems in different guises and come up with more or less the same solutions? Or does it mean that an earlier feature of language teaching has some historical or causal connection with some later manifestation under the same heading? Is it not possible that, by searching history for some evidence of an earlier manifestation of a modern idea, as Kelly has done, we merely impose on the past the linguistic and pedagogical conceptualizations of the present? Moreover, by isolating a particular aspect and studying its development 'diachronically' we may fail to see it properly in its synchronic context and thus miss its contemporary significance and view it too much in the light of twentieth-century preoccupations.

Questions of this kind suggest that language teaching history needs both approaches to complement each other, i.e., the synchronic study of language teaching and learning at a given stage in history in its social and educational context, and the 'diachronic' description of the development of different features and aspects. They further suggest that any truly satisfactory panorama must ultimately be based upon a large number of in-depth studies of more restricted scope, treating specific problems, settings or periods, or identifying events and persons whose contribution to the total picture of language teaching and learning through the ages needs more detailed and more objective investigation than is available at present.

Studies of historical aspects

At the present state of our knowledge, the second approach, the study of particular aspects, is perhaps more fruitful than further global studies. By selecting a restricted field historians have a better chance of discovering and analysing a manageable body of data and thus of contributing to an understanding of language teaching in general. The

Belgian scholar Closset (1949), who had himself included a general account of historical development in his work on language teaching theory, recognized the need for more specialized studies. At his instigation, Maréchal (1972), one of his collaborators, embarked upon a history of language teaching in Belgium. In the course of his enquiries, Maréchal soon discovered that it would be necessary to restrict himself. His study eventually became an investigation on the history of modern languages in the secondary schools in the Belgian public educational system. Apart from an introductory chapter on earlier periods, the study deals principally with the period beginning with the foundation of Belgium as an independent nation in 1830 and ending at the start of World War I in 1914. This very thorough study, however, covers in detail the impact of the reform movement in language teaching on one educational system and offers points of reference for similar studies of other European countries, or for other parts of the same educational system. Maréchal's work could also serve as a basis for a follow-up study covering the next stage of development down to the present time. Finally, it documents the role of language teaching in a bilingual country. For all these reasons, in spite of the restrictions of the topic under investigation, a study of this kind is of importance well beyond its limits of time, place, and specific area of enquiry.

Another classic illustration of the kind of specialized study needed as a basis for a better historical perspective is offered by an investigation on the teaching and cultivation of the French language in England during Tudor and Stuart times by Lambley (1920). This case study of second language teaching and language use in a given period within the sociopolitical context of one country is of particular interest to the history of language teaching because its central topic is the period of transition from Latin as the main vehicle of communication among European nations to the use of the vernaculars, a phase in the development of language teaching, to which Mackey and Kelly have attributed so much importance.

Confining herself to an introduction to French in medieval England, followed by an English linguistic history of the sixteenth and the seventeenth century, Lambley used as documentation for the medieval period some twenty manuscripts on language aspects, and, for the Tudor and Stuart times, over one hundred and fifty manuals for the teaching of French, published between 1521 and 1699.

According to Lambley's account, medieval England offered a sociolinguistically interesting example of trilingualism. Since the Norman Conquest, French was widely used in England; it was the language of the royal court, the law courts, and the nobility. English was spoken by the masses; and the language of learning and scholarship was of course Latin. Although the use of English became more widespread throughout society in the fifteenth century, French, right into Tudor and Stuart times, remained the *lingua franca* for contacts with foreigners, particularly in court circles. Consequently, as English spread as the common medium of communication, the learning of French as a second language became important in the education of the nobility. That is why it was customary for the royal court and the aristocracy to employ French tutors. Latin continued to be important as the main avenue to literacy and scholarship. The reason, then, for learning French—to use Kelly's analysis of aims—was 'social'. As a means of communication French was not only needed by courtiers, but also by the merchant class, trading with Western Europe, especially France and the Netherlands, and by other travellers and soldiers—'soit que quelcun face merchandise ou qu'il hante la court, ou qu'il suive la guerre, ou qu'il aille par villes et champs', as it was expressed in a sixteenth-century book of dialogues.[9] Furthermore, religious persecution in the course of the two centuries led to movement across the Channel in both directions: for example, in the sixteenth century, French protestants fled to England, while, in the following century, during the period of the Civil War and the Commonwealth, English upper class families willingly sent their children to be educated in France. Lambley shows how such social, political, and religious developments in France and England influenced the role and teaching of the French language in England during the period under investigation.

The interest in learning French in Tudor and Stuart times is reflected in the large number of French grammars and other guides on French which appeared at that time and which have been perceptively analysed in Lambley's study. Her enquiry lends support to Kelly's view that the parameters of the discussion on teaching methods have remained surprisingly constant. Questions of learning by practice versus learning by rule, of methods of formal study versus informal use, which have been prominent in recent discussions, already exercised the minds of French teachers four hundred years ago. Because of the practical value of French as a second language in England, the methods included, besides formal study under a tutor and with the help of a manual, study of dialogues on supposedly relevant topics, contact with French native speakers, travel abroad, living in a French-speaking family, attending French church services, or reading French romances. The different methods which were advocated for learning French provided food for thought about how to improve the teaching of Latin.

Two of the most popular French teaching grammars of the earlier part of the period in question, had been written by two French tutors at the court of Henry the Eighth, Giles Duwes, and John Palsgrave. They illustrate differences in approach to the study of a language in the sixteenth century which appear quite familiar to the modern reader.

Lambley describes Duwes' *An Introductorie for to learne to rede, to prononce, and to speke French trewly* (1534) as a practical small teaching grammar which enjoyed great popularity. Palsgrave's work, *L'Esclarcissement de la langue françoyse* (1530), on the other hand, was an immense work of scholarship, an enormous folio of over 1,000 pages divided into three books, which included a guide to French pronunciation, grammar, vocabulary, and practical exercises with interlinear translations in the form of 'letters missive in prose and in rime, also diverse communications by way of dialogue, to receive a messenger from the emperor, the French King or any other prince, also other communications of the propriety of meat, of love, of peace, of wars, of the exposition of the mass, and what man's soul is, with the division of time and other conceits' (Lambley 1920:90). The methodological conflict between teaching by 'rules' or by 'practice' to which, a century later, Comenius drew attention and which has been a matter of argument down to the present, characterized the difference in approach between Duwes and Palsgrave. Duwes, it appears, laid emphasis on a good vocabulary and a thorough knowledge of verbs acquired through practising such transformations as 'I have, have I? Why have I?' 'I have not, have I not? Why have I not?' with rules of grammar reduced to a minimum. Palsgrave, on the other hand, firmly believed in the value of learning French by means of grammar rules, and translation from English into French (op. cit.:90–92).

Unfortunately, too few studies of historical aspects of the quality of Lambley's investigation exist which would help in building up a comprehensive and fully documented history of language teaching. Nevertheless, a thorough search of the literature would probably yield a certain number of studies in monographs, review articles, or chapters in books on different aspects of historical interest. Here we can only list a few examples.

Complementary to Lambley's study is an investigation of the origins of the modern school curriculum in England by Watson (1909). It deals with the same period as Lambley's study and considers among the modern languages not only French but also the interest in other languages—Spanish, Italian, German, and Dutch—and the question of polyglottism. Watson was able to show that there was indeed a considerable interest in learning languages; but such language study was not yet visualized as a regular part of a school curriculum. An enquiry by Gilbert (1953, 1954, 1955) analyses nineteenth-century writings on the reform of language teaching and shows that the early beginnings of the reform movement in England go back to the middle of the nineteenth century. The influence of linguistics on language teaching in the U.S.A. between 1940 and 1960 has been traced in a masterly way by Moulton (1961, 1963).[10] Similar to Maréchal's study on the history of language teaching in Belgium, the history of language teaching in different countries have been traced: for example, we find as part of the American and Canadian Modern Foreign Language Study in the twenties, a detailed enquiry on the history of language teaching in the U.S.A. (Bagster-Collins 1930) and in Canada (Buchanan and MacPhee 1928). In the sixties, a series of studies were commissioned to investigate the development of the teaching of different languages in the U.S.A.: French (Watts 1963), German (Zeydel 1964), Italian (Fucilla 1967), Portuguese (Ellison 1969), Russian (Parry 1967), and Spanish (Leavitt 1969). From the point of view of different countries the history of the teaching of English as a second language has been the subject of several enquiries (Schroeder 1959; Martin-Gamero 1961; Marckwardt 1967; Kelly 1971; and Lee 1971). Certain special aspects of language teaching have been investigated historically: among them, the history of the language laboratory (Léon 1962); the American armed forces' language programmes in World War II (Angiolillo 1947; Lind 1948); the question of intensive language training (Frink 1967); the classical tradition in foreign language teaching (Morris 1957); the development of Spanish grammars over a two hundred year period (Jump 1961); the primacy of speech (Banathy and Sawyer 1969); and culture in language teaching in Germany (Apelt 1967). A few studies have traced and discussed the history of the teaching of languages in different educational institutions. Thus, Andersson has shown that the idea of teaching languages to younger children—the FLES movement of the fifties and sixties in the U.S.A.—is a revival of a common practice of language teaching to younger children in the history of American education (Andersson 1969). Other studies have considered languages at the secondary stage (Rülcker 1969; Maréchal 1972) and the universities (for example, Firth 1929; Schroeder 1959; Stern 1964; Rothwell 1968). Among neglected fields we note in particular the lack of biographies of great language teachers and of detailed and critical studies of their work.[11] Another neglected aspect involves the learner's perceptions; in a preliminary study Fraenkel (1969) has shown that the reactions and recollections of authors (for example, Churchill) writing on their language learning experiences could present interesting insights; they could be explored by systematic reviews of biographies and autobiographies of historical interest.

The study of primary sources

The reader wishing to gain historical perspective of language teaching should not confine himself to reading history at second hand. It is an illuminating experience for gaining perspective on present-day thought to examine primary sources directly; for example, theoretical and polemical writings, older teaching grammars, textbooks and other manuals for learning languages, early issues of language teachers' professional periodicals, government papers and reports of public commissions concerned with language questions.

Primary sources need not necessarily be documents of great antiquity. A selection might include the writings of some of the influential language teachers or theorists of the recent past, for example, Sweet (1899), Jespersen (1904), Palmer (1917), Bloomfield (1942), or Fries (1945) with whose thought the student of language teaching theory should come into contact.

From time to time, writers have surveyed the contemporary language teaching scene and have pointed out significant developments. In so far as such status studies or 'state-of-the-art' reports refer to other writings they are useful as secondary sources drawing our attention to significant events, trends, names, and publications of a given period. Because they involve in addition a strong element of selection and interpretation they can be looked upon as primary sources and theoretical statements in their own right. These status studies, which may take the form of books or articles, can give to a reader a good introduction to recent trends in language pedagogy.[12]

All the primary sources we have mentioned can be treated as 'theories' (T2s) in the sense suggested in Chapters 2 and 3, and can be analysed systematically with questions of the following kind in mind:

1 What is the subject and point of view of the document?
2 What are the historical circumstances within which the document was written? To whom is it addressed? Why was it written?
3 What view of *language* and *language learning* does the document reveal?
4 What view of *language teaching* is expressed in the document? In particular, what aims, principles, materials, methods, or institutions are proposed or assumed in it?
5 What was the importance of the document to its own age? How was it received? What was its effect?
6 How is the document to be assessed from the point of view of today?

We will now illustrate with an example how such a document can be analysed as a theoretical statement.

The IPA Articles

The six articles of the International Phonetic Association (henceforth referred to as the IPA articles) were a brief declaration of principles of L2 teaching which were formulated in the eighteen-eighties at the beginning of the modern era and appeared on every issue of the review of the IPA, *Le Maître Phonétique*. The text which appeared in French reads as follows in an English translation:[13]

Article 1
Foreign language study should begin with the spoken language of everyday life, and not with the relatively archaic language of literature.

Article 2
The teacher's first aim should be to thoroughly familiarize his pupils with the sounds of the foreign language. Towards this end he should use a phonetic transcription which will be employed exclusively in the early stages of the course without reference to conventional spelling.

Article 3
The teacher's second aim should be to introduce his pupils to the most common sentences and idiomatic phrases of the foreign language. With this end in view, his pupils should study consecutive texts— dialogues, descriptions, and narratives—which should be as easy, natural, and interesting as possible.

Article 4
In the early stages grammar should be taught inductively, complementing and generalizing language facts observed during reading. A more systematic study of grammar should be postponed to the advanced stages of the course.

Article 5
As far as possible expressions in the foreign language should be related by the teacher directly to ideas and other expressions in the language, and not to the native language. The teacher should take every opportunity to replace translation by references to real objects or pictures or by explanations given in the foreign language.

Article 6
At a later stage, when writing is introduced, such written work should be arranged in the following sequence: first, reproduction of thoroughly familiar reading texts; second, reproduction of narratives orally presented by the teacher; and third, free composition. Written translations from and into the foreign language are considered to be appropriate only at the most advanced stage of the course.

In order to treat this document as a T2 'theory' of language teaching, it will be analysed under the following headings: (1) general topic and point of view of the document; (2) the historical circumstances; (3) the view of language and language learning, expressed in it; (4) the approach to language teaching; (5) an assessment of the document in the contemporary context, and (6) its significance today.

1. The topic

The IPA articles represent a concise statement of major principles of language teaching method. What is at first sight surprising is that these are the principles of a society of *phoneticians*. It suggests that phonetics was at that time viewed mainly in the context of language teaching, and not so much as a scientific study in its own right.

2. The historical circumstances

In order to understand the historical situation surrounding a particular document we may have to look beyond the document itself, read 'between the lines', and interpret the social, educational, and linguistic context from other collateral sources.

The IPA articles were written during that very productive period of language teaching history, the last two decades of the nineteenth century, when the International Phonetic Association was founded and the debate on the reform of language teaching was in full swing in several countries of Western Europe. During the second half of the nineteenth century several attempts had been made to develop a serviceable international system of writing speech sounds. The need for such a system had been felt particularly by teachers of English in France, Germany, and Scandinavia. But the value of a phonetic alphabet was also discussed in relation to shorthand systems and spelling reform. It was due to the initiative of a French linguist, Paul Passy, that the International Phonetic Alphabet, based on Sweet's 'Romic', was adopted by the International Phonetic Association and promoted through its journal, *Le Maître Phonétique* (Albright 1958).

Phonetics as the basis of language study and a phonetic transcription as an essential tool were cornerstones in the language teaching theory of several reformers. For others, however, different issues were of greater importance, for example, the role of grammar, the use of dialogue and consecutive text passages, or an emphasis on speaking rather than on the formal study of speech sounds. It is noteworthy, therefore, that in the IPA articles—in spite of the IPA's commitment to phonetics and the phonetic alphabet—the teaching of speech sounds and the use of a phonetic alphabet received no greater emphasis than any of the other principles. Another interesting fact to note is that Article 2 recommends the use of *a* phonetic transcription, not necessarily the one adopted by the IPA.

3. The view of language and language learning

For the IPA, then, speech sounds were an important aspect of language which they considered to have been previously neglected or poorly treated but no more important than vocabulary or grammar. Although the IPA articles are not very explicit regarding their underlying philosophy of language and language learning, they imply that language is an intelligible and learnable system of sounds, words, and grammar. Sounds are best described by a phonetic transcription (Article 2); the vocabulary can be divided into the language of everyday life and literary language (Article 1); and grammar, which in content appears to present no problem to the authors of the articles, can either be inferred empirically from the inspection of texts or it can be studied systematically (Article 4). The view of learning we can derive from the tenor of the articles is the assumption made in most systems of language teaching, that a language can be acquired by a process of systematic study, provided that one follows the teaching principles outlined in the articles.[14]

4. The approach to language teaching

The principles and sequences of teaching are the central theme of the IPA articles. The articles have nothing to say about aims or levels of achievement to be reached. Also the institutions in which language teaching occurs are not specifically mentioned. It must be assumed that the recommendations refer to secondary schools in European educational systems, and that language courses stretch over several years. This setting is implied in the references to the suggested teaching sequences which, from the point of view of the modern reader, are somewhat vague in their indications of what to do 'first', 'in the early stages', 'at a later stage', or 'at the most advanced stage of the course'.

The teaching recommendations themselves are precise. Article 1 recommends that spoken everyday language should take precedence over literary language, a principle which is also emphasized by other reformers. Jespersen, for example, warns against the clumsiness of schoolbooks, because 'words which belong merely to elevated or specially poetical style are bundled together with everyday words in the very beginning of the first primer without any caution to the pupil against using them' (Jespersen 1904:19).[15]

Article 2 demands the 'phonetic start', i.e., the early stages of a language course should be devoted to the teaching of the sounds of the language, and during this stage a phonetic transcription should be used in preference to conventional orthography. Sweet and Jespersen again share this point of view. Sweet, for example, says emphatically that phonetics 'is equally necessary in the theoretical and in the practical study of languages' (Sweet 1899/1964:4).

Article 3 counteracts the *Meidingerei*, as Viëtor (1882) contemptuously called the use of absurd isolated sentences and bits of language outside any meaningful context, a practice which most reformers of the period, including Viëtor, Sweet, and Jespersen condemned, with equal vehemence. Their recommended alternative was the use of coherent dialogues or prose narratives as the main vehicle of language learning.

Article 4 shows that the IPA did not taboo grammar teaching; it recommended a two-stage approach: 'inductive', observational techniques in the early stages and systematic study for advanced learners.

Article 5 enunciates the 'direct method' principle: it recommends explanation of meanings in the second language by relating the expression directly to objects, visual aids, or to familiar words in the foreign language wherever possible. Translation is to be used as a last resort. The IPA, then, did not recommend a direct method at all costs.

The sixth article defines graded procedures of teaching how to write the second language. The standard technique of the period, translation of unconnected sentences, is completely rejected; but the translation of connected passages from and into the foreign language (*thème* and *version*) is not abandoned; it is treated as an exercise appropriate only for the most advanced learners. The sequence of recommended writing techniques advances from renarrating closely studied reading texts to the reproduction by the learner of new texts orally presented by the teacher, followed at the next stage by 'free' composition.

The progression in teaching a language in accordance with the IPA articles can therefore be summarized as a four-stage process:

stage 1: sounds and phonetic transcription
stage 2: elementary study with 'inductive' grammar
stage 3: continuation of stage 2 plus written composition
stage 4: continuation of stage 3 plus systematic grammar study, translation from and into the foreign language of consecutive passages and study of literary texts.

The recommendations of the six articles which in a concise form offered a neat and coherent curriculum were not new or unique in substance. The proposed procedures had been tried out by the language teaching reformers in their classes; they had also been discussed at meetings and in the contemporary literature on the reform movement. The articles constitute a cleverly conceived compromise on many of the points at issue.

5. *The contemporary significance of the document*

In order to assess the influence of a work or document upon its own age we have of course to look for circumstantial evidence. It is difficult to say how influential the IPA articles were. As we have already observed, the principles they expressed so succinctly were ideas that were current in the reform literature in general and as such they have remained an important strand of language teaching thought during the twentieth century, particularly so in Western Europe. For example, the elimination of archaic language (Article 1) from elementary language instruction—a necessary demand in the nineteenth century—developed in the twentieth into attempts at more systematic vocabulary selection. The 'phonetic start' of Article 2 was implemented in numerous school language programmes. Intensive sound practice with the help of pocket mirrors, the use of sound charts and diagrams depicting the oral cavity and vocal organs, or reading and writing phonetic transcriptions were not at all uncommon for several decades, although many practitioners were implacably opposed to 'phonetics'.[16] The use of short narrative episodes or dialogues as the basis of elementary language instruction, in keeping with Article 3, became widespread practice, as can easily be seen from an examination of language coursebooks, produced between 1900 and 1950. The avoidance of translation and of 'formal grammar' (Articles 4 and 5) was another widespread although much debated trend; and in some educational systems, the previous emphasis on translation from and into the second language was completely superseded by intensive text study, renarration, and 'free' composition (Article 6).[17]

6. *Present-day significance of the document*

Historical documents must be re-assessed periodically. The IPA articles form part of a huge reform literature of the late nineteenth century (Breymann and Steinmüller 1895–1909) which has not yet been adequately evaluated from a present-day perspective. Like so many historical documents on language teaching, the IPA articles astonish most modern readers by the relevance to our own days of principles expressed in them.

The features of the IPA document which have stood the test of time particularly well are: (a) the emphasis on the spoken language; (b) the attention to pronunciation; (c) text study and practice in the language and a lessening of the emphasis on translation as the principal or only technique of language teaching; (d) grammar teaching based on observation of language as it is used in a text, and (e) the emphasis on everyday vocabulary and common idiomatic sentence patterns. The recommendation that must have been the most important principle to the supporters of the IPA, the teaching of phonetics and the use of a phonetic transcription, is perhaps to many modern readers the least acceptable, particularly at early stages of language study. However, this may be due to the fact that in this respect the essential battle of the nineteenth-century promoters of phonetics has been won. The practical study of sounds of a language, on which they laid so much stress, developed in the twentieth century into the practice of speaking and listening with the aid of electromechanical devices, such as the tape recorder and the language laboratory. If, from a modern point of view, the insistence on phonetic transcription in early language instruction seems excessive, it must be remembered that no other convenient device for recording speech sounds for the use of language learners was then available. Moreover, in dictionaries and language courses a sound notation based on IPA principles is still widely used today as an explanatory device.

Conclusion

In this chapter we have argued in favour of giving language teaching theory historical depth. We suggested three ways of doing so:

1 by examining autobiographically our own personal background of language learning and teaching;
2 by reviewing the historical literature which we found is patchy; but which, nevertheless, contains a number of helpful studies; and
3 by studying an historical document at first-hand which was illustrated by the example of the IPA articles.

Notes

1 Rivers (1981) does not share this somewhat pessimistic view of language teaching historiography: 'As we study the evolution of language-teaching methods, we see what is most effective in each method being taken up again at a later date, elaborated and refashioned, so that the best of the past is not lost but serves the purposes of the present' (op. cit.:27).
2 As Besse (1979) in an article on *français fondamental* points out: 'L'histoire du français fondamental reste à faire ...' (op. cit.:23). See also Rivenc's retrospective essay in the same issue (Rivenc 1979).
3 Many writers refer to an episode in the life of Gouin (see p. 78, 152) which, according to his own account, was crucial in the development of his thought on language teaching: the visit to the mill with his nephew. Several writers claim that it was Gouin's son, for example, Titone (1968), Mallinson (1953), Closset (1949), Darian (1972).
4 Montaigne has written about language learning in his *Essais* (1580–1588), available in a modern French edition by Villey and Saulnier. For an English translation of his ideas on language learning, see Montaigne, *The Education of Children*. Locke, the seventeenth-century English philosopher, discusses his views on language learning in a dozen or so pages of his work, *Some Thoughts Concerning Education* (1693).
5 Quoted from the English translation of *Didactica Magna* by Keatinge (1910:206). According to Keatinge (op. cit.:14), *Didactica Magna*, probably completed in 1632 and written in Czech, was published in a Latin translation in 1657. The two principles quoted, which appear in a chapter on language teaching and learning, are

two of eight principles proposed by Comenius to make language learning easy. The eighth principle summarizes Comenius' point of view on the question of practice and rules. In an abbreviated form it reads as follows: 'All languages, therefore, can be learnt ... by practice, combined with rules of a very simple nature ...' (op. cit.: 207). Cooke (1974) has drawn attention to the frequently biased presentation of Comenius' point of view. For example, Closset (1949), Mallinson (1953), and Titone (1968) omit the important qualification to the practice principle.

6 Broadly speaking, the same applies to the other accounts referred to, for example, Closset (1949), Mallinson (1953), and Darian (1972). Diller (1978) interprets the history of pedagogy differently. He makes a distinction between two approaches, 'the empiricist' and 'the rationalist'. His division cuts across the one represented by Rivers, Mackey, and Titone. The empiricists include Jespersen, Palmer, Lado, and the audiolingualists. The rationalist position, supported by Diller, includes Berlitz, Gouin, and de Sauzé. From our perspective both divisions impose modern conceptualizations on historical developments and oversimplify the underlying theories.

7 In fairness to Titone (1968) it should be pointed out that he fully acknowledges the lack of historical documentation: 'Unfortunately, no complete monograph on the history of language teaching methods is yet available' (op. cit.:2). Moreover, in his concluding section he rejects 'overemphasis on one or a few aspects' and postulates 'a multidimensional approach' (op. cit.:109).

8 It is not quite clear what Kelly (1969) means by 'critical sciences'. He gives no examples. His explanation of this concept which appears in the Conclusion (op. cit.:395) does not help: 'Out of the reaction between these basic sciences and practice grows a science of criticism by which both performance and new ideas are judged' (loc. cit.).

9 As quoted by Lambley (1920:247) from a book of dialogues by Noel de Barlement (1557), attempting to provide an aid in several modern languages.

10 For accounts of the general historical development of language teaching in the U.S.A., see Birkmaier 1960; or Grittner 1977.

11 Exceptions to be mentioned include a biographical and critical study on Comenius and his treatment of language by Geissler (1959), and chapters on Sweet, Jespersen, and Palmer in Titone (1968) as well as a few articles and essays, for example, by Darian (1969) on Sweet, Jespersen, and Palmer, by Redman (1967) on Palmer, and a biographical study of Palmer by his daughter Dorothée Anderson (1969).

12 A few such status studies are mentioned in the different sections of Chapter 6.

13 The six articles appear with a lengthy commentary on each in the introductory part of a book of selections of French prose and poetry by Passy and Rambeau (1897). They are also briefly discussed by Albright (1958) in an historical account of the International Phonetic Alphabet. The English translation is by the present writer.

14 Contrast this view with that of Locke (1693) who recommended that for most practical purposes languages should be learnt by use rather than by systematic study. In Locke's view a systematic approach has its place in the training of professional writers and linguists. But in the education of a gentleman 'Languages learnt by roat (i.e., custom or use, *H.H.S.*) serve well enough for the common Affairs of Life and ordinary commerce ... And for this purpose, the Original way of Learning a Language by Conversation, not only serves well enough, but is to be prefer'd as the most Expedite, Proper, and Natural.' This issue, presents itself again today in discussions on communicative language teaching.

15 Sweet (1899) makes the same point under the heading of 'Limited Vocabulary' where he writes: 'Those who learn a language through its literature often have almost as wide a vocabulary as the natives, but have no real command of the elementary combinations, the phrases and idioms, so that, as already observed, they are often unable to describe the simplest mechanical operations, such as "tie in a knot", "turn up the gas". Nor when they come to study English, for instance, do they know that the antithesis of *finding* in the spoken language is not *seeking* but *looking for*' (op. cit. 1964:172).

16 'By 1920 the International Phonetic Association was strongly established. Although Paul Passy in France and Daniel Jones in Britain were the leaders of the association, a great many scholars in many countries adhered to its principles and used its alphabet and its techniques for the description and production of sounds, while thousands of teachers of modern languages employed some degree of phonetics for purposes of pronunciation teaching' (Strevens 1972:715).

17 In Britain and France, however, translation techniques have continued to be widely practised for teaching and examining purposes in schools and universities (for example, Antier 1965). But in more recent times alternatives to these techniques have been recommended (for example, Otter 1968).

6 A sketch of recent and current trends: 1880–1980

In order to put our thoughts on language pedagogy into an historical context we will indicate a few important dates, trends, names, and writings. The time span we have chosen ranges from the main period of the reform movement of 1880 of which the IPA articles were one manifestation to the time of writing (1980). The selection of items for such a brief review is necessarily subjective. Our main purpose is to put the subsequent discussions of the different disciplines into relation to each other and into the context of language pedagogy.

The events of this period of approximately one hundred years have not been identical everywhere. The picture for Europe is in many ways different from that of North America. There are even considerable differences within Europe. Studies such as those by Maréchal (1972) on Belgium or by Apelt (1967) and Rülcker (1969) on Germany will contribute to a better understanding of similarities and differences among European countries. Next it must be borne in mind that the history of English and French as second languages in Africa and Asia has again unique characteristics which make it different from the history of foreign language teaching in European and North American school systems.

The picture is further complicated by the fact that language teaching theory has tended to develop within single language traditions and within different kinds of educational institutions. Thus, British teachers of English as a second language overseas in the twenties and thirties had relatively little contact with the teaching of French in schools in Britain; and different institutions—primary schools, secondary schools, universities, adult education—evolved their own patterns of language teaching. In short, if we do not want to oversimplify the record unduly, we must bear in mind that, from an historical point of view, there are different strands of development according to countries, languages, and institutions. Nevertheless, there are common features which will be emphasized in this summary. The entire time span can be roughly divided into four periods. Each period is briefly characterized and a selected list of names, writings, or events with appropriate dates and a few comments is added. Many of the items will be more fully explained in subsequent chapters.

Period I: 1880 to World War I

The last decades of the nineteenth century witnessed a determined effort in many countries of the Western world (a) to bring modern foreign languages into the school and university curriculum on their own terms, (b) to emancipate modern languages more and more from the comparison with the classics, and (c) to reform the methods of language teaching in a decisive way. As Gilbert (1953, 1954, 1955) has shown, this period of reform is itself the culmination of long-standing criticisms, discussions, and attempts at reform that reach back into the middle of the nineteenth century and earlier. The reform movement involved academic scholars (for example, Sweet, Viëtor, Passy, and Jespersen), language teachers in secondary schools (for example, Walter and Klinghardt in Germany, or Widgery, and MacGowan in England),[1] and promoters of language teaching as a commercial venture (for example, Berlitz). The movement had its radicals, moderates, and opponents.[2] It affected school systems, led to administrative action on the part of ministries of education, brought about the creation of new organizations, such as the International Phonetic Association and associations of language teachers, and led to an intensive debate on language teaching which has gone on ever since. Among significant dates we select the following:

1878 First Berlitz school opened in Providence, Rhode Island, U.S.A.
Among nineteenth-century pioneers of the reform movement Maximilian Delphinus Berlitz (1852–1921) is a fascinating but neglected figure. Born in Germany, he lived mainly in the U.S.A., but travelled constantly founding language schools in many countries. After establishing his first school in the U.S.A. in 1878, by 1900 there were about seventy schools in operation in the U.S.A., France, England, and Germany (Stieglitz 1955).

1880 François Gouin. *L'art d'enseigner et d'étudier les langues*. The English translation was published in 1892.
Kelly (1969:115): 'The method gained few followers.' Titone (1968:33): 'It took England and America by storm.' Gouin's influence obviously needs further investigation.

1882 Wilhelm Viëtor. Quousque tandem? *Der Sprachunterricht muss umkehren: ein Beitrag zur Ueberbürdungsfrage.*
Viëtor was a German specialist in English studies. His pamphlet, demanding a complete reorientation of second language instruction in order to deal with the academic overloading in high schools, written by Viëtor under the pseudonym 'Quousque tandem?', is widely regarded as 'the real impetus towards the reform movement' in Germany (Gilbert 1954:9).

1883 Foundation of the Modern Language Association of America.

1886 Foundation of the International Phonetic Association and its· journal, *Le Maître Phonétique.*

1892 Foundation of the Modern Language Association of Great Britain.

1899 *De la méthode directe dans l'enseignement des langues vivantes.*[3]

1900 *Report of the Committee of Twelve* of the Modern Language Association of America.
    The Committee had been appointed in 1896 at the suggestion of the National Education Association. The Report on modern language teaching, which recommended a compromise solution on the method controversy, was submitted to the MLA at a meeting held in 1898 (Modern Language Association 1901).

1904 Otto Jespersen. *How to Teach a Foreign Language.*
    The English translation of this work, originally published in Danish by an outstanding and internationally respected Danish scholar of English language studies of his time under the title *Sprogundervisning*, has been one of the most widely read books on language teaching in this century.

Period II: World War I and the interwar years to 1940

The tragedy of World War I prompted efforts in many countries towards greater international understanding after the war and the promotion of language teaching in the post-war world. These trends are reflected, for example, in the British report, *Modern Studies*, a root-and-branch review of language teaching at school and university (1918). The period is characterized by attempts to resolve the debate on teaching methods of the preceding era through practical and realistic solutions, for example, the recommendation of a reading approach by West and in the Coleman Report, or of the 'Compromise Method' proposed by the *Memorandum* of the Incorporated Association of Assistant Masters in Secondary Schools in Great Britain. From the standpoint of World War II much of the theory and practice of this period was open to criticism or was at times roundly condemned, for example, by Bloomfield (1942) and by Strevens (1972). Bloomfield (1942), for example, wrote: 'Our schools and colleges teach us very little about language, and what little they teach us is largely in error.' 'The textbooks are far from perfect and some teachers have not sufficient command of the foreign language. Often enough the student, after two, three, or four years of instruction, cannot really use the language he has been studying.' On the positive side, it is during this period that the first serious attempts were made to resolve language teaching problems by research methods, for example, on vocabulary selection, or testing.[4] Among significant dates for this period, we list the following:

1917 Harold E. Palmer. *The Scientific Study and Teaching of Languages.*

Before World War II Harold Palmer (1877–1949) started as a Berlitz teacher in Belgium. He developed his own ideas on language teaching after his return to England in 1914 where he started a school of English for refugees. In 1916 he joined the staff of the Department of Phonetics of University College London (Anderson 1969). His work there prompted the writing of three major books on language teaching, the *Scientific Study* (1917), *The Oral Method* (1921), and the *Principles of Language Study* (1922). Palmer is often considered the 'father of British applied linguistics'. Some of his ideas are discussed in Chapters 8 and 15.

1918 *Modern Studies*, being the Report of the Committee on the Position of Modern Languages in the Educational System of Great Britain.

This report was based on the work of a committee, appointed by the Prime Minister, in 1916 during World War I. It is remarkable for its comprehensive treatment of language teaching. It criticized universities for their antiquarian approach to languages. It recommended the placing of languages into a cultural context. Hence, modern 'studies' (not modern 'languages').

1919 Cleveland Plan instituted.

An attempt, initiated by the language supervisor of an American municipality, Emile de Sauzé, to establish a consistent language programme in the school system of one American school district. See de Sauzé (1929/1959; and Diller 1978).

1921 Edward Thorndike. *The Teacher's Word Book.*

A landmark in word count studies. Although this work was intended as a basis for the reading curriculum in the teaching of English as the mother tongue, it was influential as a prototype for similar investigations undertaken in the interest of foreign language teaching (for background see Clifford 1978).

1921 Harold E. Palmer. *The Oral Method of Teaching Languages.*

1922 Harold E. Palmer. *The Principles of Language Study.*

During the five years in which Palmer wrote the three works on methodology that have been cited he came closest among earlier writers to the concept of language pedagogy based on theoretical disciplines, although, as will be shown later, the disciplines concerned, linguistics and psychology, were not yet well developed.

1924–1928 The Modern Foreign Language Study of the American and Canadian Committees on Modern Languages.
Under the aegis of this study several major investigations were carried out and published in 17 volumes; among these, pioneer studies on testing (Henmon 1929), word frequency counts and idiom lists in several languages (for example, Buchanan 1927; Morgan 1928; Vander Beke 1929; Cheydleur 1929). The entire study forms a valuable base line for research on language pedagogy.[5]

1926 Michael West. *Bilingualism.*

1926 Michael West. *Learning to Read a Foreign Language.* (West 1926a).
Besides Harold Palmer, Michael West (1888–1973) was one of the most influential British writers on ESL in the first half of this century. Like Coleman (see below) he advocated a reading approach. He was a school vice-principal, then a principal and later a school inspector in India, and it was in this capacity that he came to recognize the problem of learning in an unfamiliar language, English.

1923–1927 Ogden and Richards complete Basic English.
BASIC English, an acronym for 'British/American/Scientific/International/Commercial', is an attempt to simplify and rationalize the language learning problems. See below, Ogden 1930.[6]

1929 Algernon Coleman. *The Teaching of Modern Foreign Languages in the United States.* (The Coleman Report)
The findings of this report, the major conclusions of the Modern Foreign Language Study, as interpreted by Coleman, include the recommendation that the primary objective of language teaching should be reading fluency. This conclusion was not endorsed by all members of the Committee. The Coleman Report which is often treated as the *bête noire* of American language teaching has been blamed for the decline of language learning during this period.

1929 Incorporated Association of Assistant Masters in Secondary Schools. *Memorandum on the Teaching of Modern Languages.*
This British study, based on the experience of language teachers in schools, recommended the eclectic 'Compromise Method' as a solution to the language teaching method debate. The regular rewriting of this work every ten or twenty years provides an interesting record of the views of language teachers in the classroom. See IAAM 1949, 1956, 1967, and Assistant Masters Association 1979.

1930 C. K. Ogden. *Basic English: A General Introduction with Rules and Grammar.*

1933 Leonard Bloomfield. *Language.*
This classic in linguistics made its impact on language teaching at the next stage of development.

Period III: World War II and the post-war decades to 1970

The decade of World War II constitutes a 'watershed' (Strevens 1972). American wartime language programmes, initiated between 1941 and 1943, were of crucial importance in this development; they changed the approach to language teaching in the U.S.A. in a radical way. (a) Linguistic scholars were given a leading role in the solution of the language teaching problems that had to be faced, especially in the learning of less commonly taught languages. (b) The Armed Forces' foreign language training programmes demonstrated that language training does not necessarily have to be done in the conventional school-type language course, so much taken for granted during the two previous periods. Indeed, they made earlier approaches in school and university appear almost irrelevant and ineffectual. (c) They claimed to show that languages can be taught to much larger populations of ordinary learners, servicemen, and much more quickly than had previously been thought possible; and (d) they demonstrated the possible advantages of intensive language training and of an oral emphasis.

Whether in reality the American 'Army Method' was such a radical and successful innovation as was commonly believed is doubtful and was hotly debated in the post-war years. But it exercised an enormous influence on post-war thinking about language teaching in the U.S.A. and also in many other countries. Strevens (1972) rightly pointed out that similar developments took place elsewhere and also led to similar consequences. American language training experience in wartime may not have had the direct influence that is sometimes claimed for it. It would in any case be difficult to prove that it did. But the American experience was an exemplar of which note was taken elsewhere, and many practices were re-examined in the light of it. In the forties and fifties American scholarship in linguistics and psychology, and American thought on language teaching provided a challenge of which leaders in the language teaching profession were becoming increasingly aware. At the same time, there have of course also been important indigenous developments, for example, in France and Great Britain.

In the post-war era many countries in the world awakened to language learning problems in a way that could hardly have been predicted in the previous period. Language diversity was greatly increased in the post-war world. Several languages were recognized as world languages and gained official status in the UN and UNESCO. Other languages acquired status as national or regional languages. To secure inter-communication on a national or international level more languages had to be learnt as second languages by more people. Moreover, the democratization of schooling meant that language learning lost its educational elite status. Lastly, travel, trade, scientific, and cultural exchange on a world scale, and, above all, migration made language learning necessary under the most varied circumstances.

Another post-war phenomenon was an increasing intellectual aware-ness of, and an interest in the scientific study of language problems. The rapid growth of linguistics as an independent discipline is only one manifestation of this trend. The study of language from the point of view of several other disciplines also gained importance, including psychology and sociology, and vigorous efforts were made to create interdisciplinary links (for example, Osgood and Sebeok 1954). Psycholinguistics began to establish itself as a subdiscipline during the fifties and sociolinguistics gained recognition in the sixties.

It is not surprising to find that, against this background, renewed and resolute attempts were made in the fifties and sixties to tackle once more the inveterate problems of improving second language learning. They included (a) the use of a new technology (for example, tape recorder, language laboratory, radio, television, film strip projector, computer-assisted instruction), (b) new organizational patterns (for example, languages in primary or adult education, intensive and 'immersion' courses, bilingual schooling, individualized instruction), (c) method-ological innovations (for example, the 'audiovisual method', the 'audio-lingual method'), (d) the development of ambitious new language materials and language teaching programmes, (e) teacher education schemes, and (f), as already described in Chapter 4, a new research emphasis which was applied to some of these innovations.

By about 1960 many of these developments had coalesced, and it seemed as if a few highly promising and practical solutions of the language teaching problem were at long last in sight. The 'revolution' in language teaching caught the imagination of many teachers and the general public around 1960; there was an upsurge of public interest; and in Britain and the U.S.A. funds were made available for language projects. There was a great eagerness to experiment with new ways of language teaching.

The high hopes of this period were gradually eroded. The new methods did not produce spectacular results. The researches were less conclusive than had been hoped. And theoretical flaws were found in the linguistic and psychological principles that had confidently been enun-ciated. These changes led between 1965 and 1970 once more to controversy and renewed search for a more adequate basis for language teaching in the next period.[7]

Some dates which are landmarks in the development of language teaching in this third period include:

1941 Foundation of the English Language Institute (ELI), University of Michigan, directed by Charles C. Fries.

This was the first of several new language centres established in the following twenty years. In addition to teaching English to foreign students, ELI prepared new materials and undertook linguistic research. Charles Fries and his student and successor Robert Lado between 1941 and 1950 developed a language pedagogy which was based on linguistic research and embodied psychological principles of language learning which were derived from the prevailing behaviouristic psychology of the time.

1941 Intensive Language Program of the American Council of Learned Societies.

An important role in this programme was accorded to the Linguistic Society of America. It led to the publication of the two booklets below (Bloomfield, Bloch and Trager) which were seminal in the development of wartime programmes. Linguists began to play an active role in wartime language training in the U.S.A. (Moulton 1961/1963).

1942 Leonard Bloomfield. *Outline Guide for the Practical Study of Foreign Languages.*

1942 Bernard Bloch and George L. Trager. *Outline of Linguistic Analysis.*

1943 Army Specialized Training Program (ASTP) initiated in the U.S.A.

After the war the significance of ASTP was discussed, among others, by Angiolillo (1947) and Lind (1948).[8]

1946 *English Language Teaching Journal.*[9]

1948 *Language Learning: A Journal of Applied Linguistics.*[10]

1951 The commission on *français élémentaire* established at St Cloud the *Centre d'étude du français élémentaire* (Gougenheim *et al.* 1964).

1953 UNESCO-sponsored International Seminar on the Contribution of the Teaching of Modern Languages towards Education for Living in a World Community at Nuwara Eliya, Ceylon (UNESCO 1955).

In this seminar, for the first time, the language learning problems of the Third World were considered in conjunction with language teaching in developed countries.

1953 U.S.A. National Conference on the Role of Foreign Languages in American Schools, called by Earl J. McGrath, United States Commissioner of Education.

This was the first of periodic efforts in the U.S.A. to grapple with weaknesses in American foreign language capability.

1953 Theodore Andersson. *The Teaching of Foreign Languages in the Elementary School.*

A classic published in conjunction with the National Conference, referred to above, made an eloquent plea for an early start in language learning as a means of improving foreign language learning in the U.S.A. The author, Theodore Andersson, a professor of French himself and of Swedish extraction, has been one of the staunchest advocates of language learning in the early years of childhood. Foreign Languages in the Elementary School (FLES) as a distinct movement in American education began around 1955 and gained momentum in the late fifties. Interest in FLES waned from around 1965–1970.

1954 Charles E. Osgood and Thomas A. Sebeok (eds). *Psycholinguistics: A Survey of Theory and Research Problems.*

The publication of this monograph which was based on interdisciplinary meetings held in the early fifties was seminal in the development of psycholinguistics. See Chapter 14.

1954 Publication of *Le Français Elémentaire*. (France 1954).

1957 Robert Lado. *Linguistics across Cultures: Applied Linguistics for Language Teachers.*

The first systematic statement of contrastive linguistics.

1957 B. F. Skinner. *Verbal Behavior.*

1957 Noam Chomsky. *Syntactic Structures.*

These three influential books which were published in the same year are discussed in Chapters 7, 8, and 15.

1957 The School for Applied Linguistics founded at the University of Edinburgh.

The founding of this centre, later merged with the University Department of Linguistics, initiated systematic studies in applied linguistics in Britain culminating in the seventies in the *Edinburgh Course in Applied Linguistics* (Allen and Corder 1973–1977).

1958 National Defense Education Act (NDEA).

Under this U.S.A. Act which was prompted by the Sputnik crisis of 1957 a large number of projects, related to linguistics, languages, and language teaching, were funded, for example, teaching materials development projects, test development, language 'institutes', and research.

1958 First experiment in a British grammar school with an audiovisual language course (Ingram and Mace 1959).

1959 Basic audiolingual materials in French, German, Italian, Russian, and Spanish produced under the direction of Mary Thompson by the Glastonbury Materials Project (later the A-LM materials).
The introduction of the tape recorder, the language laboratory, and the film strip projector in the fifties led to new types of programmes in which the mainstay was no longer the printed textbook.

1959 Center for Applied Linguistics (CAL) founded in Washington, D.C. In the same year its newsletter, *The Linguistic Reporter*, was established. See Chapter 4:55.

1960 Nelson Brooks. *Language and Language Learning.*
Nelson Brooks' views were influential in defining the new audiolingual approach. This book which was held in high regard for many years expressed the audiolingual theory most persuasively.

1960 Edward Stack. *The Language Laboratory and Modern Language Teaching.*
Another influential book: it provided detailed guidance on how to install, organize and use a language laboratory most effectively.

1961 Scherer-Wertheimer psycholinguistic experiment at the University of Colorado (Scherer and Wertheimer 1964).
See Chapter 4:56 on the context of this experiment.

1961 First language laboratory established in an educational institution in Great Britain, the Ealing Technical College.
By 1962, twenty language laboratories had been installed, in 1963 a hundred and sixteen, and by 1965 five hundred were in use in Britain (Stern 1966).

1961 CREDIF. *Voix et Images de France.* See Chapters 4:55 and 8:161.

1962 International meeting on languages in primary education, UNESCO Institute for Education (Hamburg) (Stern 1963, 1967).

1963 French Pilot Scheme and the Nuffield Language Project launched in Great Britain.

1963 Keating Report.
Research in the U.S.A. critical of the effectiveness of language laboratories (Keating 1963). See Chapter 4, Note 11.

1964 The Council for Cultural Co-operation of the Council of Europe initiates 'Major Project—Modern Languages'.

1964 International Conference on Modern Foreign Language Teaching, Berlin. (Müller 1965.)
This large international conference reflected many of the new trends of development in language pedagogy. At this conference Carroll (1966) expressed misgivings about the current language teaching theory and contrasted the audiolingual habit theory with the cognitive code learning approach. This distinction unwittingly contributed to the acrimonious controversies about the two approaches in the succeeding years.

1964 Committee on Research and Development in Modern Languages established in Great Britain. See Chapter 4, Note 8.

1964 M. A. K. Halliday, Angus McIntosh, and Peter Strevens. *The Linguistic Sciences and Language Teaching.*
The first major British work since Palmer bringing linguistics and language teaching into contact. See Chapters 8:164–5 and 21:482–5.

1964 Wilga Rivers. *The Psychologist and the Foreign Language Teacher.* See Chapter 15:324–7.
The first major work of a writer on language pedagogy who has influenced the thinking of many language teachers across the world for nearly two decades.

1964 International Association of Applied Linguistics established at a meeting in Nancy (France). (Actes du premier colloque, etc.)

1965 William F. Mackey. *Language Teaching Analysis.*
This work which re-interpreted the concept of method introduced a new analytical approach to the study of language pedagogy. See also Chapters 8:166 and 21:482–5.

1965 First French 'immersion' kindergarten class started in an anglophone elementary school in St Lambert, a suburb of Montreal, Canada, on the initiative of a parents group.
In the following years this experiment was extended upwards within the school; from about 1969 it also spread to a wide range of schools in other parts of Canada. From 1966, the immersion experiments were regularly evaluated. See Chapter 4 Note 13.

1966 Centre for Information on Language Teaching and Research (CILT) established in London.

1966 TESOL Association (Teaching of English to Speakers of Other Languages) founded in the U.S.A.

1966 Second international meeting on languages in primary education, UNESCO Institute for Education (Hamburg) (Stern 1969).

1966 Chomsky's address to language teachers at the Northeast Conference.
'I am, frankly, rather sceptical about the significance, for the teaching of languages, of such insights and understanding as have been attained in linguistics and psychology' (Chomsky 1966:43). See also Chapters 7, 14, and 15.

1967–1970 Report of the Royal Commission on Bilingualism and Biculturalism (Canada).
This report of a national commission attempted to resolve the differences between English and French population elements in Canada by means of rational enquiry and planning. As a result of the policy implications of this report, second language learning and bilingual education became important educational and policy issues in Canada between approximately 1969 and 1978.

1968 Bilingual Education Act (U.S.A.).

1968 Report on Pennsylvania Project completed and published (Smith 1970).

1968 Modern Language Centre of the Ontario Institute for Studies in Education established in Toronto (Canada).

1968 Wilga Rivers. *Teaching Foreign Language Skills.* See Chapters 5:76 and 21:477–82.

1969 Official Languages Act (Canada).
This Act established English and French as official languages at the Federal level across Canada.

Period IV: seventies and early eighties

The upheaval in linguistics and psycholinguistics created by Chomsky's transformational generative grammar had begun to affect language pedagogy by the mid-sixties. Around 1970 theorists were acutely aware of the loss of direction and the confusion of thought that had ensued. 'Where do we go from here?' was the title of an address by Rivers (1972) and around the same time Wardhaugh (1969a), the Director of the English Language Institute, Ann Arbor, Michigan, summarized his opinion on teaching of English as a second language in the following manner:

'... the present state of the art may be characterized by the word uncertainty. This uncertainty arises from the current ferment in those disciplines which underlie language teaching: linguistics, psychology, and pedagogy.' (op. cit.:6)

and he expressed his hopes for the future in these terms:

'Perhaps a new method will develop which will achieve the same kind of general approval as the Audiolingual Method, but at the moment there is no consensus as to what it would be like ...' (op. cit.:20).[11]

For some teachers the disorientation and the sense of decline in foreign language teaching persisted right through the decade.[12] Others, however, explored new directions. At least five major trends of development can be detected as characteristic of the seventies.

1. New methods
The developments of the decade of 1970–1980 can be interpreted as various reactions against the 'method concept' as the central issue in second language learning. The four trends we will consider below can be explained that way. In spite of the strong reaction against methods, however, and rather surprisingly, several new methods have aroused interest among teachers and the general public. The Silent Way, a language teaching method developed by Gattegno in the sixties, received more recognition in the seventies than before. Community Language Learning, a method also developed in the early sixties by Curran, found an equally receptive response in the seventies. Lastly, language learning by Suggestopaedia, a system developed by a Bulgarian psychiatrist, Lozanov, was widely discussed. Various experimental programmes, for example, in the Canadian Public Service, gave the suggestopaedic method a great deal of public attention and publicity in the newspapers and magazines under such sensational titles as 'superlearning'.

The sudden interest in these different methods was unexpected in that it ran counter to the break with the method concept manifested in the other developments of the decade.

2. New approaches to language curricula
One of the most powerful trends of development of the decade was a shift from a concern with teaching methods to one with language teaching objectives, language content, and curriculum (or syllabus) design. In Britain in particular, a number of applied linguists, such as Allen, Candlin, Corder, Widdowson, Wilkins, and others, experimented with a variety of new ideas, mainly derived from discourse analysis, speech act theory, and other new developments in linguistics and sociolinguistics. A novel and influential approach to the language curriculum was made by an international group of scholars meeting regularly throughout the seventies under the auspices of a committee of the Council for Cultural Co-operation of the Council of Europe. Their work culminated in the publication of the *Threshold Level* syllabuses in

English (van Ek 1975), French (Coste *et al.* 1976), Spanish (Slagter 1979), and German (Baldegger *et al.* 1981) as well as in various writings which proved seminal, for example, Wilkins (1976), Richterich and Chancerel (1978/1980), Trim (1980), and Trim *et al.* (1980). See also Chapter 4:66.

Other promising changes to the language curriculum were tried as well. The Canadian experiment on French immersion between 1965 and 1980 illustrates one such new approach. While it seemed at first a mainly Canadian response to a Canadian language problem, its wider implications were increasingly recognized by the end of the seventies (for example, Stern 1978). In Britain and other European countries the concept of *languages for special purposes* gained momentum as a way of catering for the language needs of professionals and university students (Strevens 1977a). Through individualized learning activity packets, 'modules' and the like, through graded examinations, through differentiated proficiency objectives and needs analyses, attempts were made to meet the varying language needs of many students in a more flexible and diversified approach to the curriculum.

3. Human relations and individualization in the language class

Another reaction to the inconclusive teaching method debate of the sixties was to focus more on the learner as an individual and as a person. In the U.S.A. the concern about declining enrolments and the general unrest among student populations in many western countries between 1968 and 1972 prompted experiments with individualization of instruction as a way of language teaching. Others, reacting against the mechanical and 'cold' drill techniques of language training of the previous era, attempted to sensitize teachers to human values and human relations in the language class, and to create an awareness of the hidden curriculum of the social and affective climate created by the interaction among students and between students and the teachers. This interest in human relations explains why, during this period language learning systems, which more or less deliberately manipulate this teacher-learner relationship, aroused such widespread interest, particularly in North America: Gattegno's Silent Way, Curran's Community Language Learning, and Lozanov's Suggestopaedia.

4. Language learning research

A fourth response of the seventies to the method polemics was already mentioned in Chapter 4: the disillusionment over the teaching method debate and the inconclusiveness of the method research prompted a number of theorists to demand a search for a deeper understanding of the nature of the second language learning process itself. Research on second language learning was initiated with great vigour and enthusiasm especially in several North American university centres.[13]

5. *Communicative language teaching*

From the mid-seventies the key concept that has epitomized the practical, theoretical, and research preoccupations in educational linguistics and language pedagogy is that of communication or communicative competence. The term 'communicative competence', first used by Hymes (for example, 1972) in deliberate contrast to Chomsky's 'linguistic competence', reflects the social view of language which has found increasing acceptance since the middle of the sixties. The various trends, outlined above, and the concept of communicative competence have merged in the idea of communicative language teaching as a central focus for new thought and fresh approaches in language pedagogy in the early eighties.[14]

The following names, dates, and events characterize this period:

1970 *Language in Education in Eastern Africa* (Gorman 1970).
One of several language surveys which were carried out in Africa during this period. See Chapter 11, Note 16.

1971 Stanford Conference on Individualizing Foreign Language Instruction (Altman and Politzer 1971).

1971 Rüschlikon Symposium.
First of several meetings organized by the Council of Europe to start a project on a flexible European language curriculum for adult learners. For further meetings see below 1973 St Wolfgang and 1977 Ludwigs-hafen-am-Rhein.

1972 Savignon publishes a seminal experiment on a communicative approach to foreign language teaching (Savignon 1972).

1972 Lambert and Tucker (1972) review the first five years of the St Lambert project in bilingual education ('immersion').

1973 St Wolfgang Symposium, the second meeting on European language projects.

1973–1975 A major research project in Canada on immersion and other alternative approaches to teaching French as a second language (Stern *et al.* 1976a; Harley 1976).

1974–1975 OISE Modern Language Centre undertakes research on the good second language learner (Naiman *et al.* 1978).

1974 NFER completes ten-year research on languages for young school children with controversial report, *Primary French in the Balance* (Burstall *et al.* 1974).

1975 Symposium at University of Michigan on language learning research (Brown 1976).

1975 International comparative studies on English (Lewis and Massad 1975) and French (Carroll 1975) as second languages completed under the auspices of the International Association for the Evaluation of Educational Achievement (IEA).

1975 Jan van Ek, *Threshold Level* English syllabus is published.

1976 David A. Wilkins. *Notional Syllabuses.*
A small but influential book on notional-functional approaches to language learning.

1976 A French team, led by Daniel Coste, produces the French equivalent to van Ek's English curriculum: *Un niveau-seuil* (Coste *et al.* 1976).

1977 Third meeting, held at Ludwigshafen-am-Rhein, on the European Modern Language Project as an information session on achievements to date and on plans for future development.

1978 Henry G. Widdowson. *Teaching Language as Communication.*

1978–1979 U.S.A.: President's Commission on Foreign Language and International Studies.
This Commission was formed because of a public concern over the lack of American human resources in foreign languages and international studies. The report makes sweeping policy recommendations to remedy weaknesses in this area.

1980 Three scholarly new journals initiated: *Applied Linguistics*; *Applied Psycholinguistics*; and the *Journal of Multilingual and Multicultural Development*, reflecting the intense theoretical and empirical research interests in the language area, and the intention to back up policy with language research.

Conclusion

The developments we have briefly sketched can be summarized in the following chart. The table suggests that innovations which began about 100 years ago and have been going on ever since led to intensive theoretical debate and experimentation in the sixties, bringing about in the seventies four different strands, one of which continues the search for new methods, while the others, following the lead of Mackey's Method Analysis and the critique of methods implied in the research studies on teaching methods, looked for new emphases in curriculum design, human relations, or in the lessons of learning research. Towards 1980, the concept of communication was a rallying point for these different strands. But this does not mean that this concept has given us a genuine synthesis. In any case, it may not be desirable to attempt to build a language teaching theory around a single concept.[15]

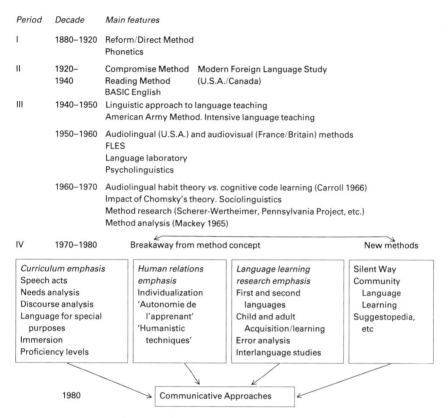

Period	Decade	Main features	
I	1880–1920	Reform/Direct Method Phonetics	
II	1920– 1940	Compromise Method Reading Method BASIC English	Modern Foreign Language Study (U.S.A./Canada)
III	1940–1950	Linguistic approach to language teaching American Army Method. Intensive language teaching	
	1950–1960	Audiolingual (U.S.A.) and audiovisual (France/Britain) methods FLES Language laboratory Psycholinguistics	
	1960–1970	Audiolingual habit theory *vs.* cognitive code learning (Carroll 1966) Impact of Chomsky's theory. Sociolinguistics Method research (Scherer-Wertheimer, Pennsylvania Project, etc.) Method analysis (Mackey 1965)	
IV	1970–1980	Breakaway from method concept	New methods

Curriculum emphasis	Human relations emphasis	Language learning research emphasis	Silent Way
Speech acts	Individualization	First and second	Community
Needs analysis	'Autonomie de	languages	Language
Discourse analysis	l'apprenant'	Child and adult	Learning
Language for special	'Humanistic	Acquisition/learning	Suggestopedia,
purposes	techniques'	Error analysis	etc
Immersion		Interlanguage studies	
Proficiency levels			

1980 → Communicative Approaches

Figure 6.1   Change and innovation in language teaching: 1880–1980

Finally, it should again be pointed out that what we have presented is a highly selective sketch which of necessity is interpretive and subjective. Nevertheless, it gives our theorizing some perspective. It is imperative that such personal reviews are matched by historical research studies. The kinds of study one would like to see done include:

1 bibliographical enquiries to establish and evaluate existing historical studies;
2 detailed and well documented studies of language teaching and learning in given periods in particular countries within the European language tradition;
3 similar studies of countries outside the European tradition, including both studies of language learning *before* the European approach to language teaching exercised its influence, as well as studies of the influence of the European tradition (for example, French or English teaching in African and Asian countries);
4 studies of major trends or events in the recent history of language

teaching, for example, the reform movement at the turn of the century; the history of the direct method; American language experience during World War II; the development of *français fondamental*; audiolingualism in the early sixties; the history of the British Pilot Scheme on French in primary education;

5 following Kelly's work, in-depth studies of particular aspects of language teaching;

6 biographical and critical studies of the personalities, ideas, and influence of great language teachers and thinkers in this field;

7 a critical review of historical introductions to writings on language teaching;

8 following the idea expressed by Fraenkel (1969), historical studies of language *learning*, based on a systematic review of historical biographies and autobiographies;

9 lastly, based on the types of studies suggested in (1) to (8), a well-documented, research-oriented critical general history of language teaching and learning.

In conclusion, let us remind ourselves that the main purpose of an historical approach is to ensure that the totality of past and present developments in pedagogy—theory, research, and practice—is not lost but constitutes a constant source and resource for our theory of language teaching.

Notes

1 For Germany see Rülcker (1969) and for England, Gilbert (1954).

2 Rülcker (1969), for example, includes a table, covering the period 1880–1900 and after, of thirty-one names of exponents of the reform movement, divided into early and later 'radicals' and 'moderates' as well as opponents of the movement after 1900.

3 Gilbert (1955:8) writes about Paul Passy, one of the co-authors of this book: 'Passy was perhaps the most famous French phonetician. His book, *Les Sons du Français*, first published in 1887 and since translated into many languages, has become a classic. He initiated in 1886 *Le Maître Phonétique*, a monthly journal which soon became the organ of the International Phonetic Association, also founded by him in the same year. The principles which this body pledged itself to support resemble closely those of the German reformers and of Gouin. They are still printed on the back of *Le Maître Phonétique*. Passy, in the first number of this journal in 1886, says that the object is to further the spread of the New Method, as he calls it, to discuss its principles, and to give specimens of foreign languages in the "International Phonetic Alphabet", drawn up by him after consultation with the members of the International Phonetic Association ...

Passy developed his ideas in more detail in his section of the book, *De la Méthode Directe dans l'enseignement des langues vivantes*, written by Laudenbach, Passy, and Delobel.'

4 A useful status study for this period and somewhat beyond is a three-part review of language teaching between 1928 and 1948 in English secondary schools made by Ewing (1949–50).

5 For a comprehensive bibliography on the Modern Foreign Language Study see Fife (1931, 1933).

6 For an interesting review and assessment of Basic English see Chapter 2 'Les origines philosophiques du Basic English' in Gougenheim *et al.* 1964.

7 Among several status studies for this period an outstanding one for 1940–1960 is Moulton (1961/1963). The excitement of promising new developments in Britain in the early sixties is conveyed by Stern (1966). Halls (1970) reviews language teaching in nineteen European countries. A European perspective is also provided by Strevens (1972). The crisis in language teaching theory of the late sixties is analysed by Norris (1971) and Wardhaugh (1969a).

8 For a concise discussion of American wartime language training and its influence consult Moulton (1961/1963) who also provides the main references.

9 Published by the British Council from 1946–1960 and since 1961 by the Oxford University Press in association with the British Council.

10 The significance of the creation of this journal for a research approach was mentioned in Chapter 4.

11 For explanations of this change in intellectual climate surrounding language teaching between 1960 and 1970 see the writer's AILA paper 1972 'Directions in Language Teaching Theory and Research' (Stern 1974).

12 An editorial in the *Audio-Visual Language Journal* commented in 1978: 'The seventies have not, in some ways, been the happiest in Britain.' A stock-taking study in 1976 talked about 'a serious and ironically inopportune crisis in language learning in the U.K.' (Bearne and James 1976).

13 This research (see also Chapter 4:57), will be explained in greater detail in Part 5: see particularly Chapter 15.

14 Breen and Candlin (1980, forthcoming) have interpreted language pedagogy in its entirety—curriculum, classroom activities, teacher training—in communicative terms. Several other theorists reject the idea of a single concept becoming once again the overriding preoccupation of language pedagogy. The advocacy of an eclectic approach (for example, Grittner 1977; Rivers 1981) or a multi-dimensional theory, suggested by the present work, counteracts this tendency while recognizing the contribution of the communicative component.

15 For the fourth period, 1970–1980, the following are suggested as status studies: Diller (1975) and Stern (1979). Several among the *Background Papers and Studies* for the President's Commission on Foreign Language and International Studies (U.S.A. 1979a) are useful as status studies for this period, in particular a paper by Warriner (1979) and one by Benseler and Schulz (1979). See also Alatis, Altman, and Alatis (1981). For documentation on the Council of Europe project, see, for example, Trim *et al.* (1980). In Britain the National Congress on Languages in Education provides overviews, although those that were published after the first assembly of this congress tended to be policy statements rather than status studies; however, they give impressions of the state of affairs as it was in Britain around 1980 (Perren 1979, 1979a). Certain concerns about language teaching in Britain at that time are reflected in a study about modern languages in comprehensive schools undertaken by H.M.I.s (H.M.I. Series 1977). Communication as a key concept in language teaching is discussed, among others, by Widdowson (1978), Brumfit and Johnson (1979), Canale and Swain (1980) and in several articles in Alatis, Altman, and Alatis (1981).

PART THREE

Concepts of language

7   Trends in linguistic theory

As soon as we try to learn a language, we come up against the most fundamental questions about the nature of language. What is 'language'? How should we set about learning a language? What is the best way of dividing up this enormous task and of arranging the various features which we recognize as parts of a language? One cannot teach or learn a language for long without being faced with some of the great puzzles about the nature of language that have baffled the great thinkers since antiquity. Even the youngest pupil may sometimes present his teacher with the most profound issues: How long will it take us to learn the *whole* language? Are all the words in the dictionary? Why are there so many exceptions? The 'theory' of language with which the teacher operates may not be consciously formulated; it may simply be implicit in the teaching traditions, in the concepts employed to talk about languages, in the way textbooks are arranged, or in the content and format of dictionaries and grammars; but it is hardly imaginable that a language could be taught without *some* underlying conception of the general nature of language.

Linguistics constitutes the most systematic study of language at our disposal. The obvious reason, then, for considering the role of linguistics in relation to language teaching is that both in different ways have to do with language. It would be unreasonable for language teaching theory to disregard what linguistics has to say about language. Whether the teacher accepts what the linguist has to offer and how the relationship to linguistics is best regulated is another matter. To explore this issue is what we set out to do in this and the next two chapters. In the course of the review of recent trends we observed that language teaching theory has been strongly affected and, at a certain stage, even thrown into confusion by recent developments in linguistics. That is why the role of linguistics needs clarifying. In the present chapter linguistics will be considered as a study in its own right. Points of contact with language teaching will be mentioned. We will see that there are sometimes differences in the ways linguists and language teachers view language, and sometimes there are similarities. There is no suggestion here that linguistics provides the 'right' way of treating language and that language teachers should necessarily follow it. Nor is there any suggestion that where language teachers see things the same way as linguists do that they have followed the lessons of linguistics like obedient pupils. The whole complicated question of the relationship of linguistics to language teaching will be examined in Chapters 8 and 9.

Beginnings of modern linguistics

Linguistics as an independent field of study, a university discipline with different specializations within it and areas of application, with its own professional organizations, journals, and scholarly meetings, is a creation of the twentieth century, and more specially a phenomenon of the period after World War II. The study of language in the Western world—not to speak of the East—is of course not at all new; it goes back many centuries to Greek and Roman antiquity and biblical times. Indeed many of the concepts we use today in the language classroom as simple technical terms of language instruction such as 'gender', 'number', 'case', or 'person', ultimately derive from Greek and medieval linguistic philosophy. But in past ages questions about the nature of language were studied as part of other scholarly activities, in connection with philosophy, theology, rhetoric, and not unexpectedly the teaching of Latin, Greek, and Hebrew.[1]

It was from the late eighteenth century that language in general and languages other than the great classical ones, Greek, Latin, and Hebrew, became objects of scientific enquiry. Historical and comparative linguistics attempted to describe and explain the historical changes which languages undergo and to build up scientifically attested knowledge of the evolution of languages and dialects and the relations among them. The scholars compared language forms of ancient and modern languages, described the changes ('sound shifts') that occurred and formulated explanations or 'laws' to account for these changes. Ultimately it was hoped to reconstruct from comparisons among different languages of Europe and Asia an Indo-European protolanguage or *Ursprache* from which many of the Indo-European languages could then be said to have descended. The linguistic scholar thus became aware, above all, of the modern form of languages as the result of a long process of historical evolution. Comparative philology—like modern linguistics—studied natural languages as objects of scientific enquiry, formulated hypotheses, looked for empirical evidence, and in so doing gathered an enormous body of information on the natural languages of the world. A new science of language was clearly in the making. Although future language teachers as students in European universities, towards the end of the nineteenth century, were trained in comparative philology, there was little in this new knowledge that was directly relevant to second language learning. Some language teachers felt encouraged to include in their teaching historical information, for example, on the etymology of words, or to draw attention to regularities in the relations among languages by making comparisons between the student's language and the target language or by comparing two second languages. Mostly, however, philological scholarship had little bearing on the teaching of modern or classical languages and teachers relied principally on prevailing traditional forms of language study.

Towards the end of the century the emergence of phonetics introduced several new elements of particular interest to language teachers. First, it expressed a recognition of the importance of *speech* in language study. Second, it offered a scientific approach to the *contemporary* form of the language. Third, it was a study applicable to *any* language; phonetics therefore opened up the possibility of an empirical study of language in general. The idea of an *international* phonetic script was a tangible expression of the desire to develop an appropriate tool for linguistic investigations across different languages. Lastly, as was already seen in the example of the IPA articles in Chapter 5, phonetics was seen as directly relevant to second language learning.

Around the same period several linguists recognized as an important step in linguistic scholarship to transcend the knowledge that had accumulated about the evolution of different languages and language families and to formulate general statements about the nature of language.[2] In 1906, the Swiss linguist Ferdinand de Saussure was asked to offer a course in 'general linguistics' at the University of Geneva where he had previously taught Sanskrit and comparative philology. We are told that he was terrified by this assignment because he felt inadequate to this task. He offered the course three times, for the last time in 1910–1911. He died in 1913, without having written any book or monograph on general linguistics. Two of his former students, however, Charles Bally and Albert Sechehaye, published in 1916 the *Cours de Linguistique Générale de Ferdinand de Saussure* on the basis of notes taken by students during the three courses. The book by Bally and Sechehaye is considered by most linguists today as the work that has initiated modern linguistics. It defines the nature of language and sets out principles of language study.[3]

Characterization of linguistics today

We have mentioned only a few names and events in order to suggest the background of scholarly study against which modern linguistics has gradually evolved. In the period between 1920 and 1970, it acquired certain characteristics to which linguists commonly draw attention. In describing them it is useful to compare them with views of language that are not infrequently found among language educators.

Linguistics is usually defined as 'the science of language' or 'the systematic study of language'. As a science it cultivates a rational outlook upon language. The linguist takes an objective view of language and all linguistic phenomena. In that respect linguistics follows the tradition set by the study of comparative philology in the nineteenth century. But it differs from the approach to language often cultivated in schools. Educators frequently recognize the 'good' or 'bad', the 'right' or 'wrong' in language and point out the value of a creative approach to the use of language. They express respect for language in works of literature. They may also appreciate the therapeutic and releasing value of the use of language. Value judgements about languages are quite common: 'French is a beautiful language.' 'Language X sounds ugly.' An objective approach to language is often condemned. The study of grammar is frequently described as 'dull' or 'arid'. Linguists do not deny that language use has a strongly emotional component and that language can be valued aesthetically. But as linguists they study language and reflect on it in a detached and dispassionate way: 'This is the way L_x functions.' 'This is the way L_y is.' 'This is a characteristic of all languages. It is a language universal,' and so on.

Linguistics is a *theoretical* science. It formulates explanations which are designed to account for the phenomena of language. For many linguistic scholars the central purpose of linguistics is the development of theories on aspects of language and a general theory of language. The nineteenth century linguists, too, had been interested in making general statements about language; but these tended to be laws accounting for phenomena in particular languages or groups of languages rather than about the nature of language in general.

Here is an obvious difference between a language teacher and a linguist. The language educator is concerned with the teaching of a particular language, for example, French, English, or Chinese, or some aspect of the language, for example, reading in English. His main concern usually is not language in general, although teaching a particular language offers good opportunities for making observations on the nature of language.[4] It has in fact been said that one of the best ways of understanding the nature of language is to try to teach (or learn) a language!

Theories in linguistics, as in other disciplines, demand verification: do the statements made about language explain the phenomena encountered in natural languages? Linguistics is not only theoretical. It is also an *empirical* science making detailed observations on particular languages to confirm or refute generalizations. Linguistics, therefore, observes and analyses data found in natural languages, following the general principles of empirical research procedures that have already been discussed in Part 1. Linguistics is accordingly not only a *theoretical* but also a *descriptive* discipline.

These two characteristics are in no way antithetical; on the contrary, they support each other. But the emphasis on theory or description has varied among the scholars. Some regard the descriptive tasks as the primary object of linguistics. Linguistics is for them a largely 'taxonomic' science like botany, concerned with the identification and ordering of many observations—of plants in botany or language data in linguistics. Others regard the theoretical statements about language, the discovery of language 'universals', and, thus, the creation of an understanding of the essential nature of language as the most important preoccupation of linguists. As we shall see, these two strands, the theoretical *and* the descriptive, are both of importance to language teaching, too.[5]

The descriptiveness of linguistics is not only constrasted with *theoretical* concerns. It stands also in contrast to the *normative* nature of much language study. As a scientist the linguist accepts language as he finds it. His job is to observe what is and to explain why it is so. It is not his function to improve the language, to prevent deterioration, to warn against its corruption by the cultivation of 'good usage'. 'The study of linguistics is a descriptive, not a prescriptive, science' (Lyons 1968:42). This feature which is commonly stressed in introductions to the subject contrasts a scientific study of language with a normative approach to it— perfectly legitimate in its place, for example, in language teaching and other forms of language education, but not one that linguistics as a science adopts. From the linguist's point of view 'a language is what the speakers do and not what someone thinks they ought to do' (Bloomfield 1942:16). 'Prescriptiveness', however, cannot altogether be dismissed from linguistics in that the native speaker's right ('grammatical') or wrong ('ungrammatical') usage is the yardstick by which linguistics must be guided. The native speaker's judgement also constitutes the norm which must guide (and is therefore prescriptive for) the second language teacher and the second language learner.[6]

Synchronic versus diachronic treatment
In the nineteenth century the dominant approach to any scientific study of language was historical. Saussure was the first to formulate clearly an alternative approach, namely that a language can and should also be studied at a particular point in time with an emphasis on how the different parts of the language hang together and interact. He therefore advocated that the 'diachronic' or evolutionary approach be matched by a static or 'synchronic' study of a given state of the language. Twentieth century linguistic studies are characterized by the predominance of synchronic treatment. Implicit in most second language teaching is the approach to a given state of the language, mostly its contemporary form.

The view of language in modern linguistics

In principle, linguistics is concerned with all languages and every aspect of language. The linguist makes no value judgements about languages.

A 'local' vernacular[7] which has few native speakers may be of no less interest to his investigations—it may even be more so—than a world language.[8]

Within a language he acknowledges the existence of the spoken or written mode. According to older school traditions, the written form was regarded of greater worth, because it was more permanent and more clearly defined and regular. Literacy was (and still is) a key issue for schooling; and as a vehicle of literary expression the written form received most attention. By contrast, modern linguistics has stressed the priority of speech because '[it] is the "natural," or primary, *medium* in which language is manifest, and written language derives from the transference of speech to a secondary, visual medium' (Lyons 1970:18). The importance of written language is not denied. Especially in literate societies the written language may acquire a considerable independence from the spoken language. Again, however, the linguist attempts to deal with this aspect of language as he finds it: as speech and writing, independent of each other, or in relation to each other. The complexity of the relationship between language as speech or writing has in recent years also been widely recognized in language education.[9]

Language varieties
The linguist also recognizes, and accepts without value judgement, the existence of language varieties, such as regional dialects and social dialects (or sociolects). Here again school traditions—certainly in the past, perhaps less so today—have tended to emphasize a single 'correct' standard form, to inculcate that standard, and to downgrade variations. Linguistics acknowledges as a social fact that a certain dialect may be treated by society as a standard form (for example, standard British English, standard North American English) or is regarded as prestigious by some members of a society (for example, 'King's English', 'Oxford accent'), whereas another is treated as socially inferior or condemned as 'provincial', 'lower class', or 'vulgar'. But the interest of the linguist can be focused, without condescension or condemnation, on non-prestigious as well as prestigious language varieties.

In this connection, it is worth noting that linguists in recent decades have become more and more interested in the language of people who, by a rigid conception of a standard language, do not talk 'properly': the language of small children and foreigners. The study of child language has therefore a *linguistic* interest quite apart from its psychological interest as the development of speech in infancy. In the same way the 'mixed' languages of former European colonies, pidgins and creoles, for example, Jamaican Creole based on English or Haitian Creole based on French, have been studied with the same interest as can be studied standard French or English (for example, Valdman 1977).

Since about 1970, a language variety that has been examined as a language system with its own rules and characteristics is the variety that second language learners develop. Such studies are usually referred to as 'interlanguage' studies or the study of 'learner languages'. The concept of interlanguage was suggested by Selinker (1972) in order to draw attention to the possibility that the learner's language can be regarded as a distinct language variety or system with its own particular characteristics and rules. As teachers, we have been accustomed, in the past, to look upon the learner's language merely as 'wrong' English or 'wrong' French to be eradicated without paying too much attention to the characteristics of the 'interlanguage'. Whether it is right to consider the learner's language as a 'language' is debatable, but the attempt to do so illustrates the linguist's intention of understanding all kinds of language varieties. (See Corder 1981).

Another relevant language variety that has lately also been examined is the language use which native speakers adopt when talking *to* babies and *to* foreigners: 'baby talk' and 'foreigner talk' are characterized by certain simplifications of language that may have universal features (for example, Ferguson 1975).

Different situations, interests, occupations, or social roles demand different uses of language. A number of concepts are employed in linguistics—especially in that branch of linguistics which relates the study of language to the study of society, sociolinguistics—to indicate these functional variations and choices within one language: style, register, domain, and code. *Styles*, for example, have been classified from 'high' to 'low' on a five-point scale: frozen, formal, consultative, casual, and intimate (Joos 1961). *Register* refers to varieties of a language according to differences in uses demanded by specific *social situations*, such as advertising, church service, political journalism, shopping, or academic discussion (Halliday, McIntosh, and Strevens 1964). Linguists have also observed that different topics, for example, nuclear physics, detective stories, or knitting, impose characteristic uses of the language; accordingly attempts have been made to identify the language appropriate to different *domains* or *fields of discourse*.

A native speaker is of course at home in various styles, registers, or domains. Collectively the different varieties of language may be looked upon as different *codes*; in analogy to bilingualism it is reasonable to describe native speakers who master more than one such code as 'bicodal' or 'multicodal'. According to function and situation, the native speaker will intuitively engage in *code-switching*. The 'foreigner talk' or 'baby talk' that has just been mentioned can be regarded as a 'code' we use in the right circumstances.

Questions of the choice of dialect or other variety arise regularly in language teaching. Should the English class be taught American or

British English? Which variety of French or Spanish or Arabic should be selected?[10]

The recognition of relatively distinct linguistic varieties has brought about in language pedagogy many attempts to make a deliberate choice of a variety of language which is most relevant to particular groups of learners. The so-called LSP approach (language for special purposes: for example, English for Special Purposes, English for Science and Technology, English for Academic Purposes) is in part an application of this view of language varieties (for example, Strevens 1977a).

Language as a system or structure

A consequence of the synchronic approach, advocated by Saussure, has been that language in modern linguistics is looked upon as a system of relationships or as an elaborate structure of mutually supporting parts, arranged in some hierarchical order. 'A language is a highly integrated system' (Langacker 1972:18). In that sense all modern linguistics, regardless of the particular school of thought, is 'structural'. A linguistic description identifies and explains the units or constituent elements that make up the language and shows how they interrelate and interact. It is therefore not enough to accumulate and enumerate observations on the language. The linguist aspires to reveal the workings of a language as a unified system, and it is here that the arguments among different schools of thought arise.

As language teachers we equally are interested in viewing a language as a coherent and well-defined system because, unless we have a conceptual scheme of what a language is, we cannot plan to teach it. It is beside the point whether the scheme is to be understood by the learner; that is an issue which presents itself as a question of methodology. But for planning language teaching, a view of a language as a coherent structure is unavoidable and therefore the linguist's effort to develop schemes of this kind is of great interest to language pedagogy.

A consequence of the view of language as a structure is that linguistics operates largely with relational concepts. Among these the principle of *contrast* or *opposition* is of particular importance in linguistic theory. This principle was first developed in phonology but it is equally applicable in other areas of linguistics. For example, in the following words— to borrow Lyons' (1968) example—

bet, pet, bed, pit, bid, bit

it is not the absolute quality of each sound unit that distinguishes one from another but the opposition of /b/ to /p/, /d/ to /t/, /b/ to /d/, /p/ to /t/, of all consonants to all vowels, and within the vowel system the distinction between /i/ and /e/ which signal the differences in meaning. 'Dans la langue il n'y a que des différences' (Saussure 1916:166).

Another relational set of concepts, *syntagmatic* versus *paradigmatic* relations, has also acquired much importance in linguistics.

Saussure offers as examples of the syntagmatic relationship combinations of morphemes, words, and clauses, for example, *re-lire, contre tous, la vie humaine, s'il fait beau temps, nous sortirons*. The quality of language units to combine is *syntagmatic*.

Within an utterance a particular item, for example, 'he' in 'He is coming' forms part of a system of pronouns ('she', 'you', 'they', etc.) which constitute a paradigm. In the same utterance 'is' forms part of another paradigm consisting of the items 'am', 'is', and 'are'. Or to use Saussure's illustration, the French word *enseignement* can form part of a number of paradigms. It may be associated with *enseigner, renseigner* or with *armement*, and *changement*, or with *éducation* and *apprentissage*. These *paradigmatic* relationships are associative; that is they may be evoked in the mind of the language user, whereas the syntagmatic relationship is visible or audible in the utterance. Saussure has compared the distinction between these two concepts to looking at a pillar in a building. We can study the function of the pillar in the construction, i.e., what part of the building it holds up (syntagmatic); or it may evoke in the beholder the idea that it is a Doric and not a Corinthian pillar (associative or paradigmatic).

Language teachers have employed practice techniques which indicate that intuitively they are familiar with this duality in language. Traditional practice tended to emphasize the paradigmatic aspect, particularly in the teaching of grammar (*je suis, tu es, il est*). Since the forties, practice techniques have shifted towards an emphasis on syntagmatic relations, particularly through sentence pattern drills to the point of tabooing the paradigm as a legitimate teaching device.

Langue and parole

A distinction of great importance to modern linguistics—and also to language teaching theory—that, like the previous set of terms, was first developed in Saussure's course, is that between language as a system or structure, *langue*, and the use of that language in utterances, *parole*. So far, we have taken for granted the object of linguistic study, language. But we must ask what precisely does linguistics study when, following Bloomfield (1942), we say that linguistics studies 'what the native speaker says'? Which native speaker? Any or all? We have already noted that linguistics is prepared to recognize varieties within languages, social and regional dialects, registers, styles, and so on. Suppose we wish to undertake a synchronic study of the *état de langue* of one language, say, French today: does the 'corpus' of utterances to be investigated comprise everything that all native speakers have uttered in speech and writing in French on one day? The sheer impossibility of this undertaking helps us to understand the usefulness of the distinction between *langue* and *parole*.

The object of study for linguistics is not principally the mass of individual utterances, *parole*, but the underlying system, *langue*, shared by all the speakers of the language as a first language or of the variety of the language under investigation.

Similar pairs of concepts have been developed by a number of theorists; they can be tabulated as follows:

Langue	*Parole*
system	use
code	message
language	verbal behaviour
competence	performance
·form	function

Information theory operates with the concept of the *code*, i.e., the system of communication which is employed, for example, Morse code, semaphore, linguistic code, in order to send *messages*. As this simplified model of the act of communication indicates (adapted from Osgood and Sebeok 1954/1965:1–3), both sender (source) and receiver (destination) must already be familiar with the code if the message to be sent is to be encoded at the source and to be decoded and understood by the receiver.

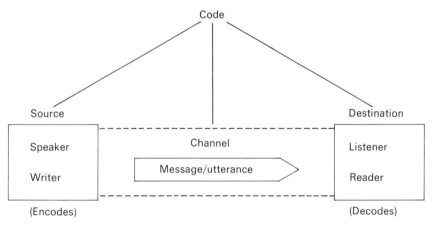

Figure 7.1   Model of the communicative act (adapted from Osgood and Sebeok)

A language as a system of communication can, minimally, be likened to a 'code' which is shared by individuals for the purpose of transmitting 'messages'. According to this analogy, linguistics—if we adopt Saussure's emphasis on *langue*—is principally concerned with describing the code, the system of formal rules, which manifests itself in the utterances or messages. Applying the same analogy to language teaching, the purpose of the language class is to teach the 'code', i.e., the second language, so that the learner can encode (speak/write) or decode (listen/read) the second language.

Rejecting the *parole-langue* distinction, Skinner (1957) in a challenging book on verbal behaviour adopted a strictly behaviouristic point of view and argued that the only observable object of scientific study is the verbal behaviour, the speech utterances and texts (i.e., *parole*). *Langue* according to Skinner, is a mentalistic and unscientific abstraction. His work on verbal behaviour is an attempt to account for all linguistic activities entirely within terms of overt and observable events without any appeal to an 'underlying system'.

The *competence-performance* distinction was introduced by Chomsky. 'Performance' refers to the infinitely varied individual acts of verbal behaviour with their irregularities, inconsistencies, and errors. The capacity of the individual to abstract from these acts of performance and to develop system and order is competence. Chomsky has made the point that the language user himself must possess intuitively and unconsciously this capacity to abstract from the concrete manifestations of language. According to Chomsky, the task of linguistics is to study competence, the knowledge of the language, or 'the underlying system of rules that has been mastered by the speaker-hearer' (Chomsky 1965:4).

It is a debatable issue in linguistics whether to lay emphasis mainly or exclusively on *langue* or equally on *parole*, or perhaps on the relationship between the two. The Chomskyan emphasis on competence has been questioned: to what extent, it has been asked, can an underlying language 'knowledge' be separated from language use? In language teaching theory, too, the question of language system versus use goes to the heart of the debate on teaching methods where, as we shall see, the distinction between a 'formal' treatment of the language as an abstract system and a 'functional' or communicative treatment of the language in use is a crucial issue.[11]

Aspects of language study

The basic problem for linguistics—as for language teaching—is how to come to grips with this vast totality that we call a language. We can hopefully represent it as a 'system' or 'structure'. But to make the system or structure accessible, visible, and learnable is quite another matter. It is clear that a scientific approach demands some ordering and restricting of the events to be investigated. Which aspects of language need the most intensive study? What construct or model would reveal most clearly and economically the structure of language and its parts? How do different parts relate to each other? What concepts are needed in language description? In trying to answer these questions, linguistics sets out from simple concepts which are quite familiar to language teachers, and even to the layman as a language user, such as 'speech sound', 'word', 'sentence', 'meaning', and 'text'. These common-sense features correspond roughly to the major areas of linguistic investigation and each is represented in one or the other of the branches of linguistics:

1 speech sounds   in phonetics and phonology
2 words   in lexicology, semantics, and morphology
3 sentences   in syntax
4 meaning   in semantics
5 text (dialogue,
  narrative, poem)   in discourse analysis

In the course of the twentieth century the scientific emphasis has gradually shifted from the study of speech sounds (phonetics and phonology) to grammar (morphology and syntax) then to meaning (semantics) and the study of texts (discourse analysis). Linguists have of course always been aware of the fact that in language all aspects are involved. But the answer to the question which it is necessary or most rewarding to investigate *scientifically* has varied in emphasis over the decades. But there has been a cumulative development so that one may find today that, collectively, there are scholars interested in any of these aspects.

Phonology

It is understandable that, in the early stages of modern linguistics, the most noticeable features of language, the speech sounds, were the first to be studied in the new science which had to find out how to study language empirically. Today *phonetics* and *phonology* are two well established sub-disciplines of linguistics or are considered disciplines in their own right. A distinction between phonetics and phonology has gradually emerged. Phonetics studies the articulatory and acoustic phenomena which make it possible to produce and perceive speech sounds. It provides us with a tool, a set of descriptive terms, by which we can describe, as minutely as is necessary for the task in hand, a particular physical sound and the gestures which produce it (Brown 1975:99). Phonetics studies speech sounds as such regardless of particular language systems. In methods and concepts it draws on a wide range of relevant disciplines, including anatomy, physiology, physics, and psychology. Phonology is a more strictly linguistic discipline which investigates the sound *systems* of particular languages and develops general principles applicable to the sound systems of all languages. Phonology is less concerned with the analysis of concrete and individual manifestations of sounds (*phones*), the performance, or *parole* element produced by different speakers than with the systematic distinctions, the *langue* or competence element, produced by the meaning-carrying sound units (*phonemes*) which characterize the sound systems of particular languages. Phonetics can be considered as helpful to pronunciation teaching in that it provides the teacher with a diagnostic understanding of how speech sounds are produced. Phonology is needed to understand what constitutes the sound system of a particular language.[12]

Grammar

During a major part of the twentieth century, approximately between 1925 and 1965, linguistics gave attention increasingly to the second theme, *grammar*, which proved to be one of the most productive and most controversial areas for linguistic analysis. Grammar, a somewhat ambiguous term today, has been defined as 'that branch of the description of languages which accounts for the way in which words combine to form sentences' (Lyons 1971:63). It is traditionally divided into morphology and syntax. Morphology studies the internal structure of the forms of words, while syntax is the study of sentence structure. In older school grammars morphology usually received extensive treatment, whereas syntax was given only limited coverage. In recent linguistic studies the roles have been reversed; morphology has tended to receive less attention than syntax.[13] The importance of grammar will hardly be questioned by teachers. Most language courses and textbooks are organized along grammatical criteria. Language teachers for generations have operated with grammatical concepts and categories which have been considered as a self-evident and simple basis of language. It is often handled in school in an authoritarian manner, and children are sometimes chided for 'not knowing their grammar'.

Over a period of about forty years, linguists have taken a fresh look at grammar and have attempted to rethink grammatical analysis from first principles. A review of modern grammatical theories (for example, Allen and Widdowson 1975) reveals an extraordinary variety of different systems. For language pedagogy, as we shall see later, the shifts of categories, concepts, terminologies, emphases, and approaches have been confusing and frustrating. At the same time these changes have created a sense of the complexity of grammar, counteracting the views of grammar as simple and self-evident. Instead, they are an invitation to teachers to treat the grammar of a second language as a puzzling and challenging phenomenon and as a subject of worthwhile and fascinating study.

Lexicology

Lexicology, the study of lexis or vocabulary, apart from its treatment under morphology as a sequence of morphemes, has received relatively little systematic attention, at least from English-speaking linguists.[14] It has received somewhat more in Germany and in French-speaking countries. One reason for its relative neglect may well be that it does not lend itself easily to the structural and systematic treatment in the way syntax and phonology have done. Another may be that the formal analysis of words has been absorbed by morphology and the study of word meaning by semantics. Yet, for language instruction, lexicography, and other practical activities a systematic understanding of lexis is important, and the neglect is all the more curious and unjustified. During the interwar years, largely outside the framework of linguistics, a number of word frequency studies in English, French, German, and Spanish were undertaken by educationists and psychologists to meet the need for vocabulary control in schoolbooks and language courses. Because of the importance of some form of ordering of lexis in language teaching, lexicological studies have come more into prominence since the fifties. But they have not been integrated into linguistic theory in the way syntax and phonology have been nor have they given rise to much imaginative and searching theorizing.[15]

Semantics

Semantics, the study of meaning, as a distinct field of investigation has a history of over a hundred years (Ullmann 1971:77). Yet, linguistics in its recent history has approached semantics with great caution and for a period had rejected it almost completely as a study within the framework of linguistics. Between about 1930 and 1955 many linguists, particularly in America, argued that linguistics should confine itself to the study of the observable linguistic forms so much so that one linguist, Charles Fries, complained that for many students of linguistics meaning had almost become anathema (op. cit.:86). Linguists have never denied that it is the essence of language to be meaningful. The question was whether meaning was a proper subject for scientific enquiry. During the sixties it was increasingly recognized that, since language cannot function without meaning, linguistics must pay attention to the problem of meaning. But the questions of meaning which relate words and sentences to each other and to 'states, processes, and objects in the universe' (Bierwisch 1970:167) are so complex that they deserve special consideration. Once this was recognized the interest in semantics and in the relationship between semantics and other branches of linguistics grew rapidly (Lyons 1977). Some of the curriculum reforms in language teaching, particularly those advocated in Europe in the seventies, referred to in Chapter 6, such as the notional syllabus, proposed by Wilkins (1976), are attempts to organize second language curricula on semantic rather than grammatical principles. In other words, instead of arranging a language course primarily in terms of the noun, the article, verb tenses, argeement of adjectives, and the like, Wilkins suggested that basic categories of *meaning* should constitute the essential framework of the course. His scheme includes *notions* of time, space, quantity, and so on, as well as the communicative *functions* which learners need in the foreign language, such as enquiring, informing, requesting, greeting and so forth.[16]

Discourse
The field of linguistic study has for long been bounded at one end by the concept of the sound and at the other by the concept of the sentence. Recent work in syntax and semantics has made it clear that linguistic investigation can no longer treat the sentence as the ultimate unit. 'Language does not occur in stray words or sentences, but in connected discourse' (Harris 1952:357). Since about 1970 linguistics has moved towards the study of aspects of language beyond the sentence through *discourse analysis*. To a certain extent, this is no more than a move in language teaching from isolated sentences to connected text passages, dialogues, descriptions, and narratives. However, simultaneously linguists, as we shall see shortly, have been led to the realization that language cannot be studied in isolation from the communicative intentions of language users and the context within which they use language. We will return to this view of language, because the context of language use is as important for language teaching as it is for linguistics. Discourse analysis and speech act theory, the study of communicative functions, began to develop as a new approach to linguistic study, and in this instance the promptings for a move into this new theoretical direction came largely from the demands voiced by practitioners.[17]

Directions in linguistics

Linguistics has advanced in two main directions. One is the detailed study of the different branches of specializations, for example, phonetics or syntax. The other is the study of language as a whole, the attempt to discover how the different parts of language interact and how the total language as a 'system of systems' can best be grasped. Linguistics has thus faced the dual problem of precise analysis down to the simplest unit while at the same time keeping sight of the general pattern of language which enables the linguist to provide a synthesis of the many features of a language.

Following the first direction, each of the different branches in linguistics had in the first place been concerned with developing basic concepts and theories. Second, studies have analysed features of particular languages, partly to advance the knowledge about these features in the language under investigation and partly to elucidate the general nature of language. Third, linguists, from within their specialization, have attempted to relate their particular field of enquiry to any of the other areas, for example, phonology to syntax, or syntax to semantics.

This last interest is intimately linked with the second major direction of linguistics, implicit in the notion of Saussurian structuralism, i.e., to represent the entire language as a coherent and unified system or structure in which the different parts have their place, and their relationships are adequately accounted for. An ideal general theory of language would provide us with a scheme of analysis and synthesis in which the specialist studies could take their place and which could be applied to the full description of any natural language. Such a theory would provide an exhaustive guide to the study of any language and it would give information on how the different elements interact. In short, it would give a completely satisfactory conceptual representation of language in general which could then be applied to the description of particular languages.

Linguists are aware of the immense complexity of all these tasks and of the insufficiency of our present knowledge. The conceptual framework in each branch of linguistics is still developing. The descriptive analysis of particular languages is far from complete and, in most cases, very tentative. The overall design of a general theory of language is the subject of controversies. The unsettled nature of the entire field and the awareness of ignorance on the part of the scholars themselves have made linguistics a promising and exciting field of enquiry. But it is not an area from which one can extract a ready-made doctrine, and, consequently, the application of linguistics to language teaching is fraught with difficulty. Nevertheless, it is important not to underestimate what has already been achieved: a vast amount of carefully attested information on many languages has been gathered; and the theories, concepts, and techniques of investigation that have been developed can be said to have considerably advanced our understanding of the nature of language.

Schools of thought

The expansion of knowledge in so many directions has led, since the thirties down to the present, to several attempts to make a synthesis and to develop a unified theory of language. Several schools of thought have emerged round a few prominent linguists (for example, Bloomfield, Firth, Halliday, Hjelmslev, or Chomsky), major centres of linguistic study (for example, Prague School, Geneva School, American Structuralism, London (or British) School, Copenhagen School), and leading concepts (for example, structuralism, tagmemics, scale-and-category, transformational generative grammar, generative semantics, speech act theory).

The main problem that linguistics has faced in this century in the study of language can be illustrated by Figure 7.2, which elaborates Figure 7.1. The language user operates in a given context or

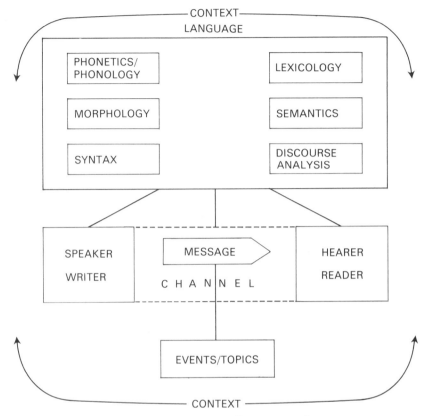

Figure 7.2   Categories of linguistic analysis

situation. As a speaker/writer he communicates with someone (listener/ reader) about events and topics in the world in which he lives. The language use in the acts of communication can be divided into the components which we have already described. The main questions that the linguistic system builders have faced are: (1) to what extent can language be studied abstractly without taking into account the context, the topics, and the speaker/listener? (2) How do these different aspects of language—phonology, grammar, semantics, lexis, etc.—relate to each other? In language teaching the same issues arise in a similar manner: (1) to what extent should the teaching of a second language mainly concentrate on the language as a formal system or adopt a broader view and take into account social context and language use by hearers and speakers? (2) If we study the language in relative isolation as a formal system, what should be our main emphasis—grammar, words, meanings, or the sound system? And how can we best integrate these different aspects with each other, and eventually with the real world of language use?

In order to illustrate how linguistics has come to grips with these issues, we will by way of example briefly sketch three of the schools of thought which have in one way or another had some influence on language teaching theory between the thirties and the early seventies.

Bloomfield and American structuralism

Of the schools of linguistics which have exercised a marked influence on language teaching theory, American structuralism is probably the most important. It has had adherents in many parts of the world; its influence can be observed in almost every aspect of language teaching since 1940. From the mid-sixties it has aroused violent opposition, and since the seventies it has been overshadowed by linguistic theories with a different emphasis; but its influence is still present. Without understanding it, it is hard to grasp later developments.

American structuralism as a school of thought ultimately derived from a single work which is widely acclaimed as a classic in modern linguistics, Bloomfield's *Language*, published in 1933. Although its author regarded it merely as a revised and expanded textbook version of his earlier *Introduction to the Study of Language* (Bloomfield 1914), it meant much more to the younger contemporary linguists. Bloch, one of Bloomfield's students, writing in 1949 on the occasion of Bloomfield's death, recalled its influence in these terms:

> 'It is not too much to say that every significant refinement of analytic method produced in this country since 1933 has come as a direct result of the impetus given to linguistic research by Bloomfield's book. If today our methods in descriptive analysis are in some ways better than his, if we see more clearly than he did himself certain aspects of the structure that he first revealed to us, it is because we stand upon his shoulders.'
> (Bloch 1949:92)

From the state of linguistics today it is not easy to recapture the intellectual climate of the interwar years when the ideas expressed in *Language* came to fruition. But it must be remembered that linguistics was still ill-defined. Bloomfield's predominant concern was to establish linguistics truly as a *science* of language. The task that he saw was needed was twofold: (a) to delimit the role of linguistics in relation to other sciences, and (b) to develop the principles and concepts of linguistics into a well balanced and unified structure.

(a) Language is so pervasive that one of the most important things to do for the early systems builders, such as Saussure and Bloomfield, had to be to delimit the role of linguistics. 'As students of language ... we are concerned precisely with the speech event ..., worthless in itself, but a means to great ends' (Bloomfield 1933:26–27), i.e., 'the message' in Figure 7.2. It is often said that Bloomfield denied the existence of meaning; but this is not so. He deliberately and advisedly restricted the object of linguistic enquiry to the formal characteristics of linguistic utterances. 'In the division of scientific labour, the linguist deals only with the speech signal' (op. cit.:32).

The data for a linguistic science, then, are a given set of verbal utterances which constitute a corpus. The task of the linguist is to study the corpus of utterances and to discover regularities and structures, in other words, the *langue* in the specimens of *parole*. The severe restriction in the field of enquiry that Bloomfield's thesis imposed helped linguistics to establish iself as an autonomous field. Much detailed and accurate linguistic research work was carried out in the subsequent years largely within the confines set by Bloomfield. Some investigators (for example, Harris 1947) went further than Bloomfield in analysing linguistic phenomena as much as possible only in relation to each other without reference to anything except formal linguistic criteria. Others came to the conclusion that a language analysis that abstracts too severely from the social context cannot be sustained and is in any case unprofitable. Pike (1960), for example, has attempted to place the formal 'Bloomfield-ian' study of language into a wider theory of behaviour and thus to restore as the area of investigation the broader frame of reference that was recognized by Bloomfield but which he considered as too broad to study *scientifically* as part of a science of language. Recent developments have tended to lend support to such a broader interpretation which takes into account psychological and sociological factors.

(b) Bloomfield wanted linguistics to become an empirical, descriptive science. The scientific philosophy which he advocated was formulated in these terms:

> 'that science shall deal only with events that are accessible in their time and place to any and all observers (strict behaviorism) ... only with events that are placed in co-ordinates of time and place (*mechanism*) ... that science shall employ only such initial statements and predictions that lead to handling operations (*operationalism*) ... only such terms as are derivable by rigid definition from a set of every day terms concerning physical happenings (*physicalism*).'
> (quoted in Fries 1961:209)

The principal value of *Language* lies in the closely argued and balanced presentation of the essential concepts which enable the linguist to analyse a language from sound to sentence (Hill 1958). It is balanced in that it gives approximately equal weight to the different levels of the analysis: phonology, morphology, and syntax. It omits, however, the semantic component indicated in Figure 7.2.

Linguists in the Bloomfieldian tradition continued to operate with the concepts developed by Bloomfield, to refine them, and to use them for more rigorous descriptions of languages. The outcome was, in the forties and fifties, many well-ordered, objective, detailed, and informative presentations of linguistics or of particular aspects of language by such writers as Fries, Joos, Pike, Nida, Harris, Gleason, and Hockett. A review of work in American structural linguistics in the fifties listed over four hundred and fifty studies and ended with the conclusion: 'Linguistics has come of age' (Hamp 1961:180). It was a period of confidence in what had been achieved. It is not surprising that structuralism influenced language teaching.[18]

Neo-Firthian theory

To illustrate an alternative to Bloomfieldian linguistics we select an early version of a theory of a British linguist, Michael Halliday, known as scale-and-category theory, which in the sixties was offered as a linguistic basis for language teaching in a work by Halliday, McIntosh, and Strevens, *Linguistic Sciences and Language Teaching* (1964). Halliday elaborated and systematized the theoretical concepts originally suggested by Firth who had led the development of linguistics in Britain at about the same period during which structuralism made headway in America (Robins 1961). As in the U.S.A. there was a close association in Britain between linguistics and anthropology. Firth, who was Professor of Linguistics at the School of Oriental and African Studies in London, was strongly influenced by the anthropologist Bronislaw Malinowski whose work and influence will be discussed in more detail in Chapter 10.

In his anthropological work in the South Seas, Malinowski had observed that the language of the South Sea Islanders whose cultures he had studied could only be understood in closest association with an interpretation of their culture. 'To us, the real linguistic fact is the full utterance within its context of situation' (Malinowski 1935 Vol. II:11). This view is basic to Firth's conception of the study of language. At the point at which Bloomfield argued that linguistics must restrict itself to the study of the speech signal, Firth, following Malinowski, argued that language must be studied at all levels in its context of situation and with an emphasis on meaning. The linguist has to study the 'text', i.e., the corpus of utterances, (a) in their linguistic environment or context, i.e., in relation to surrounding language items, and (b) in their context of situations, i.e., in relation to nonverbal constituents which have bearing on the utterance, such as persons, objects, and events.

On the basis of Firthian ideas, Halliday presents a synthesis of concepts which aims at being theoretically powerful and at the same time useful to apply in the description of natural languages. In his view a linguistic description is on three levels: substance (phonic or graphic), form, and context. Three branches of linguistic study correspond to these three levels: phonetics and phonology examine the phonic substance (graphology the graphic); grammar and lexicology study linguistic forms; and semantics studies the context which relates linguistic form to non-linguistic events. In principle, then, this theory attempts to account for a much broader range of linguistic phenomena than Bloomfieldian structuralism. But the problem that the theory attempted more particularly to resolve was to distinguish concepts which are appropriate for the description of particular natural languages from those concepts which are universally applicable to all languages.

Two fundamental concepts underlie the entire theoretical framework, i.e., the concept of 'category' and the concept of 'rank scale'. According to Halliday, the description of any language requires four fundamental theoretical categories: unit, structure, class, and system. 'With these four basic categories ... it is possible to describe the grammar of all languages' (Halliday, McIntosh, and Strevens 1964:31). A 'unit' is a stretch of utterance that carries a grammatical pattern; in English, for example, 'sentence' or 'phrase' are grammatical units. 'Structure' is an arrangement of elements in relation to other elements, for example, 'subject' and 'predicate'. 'Class' is illustrated by such paradigmatic concepts as 'nouns' and 'verbs', and 'system' is applied to closed sets of items, such as 'the personal pronouns', 'tenses', or 'aspects'. It is conceivable that a particular language does not have a grammatical unit one can identify as 'word' or 'sentence', or a 'subject-predicate' structure, or classes of items which can be distinguished as 'verbs', or a system of 'personal pronouns'; therefore, these may be descriptive categories of certain languages only. But all languages have identifiable units, structures, classes, and systems of some sort.

Moreover, the concepts subsumed under the four universal categories can in all languages be arranged in a rank order from lowest to highest, a 'rank scale'. Thus, in the grammar of English we can identify in ascending order 'morpheme', 'word', 'phrase' (or 'group'), 'clause', and 'sentence'; in phonology the rank scale has the units 'phoneme', 'syllable', 'foot', and 'tone group'. In Halliday's view, a Bloomfieldian analysis mixes phonological and grammatical units by advancing from 'sound' to 'sentence'; for 'sound' (for example, 'phoneme') is a unit of phonology and 'sentence' a unit of grammar. An analysis in terms of both, phonology and grammar, is needed, but they look at language from different perspectives. 'We have to separate the different levels, in order to say anything useful at all ... But this separation is never rigid or opaque ... We are describing language as used by human beings, and they do not use just one level of it at a time' (op. cit.:47).

Halliday's scheme was an ambitious attempt to develop a theory of a high degree of universality, but which at the same time included concepts close to the realities of natural languages, omitting nothing of importance in a particular language system. It developed categories which helped in the analysis of the flow of speech and intonation ('prosody') and speech varieties ('register') which a Bloomfieldian analysis was not equipped to handle. Its emphasis on meaning at all levels of linguistic analysis anticipated recent developments in linguistics.

Yet, scale-and-category theory has not evoked the resonance among linguists one might have expected from such a comprehensive and sensitive scheme of analysis. We can only speculate about the reasons for this relative lack of response. One may be that the multiplicity of concepts has not always been explained as fully as necessary nor has it been sufficiently related to other theories so that one could have compared the advantages of one scheme with another. Another reason may be that Halliday's theory was never set out clearly enough as an alternative theory of language description in the way in which American structuralism had been presented in Bloomfield's *Language*. Moreover, within a few years Halliday changed his theoretical position and emphasized 'system' as the key concept in his scheme in which system meant 'a set of things of which one must be chosen' (Kress 1976:3). And, finally, before scholars had time to work with and apply the scale-and-category theory, another different approach, Chomsky's transformational generative grammar, claimed the attention of linguists and the valuable contribution that scale-and-category theory would have been able to offer were not fully enough appreciated at that time nor were they ever sufficiently developed. From the point of view of linguistic theory, the story of scale-and-category theory reveals vividly the problems of analysis and synthesis, of generality and specificity that any comprehensive linguistic theory has to cope with. Halliday's theory will be referred to again in relation to language teaching in the next chapter.[19]

Transformational generative grammar
No theory has probably ever created quite such a stir in the study of language as transformational generative grammar (TG for short) did around 1965. The central figure in this approach is Noam Chomsky, a student of the structural linguist, Zellig Harris. In a study on Chomsky we read that his position 'is not only unique within linguistics at the present time, but is probably unprecedented in the whole history of the subject ... Right or wrong, Chomsky's theory of grammar is undoubtedly the most dynamic and influential; and no linguist who wishes to keep abreast of current developments in his subject can afford to ignore Chomsky's theoretical pronouncements. Every other 'school' of linguistics at the present time tends to define its position in relation to Chomsky's view on particular issues' (Lyons 1977a:9).[20]

The 'Chomskyan revolution' falls approximately into three phases; here we shall refer only briefly to the third. The first phase from about 1957 to the early sixties was marked by the publication of Chomsky's first major work, a small book, entitled *Syntactic Structures* (1957), and a violent attack on the behaviourist view of language, as exemplified in Skinner's work, *Verbal Behavior* (1957; Chomsky 1959). In the next phase, from the early sixties to about 1967, transformational generative grammar widened its scope, and the newer developments are represented in Chomsky's second major work, *Aspects of the Theory of Syntax*(Chomsky 1965). In the third phase, 1967 to the early seventies, a new generation of linguists and former students of Chomsky, notably Lakoff, Fillmore, and McCawley, critically examined transformational generative grammar and developed new directions by a shift of emphasis from syntax to semantics ('generative semantics').

At first sight, Chomsky's first work, *Syntactic Structures,* did not look like a revolutionary manifesto at all. Here was no grand new scheme repudiating completely what twenty-five years of structural linguistics had built up. Like his teacher, Zellig Harris, Chomsky was interested in linguistic analysis, and he believed with Harris that a linguistic analysis could be done without reference to meaning. The primary purpose of *Syntactic Structures* was to investigate an area in which structural linguistics had hitherto made only limited progress, namely syntax. Structural linguistics had built up an impressive technical apparatus for the study of phonology and morphology, but its treatment of syntax was far less assured. As Palmer wrote 'It is reported that one American linguist of the 1950s remarked that syntax was that part of linguistics that everyone hoped the other fellow would do' (Palmer 1971:124). It was a field which demanded a 'new look'. In his approach to syntax, Chomsky changed the perspective of linguistic enquiry. Instead of examining a 'corpus of speech events' as given, he set out the grammatical statement from the standpoint of the language user who produces or understands utterances of which the minimum unit— grammatically speaking— is the sentence. The question he asked was: what linguistic 'knowledge' must be presupposed in a native speaker to produce and interpret sentences? In his view, a statement about syntactic structures should therefore not be a summary of generalizations about specimens of 'parole', a collection of utterances already produced. Instead, the grammar statement should be a set of instructions or rules which, if followed rigidly, ends up with grammatically correct sentences in the language. An adequate grammar generates these rules and makes them as explicit as possible, and thus displays the workings of the 'mechanism' underlying language use. A grammar must be so designed that 'by following its rules and conventions we could produce all or any of the possible sentences of the language' (op. cit.:150).

Testing the validity of the rules is an important step in the development of the grammar statement; for the grammar must only contain recipes for sentences which structurally do not offend the native speaker's intuition: 'grammatical' sentences. As long as the instructions can also be used to produce ungrammatical sentences the grammar statement is imperfect.

The *generative* approach opened a new perspective. Linguistic theories from Saussure to Harris and Halliday had treated language as a static entity or finished product which can be objectively examined, analysed, and described. The Chomskyan approach reflected what he called the 'creativity of language', the *process* of linguistic production and interpretation, which structural linguistics had disregarded. Chomsky did not claim that it was a new approach. It was in his view merely a rediscovery of Humboldt's famous observation that 'language makes infinite use of finite means' (Chomsky 1965:v).

By examining current models of syntactic analysis from a generative perspective, Chomsky found them deficient. Up to a point the 'immediate constituent analysis' of sentences, used by structural linguists, proved useful and lent itself to a conversion to generative rules, and immediate constituent analysis became an essential basis of a generative grammar as its phrase-structure base component. But in *Syntactic Structures* Chomsky was able to show that it bogged down in the treatment of anything beyond the simplest type of sentence; it was unable to handle economically such changes of sentences as those from active to passive. Chomsky resolved this problem by introducing a *transformational component* and concluded that two sets of rules, phrase structure rules and transformational rules, would be necessary elements of syntax.

By this novel generative and transformational approach Chomsky created a new interest in syntax, hitherto regarded as one of the most unattractive and recalcitrant fields of linguistic enquiry. Empirically, language teachers had known for centuries that different sentence structures can be related to each other. Language learning exercises have involved transformations such as changing sentences from active to passive, from direct to indirect speech, from affirmative to negative, from affirmative to interrogative, from sentence to nominalized phrase, and so on. But linguistic theory which, up to a point, had been able to cope with the sentence in isolation was not equipped to handle satisfactorily the relationships among sentences. Thus, before transformational generative grammar linguists—like language teachers and language users—had noted the relationship of meaning between sentences such as these three:

The men built the tool house very slowly.
The tool house was built by the men very slowly.
Their building of the tool house was very slow.
(Fries 1952:177)

but grammatically they could only treat them as three different sentence patterns. Likewise structural linguistics lacked the capacity to uncover the ambiguity of the phrase

The shooting of the rebels

because the different syntactic relationships of the elements of this phrase, can only be displayed by relating them to two possible underlying 'strings':

Either X shoots the rebels
or
The rebels shoot X
(Quirk *et al.*:1972)

The fact that a given sentence or phrase can be regarded as resulting from transformations of underlying strings led Chomsky to the notion of *deep* and *surface structure* which has become an important principle in modern syntax. If, for example, we read on the side of a delivery van of a firm of nursery gardeners

Our business is growing

we can intuitively relate this surface structure to two different underlying strings which might be paraphrased

Our business is flourishing (or expanding)
It is our business to grow plants.

As Chomsky was only too ready to point out, the notion of deep and surface structure was not invented by him. Humboldt, Wittgenstein, Harris, and Hockett had used similar concepts. But it is due to Chomsky that the idea of a grammar on two levels which are dynamically interacting through the process of transformation became an important, although not undisputed, feature of linguistic analysis. Once it had been 'rediscovered' by Chomsky the observer will note so many instances that it seems surprising that this important distinction, which is intuitively employed by the language user regularly, had hitherto found so little recognition among theorists.

The theory that in 1957 had begun as a study of syntactic structures had, by 1965, become a much more elaborate scheme embracing the whole of linguistic analysis. For example, in 1957, Chomsky—in line with the extreme structuralism of Harris—tried to demonstrate that the grammar operates independently of semantic considerations by comparing two much quoted sentences

Colourless green ideas sleep furiously.
Furiously sleep ideas green colourless.

Both of them are equally meaningless, but 'any speaker of English will recognize that only the former is grammatical' (Chomsky 1957:15). By 1965, a generative grammar had become a more complex affair. It had a syntactic, a phonological, and a semantic component. The syntactic component now included a lexicon as well as deep structures and transformations. Consequently, meaningless sentences such as 'Colourless green ideas ...', which the 1957 syntax could generate, would now be eliminated by lexical restrictions in the syntax before they reached the surface structure. However, syntax and semantics are still viewed as distinct components and the primacy of syntax is undiminished.

In later developments of generative theory between 1967 and the early seventies the importance of the role of semantics became the central topic of controversy.[21]. The argument was put forward that, instead of assuming a two-level syntax with rather complex relations to semantics, the deep-level syntax can in fact be considered identical with the semantic component which can then be directly related to the surface structures, thus simplifying the representation of linguistic processes. In other words, for some scholars it became a question of the primacy of semantics versus the primacy of syntax in linguistic analysis.

Transformational generative grammar and structuralism

The new perspectives of language offered by transformational generative grammar led to a violent rejection of structuralism and everything it stood for. As we shall see in the next chapter, these radical changes in linguistic theory had important implications for the view of language in language teaching. We summarize the main points at issue.

1 Transformational generative grammar recognizes language as a 'rule-governed' system. These rules which are 'not only intricate but also quite abstract' (Chomsky 1966:47) are made explicit by a transformational generative grammar. 'Learning a language involves internalizing the rules' (Saporta 1966:86). Structural linguistics, it was argued, does not lead to an understanding of a language as a system of *rule-governed relationships*. It treats a language merely as a collection of habits. In language teaching, therefore, it sanctions imitation, memorization, mechanical drill, and practice of sentence patterns as separate and unrelated items. 'Having somehow stored a very large number of sentences cannot be equated with having learnt a language' (loc. cit.). Chomsky accused linguists of having had their share 'in perpetuating the myth that linguistic behaviour is "habitual" and that a fixed stock of "patterns" is acquired through practice and used as the basis for "analogy"' (Chomsky 1966:44).

2 Structural linguists considered as a virtue of their approach that language descriptions were based on the analysis of a given corpus. In the eyes of transformationalists this feature was a cause for critical

comment: 'I think there are by now very few linguists who believe that it is possible to arrive at the phonological or syntactic structure of a language by systematic application of "analytical procedures" of segmentation and classification' (op. cit.:45). The strongly entrenched empiricist and scientifically descriptive approach came thus under attack. Structural linguistics, by basing itself inductively on the utterances (the 'performance' or *parole*) of informants ('what its native speakers say') was accused of lacking criteria by which to distinguish the regular from the accidental, the grammatical from the ungrammatical. Transformational generative grammar, instead concerns itself with the native speaker's norm, i.e., what he considers as grammatical or rejects as ungrammatical (the native speaker's 'competence') rather than with the extent to which he obeys the norm, his performance (Anisfeld 1966:110).

3 Structural linguistics was found wanting for another reason. It was only concerned with surface structure and important distinctions that a deep-structure analysis revealed remained unrecognized. Consequently pattern practice in language teaching was often criticized for being misleading. Examples were cited which revealed the insensitivity of structuralism to deep structure. Because transformational generative grammar emphasizes the difference between deep and surface structure it was believed that it can deal more effectively than structuralism with structural similarities, differences, and ambiguities, and can provide better insight into language. 'The learning of fundamental syntactic relations and processes will not be accomplished by drill based on analysis of surface structure alone' (Spolsky 1970:151).

4 Because of its emphasis on formal aspects structural linguistics was accused of neglecting meaning. This criticism could equally well have been made of the 1957 version of transformational generative grammar, but by the mid-sixties, when these criticisms were expressed, transformational generative grammar had incorporated a semantic element, and it was therefore able to meet the charge against structuralism of an excessive concern with the purely formal characteristics of a language. 'When you learn a language, you have to learn its semantic system too' (loc. cit.).

5 Because transformational generative grammar was more interested in the native speaker's competence than his performance, the question of the phonetic manifestations of language was no longer so central. The primacy of speech, a cardinal tenet of structuralism, was called into question. 'The spoken language and the writing system do not correspond directly, and their complex relationships will receive the careful scrutiny they deserve only after linguists and language teachers abandon the notion that one is a direct representation of the other' (Valdman 1966a:xvii).

6 An important feature of transformational generative grammar was its emphasis on the productive or creative character of language, an aspect of language which had no place in structuralism and other contemporary linguistic theories. 'The most obvious and characteristic property of normal linguistic behaviour is that it is stimulus-free and innovative' (Chomsky 1966:46). 'An infinite number of sentences can be produced by what seems to be a rather small finite number of grammatical rules. A speaker does not have to store a large number of ready-made sentences in his head; he just needs the rules for creating and understanding these sentences' (Diller 1978:25).

7 Lastly, structural linguistics was accused of over-emphasizing the differences between languages and the unique characteristics of each language. Transformational generative grammar, on the other hand, concerned itself with the common elements, the universals, underlying all natural languages. As we shall see in Chapter 8, this viewpoint had obvious implications for contrastive analysis.

Towards a more semantic and more social view of language

Needless to say linguistics did not stand still even after this period of upheaval. The problem that Bloomfield faced in the thirties as to how to restrict linguistic enquiries without distortion is perennial. The dilemma for the linguistic systems builder is that he either attempts to take in everything that plays a part in language and risks making his system unwieldy and too complex to handle, or he makes a deliberate choice and abstracts from the complex reality and is thus in danger of distorting it by restricting the field of observation too severely.

In Chomsky's view linguistic theory is a very abstract affair. '(It) is concerned primarily with an ideal speaker-listener, in a completely homogeneous speech-community, who knows its language perfectly ... This seems to me to have been the position of the founders of modern general linguistics, and no cogent reasons for modifying it has been offered.' (Chomsky 1965:3–4).

In this dilemma many linguists, however, did not go along with this highly abstract view of linguistic enquiry. They became more and more convinced that the different restrictions that first Bloomfield and later Chomsky had imposed upon the study of language were no longer tenable. In spite of the difficulties in finding valid methods of enquiry, linguists were led to take into account the social and situational contexts, and the language user's intentions and perceptions. Some questioned the validity of a rigid distinction between linguistic competence and performance which for Chomsky had been axiomatic, and others postulated a more socially oriented communicative competence (Hymes 1972). New approaches began to develop which, under various labels and with new techniques of enquiry, attempted to relate the study of language to the external reality and to the language user's psychological situation. Such new fields of study which were initiated from the mid-sixties included sociolinguistics, pragmatics, ethnomethodology, and the ethnography of speaking. All of these new fields, in terms of Figure 7.2, connect the study of language with the speaker-hearer, the context, and the topic. They are less concerned with the analysis within the box labelled language, than with the relations between language and context and between language and language user.

For some linguists this wider view of language became linguistics in its new guise. They argued language cannot be studied any more in isolation from the user and the context. For others this social orientation of language study constituted new sub-fields of the study of language somewhere between linguistics and anthropology and sociology which can best be treated under the headings of sociolinguistics or pragmatics. This is what we have done. Valuable as these new approaches to language may be it would be misleading to treat the fields of linguistic study 'within' the 'language' box of Figure 7.2 which had been opened between 1890 and 1960, as superseded. The formal study of language—phonology, grammar, and lexicology—continues to be important for linguistics and language pedagogy. How to integrate them with the semantic and social approaches, however, is an important question which will have to be considered at a later stage. See Chapter 10.

Conclusion

To sum up from the point of view of language teachers this review of trends in linguistics up to this point:

1 A new situation was created for language pedagogy by the development of a science of language in the course of the present century.
2 Language teaching theory cannot disregard a discipline which shares with it its central concern for language.
3 We have found much common ground between the problems faced by linguistics and those faced by language pedagogy.
4 Linguistics is an active and growing field of study, far from approaching a state of finality. Theories battle with each other. New concepts, new models and changes in emphasis come and go. It is not surprising to find that this prolonged state of unrest and agitation creates problems for a language pedagogy that attempts to take linguistics into account.
5 In certain respects the perspectives of linguistics and pedagogy are different. A major preoccupation of linguistics is the development of *theory* of language. Another is the creation of conceptual tools for the description of natural languages in general. Language pedagogy has a

practical objective, effective language learning: and it is committed to the teaching of *particular languages*. There is therefore a difference in purpose and function between the role of linguist and language educator, and we must expect to find that the practical needs of language teaching as an applied activity and the theoretical interests of linguistics as a science do not always coincide. How language pedagogy and linguistics have, in fact, attempted to interact with one another will be considered in the next two chapters.[22]

Notes

1 See Simpson (1979: Chapters 3–5) for a brief historical introduction. He writes: 'The first Greek grammarians were philosophers, for philosophy embraced all scholarly investigation.' (op. cit.:6). For a history of linguistics see Robins (1951, 1979), or Dinneen (1967: Chapters 4 and 5). For a detailed treatment of historical and comparative linguistics in the nineteenth century, see Dinneen (1967: Chapter 6). For general introductions to linguistics see Note 22.

2 Among several earlier works an influential book on language was *The Life and Growth of Language: an Outline of Linguistic Science*, by Whitney, Professor of Sanskrit and Comparative Grammar at Yale College (1875) (Godel 1966).

3 For guidance on this fundamental work and a critical appraisal of its composition, see Godel (1957, 1966). Saussurian ideas are referred to below in the next section of this chapter. See also Dinneen (1967: Chapter 7).

4 One should add that some language educators have in recent years advocated a greater emphasis on general language questions in language teaching in order to create an awareness of language among students at the school or college level (for example Hawkins 1981). See also the curriculum model (Figure 22.4) in Chapter 22.

5 Thus, one school of linguistics, American structuralism, saw as one of its main contributions the development of scientific discovery procedures which would lead to accurate descriptions of different languages. By contrast, another school of thought, Noam Chomsky's transformational generative grammar, was more concerned with theory development and regarded the preoccupation of the structuralists with empirical data as irrelevant.

6 Hudson (1980:191–2) makes the valid point that the slogan 'linguistics should be descriptive, not prescriptive', raises problems: 'It is harder than many linguists realize to avoid prescriptivism, since the historical development of linguistic theory has been so closely linked to the description of prestigious varieties, such as standard languages'.

7 On dialects, see, for example, Lyons (1981:24–27, 181–3, 269–271) who points out that 'both Latin and English were in origin nothing other than local dialects of small tribes' (p. 183). For a more detailed and comprehensive study of dialectology see Chambers and Trudgill (1980).

8 A textbook of linguistics, such as *Fundamentals of Linguistic Analysis* (Langacker 1972), gives as examples problems from a large number of languages which include, besides French, German, English, Spanish, or Latin, such languages as Papago, Mohawk, Tamil, Maori, Swahili, Eskimo, and so on.

9 Under the impact of the tenet of the primacy of speech, many language teachers in the sixties became very dogmatic in withholding the written form during early second language teaching. Two modern criticisms of the primacy of speech have been offered: one is that it was exaggerated by modern linguistics, particularly by structuralists. The other is that the discovery of the spoken language as a proper subject of linguistic investigation has quite falsely been regarded as a modern development. Chomsky has argued that phonetics was a major concern of universal grammarians (i.e., of the seventeenth and eighteenth centuries).

10 For example, in Canada French departments in English-speaking universities have been accused of giving preference to French from France and, in the words of a professor of French language and literature in one of these universities writing in a newspaper about Quebec French, subtly 'disparaging the idiom of Quebeckers' (Ages in the *Globe and Mail*, July 26, 1980). In a similar way European teachers of English often discuss at length whether to give preference to British or American varieties of English.

11 Recent discussions on 'communicative' language teaching have been concerned with this issue; see Chapter 6, especially Figure 6.1. See also Chapter 9 (in particular Widdowson's distinction between linguistic and communicative categories) and Chapters 11 and 12.

12 For an introduction to phonetics and phonology see Brown (1975), Simpson (1979: Chapter 7–8), Wilkins (1972: Chapter 2), Lyons (1981: Chapter 3); also articles by Fudge (1970) and Henderson (1971). For a more detailed treatment of phonetics see O'Connor (1973) and of phonology see Fudge (1973).

13 For an introduction to modern thought on grammar see, above all, Allen and Widdowson (1975); other useful references are Lyons (1971), Crystal (1971:187–231), Wilkins (1972: Chapter 3), Simpson (1979: Chapters 9–12), Lyons (1981: Chapter 4). For a readable introductory monograph see Palmer (1971). Developments in morphology are discussed by Matthews (1970). For a very clear introduction to syntax see Brown and Miller (1980).

14 'For some years now the study of second language lexical acquisition has been languishing in neglect ... "Neglect" is perhaps an understatement; one might almost say that second language lexical acquisition has been a victim of discrimination' (Levenston 1979:147).

15 As a qualification to this generalization about lexicology, it should be pointed out that sophisticated lexicological knowledge is embodied in lexicography, represented by the great dictionaries such as the 'Oxford' or the 'Webster'. Among language teachers, as Strevens (1978) has pointed out, A.S. Hornby is perhaps an outstanding example of a practitioner who has filled this gap, particularly through his Oxford Advanced Learner's Dictionary of Current English. For an introduction to the treatment of vocabulary see Wilkins (1972: Chapter 4); for an up-to-date discussion of lexicography in relation to language teaching, see Cowie (1981).

16 For further discussions of Wilkins' work on notions and functions see Chapters 9 and 11. For an introduction to the treatment of semantics see Ullmann (1971), Bierwisch (1970), Leech (1974), van Buren (1975), Palmer (1981), Simpson (1979: Chapter 15) and Lyons (1981: Chapter 5).

17 On discourse analysis see Coulthard (1975, 1977), Widdowson (1979: Section 4), and Sinclair (1980). See also Chapters 9 and 11.

18 The classic presentation of structural linguistics is Bloomfield's Language (1933). For a detailed discussion of this work, see Dinneen (1967: Chapter 9). Fries (1961) has analysed and assessed Bloomfield's contribution.

19 For an introduction to Halliday's views on language see Allen and Widdowson (1975), Kress (1976), and a well documented review of the entire development of systemic linguistics by Butler (1979). For a valuable appreciation of Halliday's recent thought in the context of modern linguistics see Gregory (1980).

20 Several helpful introductions to Chomsky and transformational generative grammar can be consulted: Lyons' brief study of Chomsky (Lyons 1977a); a selection of well arranged readings with useful introductory comments (Allen and van Buren 1971); an analysis of Syntactic Structures and Aspects in Dinneen (1967: Chapter 12); see also Part I of Greene (1972). A lucid introduction to the purely grammatical problems may be found in Palmer (1971: Chapter 4); Allen and Widdowson (1975); Simpson (1979).

21 For a helpful introduction to the issues involved in generative semantics see Steinberg and Jakobovits (1971); in particular, the introductory overview to Part II, Linguistics, by Maclay. See also Palmer (1981:118–54), Leech (1974:325–45).

22 Among several excellent general works on linguistics, only a small number can be suggested here. Readers with no previous back-

ground might begin with Allen and Corder (Vol. 2:1975) or Wilkins (1972), both written with language teaching in mind. General introductions addressed to non-specialists are: Lyons (1981), Bolinger and Spears (1981), Robins (1980), Simpson (1979), Langacker (1973), Wardhaugh (1977), and Crystal (1971). More advanced introductions are Akmajian, Demers, and Harnish (1979), Lyons (1968), and Dinneen (1967).

8 Linguistic theory and language teaching: emergence of a relationship

Uncertain beginnings

The problem of linguistics in language teaching was well posed by Gouin in *The Art of Teaching and Studying Languages* (1880/1892). Like anyone who thinks seriously about language teaching Gouin, to begin with, tried to understand the nature of language and language learning in order to derive his method of teaching from his interpretation. He set out from the contrast between his own failure to learn German by 'the classical method, with its grammar, its dictionary, and its translations' (1892:35), which was to him nothing but a delusion, and 'nature's method' by which a child learns its mother tongue. During the crucial episode in his life which inspired him to develop his method, the visit to the mill, Gouin had observed that his little nephew, with whose language development he compared his own simultaneous failure to learn German, 'manifested an immense desire to recount to everybody what he had seen' (1892:37). This observation suggested to him that the child was attempting to order the impressions that had crowded in on him. Later, the child recreated the sequence of events in play and talk.

From these observations Gouin developed a psychological theory of language learning and a linguistic theory of language. It is the latter which interests us in the present context. According to Gouin, verbal expression is intimately linked with thought about real events. The child translates every observation or perception into an utterance. In other words, we do not verbalize without thinking. Thoughts and corresponding utterances do not occur randomly or singly; they come in sequences and ends-means series. The verbal expression of an event is not just a word but a sentence. The sentences are spoken; and the event is expressed, above all, by a verb. At this point Gouin makes an extraordinary leap from personal observation to pedagogical application. Therefore, he argues, the verb is more important than the noun. The teaching technique that he based on it was a purposeful action series expressed in sentences in which the verbs reflect the progression of events or actions, as in this example:

	J'ouvre la porte
marche	Je marche vers la porte.
m'approche	Je m'approche de la porte.

arrive	J'arrive à la porte.
m'arrête	Je m'arrête à la porte.
allonge	J'allonge le bras.
prends	Je prends la poignée.
	etc.
	(Gouin 1892:171)

But the language of objective events, which is 'the expression of the phenomena perceived by us in the exterior world' is only one aspect of language. The individual also comments upon events or takes up an attitude: 'the subjective language is the expression of the play of the faculties of the soul', for example,

Très bien!	I am glad that . . .
Courage!	Try to . . .
That's right.	Please pass me the bread.

Besides these two a third division is figurative language, the language of metaphor and abstraction: 'the expression of the purely ideal, that is, of the abstract idea by means of symbols borrowed from the exterior world' (op. cit.:60). For each of these three language uses, Gouin considers the 'theoretical organization' and 'the practical art of teaching them' (op. cit.:61). In his view, these three, the objective, subjective, and figurative use of language, make up 'the three constituent parts of the whole human language'.

Gouin's effort illustrates the problem faced by the language teaching theorist who wished to take into account the nature of language. Because no accessible theory of language was available, he had to construct his own and to apply it. Gouin was by no means unsophisticated. Like the linguists whose systems we considered in Chapter 7 he recognized that he had to abstract from the full reality of language, to interpret it, and to create a construct, but he was convinced that his interpretation had picked out the essentials which were pedagogically appropriate.[1]

As occurs in so many language teaching theories, in his theory of language Gouin drew attention to certain important aspects: he related language use to thought, meaning, and action. His main principle of linguistic organization can be described as semantic. In his view, semantic ordering of the items to be learnt can be theoretically justified and pedagogically helpful. He also expressed the belief that the sentence can be regarded as a more useful unit of language instruction than the word, and that the verb is no less important than the noun to which language pedagogy had previously paid much more attention. But these observations are not in themselves sufficient as a basis for a whole theory of language instruction. His attempt to subsume all language under the three categories he had noted—objective, subjective, and figurative language—was risky, and the fiction that the verbalizations of perceptions in sequences represent either a typical or pedagogically useful construct was, to say the least, questionable. Nevertheless, Gouin's attempt to understand the nature of language and to base teaching techniques on his interpretations can be admired. From our point of view it is instructive, because it shows with great clarity the difficulty of relating language theory to language teaching.

Ever since philology and phonetics were systematically studied during the nineteenth century, repeated attempts were made to apply some of the findings of the linguistic sciences. Thus, Breul (1898), a professor of German at Oxford University, writing on the teaching of languages and the training of language teachers, in line with the reform movement, recommended phonetics for pronunciation teaching. In grammar he insisted that the teacher should, of course, be well grounded: 'moreover—and this is important—he should be able to give, wherever it may be desirable, the "why" not less than the "what". He should know the historical and phonetic reasons of the chief grammatical phenomena— but it would be a great mistake if he were to introduce much of this special knowledge into his class teaching' (Breul 1898:26). Breul made a clear distinction between the linguistic background of the teacher and what the pupil should learn. In the training of a teacher of German as a second language, Breul believed, 'a historical and philological study of German is indispensable' (op. cit.:89); and he also demanded a training of teachers in phonetics, although he regarded it as less important than a general philological training: 'a teacher need not be a phonetic specialist' (op. cit.:99).

For the development of language teaching in Europe it was fortunate that a number of scholars of the calibre of Sweet, Viëtor, Passy, and Jespersen had set an example of combining their interest in the philology of European languages and in phonetics with a serious concern for language teaching.[2] The way was thus prepared for a linguistic component in language teaching theory. Language teachers had access to the work of several European linguists whose writings appeared during the first three or four decades of the twentieth century, for example, Bally, Meillet, Brunot, Dauzat, and Martinet in France; Glinz, Weisgerber, and Trier in Germany; Sweet, Jones, Palmer, and Firth in Britain; or Jespersen, Hjelmslev, and Brøndal in Denmark. These authors and their writings were not unknown among language teachers.

Yet, in spite of this steady stream of linguistic thought, the activities of language teachers, and the writings of language teaching theorists in Europe and in America until about 1940, i.e., to the end of the second period of our historical survey, did not reveal any distinct awareness of linguistics in language teaching. Language teaching theorists hardly asked basic linguistic questions: what is the nature of language? Where does the linguistic information come from on which the teaching of language X or Y is based? How reliable is this information? The training of language teachers in the university was oriented towards literary scholarship and fostered a command of the language as a practical skill. Questions of the nature, function, and structure of languages were somehow outside the theorist's range of vision. For example, the *Memorandum on the Teaching of Modern Languages* (I.A.A.M. 1929), which reflects the considered views of language teachers in England in the twenties, deals extensively with questions of methodology and organization. But the view of language, implied in the pedagogical treatment, is nowhere made explicit. Questions of language description, of theory of language, or of the contribution of linguistics simply did not arise. The only exception was the case for or against phonetics which was discussed at length, but purely as an aid to pronunciation teaching.[3] The strange anomaly, why one aspect of language should be considered in the light of linguistic science and no other, is not even mentioned.[4]

In the early decades of the twentieth century language teaching theorists in America were inclined to turn to psychology much more than to linguistics in the attempt to establish a scientific foundation for language teaching. Thus, Handschin (1923), who wrote a comprehensive and well documented book on pedagogy, in a chapter on the scientific bases of foreign language teaching considered only studies on the psychology of memory or learning. The searching enquiries of the American and Canadian Committees of the Modern Foreign Language Study included no study of fundamental linguistic issues. Admittedly, this project sponsored pioneer work on word frequency counts in French, Spanish, and German; but these were treated as *ad hoc* statistical studies in curriculum development to be solved by the strictly empirical methods of contemporary educational science or educational psychology for which Thorndike's *The Teacher's Word Book*(1921) had set the example. They were not viewed as investigations to be related to linguistic theory. Consequently, basic issues of any lexicological study, for example, the concept of 'word' to be used, the role of a statistical approach to linguistic problems, the question of register, the sampling procedures, or the relationship of other linguistic issues to the question of vocabulary control, did not enter into the discussion. The purely statistical word count studies were based on no recognizable theoretical foundation in linguistics. An exception to the non-linguistic approach was the work of Palmer who, as early as 1917, had interested himself in the linguistic analysis of the popular concept of the 'word'. In subsequent years he tried to develop rational principles of vocabulary selection. Quite apart from the word counts and Palmer's work, there was a widespread concern about the vocabulary question. Theoretical linguists, however, appear to have taken no part whatever in this essentially linguistic issue, and they offered no help on the question of vocabulary control. The development of word frequency studies in the interwar years epitomizes the relationship between linguistics and language teaching during that period.[5]

As late as 1949, Closset, a Belgian language teaching theorist, whose work on language teaching was written in a scholarly spirit and with ample references to supporting studies, included chapters on grammar and vocabulary which made no direct reference to the linguistic origins of his recommendations.[6]

There were a few exceptions to this lack of linguistic awareness in pedagogy. Notably, Palmer (1917, 1922) was among a small number of theorists who openly accorded a place to linguistics which, in his view, should constitute the scientific basis of language teaching. In his first major work, *The Scientific Study and Teaching of Languages* (1917), Palmer outlined in some fifteen pages a theory of language which was to provide the necessary linguistic concepts and systematizations for a comprehensive treatment of language pedagogy. In Palmer's theory, the study of language comprises the study of sounds (phonetics), phonemes (phonology), letters (orthography), etymons (derivation or etymology), semanticons (semantics), and ergons (syntactical units, studied by syntax or ergonics). To the different subdisciplines, which correspond to each of the units of analysis, can be assigned a number of teaching techniques intended to develop in the learner the particular aspect of language. The reader will recognize in Palmer's comprehensive approach to language, a close affinity to Firthian and Halliday's neo-Firthian ideas (see Chapter 7:138–40). Palmer's scheme offers a language teaching theory on the basis of an explicit theory of language. Contemporary writers on language pedagogy made little or no use of Palmer's well-conceived scheme. Neither accepting nor rejecting it, they simply ignored it, because presumably language teaching theorists did not see the necessity for establishing a language teaching theory on a deliberately formulated theory of language.

By and large, then, apart from a few exceptions, language teaching theory until about 1940 (and in many instances much later) simply took for granted the concept of language; and such specifically linguistic problems, as the role of phonetics, word frequency control, or grammar topics, were treated as purely empirical questions of pedagogy. The linguists who succeeded Sweet, Viëtor, and Jespersen did not consider foreign language teaching as a particular concern of theirs or as presenting problems of outstanding linguistic interest.[7]

The confident application

The role of American structuralism

It was not until the early years of World War II that linguistics was recognized as an important, perhaps even as the most important, component in a language teaching theory. The growth of structural

linguistics in America played a crucial role in this change of attitude.[8]
Round 1940, the needs of an impending war had opened the eyes of
American administrators to language problems that Americans, particularly in the armed forces, might be called upon to face. A group of
linguists, under the leadership of the Linguistic Society of America,
undertook to turn their experience in language description to the task of
a 'linguistic analysis of each language to be taught, followed by the
preparation of learning materials based on this analysis' (Moulton
1961:84). Within a few years manuals with such titles as *Spoken
Burmese* or *Spoken Chinese* were composed. Many of the leading
American linguists of this period were involved in the preparation of
texts in this series, for example, Bloch (Japanese), Hall (French), Haugen
(Norwegian), Hockett (Chinese), Hodge (Serbo-Croatian), Sebeok
(Finnish, Hungarian), Hoenigswald (Hindustani), Moulton (German),
and of the older generation Bloomfield (Dutch and Russian) (op. cit.:86).
General principles were expressed in Bloomfield's *Outline Guide for the
Practical Study of Foreign Languages* and Bloch and Trager's *Outline of
Linguistic Analysis*.

Linguists in the forties in America were fully aware of the fact that
their role in language teaching and language course writing was a new
experience for linguistics as well as for language pedagogy. There was
little doubt in their minds that one must break with the traditions of
conventional language teaching, especially in the teaching of 'exotic'
languages. 'Start with a clean slate' wrote Bloomfield in his *Outline
Guide* (p. 1). Bloomfield's severe criticism of conventional language
teaching in American schools and colleges was already mentioned in the
historical review (Chapter 6:99). Drawing on his experience of linguistic
field studies, Bloomfield suggested a professional and almost technical
approach. A language, he argued, can only be learnt from a native
speaker who acts as an informant, and who must be closely observed
and imitated. The less selfconsciously the informant can show the
student what to say and how to say it, the better it is. The more he
theorizes and sets himself up as a teacher, the worse it is. Is there then no
place for instruction? Indeed there is; but good textbooks, serviceable
grammars and dictionaries are rare; and teachers often have an
insufficient command of the language. Therefore 'the only effective
teacher' is the trained linguist working alongside the student, prompting
him what questions to ask from the informant and how to study the
forms of the language. Bloomfield does not favour unconscious soaking
up. Language learning involves conscientious recording, conscious
imitating, patient practising and memorizing, as well as analysing what
the native speaker does and says. The set of techniques that crystallized
out of these arguments was: (1) a structural analysis of the language,
forming the basis for graded material; (2) presentation of the analysis by
a trained linguist; (3) several hours of drill per day with the help of a

native speaker and in small classes, and (4) emphasis on speaking as the first objective (Moulton 1961:93). In this scheme the linguist was therefore accorded an important dual role: (a) he had to undertake the description of the language; and (b) he had to explain the linguistic system to the student.

These ideas were not 'applied' integrally in language teaching, nor did linguists oust the teacher everywhere in the drastic manner suggested by the *Outline Guide*. Nevertheless, ideas derived from structural linguistics became the accepted doctrine which was more or less implemented in the American wartime language programmes. They were commonly expressed in five slogans which reflect the influence of structural linguistics.[9] The principles expressed in some of these are already familiar to us from our previous discussion of the characteristic features of modern linguistics:

1 Language is speech, not writing.
2 A language is what its native speakers say, not what someone thinks they ought to say.
3 Languages are different.
4 A language is a set of habits.
5 Teach the language, not about the language.

The fifth slogan expresses more a pedagogical than a linguistic principle. It emphasizes the need for practice rather than for explanation. It is a reminder to the teacher-linguist not to confuse his primary interest as a linguistic scientist in the language as a formal structure with that of the student whose principal aim is to learn how to use the language as a means of communication. All five principles became tenets of language teaching doctrine during the two post-war decades. Their influence was felt in teacher training, in classroom practice, and the design of teaching materials. It was not until the mid-sixties that, under the influence of transformational generative grammar, the linguistics of these tenets was seriously questioned.

At the same time as one group of American linguists demonstrated the usefulness of linguistics in the teaching of exotic languages, another group made the same point with regard to English as a second language. From its foundation in 1941, the English Language Institute of the University of Michigan, under the leadership of Charles Fries, approached the teaching of English as a second language from the point of view of structural linguistics. In the preparation of new teaching materials at this institute the attempt was made 'to interpret, in a practical way for teaching, the principles of modern linguistic science and to use the results of scientific linguistic research' (Fries 1945:i). In a study on teaching English as a foreign language, based on this institute's experience, Fries (1945) showed how the sound system, the structures, and the most useful lexical material could be derived from available linguistic knowledge and organized for language teaching purposes. Fries repeatedly insisted on pointing out that the fundamental contribution of linguistics to language teaching was not so much the oral emphasis, intensive practice, or smaller classes, but 'the descriptive analysis as the basis upon which to build the teaching materials' (Fries 1949). Fries himself undertook, for example, an analysis of English sentence structure in which he used as descriptive data recorded conversations amounting to a corpus of 250,000 running words (Fries 1952). For the teaching of foreign languages, Fries further demanded 'an adequate descriptive analysis of both the language to be studied and the native language of the student' (Fries 1945:5). [10]

In accordance with this contrastive linguistic principle, as it became known, the English Language Institute produced an English course for Latin-American students and another for Chinese students. In 1948, three members of the Institute's staff wrote about 'The importance of the Native Language in Foreign Language Learning' in the first issue of *Language Learning, a journal of applied linguistics*, which had grown out of the work of the Institute. In 1957, Lado, who had succeeded Fries as the director of the English Language Institute, published the first major systematic study on the methods of a contrastive linguistic analysis as the basis for the preparation of language teaching materials and language tests.

Lado's approach to contrastive linguistics
Lado (1957) was concerned with the concept of difficulty in language learning. Starting out from the common-sense observation that the learner will find some features of a new language difficult and others easy, he argued that the key to degrees of difficulty lies in the comparison between the native and the foreign language. Since an individual tends to transfer the features of his native language to the foreign language, a comparative study will be useful in identifying the likenesses and differences between the languages and thus enable the linguist to predict areas of difficulty for the second language learner. The principle of such language comparisons was not new; it was implicit in much traditional language practice. But Lado, following Fries, was the first to apply the principle systematically and to make it the central feature of a dual description of two languages in parallel. Contrastive analysis was not intended to offer a new method of teaching; but it was a form of language description across two languages which was particularly applicable to curriculum development, the preparation and evaluation of teaching materials, to the diagnosis of learning problems, and to testing. Lado's study was programmatic; it outlined procedures of how to make such comparisons in phonology, grammar, vocabulary, and in the cultural aspects of a language.

The detailed work remained to be done. Soon after the Center for

Applied Linguistics had been founded in Washington in 1959, it sponsored a series of contrastive studies, which, it was thought, would give American teachers the most vital linguistic information on a number of languages in comparison with English as the native language. They included studies on the phonology and grammar of German, Spanish, Italian, Russian, and French.[11] Thus, in the early sixties contrastive linguistics had become one of the most important means of relating linguistics to language teaching. As we shall see shortly, the continuation of the development of contrastive linguistics is linked up with the evolution of the role of linguistics in language teaching generally (see p. 168 below).

By about 1960, the influence of structural linguistics upon language teaching had reached a peak, at any rate in the United States. In association with a behaviourist theory of language learning it provided the principal theoretical basis of the audiolingual theory and in this way influenced language teaching materials, teaching and testing techniques, and teacher education.[12]

Stack, the protagonist of the language laboratory in the United States, wrote in 1964: 'Today's foreign language teaching is achieving success unknown under the traditional methods. This has been accomplished by the application of structural linguistics to teaching, particularly in the realms of proper sequence, oral grammar, inductive grammar, and the use of pattern drills to give intensive practice' (Stack 1964:80–81).

Linguistics and language teaching in Europe
The trend outlined in the foregoing paragraphs referred particularly to America; but similar developments took place in Europe (1940–1960). Indeed, underlying Bloomfield's criticism of American foreign language teaching was a comparison with Europe. Bloomfield believed that in Europe a linguistic basis was part of the culture and background of the language teacher.[13] No doubt, as was already indicated at the beginning of this chapter, a considerable volume of linguistic scholarship was accessible to European language teachers since the early part of the century, perhaps more so than in the United States, and therefore the infusion of a linguistic component was even more important in America than in Europe. The linguistic influences we have referred to brought about a reorientation and updating of American language teaching theory which, to a certain extent, had already taken place in Europe at the turn of the century through the influence of Sweet, Viëtor, Jespersen, and Passy. The belief, expressed at times, that American language teaching theorists in the forties first 'discovered' linguistics, is, as Strevens (1972) has rightly pointed out, false.

Nevertheless, the impact of linguistics on language teaching in the U.S.A. between 1940 and 1960 gradually transformed the ideological climate not only in North America but in many other countries as well, and this trend had a distinct influence also on language pedagogy in Europe. Without the example of American structural linguistics, it is extremely unlikely that European linguistics alone would have brought about the changes in language teaching theory to which language teachers everywhere were increasingly exposed in the fifties and sixties.

In Britain the most determined effort to give language teaching a foundation in linguistics was made by teachers of English as a second language. Several university centres, especially London, Manchester, Leeds, Edinburgh, and Bangor, became active in this respect. But in some of them the approach to linguistics was much more cautious than in America. It prompted the well-known British applied linguist, Strevens (1963a), to characterize the American view as 'make them good structural linguists and the problems will be solved', while the British view was 'make them good teachers and the problems will be solved'. Strevens, who was one of the foremost theoreticians in Britain to make linguistics known to language teachers, advocated a synthesis of these two approaches:

> 'The teaching of English as a foreign language has become a joint activity, containing on the one hand both education and method-ology ..., and on the other hand, a sound background of linguistic thought and up-to-date descriptions of the present-day language ...'
> (op. cit.:19)

Linguistics influenced European language teaching particularly by a new emphasis on description and authenticity of language data in the development of language teaching materials. The pioneer effort in Europe was the linguistic research project on *français fondamental*, begun in France in 1951. (See also Chapter 4:55).

Français fondamental was developed as an 'initial teaching' French; in contrast to Basic English, planned in the thirties by Ogden as a self-sufficient international auxiliary language, which had to be learnt even by native speakers of ordinary English if they were to make themselves understood by 'fluent' speakers of Basic English. *Français fondamental* was envisaged only as an early stage of French for learners of French as a second language. It was based on the thought that, at an elementary level of language use, a learner requires above all the spoken language of everyday life in concrete situations. At a second level the language required for non-specialized reading would be added. Thus, a functional distinction between the linguistic requirements of stages of language learning was introduced to be reflected in the selection of language items.

The research was based on the following principles. (a) It focused its main attention on word frequency; and, in this respect, it followed the example set by the numerous word-counts undertaken during the interwar years, particularly in the U.S.A. Like in these studies, a given corpus was analysed. (b) While the majority of American studies had been based on a corpus of written or printed materials, the French team broke new ground by analysing recorded conversations so as to establish a frequency vocabulary of spoken French. Some care was taken that the 275 informants (138 men, 126 women, and 11 children of school age) represented different social and educational levels. (c) The research further included a study based on the new concept of *disponibilité* or availability, i.e., an analysis of words which, although not in frequent use, are readily accessible to the native speaker. They were elicited by asking groups of school children to write down words on a given topic or centres of interest, by a process of free association. (d) Lastly, the study did not rely entirely on the mechanical application of statistical analyses of the items collected. The final selection of words was considered in the light of a 'rational empiricism'. A somewhat less clearly defined grammatical analysis was also undertaken. The findings were first published in 1954. A revised list of *français fondamental* (first stage), appeared in 1959. It consists of 1475 entries composed of 1222 lexical words and 253 grammatical words.

For the second level, the investigators made use of the American French vocabulary frequency analysis by Vander Beke (1929) in conjunction with an analysis of modern written materials taken from newspapers, reviews, and a textbook of civic education. The two stages together constitute the 'common core' (*tronc commun*); it was envisaged that they would be followed by a number of specialized vocabularies, based on the analysis of different registers, such as literary criticism or scientific writing. *Français fondamental* illustrates well the intention of many linguists both in America and in Europe to base language teaching materials on the analysis of carefully selected, authentic samples of language use.[14]

Several other similarly motivated studies were undertaken in subsequent years, some simply descriptive, and others descriptive as well as contrastive, some laying emphasis on lexis, others on grammar, but all with the purpose of providing coursebook writers and language teachers with adequate and serviceable descriptions of the contemporary language.[15] In the report on an international conference on modern foreign language teaching held in Berlin in 1964, the position in the early sixties was summed up as follows: 'Gone is the day when a language course was simply the outcome of the inventive inspiration of an author. Course material has to be based on a linguistic analysis of the language to be taught, studied as far as possible *in situ* ... Field studies of language and systematic analyses of languages are needed' (Stern 1965:49).

Linguistic influences on teaching methods
Besides the direct contribution that, by 1960, linguistics had made to
language teaching through various descriptive and contrastive analyses,
there was another perhaps even more important aspect to its influence.
Although many linguists strenuously denied that linguistics had anything to say about how to teach a language, the effect, directly or
indirectly, of linguistics upon the design and content of language courses
and upon teaching methods was considerable, even if we set aside the
psychological theories of language learning.[16] As we observed in the last
chapter, it is an essential characteristic of linguistic enquiry to abstract
from the total reality of language and language use, and, depending on
the purpose of a study, to focus on selected features. Thus, in phonetics
and phonology, the sounds of the language are in the centre of attention,
while in syntactical studies the relationship of words within a sentence is
examined. The manipulation and close study of formal properties of
language samples has been an important tool of descriptive linguistic
enquiry. The structural linguist brought to language teaching the skill of
isolating, closely observing, and analysing specific linguistic patterns.
The methods of analysis of structural linguistics are reflected particularly in pattern practice and in language laboratory drills which focus, one
by one, on particular features of the language in syntagmatic relationships. Language teachers around 1960 were prepared to adopt techniques for language teaching which linguistic research had evolved, just
as sixty years earlier many language teachers had been prepared to
adopt the phonetician's analysis of speech sounds and the international
phonetic alphabet for pronunciation training. Whether techniques of
linguistic analysis—however well they may lend themselves to linguistic
research—are equally applicable to language teaching is of course open
to question.[17]

Application to testing
Structural and contrastive linguistics—in combination with principles
derived from psychometrics—also influenced the construction of language tests. A pioneering study by Lado (1961) was among the first to
suggest that the content of language tests should be based on a linguistic
analysis; and language tests produced during that period clearly
reflected the analytical procedures of descriptive linguistics.

The primacy of speech
Likewise, the primacy of speech in language teaching can, to some
extent, be attributed to the influence of linguistics, although this
emphasis has partly also other origins. In many ways it is the oldest of
the reform trends. Irrespective of modern linguistics, the nineteenth
century reformers counteracted the exclusive emphasis on literary

expression. There were also strong practical motives for learning how to speak and understand the spoken language which, for over a century, have prompted the demand for an oral emphasis. But linguistics backed up this demand by its stress on the primacy of speech; and the interest in the descriptive study of the spoken language in its own right led to a clearer understanding of the linguistic characteristics of the spoken medium.[18]

Alternatives to American structuralism

In the early sixties two major works appeared which promised a reorientation towards structural linguistics: *The Linguistic Sciences and Language Teaching* by Halliday, McIntosh, and Strevens (1964) and *Language Teaching Analysis* by Mackey (1965). In the face of the overwhelming weight of American writings on linguistics in relation to language teaching, Halliday, McIntosh, and Strevens (1964) endeavoured to present a broader viewpoint which was derived from European, and mainly, British linguistic traditions.[19] Like American structuralists these three linguists sought an alternative to the unformulated and traditional linguistic conventions in language teaching. An analysis of published English courses led them to criticize school grammars for their unclear categories, heterogeneous criteria, misapplied conceptual formulations, value judgements, fictions, inaccurate phonetics, and confusions between speech and writing. Again like Fries and other structuralists, Halliday, McIntosh, and Strevens regarded adequate language descriptions as the principal contribution that linguistics could make to language teaching. But descriptions, based on structuralism, in their view, are 'unsatisfactory largely because of their neglect of contextual meaning and their inability to present an integrated picture of a language as a whole' (op. cit.:149). Equally transformational grammar (the 1957 version), although fully acknowledged by them as a powerful theory, was also rejected as a theory for language teaching because it does not 'present an integrated theory to cover all levels of language' (op. cit.:150). The study adopted the neo-Firthian scale-and-category theory for two reasons: one was that it gave an adequate place to meaning at all levels of language: 'meaning cannot be isolated from form' (op. cit.:154); the other that it was 'polysystemic', that is, it gives equal weight to the different levels of language, the material substance of language (sounds and writing), the internal structure or form (grammar and lexis), and the environmental context (meaning). The implications of this theory for language teaching are indicated in the following diagram which associates the different levels of language with a series of pedagogical steps or 'methodics' (Figure 8.1, op. cit.:222). Once a language description is available, a choice ('limitation') of variety or register ('restriction') and language items ('selection') has to be made. The selected repertoire must then be 'graded' in large steps ('stages') and then subdivided into sequences at each stage. After that, 'presentation' represents the pedagogical treatment of the ordered repertoire, followed by evaluation ('testing'). The diagram indicates that at each pedagogical step the four levels of language indicated are relevant.

	Levels of language and their equivalents in methodology			
Procedures of methodics	Phonology 'sounds of speech'	Grammar 'structures' 'grammatical patterns'	Lexis 'vocabulary'	Context 'situations'
Limitation — Restriction / Selection				
Grading — Staging / Sequencing				
Presentation — Initial teaching / Repeated teaching				
Testing — Formal/Informal / Objective/Subjective / Tests/Examinations				

Figure 8.1   Methodics and linguistic analysis,
after Halliday, McIntosh, and Strevens

Thus, Halliday, McIntosh, and Strevens offer a coherent and comprehensive statement of linguistic theory and its application to language teaching. Although this work was widely read and is justifiably used even today as an outstanding source for the study of the relationship between linguistics and language pedagogy it did not bring about the expected reorientation. One reason for this failure, already referred to in Chapter 7, may be that scale-and-category theory offered no clear alternative to structuralism. Another was that the application of the linguistic theory to language teaching was not sufficiently developed to enable teachers to judge its worth. In the diagram the boxes which relate the pedagogical steps (methodics) to the levels of language were left empty; and the accompanying text did not offer sufficiently detailed illustrations of how to relate the linguistic theory to the system of methodics. Nor, to the writer's knowledge, have any attempts ever been made to translate this scheme into a curriculum. However, in many respects the scheme represents what language curricula attempt to do, i.e., to cover the different facts of language and to present them in some graded fashion. The problem, however, is what are the relationships between the linguistic divisions? And how can language items be selected and arranged to do justice to language?

The object of the other major work to challenge structuralism, *Language Teaching Analysis* (Mackey 1965), was different: it was not merely concerned with linguistic theory in relation to language teaching. It aimed at developing a broad and systematic framework for an analysis of language teaching. This framework consists of three interrelated areas: (1) language, (2) text or 'method', and (3) teaching. The first of these, language, concerns us here. According to Mackey (1965:x), language analysis comprises language theory, language description, and language differences; in other words, theoretical, descriptive, and contrastive linguistics. The recognition of the relevance of these three areas for language teaching accords with both the structuralist and the neo-Firthian positions. But unlike these, Mackey does not select a linguistic model for application to language teaching. Instead, he defines the different positions that different linguistic theories adopt in terms of different approaches to language: mechanistic or mentalistic, inductive or deductive, substance or form, content or expression, state or activity. Accordingly, there are, among different theories, differences in approaches at all levels of language description: phonetics, grammar, vocabulary, and meaning. While Mackey's highly condensed presentation does not allow for an explanation of the motivation of these different viewpoints, the range of theoretical and descriptive ideas is succinctly and impartially mapped out. The implication is that differences in language teaching can be related to these different linguistic theories. Although this analysis is not designed to direct the teacher to any one theory or description of language, it implies as a viewpoint that language teaching can find support in a number of different theories, and that in an analysis of language teaching the linguistic theory underlying it must also be clearly identified. On the whole, as will be seen in Chapter 9, it was this relatively detached position towards language theories that was widely adopted in the subsequent years.

Review

In summary, during the period 1940–1960 the idea that language teaching theory implies a theory of language and that linguistics had a direct contribution to make to language pedagogy became more and more accepted. The main impact of linguistic theory can be seen in (1) language description as an essential basis of the language curriculum and corpus selection (for example, *français fondamental*); (2) emphasis on linguistic forms reflected in the divisions into phonological and grammatical exercises and gradation of linguistic items; (3) contrastive analysis as a principle of curriculum development; (4) primacy of speech; (5) linguistic patterns as units of instruction (pattern practice, pattern drill) and of testing.

Most of these features were severely criticized in the subsequent period along with the underlying psychological assumptions that had been made. In retrospect, however, it is important to recognize the main contributions of this phase of linguistics. The first is to have created a linguistic awareness which, as we have seen, had previously been absent. The second is the recognition of the importance of descriptive data for the language to be taught. Formal structural analysis provided language teaching with an entirely new, simple, down-to-earth way of handling the complexities of a language system. The need for such well attested information on the second languages to be taught was somewhat lost sight of in the turmoil of subsequent theoretical debates. A third positive development was a new type of exercise, pattern drills. While the overemphasis on pattern drills was rightly criticized in later years, pattern practice as such can nonetheless be regarded as an important step forward in language teaching techniques because of its simple, systematic, and potentially flexible approach to relevant language features.[20]

The disorienting impact of new theory: 1965 to 1970

Even as principles of structural linguistics were being translated into practice in the classrooms, transformational generative grammar appeared on the scene. It shook the foundations of structuralism in linguistics and by implication of audiolingualism in language teaching. The 1957 version of Chomsky's theory was hardly taken note of by language pedagogy for some years. Its applicability to mother tongue teaching was recognized from about 1960 when it appeared to some as an interesting alternative to the conventional treatment of syntax (for example, Roberts 1964). About the same time transformational generative grammar began to be acknowledged by some language teaching theorists as an addition and possible modification of the structural theory and, therefore, relevant to language teaching. But as was just noted, Halliday, McIntosh, and Strevens (1964), although opposed to structuralism for their own reasons, considered transformational generative grammar as too limited to offer an alternative *general* linguistic theory for language teaching. Mackey (1965), too, treated transformational generative grammar as merely one of several possible approaches to the description of syntactical patterns.

But from about 1964, with closer acquaintance of the newer developments in transformational generative grammar, it became clear to a few linguists that this theory of grammar might well upset many of the prevailing tenets of contemporary linguistics and of the new approach to language teaching. Three discussions of these issues (Saporta 1966; Anisfeld 1966; Chomsky 1966) opened a prolonged debate on the implications of transformational generative grammar for language teaching. Bitter attacks, as scathing as those made by structural linguists on traditional grammar, were now beginning to be made on structuralism and the audiolingual theory of language teaching. Many of the criticisms were directed against the behaviouristic psychology of the audiolingual theory; but, as was shown in Chapter 7, the linguistic principles, too, came under attack, and the view of language, adopted by language teachers only a few years earlier, suddenly appeared wrong and outmoded.

Contrastive analysis and transformational generative grammar
Constrastive analysis, too, was seriously affected by these radical changes in linguistic theory. It had come into prominence in the heyday of descriptive and structural linguistics and was therefore vulnerable as the fortunes of structuralism declined. The issues and prospects of contrastive analysis in a world of changing linguistic theories were discussed repeatedly during the period under consideration (for example, Alatis 1968; Nickel 1971). Indeed, some transformational generative theorists were ready to dismiss contrastive analysis as a comparison of mere surface structures and therefore of little further interest to linguists in the Chomskyan era. However, a transformational generative approach to contrastive linguistics which 'inter-relates the semantic, syntactic and phonological components of language while providing for a distinction of surface and deep levels in each of the three components' was developed by Di Pietro (1968, 1971). Di Pietro ingeniously argued that, in order to make comparisons between languages and to find likenesses and differences, languages must have something in common, otherwise comparisons could not be made. He found the transformational generative distinction between deep and surface structure useful as a means of reinterpreting contrastive linguistics. Thanks to this newer statement, the theoretical basis of contrastive analysis, which had been clearly structuralist in Lado's work (1957), was brought into line with these later developments in linguistic theory. Although contrastive analysis has never recovered the place it held in language pedagogy in the early sixties, its value has been reassessed and its continued importance is hardly disputed today (for example, James 1980; Fisiak 1981).

Impact of transformational generative grammar on language teaching
While the influence of structuralism on language pedagogy was pervasive and powerful and can be clearly identified in teaching materials, teaching methods, language tests, and in the writings of language teaching methodologists (for example, Brooks 1960/1964; Lado 1964), the influence of transformational generative grammar was of a different kind. Admittedly, 'transformations' and 'rules' began to appear in some language courses, and a few textbook authors made serious attempts (for example, Rutherford in *Modern English* 1968) to devise teaching programmes which embodied insights from transformational generative

grammar. In the main, however, transformational generative grammar became a rallying point for all the misgivings and criticisms concerning structural linguistics and the audiolingual method that had previously been felt here and there but had not been expressed systematically. As a negative force, freeing language teaching theory from the weight of behaviourism in psychology and structuralism in linguistics, transformational generative grammar exercised a liberating impact. It created an intellectual upheaval the like of which language pedagogy had not previously experienced. Phonetics in the early part of the century and structural linguistics in the forties and fifties can be said to have exercised an influence on pedagogy; they had offered innovations that had given language pedagogy new concepts, new information, new perspectives and additional techniques. But transformational generative grammar, especially by the suddenness of the change in linguistic thought, forced language teaching theory to re-examine the entire view of language no less than the psychological side of language learning. During the late sixties and early seventies certain new developments in language pedagogy occurred which can be regarded almost entirely as resulting from the impact of transformational generative theory.

A rationalist theory of language learning

A 'rationalist' or 'cognitive' theory emerged in which transformational generative concepts represented the linguistic component and became associated with a 'cognitive' view of the psychology of language learning. This theory was placed in opposition to an 'empiricist' theory; that is, pedagogically audiolingualism, psychologically behaviourism, and linguistically structuralism. For example, Diller (1970, 1971, 1978) contrasted these two theories and openly declared his preference for the rationalist position.

Other theorists, in a more conciliatory frame of mind, held that the two theories were complementary and served different types of learners or teachers (for example, Chastain 1971, 1976) or represented different phases of the language learning process (for example, Rivers 1968). Others again argued that neither conceptually nor practically was the distinction between the two theories as clear as the juxtaposition of empiricism (audiolingualism) and rationalism (cognitive theory) would suggest (for example, Carroll 1971; Rivers 1972; Stern 1974a). In the context of this discussion it is important to note that around 1970 language teaching theorists argued fiercely about theories of language, and the choice of a linguistic theory played a major role in the polarization of methodological issues. It is not surprising to find that many observers of the language teaching scene were unhappy about this ideological rift and began to question the role of linguistics in language pedagogy.

Notes

1 'A method can never, and must never repeat Nature, or it is no longer a method ... Let us therefore confess it from the first, and declare it aloud: our method does not admit, it refuses, this qualification of "natural"; and if it is not yet an art, it is the roughed-out model of an art' (Gouin 1892:85).

2 For example, Sweet (1899/1964) believed that a good training for language teaching 'must be based on a thorough knowledge of the science of language—phonetics, sound-notation, the grammatical structure of a variety of representative languages, and linguistic problems generally' (op. cit.:3).

3 It is interesting to note, however, that the bibliography of the 1929 I.A.A.M. *Memorandum* has a brief section with twelve titles on linguistics, including works by Jespersen, Bally, and Brunot. The 1949/1956 successor volume, *The Teaching of Modern Languages*, which contains a more extensive general bibliography, includes a short section, entitled 'General Linguistics'; and in those parts of the bibliography which deal with the separate languages, there is always one section on 'linguistics' and another on the phonetics of the language. It is all the more astonishing that this had not prompted the authors to attempt a more explicit treatment of the view of language with which to operate.

4 Palmer (1922) was aware of this discrepancy in scientific development when he wrote about phonetics: 'The remarkable advance in this comparatively new science is one of the most hopeful signs of progress, and a pledge of eventual perfection ... A similar advance in the sister sciences such as grammar and semantics is not yet apparent, but there are signs that ere long the many isolated workers in these domains will be able to do what the phoneticians did twenty or thirty years ago ... and we shall witness the coming into existence of the general science of linguistics' (1964:36)

5 The chronic neglect of vocabulary in linguistic (and psycholinguistic) studies was mentioned in Chapter 7. For the history and principles of vocabulary control see Bongers (1947) who described Palmer's efforts in 1931 to make contact with research workers in this area. Palmer took up an intermediate position between the purely quantitative studies of American research workers and the highly subjective approach of Ogden, the creator of Basic English. Bongers writes about Palmer's visit to Sapir: 'At the *Institute of Human Relations* (Yale University) he renewed the acquaintance with that linguistic genius, the late Professor Sapir, who approved his attitude towards the ultra-subjectivism of Ogden at the one extreme, and the objectivism of those who relied entirely on quantitative statistics' (Bongers 1947:81). In 1934 and 1935 the

Carnegie Corporation sponsored a conference and a study on vocabulary control. In spite of the lively interest that was aroused by the question of vocabulary control, theoretical linguistics contributed little to this discussion.

6 However, Closset's bibliography includes titles in linguistics.

7 Bloomfield, however, appears to have felt very strongly that a well developed science of linguistics would be of benefit to language education generally. In *Language* (1933) he included foreign language teaching among possible fields of application. But his remarks there hardly indicated in what way linguistics would be applied so as to remedy the 'appalling waste of effort' (op. cit.:503) which he noted.

8 The influence of linguistics on language teaching in the U.S.A. between 1940 and 1960 has been fully documented and analysed by Moulton (1961/1963).

9 These five slogans have been explained by Moulton (1961:86–90).

10 Several other linguists collaborating with Fries at the English Language Institute or in the same university, for example, Pike, Nida, Marckwardt, and Lado, as well as linguists at other institutions at that time produced valuable studies in descriptive linguistics; among them, for example, Pike's pioneering work on the intonation of American English (Pike 1945).

11 For details of this Contrastive Structure series, see Alatis (1968). The *Report of the 19th Annual Round Table* on contrastive linguistics (Alatis 1968) represents an excellent review and assessment of contrastive analysis at a critical stage in its development in the mid-sixties.

12 Writings on language pedagogy, for example, Brooks (1960) or Lado (1964), increasingly specified their view of the nature of language and drew on structural linguistics.

13 In his *Outline Guide* Bloomfield (1942) recommended as background books mainly the writings of such European linguists or phoneticians as Sweet, Palmer, Passy, Ripman, Jespersen, and Noël-Armfield.

14 For further details on *français fondamental* see Gougenheim *et al.* (1964).

15 A European survey of research into spoken language, made in 1968, was able to list a number of such descriptive studies (CILT 1970).

16 Saporta (1966) went so far as to say that 'the impact of the descriptive linguistics of the forties and fifties on language teaching was primarily on the form and only incidentally on the content of pedagogical grammars' (op. cit.:82).

17 From the standpoint of 1965–6 Valdman (1966a) described and criticized this development in these terms: 'The Linguistic Method of organization of subject matter and instruction followed literally the order of descriptive fieldwork: first, phonemic contrasts; then,

assimilation of forms through pattern drills; and last, presentation of syntactic arrangements'; 'Coupled with a disinterest in the semantic aspect of language, this emphasis on drill resulted in unthinking and mechanical manipulation of linguistic features' (op. cit.:xvii-xix).

18 See, for example, Wilkins (1972, Chapter 1:5–10).

19 'Where we have represented a particular approach, one in which ideas developed in Britain play a prominent part, this is not because there is any virtue in their being British but because this approach seems to us to combine, better than any other, the requirements both of theory and of application' (Halliday, McIntosh, and Strevens 1964:307).

20 At their best, pattern drills isolate language features and practise them in various ways by grading the difficulties. In the next phase, the decontextualized character of such practice was criticized. Yet, isolating a difficulty and decontextualizing it can be a pedagogically useful device. In many language courses, however, pattern practice became almost a ritualized routine. Exercises were devised in excessive numbers and their contribution to proficiency was often vague. In short, this excess of pattern drill was subject to somewhat the same criticism as, a hundred years earlier, the translation exercises which Viëtor had condemned as *Meidingerei*.

9 Linguistic theory and language teaching: reassessment and current status

Reassessment of the relationship

The sudden ideological changes, coupled with the abstract formalism and frequent obscurities of writings on transformational generative grammar, reopened the entire question of the contribution of linguistics to language teaching. The development of transformational generative theory in the late sixties made it very clear that the Chomskyan revolution was not the end of the upheaval. Because of the continued agitation language teachers were urged by some linguists, including Chomsky himself (1966), but also by Bolinger (1968), Corder (1973a) and others, to adopt a position of independence vis-à-vis linguistic theory. 'A professional is entitled to a mind of his own' (Bolinger 1968:41). Disclaiming any expertise in language teaching, Chomsky (1966:45) in a major conference presentation (see also Chapter 6:108) appealed to teachers to accept the 'responsibility to make sure that ideas and proposals are evaluated on their merits, and not passively accepted on grounds of authority, real or presumed' (op. cit.:45).

Two viewpoints emerged. One was to say that linguistics had been misapplied and that its importance had altogether been overrated. From playing no part at all in the interwar period, linguistics had risen to an exaggerated position of influence in language teaching theory. The disillusionment with linguistics was reflected in such article titles as 'The failure of the discipline of linguistics in language teaching' (Johnson 1969), or 'On the irrelevance of transformational grammar to second language pedagogy' (Lamendella 1969). These two articles did not reject linguistics as such, but pointed to 'the dangers in too readily accepting the explanations of the linguists as the basis of a strategy of learning' (Johnson 1969:243). Lamendella thought that it was 'a mistake to look to transformational grammar or any other theory of linguistic description to provide the theoretical basis for ... second language pedagogy ... what is needed in the field of language teaching are not applied linguists but rather applied psychologists' (op. cit.:255).

The other point of view that emerged was to recognize the general contribution of linguistics but with the proviso that language teaching is by no means bound to abide consistently by one theory. As was pointed out at the end of Chapter 7, the perspective of language teaching is different from that of linguistics. The linguist may seek validity in a coherent and consistent linguistic theory, while a language teacher judges a theory for its usefulness in the design of materials, in curriculum development, or in instruction (Valdman 1966a:xxi; Corder 1973a:15). Different linguistic theories may offer different perspectives on language, and they can be treated as equivalent resources. Ingenious examples were offered of a frankly eclectic application of several linguistic theories for different purposes in language teaching. Thus, Levenston (1973) showed how the description of linguistic items, such as indirect object structures in English, can be illuminated from different angles by deliberately shifting from one theoretical position to another. 'No one school of linguistic analysis has a monopoly of truth in the description of the phenomena of speech ... Traditional school grammar, the matrix techniques of tagmemic theory, the rule-ordering of transformational generative description, the systemic choices of scale-and-category grammar—all these and more can be shown to have their own particular relevance to the language teaching situation' (Levenston 1973:2). Likewise, Allen (1973), in a revision course for advanced learners of English as a second language in a university, devised practice materials based on two different linguistic models. In his view, the taxonomic model of different grammatical surface structures was appropriate for classroom practice, but only transformational generative grammar was able to relate different sentence patterns to each other: 'We have attempted to solve this dilemma by using a taxonomic, surface-structure model for the basic presentation, but at the same time utilizing transformational insights whenever this can be done informally without incurring a large number of abstract rules' (Allen 1973:94). In other words, a shift was taking place from 'applying' linguistics directly to treating linguistics as a resource to be drawn on for the benefit of pedagogy with complete independence of mind.

Another distinction was suggested by Spolsky in 1970. He described the relations between linguistics and language teaching as dual: 'applications and implications'. That is, the descriptions of language made by linguists can be 'applied' in the sense that they provide the data needed for writing teaching grammars, course books, and dictionaries. But the discussions that linguistics has initiated about the nature of language may provide new insights which in turn have implications for the teaching of languages.

Thus, the Chomskyan notion that language is creative would imply that teaching techniques which make learners respond automatically or repeat mechanically are less appropriate than techniques which lead to creative language use (Spolsky 1970:150). Such implications that could be derived from insights about the nature of language were considered by some theorists to be the most valuable contribution that should be expected from linguistics. Corder (1973a:15) summed it up by stating that 'there can be no systematic improvement in language teaching without reference to the knowledge about language which linguistics gives us.'[1]

The concept of a pedagogical grammar

It can be argued that it was a fault of past efforts to attempt to apply too directly the findings of phonetics, structural linguistics, or transformational generative grammar. The conviction that linguistic studies cannot be applied to language pedagogy without modification and interpretation led to the formulation of the concept of a 'pedagogical grammar' as an intermediary or link between linguistics and pedagogy, represented in the model in Chapter 3 (Figure 3.7) as level 2. If linguistic theory and description lead to a specific statement about a language L, this statement constitutes a 'formal', 'scientific', or 'linguistic' grammar or part of such a grammar of L. What the teacher or course writer needs, or what can be presented to the learner is not the scientific grammar. The teacher, the textbook writer, or student should have a selection of linguistic data, derived from the scientific grammar, modified in accordance with the purposes and conditions of language learning. 'If we accept the need for a filter between these formal grammars and the classroom, then the role of the pedagogical grammar is that of an interpreter between a number of formal grammars and the audience and situation-specific language teaching materials' (Candlin 1973:57).[2]

What factors should be taken into account in writing the pedagogical grammar? How much of the scientific grammar should appear in it, and how can the information the pedagogical grammar is to offer be presented most effectively? The pedagogical grammar need not be rigidly tied to one theory of language. Moreover, other than purely linguistic factors, in particular psychological and sociolinguistic factors, must determine the content.[3]

Noblitt (1972), for example, bases his conception of a pedagogical grammar on linguistic, psychological, and educational considerations and includes a fivefold analysis: a pedagogical grammar requires descriptive and contrastive data and concepts, an ordering of the information in terms of skills (listening, speaking, reading, and writing) and in terms of levels of achievement (elementary, intermediate, and advanced), and evaluation procedures, bearing in mind objectives and educational settings for which the pedagogical grammar is intended. 'A pedagogical grammar ... is a formulation of the grammar of a foreign language with the objective of the acquisition of that language; it embodies those considerations which are relevant as the learner is put in contact with that which is to be learned' (op. cit.:316). In other words, Noblitt makes the valid point that a language curriculum cannot be founded on linguistic considerations alone and he specifies what other factors have to be borne in mind in composing a pedagogical grammar.

From a slightly different perspective Corder (1973:156) has suggested what specific contribution to pedagogy can be expected from theoretical linguistics. He recognizes three orders of application as in Figure 9.1.

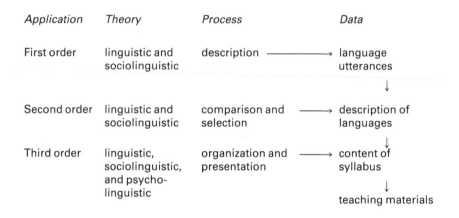

Figure 9.1   Corder's view of the applications of linguistics

At the first level of application the concepts of theoretical linguistics are used to analyse language data leading to the description of the second language. On this basis, the 'second-order applications' determine the selection of items. Such selection will be helped by contrastive analysis and error analysis, and will yield an inventory from which the linguistic content of the syllabus, equivalent to the level 2 of our model (Figure 3.7), as well as in the teaching materials can be determined at the 'third level of application' (i.e., our level 3). Although linguistics has still a contribution to make at this level in the development of a syllabus, on the composition of teaching materials, and in tests, the linguistic component has progressively declined in favour of psycholinguistic and sociolinguistic considerations.

In a similar vein to Noblitt's and Corder's proposals, Bausch (1979) analysed different attempts that have been made to relate linguistics constructively to pedagogy: direct application, 'filter', simplifications, and eclecticism. His main conclusion is that the conditions of teaching and learning must be taken into account in composing a pedagogical grammar. The findings of interlanguage studies, language acquisition research, as well as the condition of teaching itself, should be considered as legitimate input in determining the content of a pedagogical grammar. In other words, Noblitt, Corder, and Bausch agree that linguistics alone cannot say what should go into a pedagogical grammar.[4]

Conclusion
The net outcome for language pedagogy of this stage of re-assessment of linguistics has been (1) a clearer definition of specific contributions to be expected from linguistics, i.e., (a) insights into the nature of language and (b) empirical data on different languages; (2) the recognition of the need for a buffer or filter between linguistic theory and educational practice of which the pedagogical grammar is an outstanding example; and (3) awareness of the inter-disciplinary character of language peda-gogy: linguistics cannot be regarded as *the* discipline to sustain practice by itself.

The emancipation of educational linguistics: 1970–80

During the past decade a new generation of educational linguists became active who had learnt the lesson of this reassessment. This group of scholars no longer waited for the pronouncements of theoretical linguists; instead they used their own judgement and initiative in giving language pedagogy the linguistic direction they regarded as necessary.[5] They were linguists in their own right but at the same time experienced practitioners or closely in touch with practice. They were therefore in a good position to create the link between theory at level 1 and practice at level 3 in terms of the model in Figure 3.7. In some instances a team approach between a theoretically oriented linguist and a practically experienced language educator created the right conditions and led to productive co-operation.

Without waiting for the dust between structuralists and transform-ationalists to settle, they found both these linguistic theories too narrowly concerned with the purely formal aspects of language. While not repudiating a formal linguistic analysis, they welcomed the shift of interest in linguistic theory towards discourse analysis, semantics, speech act theory, sociolinguistics, and pragmatics.

For example, in a detailed and systematic attack on transformational generative grammar, reminiscent of the attacks of transformational generative grammar on structuralism and of structuralism on traditional grammar, Oller (1970) questioned the validity and usefulness of such concepts as 'competence' and 'deep and surface structure', and offered 'pragmatics as an alternative', because it placed emphasis on real language in use. He wanted to see the notion of deep structure re-interpreted as 'meanings: relations between situational settings (refe-rents, actions, events, abstract concepts, etc.) and linguistic forms, rather than relations between sentences and underlying sentences' (op. cit.:507). Pragmatics, he claimed, has implications for language teaching; for example, it indicates that 'pattern drills should be designed so that instead of manipulating purely abstract elements of a calculus— usually a paradigm of totally unrelated sentences illustrating a point of syntax—the student should be using language in response to a paradigm of situations ... Pragmatics defines the goal of teaching a language as inducing the student not *merely* to manipulate meaningless sound sequences, but to send and receive messages in the language' (loc. cit.).[6]

From a similar point of view, a number of linguists in Britain and other European countries, from about 1970, took a lead in advancing a more semantic, more social, or more communicative view of language. They were aware of the fact that the practical demands of a communicative approach to language teaching ran ahead of existing theory and research. Thus, Wilkins in his notional syllabus studies admitted that 'there is no available semantic (notional) framework' on which to base such a syllabus. Therefore he stepped in and boldly outlined a taxonomy of concepts for this kind of syllabus (Wilkins 1976:20).[7] His semantic classification was based on a tripartite theory of meaning: semantico-grammatical categories, categories of modal meaning, and categories of communicative functions.

In the same way, the group of scholars in the Council of Europe Modern Languages Project had no ready-made theoretical foundations to draw on. Instead, basing themselves on current semantic and sociolinguistic concepts, including Wilkins' notions and functions, they developed their own schemes and produced inventories which specified situations, in terms of learner roles, settings, and topics, and listed language activities, functions, and notions (van Ek 1975).[8]

In a British project Candlin and his colleagues collected sociolinguistic data in medical interviews in a hospital casualty ward, undertook discourse analyses of the recorded interviews and later developed curriculum materials for overseas doctors, based on the previous sociolinguistic research (Candlin, Bruton and Leather 1976). Discourse analysis was also used by Allen and Widdowson in the preparation of materials for the teaching of scientific English (Allen and Widdowson 1974).

Widdowson (1978) defined a set of contrasting concepts which distinguish between language as a formal system and language use as communicative events. The point of view that Widdowson advocated was that it is important for language teaching to make these distinctions and that a shift of emphasis is needed from teaching a second language as a formal system to teaching a second language as communication. The distinctions themselves can be regarded as contributions to linguistic theory. Examples of these concepts are:

Linguistic categories	Communicative categories
correctness	appropriacy
usage	use
signification	value
sentence	utterance
proposition	illocutionary act
cohesion	coherence
linguistic skills	communicative abilities
(for example, speaking and hearing)	(for example, saying, listening, talking)

Widdowson, like Wilkins, was aware of the fact that the demands of language pedagogy in terms of such distinctions may run ahead of linguistic theory. But he was not perturbed by this development. In his view, practical needs may stimulate the development of new linguistic theory, in line with the desirable reciprocal flow of ideas that we discussed in connection with the theoretical models. (See Chapter 3:46). Widdowson expressed a similar point of view on the relationship between practice and theory when he said: 'The applied linguist does not always have to wait, indeed, he cannot always wait, for the linguist to provide him with something to apply. He may follow his own path towards pedagogic application once the theorist has given a hint of the general direction. He may even, on the way, discover a direction or two which the theoretical linguist might himself explore with profit' (Widdowson 1979a:100).

This convergence between theory and practice is encouraging. However, we must not be blind to the risk that the educational linguist runs in operating at too many levels at once:

1 at the *theoretical level* of defining categories (for example, Wilkins' notional-functional taxonomy or Widdowson's linguistic and communicative categories);
2 at the *descriptive level* of gathering language data on the sociolinguistics and pragmatics of particular languages (a few discourse studies exist but these commonly combine aspects of (1) and (2), for example, Sinclair and Coulthard (1975) and Labov and Fanshel (1977));
3 at the *curriculum and syllabus level* of selection for language teaching purposes (for example, the Council of Europe Threshold Level syllabuses in English (van Ek 1975), French (Coste *et al.* 1976), Spanish (Slagter 1979), and German (Baldegger *et al.* 1980), combining aspects of (2) and (3));
4 at the *materials development level*. (The transition from (2) and (3) to (4) has not been easy. For extracts from teaching materials see Brumfit and Johnson 1979);
5 and at the *level of teaching methodology*. (Here Widdowson (1978) is relevant; see also Littlewood (1981).)

The dangers of not allowing a communicative approach to evolve more gradually at all levels with different people working at these different levels are obvious. Nevertheless, there is also promise in the scope of the activities in which educational linguists have become involved and in the more balanced relationship that is establishing itself between linguistic theory and educational practice.

Review

To sum up, the overview in this and the preceding chapter has made clear that the relations between linguistics and language teaching have moved through different phases. In spite of the early interest in phonetics round the turn of the century, and a considerable amount of scholarship in the linguistics of European languages and in general linguistics, language teaching, as late as the interwar period, remained unaffected by these developments. Equally, linguists, eager to establish linguistics as a discipline in its own right, tended to ignore the promptings and needs of such applied activities as language pedagogy. From about 1940 there was an increasing awareness among linguists of language teaching and among language teachers of linguistics. By 1960 the influence of linguistics on language pedagogy was considerable. The subsequent violent changes in linguistic theory led to questioning of this powerful influence. Even linguists themselves felt impelled to express warnings against attempts to 'apply' linguistics too directly or too hastily to the problems of language teaching. The idea of an independent stance on the part of the language teacher who should feel free to use linguistics as a resource was advocated. Yet, there are difficulties in carrying out this advice, because it presupposes a depth of understanding of both linguistics and language pedagogy, which is rare. In this predicament the notion of a mediating stage between theoretical linguistics and language pedagogy, has received attention. During the last few years a number of educational linguists with expertise in linguistics and pedagogy have emerged who can fulfil this mediating function and who can influence pedagogy as well as theoretical linguistics.

Language, linguistics, and language teaching—some conclusions

Now that we have traced the development of the relations between linguistics and language teaching we will attempt in the final part of this chapter to draw some lessons for the development of our own view of language within a language teaching theory. It is useful to remember the distinction which Spolsky and others have made between implications and applications and to recognize a twofold connection.

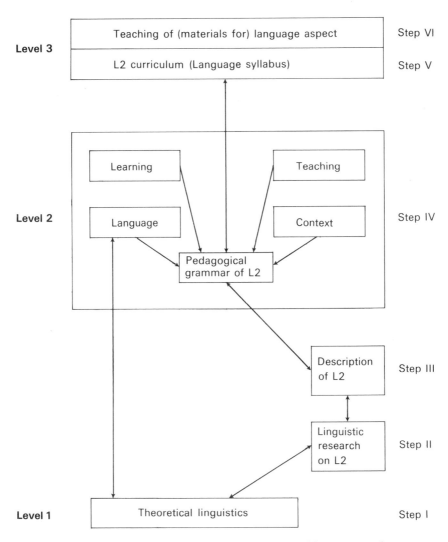

Figure 9.2   The interaction between linguistics and language teaching

1 A language teaching theory incorporates *a theory of language*—in terms of our discussion on theory (Chapter 2) most likely a working theory (T2) or, perhaps, in some instances a more rigorous scientific theory (T3). This direct relationship is indicated on the left side of the diagram by an arrow which links theoretical linguistics with language as a key concept in educational linguistics and in language teaching theory.

2 Of equal importance is the other relationship which is indicated on the right side of the diagram as a series of steps through which the *description of particular languages* is brought to language teaching.

1 Theory of language

A language teaching theory expresses or implies answers to questions about the nature of language. These questions relate language teaching theory directly to theoretical linguistics. As we reminded ourselves at the beginning of Chapter 7, the task of language teaching or learning prompts the teacher almost invariably, and the learner not infrequently, to think about the nature of language. The view of language in a language teaching theory has bearing on what we teach when we say 'we teach language X' and on the way we teach it, just as much as it can influence a learner's approach to the language. The development and controversies we have delineated in these chapters can help us to identify views of language implicit in language teaching theories.

1. Analytical and non-analytical approaches to language
A basic question to ask is to what extent the language teaching theory treats the language analytically and therefore adopts a 'linguistic' point of view, or whether it presents the language non-analytically. In this case, the teaching approach avoids any deliberate study of the language; instead it attempts to involve the learner as a participant in activities demanding the use of the second language, and the learner simply experiences the language globally in natural or quasi-natural settings, for example, through residence or in an 'immersion' setting. In that case the focus is not on language at all and linguistics is not particularly relevant, but the rationale underlying this teaching approach still implies a view of the nature of language or a theory of language.

As soon, however, as we treat language as an object to be studied, practised, or manipulated in any way, we must conceptualize it and analyse it, at least to a certain extent. In that case, and that applies to most instances of language teaching, we are bound to adopt a 'linguistic' point of view. This, of course, does not mean that we must give allegiance to a particular school of thought—structuralism, transformational generative grammar, or a systemic approach, for example. But the issues, concepts, and distinctions that linguistics has examined and argued about are also relevant to language pedagogy. Linguistics is by definition an analytical study of language. For language pedagogy it is much more a question of choice to what extent it treats language analytically or non-analytically. The language teacher may, of course, attempt to do justice to both approaches either by emphasizing both equally or by laying more weight on one while making at least some allowance for the other; but to the extent that language is treated analytically, linguistics becomes relevant through its 'insights' (Wilkins 1972) or its 'implications' (Spolsky 1970).

2. The complexity of language

Linguistic theory has not presented us with a simple and unified picture of language. Different theories of language and the theoretical debates reveal what many language teachers have intuitively known from personal experience: the inherent complexity of any language. What linguistics has done is to identify the elements or components or aspects to consider in analysing a language. The second question to ask is: *What aspects of language does our language teaching theory include or exclude, and among those that are included, which of these are especially emphasized?* The kind of diagram we considered in Chapter 7 (Figure 7.2) or the following grid (Figure 9.3) can help us in answering this question. The diagram that described the framework developed by Halliday, McIntosh, and Strevens (1964, see Figure 8.1) in a similar way illustrates a theory of language within a language teaching theory.

	Linguistically how does it work?	Semantically what does it mean?	Sociolinguistically how is it used?
Sound system			
Grammatical system			
Lexical system			
Discourse system			

Figure 9.3   Categories of language analysis

We can ask ourselves to what extent the language teaching theory gives priority to phonology, grammar, vocabulary, or discourse aspects. Going on from these, we can further ask how it handles these different components of language. Does it deal with them entirely as language forms or structures? Or does it teach them as meanings? And does it place language features into a social context and thus relate the language to the 'real world'?

3. The humpty-dumpty effect

It is one thing to isolate and analyse different aspects of language, it is quite another to bring the different aspects of the language together. This is a problem for language teaching as much as for linguistics.

Isolating features of a language distorts them to some extent because in real life they interact with other features. The categories which linguists have devised in order to study an aspect of language more effectively can become troublesome barriers. To overcome these, linguistics, as we have seen in Chapter 7, has not only concerned itself with analysis but has also aimed to make a synthesis between the different parts of language. In the same way the language teacher wishes to teach language as a whole—not just sounds, words, or sentences. Both the linguist and the language teacher find that, once a language has been taken to pieces, it cannot easily be put together again. Without analysis of some kind a language is too massive to be studied scientifically or learnt practically; without synthesis we are left with pieces which are not very serviceable for a theory of language or for language learning. *How does the language teaching theory deal with this issue?* A language teaching theory which ignores the problem of linguistic analysis and synthesis, is linguistically less satisfactory than one which acknowledges it.

4. Rule versus creativity
Another inherent opposition in language, which has been observed by linguists and by language teachers, is that *language is both rule-governed and creative.* It involves order, regularity, lawfulness, habit, and repetition. It also provides the opportunity, within the rules and regularities, to go beyond the given, to innovate and to be creative. A language teaching theory, like a linguistic theory, must take into account the regularities (rules, patterns, structures, habits) as well as the possibility of making use of the regularities in varied, novel, and sometimes unique ways as demanded by a given situation (the creative aspect). *To what exent and in what way is this dilemma reflected in our language teaching theory?*

5. A theory of language—a necessary artefact
The final question to ask is of a more general nature: *what are the main characteristics of the view of language in this language teaching theory?* It attempts to bring together the answers to the other four questions in a comprehensive statement. It we accept the view that language is complex by nature and presents certain inherent contradictions, both linguistics and language teaching must come to terms with these complexities and contradictions. A theory of language which disregards them, glosses over them, or otherwise indicates a lack of awareness of these characteristics is to that extent naive or unsophisticated and cannot provide a satisfactory solution to problems of language or language teaching.

This does not mean to say that a theory of language or a language teaching theory cannot simplify, stylize, or emphasize certain features. In fact, because of the intricacies of language it will almost always be essential to do so. But it is one thing to sacrifice with intent certain aspects and highlight others for the purpose of research in linguistics or for instruction in language pedagogy, in the knowledge of creating an artefact; it is quite another if the theory of language teaching or the linguistic theory presents its particular emphasis as 'God's truth' which other theorists have missed.

Since it is impossible, in language instruction, to do justice to the whole of language, a language teaching theory inevitably demands choices based on an interpretation of language. *All language teaching theories are artefacts which highlight some aspects of language at the expense of others.* If we can identify those aspects of language that characterize our language teaching theory and know why they are there, we will have established a sound linguistic foundation for the treatment of language in our language teaching theory.

Theoretical linguistics cannot be expected to present us with definitive interpretations, but it can provide us with concepts, models, and ideas on language and it offers a protection against oversimplification. Linguistics can help the language teaching theorist to think critically and constructively about language; without it the views on language in language teaching theory would be greatly impoverished.

2 Description of languages

The second major function of linguistics in language teaching is language description. 'There is no question but that teaching needs to be based on the best possible description of the language being taught' (Spolsky 1970:149). This aspect has been recognized by most linguists, but the concern on the part of linguists with theoretical issues may have had the effect of not placing sufficient emphasis on description.

Language teachers, too, at least until the sixties, often tended to overlook the need to base teaching on sound language descriptions. The availability in the major European languages of scholarly grammars and dictionaries had obscured this need which is more obvious as soon as we approach less commonly taught languages. A first recognition of descriptive accuracy and authenticity was indicated by the word frequency studies of the twenties and thirties which were empirically established from the analysis of specified texts. But the importance of comprehensive descriptions of languages was not clearly acknowledged before descriptive linguistics in the forties and fifties provided both methods and results of language analysis. Likewise, the contrastive studies of the late fifties and early sixties were founded on principles of (comparative) language description. Halliday, McIntosh, and Strevens (1964) and Mackey (1965) recognized that the *selection* of language items presupposes a previous 'full' description. In recent years the demands of a curriculum, based on semantic and pragmatic criteria, have outstripped the available descriptive resources.

There is often a discrepancy between descriptive information on a second language and the needs of pedagogy. Sometimes linguistic descriptions are too detailed, too technical, and too theoretical. At other times descriptions have not kept pace with the demands of the practitioner. Therefore an intermediate device, the pedagogical grammar, has been suggested and the following conceptual steps which link theoretical and descriptive linguistics with the development of a language curriculum can be indicated.

As Figure 9.2 shows, the descriptive relationship can be divided into six steps, corresponding to levels 1, 2, and 3 of the principal model. Theoretical linguistics at step I is concerned with the development of universally applicable general categories and research strategies for studies of particular languages. Research at step II can be visualized as the body of specialized and detailed studies of linguistic features of particular languages. Together, these studies constitute the data for overall scientific descriptions of given languages at step III, sometimes referred to as 'formal', 'linguistic', 'descriptive', or 'scientific' grammars. These descriptions provide the basis for a 'pedagogical' grammar at step IV. According to this definition a pedagogical grammar is an interpretation and selection for language teaching purposes of the description of a language, based not only on linguistic, but also on psychological and educational criteria.[9] It includes inventories of language items, suggestions for pedagogical presentation and arrangement, essential linguistic concepts, and other relevant information on the language. The pedagogical grammar thus forms the linguistic resource for curriculum development, the making of teaching materials, or the evaluation of language programmes, which takes place at step V, with the specific educational needs of teaching in a particular type of educational institution in mind as step VI.

Maintaining the dual relationship between linguistics and language teaching is important for langage pedagogy, but it is a complex undertaking. Neither the theoretical link nor the descriptive link can be adequately sustained by a sporadic or casual interest on the part of linguists in language teaching or on the part of language teachers in linguistics. Therein lies the justification for a mediating discipline, educational linguistics, and the creation of institutions which perform the role of intermediary between linguistic theory and language pedagogy, often referred to as language centres. The continuing developments in linguistic theory and in language pedagogy as well as the constant changes in the languages themselves, demand the permanent study of language and languages and a review of the relations between linguistic theory and language pedagogy.

Notes

1 Wilkins (1972: Chapter 8) described the relationship as one of application, insight, and implication. Applications refer to descriptive data, insights in Wilkins' view are 'linguistic notions that increase one's understanding of the nature of language' (op. cit.:217), in other words what Spolsky has called implications. Wilkins calls implications views about language learning which can be derived from the psychology of language acquisition.

2 The literature reveals a certain confusion of terminology in that sometimes the classroom textbook is called a 'pedagogical grammar', and sometimes 'pedagogical grammar' is a reference guide for the curriculum planner, teacher, or course writer, distinct from the 'teaching grammar' or 'the learner's grammar'. In our presentation we have followed a widespread practice of making a distinction between a 'scientific grammar' at level 1, the 'pedagogical grammar', at level 2, and the 'teaching grammar' (for example, a course book) at level 3.

3 Some practical guides for the teaching of French (Rivers 1975), German (Rivers, Dell 'Orto, and Dell 'Orto 1975), English (Rivers and Temperley 1978) and other languages (see Introduction, Note 3) may be regarded as fulfilling many of the functions of a pedagogical grammar. Equally, *A Grammar of Contemporary English* by Quirk, Greenbaum, Leech, and Svartvik has certain features of a pedagogical grammar. While it is organized for reference rather than for pedagogical purposes, it represents a remarkable achievement in presenting information derived from a survey of English usage and other scientific grammars, and drawing on traditional grammar and several contemporary schools of linguistics.

4 A similar view was developed in a valuable study by Roulet (1972).

5 The writings of the following illustrate this position: Allen, Bausch, Brumfit, Candlin, Corder, Coste, Oller, Paulston, Roulet, Spolsky, Trim, Widdowson, and Wilkins.

6 These ideas have received further development in Oller and Richards (1973) and Oller (1979).

7 Wilkins developed these ideas in the early seventies in conjunction with the Council of Europe project seminars (Wilkins 1973). He also presented them at the third AILA congress, 1972 (Wilkins 1974).

8 The Council of Europe project was referred to in Chapter 4 as an example of long-term research. See also Chapter 6 where it is mentioned as one of the significant developments of the seventies.

9 Corresponding to it, as we shall see in Chapter 12, is a sociolinguistic guide which, according to particular needs, may be kept apart from or merged with the pedagogical grammar. If they are combined they may be referred to as a *pedagogical language guide*.

PART FOUR

Concepts of society

10 Society, culture, and language

Language teachers have not waited for sociolinguistics to come along in order to become aware of a relationship between language, culture, and society. Indeed to many of them some of the issues in sociolinguistics have a familiar ring. Teachers have faced the same dilemma that has worried the linguist: if they concentrate too hard on linguistic forms and forget the people who use the forms in ordinary communication, they distort the reality of language use. On the other hand, if they overemphasize people and country and disregard the details of linguistic forms their teaching tends to become superficial and unserviceable. This dilemma, on the applied level, reflects the issue that in theoretical linguistics has produced a separation of the areas studied by 'linguistics proper' ('microlinguistics', 'linguistic linguistics') from the study of language in the social context. Concentration on the formal aspect, so vividly evident in Bloomfield's *Language*, has also dominated language pedagogy and has created similar problems. For over a century language teachers have repeatedly been drawn to teach language as a purely formal system, and then had to remind themselves that their students need contact with native speakers, and that the language class should provide an introduction to a country and its people.

We cannot teach a language for long without coming face to face with social context factors which have bearing on language and language learning. That language and society are in many ways closely linked, is not questioned, either in language education or in social science. Yet, while language teaching has interacted for a long time with linguistics and with psychology, social science and language teaching have only recently come into contact with each other. The reason for this belated recognition lies partly in the history of the disciplines themselves and partly in the development of language teaching theory. In our treatment of this topic, we will follow the same procedure as we did with linguistics. We consider first the social sciences as studies in their own right (in this and the next chapter) and look more specifically at the relations to language pedagogy in Chapters 12 and 13.

The social sciences

Many disciplines are concerned with aspects of society, for example, history, law, economics, and political science. The most general studies of social life that interest us here, however, are sociology, ethnology, ethnography, social and cultural anthropology, and sociolinguistics. A distinction between these disciplines cannot always be clearly made, and from the point of view of language pedagogy it may not be too important to attempt to do so. Nevertheless, there are certain differences in historical development, in the areas of investigation, and in the problems, theories, and concepts studied by sociology on the one side and by social and cultural anthropology, ethnology, and ethnography on the other. Sociolinguistics, the most recent arrival on the scene of the social sciences, can be treated later (Chapter 11) as an outcome of approaches to language that have gradually evolved in linguistics and all the sciences of society.

Sociology

'For thousands of years men have observed and reflected upon the societies and groups in which they live. Yet sociology is a modern science, not much more than a century old' (Bottomore 1971:15). As a science it is somewhat younger than psychology and a near contemporary of linguistics.[1] Perhaps more than any other discipline sociology has been the intellectual answer to the social development of modern industrialized nation states in the Western world during the nineteenth century. It has arisen as a self-examination of man in the ever-changing industrial world which constitutes the environment in which he lives. Like most human sciences sociology has changed its emphasis and perspectives as it has evolved. In the first stage of its growth from about 1850 to 1900, influenced by the social philosophies of Comte, Spencer, and Marx who can be considered the 'fathers' of sociology and anthropology, it began with encyclopaedic ambitions to embrace the whole life and history of human society. As might be expected in the Darwinian era, its early orientation, following the model of the natural sciences, was evolutionary and scientific. Towards the end of the century, in a second stage of its growth, sociology emancipated itself and developed its own characteristic approach to all studies of society: law, history, politics, religion, and so on. Major social theories and principles were formulated in the last quarter of the nineteenth and the first decades of the twentieth century by a few great teachers of sociology, particularly Durkheim (1858–1917) in France and Weber (1864–1920) in Germany. The abiding theme of Durkheim's thought was the reality and power of 'social facts' and the effect of social forces upon the individual. Social facts exist regardless of the life of any individual, but they have a coercive power upon each person in a society. Durkheim postulated a *conscience collective*, the totality of beliefs and sentiments, common to ordinary citizens of the same society. It is due to Durkheim's influence that Saussure very ingeniously came to recognize the social or supra-individual nature of language (langue) and to contrast it with the language use by the individual (parole).[2] Weber's approach to the study of society was more historical and comparative. He analysed modern capitalist society by comparing it with other social systems, for example, medieval feudalism or the great civilizations of the East.

Other avenues to modern sociology were more descriptive, empirical, and fact-finding and led to the social survey and sociological descriptions of groups or communities. The social survey represented an objective and scientific approach to certain social conditions which demanded policy decisions. Such surveys, which had already begun in the nineteenth century, led to studies in Britain which have become classics of social investigations, Booth's survey of poverty in London (1889/1891), Rowntree's studies of poverty in York (1901, 1941), and *A Survey of London Life and Labour*, published between 1930 and 1935. The descriptive study of groups and communities was developed particularly in the United States. Thus, Thrasher's well-known investigation *The Gang* (1927) described the behaviour of 1313 Chicago gangs in psychological and environmental terms. Another sociological case study which became a classic attempted to describe and explain the life and society of Polish peasants, first in Poland and later as immigrants into the United States (Thomas and Znaniecki 1918–1921). A third group of studies (Lynd and Lynd 1929, 1937), are descriptions of an urban community in the Midwest which are considered pioneer attempts 'to deal with a sample American community after the manner of social anthropology'.[3] Language surveys which interest us especially and to which reference will be made later can be regarded as a sociolinguistic offshoot of the social survey. It is, however, interesting to note that the social surveys and sociological studies of communities which have been referred to usually made little or no mention of linguistic aspects, although the methods of enquiry most certainly must have involved verbal communication. Another observation to make is that it is only in the last few decades that it has been recognized at all that such descriptive accounts of societies might have something of value to contribute to the understanding of foreign countries in second language pedagogy.

Like psychology and linguistics, sociology grew in the interwar years as an academic discipline with chairs in the universities, professional associations, and learned journals; and after World War II, as a result of the growing influence and importance of the social sciences during the war years, sociology continued to grow and expand. In the late sixties the state of sociology was described in the following terms: 'The twenty-year period from 1947 represents the general acceptance of sociology into the universities, the awareness of substantial financing of research, mainly multidisciplinary in nature, and the increasing awareness by other disciplines of the necessity of sociological research to complement their own work' (Mitchell 1968:232).

The efforts of sociologists—not unlike those of psychologists and linguists in their fields—to establish the autonomy of their discipline has no doubt been successful. But round 1960 some sociologists, reacting against the scientific apparatus of a successful social science (for example, Mills in *The Sociological Imagination* 1959), urged that sociology abandon the direction in which it was heading; instead of becoming the victim of its own academic respectability it should try to respond more imaginatively to the great social issues of the time.

A recent trend in sociology reflects a lack of confidence in the advances of science and technology and a search for meaning in the study of simple personal relationships. A group of studies has gained prominence, concerned primarily with face-to-face interaction and the process of understanding in interpersonal communication in everyday talk, in medical interviews, in psychiatric examinations, or in marriage (Dreitzel 1970). This trend of thought, sometimes described as ethnomethodology (Garfinkel 1967), has been particularly concerned with speech in personal interaction. It will be referred to in our discussion of sociolinguistics, and as we shall see in Chapter 12, it is of importance to recent developments in language teaching.

In essence then, sociology today consists of a body of theory with a set of basic concepts for the analysis of society and schemes of classification. The sociologist operates with such notions as social institution, role, status, group, function, social structure, culture, social class, kinship group, bureaucracy, and stratification. Sociology has at its disposal essential research techniques and has gathered factual information about modern industrial societies, particularly in Western countries, such as France, Germany, Great Britain, or the U.S.A. Sociology attempts to explain aspects of social life, for example, the changing role of the family or the organization of work in industrial society. It seeks to discover lawful relationships between different social phenomena, as for instance, the relations between religious values and economic structure, or between social class and educational advancement. Sociologists recognize that sociology is concerned with the great issues of social life and development and with universal abstractions as well as with the concrete problems of large or small communities, with particular problems of social groups, and face-to-face interaction, and accordingly make the distinction between 'macrosociology' and 'microsociology', but both trends of development are considered rightful and complementary directions of sociological enquiry.

A modern statement summarizes the sociological approach in these terms: 'What we may claim for sociology at its best, is a distinctive *perspective* rather than, say, any specific substantive subject matter or type of human behaviour: it is a way of looking at Man's behaviour as conditioned by his membership of social groups ...' (Worsley 1970:31). Sociological enquiries may thus provide an approach, too, for the study of aspects of the countries whose languages we teach.

Anthropology

The development of anthropology in part parallels that of sociology, and in part is so intertwined with it that it is difficult to distinguish one from the other. In a certain sense, anthropology is wider than sociology. Its domain has been defined as 'the description and explanation of similarities and differences among human ethnic groups' (Greenberg 1968:305), or as Sapir (1921:207) has expressed it, anthropologists 'have been in the habit of studying man under the three rubrics of race, language, and culture'. It includes the study of physical variations among human races. It is not concerned with the individual human organism as such (otherwise it would comprise physiology and psychology) but the individual only as a representative of a race or ethnic group. However, the main distinguishing mark of anthropology lies in the types of groups investigated. If sociology studies aspects of large-scale industrialized modern societies, anthropology has traditionally focused its principal attention on smaller pre-literate and pre-industrial societies, whether existing today and studied by *ethnology* and *ethnography* or existing in a distant pre-historic past and studied by *archaeology*.[4] Ethnography refers specifically to the descriptive study of particular tribes or societies. The distinction between ethnography and ethnology is slight; it is analogous to the distinction between descriptive and theoretical linguistics. The wide range of anthropological interest can be illustrated by the topics covered in books on general anthropology, as, for example, a work edited by the great American anthropologist and linguist Boas in 1938: it treats geological and biological premises and race; human origins, early man, and pre-historic archaeology; language; invention; subsistence; economic organization of primitive people; social life; government; art, literature, music, and dance; and, finally, mythology, folklore, and religion (Boas 1938).

The distinction between 'social' and 'cultural' anthropology indicates differences in topic and approach chosen by different schools of anthropology. By and large, British anthropologists, under the influence of such scholars as Radcliffe-Brown (for example, 1952), have viewed anthropology as a science of social structure and function or as a sociology of primitive societies, hence *social* anthropology, while American anthropologists, following Boas, regarded their task as one of a description and interpretation of primitive cultures, hence *cultural* anthropology. Naturally, for anthropologists who make no clear distinction between the concepts of 'society' and 'culture' or regard these as complementary concepts the distinction between 'cultural' and 'social' anthropology is less significant.[5]

Historically, anthropology has a dual ancestry. First, it is intimately linked with philosophical speculations on mankind's origin, diversity, and development. As such it has much in common with sociology and history. Its second origin lies in the ethnographic reports on 'primitive' and 'savage' people brought back to Europe by European white conquerors, traders, travellers, and missionaries. In this respect, it is bound up with the expansion of European power and the conquest by the white man of other continents, the Americas, Africa, and Asia. Thus, as early as 1776 Demeunier in *The Customs and Manners of Different Peoples* was able to draw on reports on several dozens of ethnic groups, including Mexicans, Ethiopians, Japanese, Peruvians, Chinese, and many others, in order to give a panorama of the enormous varieties of customs under such headings as: Food and Cookery, Women, Marriage, Birth and Education of Infants, Chiefs and Rulers, Distinctions of Rank, Nobility, Warfare, Servitude and Slavery, Standards of Beauty, Modesty, Body Adornment and Disfigurement, Astrology, Magic, Society, Domestic Manners, Penal Codes, Trials, Punishment, Suicide, Homicide, Human Sacrifice, Sickness, Medicine, Death, Funerals, Sepulchres, and Burials.[6]

In short, there is a long tradition of observations on differences of customs and manners. But it was not until the nineteenth century that thought and observations on such widely divergent societies became a subject of sustained systematic study and a discipline in its own right. The anthropologist's approach has changed since the nineteenth century and has become the subject of controversy. About one hundred years ago, hardly distinct from sociology, it was evolutionary; and the method of study comparative. 'Primitive' or 'savage' societies were viewed as examples of earlier developments in the evolution of man. By comparing societies at different stages of development the anthropologist attempted to interpret the principles, laws, or stages which governed the development of the human race. The sequence of technological invention, the growth of the family, or the development of religious beliefs and practices were viewed as advancing from stage to stage culminating in modern European civilization. Thus, Morgan (1877) distinguished three ethnic periods in human history: savagery, barbarism, and civilization.

In the first half of the twentieth century a reaction against the grand comparative schemes and their mixture of theory, fact, and fiction, led to an emphasis on scientific restraint and accuracy in ethnographic descriptions. A key figure in this development was Boas whose scholarly influence dominated American anthropology for over forty years. Boas demanded that each society (and its language) be studied on its own terms and in its own historical setting by the best empirical means available, avoiding speculative explanations about the evolution of mankind. The object was to penetrate into the culture, to understand it against its own history, to describe it objectively and to interpret it sympathetically. Not that theoretical discussion beyond the descriptive account was to be altogether avoided but, against the background of bold and often irresponsible speculations, the immediate task for Boas and his students appeared to be to collect accurate ethnographic data on tribes which soon were likely to become extinct before the relentless march of Western 'civilization'. Boas insisted that a culture be studied in such a way that the anthropologist came to understand it from the perspective of the native participant. The distinguished anthropologist Mead, who was one of his students, described her apprenticeship under Boas as follows: 'To get the depth of understanding he required meant submerging his thinking in that of another. It meant learning to think in another's terms and to view the world through another's eyes. The most intimate knowledge of an informant's thought processes was mandatory and could only be obtained by intensive work over a long period. Important concepts and strange viewpoints had to be checked with other material and with a number of informants; supplementary information had to be obtained elsewhere. But Boas conceived of his main task as the adoption of an informant's mode of thought while retaining full use of his own critical faculties'.[7]

During the interwar years anthropology was deeply affected by developments in psychology. In fact there was much cross-fertilization between anthropology and certain areas of psychology, especially child psychology, social psychology, personality and clinical psychology, and psychoanalysis. This new direction of interest had been given a tremendous impetus by Freud's writings on anthropology and religion. In *Totem and Taboo, Civilization and its Discontents*, and *Moses and Monotheism* (Strachey 1955–64) Freud applied his interpretation of the stages of psychological development to the evolution of the human race. Although his speculations about the Oedipus complex and the 'oral', 'anal', and 'phallic' stages in the development of human societies came up against the scepticism of an empirically orientated anthropology, they provided challenging hypotheses and a new theoretical direction for ethnographic studies. The fusion of interests between psychology and anthropology was expressed by Sapir in an essay on the emergence on the concept of personality in anthropology: 'The more fully one tries to understand the culture, the more it seems to take on the characteristics of a personality organization' (Sapir 1934/1970:201).

The culture, Sapir argued, is carried by individuals as members of the society; henceforth, he predicted, anthropologists would be less concerned with exotic kinship patterns than with ordinary social relationships, for example, 'such humble facts as whether the father is in the habit of acting as indulgent guide or a disciplinarian to his son' (op. cit.:204). Sapir's approach represents a view in which language, the individual, society, and culture are studied in close association with each other—an approach which is likely to be congenial to language teachers.

In the same year, Benedict in a seminal book, *Patterns of Culture*, was able to demonstrate that the customs in a society formed a discernible pattern and gave a culture a distinct life-style which was different from the pattern of culture in another society. Benedict believed that three simple societies—the Zuni Indians of New Mexico, the Dobus of New Guinea, and the Kwakiutl of the American North West—could vividly illustrate the idea of a coherent organization of behaviour which constitutes its culture.[8] Benedict's *Patterns of Culture* has influenced modern ideas on culture in language teaching.

In a similar way, Mead in two celebrated studies, *Coming of Age in Samoa* (1928) and *Growing Up in New Guinea* (1930), related child and adolescent development to different cultural training processes and showed that Western views of adolescent problems are a product of training processes and social expectations during the process of growing up rather than an inevitable stage of adolescent biology. In *Sex and Temperament in Three Primitive Societies* Mead (1935) was further able to show that the roles attributed to women in society are culturally determined and may vary from one society to another.

During and after World War II a number of studies analysed the culture of advanced nations in the manner in which Benedict and Mead had analysed tribal societies. These studies claimed to show a relationship between aspects of child training and basic personality patterns among different nations, such as Japan, Russia, and Germany. Thus, tight swaddling of Russian babies, early and severe toilet training in Japan, and a mixture of paternal harshness and maternal softness in child treatment in Germany were said to account for characteristic personality patterns which in turn affected the political behaviour of these nations.[9] While in particular instances these sweeping conclusions have not been confirmed by later studies the general line of argument has been maintained: culture determines child training; child training influences personality; and personality characteristics, in turn, reflect on prevailing beliefs and values (Whiting and Child 1953). All these studies have influenced modern conceptions of culture and 'national character' and they are therefore important for an understanding of the treatment of culture in language pedagogy.[10]

Anthropology in Britain during the interwar years was dominated by two great figures, Radcliffe-Brown and Malinowski, who differed in their approach to the study of a primitive culture. No ethnographer can attempt to describe and to account for every feature of a society. The theoretical issue therefore is to decide which are the important features and what is the best scheme which gives the observer the greatest insight into different societies. Radcliffe-Brown and Malinowski were in agreement in believing that a culture should be treated as a coherent system in which different parts have certain functions; and both approaches have been described as 'functionalism'. For Radcliffe-Brown the basis of the analysis is the society under investigation viewed as a social structure or network, analogous to the structure of a biological organism. The task is to investigate the working and functioning of different parts of that society in relation to the whole. In short, his approach is sociological; its aim is to make comparisons between different societies in order to arrive at scientific generalizations about social structures and processes. According to this view, social anthropology can be described as comparative sociology; and as such it can be carried out together with a geographical and historical study of peoples, described by him as ethnology and archaeology.

Malinowski, seeking perhaps a more comprehensive approach to cultures and societies, included in his studies of primitive peoples the biological, intellectual, and emotional life of the individual. He believed that a culture must meet three sets of needs: the basic needs of the individual, the instrumental needs of the society, and the symbolic and integrative needs of both the individual and the society; the responses to these three sets of needs constitute its culture. An anthropological study must be made at all three levels and above all it must include the study of the individual. Because of his emphasis on the individual in the culture, Malinowski was prepared to focus on psychological issues and, like anthropologists in the U.S.A., became interested in Freudian theory. He recognized that it would be particularly valuable to study sexual and family relations in primitive culture and to find out whether such investigations would confirm or deny Freudian theories. The differences between Radcliffe-Brown's structural functionalism and Malinowski's functionalism led to a somewhat acrimonious partisanship in British anthropology in the thirties. In retrospect it appears that these two approaches—one more sociological and the other more psychological—are complementary rather than in conflict with each other. Together they have contributed schemes and concepts to modern interpretations of different cultures and societies.

In the post-war world sociopolitical changes have modified the political premises of anthropology. No longer associated with colonial empires and the white man's domination, anthropology has moved closer to sociology. It is increasingly recognized that western communities can be studied by the methods of social and cultural anthropology; and the techniques of sociology as well as anthropology are needed to study the impact of western civilization on the Third World.

The impetus that was given to anthropology during the first half of the twentieth century has led in more recent decades to a search for a renewed theoretical synthesis and to a more rigorous approach to empirical data about cultures and societies, collected through field studies. As theoreticians, anthropologists today no longer dismiss as a thing of the past the evolutionary principles, developed in the nineteenth century. There is again an interest in the grand design of sociocultural change, and a desire to understand the relations between technological and economic development, social structure, culture, and man's adjustment to his natural environment. Such theoretical enquiries are now strengthened by a century of thought and research both in anthropology and sociology. Moreover, a growing number of field studies and improved techniques of record keeping have extended the data base for comparative studies. Thus, in 1937 a data bank of indexed ethnographic information was set up at Yale University in the U.S.A. Known since 1949 as the Human Relations Area Files this data bank offers a comprehensive classification and record of anthropological information. The classification alone with its eight hundred and eighty-eight categories reveals the extraordinary complexity of a cultural description, and it makes the inclusion of culture in language teaching appear somewhat daunting.[11]

Nevertheless, the study of society and culture embodied in sociology and anthropology has an obvious relevance for a language curriculum which aims to relate language teaching to the sociocultural context. From this point of view, however, it is unfortunate that, while anthropologists have studied in detail the social structure and culture of tribal societies, whose languages are only rarely taught, sociologists dealing with the large and complex modern societies whose languages are most widely learnt have found it 'much more difficult to portray and analyse the total social structure' (Bottomore 1971:126).

Language in anthropology and sociology

Social scientists have always been aware of language as an essential factor in social life. In a comparison between human society and societies among non-human species it has been observed that 'it is this inability to produce language ... that keeps the apes as they are. For culture is only transmissible through coding, classifying and concentrating experience through some form of language. A developed language, therefore, is a unique and distinctive human trait, and human society is a higher level of organization of behaviour than merely instinctive or animal behaviour' (Worsley 1970:25). Equally, according to Bottomore, the minimum requirements for a society are: (i) a system of communication; (ii) an economic system dealing with the production of goods; (iii) arrangements for the socialization of new generations, such as the family and education; (iv) a system of authority and power; and (v) a system of ritual serving to maintain and increase social cohesion and to give recognition to significant personal events such as birth, puberty, courtship, marriage, and death (Bottomore 1971:115–16). In spite of this clear recognition of language or a system of communication as important factors in society in the sociological literature illustrated by these two examples, in neither of these two introductory books is there any further mention made of language and its role in society. In this respect the development of sociology and anthropology diverge.

Anthropology
In anthropology the importance of language has been widely acknow-ledged throughout the present century. Among anthropologists the principle is well established that it is necessary to study the languages of ethnic groups and to examine the relations between language and culture. The growth of linguistics and of anthropology as modern human sciences in the twentieth century are closely bound up with one another. Anthropologists have recognized that, up to a point, language can be studied as a self-contained system and requires an expertise of its own. But the study of a language constantly demands an interpretation of socially determined meaning, and, vice versa, the study of different aspects of culture requires an understanding of the verbal aspects of that culture. Linguistics, therefore, is an important tool in anthropological investigation. The interaction between the two disciplines is reflected in the development of a border field, sometimes referred to as 'linguistic anthropology' (i.e., the systematic investigation of the relations between language and culture from the point of view of anthropology) and sometimes as 'anthropological linguistics' (i.e., the expertise of the linguist in dealing with language problems in anthropological research). The closeness of the relationship is exemplified in the interests and activities of a number of scholars in America and Europe.[12]

The great figures in American anthropology of the first half of the twentieth century are equally great figures in linguistics: Boas, Kroeber, and Sapir. As anthropologists they recognized the importance of recording the fast disappearing Indian languages. They and their students did not only learn the languages of the ethnic groups they investigated but recorded and analysed a large number of languages through intensive work with native informants. Such studies were published, for example, in the *Handbook of American Indian Languages* (1911/1922) under the editorship of Boas.

As these anthropologists had become familiar with widely divergent cultures and had learnt to accept them as different patterns of living, they simultaneously learnt to recognize and accept the divergences among languages. The writings of Boas and others constantly em-phasized that the vocabulary and grammatical categories of primitive languages were totally different from Indo-European languages, and the grammar of a primitive language must be described on its own terms, not as a deviant from the more familiar grammars of English or Latin: 'No attempt has been made to compare the forms of Indian grammars with the grammars of English, Latin, or even among themselves; but in each case the psychological groupings which are given depend entirely upon the inner form of each language. In other words, the grammar has been treated as though an intelligent Indian was going to develop the forms of his own thoughts by an analysis of his own form of speech' (Boas 1964:123).

Kroeber, like Boas, was as interested in language as in culture and his research and writings have contributed to both. According to Hymes (op. cit.:689), Kroeber was 'probably the greatest general anthropologist that American anthropology has known. His contributions to linguistics, archaeology, ethnography, and ethnology could each have earned him an enviable reputation as a major figure'.[13]

Sapir, who is often described as the originator of modern American linguistics, was intellectually at the intersection between linguistics, anthropology, and psychology. With an M.A. in German and a Ph.D. in Anthropology under Boas at Columbia University, he ended his distinguished career as a professor of anthropology and linguistics at Yale. His studies ranged over language, culture, personality, and society, and his writings appeared in psychological, linguistic, and sociological journals. In defining the specific role of linguistics he always viewed it in relation to psychology and other social sciences. His name is associated with the theory of linguistic relativity which argues that language determines thought and world view, and that, therefore, culture and thought are dependent upon language. However, it would be wrong to assume that Sapir saw the relationship between culture and language as amenable to a simple formula. On the contrary, he was insistent that such concepts as 'race', 'culture', and 'language' should not be confused or identified with each other. 'Language, race, and culture are not necessarily correlated. This does not mean that they never are' (Sapir 1921:215). He even went so far as to say that '. . . all attempts to connect particular types of linguistic morphology with certain correlated stages of cultural development are vain. Rightly understood, such correlations are rubbish' (op. cit.:219).

Sapir always saw the relationship between language and culture as an important problem for anthropology, linguistics, or psychology. In his later writings he expressed himself more positively about this relationship than in the earlier quotation. For example, in an assessment of the value of linguistics for anthropology he acknowledged language as a valuable guide to the scientific study of a given culture, because 'the network of cultural patterns of a civilization is indexed in the language which expresses that civilization' (Sapir 1970:68). Language, he said, is 'a guide to social reality' (loc. cit.) and a 'symbolic guide to culture' (op. cit.:70). A persistent theme that runs through his writings on language and society is expressed, for example, as follows: 'The tendency to see linguistic categories as directly expressive of overt cultural outlines, which seems to have come into fashion among certain sociologists and anthropologists, should be resisted as in no way warranted by the actual facts' (op. cit.:34). As will be seen shortly, it was largely due to Sapir's influence that Whorf studied the relations between language, culture, and thought more closely.

Like Sapir, Bloomfield, although remaining more strictly within the confines of linguistics than Sapir did, was also close to ethnology. He considered himself a student of Boas, and his research included field studies in anthropological linguistics. In his earlier work he insisted on a close link between linguistics and ethnology. Considering this strong bias towards a linguistically oriented anthropology and an equally strong anthropological interest among linguists in the second and third decades of the twentieth century it is surprising to observe that American linguistics—mainly under the influence of the astringent direction recommended by Bloomfield in 1933—demanded a development of a study of linguistics which deliberately abstracted from meaning and the sociocultural environment of language. It is only in the sixties that the mainstream of American linguistic thought rediscovered meaning and sociocultural relations: a renewed interest in semantics and the sudden rise of sociolinguistics have redressed the balance.

Although the dominant linguistic interest in America in the thirty year period between the thirties and sixties was more narrowly restricted to the theory and description of linguistic forms, the continuity with the earlier broader issues was never broken, and in spite of the emphasis on a study of linguistic structure apart from culture and society, interest continued to be expressed in the interaction between culture, society, and language, or between linguistics and ethnology.

The Whorfian hypothesis
The writings of Benjamin Lee Whorf were particularly influential in keeping the lines open to a wider conception of language in relation to culture, society, and the individual. Among the great themes that have linked linguistics to anthropology (and psychology) was that which was associated with Whorf's name, sometimes referred to as the principle of linguistic relativity, the Whorfian (or Sapir-Whorf) hypothesis, or the linguistic *Weltanschaung* (world view) problem. Language learners are only too well aware of the fact that certain aspects of a new language— items of vocabulary, or grammatical features—often imply concepts for which the native language has no equivalent. Contrastive analysis is founded on such comparisons. One language has separate vocabulary

items for concepts which are left undifferentiated in another language. A famous illustration of this fact, given by Boas and later vividly illustrated by Whorf in a drawing in one of his papers, was that Eskimo has four different expressions for the one English word 'snow': snow on the ground (*aput*); falling snow (*quana*); drifting snow (*piqsirpoq*); and a snow drift (*quiumqsuq*). Likewise, differences between grammatical categories suggest that in different speech communities differences in categorizations are related to differences in grammatical forms. 'Some languages recognize far more tenses than do others. Some languages recognize gender of nouns ... whereas others do not. Some languages build into the verb system recognition of certainty or uncertainty of past, present, or future action. Other languages build into the verb system a recognition of the size, shape, and colour of nouns referred to' (Fishman 1972:156).

One of the major preoccupations of some scholars for more than a century has been to understand the relationship between this diversity in languages and human diversity of thought and culture. Questions about its significance have been asked in different ways by philosophers, linguists, psychologists, and anthropologists. In the present context we recognize it as of interest particularly to anthropologists and linguists, because it relates linguistic forms to culture. The interest in the problem originated in German romanticism and its conception of the individuality of nations and races. The nineteenth century German linguist von Humboldt suggested that the different ways in which a language categorizes reality imposes on the mind ways of organizing our knowledge; the diversity of languages, therefore, 'is not one of sounds and signs but a diversity of world perspective' (Weltansichten). While the problem of this relationship was known throughout the nineteenth century it was once more developed in the twentieth by German linguists (Weisgerber and Trier) in lexicological studies, and in America by Boas and Sapir in their studies on languages in relation to cultures. It found a most vivid expression in Whorf's writings.

Whorf is one of the most unusual figures in modern linguistics. Trained as a chemical engineer at the Massachusetts Institute of Technology he professionally worked for a fire insurance company as an investigator of reports of circumstances surrounding industrial fires and explosions. Without any formal training in linguistics or anthropology he pursued studies on archaeology and Amerindian languages. He was particularly interested in the Aztec and Maya Indians of Mexico, believing that studies on these ancient languages would lead eventually to uncovering the principles underlying human speech behaviour. When Sapir went to Yale in 1931, Whorf enrolled in his course on American Indian Linguistics. Thus, in the last decade of his short and full life (he died in 1941 at the age of 44), he came under Sapir's influence and made contact with other younger linguists and anthropologists. In 1937–38 he was appointed to a part-time post in the Department of Anthropology at Yale to lecture on problems of American linguistics. His writings fall into two groups: papers on American linguistics (Hopi, Shawnee, and Maya) and on the theoretical problem with which his name is closely associated, the principle of linguistic relativity, that is, the relationship between language, mind, and reality.[14]

Whorf was deeply impressed with the power of language over man's mind. Drawing on his professional experience as an investigator of causes of fires, he gave this illustration: '... In due course it became evident that not only a physical situation *qua* physics, but the meaning of that situation to people, was sometimes a factor, through the behavior of the people, in the start of the fire. And this factor of meaning was clearest when it was a LINGUISTIC MEANING, residing in the name or the linguistic description commonly applied to the situation. Thus, around a storage of what are called "gasoline drums", behavior will tend to a certain type, that is, great care will be exercised; while around a storage of what are called "empty gasoline drums", it will tend to be different—careless, with little repression of smoking or tossing cigarette stubs about. Yet the "empty" drums are perhaps the more dangerous, since they contain explosive vapor' (Whorf 1956:135).

Influenced by Sapir's view that 'we see and hear and otherwise experience very largely as we do because the language habits of our community predispose certain choices of interpretation' he argued that language organizes experience. His manner of demonstrating it was by comparing the differences in the way in which the grammar of European languages, collectively referred to as SAE (Standard Average European), analyses experience in one way while an American Indian language, such as Nootka, Hopi, or Shawnee, emphasizes totally different aspects. For example, the emphasis on time (past, present, and future) and the objectification of time in terms of space ('before' and 'after') predisposes the SAE speaker to history, records, diaries, clocks, and calendars. These comparisons led Whorf to the belief that a study of grammatical categories of languages would lead to deep cultural insights and was therefore of tremendous importance to the development of ethnology, and in turn would uncover unconscious predispositions in our own thinking.

Whorf's writings, especially a few popular articles, aroused widespread interest and led in due course to many debates and studies on the validity of his thesis. Thus, Hoijer, an anthropologist, following in the tradition of Sapir and Whorf, in an intensive investigation of Navaho language and culture, observed that the Navaho language emphasizes movement and specifies movement in detail. Navaho culture parallels this semantic theme: 'The Navaho are fundamentally a wandering

Nomadic folk, following their flocks from one pasturage to another. Myths and legends reflect this emphasis most markedly, for both gods and culture heroes move restlessly from one holy place to the next' (Hoijer 1964:146).[15] Hoijer suggests that this phenomenon 'connotes a functional interrelationship between socially patterned habits of speaking and thinking and other socially patterned habits'. In 1956 Carroll summed up the view of the Whorfian hypothesis by saying 'the validity of the linguistic relativity principle has thus far not been sufficiently demonstrated; neither has it been flatly refuted' (Carroll in Whorf 1956:27).

Over the last two or three decades several investigators have tested the Whorfian hypothesis with conflicting results by studying different aspects of language in relation to extra-linguistic factors in different cultures, such as kinship terms, colour terms, number words, disease terminologies, or modes of address. The consensus on this question is well expressed in the following three statements:

1 'Languages primarily reflect rather than create sociocultural regularities in values and orientations.'
2 'Languages throughout the world share a far larger number of structural universals than has heretofore been recognized.'
   (Fishman 1972:155)
3 'If we can put aside the issue of "what first causes what", we are left with the fascinating process of ongoing and intertwined conversation and interaction. In these processes languages and societal behaviour are equal partners rather than one or the other of them being "boss" and "giving orders" to the other.'
   (op. cit.:171)

For language pedagogy, these studies have been extremely important. They have led to the widespread conviction that the language learner should not only study the cultural context ('language AND culture') but that he should be made aware of the interaction between language and culture ('language IN culture', 'culture IN language').[16]

In Britain[17], the prevailing view of the thirties about the relationship between anthropology and linguistics was well expressed by Radcliffe-Brown in his work *Structure and Function in Primitive Society*. Radcliffe-Brown recognized 'a certain very general relation between social structure and language' (1952:196). Language was one of the phenomena, besides the economic institutions, and the rules of etiquette, morals, and law, which make up the social structure. But in his view there was no direct connection between characteristics of the social structure of a community and the language it speaks. Accordingly, he believed that 'linguistics is ... the branch of social anthropology which can be most profitably studied without reference to social structure' (loc. cit.). He saw of course that languages and societies are not completely unconnected: 'Thus the spread of language, the unification of a number of separate communities into a single speech community, and the reverse process of subdivision into different speech communities, are phenomena of social structure. So also are those instances in which, in societies having a class structure, there are differences of speech usage in different classes' (loc. cit.).

In spite of this recognition, in a few lines, of essential features of what later became sociolinguistics, Radcliffe-Brown did not appear to regard it as profitable for social anthropology or linguistics to study aspects of language in relation to society. This separation of linguistics from anthropology is reflected in his research interests, which almost entirely disregarded the language aspect.[18]

By contrast, Malinowski, whose influence on the British linguist Firth was briefly mentioned in Chapter 7, represents in Britain an anthropological school of thought in which language played a much more significant role. His position is in some ways similar to that of Boas, Kroeber, and Sapir in the U.S.A., although as a linguist he is often regarded as a less sophisticated investigator. Like Boas he was convinced that field work demanded familiarity with the tribal language. At the same time he believed that an understanding of the language was impossible without constantly relating it to the culture in which it was operative. A characteristic example of Malinowski's views on language and culture can be found in Ogden and Richards' *The Meaning of Meaning*, an influential philosophical work of the early twenties which explored the relations between language, thought, and reality. At the suggestion of the two authors, Malinowski had contributed in a famous supplement to their lively philosophical study his views on meaning in primitive languages.

Using as an illustration an utterance of a native in the Trobriand Islands who was talking about a canoe trip and the superiority of his canoe, Malinowski observed that such an utterance in a primitive language is totally incomprehensible unless it is placed into its cultural setting and related to the circumstances in which it occurs. He eloquently argued for this point of view:

'Language is essentially rooted in the reality of the culture, the tribal life and customs of the people, and ... it cannot be explained without constant reference to these broader contexts of verbal utterance.' (1923:305)

'An utterance becomes only intelligible when it is placed within its *context of situation*, if I may be allowed to coin an expression which indicates on the one hand that the conception of *context* has to be broadened and on the other that the *situation* in which words are uttered can never be passed over as irrelevant to the linguistic expression.' (op. cit.:306)

'The study of any language spoken by a people who live under conditions different from our own and possess a different culture must be carried out in conjunction with a study of their culture and of their environment.' (loc. cit.)[19]

He rejects the 'philological' approach to language as 'fictitious and irrelevant' because it looks at written language in isolation; the ethnographer's approach, on the other hand, is 'real and fundamental'. The uses of language that Malinowski observed in a primitive community are fourfold: First, he identifies the *speech of action* as for example in the use of speech during a fishing expedition in the Trobriand Islands: 'language in its primitive forms ought to be regarded as and studied against the background of human activities, and as a mode of human behaviour in practical matters' (op. cit.:312). Another is *narrative*, language used 'in primitive communities as a mode of social action rather than as a mere reflection of thought' (op. cit.:313). A third use, named by him in a memorable phrase, *phatic communion,* is 'a type of speech in which ties of union are created by a mere exchange of words' (op. cit.:315). In short, Malinowski viewed language in its primitive function and original form as essentially pragmatic in nature, as 'a mode of behaviour, an indispensable element of concerted human action' (op. cit.:316). As a result of the close association of words and actions emerges a fourth use of language in primitive society: *the ritual use of words* in word magic and the use of spells.

Malinowski contrasts these four functions of language in primitive societies with civilized language which includes, besides all those functions already described, complex and abstract activities such as writing or reading a scientific book, detached from the exigencies of an immediate situation. These however are advanced and derived uses of language and therefore must not be treated as prototypes of linguistic activity. In a highly speculative concluding part to the essay Malinowski sketches a genetic sequence of the growth of grammatical categories in language development in the child in keeping with these functions and draws a parallel with the development of the functions of language in the growth of primitive societies. He sees the development of meaning in primitive language as the prehistoric antecedent to the use of meaning in the kind of philosophical discourse that was discussed by Ogden and Richards. His argument presupposes a view of language in primitive societies as functionally and structurally more 'primitive' than language use of advanced societies—a view which is contrary to present-day beliefs, and contrary also to the approach to language by the American contemporaries of Malinowski. However, Malinowski's recognition of four pragmatic functions of language use and the relationship between language use, context of situation, and culture anticipate present-day sociolinguistic thought.

The context of situation, to which Malinowski attributed so much importance became, as was mentioned in Chapter 7, a central concept in the development of linguistics in Britain by Firth who acknowledges his indebtedness to Malinowski: 'A key concept in the technique of the London group is the concept of the *context of situation*. The phrase "context of situation" was first used widely in English by Malinowski. In the early thirties, when he was especially interested in discussing problems of language, I was privileged to work with him' (Firth 1957:181).

By including the social context in linguistic analysis the Firthian or London school of linguistics has always—at least in theory—looked at language in a broader perspective than its American counterparts. Descriptive linguistics, according to Firth, is 'an autonomous group of related disciplines—such as phonetics, phonology, grammar, lexicography, semantics, and what may be called the "sociology of language" (Firth 1957:177). The basic unit of linguistics for Firth is the language event, and the context of situation brings it into relation to:

(a) the relevant features of participants: persons, personalities
   (i) the verbal interaction of the participants,
   (ii) the non-verbal interaction of the participants;
(b) the relevant objects; and
(c) the effect of the verbal action
   (op. cit.:182).

To sum up, these ideas on the social function of language, expressed by Malinowski in the twenties and by Firth at least since the thirties, have been rediscovered in the sociolinguistics of the sixties and seventies.[20]

Sociology and social psychology
In contrast to the intense interest of anthropologists in language, sociology in the first half of the century—in spite of its recognition of the importance of language and communication in society—was strangely silent on the relationship between linguistic and social phenomena. Thus Carroll in his review of the study of language in 1953 noted that the implications of linguistics for social problems remain 'almost completely unexplored' (op. cit.:118). Among a few exceptions is a work of the American social psychologist Mead, *Mind, Self, and Society* (1934), which developed the theory that the mind of the individual and the individual's perception of himself are formed by the social relations between the individual and his social environment, and that the individual's role is defined by verbal symbols. Mead's theory influenced a number of American social psychologists and psychiatrists who recognized that verbal 'labelling' and the use of language in interpersonal relations had a profound influence on the individual's self-image. [21]

A number of linguists for their part began to interpret the social aspects of language, and in view of Firth's clear sociological perspective it is indeed surprising that there was no more definite development of a 'sociological linguistics' as Firth had projected. Thus in Britain, shortly after World War II, Lewis (1947), an educationist and psychologist with a particular interest in child language, in a somewhat neglected study asked some fundamental questions about the functions of language in society, largely prompted by the experience of the use and misuse of language in wartime. Western society, Lewis argued, had gone through a *linguistic revolution* due to the technological inventions of the book, the newspaper, the telephone, and the radio, and the resulting emphasis on mass literacy and mass education. What were the consequences of these developments? Drawing on psychology, anthropology, and philosophy, Lewis tried to define the functions of language in the individual: mental life is closely bound up with language, because 'mind is behaviour mediated by symbolization', and society equally cannot exist without the use of symbols. But different societies use language in different ways. Thus, smaller primitive societies may make more use of ritual but less of language in managing their group activities than larger western societies do. Western societies, by the extensive use of verbalization, become more highly organized in industrial and political enterprises and more integrated into larger, more powerful, and more cohesive units; but because of their reliance on verbal symbols they can also use (and, thereby, misuse) language for social or racial conflict and for warfare. Thus, the linguistic revolution has great potential but also great dangers. 'The society that seeks the full benefits of full communication must guard, foster, and direct its growth. How is this to be done? ... How are societies to use symbolic communication not to destroy but to build, not as a weapon of war but as the chief means of achieving unity of thought, feeling, and action? How?' (op. cit.:230). In order to understand language, he argues, 'we must study its working in society' (op. cit.:239).[22]

That language problems could be considered from psychological or sociological perspectives as well as from a linguistic one and that the three approaches could well support each other was the message of a seminal study of the early fifties, *Languages in Contact* (Weinreich 1953). Under the concept of language contact Weinreich considered first the linguistics of language contact, interlingual interference, i.e., the influence of one language, dialect, or other linguistic variety upon another, its phonology, grammar, and vocabulary. He, then, viewed the same problem from the point of view of the individual in a situation of language contact, in other words, the psychology of the bilingual person. Lastly, he studied contact as a social problem of communities in language contact. The object of the study was to analyse 'the mechanisms of linguistic interference, its structural causes and its psychological and sociocultural co-determinants' (op. cit.:111). By bringing together evidence from a great variety of linguistic and sociocultural sources, Weinreich's study ushered in a new and sympathetic treatment of a host of problems of language contact, which over the subsequent decades became one of the preoccupations of sociolinguistics.[23]

In the same year as Weinreich's work on languages in contact was published (1953) another study on bilingualism appeared which was equally influential in paving the way to a sociology of language, *The Norwegian Language in America* by Haugen. This case study of bilingual behaviour consists of a social history of the linguistic adaptation of Norwegian immigrants to American life and language and a linguistic study of the resulting American dialects of Norwegian. Haugen, himself the son of Norwegian immigrants to the U.S.A., has made a life study of bilingualism and other questions of language in relation to its social environment, an area to which he gave the name of 'ecology of language'. He defines language ecology as the study of interactions between a given language and its environment and describes it as the kind of study that 'has long been pursued under such names as psycholinguistics, ethnolinguistics, linguistic anthropology, sociolinguistics, and the sociology of language' (Haugen 1972:325, 327).[24]

In the late fifties, beginnings of a sociological investigation on the role of language in relation to social class and education in Britain created a new awareness of the language factor in society. In post-war British education a supreme effort was made to provide equality of educational opportunity to all, regardless of social origin. Ability, not social background, was to be the decisive principle in educational choice. However, the statistics of class distribution in schools and universities showed clearly that, in spite of the best intentions on the part of the educational policy makers, the working class was under-represented in grammar school and higher education.

Bernstein, a British sociologist, who studied this problem set out from his own experience as a teacher at the London City Day College where he taught GPO messenger boys in a one-day-a-week release class. His main responsibility was to teach English, arithmetic, and civics to a large group of students whose formal attainments 'was one of the best indictments of the educational system' (Bernstein 1971:4). His training in sociology, his experiments in teaching English to these pupils, together with his reading of Sapir, Whorf, Vigotsky, Luria, as well as Cassirer's *Philosophy of Symbolic Forms* led him in the late fifties and early sixties to a first formulation of ideas on the relations between social factors and language.

Bernstein's contention was that there is a systematic relationship between social class and language use. The middle class tends to use what he described as a *formal* or *elaborated* code, while the working class is inclined towards the use of a *public* or *restricted* code. 'Code' is understood as 'form of usage'; it is, therefore, a variety of language. But Bernstein rejected the idea that these codes are simply standard and non-standard dialects or 'sociolects' each identifying a social class by a number of speech characteristics. The distinction between a public and a formal code is roughly equivalent to a distinction between a stereotyped, or undifferentiated use of language, as in talking about the weather or the 'opening gambit at a cocktail party' (Bernstein 1964:252), and the flexible, individualized, often more abstract and objective use of language by a speaker who is attempting to solve a problem by verbal exchange. The restricted code requires a context of intimacy, of shared or implicit meaning (it is 'context-dependent'), while the elaborated code is more explicit, or more 'context-independent'.[25] Any speaker, irrespective of social class, is likely to use either code, depending on the situation which requires linguistic expression. Moreover, the allocating of an utterance to the two codes is a question of degree rather than of absolutes. In Bernstein's view, however, working-class life at home and at work predisposes individuals towards the habitual use of a restricted code and middle-class life towards the use of the elaborated code. Schooling, in turn, transmits a middle-class culture and favours an elaborated code. Consequently, the middle-class child, more trained in the elaborated code by his home life, has an advantage over the working-class child at school. Bernstein's theory thus explores the relationship between social class, language use, and education. In the sixties Bernstein became increasingly interested in the social characteristics of different families, the control and regulation families exercise over their children, the characteristic forms of communication within the family, and the effect of such control and communication on the cognitive development of their children.

British educators recognized the potential value of Bernstein's ideas for education, and in 1964 a Sociological Research Unit was set up at the London Institute of Education under Bernstein's direction, and a number of studies were made by Bernstein himself, his colleagues, and students to explore and substantiate the relationship between the different factors. At the same time, the conviction that language had played a crucial role in preserving social class barriers led to attempts to overcome the resulting social injustice by deliberate language education.[26]

Bernstein's thesis became a subject of controversy because it was considered to be an example of a linguistic 'deficit theory'.[27] That is, Bernstein's theory was said to be based on the assumption that the elaborated code is preferable, and that the working-class child using the restricted code is to a certain extent 'linguistically deficient' rather than simply different. Against this, the critics claimed that the school did not exploit the linguistic resources of the working-class child nor that the research in support of Bernstein's thesis had adequately explored these resources. In the early stages of these studies, Bernstein's research certainly lacked the rigour and sophistication of a convincing linguistic investigation. The history of Bernstein's research, which was motivated by the wish to overcome social injustice, ironically became tainted with the accusation that it treated lower-class children as linguistically inferior. Whatever the justification for this criticism, the entire research area offers an interesting example of the close interaction of linguistics with social and cultural factors in the study of problems of language use and educational opportunity. It also reveals the theoretical and technical difficulties in undertaking valid studies of language in relation to society. Such studies, no doubt, needed more specific attention and in some instances greater sophistication than had perhaps been previously recognized. It was in this climate of thought on language and society that sociolinguistics began to develop as a distinct discipline in its own right.

Notes

1 For a general introduction to sociology see, for example, the readable guide to problems and literature by Bottomore (1962/ 1971), or the historical account by Mitchell (1968). Problems of sociology are also vividly presented in an introductory work by a team of sociologists from the University of Manchester (Worsley 1970/1977).
2 For a brief introduction to Durkheim, his life and work, and pages of his major writings, with critical comments, see Bierstedt (1966).
3 Quoted from the foreword to *Middletown* by Clark Wissler (Lynd and Lynd 1929).
4 As will be pointed out later, anthropology today is no longer confined to the study of 'primitive peoples'. (See p. 198).
5 Hannerz (1973) explains his preference for 'social' anthropology as follows: 'The two master concepts which go with this broad view are "culture" and "society". It is at this point that the particular characteristics of social anthropology begin to appear, for anthropologists have a preference for one or the other of these concepts. Some of those who label themselves cultural anthropologists emphasize the integration of beliefs, values and their behavioral expressions but pay less attention to the distribution and organization of these in the society. If it is not assumed that the society is culturally homogeneous, then at least there may be a relative neglect of how the diversity is made to work. The resulting image may be a rather uncomplicated one of "one society—one culture", parallel to

the conception of the undifferentiated speech community which has presently been the target of some criticism in linguistics (cf. Gumperz 1968). The kind of social anthropology I want to draw on here does not in its turn neglect the cultural dimension but ties it to the structure of social relationships: an individual learns his beliefs, values, and modes of behavior in these relationships, and it is also in these that he uses many of them' (op. cit.:236–7).

6 Harris in his history of anthropology refers to a study by van Gennep (1910) who found Démeunier's book at a *bouquiniste's* on a Paris quay (Harris 1968:18).

7 Mead, 'Apprenticeship Under Boas' in Goldschmidt, (1959:29–45; quoted from Harris 1968:316–17). This approach foreshadows the notion of empathy with a culture which will be met again in Benedict's work on patterns of culture (see Note 8 below) and in most recent work on the teaching of culture in language pedagogy. It derives largely from the nineteenth-century German philosopher Dilthey.

8 In her analysis of cultures Benedict was influenced by German philosophy as much as by psychology: by Dilthey's concept of *Weltanschauungstypen*(types of world views) and the notions of dominant approaches to life in different civilizations, first developed by Nietzsche and later by the historical philosopher Spengler in his influential work *The Decline of the West*. But while Spengler analysed large and complex civilizations of East and West, Benedict believed that the three simpler societies she had studied in *Patterns of Culture* could illustrate the idea of a coherent behavioural organization and culture more vividly.

9 Examples of such (often speculative and tendentious) studies are one on Japanese culture by Benedict (1946), another on American national character by Gorer (1948), and a third on Russian psychology by Gorer and Rickman (1949). In a similar way the etiology of Nazi mentality in Germany was investigated by Dicks (1950) in a wartime study of German prisoners of war, and Adorno and his colleagues (1950) attempted to account for anti-semitism and racial prejudice in a monumental investigation on *The Authoritarian Personality*.

10 A general review of these investigations of the forties and early fifties on national character, basic personality, and culture may be found in the *Handbook of Social Psychology* (Inkeles and Levinson in Lindzey and Aronson 1969). The concept of culture has been critically reviewed in a fascinating work by Kroeber and Kluckhohn (1952) which cites and discusses one hundred and sixty-four definitions of culture and numerous statements about culture.

11 The classification system, *Outline of Cultural Materials*, was originally designed to serve a vast cross-cultural survey, established

in 1937 by the Institute of Human Relations at Yale University. This survey collected and classified information on a sample of the peoples of the earth. In 1949, the Cross-Cultural Survey became an independent organization, Human Relations Area Files, Inc., under the auspices of twenty-three universities. The *Outline*which, since its inception in 1937, has gone through four revisions has 'come to represent a sort of common denominator of the ways in which anthropologists, geographers, sociologists, historians, and non-professional recorders of cultural data habitually organize their materials' (Murdock *et al.* 1964).

12 An outstanding guide to trends of thought and research on language in anthropology is *Language in Culture and Society* (Hymes 1964). In an earlier paper Olmsted (1950) reviewed the relationship between ethnology and linguistics, as seen by the leading authorities in linguistics and anthropology: (a) the use in ethnology of the findings of linguistics, (b) the use by linguistics of the findings of ethnology, (c) a comparison of methodology of both, (d) the study of problems requiring the techniques of both linguistics and ethnology, and (e) the development of ethnolinguistics as an integrating approach to the social sciences.

13 Kroeber introduced the preface to Hymes' book on *Language in Culture and Society* with the remark: 'As an anthropologist who found his way into his profession by being shown how to analyse Boas' *Chinook Text* into grammar and whose first remembered purely intellectual pleasure, as a boy of ten, was the demonstration of pattern in the classes of English strong verbs, it is a pleasure to say something about Professor Hymes' reader' (Hymes 1964:xvii).

14 Whorf's papers have been collected and edited by Carroll who has also introduced Whorf's writings by a biographical account and an appreciation. The present account of Whorf is based on Carroll's study (Whorf 1956).

15 Hoijer's study was carried out in the forties. The quotation is based on a paper given in 1950 and published in Hymes, 1964, under the title of 'Cultural implications of some navaho linguistic categories' in Part III of Hymes' work which deals comprehensively with 'world view and grammatical categories'.

16 The relations between language and culture are regularly referred to by theorists who advocate the teaching of culture. See Chapter 12.

17 For a fuller appreciation of the relations between linguistics and anthropology in Britain see Ardener (1971).

18 This is particularly striking in one area of investigation in which Radcliffe-Brown was active, an area which has a strong linguistic component: the study of joking relationships. Anthropologists had noticed that in certain societies it is customary and often *de rigueur* to tease and joke with certain people, for example, a man with the

brothers and sisters of his wife, while in relations to other persons such conduct would be completely ruled out. Such studies, today, would be treated as illustrations of communicative competence under the heading of ethnography of communication. Radcliffe-Brown's treatment of this subject is entirely concerned with the principle and significance of joking in contrast to the relationship of respect towards other types of persons. It makes hardly any mention of the verbal manifestations of this relationship.

19 These views would no doubt be very acceptable to language curriculum developers today.

20 The development of the concept of 'context of situation' by Malinowski and Firth has been discussed by Robins (1971).

21 In psychiatry, for example, Cameron (1947) adopted Mead's theory to account for the development of personality and personality problems, and therefore attributed crucial importance to language in the etiology of mental illness. A similar point of view is expressed in a famous and influential book of its time by Dollard and Miller (1950). This point of view extends Whorf's claim of the effect of language upon cognition to the effect of language upon affect and personality. See also Chapter 14:292.

22 Lewis' view of language in society, thus, reaches back to Malinowski's distinction between the functions of language in primitive and in developed society. At the same time he seems to anticipate the need for conscious social language planning.

23 It should be noted that linguistics—at any rate since Saussure—was based on the conception of a single language as a coherent and self-sufficient system. Such a view of language cannot easily accommodate bilingualism, diglossia, contrastive linguistics, etc. which relate two or more language systems to each other. Weinreich's work is one of the first to overcome this ideological handicap of modern linguistics. See also Chapter 11:230–1 on the 'monolingual illusion'.

24 Other important works by Haugen in the fifties and sixties include *Bilingualism in the Americas: A Bibliography and Research Guide*(Haugen 1956), and*Language Conflict and Language Planning: The Case of Modern Norwegian* (Haugen 1966).

25 Bernstein gives this example: 'A mother who can just see out of the corner of her eye her child intent on some piece of domestic sabotage suddenly shouts "Stop that! You do that again, and you're for it!" If we heard that imperative and threat on a tape recorder, it would be difficult to infer what it was that evoked the imperative, and what, specifically, would happen if the child continued'. (Bernstein 1971:13)—hence this would be an illustration of the (context–dependent) restricted code.

26 Bernstein's work in the fifties and sixties has been collected in two volumes of studies (1971, 1973). For a review of his work see

Lawton (1968) or Robinson (1972). The reader who wants to understand the development of Bernstein's thought should read the introduction to Bernstein (1971) which traces it against the background of his life. He is very much aware of changes and inconsistencies: '... guiding ideas were constantly developing' (Bernstein 1971:1). In another paper, written in 1973, he has explained the development of his ideas on the sociolinguistic codes (Lee 1973). For a later assessment of Bernstein's work, see Hudson (1980).

27 To be accused of advocating a linguistic 'deficit theory' is in the same order as being accused of racism or sexism.

11 Aspects of sociolinguistics

In sociolinguistics converge all the earlier efforts in anthropology, sociology, social psychology, and linguistics to relate language systematically to society and culture. We saw in Chapter 7 that linguistics had restricted its focus upon the formal aspects of language. It treated each language as a coherent, autonomous, and self-sufficient system. Linguistics was concerned principally 'with an ideal speaker-listener, in a completely homogeneous speech-community' to quote again Chomsky's famous statement (1965:3). This concentrated attack on the formal features of an idealized *langue* had been extremely powerful in the analysis of language. But it was unable to account for linguistic realities with speakers who were not ideal and speech communities which were not homogeneous. Towards the end of Chapter 7 we had noted that the messy realities of language use clamoured for attention. Moreover, as we saw in Chapter 10, a number of questions about the relationship between language, society, and culture were asked again and again. The concept of sociolinguistics had already tentatively appeared in the fifties. Firth, we saw, as early as the thirties proposed a study of 'sociological linguistics'. But it was probably due to the success of structural and descriptive linguistics in the forties and fifties, and to the dominance of transformational generative grammar and psycholinguistics in the sixties, that it was not until then, i.e., in the sixties, that sociolinguistics began to develop as a distinct field of study. From about 1963 some linguists resolutely tackled the complex realities of language in use in society, and social scientists and linguists collaborated more closely on common sociolinguistic problems. Studies on language in society were gathered in symposia and books of readings (for example, Hymes 1964; Bright 1966; Fishman 1968, 1971); and new specifically sociolinguistic research was initiated.[1]

Three major directions characterize the development of sociolinguistics as a distinct discipline. One is a redirection of general or theoretical linguistics into a study of language in society. The second has extended the concept of the native speaker's linguistic competence into the concept of communicative competence by changing the focus from an abstract study of language to concrete acts of language use: an 'ethnography of speaking'. The third derives more distinctly from sociology and is often referred to as 'sociology of language': it is the study of speech communities. The three orientations cannot be kept strictly apart, but they provide convenient headings for characterizing the principal directions in sociolinguistics, and, as will be seen in Chapters 12 and 13, all three have relevance for language pedagogy.

The study of language in its social context

Nearest to the kind of linguistics, described in Chapter 7, is the first trend, the study of language in its social context—to borrow the phrase used by one of its chief exponents, William Labov (1971, 1972). In Labov's view, shared by several other sociolinguists, the study of language within the context of a speech community *is* linguistics. The common topics of linguistic analysis, phonology, morphology, syntax, discourse analysis, and semantics, continue to be the areas to be investigated; but studying them in a 'pure' and 'abstract' form, as linguists from Saussure to Chomsky have done, leaves out from linguistic enquiry what is most interesting, the infinite varieties of language use. In the choice between *langue* and *parole*, or *competence* and *performance*, in which Saussure opted for the study of *langue* and Chomsky for the study of *competence*, as the proper subject of linguistics, the sociolinguists made the opposite choice. For them it is the variability of *parole* or *performance* that constitutes the substance of linguistics: 'It seems natural enough that the basic data for any form of general linguistics would be language as it is used by native speakers communicating with each other in everyday life' (Labov 1971:153).

The study of language in its social context starts from the assumption that speech varies in different social circumstances and that there are speech varieties within a speech community. It is the business of linguistics to account for these and to study the rules of these variations as normal phenomena of language use. Labov himself, for example, has investigated quite specific phonological features in the use of English in New York, such as varieties of /r/ or the voiceless interdental fricative /θ/ as in *thing* or *thick*. The 'prestige form' of this phoneme appears sometimes in the stigmatized form of an affricate or stop (*fing* or *ting*). Labov has been able to show that individual New Yorkers do not use one or the other form of /θ/ exclusively but may vary in their speech habits according to the formality of the situation: thus they use different variants of /θ/ in casual speech, careful speech, in consecutive reading style, or in reading a word list. In other words, there is a stylistic gradient. But there are also social differences. There is less stylistic differentiation among upper-middle-class speakers than among work-ing-class or lower-class speakers. According to Labov, a sociolinguistic variable is a linguistic feature which can be systematically related to some non-linguistic feature in the social context: the speaker, the addressee, the audience, or the setting. Thus, some features such as /θ/ in

New York vary systematically according to the degree of formality of language use and the social class of the speaker.[2]

It is clear that taking into account the many social and regional variations of language use makes the description of a language an even more complex task than if they are disregarded. The language teacher faces a similar problem when he asks himself whether to teach a language as it is spoken or whether he should confine his teaching to an idealized 'standard' variety. In the latter case the task is simplified, but the student may find that no native speaker uses the language quite the way he was taught: the student is not sensitized to the differences among groups of speakers and to the social significance of these differences. Language in social context is closer to real life, but variations make the teaching-learning task more complex.

The effect of this trend in sociolinguistics is a socially more differentiated description of linguistics: a phonology, morphology, syntax, and lexicology in which the distinctions in the use of language by different groups in society and by individuals in different situations are not rubbed out.

Ethnography of communication

A second major direction of sociolinguistics has been the study of the individual's communicative *activity* in its social setting, referred to as 'ethnography of speaking', or more widely as 'ethnography of communication' (Sherzer 1977). This approach to sociolinguistics extends the area of linguistics beyond the study of formal properties of utterances to the study of the social contexts and of the participants in acts of communication. The model of the speech act (see Figures 7.1 and 7.2) can again be used as a starting point but this time with less emphasis on either the formal properties of the message (linguistics in the more specific sense) or on the mental processes of language use (psycholinguistics), instead with more stress on the interpersonal functions of speech acts and on the relationships between linguistic form and social meaning.

This concern with social function of speech implies that the model for the analysis of languages is shifting from the utterance in isolation and the study of a 'context' into which this utterance must be placed towards an attempt to regard the interpersonal social *act* as the primary event and the speech forms as secondary. The act of communication is therefore seen not as basically an exchange of linguistic messages, but rather as a socially meaningful episode in which the use of language plays a part only inasmuch as the social rules and functions are already previously agreed upon or are known by the participants in the verbal exchange. Thus, in a given situation, it is the sequence of interpersonal events that sets the stage (or provides the context) for given messages. It has been demonstrated that if an individual breaks the rules of a social act by saying something unexpected he can cause confusion or annoyance in the speech partner in the episode. Experiments to prove this point, which have been conducted by Garfinkel (1967:38–44), can be illustrated by this example:

'The victim waved his hand cheerily.
S "How are you?"
E "How am I in regard to what? My health, my finances, my school work, my peace of mind, my ...?"
S (Red in the face and suddenly out of control.)
  "Look! I was just trying to be polite. Frankly, I don't give a damn how you are."'

The characteristics of language use are looked at more as indicators of a social relationship or as markers of individual interpretations of the events than as examples of syntactic constructions.

An early task of the ethnography of communication was to develop a conceptual scheme for the analysis of speech events in their social setting. If we take as examples models developed by a linguist, Jakobson, a social psychologist, Robinson, and a linguist and anthropologist, Hymes, we can see that they have much in common (Figure 11.1)

	Jakobson (1960)	Robinson (1972)	Hymes (1972, 1972a)
1	addresser	addresser/emitter	speaker/sender/addressor
	addressee	addressee/receiver	receiver/audience/addressee
2	message	message/message form verbal act	speech act/message (key/genre)
3	contact	contact social relationship control	channel
4	context	extralinguistic world situation	situation/setting/scene
5		topic/prime focus of verbal act	topic/message content
6	code	language	code/forms of speech: language/dialect/variety
7	functions	functions	purposes/outcomes/goals/ends

Figure 11.1   Categories of language events

1 One essential set of concepts in these models always identifies the *participants* in the speech act: the speaker and listener, writer and reader, or, in more general terms, addresser and addressee, or performer (emitter) and receiver. Hymes rightly points out that some speech acts are not dyadic, that is, they do not require an addressee: the monologue, thinking aloud, or prayer. In other cases, the relationship is triadic involving a third participant, hearer, or audience. Another type of triad is source, speaker (spokesman, interpreter, 'ghost writer') and addressees.

2 The next major concept is the *message* itself, in most cases a verbal utterance, but sometimes a non-verbal act of communication in its own right or accompanying the verbal utterance. The smallest unit of speaking is usually referred to as the *speech act*. The next larger socially recognized unit of speech activity—conversation, discussion, lecture, etc.—constitutes a *speech event*, which occurs in a speech situation (see 4 below). Hymes uses the literary term *genre* to describe generically different speech events such as 'poem, myth, tale, proverb, riddle, curse, prayer, oration, lecture, commercial, form, letter, editorial' (Hymes 1972a:65). Speech acts and events can also be distinguished by their tone or style, or in Hymes' terminology, the *key*, for example, serious, solemn, ironic, comic, formal or informal.

Looking at utterances as speech acts owes much to the penetrating studies on ordinary language that linguistic philosophers undertook in the forties and fifties. The impetus came from Austin who in his *Harvard Lectures on How to Do Things with Words* (1962) showed that certain utterances are acts in themselves as opposed to utterances which are statements about something; for example, 'I bet', 'I promise', and 'I pronounce you man and wife' fall into the first category. Austin began by distinguishing these verbal acts ('performatives') from other utterances which can be either true or false ('constatives'). But going beyond that, he argued that any utterance can be considered as a speech act. Thus, if I say 'It's cold here' this may be simply a statement or a proposition (a 'locutionary act') but it may at the same time be an invitation to someone to shut the window (in Austin's terms an 'illocutionary act') and therefore function as a speech act, that is, in this case as a request. In other words, an utterance can fulfil a number of functions simultaneously.[3]

3 A speech act is carried by a medium or *channel* (air, paper, or wire) which in physical terms establishes a relationship between participants. But the relationship can also be viewed psychologically as a social *contact* or *role relationship* between the participants. Talk reflects differences in social role between individuals: thus, a child is likely to talk differently to his parents, a friend, or a teacher.

4 The speech event takes place in a setting or scene, the *speech situation*. The situation, as interpreted by the participants, may

determine the topic, the verbal behaviour, and expectations of the participants. Thus, characteristic uses of language and language behaviour go with a classroom lesson, a committee meeting, a funeral, an evening party, or, as so vividly portrayed by Malinowski (1923), a fishing expedition. Malinowski, as we already observed, long ago emphasized the importance for an understanding of language of 'the context of situation', the concept adopted by Firth and many other British linguists.

5 A message is further distinguished by its *topic*, or content, which often but not always relates to the external non-linguistic reality, the situation, or context in which the speech event occurs.

6 In a given situation participants select a particular *variety of speech*, dialect, language, code, or register, which is likely to depend on the situation and the relationship between the participants or the topic. As we have seen, sociolinguistics differs most clearly from linguistics in the Saussurian sense by the importance it attributes to varieties of speech and the systematic speech variations among speakers and within speakers. The study of the social roles, situations, or functions that control the use of different speech varieties in predictable ways, has therefore become of particular significance to the development of sociolinguistics.

7 The conceptual schemes acknowledge that different speech acts have different *purposes* or *functions*. Several attempts have been made to define exhaustively the functions of speech. Figure 11.2 (*overleaf*) represents five such schemes.

One of the oldest and simplest categorizations is Bühler's threefold division of the functions of speech into expressive, representational, and conative. Searle's (1969) functional analysis distinguishes five categories. Jakobson's six categories of functions (1960) were outlined in a paper which was specially concerned with the stylistic or poetic function. Halliday's scheme, developed in a book on functions of language (1973), has seven categories. Robinson's (1972) scheme with fourteen categories is probably the most detailed and elaborate one.[4] Wilkins (1976) offers a similar set of categories. It has not been included in the tabulation in 11.2, but will be referred to in the text. As was already pointed out, any utterance may fulfill more than one function at a time. What functional elements, then, can be identified?

(a) The first category, common to most schemes, recognizes that a speech act serves to *express* the speaker's personal state of mind or attitude, for example, a child's cry, exclamations (ooch!), grunts, or sighs. Some of Labov's studies provide ingeniously devised evidence in speech behaviour for the speaker's perceptions of his identity in the social structure and even his aspirations and assessment of a situation (as more casual or more formal). In Robinson's analysis a speech act is

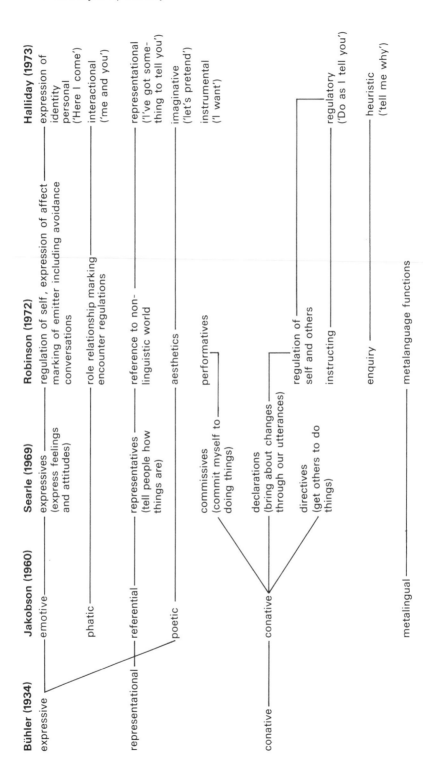

Figure 11.2 Functional categories of speech acts (lines indicate approximate conceptual equivalence)

said to mark the emotional state, personality, and social identity of the speaker. Wilkins identifies personal emotions (positive and negative) as one functional category.

(b) Another function of a speech act is to bring the participants in contact or in relationship to each other. This function has been described by Halliday (1973:17) as *interactional* or as the 'me and you' function. It may therefore serve to mark role relationships or regulate encounters (Robinson). One important aspect of this function is simply to open up and maintain social contacts, the 'phatic communion', referred to by Malinowski (see Chapter 10:208), a concept adopted by Jakobson. Probably Wilkins' category of emotional relations (greetings, sympathy, gratitude, flattery, and hostility) covers the same ground.

(c) The *referential* or *representational* function of speech (Searle's 'representatives') figures in all the schemes. Even a child intuitively knows and can convey 'a message which has specific reference to the processes, persons, objects, abstractions, qualities, states and relations of the real world around him' (Halliday 1973:16). The referential function relates the speech act specifically to the context (Jakobson), or the non-linguistic world (Robinson). Wilkins includes this speech function partly under Argument ('information') and partly under Rational Enquiry and Exposition.

(d) Language is often used with the purpose of making the recipient do something (*instrumental use*), for example, requesting, commanding, urging, or in some other way of regulating his conduct (regulatory use or Searle's directives). Instructing or teaching can be regarded as a type of communicative behaviour intended to cause the addressee to do something (i.e., to learn). Wilkins has a broad category 'Suasion' which includes advising and suggesting.

(e) Following Austin (1962) Robinson (1972) has identified as *performatives* certain speech acts which in themselves fulfill the role of actions such as advising, warning, congratulating, cursing, or promising. These are categorized by Searle as declarations and commissives.

(f) The use of language for enquiry or questioning is treated as a separate category by Halliday and Robinson. Halliday refers to it as the *heuristic* function. Wilkins' category 'Rational Enquiry and Exposition' partly covers the same ground.

(g) The use of language for its own sake, to give pleasure, i.e., imaginatively and aesthetically, is recognized by some schemes. In Bühler's model this function is subsumed under the expressive category.

(h) Lastly, Jakobson and Robinson treat as a separate category the use of language to talk about language (*the metalingual function*), i.e., explanations and comments about speech acts (for example, 'I repeat', 'I must emphasize', 'What does this word mean?').

The 'constitutive elements' in Hymes (1972a) of the speech act which provide the categories of the first model and the functions in the second are complementary and can be related to each other. Jakobson (1960) thus co-ordinates six functions and six elements in the following elegant and ingenious way (see Figure 11.3)[5].

                        CONTEXT
                        referential

ADDRESSER   MESSAGE   ADDRESSEE
emotive   *poetic*   *conative*

                        CONTACT
                        phatic

                        CODE
                        metalingual

*Figure 11.3   Jakobson's analysis of the speech act
and speech functions*

Robinson (1972), expanding Jakobson's scheme into a taxonomy of fourteen functions, relates each to a particular concept or focus of the speech act. The diagram and corresponding table of Robinson's scheme requires little explanation (see Figure 11.4).

Robinson's book (1972) elaborates this classification. It relates a language function to social situations, role, class, and personal characteristics of the individual, and characterizes the main uses of language: encounter regulations (for example, greetings, leave taking), performatives (for example, promising, betting, naming), regulation of self (for example, talking to oneself, praying), regulation of others, expression of affect, reference to the non-linguistic world, instruction, enquiry, and metalanguage use.

Searle has succinctly summarized many speech functions in these terms:

'... we tell people how things are, we try to get them to do things, we commit ourselves to doing things, we express our feelings and attitudes and we bring about changes through our utterances. Often, we do more than one of these at once in the same utterance.'
(Searle 1976:23)

The studies by Wilkins on notional syllabuses (for example, 1976) and the Council of Europe schemes to develop inventories of speech functions (for example, van Ek 1975 and Coste *et al.* 1976) constitute attempts at detailing categorizations of this kind and applying them to the development of language curricula. But it must be remembered that the functional categories are still very tentative and supported by relatively little empirical research.

The various conceptual schemes recognize that the different elements

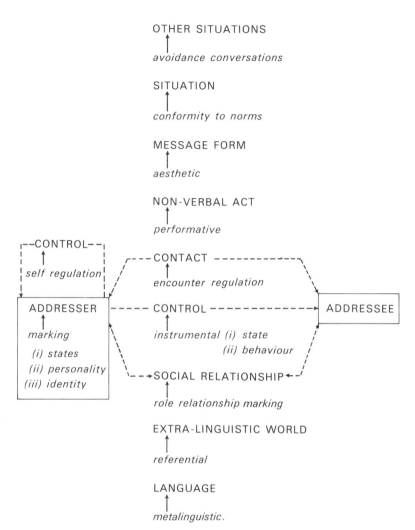

*Figure 11.4   Functions of language. Capital letters mark the focus,
italics are used for functions (Robinson 1972)*

represented by these categories in a given culture are interrelated in a
rule-governed way, so that one can say that there are *norms of
interaction* or *norms of interpretation*, appropriate to participants in a
particular situation. The ethnography of speaking aims to discover these
rules and thus to extend the systematic knowledge of language *use*. The
American linguist Ervin-Tripp (1971) has been particularly skillful in
drawing together studies which lead to the formulation of sociolinguistic
rules. For example, the forms of address which participants can use, first
or family names, the 'tu' or 'vous' forms of address, are subject to clearly

defined choices ('alternation' rules, i.e., *selection rules*). Equally, the sequencing of speech acts in a given situation, for example, in a telephone call (see below), or the co-occurrence of style elements in a given situation are subject to definable *rules of sequence*or *rules of co-occurrence*. Garfinkel's example, quoted on p. 221, illustrates the effect of the failure to observe a sequence rule.

An example to illustrate the kind of research that has been done on ethnography of communication is offered by a group of studies that has focused on communication in everyday life. The attempt has been made to develop what has been described as a social syntax of communication, in other words to discover the 'norms of interaction' as in Hymes' scheme. These studies are particularly illuminating because they show sociology and linguistics investigating a new area of common-sense experience from two different theoretical perspectives. Linguists who have hitherto confined themselves to the formal analysis of sentences have moved outward to discover the rules of communication. Sociologists who have in the past largely concerned themselves with the broader issues of social structure and social class have moved closer to the fundamentals of face-to-face interaction. For example, in one such study the investigator (Schegloff 1968) examined the sequencing in conversational openings. Traditional linguistic science had previously completely neglected the rules of such verbal interactions. Schegloff's unit of analysis is a conversation, in particular a two-party conversation in which the sequence of talk is alternating. He has closely examined openings of conversation, using as his corpus tape-recorded phone calls to and from a police department of an American city. On the basis of a careful examination of the opening sequence Schegloff has developed rules which make conscious the presuppositions and expectations of participants in telephone conversations. Thus, the ring of the phone acts as a 'summons'. The called person normally establishes his identity; i.e., the answerer speaks first. The summons-answer sequence is conducted in such a way that the conversation continues. The rules thus established are rules of communication which form part of a whole network of social rules governing speech acts, communicative acts generally and, beyond that, other forms of social interaction. Violations of these rules, as in non-response to the summons of the ring of the telephone, immediately prompt the summoner to an interpretation, as in this example by Schegloff:

Summoner: Are you mad at me?
Summoned: Why do you think that?
Summoner: You didn't answer when I called you.
Summoned: Oh. No, I didn't hear you.
(Schegloff 1972:367)

In the last decade several thorough and perceptive studies on language use in particular situations or of a particular speech act have been made, for example, classroom discourse (Sinclair and Coulthard 1975), medical diagnostic interviews (Candlin, Bruton, and Leather 1976), a therapeutic psychiatric session (Labov and Fanshel 1977) and analyses of the speech act of explanation (Weinstock 1980). Such studies reveal the extraordinary complexity of ordinary language use in that utterances fulfil several functions simultaneously. In the light of these studies the idea of 'ordinary everyday conversation' as a simple and modest objective of language teaching must today be tempered by the knowledge that ordinary everyday conversation is a very subtle and intricate form of language behaviour.

Communicative competence

A native speaker's language proficiency implies the ability to act as a speaker and listener in the diverse ways that the different categories we have outlined attempt to grasp. The intuitive mastery that the native speaker possesses to use and interpret language appropriately in the process of interaction and in relation to social context has been called by Hymes (1972) and others 'communicative competence', a concept which has in recent years been widely accepted in language pedagogy. In Hymes' much quoted formulation, it is a competence 'when to speak, when not, and as to what to talk about with whom, when, where, in what manner' (Hymes 1972:277).

This concept constituted a definite challenge to Chomsky's 'linguistic competence' which is confined to internalized rules of syntax and abstracts from the social rules of language use. Communicative competence no doubt *implies* linguistic competence but its main focus is the intuitive grasp of social and cultural rules and meanings that are carried by any utterance.[6] It further suggests that language teaching recognizes a social, interpersonal, and cultural dimension and attributes to it just as much importance as to the grammatical or phonological aspect.

On the other hand the complexity of the entire rule system is such that it might appear almost impossible for anyone except a native speaker to acquire communicative competence. This observation leads to the conclusion that communicative competence of a second language learner must be conceived somewhat differently from that of a native speaker. It suggests, besides grammatical and sociolinguistic competences which are obviously restricted in a second language user, a third element, an additional skill which the second language user needs, that is to know how to conduct himself as someone whose sociocultural and grammatical competence is limited, i.e., to know how to be a 'foreigner'. This skill has been called by Canale and Swain 'strategic competence'.[7] Naturally, as the second language user's communicative competence increases in the other two respects this third element becomes less and less important.

Whatever conclusions language pedagogy draws from this more intricate sociolinguistic analysis of language, the categorizations and studies in the ethnography of speaking are likely to play an increasingly important role in second language curriculum development. Theoretical and descriptive studies in this area are needed if pedagogy is not to operate with these concepts in the abstract.

The sociology of language

The first and second direction of sociolinguistics can be said to operate at the 'micro' level of language use and language behaviour. The sociology of language operates at the 'macro' level (Fishman 1972). This direction of enquiry focuses on speech communities and on languages as social institutions. From this perspective sociolinguistics looks at countries, regions, cities, and so on, and relates social structures and social groups to the languages and varieties of language used in the society in question. This approach is close to the traditional interests of sociology and merges into history and political science.

It is not always sufficiently realized how much our view of language and languages in society has been determined by the position occupied by a handful of European languages which, over a period of a few centuries since the Renaissance, had established themselves as standardized national languages in the growing nation states of Europe. The development of printing, schooling, literacy, the growth of the concept of the nation state, and the use of a standard language as the medium of communication throughout the country created a unity and uniformity of language use which more and more came to be regarded as right and normal. Language standardization and unilingualism were dominant characteristics of the Western world, a view of language which prevailed certainly until World War II.

Certain deviations from such national unilingualism, above all local and regional dialects, were tolerated. Most unilingual countries have always had minority groups of immigrants or other exceptions to the linguistic uniformity, especially in frontier regions between countries, such as the Sudetenland on the border between Czechoslovakia and Germany, the region of Alsace between Germany and France. Dialects offered no political challenge. Multilingualism in society and in education, however, tended to be regarded as an irritation, a residue of the past, often as a retrograde form of regionalism, or as politically dangerous irredentism or separatism. Sometimes the struggle among different language groups to achieve pre-eminence or recognition caused riots and civil strife. As a consequence of this unilingual view of society, bilingualism or multilingualism was regarded as 'a problem' and as detrimental to society or to the individual rather than as a normal state of affairs and an asset.

The study of languages and literatures in schools and universities and even the more recent study of linguistics were largely founded on the position that languages had attained in the major European nation states: a position of uniformity, standardization of use, and homogeneity throughout the society. The ideological reflection of this sociopolitical view of language has been the language in isolation, treated as a complete and independent entity which provided the frame of reference for the majority of linguistic studies from Saussure to Chomsky. Most modern schools of linguistic thought tend to look at a language as an internally coherent system of contrasts and relations. They are not directly equipped to cross language boundaries, to relate one language to another or to deal with multilingualism.[8]

School systems also reflected this view of language; but they did not only reflect it, they cultivated unilingualism through education. The idea of a single-medium education in a unilingual nation state, transmitting the cultural values of that state through its literature and folklore and legitimizing only that language as the language of education, was roughly suited to the development of France, Germany, and England, whence it spread to the rest of Europe and throughout the world.[9]

Since World War II the profound social and political changes in the world have led to a recognition that the reality of the language situation can no longer be forced into the simple mould of the single-language nation state with its single-medium school as inevitably right in all circumstances. All over the world linguistic, ethnic, cultural, and religious minorities have begun to assert their language rights and to maintain their cultural distinctiveness. The countries of Africa and Asia present obvious examples of complex language and dialect situations to which the European unilingual model of the nineteenth century cannot be applied without modification. Language and dialect diversity has become accepted as a reality of life in most societies, and a more diversified approach to language issues characterizes national policy in many countries of the world today.

The sociology of language has been the intellectual response to this new interpretation of the role of languages in society. Of course linguists since the nineteenth century have studied regional differences within a speech community; dialectology has always been an important branch of linguistics; and for many years scholars have investigated the specialized languages of certain social groups, such as the slang of thieves and soldiers, craft jargons, and secret argots. But dialects and slangs tended to be regarded as linguistically interesting deviations from the language norm rather than as the socially significant range of normal linguistic diversity.

Today, the dialects and languages of groups, of interest to linguists in previous decades, are much more recognized as examples of a regular social phenomenon: sociolinguistic groupings. The work of Weinreich on languages in contact in Switzerland, Haugen's studies on the Norwegian language in America, and Bernstein's sociolinguistic codes of social classes in Britain in the fifties are now seen as the beginnings of a new view of normal language diversification in society. (See also Chapter 7:124–6).

Varieties of language situations

Around 1960 the new view of the role of languages in society attracted the attention of linguists, anthropologists, and sociologists. In a study on the role of second languages in Asia, Africa, and Latin America (Rice 1962), Ferguson observed that 'no satisfactory classification has yet been worked out which can be used to characterize either a language or a language situation from a sociolinguistic point of view' (op. cit.:3).

The sociolinguists and linguists in the sixties set about to define or redefine a number of basic concepts of the sociology of language. One such a central term is *speech community*. In the past this term might have been defined as a community that shares the same language.[10] But in the sociology of language a speech community is redefined as a group of people (face-to-face group, gang, region, nation) who regularly communicate with each other (Gumperz 1968). It is therefore left open in this definition whether the group is large or small, and whether the medium of communication they use is one language or dialect, or several dialects, codes, or languages. A speech community may be uniform or homogeneous, or diversified in its *verbal repertoire*. Another set of basic concepts has been that which describes varieties of language used in the speech community. *Dialects* are regular regional varieties within a speech community. Regular social variations of language are often referred to by analogy as *social dialects* or *sociolects*. In many speech communities a functional differentiation occurs between two different dialects of the same language. Thus, one dialect may be used for literary, official, or educational purposes, while the other is used for familiar or informal talk. The observation that some languages have developed a high (H) and a low (L) form of the same language has prompted Ferguson (1959) to adopt for this particular diversification the term *diglossia* (from French *diglossie*). Examples of diglossia are classical Arabic and Egyptian Arabic in Egypt or Standard German and Swiss German in Switzerland.[11]

Within a speech community two or several languages (bilingualism or multilingualism) may be in use. In order to analyse the possible diversifications, attempts have been made to define language types. In a widely used typology (Stewart 1962, 1968) languages, including dialects, are distinguished by four sociohistorical attributes:

Historicity (I), i.e., whether or not the language is the result of a process of development through use. What makes a language obviously historical is its association with some national or ethnic tradition.

Standardization (II), i.e., whether or not there exists for the language a codified set of grammatical and lexical norms which are formally accepted and learnt by the languages users . . .

Vitality (III), i.e., whether or not the language has an existing community of native speakers . . .

Homogenicity (IV), i.e., whether or not the language's basic lexicon and basic grammatical structure both derive from the same pre-stages of the language.[12]

With these four characteristics Stewart has been able to define seven language types as in the following figure:

	Attributes			Language type	Type symbol
I	II	III	IV		
+	+	+	+ / −	Standard	S
+	+	−	+	Classical	C
+	−	+	+	Vernacular	V
+	−	+	−	Creole	K
+	−	−	−	Pidgin	P
−	+	−	+ / −	Artificial	A
−	−	−	+ / −	Marginal	M

Figure 11.5   Stewart's classification of language types

A *standard* language (S), such as English or French spoken by educated native speakers, has all four attributes. A *classical* language (C), such as Latin or Classical Arabic, has three but lacks the attribute of 'vitality'. A *vernacular*, for example, tribal languages of America or Africa, has three, but lacks the formal standardization of grammar and lexicon. A wide definition of vernacular can include dialects. *Creoles* and *pidgin* languages are 'the result of the development of a secondary language for wider communication in . . . contact situations where grammatical and lexical material from different sources became fused' (Stewart 1962:19–20). A pidgin is only used as a secondary language. Its only defining characteristic is historicity. If it becomes a native language it develops into a creole. Esperanto is an example of an *artificial* language (A). *Marginal* languages (M) describe household languages or codes, developed among small groups.

In addition to language types (marked by capitals) the scheme developed by Stewart recognizes seven different societal functions (marked by lower-case symbols) by which the language can be distinguished:

Official (o): The legally recognized use of a language, for example, use as the language of education and government.

Group (g): The use of a language by the members of an ethnic or cultural group.

Wider Communication (w): The use of a language for communication across language boundaries. Another term used for a language of wider communication is *lingua franca* (Samarin 1962).

Educational (e): The use of a language for educational purposes.

Literary (l): The use of a language for literary or scholarly writing.

Religious (r): The use of a language in connection with religious practice.

Technical (t): The use of a language for technical and scientific communications.

With these concepts and symbols it is possible to indicate briefly the language position in a multilingual country as far as it is known.

Studies in the sociology of language over the last decades have attempted to find out about the way in which the verbal repertoire—whether it consists of different languages or different dialects—is used by social groups. Such studies range from enquiries on individuals and their choice of language in given circumstances to enquiries on attitudes of social groups to language diversity, and beyond that to language surveys in large regions or nations (see also p. 236). In the sixties it was increasingly recognized that the presence of more than one language or language variety in one speech community must be accepted as a normal feature of social life and not as an exception to linguistic uniformity.

The intricate patterns of language use in multilingual speech communities and the relationship of bilingualism to social factors has been investigated in several countries. Again a preliminary task had to be to create concepts as well as to describe and analyse diverse situations. But another task was to try to explain the phenomena of *language maintenance* and *loyalty* often in the face of pressure towards linguistic uniformity, or the *language shift* from the dominance of one language to another.

Extending the concept of diglossia, developed by Ferguson (1959),

Fishman, who has been foremost in the investigation of language patterns in multilingual societies, has evolved categorizations for the diversity of language situations. He uses the term *bilingualism* for the dual language command of the individual and the term *diglossia* to characterize 'the social allocation of functions to different languages or varieties' (Fishman 1972:102). Accordingly, four possible patterns can be recognized: (1) both diglossia and bilingualism (2) bilingualism without diglossia (3) diglossia without bilingualism (4) neither diglossia nor bilingualism.

The first type, both diglossia and bilingualism, can be illustrated by Paraguay where, according to a well known study by Rubin (1968), a majority of the population came to be bilingual in Spanish and the aboriginal language Guaraní. Spanish is the official language (o) and the language of education (e), but Guaraní is widely used for informal communication especially in rural areas, and among speakers with little formal education (g). It has therefore the status of a vernacular (V), but although Guaraní is often referred to as a boorish and uncultured form of speech, it has maintained itself and has even produced a literature.

> 'The large majority of rural Paraguayans have Guaraní as their first language and are first exposed to Spanish in the classroom. Whereas one could live in the rural areas today without ever speaking Spanish, lack of knowledge of Guaraní would be a real handicap. Although the reverse is true for the major cities, there are numerous occasions when lack of knowledge of Guaraní would isolate a person from casual speech—for example, at even the most formal dinners after-dinner jokes are usually told in Guaraní.'
> (op. cit.:477)

The second type, bilingualism without diglossia, occurs where there is no clear functional separation between the languages in use. This situation arises not infrequently in the case of second-generation immigrants. The newly arrived first-generation group of immigrants commonly uses the first language in the home and neighbourhood, and second languages in contact with government offices, in education, or for intercommunication with other members of the society. The second generation, however, through schooling and wider social contacts, frequently brings the language of the school into the home. No clear functional differentiation occurs, but a command of the ethnic language persists. In this transitional situation there is bilingualism without diglossia.

The third type, diglossia without bilingualism, can be illustrated by the position of English in India in colonial days. The expatriate English officials operated through the medium of English without, as a rule, using the languages of India for the conduct of administration; hence, in this diglossic society the English expatriates were monolingual, and most of the populations which they governed were monolingual in an Indian language. In Canada, in the largely French-speaking province of Quebec, one may find groups of English native speakers who know no French and French native speakers without a knowledge of English, i.e., diglossia without bilingualism.

Lastly, neither bilingualism nor diglossia, is the position cultivated as the nineteenth century ideal of the unilingual state in which the notion prevailed that a single standard language should be the only means of all communication at all levels.

The combination of bilingualism and diglossia offered by patterns 1 to 3 may or may not be stable. The phenomena of change and stability have been categorized as the problems of *language maintenance, language shift,* and *language conflict.* Haugen's study of the Norwegian language in America, referred to in Chapter 10, illustrates the vicissitudes of a bilingual existence for an immigrant minority. Fishman *et al.* (1966) have gathered a number of studies which portray the maintenance of non-English mother tongues in American ethnic and religious groups. In spite of the tremendous pressures since the early part of the twentieth century to lose an ethnic identity which did not seem to fit life on the new continent and to merge more consciously with an English-speaking majority, language groups have maintained themselves: indeed in recent years there has been a considerable revival and cultivation of ethnic life and language throughout North America.[13]

The idea of language shift is illustrated by '(a) the vernacularization of European governmental, technical, educational, cultural activity, (b) the Anglification/Hispanization of the populations of North/South America, (c) the adoption of English and French as languages of elitist wider communication throughout much of the world, but particularly in Africa and Asia, (d) the Russification of Soviet-controlled populations, and most recently (e) the growing displacement of imported languages of wider communication and the parallel vernacularization of governmental, technical, educational, and cultural efforts in many parts of Africa and Asia' (Fishman 1972:107). The presence of linguistic minorities, of migrant workers and their families, and the movement of populations across the world as refugees or immigrants has presented language problems and questions of an educational language policy almost everywhere in the world.[14]

It is not surprising to find that India with its many languages and dialects and corresponding regional, religious, and social divisions faces a particularly difficult language situation (Das Gupta 1970). The awareness shared by policy makers and sociolinguists of the complexity of language in a society has led to a demand for comprehensive reviews of language use in the society and, on the basis of this information, to plans for policy decisions. Recent decades have thus witnessed, as applications of sociolinguistic concepts, language surveys and the growth of a new subfield of the sociology of language, *language planning*.

Particular attention has been paid to the language questions of developing nations in Africa, Asia, and South America (for example, Fishman, Ferguson, and Das Gupta 1968; Das Gupta 1970; Spolsky 1978). Language surveys, for example, in Canada and East Africa, provide the basis of information on language use in the home, at school, in towns and villages, in government, on radio and television, in industry, in administration, and law.[15] The differences among age groups, the sexes, social groups, rural and urban populations, speakers of different educational levels suggest that national language profiles cannot be drawn easily by simply applying a few basic categories of type and function, even though the categories developed by Stewart (1962, 1968) form a useful basis.[16]

Sociology and social psychology of speech communities
An important aspect of the complex sociology of speech communities is the intellectual and emotional response of the members of the society to the languages and varieties in their social environment. It is part of the native speaker's communicative competence to be able to distinguish his first language from all other languages and to identify different language varieties. Different languages and language varieties are not only identified but they are often associated with deep-rooted emotional responses in which thoughts, feelings, stereotypes, and prejudices about people, social, ethnic and religious groupings, and political entities are strongly associated with different languages or varieties of a language. Feelings about languages can run high, and if languages or varieties of a language become an issue of language policy or educational policy they can lead to language conflicts.

Social attitudes towards languages and speech communities, including one's own, and the language perceptions of members of speech communities have been studied by social psychologists for several decades. Pioneer work was done by a group in Canada round Lambert of McGill University in Montreal, and Gardner (for example, 1979) at the University of Western Ontario in London, Ontario. Their work which explored cultural and language stereotypes is a continuation of studies on prejudice and personality which in the forties had culminated in the *Authoritarian Personality*(Adorno *et al.* 1950), mentioned in Chapter 10, Note 9. In the seventies another group of social psychologists at the University of Bristol round Giles expanded this research on language prejudice.[17] All these studies have documented that individuals have strong feelings about their own language or language variety and relate it cognitively and affectively to other languages or other language varieties. For example, d'Anglejan and Tucker (1973) investigated the reactions of French Canadian students, teachers, and workers from three regions of Quebec to the French speech variations in Quebec. This group of subjects perceived weaknesses in the Quebec speech forms compared to what they regarded as a more desirable form of European French. While this study reflects the peculiar situation of French in Canada and certain attitudes of French native speakers to their own dialect, other investigations have shown that social and emotive judgements about ways of speaking form part of the language situation in any speech community (Hudson 1980: Chapter 6).

Schumann (1978) has developed a theory, the 'acculturation' model, to explain the differences in social perceptions between groups and individuals who are prepared to learn a second language, and those who are unwilling or unable to do so. According to Schumann, it all depends on how the groups view each other and their languages. Thus, higher status groups will tend not to learn the languages of lower status groups. For example, during the days of the British Empire, Britons in India or Africa did not intend to learn the languages of India and Africa. In other words, the pattern of social dominance is likely to influence the willingness to learn a second language. A minority language group which views itself as a subordinate group tends to adopt one of three integration strategies. If it gives up its own life style and values, as some immigrant groups do, the group is likely to learn the language well ('assimilation'). If it rejects the culture of the dominant group, language learning is unlikely to occur ('rejection'). If the group takes a positive view of its own culture and an equally positive view of the target group, second language acquisition is likely to vary ('adaptation'). In a study among francophone university students, learning English in Quebec, major predictors of proficiency were the degree of contact with the anglophone community and the students' perceived threat to the group identity or fear of assimilation.

From the point of view of language pedagogy surveys and analyses of language situations in a speech community are significant in two ways. First, they provide teachers with information on the language situations within which they teach and to which their efforts contribute by extending the language competence in certain directions. Second, the target language as the language of another speech community can be viewed by teachers against the background of the language situation in that speech community. By adopting this sociolinguistic perspective teachers can understand and interpret more effectively the languages they teach, and the sociolinguistic situations in which they operate.[18]

Language planning
Language planning consists of organized efforts to find solutions to language problems in a society (Fishman 1972:186, after Jernudd and

Das Gupta 1971). It is therefore an application of sociolinguistic concepts and information to policy decisions involving languages. Language planning—like social, economic, or educational planning—is a process of decision making based on 'fact-finding, the consideration of different plans of action, the making of decisions, and the implementation of these in specified ways' (Haugen 1966a:52). Examples of language planning are: developing a writing system for a hitherto unwritten language; introducing a spelling reform; the revival of a language (for example, the case of Hebrew or Irish); the choice and introduction of a language as a medium of wider communication or instruction; standardization of language usage; extension of the vocabulary in order to meet needs of modernization.[19]

The idea of social measures to influence and control language use is in itself not new. Historically, most European languages have gone through forms of language planning in which government agencies or the intellectual prestige of certain writers exercised the function of language planner and policy maker. Educational systems, books, newspapers, and other media involve the application of standards or norms of language use. An outstanding example of an institution making systematic decisions on language questions has been the *Académie française* which was founded in France in the seventeenth century. In the English-speaking world, the great dictionaries, for example, the Oxford dictionary in Britain and Webster's dictionary in North America, have exercised a similar influence.

Modern linguistics has explicitly rejected the role of decision maker: the linguist, as was pointed out in Chapter 7, takes language as he finds it and does not claim to legislate language use. Does language planning mean that the linguist adopts again the role or arbiter and norm maker? Not quite. For, as Haugen points out, it is not the function of the language planner to take up an *a priori* position on the main issues of controversy. Thus, he does not either promote or prevent change; he does not advocate uniformity or diversity among groups of speakers; he does not resist or encourage linguistic borrowing nor does he work for 'purification' or 'hybridization'. Language planning 'is not committed to EFFICIENCY at the expense of BEAUTY; it may work for ACCURACY as well as EXPRESSIVENESS. It is not even committed to the MAINTENANCE of the language for which it plans: it may work for a SHIFT to some other language' (Haugen 1966a:52).

Language planning is a means to arrive at more informed decisions about language in society. It comprises at least two sets of activities: in the first place, the planner can assist in making basic policy decisions on such questions as to which language should be used for wider communication, which language should be used for instruction, etc.—in short, the fundamental decisions of language choice, language emphasis, and language tolerance. The decisions are particularly important in newly formed nation states which are in the process of modernizing their society and which have to select a convenient means of wider communication. But in older countries basic decisions may also have to be taken: to what extent and by what means should the French language be strengthened in Canada? What should be the place of Welsh in Britain? What should be the place of minority languages in the U.S.A.?[20]

From another point of view language planning is more directly linguistic. Assuming that the selection of languages is settled, planning in this second sense is concerned with the development or cultivation of the language itself: questions of standardization, determination of norms of pronunciation, establishment or reform of the orthography, extension of the vocabulary, and so on—in short the tasks of shaping and refining the language as an effective means of communication. In this kind of language planning the skills of the linguist come into play; but different from linguistics, language planning at this stage is necessarily to a certain extent 'prescriptive' or 'normative'. There are differences of views among language planners as to the degree of prescriptiveness on the part of the planner at this level. On the whole, language planners today regard their function as a discreet and cautious one, and, ideally, the criteria they employ in coming to decisions on points of language should be openly stated and subject to revision.

Whether language planning is conceived as planning the selection and determination of a language, or whether it is understood as development and cultivation of aspects of the particular language already in use, the planning process is likely to go through a necessary series of stages (Rubin 1971, 1973):

(a) *Fact-finding*. The planning must be based on a survey and review of the language situation for which the plan is developed. From this point of view, the Canadian *Report on Bilingualism and Biculturalism* or the East African language survey are part of language planning.

(b) *The selection stage*. At this stage the planner will attempt to identify language goals and choices open to the society in question or to its policy makers and suggest strategies for reaching these goals. During this phase fundamental decisions are recommended on such questions as: which language is to be the medium of wider communication? What is the appropriate language for education? What is to be the role of different languages and dialects in that society? In many countries these questions do not arise because the basic decisions of language choice have been taken long ago and are not open to revision. In some cases, however, even if these issues *seem* settled, modifications of the status quo may be regarded as desirable. Thus, in many countries which had previously adopted a policy of unilingualism, policy is shifting towards bilingualism or multilingualism. In Canada, for example, the Official

Languages Act of 1969 has enhanced the status of French vis-à-vis English in many sectors of public life. In French-speaking Quebec the maintenance and development of French and its protection against the inroads of English on a largely English-speaking continent has led to numerous measures involving planning, policy, and legislation. In the U.S.A. the Bilingual Education Act of 1968 has opened the possibility of using languages other than English as languages of instruction in schools.

(c) *The development stage*. At this stage, the traditionally recognized forms of language planning are employed: the cultivation and development of the language or languages that have been selected at the previous stage. Planning as development will focus on the preparation of an orthography, the making of a pronunciation guide, the preparation of technical vocabularies, and so on.

(d) *The implementation phase*. The selection of a language is not enough nor is the setting up of the orthography, lexical list, pronouncing dictionary, or grammatical guide. The planning decisions must eventually become part of the language behaviour of the speech community. Defining the steps to take—information, dissemination, and instruction—constitute the fourth phase of the planning process.

(e) The final phase is one of *feedback and evaluation*. This aspect of planning can be regarded as concurrent with, as well as subsequent to, the other phases. Evaluation will relate each phase to goals and effects of a language policy. It will also represent the follow-up part of the implementation. Has the plan achieved its object? What modification in objectives, methods or treatment are needed? In other words planning becomes part of a cycle of activities which can be represented as follows:

fact-finding survey—language selection—cultivation and development—implementation—evaluation—revision of plan, etc.[21]

Conclusion

From this survey of sociology, anthropology, and sociolinguistics in this and the last chapter it is evident that the role of language in society and the relationships between language, society and culture have become a central subject of study, whether it has been approached from the point of view of anthropology and sociology or the point of view of sociolinguistics or social psychology. Scholars are seeking more and more to integrate their views of language and society. That is to say they are not merely seeking to find parallels between language and society or cause-and-effect relations between them but to create concepts in which language is not isolated from society, or society looked at as if verbal communication could be ignored.

In our exploration of concepts of society for language pedagogy, the social sciences can be said to offer a threefold contribution:

1 Sociology and anthropology provide the tools for the systematic study of societies and cultures which form the necessary contexts for a study of language.
2 Sociolinguistics provides concepts, mechanisms, and systematic information for a study of language in a social, cultural, and interpersonal matrix. Both these contributions can be said to have bearing on curriculum objectives and content.
3 The sociology of language suggests ways of looking at languages and language teaching in a sociological way and may lead to an interpretation of second language teaching and learning as one of society's ways of establishing crosslingual and ethnic group contact.

In the next two chapters we will consider how language pedagogy has, in effect, dealt with the social and cultural aspects of language and what role the social sciences, particularly sociolinguistics, have played or might play in language education.

Notes

1 For introductions to sociolinguistics, see for example, Fishman (1972), Trudgill (1974), Dittmar (1976) and Hudson (1980), and a wide-ranging bibliographical review article by Le Page (1975). For a fairly recent statement of anthropological approaches to language, see Saville-Troike (1977).
2 For a detailed and readable introduction to research by Labov and similar studies see Hudson (1980: Chapter 5).
3 Austin distinguished three aspects of a speech act: the *locutionary* act, i.e., the overt utterance and its surface meaning; the *illocutionary* act, the underlying intention in making the utterance, and the *perlocutionary* act, the effect of the act on the recipient.
4 However, Robinson's scheme (see Figure 11.4) contains some categories which, in our view, cannot be regarded as 'functions' and which have therefore been omitted from Figure 11.2.
5 Jakobson's model has been developed in the context of a discussion of poetics in relation to linguistics. In my view, it is the 'classical' statement of the act of communication and of communicative functions.
6 See Chapter 6:111 above, in particular Figure 6.1, and also Chapter 16:342 below for further explanations of communicative competence. Pedagogical implications are discussed in Chapter 12:258–62. On the development of the concept of 'communicative competence' see also Canale and Swain (1980).

7 Canale and Swain (1980) describe 'strategic competence' as the knowledge of 'communicative strategies', that is strategies that second language learners intend to make use of in order to get meaning across in spite of their imperfect command of the language: paraphrasing, avoidance of difficulties, simplifications, coping techniques, and so on.

8 The same applies to the treatment of literature which was also frequently designed to enhance the national self-image through contact with the great literary monuments of the speech community.

9 Second language learning in school systems is compatible with educational unilingualism. Our modern approach to teaching languages as subjects has largely developed in basically unilingual educational systems: other languages play a more or less important role but remain secondary in school curricula to the major unilingual educational philosophy.

10 For example, Bloomfield (1933): 'A group of people who use the same system of speech-signals'. Other definitions of 'speech community' are discussed in Hudson (1980:25–30).

11 Ferguson has defined diglossia as follows: 'Diglossia is a relatively stable language situation in which, in addition to the primary dialects of the language (which may include a standard or regional standard) there is a very divergent, highly codified (often grammatically more complex) superposed variety, the vehicle of a large and respected body of written literature, either of an earlier period or in another speech community, which is learnt largely by formal education and is used for most written and formal spoken purposes but is not used by any sector of the community for ordinary conversation' (Ferguson 1971:16). For a further discussion of diglossia, see pp. 234–6 below.

12 Shortened and slightly adapted from Stewart (1962:17–18).

13 The efforts made to halt the decline of ethnic languages are well illustrated by investigations on Athapaskan language maintenance and bilingualism by Spolsky in a study by Kari and Spolsky (1973). See also Spolsky (1978:43).

14 Examples are Spanish-speaking Mexican migrant workers in California, Turkish migrant workers in Berlin and Sweden, language minorities in the U.S.A. or Canada, for example, Navahos in the U.S.A and Ukrainians in Alberta, Swedes in Finland, Finns in Sweden. These situations are discussed, among others, by Spolsky (1972), Paulston (1975/1976), Skutnabb-Kangas and Tukoomaa (1976), and Spolsky (1978).

15 A useful brief review of the language problems and conflicts in relation to national development in Europe and the new multilingual

states of Africa and Asia may be found in Chapter 1 of Das Gupta (1970).

16 For a recent overview and discussion of language surveys see Cooper (1980). The Canadian *Report on Bilingualism and Biculturalism-*(Canada 1966–1970) and the *Survey of Language Use and Language Teaching in Eastern Africa* which included studies in Uganda, Kenya, Ethiopia, Tanzania, and Zambia (Gorman 1970; Ladefoged *et al.* 1972; Whiteley 1974; Bender *et al.* 1976; Polomé and Hill 1981) are outstanding examples of language surveys. Language surveys in developing nations have been reviewed by Ohannessian, Ferguson, and Polomé (1975). Other attempts to describe a national language profile include one by Ferguson (1966) and an analysis of the variables by Kloss (1966). Whiteley (1973) has described some of the difficulties encountered in attempting to apply Stewart's categories in East Africa. Recent examples of empirical (small-scale) surveys of language situations in Africa are unpublished studies by Africa (1980) on Zambia, by Ituen (1980) on Nigeria and Côte d'Ivoire and on India by Seshadri (1978).

17 Several of these studies are reviewed by Hudson (1980:195–207), although Hudson deals mainly with social rather than ethnolinguistic attitudes. For the latter see Chapter 17:378. See also Schumann (1978), Brown (1980: Chapter 6), Giles (1977), and Giles and St Clair (1979).

18 Spolsky (1978) offers a helpful general introduction to the kind of analysis needed to interpret the social context of language teaching.

19 Among introductions to language planning, see Rubin and Jernudd (1971) and Rubin and Shuy (1973), and a short but informative overview in 1979 by Rubin (1979). A useful and well arranged annotated bibliography has been prepared by Rubin and Jernudd (1979). The only international scholarly journal on language planning, *Language Problems and Language Planning*, was taken over in 1980 by the University of Texas Press from Mouton in the Hague who published the first three volumes of this journal. The East–West Culture Learning Institute at the East–West Center, Honolulu, Hawaii, publishes a *Language Planning Newsletter*.

20 For example, in Norway a longstanding struggle has surrounded the development of two forms of Norwegian, one more popular, Nynorsk or Landsmaal, and the other more literary, Riksmaal or Bokmaal (Haugen 1966).

21 The basic idea of language planning was contained in the paper by Haugen (1966a) on language planning, quoted above, and a book on *Language Conflict and Language Planning*(1966) with Norwegian as a case study. The concepts have been theoretically developed, extended, and applied in a number of studies, particularly relevant

to the emergent nations of the Third World by Rubin and Jernudd (1971), Fishman, Ferguson, and Das Gupta (1968), and Rubin and Shuy (1973). The steps in language planning suggested here have been based on a discussion of models of planning in Rubin and Shuy (1973), especially the introduction and the first paper, both by Rubin (1973, 1973a), a paper in the same volume by Jernudd (1973), as well as a paper by Rubin (1971) on evaluation in Rubin and Jernudd (1971).

12 The social sciences and the second language curriculum

The relations between the social sciences and language teaching have developed differently from the relations between language teaching and linguistics. Contacts were established later in the history of language pedagogy, and the interaction has been far less intensive. The development of the relationship has not been one of similar dramatic ups and downs. In the fifties and sixties, an anthropological and sociological view of language in connection with culture and society began to influence language teaching theory to a limited extent. Earlier thinking on language and society was directed to historical studies or philosophy. Sociolinguistics as a relative newcomer in the language sciences has only quite recently become involved in pedagogy. As a generalization one can say that language teaching theory today is fast acquiring a sociolinguistic component but still lacks a well-defined sociocultural emphasis. The present chapter and the next are in certain respects therefore programmatic rather than descriptive. In these two chapters we will delineate the four areas in which an interaction with the social sciences has been emerging or could be productive:

1 The study of society and culture;
2 the study of language in its social context;
3 the communicative approach to language teaching;
4 the sociology of language teaching and learning.

Areas 1, 2, and 3 which have bearing on curriculum are considered in this chapter. The fourth area which concerns the planning and organization of second language teaching is dealt with in Chapter 13.

The study of society and culture

In nineteenth century modern language teaching, as in the teaching of the classical languages before that, the question of relating language to society did not arise with particular urgency. Language teaching was preparatory to the study of literature, and therefore the main emphasis was upon formal language study, particularly upon its written form. Even the shift towards an attention to the spoken form, which occurred

by the end of the nineteenth century, did not bring about a fundamentally new approach to language in society. Language learning in the
classroom continued to be conceived as a training rather than as 'real'
communication or as an introduction to a foreign society. This emphasis
on learning of language forms, developing mental associations, and
acquiring speech habits in the abstract, or, to use a modern term, the
emphasis on the acquisition of *skills*, independent of communication in
society, prevailed until most recent times and in many ways is still
dominant today. This theory was greatly strengthened by the view of
language implied in phonetics (from about 1890) and, since the forties,
in structural linguistics and other recent linguistic theories. Linguistics
and psychology gave scientific backing to a relatively detached technical
approach to the teaching of language outside a social and cultural
context.[1]

Nevertheless, since the reform movement in the last century, and even
before, language teaching theorists repeatedly stated that an important
purpose of language learning was to learn about a country and its
people.[2] Writings of language teaching theorists and government reports
indicate a clear awareness of this component. For example, the British
report, *Modern Studies*, prepared by a national committee in the midst
of World War I (see Chapter 6:99), reveals, even in its title, a deliberate
emphasis on the cultural aspect: 'Modern *Studies*', not simply 'Modern
Languages'—in other words, the study of a country, its culture and
literature, not the study of language alone. A widely read book of the
same period recommended 'some knowledge of the history of the people
who speak the languages' as a necessary part of the language programme (Atkins and Hutton 1920). Equally, in France it became
customary to supplement language programmes by the study of
civilisation.

Kulturkunde in Germany
In German language teaching theory the teaching of culture (*Kulturkunde*[3]) as part of language programmes was developed with particular
vigour after World War I. The history of this fascinating movement can
serve both as a lesson and a warning when we consider present-day
attempts to teach culture. Since the days of von Humboldt the German
intellectual tradition had been accustomed to viewing language and
nation as closely related. Moreover, some German historians expressed
ideas on the culture of nations which have much in common with the
modern anthropological culture concept (Kroeber and Kluckhohn
1952). Towards the end of the century, the German philosopher Dilthey
advocated the notion of 'structure', 'pattern', or 'underlying principle' as
fundamental concepts in the humanities and social sciences in order to
interpret historical and social events, whether these occurred at the level

of the individual, the family, of society, nation, and epoch, or in historical movements. A few decades later, these early forms of a structural or *Gestalt* principle were adopted by Benedict in her concept of '*patterns* of culture' (see Chapter 10:198). In Germany, however, the concept of culture became tainted by the development of extreme nationalism. Even before World War I, and more so in the interwar years, *Kulturkunde* was increasingly understood as an assertion of German identity. German educators advocated *Kulturkunde* in mother tongue education as the unifying principle binding together the teaching of 'German subjects'; German language, German literature, German history, and the geography of Germany.

When *Kulturkunde* in the interwar period was applied to foreign language teaching in Germany, several different directions were pursued, revealing the ambivalent interpretation of the *Kulturkunde* concept. To some language educators it meant the foreign equivalent to German *Kulturkunde*: treating language quite appropriately in relation to a foreign literature, history, and geography, thus widening the scope of language teaching. Another promising interpretation was one that advocated *Kulturkunde* as the history of ideas of another country: for example, in teaching English as a foreign language, instead of reading this or that English author out of context, teachers were encouraged to focus on an era, for example, to study the Elizabethan Age and to treat Shakespeare as an example of a new form of Renaissance drama, or to study Milton as the poet of Puritan idealism. This sophisticated historical, literary, and philosophical approach, expressed in the slogan '*Kulturkunde* as "history of ideas"' ('*Kulturkunde* as *Geistesgeschichte*'), has maintained itself in Germany until today.

A further trend of thought, akin to such concepts as patterns of culture, basic personality, or cultural 'themes', a set of concepts which in later years was adopted and developed by cultural anthropologists (see Chapter 10:198), had as its aim to discover the underlying 'structure' or 'mind' of a foreign nation ('*Geist*' or '*Seele*') and to view historical events, current social facts, and literary and artistic works in the light of this underlying principle. While Benedict's empirical scholarship and critical acumen made this approach fruitful and exciting, in the climate of the Nazi ideology that gained prevalence in German education in the thirties, the search for the mind of a nation was an invitation to blatant forms of prejudice and stereotyping about the 'French *esprit*' or 'English realism'.[4]

An extreme view of *Kulturkunde* during the interwar period was entirely in the spirit of the Hitler era. It treated *Kulturkunde* in the foreign language class exclusively as a foil against which to develop a better appreciation of German culture.[5] The point of foreign culture teaching was to form in the student 'his German consciousness and

German sense of value' (Schön 1925:1).[6] It was openly ethnocentric in outlook.

German *Kulturkunde* of the interwar years, although a product of the German historical and ideological situation of that period, anticipated many of the general problems that were encountered again when the anthropological view of culture was introduced into language teaching after World War II: the scope of language teaching was widened; but expansion brought with it the question of selection and the problem of an organizing principle. Culture teaching, further, led to a search for materials and methods, and, finally, raised the question of what attitudes of mind to cultivate in the learner vis-à-vis a foreign culture.

Culture teaching elsewhere

In other countries during the same period culture teaching was not unknown either. But it was less developed and less clearly defined than in Germany. Anthropology and sociology had not yet any part in it. Culture was frequently interpreted in a dual sense: (a) as the personal development, through language learning, of a cultivated mind: the training of 'reasoning powers', 'intelligence', 'imagination', and the 'artistic faculties' (IAAM 1929); and (b) as 'the knowledge of the history and the institutions of foreign peoples and of their psychology as expressed in their ideals and standards, and of their contribution to civilization' (Fife 1931). There was no conflict between these two conceptions; indeed, they were often combined as, for example, in this expression of a cultural objective: language teaching should lead to 'a certain widening of outlook brought about by a sympathetic present-ment of the life and history of foreign nations ...' (IAAM 1929:21). Thus, culture teaching, in Britain and America, focused on history, institutions, and customs as well as on the distinctive contributions of the foreign country to human civilization. The teaching of culture in this sense was regarded as an educationally valuable addition to the customary language and literary studies, but it was recognized that in practice it played a subordinate role. In an opinion survey in the twenties which formed part of the American *Modern Foreign Language Study* half of the university modern language departments included in the survey expressed a demand for a special course in *Kulturkunde*, but only one-fifth of the departments offered such a course (Fife 1931:61).[7]

Moreover, during this period increasing efforts were made in Euro-pean school systems to back up classroom language teaching by personal links with foreign countries through student travel, teacher and student exchanges, and pen-friendships across nations.[8] In university language studies it became more and more the accepted practice for students to spend a period of time—from a few months to a year—in the country whose language they had learnt. While the primary purpose of this scheme was to help students to become proficient in the language, the advocates of residence abroad were also conscious of the fact that a stay in the country would give students direct experience of the foreign culture and society. At the same time it should be pointed out that no very clear theoretical conception of the nature of such field experience guided these contacts and visits abroad.[9]

Anthropological influences

It was not until World War II that language teaching theorists began to recognize that anthropology and sociology might offer a theoretical framework for teaching about culture and society. The exciting and varied perspectives upon different aboriginal cultures, revealed by ethnography and applied from around 1940 to Western industrialized societies, together with the findings of sociology and social psychology, gradually began to be seen as relevant to language pedagogy. However, during the same period, in the forties and fifties, the influence of linguistics and the new technology of the language laboratory encouraged an emphasis on the formal aspects of language and on the speaking of the language as a skill, overshadowing a major interest in the social and cultural context.

Nevertheless, the theory of American wartime language courses acknowledged the importance of anthropology as the other science (besides linguistics) which was needed as a scientific basis for language studies. During the same period several American universities introduced 'area studies' in which language learning was only a part of an interdisciplinary study of a region, for example, Russia, the Far East, South East Asia, the Near East, Europe, Africa, and Latin America; the main emphasis was on a political, historical, geographical, and sociocultural examination of the region.[10]

Thus, in the post-war world, the idea of a study of language combined with a study of culture and society was familiar enough to most theorists. This viewpoint is reflected in the post-war writings on language pedagogy. The leading works on language teaching theory of the last few decades (for example, Lado, Brooks, Rivers and Chastain) have all firmly stated that cultural understanding and cross-cultural comparisons are a necessary component of language pedagogy.

The principles expressed by these theorists broadly show a consensus of views. First of all, the cultural component in language teaching is given more or less equal emphasis by all of them. It is a common misconception to believe that language teaching theory of the fifties and sixties stressed only the purely linguistic side. Theory recognized that cultural teaching must be integrated with language training. Secondly, an *anthropological* view of culture was now unmistakenly given prominence.[11] The older view of culture as 'intellectual refinement' and 'artistic endeavour' (Brooks 1960/64:83)—often referred to as culture with a capital 'C'— was not rejected. But culture in the anthropological sense, the way of life of a society—culture with a small 'c'—was given preference, partly because it was less familiar to the humanistically trained teachers and therefore needed fuller explanation, and partly because it was more encompassing: literature, the visual arts, music, and so on can be regarded as part of the 'way of life'.

On the basis of anthropological studies, language teaching theorists today point out the unity, pattern, or themes of a culture. A culture is recognized as a distinct entity in which particular items of behaviour are seen as part of a functional whole. As cultures differ, the relativity of cultural values is frequently stressed.

The theorists have been sufficiently imbued with Sapir's and Whorf's ideas to acknowledge the closeness of language and culture: 'Language and culture are not separable' (Brooks 1960/64:85); 'Language cannot be separated completely from the culture in which it is deeply embedded' (Rivers 1981:315). In 1960 an American committee on language and culture expressed the relationships which it regarded as essential in three statements. '(1) Language is a part of culture, and must be approached with the same attitudes that govern our approach to culture as a whole. (2) Language conveys culture, so that the language teacher is also of necessity a teacher of a culture. (3) Language is itself subject to culturally conditioned attitudes and beliefs, which cannot be ignored in the language classroom' (Bishop 1960:29). Seelye (1974) regards it as an important objective for the learner to understand the interaction between language and social variables, and to be able to appreciate the cultural connotation of phrases. On the other hand, the Whorfian hypothesis is usually treated with justifiable caution (for example, Rivers 1981:340–42; Seelye 1968:49–51), and writers warn against facile generalizations from language patterns to a cultural trait (Nostrand 1966:15; Seelye 1974:18–20).[12]

The goals that language teaching theorists recommend for teaching culture have also been strongly influenced by anthropological and sociological thought. Through various activities in the classroom or direct field experience the student is expected to learn something of the techniques of enquiry and insights that cultural anthropologists have developed in field work or in work with individual informants. Nostrand (1974) and Seelye (1974), for example, have argued most persuasively for ways and means of strengthening the cultural component in language teaching and have made many ingenious practical suggestions on objectives, techniques, topics, and emphases in cultural teaching and methods of testing cultural knowledge.

In spite of these advances, the anthropological concept of culture has been much more difficult to incorporate into language teaching than most of the writings have admitted so far. A number of problems remain:

(a) The first of these is the comprehensiveness of the anthropological concept of culture itself. If culture embraces 'all aspects of the life of man' (Seelye 1974:22) culture is everything and becomes unmanageable. Consequently, the ordering of the life of a society into a scheme and an enumeration of selected aspects of culture become a necessity. The theorists have based themselves on various sociological and anthropological schemes, for example, the Yale *Outline of Cultural Materials* (Murdock *et al.* 1964; see Chapter 10:200 and Note 11) or Talcott Parsons' definition of culture and society (Nostrand 1966). But the Yale *Outline* with its eight hundred and eighty-eight headings is vast and technical and Talcott Parsons' model is very abstract. Although it is claimed that culture is 'patterned' and offers an integrated whole, in effect, what is presented is often a far from integrated miscellany of categories. Brooks (1960) lists over fifty cultural topics without claiming that this list is exhaustive: some of his topics are sociolinguistic (including levels of speech, patterns of politeness, and verbal taboos); some refer to customs and rituals (for example, holidays and festivals); others describe the material culture (telephone, pets, flowers, gardens, and so on); and others again refer to health and food, to personal relations, amusements, and sports. No attempt is made to arrange them in any order, to control the degree of abstraction of the different headings, to suggest principles of selection, or to avoid the distinctly North-American flavour of several of the categories.

Nostrand who has been strongly aware of the problem of converting the sociological and anthropological concepts into a manageable scheme, has evolved an 'emergent model', based on Talcott Parsons' analysis of sociocultural systems. It is divided into four subsystems: culture, society, ecology, and the individual. Each is defined as follows:

1 *Culture*: dominant values, habits of thought, and assumptions (the 'semantic matrix' or 'ground of meaning' of the culture); its verifiable knowledge, art forms, language, paralanguage, and kinesics.
2 *Society*: social institutions and the regulation of interpersonal and group relations: family, religion, economic-occupational organization, political and judicial system, education, intellectual-aesthetic and recreational institutions, communications. Social norms, social stratification. Conflict and resolution of conflicts.
3 *Ecology*: 'the population's relationship with its subhuman environment': attitudes towards nature, exploitation of nature, use of natural products, technology, settlements and territorial organization, travel and transportation.
4 *The individual*: 'what a given person does with the shared patterns: conforming, rebelling, exploiting, or innovating.' The integration of personality (intrapersonal and interpersonal), status by age and sex.
(adapted from Nostrand 1974:276, and Seelye 1968:58)

On the basis of this model it is said to be possible to identify the culture's main *themes*, where a theme is defined as an 'emotionally charged concern, which motivates or strongly influences the culture bearer's conduct in a wide variety of situations' (Nostrand 1974:277). The model has been applied, apparently with success, in university teaching and research by Nostrand himself, in contrastive studies by Nickel, and in literature class teaching by Mueller. However, in spite of the merits of this scheme, it is questionable whether its wide categories, which may be suitable for comprehensive anthropological enquiries, are always sufficiently relevant, manageable, and applicable in the context of language teaching.[13]

(b) Another problem, treated somewhat lightly in the literature, is the interaction between language and culture. In spite of the common assertion that language and culture cannot be separated, in effect the evidence for the integration of culture and language, frequently proposed in the literature, is confined to a small number of observations. The bulk of language teaching is still described in terms which leave it largely unrelated to sociocultural contexts. Too little sociolinguistic research has as yet been presented in a form which makes it feasible to integrate linguistic aspects with their sociocultural concomitants. However, current and future sociolinguistic studies may change that (see Figure 12.1 and pp. 256–8 below).[14]

(c) The third problem is one that sociologists (for example, Bottomore 1971) have pointed out: the ethnography of the advanced industrialized societies, whose languages are commonly taught, is inadequately developed. Studies on Western societies, comparable to the studies on tribal societies, are scarce or non-existent.[15] Consequently, language teachers lack the necessary documentation or even an appropriate methodology of enquiry as to what social, cultural, and sociolinguistic data to look for, and where and how to find them. The way out, recommended by cultural theorists, is to suggest techniques by which to sensitize teachers and students to sociocultural and sociolinguistic data. Under the circumstances this is a sensible approach. But it would be as naive to believe that the teacher or student could get far in this as to suggest that teachers or students could write their own grammars and dictionaries. There are of course situations where this has to be done, but it is a difficult task; and writing the description of a society and culture and the 'grammar' of social conduct is just as complex an undertaking. The result of this state of affairs is that teachers who generally are untrained in the methods of social science are obliged to rely on their personal experience, background knowledge, and intuitions as a basis for their teaching of culture. There is a real danger therefore that such teaching has similar defects as the teaching of *Kulturkunde* in Germany of the twenties and thirties: stereotyping and prejudice.

(d) Lastly, theorists have not always kept sufficiently distinct the different aspects of culture teaching: the concept of culture and the corresponding schemes of observation as a framework for objective description; the observer's attitudes to a foreign culture; pedagogical aims in teaching culture; culture as a motivator in language learning; literature as an introduction to culture; and cultural background as a means to an understanding of literature.

The impetus to a sociocultural view of language teaching that has been given by theorists like Nostrand since the late fifties, or Seelye since the late sixties is of immense value. But the difficulties that the 'scientific' approach to culture presents should not be minimized.

In order to place the teaching of culture and society on a more solid footing language pedagogy needs ethnographic guides which parallel and intertwine with the pedagogical grammar described in Chapter 9.[16] The theoretical steps in establishing such a guide can be illustrated by a diagram which is congruent with the diagram of the pedagogical grammar in linguistics (Figure 9.2). This model can also be viewed as an enlargement of a part of the basic model (Figure 3.7).

Reading the diagram from the bottom up, the social sciences are visualized as offering fundamental concepts and studies (Step I). They develop general theories and provide the instruments for gathering information on particular cultures and societies at Step II. On the basis of studies at these two stages it is possible to develop an ethnography of a particular country or region at the next stage up (Step III). We have already noted that such systematic ethnographies of the Western countries whose languages are most widely taught are not at present readily available. Assuming, however, that studies constituting approaches to such an ethnography exist or could be compiled it would then be possible to derive from them at the next stage up (Step IV) a pedagogical guide which, in convenient form, would give language teachers information about the country, based on the available descriptive work and the theoretical concepts at the more fundamental levels. This guide would include suggestions for techniques on how to incorporate ethnographic aspects into a language teaching programme. It would then be available to language teachers as a resource at the curriculum development stage (Step V). Thus, teachers of French or English should have at their disposal sociocultural guides to Francophone or Anglophone speech communities just as teachers of Spanish should be able to refer to guides on Spain and the Spanish-speaking countries of Latin America. The final step (VI) represents the application of this component in teaching/learning activities and in materials.

As in the linguistic model (Figure 9.2) we can visualize a second more direct route from social science theory to the Interlevel (Level 2) of the basic model. The social sciences suggest concepts, schemes of analysis, and theories for the view we take of the sociocultural context of the second language.

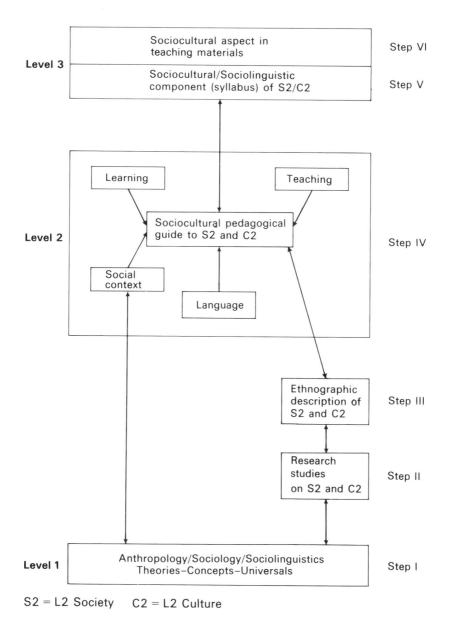

S2 = L2 Society   C2 = L2 Culture

Figure 12.1   Interaction between the social sciences and language teaching

The main problem that a language pedagogy which is context-oriented faces is the lack of systematic sociological and anthropological research and documentation on the different language communities. A greater awareness of this need at the level of practice can perhaps stimulate an interest in such research at the more fundamental levels.

In the absence of adequate documentation there is no reason—as Nostrand and Seelye have rightly recognized—why curriculum developers, teachers, and learners themselves cannot make their own ethnographic studies and observations and, through personal participation, place the language into a social and cultural context. Provided we keep in mind the limitations and biases of such a relatively improvised individual approach there is—as in all research (see Chapter 4)—no strict division between personal enquiry and systematic research. But training for teachers and a background in anthropological theory and field work could introduce a certain sophistication into this treatment of the sociocultural context.[17]

The study of language in its social context

The treatment of culture in the language programmes largely—and, we suggest, quite legitimately—concentrates on non-linguistic features in the life of the society. But, as we have seen, the theorists also include the interaction between language and culture among the various aspects of cultural teaching, and from the point of view of language pedagogy it is important at any time not to separate too rigidly language from society and culture. In practice, the integration of language with its sociocultural context has not been an easy matter. The descriptions of language on which language pedagogy is based are generally 'a-social' and 'culturally neutral'. The social significance of linguistic forms or the linguistic implications of social facts have until recently not been sufficiently taken into account in textbooks nor have they played a significant part in the language teacher's own education to be adequately represented in language teaching. At the present stage of the development of a socially oriented linguistic science we recognize that teachers are beginning to become sensitive to the implications of a social orientation in linguistics and to the growth of sociolinguistics.

1 Language pedagogy is taking a more positive view than it did in the past of the existence of *varieties of language*, dialects, and sociolects, within a speech community. In the past, the selection of a standard or norm in teaching a foreign language tended to be in absolute terms. It was based on an unquestioned tradition and was often coloured by prejudice for or against different varieties. In many European countries it is not uncommon for teachers of English as a second language to insist on teaching what they often naively refer to as 'Oxford English' or the 'King's English' and to reject indignantly American English as 'less pure'. In Canada French teachers are sometimes urged by parents to teach 'Parisian French' and to avoid Canadian French (see Chapter 7:125–6). Linguistics and sociolinguistics have provided a scholarly basis for applying more flexible and

rational criteria for the choice of standards or norms for teaching a second language. It is obviously too difficult for a language learner to be constantly aware of the full potential (Halliday) of variations offered by a language. The definition of a pedagogical norm must presumably be based on several criteria: (a) the variety of language learnt must be acceptable to native speakers as appropriate for a non-native to use; (b) it must facilitate communication between native speakers and the learner; (c) it must be adapted to the probable uses of the language by the learner; (d) it should also make the learning task initially simple without distorting the language used; and (e) as the learner progresses the social meanings of different language varieties or of particular features in the language should increasingly have a place in the teaching of the language. The finer distinctions of social uses of the kind Labov has studied in New York English may be too subtle for early stages of ESL. Nevertheless, at any stage in language learning it should be possible for the language student to find out about the social significance of variations in language use.

2 The learner will also progressively be made aware of those *variations in language use* that are determined by role relationships, situations, topics, or modes of communication (speech or writing). In some languages role relationships, for example, deference or equality of status, or the sex of the speaker or addressee, are clearly marked in linguistic forms. Some language uses—as Bernstein has rightly pointed out—are more 'context-dependent'; for example, so-called everyday conversation forms part of social encounters, while other forms of communication with less situational support (more 'context-independent') have to be more explicit. Many language teachers have had an intuitive understanding of some of these distinctions in communicative situations but sociolinguistic studies systematize them.

3 The different social meanings, decribed in (1) and (2) above, have different *linguistic manifestations*. Sometimes they are expressed by phonological features, sometimes by grammatical differentiations, often in the selection of words, and at times by certain general stylistic qualities of the entire discourse. Learning a language involves learning some or many of these distinctions; but it all depends on the level of competence of the learner to what extent he can be expected to master these differentiations.

4 From the point of view of *pedagogical treatment*, it is possible to proceed in one of two ways so as to place language into a social context: one is to start out from linguistic features (for example, the *tu* and *vous* distinction, or a phonological feature such as variations of English /θ/) and to differentiate between various social meanings. Thus, in studying a play or a narrative in the language class the teacher may draw attention to language features which signal these

meanings.[18] The other possibility is to start from social institutions, social structures, a role relationship, or a culturally significant event, and to examine its manifestations in language use. This second approach is however much more difficult to handle, because the linguistic manifestations of social facts have not been documented in a sufficiently systematic fashion.[19]

The Orléans Project

To overcome the lack of sociolinguistic data an early pioneer effort illustrates the kind of sociolinguistic data base that can be created: a sociolinguistic study of the spoken French in the city of Orléans (Blanc and Biggs 1971). The object of this enquiry, begun in the late sixties at the instigation of a group of British university teachers of French, was to record the spontaneous speech of different generations, different regional and social groups, and different language uses and situations. The outcome of this project was a set of carefully prepared tape recordings with transcriptions which provide (1) data for a linguistic and sociolinguistic analysis, (2) materials for teaching spoken French, and (3) sociocultural information. The tape recordings consist of interviews with a representative sample of the inhabitants of Orléans, interviews with leaders in various walks of life in this French city, formal discussions such as work-council meetings, and informal table talk, telephone conversations, counselling interviews, and the language used in shops, markets, and in industry. The material collected in this study, therefore, presents a *portrait sonore* of a French town around 1970. It abounds with cultural information; it is also a rich source of linguistic data on spoken French, of sociolinguistic data on different social groups of native French speakers, and of sociolinguistic information on the differences in the use of French in different social contexts. A tape collection of this kind can be used as source material for linguistic, sociolinguistic, and sociocultural research, or it can directly serve as material for teaching at an advanced level in schools or universities.[20]

The communicative approach to language teaching

Through such concepts as 'communicative' or 'functional' language teaching or 'communicative competence as a goal of language teaching' theorists have attempted to bring into language teaching insights which they have derived from speech act theory, discourse analysis, and the ethnography of communication. As a development in educational linguistics this new trend was already described in Chapter 9. Here we want to characterize only some of the effects on pedagogy.

In the literature on language pedagogy of the last decade we find references to Austin, Searle, Hymes, and Halliday (for example, Brumfit and Johnson 1979; Canale and Swain 1980). In Germany the writings of Habermas have been used as an additional theoretical basis. The sociolinguistic emphasis is expressed by contrasting a 'communicative' or 'functional' approach with 'linguistic', 'grammatical', 'structural', or 'formal' approaches to language teaching. Widdowson's distinction of linguistic and communicative categories has helped to clarify the difference between these two approaches (see Chapter 9:178–9).

The main distinction is seen in the fact that the formal or structural theories view language outside a particular context of language use while the communicative theory presents the second language in a more clearly specified social context and situation. It should be pointed out though that advocates of a structural approach were not unmindful of situations of language use. But the situations were left open and relatively undefined. Theorists talked about speaking and listening as skills in general. Provided emphasis was laid on 'the primacy of speech' and opportunities for skill practice existed, it was thought enough was done to make language teaching realistic and relevant for potential language use.[21]

By basing themselves on speech act theory and the analysis of discourse and by introducing perspectives of sociolinguistics generally, theorists since the last decade have attempted to come closer to the reality of language use. Henceforth, uses of language were to be specified in social settings much more precisely, in the expectation that language pedagogy would thereby become more relevant to the declared or putative needs of language learners. The theorists' energies have been directed to bringing these sociolinguistic perspectives into the language curriculum through new curriculum designs, and through new materials, teaching techniques, and testing with a communicative orientation. Several educational linguists and language teachers in different countries, since about 1970, have been actively involved, in efforts to give concrete shape to this direction of language teaching.[22]

Much thought went into the design of a curriculum based on communicative principles (for example, Munby 1978; Shaw 1977). The Council of Europe Modern Languages Project, referred to in previous chapters, was one of the main pioneering endeavours in this respect. The rationale of this project and others of a similar nature was that in order to determine what language functions to include one has to set out from the *language needs* of language learners. The definition and identification of these language needs has constituted a first and important stage in the procedures to make language teaching communicative (Richterich 1980; Richterich and Chancerel 1977/80; Savard 1977; Munby 1978). The second stage has been the definition of language categories in semantic and sociolinguistic terms accompanied by examples of language items. While these procedures have stimulated a great deal of interest among practitioners, the gap between the inventories of language items in a 'syllabus' and the teaching materials, teaching techniques, and testing procedures which carry these syllabuses into effect has been difficult to bridge (Johnson 1977), and even now these difficulties have not yet been entirely overcome.

Teaching materials and techniques which are based on sociolinguistic principles usually identify learners in a specific role of language use, for example, as tourists, or university students, or migrant workers. Often the interactants are specified: shop-assistant–customer; foreign traveller–policeman; physician–patient, and so on. Situations of language use are indicated and sometimes described in a detailed scenario: for example, visiting a city; arriving at a hotel; reading academic papers; participating in seminar discussions; asking a neighbour for help; visiting a doctor's surgery. Next, speech acts are analysed which regularly occur in the given situation: introducing oneself, enquiring, gathering information, asking permission, asking for help, giving reasons or explanations, and the like. Eventually the linguistic manifestations of the speech act or acts are presented in a text, a dialogue, a flow-chart, a table with explanations or an excerpt from a newspaper, etc. Learners are usually invited to enter vicariously into the situation so that they become participants. The learning tasks, therefore, frequently involve problem solving, simulation, or role playing. There may be conventional drill-type exercises, but the difference from structural practice lies in the fact that the linguistic forms to be practised have an identifiable place in a sociolinguistic context which is presented to learners as a concrete, practical situation in which they can feel at home and in which they need the language items to be learnt. Ideally, the practice is never entirely repetitive or imitative but offers natural options of language use which reproduce the kinds of choices that occur in spontaneous communication.

Similar principles have been applied to testing. Although communicative testing as an idea has appealed to language teachers for several years (for example, Levenston 1975), the construction of such tests has proved troublesome. The aim is not to test only formal correctness, but also social appropriateness in a given context. The test items usually define a situation, say, a crowded bus, a role or the roles of two or more interactants, such as travellers on the crowded bus, and a problem requiring a speech act, for instance, an appropriate, polite request: 'You want to get to the exit. What do you say?' The test item consists of the response the learner is expected to make. It can be formulated as a multiple-choice or as an open-ended test item.[23]

In the development of this communicative orientation some of the schemes of the communicative event (see Chapter 11) have been useful, but the absence of empirically established descriptive data of ethnographic information has created difficulties of a similar kind to the lack of cultural information we noted previously. However, the sociolinguistic orientation has opened new perspectives in language teaching which have only recently begun to influence language pedagogy. The consensus among theorists and practitioners is that this sociolinguistic component complements and modifies a 'structural' or 'grammatical' approach to language but does not supersede it. The problem that has engaged the attention of several linguists is how to combine for teaching purposes a structural and a sociolinguistic approach to language most effectively.[24]

Some language teaching theorists have derived a different conclusion from the sociolinguistic expansion of the view of language from the one we have just described. They see in it further proof, in addition to the evidence provided by structural linguistics and transformational generative grammar, that language is too complicated to be taught by mainly analytical methods, structural or sociolinguistic. Instead they recommend ways which systematize and supplement language 'acquisition' processes, that is, natural language learning without formal tuition. While these considerations are best examined as psychological or methodological questions in pedagogy, it can be pointed out that these views have been reinforced by a sociolinguistic interpretation of language because sociolinguistics has placed language and language learning into a social context of interaction, and non-analytical approaches to language learning are based on the principle that the learner must become a *participant* in a real-life context of language use as a condition of effective language learning.[25]

Attempts have recently been made to combine analytical and non-analytical approaches in a multilevel curriculum as in this scheme by Allen (1980):

Level 1	Level 2	Level 3
Structural	*Functional*	*Experiential*
Focus on language (formal features)	Focus on language (discourse features)	Focus on the use of language
(a) Structural control	(a) Discourse control	(a) Situational or topical control
(b) Materials simplified structurally	(b) Materials simplified functionally	(b) Authentic language
(c) Mainly structural practice	(c) Mainly discourse practice	(c) Free practice

Figure 12.2   An adaptation of Allen's three levels of communicative competence in second language education

This model expresses the view that a language curriculum must have a structural level, as recognized in most conventional language programmes, but the structural component by itself is insufficient. Discourse analysis and speech act theory provide the basis for a second-level component of the curriculum. Both of these must, however, become integrated at a third level where the language is used instrumentally in real-life activities. According to this conception the language curriculum must have all three components. Although the emphasis at different stages of the curriculum may shift from level 1 to level 2 and then to level 3, in Allen's view the curriculum at all times should include all three components. In other words, a curriculum should be based both on a formal and functional analysis and at the same time offer opportunities for experiential participation in real-life communication which by its very nature is non-analytical.

If we recognize, as we have done in this chapter, that a language curriculum must also have a sociocultural component, we could modify Allen's scheme and suggest as a synthesis a fourfold curriculum framework as follows:

Structural aspect	Functional aspect	Sociocultural aspect	Experiential aspect
mainly analytical (involving language *study* and *practice*)			mainly non-analytical (involving language *use* in authentic contexts)

Figure 12.3   Sketch of a fourfold curriculum framework for second language teaching

In other words, we are saying that language teaching can and should approach language learning objectively and analytically through the study and practice of structural, functional, and sociocultural aspects, and it should offer opportunities to live the language as a personal experience through direct language use in contact with the target language community. (See also Chapter 22:504; Figure 22.4 and Note 7).

In pursuing these implications of a communicative perspective for practical language pedagogy we must remind ourselves that, for the present, many of these ideas are largely programmatic and are as yet relatively untried. They are only beginning to be implemented and with the exception of 'immersion', they have not yet been the subject of systematic empirical research. They can be put forward only tentatively as suggestive ideas for giving language teaching a sociolinguistic direction. As such they appear promising and invite experimentation as well as dispassionate enquiry.

Conclusion

To sum up, the three areas discussed in this chapter, (1) cultural information, (2) sociolinguistic findings, and (3) communicative approaches, constitute the sociocultural and sociolinguistic component of the curriculum. This component could form the content of an ethnographic guide which would serve as a companion to the pedagogical grammar referred to in Chapter 9. The guide and the grammar, represented in Figure 12.1 and 9.2 respectively, should not be thought of as rigidly separate. As linguistics and sociolinguistics merge one would expect the grammar and the guide to become more and more integrated. Together they would be a resource of authentic and accessible material for curriculum development and for teaching the second language in its sociocultural and sociolinguistic context.

Notes

1 Sweet's *Practical Study* (1899), wide-ranging though it was, makes no reference to anything that might be described as the 'cultural' aspect of language teaching.

2 The argument for relating language to culture was often presented in this form: 'Without knowing the language of a people we never really know their thoughts, their feeling and their type of character' (John Stuart Mill, quoted by Hall 1947:14). For examples of modern thought on the teaching of culture, see Seelye (1974), Lafayette (1978), and Rivers (1981: Chapter 11); see also Note 11 below for further references.

3 This sketch of *Kulturkunde* in second language instruction is based on the informative discussion of this subject by Rülcker (1969:47–70) who reviews the history and current significance of the *Kulturkunde* movement. Discussions on *Kulturkunde* in language teaching are illustrated by a few studies of the twenties reprinted (in German) in Flechsig (1965). For an explanation of the concept of culture in Germany see also Kroeber and Kluckhohn (1952).

4 During World War II a similar approach in Britain and the U.S.A. also lent itself to stereotyping of the 'national character' of the Germans, the Japanese, and the Russians. See Chapter 10:198 and Notes 8 and 9.

5 'Als Folie für unser eigenes Vokstum' (Hübner 1925).

6 'Seine deutsche Bewusstheit, sein deutsches Wertgefühl zu bilden, sind *nach* dem Deutschen, neben der Geschichte die fremden Sprachen berufen.' (Schön 1925: in Flechsig 1965:192.)

7 The American *Modern Foreign Language Study* included investigations on cultural data in foreign language teaching materials. Reading texts were examined with regard to their references to

cultural items: 'Concrete *realia* like bridges and canals, weights, and measures; institutions, such as the church, hospitals, prisons, railroads, theaters, and customs administration; contacts with daily life, such as clothing, cost of living, food, hotels; or general aspects of national culture, such as education, finance, literature and superstitions, as well as geography, history, and political life' (Fife 1931:177). The count revealed 'very little material bearing explicitly on the foreign country and its civilization'; 'it is surprising to note ... how little light they throw on life in France or in Spain' (Coleman 1929:101).

8 It is interesting to note that some language teaching reformers in Germany, well before World War I and before the *Kulturkunde* movement, had already initiated class visits abroad and correspondence exchanges among pupils in order to cultivate better international understanding through language learning (see Flechsig 1965:20).

9 The picture presented here of the teaching of culture can be illustrated by the *Memorandum on the Teaching of Modern Languages* by the Incorporated Association of Assistant Masters (IAAM/AMA). As was explained in Chapter 6:101, this work, which was first published in 1929 and rewritten four times in subsequent decades (1949, 1956, 1967, 1979), reflects the development of thought of successive generations of experienced language teachers in Britain. A comparison of the five versions indicates the following trend of development in the teaching of culture:
In 1929 (IAAM 1929) the aims of the modern humanities were described as useful as well as 'cultural' in the dual sense, explained on p.249. The 1949 (IAAM 1949) version includes 'culture' as one of the criteria determining the choice of a language. Culture here includes literature, art, architecture, and music. The particular contribution of language teaching is literary culture. However, the qualifications of a language specialist include 'an acquaintance with the civilization of the country' (op. cit.:43). At this stage a good deal of emphasis was laid, in sixth form studies, upon 'The Study of People and Country'. History, sociology, and geography were recognized as relevant, but difficulties were found in presenting them because of a shortage of materials and a lack of expertise on the part of the teacher. As for sociology, the 1949 report expresses itself sceptically: 'the average sociologist is no more capable than the average novelist of synthesizing the life of a people, and any work that attempts the task is likely to be either jejune or highly misleading' (op. cit.:175). This edition, however, recommends personal contact, school links, and the employment of native assistants as well as project work involving personal investigations and the use of foreign newspapers, reference books on the foreign country, and

'field work'. The bibliography includes several works on France, Germany and other countries.

The 1956 edition (IAAM 1956) is substantially the same as that of 1949. In the 1967 edition (IAAM 1967) culture as refinement is reaffirmed: 'A country's civilization often finds its finest manifestation in its literature' (op. cit.:46). But the teacher is also encouraged to know 'through works and first-hand acquaintance, about the people who speak the language he is teaching, about their country and way of life and about the finest manifestations of their spirit' (loc. cit.). The edition contains much on new types of language programme, the new technology, and a great deal on school journeys, and foreign assistants; but the approach to culture is unchanged. The 1979 edition (AMA 1979) briefly acknowledges again that 'a child learning a language would also discover something about the life and culture ... and develop a tolerance beyond national prejudice' (op. cit.:6). This edition includes a chapter on contacts with the foreign country.

Basically, throughout this half century, this work has laid emphasis on language practice and at the same time recognizes the importance of literature and opportunities for personal experience and direct contact, but the influence of anthropological or sociological thought remains, if at all present, very indirect or remote and no specific thought is given to the cultural content.

In a survey on European countries in the sixties Halls (1970:41) concludes: 'In practice most European countries do not teach about the foreign culture in any systematic fashion'.

10 'World War II was not the mother of areas studies', wrote Hall in an appreciation of area studies in American universities (Hall 1947:12). Around 1950 an American survey of area studies (Bennett 1951) noted the uneven distribution of disciplines in area studies: anthropology was poorly represented for Russia, Europe, the Near East, and South East Asia, whereas sociology was restricted to Western civilization. Literature was generally well represented, while art was well represented only for the Far East. On the other hand, area studies generally lacked contributions from law, geography, psychology, political science, and educational theory. The theory, practice, and problems of area research, as they had developed down to about 1950, were fully and perceptively discussed in a small book by Steward (1950).

In the seventies an area studies approach was adopted in many British schools under the concept of 'European studies' and 'French studies' (for example, Centre for Contemporary European Studies, 1972). The international studies recommended in 1979 by the President's Commission Report (U.S.A. 1979) appear to be demanded with similar expectations.

11 An anthropological view of culture and society has been present in the writings on language teaching theory since the forties, but perhaps more clearly so since the late fifties (Lado 1957) and the sixties (Bishop 1960; Brooks 1960; Lado 1964; Rivers 1964, 1968, 1981; Nostrand 1966, 1973, 1974; Seelye 1968, 1974; Chastain 1976).

12 Nostrand gives a good example of the misuse of the Whorfian hypothesis. He writes 'I once heard a teacher of English in a foreign country say, "In English they have an expression, "Why! That man must be worth half a million dollars, or must be worth a million dollars!" This shows how materialistic the people are." Apart from the fact that the expression is going out of date, one simply cannot find out whether a people is materialistic and in what sense materialistic by examining dead metaphors' (Nostrand 1966:15–16).

13 Chastain (1976:389–92) offers a list of over forty-four main categories without any indications where and how the information is to be obtained.

14 Seelye (1974) includes among the goals of cultural teaching awareness of the language–culture relationships: 'Interaction of Language and Social Variables' (op. cit.:40) and 'Cultural Connotation of Words and Phrases' (op. cit.:42). His examples no doubt invite an awareness of the relations between language and culture, but he does not point out the difficulties in working towards this objective nor does he direct the reader to the sociolinguistic literature that could be consulted.

15 The 1972 reports of the Northeast Conference (Dodge 1972) constituted an attempt to strengthen the approach to culture from an anthropological and sociolinguistic perspective. The volume includes chapters and bibliographies on the culture of France, French-speaking Canada, Germany, Italy, Japan, the Soviet Union, Spain, and Latin America and in an introductory chapter characterizes the culture of the U.S.A. But only in the chapter on France is any definite effort made to identify specifically sociological research. For the rest most of the portraits could largely have been written without reference to anthropology or sociology. Seelye (1974:28–32) draws attention to anthropological studies of American culture by Commager (1970), Stewart (1971), and Hsu (1969).

16 It was a similar idea no doubt that prompted Widdowson to write: 'What I have in mind is a kind of pedagogic rhetoric which will serve as a guide to rules of use in the same way as a pedagogic grammar serves as a guide to grammatical rules' (Widdowson 1979b:68). Widdowson's pedagogic rhetoric is probably more strictly sociolinguistic than the guide proposed here which is thought of more broadly as anthropological, sociological, as well as sociolinguistic.

17 Although Nostrand and Seelye recommend such a self-help approach without specifically drawing attention to it, they do not, in my view, make sufficiently clear the lack of adequate theoretical and descriptive resources.

18 For example, Adam (1959) has pointed out that in teaching English in Fiji, a reading text entitled *Beau Geste* requires explanations on many lexical items which relate to unfamiliar geographical and sociocultural facts:

Climate	'one autumn evening'
Clothing	'dressing gown'
	'bedroom slippers'
Flora & fauna	'bull-dog tenacity'
	'as proud as a peacock'
Housing	'paraffin'
	'the great drawing room'
	'deep leather armchairs'
Religion	'boulders as big as cathedrals'
	'in a circle like spiritualists'
Social customs	'preparatory school',
	'honorary degree'
	'Eton and Oxford'
	'police-court reporters'
	'be my banker in this matter'
Naval or military terms	'field glasses'
	'fatigue party'
	'garrison duty'
Literary or historical	'like Gulliver at Lilliput'
references	'a Viking's funeral'
	'a drawbridge leading over a moat'

19 At this point the reader might care to turn back to Figure 9.3 which prompted the question to what extent the different aspects of language—phonology, grammar, lexis, and discourse—are treated sociolinguistically. The present chapter suggests that this sociolinguistic perspective should pervade the entire treatment of language. However, we must stress that such a perspective cannot be introduced without some difficulty because of the lack of documentation. On the other hand, it offers an orientation for the teacher and curriculum developer which does not have to wait for definitive research results.

20 For a discussion of this project, which has never made quite the impact it should have done, see Blanc and Biggs (1971) and Ross (1974). Some teaching materials were based on it (Biggs and Dalwood 1976) and a detailed analytical catalogue of the tape

recordings was prepared by the Orléans Archives in the Department of Language and Linguistics of the University of Essex, Colchester, England (Orléans Archive 1974).

21 Contexts were not by any means ignored. For example, in the CREDIF programmes, such as *Voix et Images de France,* the visuals provided a context or scenario, but the nature of the context and the speech acts it gave rise to were far less important than the structures which were presented in the dialogue. The settings and speech acts were selected intuitively and not on the basis of the kind of analysis that a decade or so later determined the *Threshold Level* inventories of the Council of Europe Modern Languages Project.

22 See also Chapter 6:111–13 seq. and 9:177–80. In the period of approximately 1979–81 the following names and centres illustrate these developments: in Britain the applied linguists of the University of Edinburgh Department of Linguistics, Allen, Corder, and Widdowson; Trim in the Centre for Information on Language Teaching and Research in London; at the University of Reading Wilkins, Johnson, and Morrow; at Lancaster University Candlin and Breen; in the London Institute of Education Widdowson and Brumfit; in Switzerland Richterich; in France Coste; in Germany Piepho at the University of Giessen; Neuner at the Gesamthochschule Kassel; and Edelhoff at the Hessische Institut für Lehrerfortbildung; in the U.S.A. Savignon, Bratt-Paulston, Bruder and Palmer; in Canada, the OISE Modern Language Centre, the Ministry of Education of the Province of Quebec, and the language training programmes of the Federal Government and of some universities (e.g., Carleton, Ottawa). See, for example, Widdowson (1978, 1979), Brumfit and Johnson (1979), Canale and Swain (1980), Müller (1980), Alatis, Altman, and Alatis (1981), Littlewood (1981), and Yalden (1981).

23 Attempts to develop communicative tests have been described and discussed, among others, by Morrow (1979), Oller (1979), Carroll (1980), and Wesche (1981).

24 This issue is specifically discussed, for example, by Johnson (1977), Brumfit (1980), Guntermann and Phillips (1981), and Widdowson and Brumfit (1981).

25 This is, for example, the condition which has been created in the Canadian 'French immersion' programmes, referred to in Chapter 4. These programmes, which began experimentally as early as 1965, have become well established across Canada as an alternative form of schooling, and they have been evaluated by numerous studies. They are instructive as examples of a participant 'real-life' approach to second language learning. For references see Chapter 4, Notes 13 and 28.

13 The sociology of language teaching and learning

In the last chapter we considered three areas which have implications for language curricula. The fourth area demands a change of perspective from 'micro' *sociolinguistics* to 'macro' *sociology of language*:[1] we now look at the whole enterprise of second language teaching and learning in all conceivable forms as a set of activities in society. These activities are designed to influence language behaviour within that society through educational measures. The sociology of language, it will be remembered (see Chapter 11:230 ff.), describes the distribution of languages and dialects and language contacts within a speech community, relates the language situation to other social factors, accounts for such phenomena as language maintenance, language shift, and language conflict, and, by means of language planning, proposes social action in order to deal with linguistic problems. But the sociology of language has hitherto paid relatively little direct attention to a society's deliberate attempts to develop second-language competence and bilingualism by its educational policy.[2]

A sociological perspective can be considered as particularly important (1) for the analysis of the social context of language teaching and learning and (2) for second language planning.

The analysis of the social context of language teaching and learning

The social context of language learning can be regarded as a set of factors that is likely to exercise a powerful influence on language learning, and it is therefore necessary to take note of such contextual factors in analysing a given language teaching situation.

There has been a general awareness for some years of these environmental factors, and several research studies have examined some of the possible relationships. In a plan for research on language teaching, Carroll (1967, 1969) identified a number of background variables to take into account in conducting language teaching research. The factors singled out by Carroll include linguistic factors, i.e., the characteristics of the new language to be learnt in comparison with the language of origin. Here the kind of analysis that Stewart (1962/1968) has proposed is helpful (see Chapter 11:232–4). Sociocultural factors that bear upon motivation, such as the relative social status of the first language and the second language, the instrumental value of the second language, the cultural values of the second language, and political factors should be considered; they lead to the kind of interpretation of the relative status of the first and the second language in accordance with Schumann's acculturation theory (Chapter 11:238). Other aspects to bear in mind are the social opportunities for contact with the second language and the opportunities for learning the language offered in the school.

Sometimes environmental factors declare themselves very distinctly, at other times they are much more difficult to identify. For example, in the British study *Primary French in the Balance* (Burstall *et al.* 1974), the investigators found a high correlation between achievement in French and the socio-economic status of parents: 'For pupils of both sexes in each group of primary schools, high mean scores on the Listening, Reading, and Writing tests coincide with high-status parental occupation and low mean scores with low-status parental occupation' (op. cit.:24). According to this study this result confirms a general pattern of school achievement in Britain. The explanation offered is that the home influences motivation and thereby indirectly affects achievement: 'children with parents in higher-status occupations receive greater parental support when they approach new learning experiences than do those with parents in lower-status occupations' (op. cit.:31). This pattern of results is accentuated as students proceed through the educational system. Another interesting environmental influence, noted in the same study, is suggested by the fact that children in the south of England, which is geographically closer to France, take a more positive view of learning French than children in the more distant north (op. cit.:133–4; 160).

But another example from the same study shows how cautious one has to be in interpreting the relationship between environmental factors and language teaching. Intuition might lead one to assume that teaching languages in the more cosmopolitan atmosphere of a large, modern city school would lead to greater success in language learning than studying the same language in a small and often old-fashioned rural school. Yet, one of the most consistent and most surprising findings of the British study was the higher level of achievement in French in small rural primary schools. An explanation for this unexpected finding could only be found by a close comparison of the two school environments. It was discovered that the teachers in the small country schools were, on average, older and more experienced than their counterparts in larger schools and tended to live in the village in which they taught. The classroom situation in the school was much more inclined 'to encourage co-operative behaviour and to lack the negative motivational characteristics of the competitive classroom' in a large city school (op. cit.:32).

The question of the relationship between the social milieu and language learning in the school setting has become particularly acute in recent studies on bilingual schooling. Here the results are puzzlingly contradictory. In Canada bilingual schooling appears to be outstandingly successful, while in other countries, in Ireland or in the U.S.A., for example, educational failure has sometimes been attributed to bilingual schooling. Thus, Spolsky *et al.* (1974) ask 'how does one understand the success of a home school language switch for English children in Montreal, and its failure for Navajo children on the Reservation?' (op.cit.:2). Equally, Paulston (1975), attempting to account 'for contradictory data' argued 'that we can begin to understand the problems and questions of bilingual education only when we see bilingual education as the result of certain societal factors . . .' (op. cit.:4).[3]

In order to study these environmental influences students of bilingual education have looked more closely at the relationships between language in school and the social environment. Two schemes have been developed; they are designed to analyse bilingual schooling in its context. A typology of bilingual education, proposed by Mackey (1970), shows the intricate varieties that may occur when we relate the language of the school to the home, area, or nation (Figure 13.1).

Mackey identifies nine different ways of arranging the language curriculum in school leading to no less than ninety different patterns of interaction between home, school, area, and nation. The details of the scheme need not concern us here, but if we apply Mackey's categories to language teaching in general, it shows in simple and clear terms how different social variables interact with language teaching and learning.

Another scheme, developed by Spolsky *et al.* (1974), attempts to present in a single configuration all the possible factors that have bearing on bilingual education. Placing education in the centre, Spolsky and his co-workers examine six factors that impinge upon it: linguistic, sociological, political, economic, cultural, religious, and psychological (Figure 13.2). They show how this model can be used, first, in the analysis of a situation in which bilingual education is being considered; second, once established how it can help at the operational level to decide upon the curriculum; and lastly, how it can be used to evaluate the outcome of bilingual education.

With certain modifications these two models for analysing the context of bilingual schooling can be applied to language teaching situations generally; they constitute a useful scheme for the analysis of contextual factors. An adaptation of Mackey's model effectively indicates the interaction of *different social agencies*, some close to the language teaching situation and others more distant (Figure 13.3).

An adaptation of Spolsky's model can be helpful as an aid to the analysis of *different factors in society* which impinge upon language teaching (Figure 13.4).

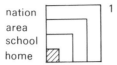

1. The school may be located in a place where the language of neither the area nor the national language is that of the home.

2. It may be in a country where the language of the home but not that of the area is the national tongue.

3. Conversely, the language of the area and not of the nation may be that of the home.

4. Both area and national language may be that of the home.

5. The national language may not be that of the home but the area may be bilingual, with both the home and national languages being used.

6. Conversely, the country may be bilingual and the area unilingual.

7. Both the area and the country may be bilingual.

8. The area may be bilingual and the national language may be that of the home.

9. Finally, the country may be bilingual and the area language that of the home.

Figure 13.1   Mackey's typology of bilingual education

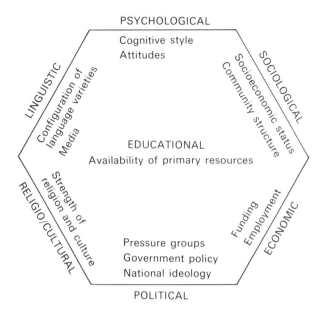

Figure 13.2   Representation by Spolsky et al. *(1974)*
of contexts of bilingual education. (Similar diagrams relate
curriculum and evaluation to social contexts.)

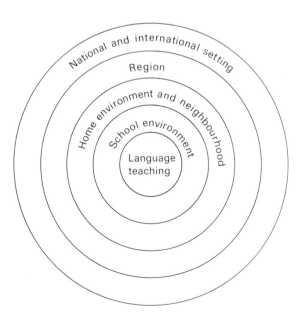

Figure 13.3   An adaptation of Mackey's scheme of
contextual analysis to language teaching

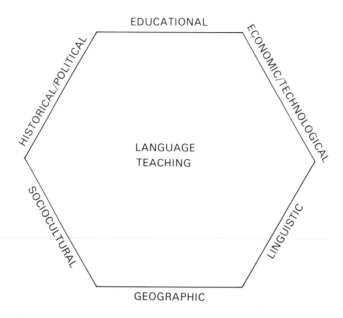

Figure 13.4   An adaptation of Spolsky's diagram to an analysis
of social variables in language teaching

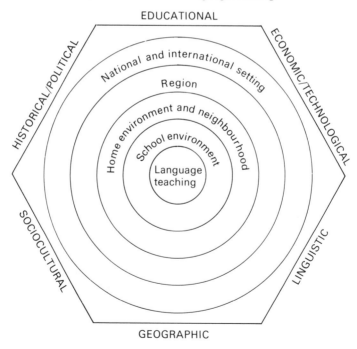

Figure 13.5   An adaptation of Mackey's and Spolsky's diagrams combined
as an inventory of contextual factors in language teaching

Since the two models are complementary, they can be superimposed (Figure 13.5).

At the centre of the diagram is the particular language teaching situation under consideration, for example, an English class for adult immigrants, French in a comprehensive school in Great Britain, English in a German primary school, Spanish in a U.S. high school. This specified language teaching situation normally occurs in a school context of some kind, in a certain primary or secondary school, in a college or university department within an educational system. This school or school system provides the immediate environment of the language teaching situation. Accordingly, the first question to ask in analysing the situation would be how language teaching fits into the given educational environment. The school or school system, in turn, is located in a neighbourhood which offers a characteristic home environment to the students. Whether these neighbourhood influences are linguistic, cultural, or socio-economic, they are the immediate background against which teaching and learning take place; as the British primary French study has shown (Burstall *et al.* 1974; see p.270 above), it can be assumed that in some situations their influence is likely to be powerful. This influence should therefore be examined. The immediate neighbourhood finds itself in a wider environment, a city, a region, or part of the country, which may be *like* the neighbourhood or *different* from it. It is these different patterns of likeness and contrast between school, neighbourhood, and region that Mackey's diagram has clearly symbolized. Beyond the region we can visualize the entire country with its language or languages in relation to the international community influencing language attitudes and language policy and thus, directly or indirectly, affecting language education at the institutional level.

The immediate or wider social context can be analysed for various factors which, we assume, have bearing on language teaching. They can be classified, as indicated in Figure 13.4 and 13.5 opposite, slightly modifying Spolsky's categories, as: linguistic, sociocultural, historical/political, geographical, economic/technological, and educational.

The influence of these factors on language teaching is not self-evident. A factor may or may not be operative in a given context. The list merely forms a convenient inventory of aspects which may sometimes act as constraints but at other times may enhance opportunities for language teaching. The analysis of the setting demands a case study which may range from the momentary, almost intuitive apprehension on the part of the teacher of factors influencing the language class, to a systematic and elaborate analysis of the language situation of a community or an entire nation, such as may be found in the six-volume report of the Canadian Royal Commission on Bilingualism and Biculturalism (Canada 1967–70).

Linguistic factors

The most obvious contextual factor against which to view language learning is the language situation. Some countries or regions in which languages are taught are linguistically relatively homogeneous, for example, Germany, France, Britain, Argentina, or Thailand. In these countries language learning takes place against a fairly uniform language background and students are likely to have many language learning problems in common. On the other hand, a uniform language environment which creates among students the illusion of universal unilinguality as a normal state of affairs, can lead to resistance to second language learning.

Other language situations are much more complex. For example, in the West Indies standard English (or French) is learnt in school against a background of various degrees of an English-based or French-based Creole.[4] This situation is further complicated if, against this background, another foreign language, such as Spanish, is learnt. In India second languages, for example, English, or in the Philippines the national language Pilipino are learnt in a sociolinguistic context of many languages and dialects. This has the advantage that students approach language learning on the basis of experience with different languages and varied language contacts in their own environment, but the diversity of language backgrounds in the language class may complicate the teaching task.

Another linguistic aspect to bear in mind is the relationship of the target language to the learner's language. The contention of early forms of contrastive analysis that differences between languages point predictably to degrees of difficulty can no longer be sustained without qualifications; but linguistic and cultural distance between the first and the second language certainly suggest some learning problems. Most of the widespread European languages, such as English, French, German, Russian, Italian, and Spanish, as Whorf recognized in his concept of Standard Average European (SAE), share common European linguistic and cultural assumptions, reflected in the vocabulary and grammar of these languages. Equally, many of the languages of India, such as Hindi or Gujarati, have much in common. On the other hand, a European learning an oriental language, such as Chinese, Japanese, Thai, or Hindi, must come to terms with many unfamiliar linguistic and cultural features. Equally, a native speaker of, say, Hindi or Japanese faces similar problems in learning English as a second language.

Linguistic similarity is no absolute guarantee that the second language will be easily learnt. One of the IEA language studies (Carroll 1975) found little relationship between linguistic closeness and achievement in French as a second language[5]. If linguistic closeness were a guarantee of good language learning, one could expect, for example, speakers of a

Romance language, such as Spanish or Rumanian, to find French easier than speakers of English. Indeed, in the IEA study, the Rumanian students reached a very high level of French, but if we jump to the conclusion that this is so because of the similarity of Rumanian and French, we would expect this argument to hold good equally for Chilean students; for Spanish can be regarded as even closer to French than Rumanian. Yet, the Chilean students did far less well than the Rumanians. Other factors may be more important than linguistic similarities. Hence the conclusion was reached that 'it is very doubtful that native language is a critical factor' (Carroll 1975:185). It must of course be remembered that all the first languages involved in the study were European (Dutch, English, Rumanian, Spanish, and Swedish) and therefore the differences between these languages were never as great as between oriental and European languages.

Social and cultural factors
Closely associated with the language situation are sociolinguistic and sociocultural factors in the learning environment. They are the social organization of the community and the different groups that constitute the society, its social classes and occupational, ethnic, cultural, and religious groups. Mackey's model draws attention to *language differences* between different social groupings. We must be equally aware of *socio-economic and sociocultural differences* which may manifest themselves in different attitudes to language in general, to particular languages, to social or regional dialects, to bilingualism, and to second language learning and which, then, become crystallized in status differences between different languages. Particular languages are sometimes held in either high or low esteem because of economic, political, or cultural values associated with them. Sometimes these views about languages reflect rational arguments about the merits of the language concerned, based on a realistic assessment of the value of different languages for a particular community; at other times, they express common stereotypes about the target language. Students, therefore, frequently come to language learning with positive or negative attitudes derived from the society in which they live, and these attitudes in turn influence their motivation to learn the second language.[6]

Relationships between socio-economic or sociocultural factors and language learning, however, cannot be treated as self-evident. Studies have sometimes found very clear associations, but at other times the relationships were far less evident. Thus, the IEA study of French categorically states that 'the student's socio-economic status as such is not a relevant consideration in foreign language achievement' (Carroll 1975:213). On the other hand, as was already pointed out, the British study, *Primary French in the Balance*, found a consistent relationship between socio-economic status and achievement in French: 'high mean scores tended to coincide with high-status parental occupation and low mean scores with low-status parental occupation' (Burstall 1975:392). This association reflects different social attitudes to learning French in different strata of British society, which indirectly affect the achievement of pupils. See also Chapter 19:424–6.

The historical setting and the national or international political situation
The choice of particular languages in the curriculum, the relative emphasis to be placed upon different languages, and the general emphasis laid on language learning are largely determined by factors beyond the immediate environment. Among these is often an almost implicit interpretation of historical and political forces in the wider community or nation. In wartime or in other periods of political upheaval or social unrest these historical and political influences become more noticeable. For example, in Western countries the teaching of German as a foreign language has fluctuated from great popularity before World War I and in the period of the Weimar Republic to almost a complete eclipse during World War II. These changes reflect changing attitudes towards another country. Shifts in the emphasis on French, English, German, Spanish, Portuguese, Russian, or Dutch as second languages throughout the world have mirrored the ups and downs of political and economic power and prestige. As we will note below, the concept of language planning could well be expanded so that the decisions on second language choices are made on a basis of a more rational analysis and more comprehensive and long-term national and international considerations than has hitherto been customary. To a new teacher, faced with the teaching of a particular language in a particular school, an awareness of these historical and political factors can be a help and give greater significance to his teaching.

Geographical aspects
If language teaching, to a certain extent, is a way of creating language contacts between linguistic communities, the geographical distance between these communities may also have some bearing on language learning. Learning French in Australia and New Zealand is likely to be questioned by students in these countries more than learning French in Great Britain, the Netherlands, or Germany. The need for learning French in Canada may be expressed more strongly in Ontario, close to Quebec and other French-speaking areas, than in the more distant province of British Columbia. Even within Ontario teachers in predominantly English-speaking areas stress the difficulties created by the distance from French-speaking parts of the province. In France, which borders on Germany in the north-east, Italy in the south-east, Spain in

the south, and Britain in the north-west, these differences in geographical locations are reflected in the emphases in language provision in the school. German tends to predominate in the north-east, Italian in the south-east, Spanish in the south, and English in the west and north. As was pointed out already, the British Pilot Scheme (Burstall *et al.* 1974) found that geographical distance between the north and the south of England was reflected in differences in language achievement.

Yet, the geography of the situation must not be interpreted too mechanically. Ease of communication has served to overcome geographical distance to some extent; but in spite of that, it makes a difference whether a second language is used within or close to the environment in which the language is learnt or is only available at increasing distances from it. The distinction that is often made between 'second language' and 'foreign language' is primarily a distinction between the geographical settings in which the language is used and the sociolinguistic and sociocultural implications of these settings for language teaching and learning. In the 'second language' situation where the language is used within the environment in which it is learnt, teachers and learners have immediate and regular access to opportunities of language use. The second language finds support in the social milieu. In the foreign language situation the environmental support is lacking and therefore has to be compensated for by special pedagogical measures.[7]

In general, it is probably less the geographical distance as such that affects learning than how the language is perceived by teachers and learners. These perceptions are usually more influenced by cultural and sociolinguistic assumptions that are current in the speech community in which learning occurs than by purely geographical factors. In short, in assessing a language teaching situation it is important to ask whether the second language is available within the learning environment or, if not, at what distance from the learning environment it is; and to assess what bearing the geographical distance is likely to have on the perceptions of learners and teachers.

Economic and technological development
Economic and technological factors are important in the environmental analysis from two points of view[8]. Language teaching may be needed for economic development. The acquisition of technological skill may depend upon the knowledge of a major world language through which these skills may be acquired. Thus, in Third World countries English as a second language is often a prerequisite to scientific or technological training.

On the other hand, language learning itself demands an economic investment, and a society may have to weigh up the importance of language learning against the importance of other educational needs.

Much language teaching in advanced industrialized societies has been characterized by an abundance of teaching materials and of electronic audio and video equipment. Many developing countries, particularly in the Third World, lack such materials or equipment and cannot afford to buy them. They may also lack the skilled manpower to install and maintain such equipment. It is therefore important for an analysis of the context of language teaching to take account of the economic and technical capabilities in determining curriculum materials or in recommending techniques or a technology. Most countries outside the highly developed areas of Europe or North America may be more interested in a simple technology of second language learning than in elaborate gadgets partly for reasons of economy and partly because of the shortage of technological skill to service equipment.

Educational framework

The final aspect to consider in the analysis of the context of language teaching is the educational framework in which the teaching normally occurs. The concepts needed to interpret the educational situation will be discussed in Part 6. Here it is sufficient to indicate by way of example how varied the circumstances may be under which languages are taught. This can be seen from the IEA studies of *The Teaching of English as a Foreign Language in Ten Countries* (Lewis and Massad 1975; see also Chapter 19:432–4). In the ten countries, the beginning age of compulsory education ranged from five years to eight years, and the period of compulsory schooling from four years in Thailand to nine years in Belgium, Germany, Finland, Israel, and Sweden. Countries differed also in the way they organized schools and distinguished between elementary/primary and secondary schools. Sweden was the only country that did not distinguish between elementary and secondary schools up to the age of sixteen. In Italy, the transfer from the primary to the secondary school occurred at ten; in Chile, Hungary, and Thailand it was as late as fourteen. Some countries introduced an intermediate or 'observation' period between elementary and secondary schooling. Most countries distinguished at the secondary stage between academic (classical, humanistic, and scientific) programmes, and vocational (technical, commercial, or agricultural) programmes. Great differences occurred between total amounts of school-time for secondary education: they ranged from 960 hours annually in Chile to 1544 hours in Israel in academic schools, and from 832 hours in Chile to 1740 in Finland for vocational schools. Consequently, there is simply more teaching time available for language study in some countries than in others. These examples, drawn from the Ten-Country Study of English as a Foreign Language, merely serve to indicate how important it is to have a detailed understanding of the total educational setting as part of the analysis of the language teaching context.

Second language planning

The creation of bilingualism through schooling presents a number of problems which can be regarded as questions for language planning: Which second language or languages should be learnt in a given society? What are the language priorities? What criteria should be employed in selecting language A, B, or C for second language learning? What levels of proficiency should be aimed at? Should everybody or only some learn languages A or B? What place should these languages be given in the educational system? What provisions have to be made to implement the language policy upon which the society has decided?

In certain multilingual speech communities the learning of a second language is of particular importance, because the second language is essential as a medium of intercommunication or as the language of schooling, for example, English in Nigeria or Zambia. Here language decisions may be vital issues of national development. In many countries of the Third World where a second language is needed as the standard language or has to be learnt as a language of wider communication, such second language planning is already happening. But even in countries where the fabric of social life is not so dependent on the choice of a second language as a medium of instruction and internal communication, the provision of second or foreign languages still presents a complex task of educational language planning. It demands major policy decisions and, following them, the education and supply of teachers, the compilation of grammars, dictionaries, and cultural and sociolinguistic guides, the development of a language curriculum, and the preparation of course materials.

Steps in the development of a second language plan are similar to those outlined in Chapter 11 for general language planning (see pp. 240–1). (1) A fact-finding survey examines the language situation of the speech community concerned, identifies the existing language provision and interprets the language needs of the society. (2) The fact-finding survey leads to a 'language plan' or several 'alternative plans', i.e., a reasoned selection and arrangement of languages in order of priority to provide for in schools, universities, language centres, and research institutions. One or two foreign languages (A or B) may be planned as universally necessary or available in primary, secondary, higher, and adult education. Other languages (X, Y, or Z) are planned to be offered only to a restricted extent in higher and adult education. Many languages will be offered only in university programmes and some are likely to remain the subject of purely specialized research institutions.[9] (3) Once a language plan has become policy the development phase of the language plan involves the more specific second-language *linguistic* planning: for each particular language a norm or norms as standards for second language proficiency must be chosen and the ground prepared for the composition of pedagogical grammars, word lists, and sociocultural and sociolinguistic guides. (4) The planning of the next phase, implementation, would lead to concrete proposals for what steps to take within the school system to provide for language instruction to the level and extent suggested by the plan: the development of curricula, the preparation of teaching materials, the planning of teacher education, and the necessary basic studies and research. (5) An evaluation phase, envisaged for language planning, is equally applicable to the development of a second-language plan. In this phase steps will be taken to assess whether the execution of the plan leads to the recommended levels of second-language proficiency among the population. In most cases a test development programme would therefore be part of the total plan. In a more general way, the plan should include regular review procedures to be carried out when the plan is being executed in answer to such questions as: Is the plan still valid? Are the proposed measures effective? The evaluation of the plan would lead to its revision so that planning, once set in motion, can be repeated at regular intervals and become part of an ongoing cyclical process of review, renewed planning, implementation, and evaluation followed by a further revision of the existing plan.

To our knowledge, this model of language planning extended to second language provision is not yet applied in its integral form anywhere but there are instances of studies which illustrate parts or aspects of the planning process. The great historical reports on language teaching can be considered surveys of second language learning and plans for the development of language instruction. An outstanding example—and probably the nearest to what has been envisaged in phases (1) and (2) in the second-language planning model—is the Canadian *Report on Bilingualism and Biculturalism* (Canada 1967–70). In this study French and English as second languages were surveyed in the context of the Canadian language situation of the sixties. A thorough study was made of language teaching in different provinces and at different levels of teaching, and the report included surveys of students and teachers. It made policy recommendations for the improvement of language teaching as part of its overall aim to cultivate bilingualism and biculturalism in Canada.

Several British examples can also be cited in addition to the previously mentioned *Modern Studies*, the Government report of World War I which influenced language teaching in the interwar years. The lack of provision for Russian and other Slavonic languages was documented by the Annan Report (1962) which made policy recommendations to overcome this deficiency. In a similar way the Hayter Report (1961) was intended to analyse deficiencies in the study of oriental and African languages and to propose improvements.

In 1969 a study of national needs in modern language was recommended by a national language committee in Britain. The difficulties in mounting such a vast enquiry, however, led to two more restricted projects, each of which illustrates well the kind of surveys needed in second-language planning. One was a survey of curricula and proficiency levels in modern languages within the state system of education. In this study several hundred syllabuses in French, German, Italian, Russian, and Spanish at school level, in further and higher education were analysed according to a uniform scheme. The study provided a map of language provision in Britain (James and Rouve 1973). The second study was a survey of national manpower requirements in foreign languages. It consisted of a questionnaire enquiry addressed to 'Advanced level' candidates and another questionnaire directed to commercial and industrial firms and employers in order to find out the language needs of industry. In a third part an analysis of the advertising columns in national newspapers was made in order to find out the number of advertisers of new posts demanding languages from applicants, and further to discover in which positions languages were required or desirable, which languages were demanded, and what particular language skills were looked for (Emmans *et al.* 1974). The National Congress on Languages in Education (NCLE) which was established in Britain in 1976 as a permanent body is a step in the direction of a planned approach to language questions in education.[10] Finally, the Modern Languages Project of the Council of Europe which, between 1971 and 1981, attempted to develop a consensus among European nations on standards of language proficiency for adults can also be considered as a pioneer effort in foreign language planning.[11]

These studies, surveys, and projects are only a beginning of second-language planning. However they suggest that the hit-or-miss approach of the past will gradually give way to a more planned process of deciding on language provision.

Review and conclusion

From the point of view of language teaching and learning, the concept of social context can be seen to be of great importance. First, we have seen that language itself must be treated in a social context. In addition, for language teaching, it is important to relate language to society, because languages are taught and learnt to establish contact and communication across language boundaries. Hence society and culture are more than background and even more than context. Society and culture are, after all, the concepts that represent people with whom the learner eventually must make contact if language learning is to have any value in human terms. Finally, language teaching can be looked upon as a deliberate intervention into ethnolinguistic relations which can be planned more or less effectively and which, in this way, can contribute to the bilingualism of a society.

From the overview of social sciences and language teaching in the last three chapters, it is evident that sociolinguistics and other social sciences have a major role to play in second language pedagogy, profoundly influencing the substantive quality of language programmes and the provision of languages in a speech community.

In concluding this part of our study, it is interesting to reflect that the relationship between the social sciences and language pedagogy has developed differently from that between linguistics and language teaching. Social scientists, unlike, linguists, have been somewhat indifferent to language pedagogy and have hardly recognized the importance of theories and descriptions of society and culture for language teaching. Instead, some educational linguists and a few language teachers have become aware of this need and have boldly moved into the social science arena. These developments are still relatively new and sporadic. In the long run, the best hope for the future lies in co-operation between social scientists, educational linguists, and language teachers.

Notes

1 As Criper and Widdowson in a brilliant paper on 'Sociolinguistics and language teaching' (1975) rightly pointed out 'these two ways of looking at society, the "bird's eye view" and the "worm's eye view" are not contradictory but complementary' (op. cit.:158).

2 In the early sixties the Center for Applied Linguistics in Washington took a lead in looking at second language learning sociologically from a world perspective in two small but significant publications which dealt with second language learning in the national development of Third World countries (Center for Applied Linguistics 1961; Rice 1962).

3 See Chapter 2, Note 13 in which this difference was referred to as an example of 'inconsistencies' which demand explanation.

4 Creoles range from a pure form ('basilect') via various gradations ('mesolect') to a form which is close to standard English or French ('acrolect') (Hudson 1980:67). See Chapter 7:124. See also Valdman 1977.

5 The IEA studies are briefly referred to in Chapter 4:56 and described in greater detail in the context of comparative education in Chapter 19:432–4.

6 Recent research studies have attributed a great deal of importance to the influence of interethnic relations upon ethnolinguistic attitudes

and on language learning. For a brief summary with references, see Stern and Cummins 1981:209–212. Refer back to Chapter 11:237–8 for a discussion of the sociology and social psychology of speech communities and see also Chapter 17:375–9 for a more detailed treatment of affective aspects of language learning.

7 See on this distinction Chapters 1:15–17 and 18:391–3. The other distinction that has been made between intranational and international is also partly geographical. As we saw in Chapter 1:17 'intranational' refers to the use of a language of wider communication within a country, for example, English in India or Nigeria, while 'international' refers to the negation of any specific geographical location (country or region). On this point see Smith (1981).

8 See also on this aspect Chapter 19, Section 5 for economics, and Section 10 for the technology of education.

9 The principles on which such a selection of languages might be based are at present not yet clear. Nearly forty years ago Peers (1945) attempted to develop rational arguments for the place of different languages in British schools and universities. More recently the National Congress on Languages in Education (Perren 1979, 1979a) has begun to tackle this task by considering foreign languages in the school in the context of language education.

10 NCLE is an independent body which is administered through the Centre for Information on Language Teaching and Research. Its first 'assembly' took place in Durham in 1978. Some of the papers prepared for this meeting, which deal with the mother tongue and foreign languages in education, were published by CILT as *NCLE Papers and Reports* (Perren 1979, 1979a).

11 See Trim 1980; Trim *et al.* 1980; Council of Europe 1981. In the U.S.A. the President's Commission report on foreign languages and international studies (U.S.A. 1979) or in Canada the work of a ministerial committee in the province of Ontario (Ontario 1974) on the teaching of French further illustrate the same direction: planning of second language provision on a regional or national scale.

PART FIVE

Concepts of language learning

14 Psychological approaches to language and learning

The fourth perspective from which to develop a language teaching theory is that of the individual language learner and the processes of language learning. The discipline that is relevant to this perspective is of course psychology.

In exploring this area it is useful to begin with introspection, retrospection, and observation and to think about ourselves as language learners and our pupils or students in that role. Recollecting our own experiences, how did we tackle language learning? Did we find it easy or hard? And what was easy or hard about it? Were we successful or unsuccessful? Did our view of language learning change as we progressed? If more than one language was involved did we approach the different languages in the same way or differently? How do we explain our own learning experiences? What did we learn from them about language learning?[1]

In a similar way we can attempt to observe language learning among our students and ask ourselves why some are successful and others seem to struggle rather helplessly, or what view of learning is implied in our teaching.

In discussing these questions we are almost bound to use psychological concepts, because our thinking on learning is inevitably influenced by the psychological knowledge that is part of the common understanding of human behaviour in our culture. No doubt, such psychological terms as 'remembering', 'forgetting', 'skill', 'motivation', 'frustration', 'inhibitions' and so on will form part of our analysis. The importance of psychology and psycholinguistics to a theory of language teaching is hardly in question today. Some of the most debated issues which have created a stir in language teaching theory in recent years refer to the *psychology* of second language learning. Thus, the debate on the role of habit versus cognition or the discussion of the relationship between first and second language acquisition are based on different psychological interpretations of language learning and on psychological arguments and counter-arguments.

Like the other disciplines we have previously considered psychology as a field of study in its own right has a history of over a hundred years. The first half of the twentieth century witnessed a tremendous expansion

Main fields of enquiry	Fields of application	Method of enquiry	Schools of thought	
			Chief exponent	Name of school or leading concept
Philosophical psychology	Applied psychology (in contrast to 'pure', 'general', or 'theoretical' psychology)	Introspective	Wundt, Titchener, Brentano, Stumpf, Külpe	Structuralism 1870–1900
General psychology: perception	Educational psychology	Experimental	James, Dewey, Hall, Woodworth	Functionalism 1890–1940
learning	Industrial psychology	Clinical	Thorndike	Connectionism 1900–1930
memory	Medical psychology: clinical psychology	Statistical	Pavlov	Conditioning 1905–1928
thinking	psychotherapy	Psychometric	Watson, Skinner	Behaviourism 1910–1965
motivation	counselling psychology		Koffka, Köhler, Wertheimer	Gestalt psychology 1912–1935
emotion			Lewin	Field theory 1935–1945
Physiological psychology			Piaget, Bruner	Psychology of cognitive development 1920–1980
Personality			Freud	Psychoanalysis
Developmental psycho-logy: infancy, childhood			Jung	Analytical Psychology
adolescence, adulthood			Adler	Individual Psychology 1900–1940
senescence			Allport, Maslow, Rogers	Humanistic psychology 1955–1980
Social psychology				
Psychology of behaviour disorders (psycho-pathology)				
Psychology of . . . art				
music				
language (psycho-linguistics)				

Figure 14.1   An overview of psychology (Dates indicate approximate periods of major development.)

of psychology. This development which occurred in several countries across the world took many different directions.[2] The accompanying table (Figure 14.1) gives an indication of the wide range of activities covered by psychology today. It includes different fields of interest and specialization, different areas of application, and different schools of thought which—as in linguistics—are identified sometimes by a prominent exponent (for example, Freud, Watson, Skinner) or a leading concept (for example, behaviourism, Gestalt).[3] Psychological ideas and psychological terms are pervasive in present-day thought, and it is therefore not surprising to find that language teaching theory and practice, too, are permeated by psychological thinking which can be traced to various branches of psychology and to different schools of thought.

For our purposes it is not necessary to analyse the possible connections between psychology and language teaching in every detail. This is the task for more specialized studies. In the present chapter two key concepts for a language teaching theory, *language* and *learning* will be considered from the point of view of general psychology so that we have the background to study second language learning more specifically from a psychological perspective in the following chapters (Chapters 15–18). The relations between psychology and language teaching theory will become evident as we proceed.

Language in psychology

Before World War I
In the history of psychology language has always played a certain role, but at no time have linguistic processes been so much in the centre of attention as they have been since the fifties and sixties. Psychology studies the behaviour, activities, conduct, and mental processes of human beings. It can be defined as the science of the mental life and behaviour of the individual.[4] Speech is one of the features that distinguishes man most clearly from other species, and therefore its function in the life of man is a necessary part of psychological enquiry. But as we can see from Figure 14.1 language is only one among many aspects of human behaviour studied by psychologists. Over the hundred years of its development as a scientific discipline, psychology has not always paid sufficient attention to speech or language. In the last decades of the nineteenth century it was more concerned with sense perception. From about 1900, questions of learning, memory, thinking, and intelligence (the 'higher mental processes') were the principal topics of investigation. In the interwar years, the studies of the emotions, personality, psychological growth of the child, and the measurement of

individual differences became prominent. Even today one may find psychologists who question whether the psychology of language is a fruitful field of enquiry.[5]

Nevertheless, language looked at from a psychological point of view has never been completely neglected. A classical work by Wundt (1877), the scholar who is often regarded as the founder of modern scientific psychology, was a monumental study of 'ethnic psychology' (*Völkerpsychologie*) which included as its first volume a study of language. Most of the early investigations in child psychology between 1870 and 1900 contained remarkably acute observations and sophisticated theoretical discussions on the development of speech in early childhood.[6] The modern interest in first-language acquisition is a renewal of earlier studies in this field. Many of the experiments in psychology around 1900, especially studies on memory and mental associations, involved the use of language. Memory experiments, for example, often tested the learning and retention of word lists. They indicated that in memorizing the subject tends to arrange and organize the verbal elements to be learnt in some recognizable pattern. Word association experiments, first undertaken by Galton (1883), demonstrated that subjects can respond spontaneously and in predictable ways to separate words (verbal 'stimuli') with words (verbal 'responses' or 'reactions').[7] Such experiments increased not only the psychologists' understanding of the human mind, they also suggested principles that govern verbal repertoires in the first language. They are therefore also studies of language behaviour.

Around the turn of the century, one of the most captivating approaches to the emotional dynamics of verbal behaviour was Freud's treatment of slips of the tongue or the pen. He was able to show that these performance errors of speakers or writers had an internal emotional 'logic', and like dream symbols were clues to stresses and internal conflicts.[8] For this reason, Jung, following Freud, was able to use verbal associations as a diagnostic tool to uncover emotional 'complexes'. The associations, evoked by a given word, although not absolutely predictable, have regularities which suggest that the words in a speech community, as Saussure had also observed, constitute a network of common associative patterns. According to Jung's theory, a person with emotional problems is likely to deviate markedly from the common verbal associations of his speech community. It was this observation that suggested to Jung (1918) to treat unusual word associations as indicators of emotional peculiarities and stresses. Thus, psychoanalysis and related schools of thought drew attention to the fact that language is not only related to thinking, but also to the affective life of man—an aspect of language which even today is still insufficiently recognized in second language teaching.

The interwar period

Behaviourism, which was advanced in America as a new approach to psychology in the early decades of the twentieth century, attributed particular importance to 'verbal behaviour', because speech enabled behaviourist theory to dispense with such mentalistic concepts as 'thinking' which was reinterpreted as 'subvocal verbalization' (Watson 1919).[9] By describing linguistic processes as verbal 'behaviour' or as vocal stimuli and responses, or as 'habits' or 'skills', behaviourists were able to apply to human speech the same principles that they applied to the description of other human and non-human modes of behaviour. The acquisition of language in infancy was explained as governed by the same mechanisms of learning that governed the acquisition of other habits.

During the interwar period child psychologists, whether they operated within the framework of behaviourism or not, gathered much factual information on language development in early childhood as part of their studies of the general growth of the individual (for example, McCarthy 1946).

What interested them particularly in these studies of mental development of the child was the question of how to account for individual differences in development. 'Nature or nurture' was one of the most hotly debated issues. In their explanations of mental growth psychologists tended to be divided. Some favoured chiefly maturational (biological, nativistic) explanations, while others saw mental development as mainly or entirely as learnt and preferred 'social' or environmental explanations. By the forties the prolonged debate between nativists and environmentalists had reached a 'biosocial' compromise: the division between the two points of view had become less rigid. Rather than expecting a clear-cut solution, the question was much more one of asking what proportion or what aspects of human functioning could best be accounted for in terms of biological growth, heredity, innate disposition, and maturation, and what proportion or aspects could be explained most convincingly as the result of environmental influences and learning. Intelligence was viewed as a good example of a feature in which the 'bio' component was perhaps stronger than the 'social' aspect. In language development, on the other hand, the weight was at that time considered to be much more on social influences and learning than on biological factors. After all, a child learns the language of its social surroundings. Nevertheless, a basis of neural development was presupposed even among those who interpreted language development almost entirely in environmental terms.

The interaction between genetic factors and environmental influences has remained a much debated issue. In the sixties, as we shall see below (p.302), a fresh controversy on this question was provoked by the claim, advanced by Chomsky, Lenneberg, and others, that language development should be viewed as biological rather than as the result of social learning.[10]

Another major issue involving language which has been thought about in psychology for many decades is the interaction between language and other aspects of human psychology. Ever since the beginnings of intelligence testing in the early decades of the twentieth century, the growth of language in the child was seen above all as an indicator of mental growth. Many of the earlier measures of general intelligence, following the lead of Binet's first effort in 1904 to measure intelligence, relied on knowledge of words in the first language and on the understanding of verbal relationships. Tests of vocabulary (i.e., tests defining word meanings) were regarded as one of the best ways of assessing the mental status attained by an individual.

How was the relationship between language and thought to be understood? Underlying the use of vocabulary tests as measures of intelligence was the assumption that language growth is dependent upon intellectual growth. The Swiss psychologist Piaget, in his first major work on language and thought in childhood (1923), advanced the thesis that language development and the functional use of language in childhood reflect the mental development of the child. Increasingly, however, influenced by the Whorfian hypothesis (see Chapter 10:203–6), language was seen to have a formative influence on perception and cognition. Eventually, it led to the theory, sometimes advanced around 1950 (for example, by Cameron 1947), that the individual's view of the world and his entire cognitive system were shaped by the verbal symbols given to each one of us by society as we learn our native language. Since our understanding of social relations is almost completely dependent upon verbal labelling, the influence of language on social roles and on the individual's perception of his own role, was considered as crucial. Further, the verbal labelling of emotional states and personal experiences came to be regarded as playing an important part in emotional development and in mental health.

On the whole, then, by the middle of the twentieth century, for some psychologists, the role of language was viewed as a central factor in determining the cognitive and affective states of the individual. Through verbalizations a decisive influence could indirectly be exercised on the way humans think, feel, and regulate their lives. Not all psychologists shared this central view of language. Some were less convinced of such a direct effect of language upon the mental make-up of the individual. They believed that there was a certain parallelism between language growth and mental growth generally, but that this was by no means perfect. Others again believed that a cause-and-effect relationship worked in the opposite direction; they regarded language as dependent upon and a part of cognitive development.

In 1968 the issue was once more reopened by Chomsky through a small book on language and mind in which he advocated the viewpoint that one should recognize in linguistic processes the reflection of fundamental ways in which the human mind is organized. Therefore for Chomsky it is not a question of the 'influence' of cognition on speech. Rather universal characteristics of languages are mirrors of the way the mind functions. In short, the place of language in relation to other psychological functions has been and continues to be a fascinating puzzle, and in dealing with this question language teachers can only be warned not to believe that these relationships can easily be unravelled and to bear in mind this opinion that ends a lucid small book on language and thought: 'If I leave you with a sense of mystery, this book will have achieved its purpose' (Greene 1975:133).

In most of the studies and discussions on the psychology of language it was tacitly assumed that the individual is a monoglot, operating in a static and unilingual environment.[11] Apart from a few exceptions, the acquisition of more than one language and bilingualism were treated as unusual, and relatively marginal phenomena like language pathology (aphasia, stammering, etc.). The aim of studying bilingualism was to find out how damaging it is to intellectual growth if a child operates with two languages rather than one. This implicitly negative approach to bilingualism has prevailed until recent times and is not uncommon even today. A study by Peal and Lambert in 1962 which claimed that bilingualism was not necessarily a disadvantage and could in fact be beneficial to the individual ushered in a major change to a prevailing view.

After World War II: the growth of psycholinguistics
World War II and the post-war era were periods of much interdisciplinary development. Psychologists had become increasingly aware of the fact that the linguistic concepts they had previously used in their investigations were simply common-sense notions of language with which they were familiar as educated persons. They were conscious of the fact that they had not adequately taken into account the more systematic thought on language that had meanwhile been developed by the growing science of linguistics. Linguists, for their part, also wanted to co-ordinate their linguistic studies with those of psychologists. These thoughts led to meetings between linguists and psychologists. The intention of these exchanges was to establish a common basis of discussion on language, to develop a body of common theory, and to study research issues. Such interchanges of ideas which took place in the U.S.A. in the early fifties led to a seminal survey on 'psycholinguistics',

as this new interdisciplinary field began to be called (Osgood and Sebeok 1954). This survey brought together a great deal of information on current thought and research problems. Starting out from Shannon's model of the act of communication (Shannon and Weaver 1949; see also Chapter 7:128 above), Osgood and Sebeok developed a theoretical model defining the role of psycholinguistics in relation to other contributing disciplines (1954/1965:3).

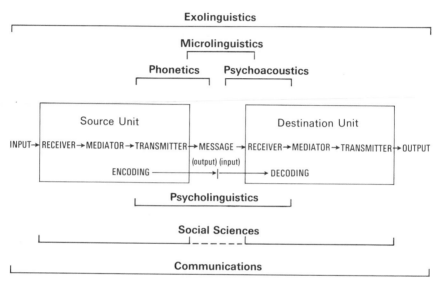

Figure 14.2   Osgood and Sebeok's representation of the place of psycholinguistics among the social and language sciences

According to this diagram, the entire field of language study is 'exolinguistics' (more recently often referred to as 'macrolinguistics'). Linguistics in the narrower sense ('microlinguistics') is given a somewhat wider range than was envisaged by Bloomfield (see Chapter 7). The place of psycholinguistics was defined in the following terms:

'The rather new discipline coming to be known as *psycholinguistics* … is concerned in the broadest sense with relations between messages and the characteristics of human individuals who select and interpret them. In a narrower sense, psycholinguistics studies those processes whereby the intentions of speakers are transformed into signals in the culturally accepted code and whereby these signals are transformed into the interpretations of hearers. In other words, *psycholinguistics deals directly with the processes of encoding and decoding as they relate states of messages to states of communicators.*'
(Osgood and Sebeok 1954/1965:4)

A second diagram (op. cit.:5), intended to map out the major divisions of psycholinguistics, (Figure 14.3), made it clear that psychology in the top half of the model analysed persons as 'communicators', while linguistics in the bottom half studied the communications or messages. Psycholinguistics, then, was the meeting ground between the two. The linguistic analysis was conceived not only as linguistic in the narrow sense but included paralinguistic features of facial and bodily gestures (kinesics) and situations. The psychological analysis of communicators was envisaged comprehensively as directed to cognition, motivation, 'anticipational and dispositional sets', and sensorimotor skills. The model extended the Saussurian distinction between synchronic and diachronic linguistics to psychology and psycholinguistics. 'Diachronic',

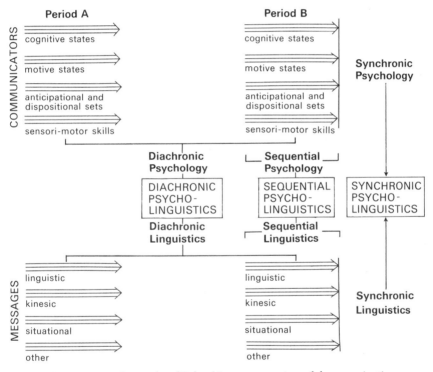

Figure 14.3   Osgood and Sebeok's representation of the organization of content in psycholinguistics

applied to psychology, referred to studies of different stages of development and learning in an individual. Diachronic psycholinguistics therefore involves 'comparison between two or more stages in language development' in the individual and in society (op. cit.:126). It includes first language learning, second language learning and bilingualism, and the phenomenon of language change. Second language learning and bilingualism were thus given a distinct place in this scheme of psycholinguistics. What, from our perspective, is particularly interesting is (a) that in this first mapping-out of psycholinguistics, second language learning and bilingualism were treated as interrelated psychological phenomena, and (b) that they were not treated separately but placed squarely (however briefly) into the theoretical framework of a psychology of language.

The main question raised in the brief treatment by Ervin and Osgood (1954/1965) of second language learning and bilingualism was how an individual, who can use two languages (the bilingual or second language learner), stores the two linguistic codes and brings them into action. Two different systems were envisaged: sometimes two languages are handled by individuals as two separate entities which operate independently. This mechanism, referred to as *co-ordinate bilingualism,* according to Ervin and Osgood, is typical of the 'true' bilingual 'who has learnt to speak one language with his parents, for example, and the other language in school and at work' (op. cit.:140). In the other case the two languages are linked, and the meanings of one language are interpreted through the medium of meanings in the other (*compound bilingualism*). The compound command is cultivated by learning two languages in the same social environment or by translation methods in foreign language classrooms, for example, learning vocabulary lists by associating a word in the second language with its translation equivalent in the first language. Different speakers of two languages do not fall absolutely into one or the other category, but they are likely to vary in degree of 'co-ordinateness'. The distinction between 'co-ordinate' and 'compound' bilingualism was the subject of much debate in subsequent years. It has bearing on the question in language teaching methodology whether to include or exclude the first language in second language learning. Brooks (1960/1964:49–52), for example, made an eloquent plea for a 'co-ordinate' treatment of languages in language classes.

Regrettably the psychologists of the time appear to have favoured a co-ordinate approach as superior to a compound one, and by this bias diminished the theoretical value of the distinction. Research on it led to conflicting results (Macnamara 1967). Eventually researchers abandoned this distinction (for example, McLaughlin 1978:8), and the whole question of the 'L1-L2 connection' in language learning was left as an open issue which, as we shall see later, has reappeared in discussions on language teaching today.[12]

Skinner and Chomsky

It is evident, then, that in the fifties language was no longer a neglected topic in psychology. Language questions received a new prominence after the publication of Skinner's *Verbal Behavior* (1957) and the review of this work by Chomsky (1959). The thesis of Skinner's book, an openly radical speculation, developed over a long period and the logical continuation of Watson's behaviourism, was that what is normally called 'language' can be described exhaustively and consistently as 'verbal *behaviour*'. To use language even in poetry or philosophy requires no new principle of explanation and no new basic concepts. Skinner's argument was that there is no fundamental difference in accounting for the fact that a rat in an experimental cage can learn to press a lever to receive a food pellet as a 'reward' and the fact that a human can learn to use vocal signals as 'operants' to satisfy his needs. Skinner's thesis accorded with the behaviourist philosophy which provided the commonly accepted ground rules in psycholinguistics of that time; but it was more extreme in that it attempted to dispense entirely with any mentalistic concepts, above all, the concept of 'meaning'.

Chomsky (1959), in a long and famous review article on *Verbal Behavior* in the journal *Language*, made a fundamental attack not only on the thesis and the concepts developed by Skinner in this book but, through this review, on the entire behaviourist position in contemporary psychology and psycholinguistics. While many psychologists, usually referred to as neo-behaviourists, had for years adopted a less anti-mentalist view of behaviour than Skinner, most of them—certainly in North America and Great Britain—had fully accepted the basic principles of behaviourism, particularly in the treatment of language. Carroll (1953) expresses a view which would have found widespread acceptance among psychologists in the fifties:

> 'I take the initial position that subjective events can be regarded as behavioral, that they play an important role in many behavior sequences, and ... that there are publicly observable indices of subjective events (not the least of which is verbal behavior) and that subjective events may be assumed to follow much the same laws as those events observable as neurological, motor, and glandular responses.'
> (op. cit.:72)

Therefore, to attack the entire behaviourist basis, as Chomsky did in this review article, required courage and conviction. What made this attack even more remarkable was that it was made in an area, the field of language, in which a behaviourist approach appeared much less assailable than in other areas of psychology, for example, personality or thinking. Because of the fierceness of Chomsky's attack, valuable aspects of Skinner's work may not have found adequate recognition, and the work demands today a thorough reassessment.[13]

The object of Chomsky's review of *Verbal Behavior* was to show that the principal concepts of a behaviourist approach to language are totally inadequate to account for language behaviour. For example, the concept of 'shaping' and 'reinforcement', which Skinner had transferred from conditioning in animal experiments to language use, was in Chomsky's view completely misleading. 'I have been able to find no support whatsoever for the doctrine of Skinner and others that slow and careful shaping of verbal behavior through differential reinforcement is an absolute necessity' (Chomsky 1959:158). The notion of 'generalization', Chomsky argued, was equally insufficient to account for the creative character of language use: 'Talk of "stimulus generalization" ... simply perpetuates the mystery under a new title' (op. cit.:158). Instead of attempting to explain language in terms of the simpler modes of behaviour of non-human organisms, psychologists, he said, had better use the evidence of language to reinterpret the characteristic workings of the human mind. A few years later, Chomsky (1966) summarized his criticism of behaviourism in such phrases as these:

'Language is not a "habit structure".' (op. cit.:44)

'Repetition of fixed phrases is a rarity ...' (op. cit.:46)

'The notion that linguistic behavior consists of "responses" to "stimuli" is as much a myth as the idea that it is a matter of habit and generalization.' (loc. cit.)

'Ordinary linguistic behavior characteristically involves innovation, formation of new sentences and new patterns in accordance with rules of great abstractness and intricacy.' (op. cit.:44)

'There are no known principles of association or reinforcement, and no known sense of "generalization" that can begin to account for this characteristic "creative" aspect of normal language use.' (loc. cit.)

Chomsky had not always made direct psychological claims for his own linguistic theory. On the contrary, he often emphasized that a generative grammar and the concept of the native speaker's 'competence' were constructs to account for the *linguistic* characteristics of a given grammar of a language. They were not to be thought of as models of how a native speaker makes up or interprets utterances. But it was obvious that the notion of competence and the concept of linguistic creativity together with Chomsky's attack on behaviourism would lead psychologists, sooner or later, to re-examine the theoretical bases of psycholinguistics. Moreover, in the course of the sixties Chomsky himself became more and more convinced that the study of language may very well 'provide a remarkably favourable perspective for the study of human mental processes' (Chomsky 1968:84) so much so that he characterized linguistics as a 'subfield of psychology' (op. cit.:24). Chomsky's work, by the beginning of the sixties, had not only initiated a revolution in linguistics but also in psychology and in psycholinguistics.

The study of language comprehension and production
Psycholinguistics, by about 1960 firmly established as a border discipline between linguistics and psychology, did not immediately follow Chomskyan directions. To a certain extent it pursued the path set in 1954 by Osgood and Sebeok's survey of theory and research.[14] But its main interest began to shift towards an exploration of the psychological implications of transformational generative grammar.[15] Two broad areas received particular attention. One was to discover the psychological correlates to transformational generative grammar among ordinary language users. What is the psychological reality of linguistic competence or grammatical transformations? Does the distinction between 'deep' and 'surface' structure in linguistics correspond to the way in which a language user makes up or interprets sentences? Subsequent psycholinguistic experiments suggested that there is no simple one-to-one relationship between linguistic constructs and psychological processes. But the search for such a relationship has 'by its very failure brought to light the influence of many unexpected factors' (Greene 1972:196).[16]

The net effect for a psychological approach to language behaviour was a recognition of the complexity of that behaviour. While these psychological studies did not produce a satisfactory explanation of how a native speaker produces or interprets utterances they made it clear that the rather simple views of language competence current among some language educators, particularly among second-language teachers who had adopted the audiolingual theory, were inadequate. This critique was in some ways salutary but at the same time it created the intellectual confusion that was so acutely felt by many language teachers around 1970.[17]

It should be noted that the impetus given by the attempts to discover psychological correlates of linguistic analysis gradually led to very insightful interpretation of language comprehension and production. In the course of time these interpretations were not based on transformational generative grammar alone, but semantics and speech act and discourse analysis were drawn in, and accounts of speech comprehension and production, exemplified by Clark and Clark (1977), brought to consciousness processes and strategies implicit in the use of language. The implications for second language teaching of the findings of psycholinguistics of the kind that Clark and Clark (1977) synthesized have not yet been developed, but these findings open up exciting possibilities of a more profound analysis of second language use which could prove to be very helpful to second language teaching.[18]

Language acquisition in childhood
Although the growth of language in the child, as was pointed out above, was studied through baby biographies since the eighteen-seventies, most

of the studies carried out between the twenties and the fifties, were simply accounts of changes from babbling to the first word and descriptions of the growing vocabulary and sentence length. Linguistically these studies were relatively unsophisticated. Their main interest lay in the fact that language development showed a trend towards increasing complexity and was therefore comparable to cognitive and social development. Explanations of language growth were also often somewhat simplistic. Most observers regarded language development as a matter of imitation, practice, and habituation; and psychologists in the behaviourist tradition looked to conditioning as the main mechanism to account for language development.

The beginnings of a more searching approach were indicated in a study by Lewis (1936), who was one of the first scholars to bring linguistics, in this case phonetics, to bear on an analysis of child language. However, the study was somewhat exceptional.[19]

It was not until the sixties that the study of first language acquisition received a new major impetus largely through transformational generative grammar. Since transformational generative grammar had revealed that the system of rules in language use is extremely complex, it became all the more puzzling how an immature child could possibly abstract these rules, even unconsciously. Chomsky and others, in particular the neuro-physiologist Lenneberg (1967), were convinced that language development could not be accounted for in terms of a learning theory in the way behaviouristic psychology had done. An innate disposition to process linguistic data, a *faculté de langage* or language acquisition device (LAD), was postulated thus re-opening the old debate about 'innate ideas' and the relative importance of biological or environmental factors in the growth of language. Moreover, the principle of linguistic creativity in transformational generative grammar suggested that the customary explanatory concepts of language development—imitation, practice, and habit formation—had to be critically re-examined.[20] Lastly, the stress on syntax indicated that a more self-conscious choice of a grammatical model in the analysis of child language might be useful. For all these reasons the study of child language and of language acquisition received more attention in the sixties than ever before and the whole apparatus of linguistics, phonology, syntax, and, since the seventies, semantics and discourse analysis, was applied to child language giving rise to fresh insights.

In spite of intensive research on language growth and the new perspectives that were thus opened on child language in the sixties, by the early seventies the understanding of language development was far from settled. The balance between environmental influences and biological growth was still not clear. Bypassing the argument between rationalists (following Chomsky) and empiricists (following Skinner), students of child language, as McLaughlin (1978) has pointed out, have focused their attention on observing how infants process language. As they grow, infants face certain linguistic tasks, and recent studies have described systematically these phonological, syntactic, semantic, and communicative tasks involved in language development. In a review of first language acquisition, McLaughlin (1978:46) points out that 'of the various ways of conceptualizing the language acquisition process, the most satisfactory is one that takes both the linguistic knowledge and behaviour of the child into account'. Secondly, he suggests that it is a *dynamic* process 'reflecting the child's changing experiences with the linguistic and nonlinguistic environment'. Thirdly, the process is *gradual* and reflects the child's cognitive growth. Finally it is a process which is not narrowly linguistic but includes besides phonological and syntactic development the acquisition of *communicative skills* through interaction with the social environment. In short, the language development of the child is more and more viewed in the context of the total psychological and social growth in infancy and childhood.

Review

This brief and selective survey of the study of language in psychology suggests that psycholinguistics, which developed as a distinct field of study in the fifties and sixties deals, broadly speaking, with two main questions: (1) What does it mean to know a language? and (2) How does a child acquire language? Although it is implicit in most of the studies that the answers refer to native speakers, the findings are relevant, and in the seventies were recognized to be relevant, to second language learning. As to the first question, the interpretation of knowing a language provides a standard or model for the concept of proficiency or competence in second language learning. In defining language teaching objectives, the teacher must be guided by some conception of what it means to know a language, and as psycholinguistics provides concepts and theories of language proficiency, knowledge, and use, the language teaching theorist must certainly consider these. The objectives of second language learning are not necessarily entirely determined by native language use but the interpretation of native language competence inevitably serves as a foil against which to set second language learning. See Chapter 16:341 ff.

Similar considerations apply to the second question. It cannot be automatically assumed that first language acquisition and second language learning are identical or even similar processes, although they may well be. But even if they are considered very different, second language learning is bound to be thought about in relation to first language acquisition. Native language growth provides a standard against which to conceptualize second language learning.

In the progress of psycholinguistics the interest of scholars in the sixties had been almost entirely focused on first language acquisition and use. In comparison, bilingualism and second language learning—in spite of the lead given by Osgood and Sebeok (1954)—received far less attention. The situation in psychology was therefore similar to that in linguistics where contrastive studies, cross-linguistic investigations, and languages in contact have been superimposed on a discipline with a basically unilingual orientation. As will be seen in Chapter 15, second language learning and bilingualism were not altogether neglected. But *systematic* theoretical and empirical studies of second language learning only began to be made in the late sixties. They continued throughout the seventies. But even today, second language learning and bilingualism are still not very well integrated into psychology and psycholinguistics.[21]

The psychology of learning

The second psychological topic of special interest in connection with language teaching theory, the psychology of learning, has been a major preoccupation of psychologists from the early part of the century to the present. The interest in learning phenomena largely arose from the wish on the part of psychologists to show that the new science had practical applications. The study of learning has obvious relevance to education. The analysis of learning became a central theme of educational psychology. But second language learning did not figure prominently, if at all, in these studies.

In a wider sense, learning is also of importance to general and theoretical psychology, because the psychologist is particularly in-terested in the interplay of stability and change in man, and learning is a general concept which refers to the modifications and adaptations of organisms to their environment. As was already mentioned in Chapter 1, learning is much more broadly conceived in psychology than in common parlance. Applicable to animals as well as humans, it is understood as a process by which individuals change in a positively valued direction as a result of experience or practice and under the influence of environmental factors including teaching. It is commonly contrasted with mainly biological concepts of change such as 'growth', 'maturation', or 'development'.

Learning has been approached in two main ways: (1) through theoretical and experimental studies (see below); and (2) through empirical studies in educational settings (see pp. 308–9). The two together constitute *the psychology of learning*.

1. The theoretical and experimental study of learning
The theoretical and experimental study of learning which developed in the first half of the twentieth century produced a whole array of theories. The related experimentation was carried out mainly with animals (dogs, rats, cats, and pigeons) as experimental subjects. The landmarks in these

studies are the so-called 'theories of learning' which can be understood as systematizations (T2s and T3s) advanced by different psychologists to account for all or the most important learning phenomena as economically and comprehensively as possible. Learning theories—like linguistic theories or schools of psychology—are known by the name of the chief exponent (for example, Watson, Thorndike, Hull) or a salient conceptual feature (for example, Gestalt, connectionism).[22]

Broadly speaking two groups can be distinguished. The first, derived from the British associationist school of philosophy (Hobbes, Locke, Berkeley, and Hume), adopts a largely environmentalist view of man. Modern milestones in the development of this position are Pavlov's studies of conditioning, Watson's behaviourism, Thorndike's connectionism, and Skinner's operant conditioning. Theories in this school of thought, so-called S-R theories, as was already noted in the previous section, are characterized by emphasis on externally observable responses (R) to specific stimuli (S), an empirical and experimental approach, and the avoidance of subjective or 'mentalist' concepts. What many psychologists in this tradition have in common is that they try not to make any assumptions about what goes on inside the individual who learns. The psychology of learning, according to this viewpoint, therefore, is a study of learning phenomena which disregards the intentions, the thinking, the conscious planning, and internal processes of the learner. Hence the tendency to demonstrate the effectiveness of a learning theory by the use of animals in experiments. The learning tasks in laboratory experiments have usually been simpler than those encountered in classroom learning or in such a complex learning task as learning a language. Some representatives of this school of thought, for example, Skinner, are radical in their rejection of mentalism; they take this view not because of a lack of sensitivity but in the interest of parsimony of explanation. The 'neo-behaviourists', for example, Woodworth, Osgood, and others—a group of psychologists particularly associated with the 1954 survey of psycholinguistics (Osgood and Sebeok 1954)—are more prepared to take internal processes into account but attempt to describe them as far as possible in behavioural terms. But it was Skinner's general view of learning that exercised a profound influence on educators.

Skinner's operant conditioning and the teaching machine. In the fifties, Skinner, working in the Psychology Department of Harvard University, applied to human learning the experience he had gained from his experimental studies on pigeons. A book (Holland and Skinner 1961) and a few seminal articles (Skinner 1954, 1958, 1961) on learning, teaching, and teaching machines captured the imagination of educators. These publications also made a profound impression on language pedagogy. Skinner argued if the lowly pigeon can be trained by skilful control of the environment, how much more could human beings learn if we only arranged the learning environment in a more deliberate manner. He describes his 'animal-teaching machine' in these terms:

> '... a hungry pigeon is permitted to move about in a small enclosed space with transparent walls. On one wall is mounted a food magazine: a magnetically operated dish of grain that can be raised within reach of the pigeon when the demonstrator presses a hand switch.'

> With these laboratory devices and 'suitable experimental methods we have learned much about the way animal behavior can be shaped into intricate patterns by the use of reward or, as we prefer to call it, reinforcement.'

> (Skinner 1961:4)

The experimenter reinforces those responses of the pigeon which he decides should lead to the food reward. For example, he can train a pigeon to turn 'clockwise in a single continuous swift movement' or to peck the brighter of two spots of light.

Applying the techniques of 'shaping' and 'operant conditioning'[23] to humans, Skinner argued that it should be possible to construct a learning environment, i.e., a teaching machine which can be programmed in such a way that a student can learn more in less time and with less effort than through conventional classroom teaching. It is of course not the machine as such but the programme devised for it that constitutes the labour-saving device which would shape students' responses more efficiently than can be done in the traditional classroom. Skinner applied his principles to his own teaching. Together with Holland, Skinner developed a teaching-machine programme on behaviour, supplementing his classroom lectures. The programme was designed to help students master 'a large repertory of concepts by presenting them in an orderly sequence of small steps' (op. cit.:10). Skinner saw no reason why the same principles could not be applied to any subject, geography, history, reading, or music. Although he did not specifically concern himself with second language learning, it was easy to see that this persuasive message could be applicable there as well.

The possibility of constructing a teaching machine had been recognized before Skinner in the twenties by Pressey, an American psychologist at Ohio State University. Pressey had developed a machine that automatically *tested* achievement by presenting the learner with questions and multiple-choice responses. Pressing the button for the correct answer would move the machine to the next test item. The possibility of using this device as a *teaching* machine was clear to Pressey, but the educational world of the twenties and thirties was not as responsive to Pressey's suggestions as it was twenty years later to Skinner's.

In his own time, Skinner was not the only one to formulate ideas for teaching machines and programmed instruction. Crowder, for example, developed programmes with larger steps; he was less concerned about avoidance of errors: as an alternative to Skinner's *linear* programme, he proposed a *branching* programme which enabled learners of different abilities to advance more slowly or more rapidly.[24]

Experiments on programmed instruction in language teaching were carried out from the late fifties. However, apart from these direct applications, Skinner's treatment of learning as a sequence of stimuli and responses, reinforced by immediate confirmation of the correct response, provided a formula for language practice in the classroom and the language laboratory. It formed the basic conceptualization for the audiolingual approach in the sixties. The critique of Skinner's behaviourism, initiated by Chomsky's review article (1959) of *Verbal Behavior* (Skinner 1957), was recognized by language teaching theorists as relevant to language teaching based on Skinnerian thought, and from about the mid-sixties it led to the questioning of this approach.

Cognitive approaches to learning. The other trend of thought on learning, of which an early representative was Gestalt psychology, had for many decades—well before Chomsky's critique of behaviourism—opposed, first, associationism and later, behaviourism. It had laid emphasis on innate organizing principles (Gestalt, pattern, or configuration) in human perception, cognition, sensorimotor skills, learning, and even in social conduct. Gestalt theory does not regard repetition or practice, the mechanical 'stamping in' or Thorndike's laws of learning, or Skinner's 'shaping', as characteristic of *human* learning. For Gestalt theory it is impossible to represent human learning without concepts of subjective experience, such as the sudden click of understanding or 'insight'. Gestalt psychology was able to throw light on perceptual and cognitive learning by describing and demonstrating the subjective cognitive experiences of the learner with such concepts as 'whole and part', 'integration and differentiation', 'figure and ground', 'field', 'structure', and 'organization'.

Without necessarily subscribing to all the concepts of the Gestalt school, some psychologists have developed a cognitive theory of learning. They lay emphasis on 'meaningful learning', meaning being understood not as a behavioural response, but as 'a clearly articulated and precisely differentiated conscious experience that emerges when potentially meaningful signs, symbols, concepts, or propositions are related to and incorporated within a given individual's cognitive structure ...' (Ausubel 1967:10). Among those who adopt a 'cognitive position' there are some who reject the behaviourist position completely (for example, Ausubel) while others (for example, Bruner and Gagné) have adopted a less extreme point of view. In their view certain kinds of learning are adequately covered by a behaviourist stimulus-response theory, but conceptual learning or the learning of principles require a cognitive theory.

Bruner's persuasive presentation of a strongly cognitive approach to school learning made a powerful impact on curriculum development in the sixties, particularly in the natural sciences, social sciences, and mathematics (Bruner 1960/1977, 1966), but its relevance to language teaching was left unrecognized until very much later.[25] Gagné distinguishes several varieties of learning. In his latest interpretation (Gagné 1977), he identifies five: learning intellectual skills, concepts, and rules; learning problem solving or cognitive strategies; verbal information learning; motor skill learning, and the learning of attitudes. In his analysis of these different kinds of learning he uses behavioural (S-R) as well as cognitive concepts. Any concrete learning task, such as learning a language might, in fact, involve several or indeed all kinds of learning.[26]

2. The empirical study of learning in educational settings
Psychology has also investigated learning problems from the applied side in practical learning situations: the learning of school subjects, especially reading and mathematics; the learning problems of children with educational or emotional difficulties; questions of work training in industry; problems of rehabilitation and re-education of individuals requiring remedial treatment; and the theory and practice of 'programmed instruction'. Psychology has brought to the study of such problems, besides theories, concepts, and the results of experimental studies, a scientific approach and a general systematic knowledge of human behaviour.

In addition, a considerable number of experimental enquiries on specific learning problems have been prompted by the practical needs of study and training in educational settings, for example, transfer of learning, memorization, retention and forgetting, the spacing and methods of practice in prolonged learning tasks.

Critics have deplored the wide gap that has developed between 'classroom learning theory' and the theoretical and laboratory study of learning. Some have argued that research on teaching (Gage 1963) would serve to overcome this cleavage between learning theory and educational practice. Others have been inclined to set aside the entire discussion and all the debates about the psychology of the learning and teaching process. Others again have made the point that it was the uncritical acceptance of learning theory that has been damaging to the development of a sound and useful psychology of learning.

'We have had more than enough wild and naive extrapolation of evidence and theory from rote, motor, animal, short-term, and

stimulus-response learning. I still cling to the opinion (fundamental in cognitive theory) that psychological processes are implicated in the individual acquisition of a body of knowledge, and that it is important for teachers and curriculum-builders to understand the nature of these processes. The task ahead demands not that we dismiss the relevance of learning processes for the activities involved in transmitting and acquiring subject-matter knowledge, but rather that we formulate and test theories of learning that are relevant for the kinds of meaningful ideational learning that take place in school and similar learning environments.'
(Ausubel 1967:5)

Concepts of learning in educational psychology
The psychology of learning in the textbooks of educational psychology usually represents a broad and to some extent intuitive interpretation of learning from these two sources: the theoretical and experimental studies of learning and the applied investigations of specific learning problems. Categories of the psychology of learning, commonly applied to formal educational activities, refer to (a) characteristics of the learner and individual differences among learners (abilities, personality, attitudes, and motivation), (b) different kinds of learning, (c) the learning process, and (d) outcomes of learning.[27]

(a) Among *learner characteristics*, factors that are frequently presented in the literature include (1) the influence of age and maturity on mental development and learning; (2) the effects of heredity and environment on abilities and achievement; (3) specific aptitudes for particular learning tasks, for example, musical aptitude, manual dexterity, and of course also language learning aptitude; and (4) the influence of home and community on motivations and attitudes that impel learners to attend to learning tasks and the degree to which the learners are prepared to persevere with it.

For example, in language teaching the question of optimal language learning age has been one of the most controversial issues. It has bearing on the entire organization of language learning in educational systems. The relative importance of general intellectual abilities (intelligence) or a special language learning aptitude has also been a much debated issue. Several attempts have been made over the last thirty years, for example, by Carroll and Pimsleur, to isolate a language aptitude factor and to relate it to other learner characteristics. The influence of the initial motivation and attitudes upon success in language learning is widely acknowledged. To substantiate it several ingenious studies have been made, especially by Lambert, Gardner, and their colleagues and students, to identify characteristic motivations that contribute in a significant way to the success or failure of language learners. See Chapter 17.

(b) *What* is being learnt has been frequently expressed as three major psychological categories. *Conceptual* and *verbal learning* includes information, knowledge, ideas, concepts, and systems of thought. *Skill learning* refers to the acquisition of sensorimotor processes, for example, sewing, drawing, writing, playing a musical instrument, or acquiring a new movement combination as in tennis; habitually performed acts, such as social habits, as greeting or leave taking, shaving, using eating implements; and biologically useful techniques, such as learning how to learn, or problem solving. *Affective* and *social learning* refers to the acquisition of emotional conduct and expression, interests, social attitudes, and values.

The three categories have been used to define educational objectives. In any concrete act of learning, particularly in such complex tasks as learning school subjects or disciplines, the three categories—cognition, skill, and affect—are likely to be represented to varying degrees. This applies also to language learning.[28]

For example, in teaching pronunciation, the teacher is usually concerned with making the student learn how to produce the appropriate sound pattern, in other words, with teaching a sensorimotor skill or part of a skill. He is far less concerned with a conceptual understanding of the articulatory description of the sound. However, if the pupil is shown how a sound in the new language differs from similar sounds in the first language and the teacher introduces a phonological explanation the learning task becomes more conceptual. A skill often demands elements of conceptual knowledge, and in conceptual learning certain techniques of analysis have to be acquired which can best be described in Gagné's terms, as intellectual skills or cognitive strategies. The controversy around the audiolingual habit theory versus the cognitive code theory hinged largely on the question of whether second language learning was more effective if it was understood as conceptual or as skill learning.

In addition, an affective component is always involved in second language learning. The student approaches language learning with certain affective predispositions; the actual learning of the language is accompanied by emotional reactions, and the entire learning experience may lead to a fixed constellation of likes and dislikes directed towards the whole language in question or features of that language, languages in general, the people speaking the language, and so on.[29]

(c) In the attempt to understand the *how* of learning, the *learning process*, a number of distinctions have been introduced all of which are relevant to language learning. One is on the time-scale of learning: there may be developmental differences between the learning of infancy ('early' learning) and adult (or 'later') learning. Related to it is the distinction between 'first learning' (for example, learning the first language) and 'second learning' (for example, learning a second language), the latter involving relearning, additions to something already learnt, or 'unlearning'. Learning processes may further differ in the degree of awareness or volitional control on the part of the learner: some learning is more or less unconscious, i.e., partially or entirely out of the awareness of the learner; often also referred to as 'blind', 'latent', or 'incidental' learning. The distinction introduced by Krashen (1978) between language 'learning' and 'acquisition' refers to the degree of awareness on the part of the learner (see Chapters 15:331 and 18:391–405). Most of the learning going on in educational settings is designed to be learning with intent or deliberate learning; it is at least to some extent under the learner's volitional control. The contrast between 'rote' or 'mechanical' learning and insightful, meaningful, or cognitive learning refers to the degree of conceptual understanding of the learning task by the learner. The opposition between sudden restructuring, single trial learning, once-and-for-all learning, and gradual learning (practice, repetition, memorization, shaping, stamping-in) indicate not only different speeds of learning but also different mental processes involved. Self-directed learning (auto-instruction, discovery learning, learning by trial and error) can be distinguished from other-directed learning (learning from a teacher, receptive learning, following a model or identifying with it, learning by imitation or suggestion).

As will be seen in Chapter 18, the fiercest arguments in the interpretation of language learning have centred round the type of learning process that most adequately represents language learning and the supporting theory to account for it.

Next, the *conditions of practice* have been investigated, including such questions as: to what extent is practice helpful to learning? How much practice is needed, and how should it be arranged? What kind of practice is most effective? An important aspect of all learning is the application or transfer of learning in the classroom to real-life situations (for example, Cronbach 1977). In language teaching, the importance to be attributed to 'drill' or other forms of practice, the nature of the practice tasks, the degree of intensity of practice, the techniques which would be helpful to transfer classroom learning to genuine communication have also been among much debated issues. In discussions on second language learning far too little notice is usually taken of the treatment of the fundamental learning processes in educational psychology.

(d) Lastly, the needs of *assessing the outcome of learning* have led to the development of tests of achievement and proficiency. See Chapter 16. Techniques of measurement and evaluation, which psychometrics has contributed to educational psychology, have an obvious relevance for the assessment of language learning. The applicability of psychometrics to language testing was recognized in the early stages of educational psychology in the twenties (see Chapter 15:320–1). Since then, language testing has been an area in which the direct influence of this branch of psychology has been clearly in evidence until the present. What language testing has lacked until the sixties was an awareness that it does not only need an input from psychometrics but also from linguistics.[30]

Conclusion

Besides the psychology of language and the psychology of learning on which we have laid main emphasis in this introduction to psychological issues, other areas of psychology have direct bearing on language teaching, in particular, child psychology, social psychology, physiological psychology, even psychopathology, and clinical psychology. For example, physiological psychology which studies the physiological correlates of mental processes in the brain and nervous system, has played a part in the debate on the question of optimal age of second language learning: does the maturation of brain functioning and lateralization which occur in the early years of life have bearing on the ability to learn languages? Some language teaching theories have based themselves on insights derived from clinical psychology and group therapy. Language pathologies, ranging from stammering to the complexities of aphasia, and studied by medical psycholinguistics, can offer interesting (although neglected) parallels to second language learning in that both the individual with a language disturbance and the foreign language learner for different reasons encounter difficulties in communication. The psychological contribution is so pervasive that there is hardly an aspect of language teaching which could not be related to psychology. The descriptive study of languages, the making of pedagogical grammars, curriculum development, the expression of objectives, teaching procedures, and the organization of language teaching in educational systems—all have psychological aspects.

Like the relationship between linguistics or social science and language teaching theory, the interaction between psychology and language teaching theory is not without its problems. In general psychology, in educational psychology, and in psycholinguistics the learning of other languages has not been used very much as an example which can illustrate general issues of the psychology of language or of learning. This is in many ways surprising, because it can be argued that second language learning epitomizes some of the most interesting questions of general and educational psychology and of psycholinguistics. In the next chapter some of the more specific attempts that have been made to develop a psychology of second language acquisition or learning and of a dual language command will be examined more closely.

Notes

1 Interesting psychological introspections about language learning have been published by some psychologists (for example, Moore 1977) and language teachers (for example, Rivers 1979). See Chapter 18:400–401 for further details. Some recent research studies have also attempted to understand the retrospective insights of language learners (for example, Naiman *et al.* 1978). A combination of 'introspection' and 'retrospection' is advocated and discussed in detail and with examples by Cohen and Hosenfeld (1981). See also Chapter 18, Note 15.

2 For an international review of psychology 'around the world' see Sexton and Misiak (1976).

3 Among many works which provide an introduction to modern psychology and would give a reader a sense of the scope and ramifications (regardless of our specific interest in its relevance to language teaching) see, for example, Lindzey, Hall, and Thompson's elegantly produced and well written work (1975). For the reader a series 'Essential Psychology', consisting of thirty small volumes, would also provide useful background information, for example, Legge's introduction to the series (1975), and Greene's treatment of thinking and language (1975).

4 Psychology is 'the scientific study of behavior' (Lindzey, Hall, and Thompson 1975:4). Miller and Buckhout (1973:10) adopt the definition first offered by William James in *The Principles of Psychology*: 'Psychology is the science of mental life'.

5 For historical treatments of psychology see, for example, Boring (1929), Flugel and West (1964), Thomson (1968), or Schultz (1975).

6 For example, Darwin's observations on his own child (1877). Other examples are Preyer (1882), and Clara and William Stern's monograph on child language (1907).

7 Galton who can be regarded as the 'father' of experimental psychology in Britain described his own word association experiments in his *Inquiries into Human Faculty and its Development* (1883).

8 Freud wrote repeatedly about slips of the tongue and pen, and the dynamics of forgetting. His *Psychopathology of Everyday Life* which first appeared in 1904 was first published in an English translation in 1914.

9 Watson made behaviourism a rallying point for psychology through an article in the *Psychological Review*, 'Psychology as the Behaviorist views it' (1913). He elaborated his position, which was revolutionary, first in *Behavior: an Introduction to Comparative Psychology* (1914) and, more specifically, in his second work *Psychology from*

the Standpoint of a Behaviorist (1919). Watson was not the only psychologist at the time to advocate an objective approach to the study of psychology. For example. Bloomfield was much more influenced by another 'behaviourist', Weiss. Many other psychologists, particularly in America, considered psychology no longer as the study of 'consciousness' or 'mental life' but of 'behaviour' and instead of introspection, experimentation with animals became a widely used technique in psychological enquiries.

10 See, for example, Lenneberg (1967). Clark and Clark (1977) rightly comment on this debate in these terms: 'The strict opposition between nativism and empiricism presents the issue as if it were an all-or-none affair. In fact it is much more a matter of degree' (op. cit.:298).

11 For example, Clark and Clark (1977), which is a recent and comprehensive work on the psychology of language, does not even mention second language learning or bilingualism.

12 See Chapter 18:402–3. For a discussion of the compound—co-ordinate distinction see also Hörmann (1979:177–178).

13 Chomsky's review of *Verbal Behavior* which appeared first in *Language* has been reprinted wholly or in parts in several publications. The page references are to the reprint in Jakobovits and Miron (1967:142–71) where it appeared with a few additional comments made by Chomsky for this edition.

14 For a characteristic collection of psycholinguistic studies of around 1960 see a book of readings on psycholinguistics, collected by Saporta (1961). A well-documented 'intellectual history' of psycholinguistics, describing the ten-year period of research following the publication of the monograph by Osgood and Sebeok (1954), can be found in the 1965 edition of that monograph, published by Indiana University Press (Diebold 1965).

15 In 1960 Miller, Galanter, and Pribram (1960) were among the first to draw the attention of psychologists to the importance of transformational generative grammar for psycholinguistics.

16 Greene (1972) has described many experiments that have been made between 1960 and 1970 to find out the psychological correlates of transformational generative grammar.

17 See on this point Chapter 6:108–9 and also Chapter 15:328–9.

18 Oller's concept of an 'expectancy grammar' (Oller 1979), for example, was helpful in adapting to second language learning the direction in which psycholinguistics has moved in its study of first language use.

19 It should however be pointed out that there were other highly sophisticated enquiries into child language, for example, Piaget (1923). From the point of view of second language learning the classical studies by Leopold of early childhood bilingualism deserve

special mention (Leopold 1939, 1947, 1949, 1949a). Lewis' contribution to sociolinguistics was pointed out in Chapter 10.

20 See for example, a paper by McNeill (1966a) significantly entitled 'The Creation of Language by Children' and the discussion of that paper by Fraser and Donaldson in Lyons and Wales (1966). The case for an innate *faculté de language* and for the construct of a 'language acquisition device' was vigorously argued, around 1965–7, by Chomsky (1965:30–37), Katz (1966:246), and McNeill (1966:38–9). See also Smith and Miller (1966: Introduction) for background. For more recent less 'nativistic' points of view see, for example, Clark and Clark (1977) and McLaughlin (1978). See also Stern (1968–69).

21 For modern accounts of psycholinguistics the reader should consult Slobin (1979), Clark and Clark (1977), Taylor (1976), or Hörmann (1979).

22 For comprehensive and balanced reviews of the psychology of learning see Hilgard and Bower (1975), or Hill (1977). For widely accepted statements on learning see Gagné (1975 and 1977).

23 Definition of operant conditioning: An operant is defined as a form of behaviour in which the behaviour of the organism leads to a stimulus which presents rewards, i.e., in the case of the pigeon, a food pellet. Only the right operant is rewarded.

24 For a brief account of programmed learning with essential references see Hilgard and Bower (1975:627–30).

25 However no sustained attempt has, in fact, been made even by those whose approach to language learning was 'cognitive' to work out in any depth the application of Bruner's ideas to language teaching.

26 Ingram (1975) has interpreted second language learning in accordance with the concepts developed by Gagné.

27 For recent examples of the treatment of learning in the literature of educational psychology see Ausubel, Novak, and Hanesian (1978), Travers (1979), Cronbach (1977), Gage and Berliner (1979). These are excellent studies; they are however primarily addressed to student teachers and are described as introductions to teaching as much as to educational psychology. Little or no reference is made in them to second language learning.

28 As we shall see in Chapter 19, Bloom and his colleagues have used these three main psychological divisions as the basis for establishing a classification of educational objectives. In a modified form these objectives have been applied, first, by Valette (for example, 1971) and later by Stern *et al.* (1980) in the definition of language teaching objectives. In Chapter 22 these psychological categories have been adopted in a modified form to identify language teaching objectives.

29 As was pointed out on p. 292 above, the affective component in second language learning is not yet adequately understood. See also Chapters

15:321 and 17:375–86 for a more detailed treatment of the language learner's affective characteristics.

30 Lado (1961) was among the first to recognize that language testing has linguistic as well as psychometric aspects. Since then, language testers have been increasingly aware of changes in linguistic conceptualizations and have tried to do justice to them, for example, Oller 1979.

15 Development of a psychological perspective in language teaching: a selective review

Early associationism

It is hardly imaginable that one could teach a language without a psychological theory of the language learner and of the language learning process; and so it is not surprising to find in the writings of most language teaching theorists reflections of a psychological nature and, not infrequently, references to contemporary thought in psychology. For example, Sweet (1899/1964) interprets language learning in terms of the associationism of his time:

> 'The psychological foundation of the practical study of languages is the great law of association to which we have frequently had occasion to allude already.
>
> The whole process of learning a language is one of forming associations. When we learn our own language we associate words and sentences with thoughts, ideas, actions, events' (op. cit.:102). 'The function of grammar is ... to sum up the associations by which we all understand and speak our own language as well as any foreign languages we may learn' (op. cit.:103).

From these observations, Sweet derived a few general principles of associative learning: (1) 'Present the most frequent and necessary elements first;' (2) 'Present like and like together;' (3) 'Contrast like with unlike till all sense of effort in the transition ceases;' (4) 'Let the associations be as definite as possible;' (5) 'Let the associations be direct and concrete, not indirect and abstract;' (6) 'Avoid conflicting associations.' Sweet emphasized the need for repetition and memorization— but with economy and always on good grounds and without facile tricks. In short, in spite of the fact, then, that Sweet's main interest was directed to *linguistic* aspects of language teaching, he certainly did not neglect the psychology of the learner and of language learning.[1]

Harold Palmer, even more than Sweet, was strongly conscious of the psychological component in a language teaching theory. He, too, considered the learner factor as much as the learning process. In his analysis of the learner he weighed up the importance of age, temperament, the student's motivation and academic background, such as his previous experience in language study and his general level of schooling, and—more doubtfully—his nationality. Palmer thus arrived at a definition of language aptitude as a composite of different elements:

'... the student of even temperament, an expert penman, an artist in mimicry, an expert in the linguistic, pedagogic, and mnemonic sciences, unspoiled by previous defective study and possessing a powerful incentive, is more likely to study a foreign language with success than one who is his antithesis in every particular.'
(1917/1968:33).

In Palmer's view, the language learning process had a natural basis in man's 'spontaneous capacities for acquiring speech' (Palmer 1922/1964). Nevertheless, this had to be combined with the use of 'studial capacities', i.e., deliberate, cognitive, co-operative learning. Palmer was firmly convinced that the learning processes most appropriate for language learning are those that lead to habit formation and 'automatic', unconscious use rather than those that lead to concept formation and systematic thought. The chapter 'Habit-forming and Habit-adapting' in *The Principles of Language Study* (1922/1964) is perhaps one of the most eloquent statements of this point of view ever composed:

'Language learning,' Palmer writes, 'like all other arts as contrasted with sciences, is a habit-forming process. Proficiency in the understanding of the structure of a language is attained by treating the subject as a *science* by studying the *theory*; but proficiency in the *use* of a language can only come as a result of perfectly formed habits. No foreign word, form, or combination of these is "known" or "mastered" until we can use it automatically, until we can attach it to its meaning without conscious analysis, until we can produce it without hesitation and conscious synthesis.'
(1964:54)

He counters the possible objections to an automatic habit theory by these observations:

'The fear of monotonous and tedious memorizing work, and the realization of the length of time necessary for each act of memorizing, induces the student to invent pretexts for avoiding such work. He declares that "parrot-work" is not education, that modern educationalists condemn "learning by rote", that the age of blind repetition is over and that the age of intelligent understanding has taken its place. He will talk of the method of discovery, the factor of interest, and will even quote to us "the laws of nature" in defence of his thesis. But we know that in reality these are but so many excuses for his disinclination to form those habits which can secure him the automatism which alone will result in sound and permanent progress.'
(op. cit.:56–7)

Palmer and Redman in the second part of their joint work, *This Language-Learning Business* (1932/1969), address a fictitious letter to language learners, teachers, parents, and headmasters in order to dramatize the different perceptions among language students of their objectives and preferences in teaching methods. The fictitious 'replies' suggest varieties of purposes of language learning needs, and of views on how to learn languages. Among these different views, Palmer and Redman single out one statement as the most adequate viewpoint to which they give their full support: it describes the essentials of the language learning process as 'fusing linguistic symbols to the things symbolized', and any device that will aid in bringing about this fusion, bond, or association as quickly and economically as possible is in their view appropriate. In other words, Palmer like Sweet subscribes to an associationist psychology of second language learning.

Educational psychology enters the scene

With the development of psychology in the interwar years, and particularly with the growth of educational psychology, several studies attempted to apply the new psychology to second language teaching. During that period, the application of psychological thought and research techniques made much more rapid strides than the application of linguistic concepts. In a first critical work on the psychology of foreign language teaching, based on educational psychology, Huse (1931) viewed the task of language learning rather narrowly as 'essentially a memory problem; it is the learning for recognition or recall of a fixed list of units of expression. This task is as precise as learning the multiplication table, and might be accomplished with equal efficiency' (1931:164–5). Huse made a plea for a more experimental approach to problems of foreign language study. In his view, educational psychologists could hardly find 'a more promising field of experimentation and educational measurement' (1931:7).

The place of psychology in language teaching in Britain in the thirties can be illustrated by a remarkable article (Findlay 1932) which appeared in the then newly established *British Journal of Educational Psychology*. Findlay's article offers in effect an entire theory of second language teaching which, besides interesting psychological insights, contains linguistic as well as pedagogical observations. In his psychology Findlay recognizes more clearly than most observers of his time, and indeed of later periods, the learner's emotional resistance to abandoning the first language frame of reference and his refusal to 'grasp the foreigner's mind by entering into *his* mode of thought' (op. cit.:319). In Findlay's view, language learning is psychologically an imitative task in which the learner 'has to copy the behaviour of the native by conscious attention, practising again and again, establishing a multitude of new habits, all of them contrary to the stream of his own vernacular habits' (op. cit.:321). Findlay is not opposed to memorization because it is important for the learner to establish a 'subconscious store'; for habit is 'unconscious memory' (op. cit.:329). The new habit system, Findlay argues, is best established by grasping it 'apart from our vernacular'. He thus makes a plea for an approach to language learning which establishes a form of co-ordinate bilingualism (see Chapter 14:298): 'All the investigations, alike of psychologists and physiologists during the last half-century, confirm the view that the establishment of a separate centre of function for every new language is the immediate purpose which the learner must achieve' (op. cit.:322). In order to meet the language as a living reality, the language should not be analysed linguistically but presented alive in situations representing actual experiences in dramatic form: 'Hence for the early months I am content to let the learner enjoy the reproduction of scenes designed to give him the real thing' (op. cit.:325). The learner's first language is not excluded; for it will always assert itself. But seeking the learner's co-operation Findlay tries to lead him to accept the second language on its own terms, in the same way as he would be prepared to acquire a new games skill. Without any specific reference to Gestalt psychology, the objectives of language learning are interpreted more in its terms than in those of associationism: 'The learner ... is concerned with patterns or structures' (op. cit.:327), and the configurations to be developed are not purely linguistic but also sociocultural: 'The essential matter is to realize *our end in view*, viz, a structure which is not merely linguistic, but essential (sic) bound up with the culture, history, geography, art, pleasures, ideals of the German people; this and nothing less is what we mean by "learning German"' (loc. cit.).[2] For a relatively new journal with scientific aspirations, the *British Journal of Educational Psychology*, whose editors at that period in the development of the discipline must have been anxious to relate psychology to various areas of educational practice, Findlay's approach to a psychology of second language learning can only have been a modest beginning. While the article indicates intuitive insights into language learning, the author never makes clear what is particularly psychological rather than pedagogical; nor does he relate his personal psychologizing to current thought in psychological theory or research. It is not surprising to find that, a few years later, in the same journal another writer remarked: 'When we pass to some subjects, of which modern languages may be taken as an example, it is doubtful whether at present psychology has much to offer' (Archer 1941:133).

Nevertheless, in the interwar years several more specific applications of psychology to second language learning should be noted. In the U.S.A. the mental test movement gave the impetus to the development of several 'objective' language tests. Some of these were employed in the surveys of language achievement for the Modern Foreign Language Study (see Chapter 6:101). The first language aptitude or prognosis tests were also developed during that time.[3] In Britain an investigator (Simmins 1930) working under Spearman, the noted British psychologist, applied to foreign language teaching the technique of control group experimentation which was popular at the time in studies on 'transfer of learning'. This experiment was designed to study the mental processes involved in learning a foreign language. Simmins compared the performance of four classes in a girls' elementary school in which different approaches to learning were explored in sets of eight German lessons. In group A no explanations were given and the 'direct method' was applied. In group B care was taken to avoid errors, and grammar was explained and demonstrated. In group C teaching was like in B; but more opportunity was given for active recall and the making and correcting of errors. In group D teaching was like in C but an additional emphasis was placed on transfer, i.e., the application of what had been learnt to new settings. The last group was found to be the most effectively taught. While the experimental controls in this rather complicated study are open to question, the underlying rationale of this experiment is interesting: advancing from group A to D the learners become more actively and more cognitively involved. Simmins draws this general conclusion on psychological experiments of this kind:

> '... it is suggested that the technique of Modern Language teaching might be modified on a basis of psychological analysis and experimental investigation in such a way that a considerable saving of time and energies might be effected in the learning of languages.'
> (op. cit.:43)

In the literature of psychoanalysis and its derivatives a few writings began to appear in which second language learning was related to the life style, personality, and affective psychology of the individual, a valuable trend of thought which was somewhat lost sight of until the seventies. Thus, Brachfeld (1936) basing himself on Adlerian Individual Psychology made the valid point that 'When I learn a language ... it is not my "linguistic talent", nor my "intelligence", nor my reasoning which does the learning: it is *I* who am learning, i.e., *the entire person*' (op. cit.:82). Brachfeld recommends that the learning of the language should be associated with an 'introduction to the ideas of Individual Psychology' (loc. cit.) so that the learner is aware of the psychological relationship between language learning and the learner's 'life style'.[4] Another interesting observation made by Brachfeld, based on introspection, is that of the 'turning point' in language learning, i.e., a moment in the development of the second language in which the language 'klicks'. After having struggled haltingly, suddenly 'the miracle happens: almost overnight all this disappears; for the first time the student speaks the foreign tongue as easily and as "naturally" as his own— though perhaps not correctly. But *what matters is not correctness* in *every detail*, but above all a *feeling for the "form"* the "structure", the "spirit" of the foreign language' (op. cit.:81).[5]

In a similar vein, Stengel, a refugee psychoanalyst who had settled in England, made observations on the emotional resistances in adults learning a foreign language in a foreign country, the 'dread of appearing comic' (1939:477), the uncertainties aroused by the idiomatic use of the second language, and the similarities between language defect in pathological conditions, such as aphasia and epilepsy, and the language difficulties of foreign language learners.

The post-war years: turning to psychology for answers

A new attempt to relate British psychological thought systematically to language learning was made by Stott (1946) in a small book on language teaching in the post-war era. Rebuking Archer (1941; see p. 320 above) for his negative view on the relevance of psychology, Stott attempts to show that psychological theory is 'capable of improving practice' (1946:24). The language teaching theory he develops draws selectively on British educational psychology and rejects the purely mechanical approach, recommended by Huse (1931). Stott develops a largely cognitive and active approach: (a) the learner is encouraged to think for himself about the language; (b) he is guided to make linguistic observations; and (c) he is given the opportunity to participate actively in language games. Stott, like Findlay, accepts the need for memorization and habituation in language learning, but he derives from the psychology of learning certain principles of learning how to learn. In a tentative way, Stott also makes observations on language and thought and on first language acquisition. The role of psychology, however, remains purely supportive. It serves as a resource for the language teacher and thus provides concepts, ideas, and parallels; but no attempt is made at this stage to develop a coherent psychology of second language learning in its own right, based on the experiences of second language learners.

As in Britain language teaching in America in the forties and fifties— in spite of its link with structural linguistics— had no clear association with any one school of psychology, nor was the possibility of different choices of 'theories of language learning' a point at issue. But, as was shown in Chapter 7, American structuralism through Bloomfield had developed close ties with behaviourism. Certain behaviouristic convictions were implicit in structural linguistics and these became widely accepted psychological tenets of language teaching. As Carroll (1953) put it, the linguist 'is enough of a psychologist to realize that language is a system of well-learned habitual responses' (op. cit.:191). Without regarding this view as controversial, scholars interpreted second language learning as a process of imitation, repetition, practice, habitua-tion, or conditioning assisted by 're-inforcement' and 'generalization'. The principal techniques of conscious learning were often referred to as mimicry and memorization, mim-mem for short.

A psychological issue that began to be discussed in the fifties was the question of the optimal age for second language learning. The ability of young children to learn languages 'easily' had, from time to time, been noted in the psychological literature (for example, Tomb 1925). But in the fifties it was the view of Penfield, a neurophysiologist at McGill University in Montreal, which aroused widespread attention. Penfield, partly on the basis of his scientific work as a neurosurgeon and partly on his personal conviction, put forward the idea that the early years before puberty offered a biologically favourable stage for second language learning, and he recommended that the early years of childhood should be used more intensively for language training.[6] This viewpoint shared by a growing number of teachers, specialists, and the general public, manifested itself in the introduction of language teaching in the early years of schooling in several countries (Stern 1963/1967). The debate on this controversial issue has gone on ever since, and in spite of experimentation, some research, and endless theoretical argumentation, the issue of the optimal age has remained unresolved even thirty years after Penfield's challenge had opened up the debate. See Chapter 17.

The need for more systematic psychological research on language learning was fully recognized and clearly expressed by Carroll in the fifties: 'we are fundamentally ignorant of the psychology of language learning' (Carroll 1953:187). Carroll believed that educational psychology might provide helpful answers to pedagogy by carrying out research on specific questions of language learning, for example: 'Should sounds and meanings be presented simultaneously or successively?' 'Can meanings be mediated just as well by verbal definitions as by pictures and concrete materials?' 'How can the transfer from speaking and understanding to reading be facilitated?' 'Under what conditions does use of the native language delay or facilitate learning?' 'When do linguistic explanations facilitate learning?' 'At what rate can new materials be introduced?' (op. cit.:188–9). Following up these and similar questions, Carroll and some of his students began to investigate a few of them. One of the most notable enquiries of that time was Carroll's own attempt, in collaboration with Sapon, a professor of Spanish, to develop a new language aptitude test (Carroll and Sapon 1959). Around the same time, studies on the social psychology of language learning and bilingualism were initiated by Lambert and his students at McGill University in Montreal. From about 1960, in the context of an emerging discipline of psycholinguistics, there was a growing interest in studying second language learning from a psycho-logical perspective.[7]

In spite of this rising interest and activity in a psychology of second language learning, psychologists did not openly question, let alone repudiate, the simplistic approaches to the psychology of language learning that were current in the language teaching profession, nor did they attempt to develop a more sophisticated alternative theory. On the contrary, authorities like Lambert or Carroll seemed to suggest that a behaviouristic or neo-behaviouristic interpretation of language learning offered a sound basis for understanding second language learning.

For example, in 1962, Lambert (1963, 1963a) in a comprehensive review, addressed to foreign language teachers, of a great variety of psychological approaches to the study of language merely underlined the value of theories of conditioning as explanations of language learning without any reference to any possible critique of this point of view and of the dangers of too limited an interpretation of the language learning process. Equally, as late as 1964, Carroll offered few hints that the psychology of language learning current in second language pedagogy might be considered as oversimplified: 'In view of the large number of new habits that must be made as highly automatic as possible, successful second language learning requires a considerable investment of time, a major proportion of which must be spent in repetitive drill' (Carroll 1964:43). The only corrective suggested was that language teachers should not 'overlook the importance of conducting drill in accordance with principles of learning' (loc. cit.).[8]

The sixties: questioning psychological assumptions

In the same year, however, in an address at the Berlin Conference on Foreign Language Teaching, Carroll began to express a more critical point of view.[9] He voiced his concern that language teaching theories had not taken adequate account of the findings of the studies of verbal learning and he demanded 'a profound re-thinking of current theories of foreign language teaching in the light of contemporary advances in psychological and psycholinguistic theory' (Carroll 1966:105).

Rivers' study on psychology and language teaching
In the same year, too, for the first time in the history of the psychology of language teaching, an experienced teacher and scholar (Rivers 1964) published a critical analysis of the psychological basis underlying a language teaching theory, the audiolingual method. The first major work by Rivers was quickly recognized as an important contribution for a better understanding of the relations between psychology and language teaching. It has often mistakenly been treated as a polemic *against* audiolingualism. In fact, this was not its intention.[10] Rivers was intrigued by the claim, frequently advanced by advocates of the audiolingual method, that this method was based on psychological

theory. She examined, therefore, a number of psychological assumptions of audiolingualism in the light of some thirteen theories of learning and research findings. In doing so, she also bore in mind the criticisms of the audiolingual method made by experienced practitioners. Rivers was able to show that the findings of psychology had often been too narrowly interpreted by advocates of the audiolingual method. A more wide-ranging awareness of learning theory among practitioners, she argued, would modify the assumptions and lead to changes in the principles of audiolingualism in line with criticisms often made by classroom teachers.

One by one, Rivers went through four basic psychological assump-tions of the audiolingual method and three corollaries attached to the first of these four assumptions:

'**Assumption 1.** Foreign-language learning is basically a mechanical process of habit formation.
    Corollary 1: Habits are strengthened by reinforcement.
    Corollary 2: Foreign-language habits are formed most effectively by giving the right response, not by making mistakes.
    Corollary 3: Language is "behavior" and ... behavior can be learned only by inducing the student to "behave".

Assumption 2. Language skills are learned more effectively if items of the foreign language are presented in spoken form before written form.

Assumption 3. Analogy provides a better foundation for foreign-language learning than analysis.

Assumption 4. The meaning which the words of a language have for the native speaker can be learned only in a matrix of allusions to the culture of the people who speak that language.' (1964:vii-viii)

In her discussion of the first assumption Rivers did not question that language learning is a process of habit formation, but instead of interpreting this process in Skinnerian terms, she urged that the neo-behaviourist position of Osgood and Mowrer could be considered as more appropriate because it is less concerned with the outward behaviour of the learner than with his thoughts and feelings. The concept of reinforcement in corollary 1 was found to be widely in keeping with the learning theories examined by Rivers, but 'a mechani-cal application of some standard reinforcement which does not take into account the student's perception of the goal of foreign-language skill cannot of itself be automatically reinforcing' (op. cit.:55). The emphasis on the right response in corollary 2 was found to be in harmony with a wide range of theories of learning; but where it is interpreted too narrowly, it can lead to fixing stereotyped responses and reducing the student's ability to select among possible alternatives (op. cit.:67). Corollary 3, in which emphasis was laid on 'inducing' behaviour, in other words on the motivational and affective aspect of language learning, Rivers found ample evidence in psychological theory and research justifying this emphasis, but audiolingual practice could be said not to have taken it sufficiently into account.

Rivers found little support in psychological research for a rigid insistence on the spoken form before the written form in assumption 2. The practical implication of this observation was that the taboo on the written symbol was called into question. Nor did Rivers find much evidence in theories of learning for assumption 3, i.e., that analogy is better than analysis. Basing herself largely on Gestalt psychology and studies of cognitive learning she concluded that the withholding of explanations and the cavalier treatment of meaning and understanding by the audiolingual method were misguided. 'By developing understanding of structure through analysis and by practicing manipulation of linguistic structures by analogy, (the learner) can achieve mastery of a foreign language both at the level of formation of correct phrases and in the more demanding area of organizing the expression of complex ideas' (op. cit.:130). The fourth assumption of learning meaning in a cultural context was found by Rivers to be in line with studies in anthropological linguistics no less than with psycholinguistic research on meaning; but audiolingual theory and practice had often overemphasized linguistic form and practice through drill at the expense of the function of language in a sociocultural context: 'language communication involves a relationship between individuals and not merely the memorization and repetition of phrases and the practicing of structures' (op. cit.:163). The practical recommendations derived from Rivers' analysis were to demand that the learner's perceptions, motivations, and feelings be taken into account more than was allowed for in the psychology of orthodox audiolingualism, and that the emphasis be shifted from linguistic form to communication in a sociocultural context.

In her second major work, published in 1968, Rivers maintained this position putting forward the idea that second language learning is fundamentally a two-stage process, a lower, manipulative early stage for which a largely behaviouristic psychology of learning is adequate, and a more advanced stage of expression which demands the exercise of linguistic choice and a more conscious understanding of the linguistic resources at the disposal of the language user; at this stage a more 'cognitive' psychology of learning would be more suitable.

In the 1964 study, then, Rivers used the psychology of learning as *a resource* for discovering the views and concepts of learning psychologists and for relating these concepts and directions of thought to the current theory and practice of language pedagogy. In summary, Rivers' interpretation of the relationship between psychology and foreign language teaching suggested that (1) the audiolingual theory had indeed oversimplified the underlying psychology of second language learning to the detriment of the teaching method; and (2) a more sensitive and wide-ranging reading of the psychology of learning would yield more differentiated conceptualizations supplementing the current Skinnerian approach and would lend support to a modified, more flexible and more workable audiolingual theory. (3) No single theory of learning, however, among the thirteen Rivers had examined could by itself adequately provide the needed conceptualizations. By drawing eclectically on different theoretical formulations—particularly on the neo-behaviourism of Osgood and Mowrer and upon Gestalt psychology—a more appropriate psychological basis than that of the mainly Skinnerian approach most widely drawn upon at that time could be developed. This questioning yet optimistic view of the current psychology as a resource for a better language teaching theory, although greatly welcomed in the mid-sixties, was however not the end of the argument.

The attack on the psychology of audiolingualism

As we saw in Chapter 8 the onslaught of transformational generative grammar on linguistics had a profound effect on the view of *language* underlying audiolingualism. But its effect was even more radical on the prevalent psychology of that time and its confident assumptions about language *learning*. Chomsky (1966), in a famous and influential address at the Northeast Conference in 1966, again took up the case against behaviourism which he had first made in his review article on Skinner's *Verbal Behavior*. In this address he nonchalantly rejected the psychology of language learning prevailing among language teachers and condemned as 'not merely inadequate but probably misconceived' (op. cit.:43) widely accepted principles of association, reinforcement, Gestalt psychology, and concept formation. Chomsky thus went much further than Rivers or Carroll had done in questioning the psychological interpretations underlying language teaching.[11] Others, too, largely influenced by transformational generative grammar in linguistics, were now emboldened to reach the conclusion that merely widening the psychological bases of language teaching theory, as Rivers (1964) had proposed, was not enough. Anisfeld (1966), still rather cautiously, in a thoughtful attempt to reconcile behaviouristic psychology with the new view of language use and language acquisition (see also Chapter 8:167 ff), advanced the theory that language can be divided into two components: specific habits (for example, the acquisition of word meaning) and general rules. For the former, behaviouristic learning principles are appropriate although not sufficient; but language rules require a different, more cognitive model of information-processing which recognizes that the learner is not passively awaiting the input of sensory data to start his interpretation 'but is active in forming hypotheses as to the category membership of a particular stimulus and looks for cues to confirm or reject them' (Anisfeld 1966:117).

Several much more radical expressions of a new psychology of second language learning began to appear (for example, Jakobovits 1968, 1970; Cook 1969; Cooper 1970; Stern 1968–69, 1970). The shift of ideas that had occurred within a few years becomes evident when one compares, for example, Lambert's analysis of psychological approaches to language in 1963 (see p. 324) with a paper of similar intentions, presented five years later to ESL teachers by one of Lambert's former students, Jakobovits (1968). The Lambert paper was entirely and unquestioningly in the tradition of Skinner, Osgood, and neo-behaviourism, whereas the Jakobovits paper was based on Chomsky, Lenneberg, McNeill, and Miller. The newer theorists attempted to work out for a psychology of second language learning (1) the implications of Chomskyan notions, such as competence and performance, language as rule-governed and creative, and the distinction between deep and surface structure, as well as (2) the implications of the new view of first language acquisition. Contrasting the new and the old view Jakobovits writes about the old approach:

'The child was merely a passive organism responsive to the reinforcement conditions arranged by agencies in the environment ... The new approach ... can be characterized by saying that ... the burden of acquisition is now placed on the child with relatively minor importance attached to the environment as a *reinforcing* agency' (1970:2).[12]

The implications that he derives from his new view are summarized in this statement:

'Rules that the child discovers are more important and carry greater weight than practice. Concept attainment and hypothesis testing are more likely paradigms in language development than response strength through rote memory and repetition' (op. cit.:15).

Like Anisfeld, Jakobovits recognized that language learning involved *some* habit formation and automatization, but it was only a secondary factor in a two-factor theory. The first factor was 'the discovery of the underlying structure of the language by means of inductive and deductive inferences ...' (op. cit.:25). Both discovery and practice are to take place in a context which exposes the learner to the total range of language from the start. He should be allowed sentences and semisentences freely, whether correct or not, and given a chance to practise in situations which demand communication; and correction should take the form of 'expansion' of the kind a mother employs in helping her child to communicate.

This 'radically new psycholinguistic theory of language acquisition' (op. cit.:24) led to much polemical argumentation and sometimes an excessive condemnation of the audiolingual theory and its underlying psychology. As a result of these debates, a few theorists in the early seventies, in particular Carroll (1971) and Rivers (1972), felt impelled to redress the balance by pointing out exaggerations and superficialities in the new 'orthodoxy'. Carroll, for example, pointed out that the concept of 'habit' which Chomsky had so severely condemned 'is much more fundamental, psychologically, than the notion of rule' (Carroll 1971:103–4) to which Chomsky attributed so much importance.[13] 'What seems to have happened is that because of Chomsky's attack on a particular variety of behaviouristic psychology, and because of the unquestioning acceptance of this attack, linguists and language teachers have overgeneralized his conclusions to all of psychology and its concepts' (op. cit.:105).

In review, the psycholinguistic studies of the period 1964–1970 had heightened the psychological awareness of language teaching theorists—a welcome result. But at the same time they contributed to intellectual conflict and a sense of disorientation. The old problem of language teaching theory of operating with rather simplistic psychological concepts had not altogether been banished by the influx of new ideas. Reading some studies of the late sixties one cannot help feeling that the dogmatism of a new school of thought had merely replaced the dogmatism of an older one.

The seventies: fresh theorizing and empirical research

In the early seventies a further radical change took place. The disillusionment with the inconclusive debate on language teaching method and the acrimonious arguments about psychological theories of language learning gradually led a number of researchers in different centres in North America and Europe to the conviction that what was needed was to study second language learning directly and empirically and not simply to extrapolate from first language acquisition or from general learning theory. In 1972 Rivers, for example, pointed to 'the need for us as teachers to know as much as we possibly can about the way the student learns and learns language' (op. cit.:73), and the present writer in the same context advised that language teachers 'should press for such sorely needed direct research on the psychology of second language learning' (Stern 1972:xi)

Second language learning as a psychological research problem was 'discovered' almost with suddenness by several applied linguists and psycholinguists as an important and uncharted area of investigation and the upsurge of research and theorizing between 1972 and 1978 or thereabouts on the psychology of second language learning was astonishing to anyone who had been aware of the lack of second language learning research in the preceding decades.

Many of the North American investigators who had begun to work on the psycholinguistic problems of second language learning met regularly for some years at the annual TESOL convention and at other meetings in Boston, Los Angeles, and Ann Arbor; and a fruitful collaboration evolved among many scholars including also a number of European scholars in Britain, Germany, the Netherlands, and Scandinavia.

An early stock-taking took place at a meeting of applied linguists held at the University of Michigan in 1975. The papers of this meeting on language learning research, which were published in a special issue of *Language Learning* (Brown 1976), dealt with many of the questions that preoccupied the researchers throughout the decade: the nature of the language learning process, the lawfulness of this process, the concept of 'interlanguage', the relationship of first to second language learning, and so on. A series of nineteen *Working Papers on Bilingualism*, initiated by Swain of the OISE Modern Language Centre, Toronto, in 1973, provided a forum for new research on second language learning during the seventies (Swain and Harley 1979). *TESOL Quarterly* and the annual proceedings of the TESOL convention (for example, Burt and Dulay 1975) gave expression to the growing interest of the TESOL Association in the psycholinguistic study of language learning. *Language Learning*, among established journals, and several new reviews have reflected the increasing interest and research activity in the area of second language acquisition, interlanguage studies, and bilingualism. [14].

Among the many theories and new concepts that were discussed during this fertile period of enquiry, a few outstanding ones should be mentioned at this point in this chronological review. The first of these is the concept of *interlanguage* which was already mentioned in our discussion of language varieties (see Chapter 7:125). It will be referred to again as one of the ways of looking at language learning processes and outcomes (see Chapters 16 and 17). Here it is mentioned as one of several new concepts which captured the imagination of researchers and gave direction to a more specific line of fruitful enquiry on second language learning. It has given rise to a whole spate of 'interlanguage studies' and a journal of its own.[15]

Another group of studies which began in the early seventies was preoccupied with the nature of the second language learning process. Several American investigators, in particular the team of Dulay and Burt, challenged the widespread conception of contrastive linguistics, i.e., that the differences between the first language and the second language are the main cause of the difficulties in second language learning. Rejecting the interference or transfer hypothesis, these investigators attempted to show that second language learning, like first language acquisition, is a lawful and creative process. The steps and sequences in second language learning, they claimed, are universal and have the same regularities that one can find in first language acquisition. This 'creative construction hypothesis' gave rise to a great deal of thought, discussion, and research on basic issues: Is second language learning like first language learning? Are there 'innate mechanisms' (Dulay and Burt 1977:97) that operate in second language learning as much as in the first language? Is this a universal process which is independent of the language of origin? What are these lawful sequences of language learning?[16]

A theory that also aroused widespread interest during the seventies was formulated by Krashen: the so-called Monitor Model. Krashen distinguished between conscious processes of language *learning* and the less conscious but equally or even more important processes of language *acquisition*, a distinction briefly mentioned in Chapters 1:20 and 14:311. Krashen postulated a Monitor as a construct to refer to the editing and controlling function that can be exercised during the study of a language or when writing or reading. Through his research and writings on learning, acquisition, and the Monitor Model, Krashen has drawn attention to a perennial problem of language learning, i.e., to what extent language learning is subject to conscious control or whether more intuitive, less deliberate ways of learning are more effective.[17]

Another fruitful line of enquiry was prompted by the researches of Schumann who drew attention to affective and sociocultural problems in second language learning. Schumann, as was pointed out in Chapter 11:238 (see also Chapter 13:277), tried to find explanations for the failure of many immigrants to learn the language of the host country, for example, many Spanish speakers who live in the U.S.A. and have difficulty in learning English. Schumann recognized that a number of different factors, such as personality, aptitude, cognitive factors, and so on, enter into language learning. But by far the most important in accounting for differences in language proficiency were, in his view, certain sociocultural and affective factors. A key concept in Schumann's interpretation of second language learning is 'acculturation'. By acculturation he means 'the social and psychological integration of the learner with the target language (...) group' (Schumann 1978:29). Among *social* factors, he lays particular emphasis on how the learner group relates to the target language group, and, among *psychological* factors, he attributes importance to the affective reaction of the learner to the language and culture of the target language group. Schumann does not claim that acculturation plays the same role in foreign as in second language learning. But in second language learning, for example, by immigrants, he regards the acculturation component as much more crucial than the effect of any teaching.[18]

Several books which appeared in the period from about 1973 to 1979 represent a visible record of the developing thought and research trends. They indicate that the focus was now clearly on the learner (for example, Oller and Richards 1973), and that research was vitally concerned with the entire *psychology* of second language acquisition and of foreign language learning (for example, Gingras 1978; Hatch 1978; McLaughlin 1978; Naiman *et al.* 1978; and Richards 1978); or with certain specific aspects, such as error analysis (Richards 1974; Corder 1981).[19]

In retrospect, the seventies can be recognized as a period in which serious and sustained attempts were made by several psycholinguists and applied linguists to study directly through theoretical debate and by methods of empirical enquiry the psycholinguistics of second language learning and bilingual proficiency, to construct theoretical models, to establish areas of research, to identify essential concepts and, in a general way, through these varied approaches to advance our knowledge of the psychology of the language learner and of language learning, and thus no longer simply to rely on psychologists in other fields to tell teachers how to understand language learning. This interest in the psychology of second language learning has continued in the eighties, although there are only few centres in the world where this particular area of enquiry is today pursued systematically and consistently.

Conclusion: The role of psychology in language teaching theory

Language teaching theory has been in contact with psychology, and more recently with psycholinguistics, for a sufficiently long period of years to draw certain conclusions from this experience. Like linguistics and social science, psychology and psycholinguistics are growing fields of study; and it would be misguided to approach them in the expectation of being able to read off, once and for all, a definitive theory of second language learning.

The general function of psychology in language teaching theory is no longer in doubt, and a broad demarcation from linguistics and sociolinguistics can be indicated. While linguistics and sociolinguistics are concerned with language or language in society in general and scientific approaches to particular languages and speech communities, psychology directs our attention to the individual person (1) as a language user, and (2) as a language learner. Since language teaching is concerned with the acquisition by individuals of a dual language command, its theory is bound to operate with psychological concepts of language use and language learning, and psychological thinking on these topics forms an essential part of any language teaching theory.

Until recently, the relationship between second language pedagogy and psychology was viewed almost exclusively in terms of receiving and applying information, gaining direction from studies carried out in other though related circumstances, and extrapolating findings to second language learning and teaching. However, the task is never one of simple application alone, and more recently the need for direct psychological studies of second language learning has been recognized. As a result a more reciprocal relationship between psychology and language pedagogy has developed.

This implies that in the future one will of course continue what had already been begun many years ago, i.e., to scan the field of psychology and psycholinguistics so as to be cognizant of theories, concepts, studies, and research findings that appear relevant, extrapolate from them, and work out their implications for language teaching theory. The other approach, which has been initiated over the last decade, is to develop a more specific psychology of second language learning: that is, to make direct empirical and experimental studies on second language learning, language teaching, the use of second languages, and bilingual language behaviour generally. These two approaches are never entirely distinct and they support each other: in order to scan the field of psychology in search of relevant information, one must be aware of the psychological questions presented by language learning, and in order to make direct studies of second language learning one must know beforehand which questions to ask that are psychological in character and which concepts and research approaches to employ that are appropriate for a specifically psychological study.

While the few years of research and theorizing have not yet provided us with definitive answers to all the puzzles of second language learning, they have given us a more differentiated understanding of the issues and have encouraged a less dogmatic approach to questions of language learning. In the following three chapters we will review some of the current questions, findings, and interpretations, and consider what the knowledge and viewpoints that have been accumulated contribute to a theory of language teaching.

Notes

1 These points are developed by Sweet in Chapter 10 of *The Practical Study of Languages* (1899/1964). Gouin, too, had a psychological theory. His main wish was to base his language teaching theory on the natural processes of first language learning (Gouin 1880/1892).

2 Findlay thus intuitively anticipates the co-ordinate bilingualism described by Ervin and Osgood (1954) and strongly advocated by Brooks (1960/1964). See Chapter 14:298. He also foreshadows some currently popular ideas of communicative teaching and communicative competence.

3 Objective achievement tests in languages, based on the new-type mental group tests, which became more widely known in the

twenties, were prepared by Henmon (1929); foreign language prognosis tests were developed by Luria and Orleans (1928) and by Symonds (1930). While objective foreign language tests did not become widespread, the objective multiple-choice format and several concepts of psychological testing, such as the concepts of validity and reliability, began to become known among language teachers and examiners and to influence their approach to language testing and examining.

4 These ideas of helping a learner to gain insight into the emotional difficulties of language learning and to understand the attitude to languages as part of one's personality have only rarely been pursued. One example is an article by Nida (1957); another—twenty years later— is the study by Naiman *et al.* (1978). See also Brown 1980: Chapter 6.

5 In my view, the experience, described by Brachfeld as the 'turning point', has been insufficiently noted and studied. See Chapter 18:400.

6 Penfield first expressed these views in 1953 in a paper addressed to the *American Academy of Arts and Sciences* and forcefully reiterated this point of view in the final chapter of a work on speech and brain mechanisms of which he was co-author (Penfield and Roberts 1959); see also Penfield (1965). He argued that use should be made of the 'plasticity' of the young brain for its educational development.

7 For example, in 1959 a conference on 'Psychological Experiments Related to Second Language Learning', held at the University of California in Los Angeles, brought together some eminent teachers, psychologists, and linguists. Their intention was to define their common interests and to discuss needed research in the psychology of second language learning (Pimsleur 1960). The famous Scherer-Wertheimer study (1964; see Chapters 4:56 and 6:106), which was begun soon after the UCLA meeting, was first discussed at that meeting as an example of one type of study that was needed. See also Lambert (1963, 1963a) whose review of psychological approaches to the study of language interprets aspects of second language learning in psychological terms.

8 It is curious to observe that authorities like Carroll (1964) or Lambert (1963,1963a), four or five years after Chomsky's attack on Skinner, did not seem to be concerned about the implications of Chomsky's critique for the psychology of language learning. For example, Carroll (1964) gives a detailed account of Skinner's view of language, but makes no reference to Chomsky's view of Skinner.

9 For a reference to the Berlin Conference 1964, and Carroll's important address, see Chapter 6:107. Carroll's paper which was delivered on September 5, 1964, was published in the Conference proceedings (Müller 1965:365–81). It also appeared in the *Modern*

Language Journal (Carroll 1965) and in *Trends in Language Teaching* (Valdman 1966:93–106).

10 In her second book (see also p. 326–7 below) Rivers (1968) gave prominence to the audiolingual method while setting out its weaknesses as well as its strengths. For a more recent expression of Rivers' views on teaching methodology see Rivers 1981: Chapter 2.

11 Chomsky's challenging address at the Northeast Conference, was already mentioned in Chapter 6:108 and 7:144–6. He was taken to task in a conference response by Twaddell for his 'dogmatic vehemence' in rejecting the notion of habit. Chomsky's paper appears in the conference report (Mead 1966:43–9). It has also been reprinted with an explanatory comment in *Chomsky: Selected Readings* edited by Allen and van Buren (1971:152-159). For a brief discussion of the Chomsky paper see also Stern (1970:62).

12 Jakobovits first presented the new view of language acquisition and its implications for second language teaching at the TESOL convention in San Antonio, Texas, in March 1968. It was published in *Language Learning* and, later, became Chapter 1 of his book on *Foreign Language Learning*, published in 1970. The quotations are taken from the book.

13 Carroll (1971) has rightly pointed out that what in linguistics legitimately appears as a 'rule' of language can in psychological terms equally legitimately be described as a 'habit'; there is no 'basic opposition between conceiving of language behaviour as resulting from the operation of "habits" and conceiving of it as "rule-governed"' (op. cit.:103). See on this point also Chapter 2, Note 4 above.

14 For example, *SLANT (Second Language Acquisition Notes and Topics*, published by the English Department of the San Francisco State University, California, U.S.A.), *Workpapers in TESL* (University of California at Los Angeles, U.S.A.), *Interlanguage Studies Bulletin* (University of Utrecht, Netherlands), *Studies in Second Language Acquisition* (Indiana University, Bloomington, U.S.A.). Three new journals started in Britain in 1980, indicate the ongoing interest and research activity in this and related areas: *Applied Linguistics* (Oxford University Press, Oxford, U.K.), *Applied Psycholinguistics* (Cambridge University Press, Cambridge, U.K.), *The Journal of Multilingual and Multicultural Development* (Tieto Ltd., Clevedon, U.K.).

15 The earlier work is well represented in Richards (1974) which contains the two 'classical' papers by Corder (1967) and Selinker (1972). For continuing work on 'interlanguage' see, for example, Selinker, Swain, and Dumas (1975); Tarone, Frauenfelder and Selinker (1976), Hatch (1978), Richards (1978), Tarone (1979), and

Corder (1981). See Bausch and Kasper (1979) for an excellent overview. See also Chapters 16:354–5 and 18:399.

16 For a concise and well-documented summary and analysis of the 'Identity hypothesis' (i.e., L2=L1) see Bausch and Kasper (1979). Dulay and Burt, the main protagonists of this viewpoint, have supported their view with a number of studies (for example, Dulay and Burt 1974, 1975, 1976, 1977). Corder's suggestion of a 'built-in' syllabus and of language learning as an active cognitive process went in a similar direction (Corder 1967). The identity thesis has been challenged, for example, by Kennedy and Holmes (1976).

17 The Monitor Model has been developed over a number of years from about 1975 (for example, Krashen and Seliger 1975, Krashen 1978). A full account of this theory with references to earlier studies and related work by other writers, can be found in Krashen (1981). For a further discussion of Krashen's views, see Chapter 18:391–3, 403–4 below.

18 Schumann's theories have been developed in articles which have appeared between 1975 and 1978. See in particular Schumann (1975, 1976, 1976a) and a detailed treatment of the acculturation model in Schumann (1978). Schumann's views have been already briefly referred to in Chapter 11:238.

19 In spite of all the research on second language learning, relatively little has as yet been written for the general reader which could be described as a 'psychology of foreign language teaching'. After Rivers' work on the psychologist and the foreign language teacher (Rivers 1964), the most prominent psychological study has undoubtedly been Jakobovits (1970). Apart from articles in books, such as Ingram (1975), Carroll (1974), and Stern and Cummins (1981), and a few collections of papers, such as Pimsleur and Quinn (1971), Oller and Richards (1973), and Richards (1974, 1978), only Brown's book on language teaching and learning (Brown 1980) can be cited as one which is written from a mainly psychological perspective, and, finally, a work specifically written as a psychology of foreign language teaching by McDonough (1981).

16 Models of second language learning and the concept of proficiency

Our goal in this chapter and the next two will be to obtain sufficient background and an overview on the psychology of the second language learner and the learning process so that our language teaching theory includes the necessary psychological perspective. This is therefore not intended to be a comprehensive study of second language learning which would require more detailed treatment than we need give here for our purposes.

To begin with, once more, the reminder that on most of the issues our present knowledge cannot be regarded as definitive. This means that practitioners who seek to be guided by research evidence must be prepared, in spite of all the research that has been done, to accept an element of caution and uncertainty. They will often find themselves in a position where decisions involving some sort of psychological judgements have to be made in the classroom or in school systems in the face of the fact that the theories we operate with are provisional and the research evidence is sometimes inconclusive, questionable, or altogether lacking.[1]

1 Models of second language learning

A synthesis

A useful result of the many recent studies on second language learners and learning has been that several researchers have proposed 'models' of second language learning which, in terms of this book, are T1s (see Chapter 2), i.e., they provide a framework or map of essential factors to be taken into account in interpreting second language learning. These models are helpful to our enquiry because they establish the kind of overview we need. They identify factors or variables believed to be essential, and they suggest ways in which the sets of different variables are likely to interact.

Without going into differences between various models which have been proposed we can consider the diagram in Figure 16.1 as an uncontroversial synthesis representing the consensus among different investigators on the main factors that play a role in language learning.[2]

In this diagram five sets of variables have been distinguished. Three of these—(1) social context, (2) learner characteristics, and (3) learning conditions— are represented as determiners of (4) the learning process and, through it, of (5) the learning outcome. The basic questions are: Why are certain groups of learners or certain individual learners successful while others are not? What factors in the model or combination of factors contribute to the success of some or the failure of others?

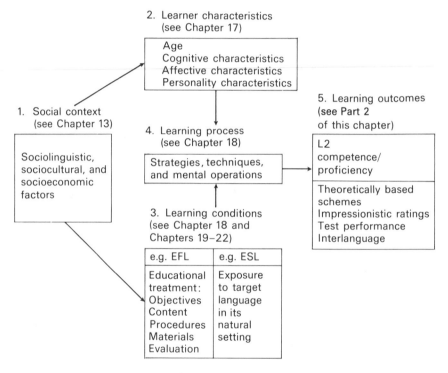

Figure 16.1   Framework for examination of second language learning

Differences of viewpoint among practitioners, theorists, and researchers have arisen from the fact that varying degrees of importance have been attributed to the various factors. The essential research problem has been to identify crucial factors and to trace their interaction. But empirical research in studying language learning has come up against a number of obstacles. The constructs used, such as 'proficiency', 'motivation', 'aptitude', 'language learning context', are ambiguous. They are difficult to describe or measure. The learning process itself is elusive, and the relationship among different factors, for example, aptitude and motivation, or the specific contribution of individual characteristics, the social context, and the effect of teaching, is hard to isolate.

Let us now look more closely at this model of language learning. If we want to understand the influence of *learner characteristics* (box 2 in Figure 16.1) on learning and learning outcomes, it seems reasonable not to restrict our field of vision *a priori*. A great number of learner variables have in fact been considered and at the present state of knowledge none can be regarded as irrelevant to language learning: age and sex; cognitive variables (for example, general learning abilities, language learning aptitude, previous language learning experience, cognitive learning styles); affective factors (attitudes and motivation); and personality (see Chapter 17).

The *learning process* (box 4 in Figure 16.1) can be looked upon as consisting overtly of strategies and techniques employed by the learner and, covertly, of conscious and unconscious mental operations. The problem is and has been how best to study them. A first approach would be one which openly examines the actual language learning behaviour: what do learners do to learn a language in the classroom or in a free learning situation? Another approach might be to tap the insights of the learners themselves and to inquire into their objectives, strategies, and techniques, their thoughts and feelings about language learning as well as steps and stages perceived by them as necessary to master the language (see Chapter 14, Note 1). Another approach might be to make experimental, observational, or introspective studies of cognitive processes involved in language learning, such as: attending, discriminating, imitating, memorizing, rehearsing, probing, matching, guessing, comparing, inferring, forming hypotheses, generalizing, verifying, and planning. It would also be valuable to explore by observation, experiment, or introspection the motivational and affective concomitants of the learning process, for example, persistence, elation, frustration, resistance, humour, and so on. Any of these suggested approaches can be repeated over a period of time in order to obtain a longitudinal account of language learning development. It should further be possible to compare different learners in the same situations or groups of learners in different situations in order to discover individual or group differences among learners in response to variations in the learning conditions. At present, we are still at the beginning of the direct study of second language learning behaviour. The approach that up to now has most commonly been applied to the study of learning processes has been referred to as the study of products, using the outcome of learning as a source of inference about the learning process (see Chapter 18).

In considering *learning conditions* a basic distinction to be made, as is indicated by box 3 in Figure 16.1, is whether the second language is learnt through exposure to the target language in a supportive language environment in which the second language is used and is, therefore, 'second language learning' in the specific sense, for example, TESL, or whether it is learnt in a language class in a non-supportive language environment and is 'foreign language learning' in the specific sense, for example, TEFL (see Chapter 1:15–17). If the second language is learnt in a supportive environment, the language class is likely to be only one among several language influences on the learner, the others coming from exposure to the target language in its natural setting. The millions of migrant workers in Europe, for example, the Turkish, Spanish, or Italian *Gastarbeiter* in Germany, frequently acquire their Pidgin German entirely through exposure to the language in the natural environment and have no formal instruction whatever (Heidelberger Forschungsprojekt 1979). But if the second language is learnt as a foreign language in a language class in a non-supportive environment, instruction is likely to be the major or even the only source of target language input. This difference in the conditions of learning a second language has led to the distinction between 'guided' ('directed') or 'unguided' ('undirected', 'natural') learning, a distinction which has been very important in the study of the learning process (see Chapter 18).

According to the model, the learning conditions and learner characteristics are influenced by the *social context* (box 1). This set of factors has already been analysed in Chapter 13 primarily as a question of sociological and sociolinguistic enquiry. In the present chapter we are more concerned with the perception of the social context by the learner than with the analysis of the social context itself. How is the social context experienced and interpreted by the individual learner? What influence has the social context on the learner's attitudes and motivations, and to what extent do they in turn affect language learning and the conditions of learning?

Learning outcomes (box 5). If the ultimate objective of language teaching is effective language learning, then our main concern must be the learning outcome. Everyone interested in second language learning, often after years of study or residence in the second language environment, faces the problem of inadequate knowledge and frequent failure. Success in second language learning is not the rule. Moreover, failure can be accompanied by a sense of isolation or alienation, by dissatisfaction, and an awareness of one's own inadequacy, and sometimes leads to resentment directed against teachers or the school system. These feelings may spill over into negative attitudes to the second language and its speakers and language learning generally.

Teaching and learning aim at what Figure 16.1 calls 'competence' or 'proficiency'. The definition and assessment of proficiency have presented problems shared by practitioners and researchers. Yet, any empirical research demands that the concept of proficiency must be clearly understood. Variations in second language learning outcome have been conceptualized in a variety of ways, ranging from conceptual schemes of proficiency through impressionistic ratings of proficiency and descriptions of different mastery levels to performance on tests and the analysis of interlanguage patterns.

Without being able to deal with all the components of the model in detail we will in Part 2 of this chapter and the next two chapters focus on a few aspects in the second language learning model.

2   Proficiency

Introduction

Beginning at the extreme right-hand end of Figure 16.1 we first consider proficiency as the learning outcome in which teachers, administrators, curriculum developers, test constructors, researchers, parents and, of course, students themselves are all equally interested. Proficiency can be looked at as a *goal* and thus be defined in terms of objectives or standards. These can then serve as criteria by which to assess proficiency as an empirical *fact*, that is the actual performance of given individual learners or groups of learners. Once proficiency has been established it can be related to the other variables in the model: context, learner characteristics, learning conditions, and learning process. The conceptualization and description of proficiency is therefore an important step in the study of second language learning.

Native-like proficiency

Among different learners at different stages of learning second language competence or proficiency ranges from zero to native-like proficiency. The zero is not absolute because the second language learner as speaker of at least one other language, his first language, knows language and how it functions. Complete competence, whatever its definition, is hardly ever reached by second language learners, and it is widely acknowledged among practitioners and theorists that in most cases it would be wasteful and perhaps even undesirable to attempt to reach it. Nevertheless, it forms an ideal goal to keep in mind. The native speaker's 'competence', 'proficiency', or 'knowledge of the language' is a necessary point of reference for the second language proficiency concept used in language teaching theory.

What has the native speaker in the first language that the second language learner lacks and wants to develop? The answer to this question is based on the totality of linguistic, sociolinguistic, and psycholinguistic studies we have considered in previous chapters. The notion of the native speaker's competence, introduced by Chomsky and later reinterpreted by Hymes and other sociolinguists, has been helpful in dealing with this question. As Chomsky has expressed it, competence is 'the intrinsic tacit knowledge ... that underlies actual performance'. (Chomsky 1965:140). But the concept of linguistic competence, was criticized for its exclusive attention to purely formal linguistic elements. Discourse analysis and sociolinguistics have added an essential pragmatic and sociocultural dimension by pointing out that what the native speaker has is not merely *linguistic* competence, but sociolinguistic *communicative* competence in the sense developed already in earlier chapters (see particularly Chapter 11:229–30 and Note 6).

The components of linguistic and communicative competence that must somehow be represented in the psychology of the language user are no longer in question; they include the phonology, lexis, syntax, semantics, as well as sociocultural, discourse, and situational features. But it is the relative importance of the different aspects and the interaction between them as *psychological processes* which psycholinguistics over the past twenty years has begun to explore (for example, Clark and Clark 1977).

The following sketch picks out from among the features which characterize what it means 'to know a language' a few of those characteristics which appear to be of particular significance for a theory of second language teaching. What recent interpretations show is that the older view of conceptualizing language knowledge or proficiency merely as a 'habit structure' or as a 'bundle of skills' reduces the complexity of proficiency too drastically.[3]

1 *The language user knows the rules governing his native language and he can 'apply' them without paying attention to them.* As native speakers we can distinguish typical, right, well-formed, or grammatical forms or utterances from atypical, wrong, ill-formed, deviant, or ungrammatical ones. We have *Sprachgefühl*, a sense for right and wrong use in the first language. As native speakers we possess norms of language against which we can judge utterances which we hear or produce. We can interpret (make sense of) deviant utterances as if they were well-formed. For example, in a telephone message, in spite of 'noise' on the line, we can often still make out the message. If a foreigner or a child produces an utterance with grammatical errors or mispronunciations we can reformulate it as if it were well-formed.

  Knowledge of the rules in this sense is an intuitive grasp; it does not mean knowing *about* the language, i.e., having a conceptual metalingual understanding of the language as a system of rules and relationships. In the area of language this intuitive first language knowledge is analogous to 'frame of reference' or 'norm' in the study of human perception and social behaviour. It provides the native speaker with a communicative constant or permanent system of orientation. In normal living it is taken for granted. The first language speaker does not ordinarily reflect on it; the knowledge remains implicit. But under certain circumstances it can be made explicit, for example, in case of breakdown of communication, in misunderstandings, also in communicative pathologies, or in the search for an expression of the kind that sometimes occurs in the 'tip-of-the-tongue' phenomenon. Although the unsophisticated native speaker does not possess (or need) concepts about his first language he is capable of singling out phonological, grammatical, or lexical features which demand special attention. Thus, he may comment on a foreign accent; and even a small child can spot and correct a grammatical deviation or a wrong word order. In a joke the native speaker can detect a lexical, semantic, syntactical or phonological absurdity or ambiguity.

This mastery of the forms of a language which is intuitive and yet can be made conscious under certain circumstances is a characteristic of first language proficiency, which second language learners in the early stages of a second language lack entirely and acquire only gradually as they progress.

2 *The native speaker has an intuitive grasp of the linguistic, cognitive, affective, and sociocultural meanings expressed by language forms.* As native speakers we can relate different sentence patterns to their underlying meanings. We can understand the semantic equivalence of two (or more) different sentences. In other words, we can keep an underlying meaning constant while changing the surface sentence structure. We can understand lexical or syntactical ambiguities such as are met in jokes or puns. We can assign two different underlying meanings to the same (or similar) surface structures.

The fusion of form and meaning which is self-evident in the first language, is lacking in a new language. Second language forms, to begin with, are meaningless to the second language learner and appear at first arbitrary and sometimes even unnatural and peculiar.

3 The aspects (1) and (2) can jointly be referred to as *linguistic competence*, i.e., competence with reference to mainly formal and semantic features of the language in question.

4 *The native speaker spontaneously uses language for the purpose of communication and has an intuitive understanding of the sociolinguistic functions of a language in use.*[4] Consider the various uses of language in communication: greeting, leave-taking, small talk, en-

quiring, teaching, learning, letter writing, reading poetry, following instructions, promising, persuading, betting, requesting, praying, commanding, joking, declaring, arguing, swearing, making excuses, and apologizing— these different language functions are second nature in the first language, but in a new language either an impossibility or an enviable art. In our first language we also spontaneously know which use of language, 'register' or style, etc., is appropriate or is incongruous in given social circumstances. Moreover, we can recognize (and often employ) more than one variety of the language, for example, a social or regional dialect. We can identify a speaker of our own dialect and mark him off against speakers of other social or geographical dialects. In a second language these sociolinguistic and stylistic varieties are most difficult to acquire and sometimes are never learnt by the second language learner. Like the linguistic component the communicative component of first language proficiency is implicit knowledge, but, again, in certain circumstances, it can be made explicit. This intuitive knowledge of social, functional, and contextual features is, after Hymes, referred to as *communicative competence*.[5]

5 *Linguistic and communicative competence manifests itself in language behaviour receptively and productively* in listening and talking, and, in literate societies, after training, also in reading and writing.

6 *The native speaker uses the first language 'creatively'*. That is to say, competence is active and dynamic, not mechanical or static. As users we do not merely possess a set repertoire of phrases and sentences. We have such a repertoire but we can—as Chomsky has repeatedly pointed out—make an infinite number of new sentences which conform to the first language and understand utterances as belonging to the first language although we have never heard them before. We can also make up new words or expressions which, though novel, still conform to the rules of the first language.[6]

Creativity, further, means that as language users we do not simply conform to an existing system, but we actively impose order and regularity on language data with which we are confronted and thus 'create' our own language system. The concept of creativity, then, can be applied to both the productive use of the system of existing rules and the creation of new rules.

In the light of this creative aspect of competence, language teaching theory has been criticized for treating second language learning too narrowly as a purely receptive process and missing this productive, active, 'creative', aspect in second language acquisition. Whether we like it or not, as second language learners we make up our own rules, impose our interpretations on the second language, and cope with communicative functions of the second language as best we can on the basis of our experiences as first language users and our imperfect knowledge of the second language.[7] See also (10) below.

7 *A child also has linguistic and communicative competence*, i.e., a system of formal and social rules which can be applied creatively and more or less unconsciously. As language development takes place the child advances from a simple and relatively undifferentiated competence level through stages of ever increasing differentiation to one in which his language use approximates and finally reaches that of the adult environment in which he lives. The study of language acquisition describes and explains the development of linguistic and communicative competence in the first language.

8 While it is a universal characteristic of being a native speaker to have linguistic and communicative competence, *different first language users are likely to have competence to a different degree.* Thus all first language speakers can use the first language 'creatively', but there are differences in the degree of creativity to which individuals make use of the linguistic potential at their disposal. Likewise, while all native speakers possess communicative competence in their first language they differ in degrees of sociolinguistic sensitivity. Moreover, in their communicative 'performance' they will at times use the language inappropriately and commit a 'faux pas' or 'drop bricks'.

9 In order to use language as described in (1) to (8) *we postulate in the native speaker an 'internal system'*, 'mechanism', 'structure', 'network', or 'schema', the first language competence or proficiency, which processes language items in such a way that the individual is able to convey meaning through utterances or to assign meaning to utterances received.

We can visualize second language competence or proficiency, likewise, as an internal system, structure, network, or schema which, to begin with, is relatively fluid, simple, unstructured, and inefficient. In the course of the learning process it becomes more structured, more differentiated, more complex and more efficient.

Should second language competence be conceived as psychologically distinct from first language competence, or should we think of language competence as unitary, manifesting itself in first and second language? In raising this question, we revive the distinction made in the fifties between co-ordinate and compound bilingualism (see Chapter 14:298). The writer favours a view which suggests that all languages have much in common and many shared meanings. However, certain parts of different languages are not shared. Proficiency in two languages can perhaps best be represented as what Cummins (1980a) has aptly called the 'dual-iceberg' phenomenon which shows underlying common as well as language-specific elements (Figure 16.2).

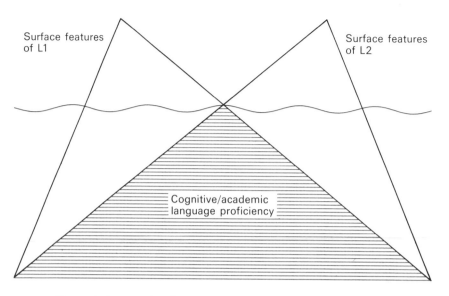

Figure 16.2 *'Dual-Iceberg' representation of bilingual proficiency*

10 *Each individual has his own competence*, i.e., his internalized system of the first language with features which he mostly shares with other first language users, but with certain more or less individual characteristics which are specific to the individual. Likewise, second language competence is, hopefully, shared with target-language first-language users, but at the same time it is likely to have certain characteristics shared with other second language learners, and others again that are specific to the individual. *Interlanguage studies*, which were initiated in the seventies, are in effect attempts to understand the characteristics of the proficiency of language learners.

11 Lastly, *the concept of competence (or proficiency) as interpreted in (1) to (10) is a construct* which is accessible only through inference from the language behaviour of the individual, his 'performance' in listening, speaking, reading, or writing. As we shall see subsequently, many different attempts have been made to capture the essentials of second language competence in a variety of ways.

In review, knowing a language, competence, or proficiency in the first or second language can be summarized as:

1 the intuitive mastery of the *forms* of the language,
2 the intuitive mastery of the linguistic, cognitive, affective and sociocultural *meanings*, expressed by the language forms,
3 the capacity to use the language with maximum attention to *communication* and minimum attention to form, and
4 the *creativity* of language use.

Let us now consider some of the approaches that have been made to conceptualize and describe second language proficiency.

Approaches to second language proficiency

Since the sixties it has become increasingly clear that a simple classification of proficiency as the 'four skills' of listening, speaking, reading, and writing, is inadequate, particularly for curriculum development and testing. A great deal of work has been done over the past two decades to offer teachers, testers, and researchers theoretically more clearly defined, descriptively more differentiated, and practically more serviceable specifications of language proficiency. Interesting conceptualizations have resulted from these different endeavours; but unfortunately they do not always match up with one another, and it is not surprising to find that practitioners are sometimes confused by the discussions about proficiency in terms of behavioural or performance objectives, linguistic or communicative competence, transitional competence, interlanguage, learner's language, approximative systems, and the like.

We can distinguish four approaches to the phenomenon of language proficiency which have characterized the past decade or two: theoretical conceptions, rating scales, standardized tests, and interlanguage studies. These form a continuum ranging from theoretically-based to more and more empirically-based schemes.

Theoretically-based conceptions of proficiency
(a) One group of concepts defines proficiency as *linguistic content*. While, until 1970 or so, phonology, vocabulary, and grammar have predominated, the more recent definitions of proficiency include semantic, discourse, and sociolinguistic features. Thus, one analysis of proficiency comprises, besides grammatical well-formedness, speech act rules, language functions, and language varieties (Richards 1978a). Proficiency is today emphatically expressed in communicative and not merely linguistic (i.e., grammatical) terms. But in defining the linguistic aspects of proficiency recent writers (for example, Canale and Swain, 1980) strongly emphasize that the stress on communication does *not* mean that the grammatical component of proficiency can be ignored.

(b) A second set of concepts is more *psychological* or *behavioural* (Figure 16.3). The descriptions of proficiency on this dimension cover relatively abstract concepts at one end of the scale: proficiency as competence (linguistic or communicative) or proficiency described more concretely as language activities in the familiar terms of 'skills', that is, the 'intralingual' skills, listening, speaking, reading, and writing, and in the less familiar terms of 'crosslingual' or 'mediating' skills of interpreting and translating. At the concrete end of the scale, proficiency has been

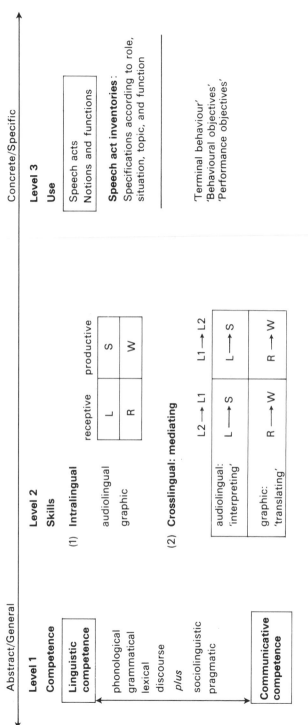

Figure 16.3   Aspects of second language proficiency: levels of abstraction

described through detailed inventories of language items, situations, psychological roles of the speaker, speech functions, appropriate semantic categories, and topics. The more abstract the behavioural specification of proficiency the more widely applicable it is likely to be. The more detailed and concrete it is the more restricted it is in its application.

Our interpretation of competence in the foregoing pages can be considered as an example of an abstract scheme. In another recent formulation just referred to (Canale and Swain 1980), prepared as a basis for test development, proficiency has also been interpreted abstractly as communicative competence and analysed into (1) grammatical competence, (2) sociolinguistic competence, and (3) strategic competence (i.e., the second language learner's ability to compensate for problems in communication).

In the Canale-Swain scheme grammatical competence is analogous to our mastery of forms and meanings; sociolinguistic competence to capacity to communicate; and strategic competence to aspects covered under creativity.

By contrast, the Council of Europe's *Threshold Level* scheme for second language English (van Ek 1975) and *niveau-seuil* for second language French (Coste *et al.* 1976), which offer specifications of English and French language learning objectives, defined proficiency in the concrete details of a syllabus of items useful for specified groups of learners, for example, travellers temporarily in contact with the target language community.

(c) A third categorization combines *behavioural and linguistic content* categories. Thus Carroll offered in the sixties several versions of a proficiency scheme which cross-tabulated language skills (auditory comprehension, oral production, reading and writing) with language aspects (phonology/orthography, morphology, syntax, and lexicon). In its most elaborated version Carroll's scheme (1968:54–5) consists of two charts (Figures 16.4 and 16.5), one detailing 'linguistic competences' and the other the corresponding 'linguistic performance abilities' (1968:57). The claim of such a scheme is that performance abilities can be tested and thus give empirical proof of specific competences.

While all the schemes which we have so far considered describe proficiency as consisting of a number of psychological and linguistic components, Oller (1976) has put forward the suggestion that proficiency is unitary and that the essential character of proficiency is what he has called *grammar-based expectancies* or an *expectancy grammar*. Oller sets out from the assumption that receptive language use is an active process in which the listener and reader anticipate what the message is likely to be and then compare the actual message received with his anticipations. It is a hallmark of being proficient that one can anticipate language use. Likewise the productive use of language in

	Phonology and orthography	Lexicon: Morphemes, words, idioms	Lexicon: Semantic and grammatical components of lexicon	Grammar: Morphology and syntax (Recognition / Ability to produce)	Grammar: Semantic components (Understanding / In appropriate contexts)
Spoken language — Receptive skills (Listening)	Phoneme recognition and discrimination; ability to discriminate words or phrases differing in one phoneme or distinctive feature [List phoneme pairs to be discriminated]	Recognition of lexical elements as belonging to the language [List lexicon]	Recognition of semantic and grammatical meanings (i.e. word class assignments) of lexical elements	Recognition — of morphological and associated phonology [List]	Understanding
Spoken language — Productive skills (Speaking)	Phoneme production; ability to produce phonemes or allophonic variants in word forms or phrases, with accuracy at either phonemic or phonetic level [List phonemes of language with variants]	Ability to produce lexical elements fitting semantic and grammatical specifications		Ability to produce — Morphological and syntactical features with appropriate phonology	In appropriate contexts
Written language — Receptive skills (Reading)	Recognition of the graphemic symbols of the language, with (as appropriate) ability to name them and give their sounds [List graphemes]	Above, plus recognition of meanings and pronunciation of written forms (including special graphemic symbols, abbreviations, etc.) [List]		Above, plus recognition of special grammar-related conventions of the written language, such as punctuation, capitalization, certain spelling changes, etc. [List such conventions]	
Written language — Productive skills (Writing)	Ability to write (by hand or other method) the graphemes of the language, state their customary ordering [List any details not covered above]	Spelling		As for receptive skills, plus ability to produce written conventions in appropriate contexts	

Figure 16.4   Carroll's chart of linguistic competences

	Phonology	Lexicon	Morphology and syntax	Integrated language performance
Speed of response	Articulation ability (speed and accuracy of speech sound production)	Naming facility (speed of responding with the names of things when presented in rapid succession)	Expressional fluency (ability to compose rapidly sentences fitting given grammatical requirements)	Oral speaking fluency
Diversity of response	'Word fluency' (ability to recall words with given phonetic-orthographic characteristics)	Ideational fluency (ability to call up names or ideas fitting given semantic characteristics)		Listening comprehension
Complexity of information processing	Auditory memory for speech sounds or sequences of sounds	Abstract reasoning ability (ability to process complex linguistically coded information)		Reading comprehension (and speed)
Awareness of linguistic competence	(No pertinent evidence)	Awareness of the structure of the lexicon; facility in giving opposites, superordinates, etc.	Grammatical sensitivity (ability to find analogous grammatical elements in sentences)	Writing ability

Figure 16.5 Carroll's chart of linguistic performance abilities (all based on underlying competences)

speaking or writing involves a corresponding process of planning messages. Both these processes constitute the necessary expectancies. This theory offers a twofold challenge to previously held views. The first is the idea of unitary language proficiency as opposed to the theory of proficiency as consisting of various components which combine differently in different individuals. Assuming that the unitary proficiency theory is right, the second challenge is that expectancy is the key concept for such a unitary proficiency theory. Oller's views have been contested by several investigators. Cummins (1979, 1980), for example, has pointed out that Oller's theory of a unitary proficiency concept is based on an interpretation of language test data. Language tests, however, have a certain academic or cognitive character. What, in fact, they test is 'a cognitive/academic language proficiency' (CALP), and small wonder that they highly correlate with each other and with intelligence tests, because they all have the same academic characteristic. What these tests fail to capture is another quality of language use, which Cummins refers to as the 'basic interpersonal and communicative skills', (BICS) corresponding roughly to aspects of what we have called the communicative capacity and creativity. In Cummins' view therefore proficiency has at least these two components: CALP and BICS. What Cummins' distinction has usefully drawn attention to is that, in school settings, proficiency is often interpreted as a conscious or explicit mastery of features of the language and that language tests are designed to assess proficiency in these terms. On the other hand, proficiency interpreted as the way language is used by native speakers or by second language users, as we have done in our analysis of proficiency, is perhaps not adequately captured by language tests commonly in use.[8]

The schemes we have so far described, including our own, illustrate definitions of proficiency based either on mainly theoretical considerations or on expressions of desired outcomes. It must, however, be stressed that they have not been empirically arrived at nor in most cases empirically tested. A somewhat more empirical approach has been used to develop descriptive rating scales of proficiency.

Description of proficiency levels on rating scales
Working on the assumption that second language proficiency ranges from zero to full bilingual proficiency, it is possible, on the basis of practical knowledge of learners at different stages, to define stages or levels of proficiency which are appropriate for specified purposes. One of the best known rating scales of this kind is that of the U.S. Foreign Service Institute and the Defense Language Institute, the so-called FSI Language Proficiency Ratings, which distinguish five classes of proficiency: (1) elementary proficiency; (2) limited working proficiency; (3) minimum professional proficiency; (4) full professional proficiency; and (5) native or bilingual proficiency.

Each of these five rating levels is described in relation to communicative roles as well as by reference to certain linguistic criteria. For example, the communicative standard of the lowest speaking level (S-1) is summarized as the ability to satisfy routine travel needs and minimum courtesy requirements. A candidate at S-3 is expected to be able 'to participate effectively in most formal and informal conversations on practical, social, and professional topics'. Council of Europe scholars who have operated with proficiency levels for some time, of which the *Threshold Level* or *niveau-seuil* is one, have suggested a scheme with seven steps ranging from 'survival', 'waystage', and 'threshold' to an ambilingual level (Trim 1978).

Rating scales are commonly divided in terms of communicative skills into listening, speaking, reading, and writing, and they often fulfil a dual function. From one point of view they indicate standards expected for given purposes. For example, for certain government positions, such as, the diplomatic service, standards of speaking, reading, or writing by reference to a rating scale can be specified. This is the task that the FSI rating scales have had to perform. From a more empirical point of view, rating scales can be used as descriptions or analyses of levels reached by second language learners. They can also be used by learners for self-assessment of their own proficiency (Naiman *et al.* 1978, Oskarsson 1978).[9]

Rating scales provide useful impressionistic descriptions of typical stages and of the development of proficiency from minimal to advanced levels, and they can usually claim to be based on practical experience with different levels of language performance.[10]

Proficiency as measured by standardized tests
Language tests, such as the MLA Cooperative Tests or the IEA French Tests (Carroll 1975) and the IEA English Tests (Lewis and Massad 1975), imply a conception of proficiency which has a certain empirical basis in the fact that they reflect what learners at school or university are expected to be able to do. But language tests represent what is taught in classrooms, and it is arguable that proficiency is more than that and that language tests only partially cover what constitutes proficiency. This is the limitation of language tests to which Cummins (1979, 1980) has drawn attention by his distinction between CALP and BICS (see p. 352 above). In this view tests typically assess those aspects of proficiency which can be taught as academic skills, for example, the grammar and vocabulary of a language. Other aspects, the communicative and creative components of proficiency (BICS) may not be adequately assessed in this way. In other words, language proficiency tests, as at present devised, seem to be able to capture certain aspects of second language proficiency, the analytical or explicit component of language use, but the intuitive mastery and the communicative or creative aspects

which form part of proficiency have so far not been adequately covered in the language tests at our disposal.[11]

Interlanguage studies
A fourth approach to the interpretation of proficiency consists of a whole area of psycholinguistic research which has been vigorously pursued since the seventies: interlanguage studies.[12] Researchers have looked closely at language learners' performance in the second language. It is the most theoretically developed and at the same time the most empirically investigated approach to the study of second language proficiency.

In 1967 Corder at the University of Edinburgh first suggested that a better understanding of language learning would come from a more systematic investigation of learners' errors by discovering the 'built-in syllabus' of the language learner. Many of the efforts of the following decade were in fact directed to discovering the natural sequences of second language learning. A key concept in these studies, as was mentioned in Chapter 15, was one advanced by the American linguist Selinker during a period of study in the late sixties at the University of Edinburgh, the concept of 'interlanguage'. Rather than studying errors in isolation, Selinker postulated the developing learner language as a system in its own right. See also Chapter 7:125. According to the interlanguage hypothesis, 'second language speech rarely conforms to what one expects native speakers of the target language to produce, that it is not an exact translation of the native language, that it differs from the target language in systematic ways, and that the forms of utterances produced in the second language by a learner are *not* random. This interlanguage-hypothesis proposes that the relevant data of a theory of second language learning must be the speech forms which result from the attempted expression of meaning in a second language' (Selinker, Swain, and Dumas 1975:140).

Many investigators have theorized about the nature, lawfulness, and changes of the interlanguage. Specific aspects of learner language development have been recorded and analysed. The fluctuating nature of the emerging language systems has varyingly been described as 'transitional competence', 'approximative system', 'idiosyncratic dialect', or simply as 'learner language' (Corder 1981).

Errors which in the language teaching theories of the sixties were seen as signals for better pedagogical grading were recognized in the seventies more and more as inevitable in the development of second language proficiency and as valuable aspects of learning: 'you can't learn without goofing' (Dulay and Burt 1974:95). For research, errors were also an indispensible data base in the study of the learner's language. In many of these investigations, the researchers closely studied the appearance of particular grammatical features and their subsequent development in the learner's repertoire, for example, morphemes, question forms, or the use of the auxiliary; and they used the findings to answer some general questions about the nature of second language learning and indeed about the nature of language in general. See Chapter 18.

In a thorough and perceptive review of much of this research Hatch (1978a) tried to estimate to what extent these studies have in fact answered the questions interlanguage research set out to answer. Hatch discusses ten such questions about interlanguage research and through a review of the most important syntax studies attempts to estimate the current state of knowledge. Some of Hatch's questions and answers deal with the learning process, as far as it can be inferred from interlanguage studies. These will be discussed in Chapter 18. Here we will only cite two questions concerned with interlanguage as stages of proficiency reached by second language learners. Her view can be summarized as follows:

Questions	*Answers*
1 'Is interlanguage real (systematic) or is it just a cover term for random fluctuation ... ?' (op. cit.:35)	'While there is a good deal of argument about the degree of systematicity ...' the move from the beginning stages to fluency is not random. (op. cit.:60)
2 If interlanguage is systematic, what is the system? How much variability is there?	While each learner's interlanguage may develop systematically, the system is not invariant.

Much of the research reviewed in Hatch's study has been concerned as yet only with linguistic minutiae in the development of a second language. The hope of understanding the interlanguage of learners in its totality, the successive stages of interlanguage, the development of proficiency at different age levels and under different conditions of learning from a hypothetical zero to an advanced stage is far from being fulfilled.

What emerges from interlanguage research is a conviction that the learner's degree of proficiency can legitimately be conceived as a 'system' created by the learner for himself.[13] This system is not invariant although it may have certain relatively fixed defects which, after Selinker (1972), are often referred to as 'fossilizations'. From the point of view of research the interplay of variation and systematicity and the causation of the interlanguage characteristics are the main questions to be investigated. From the point of view of pedagogy, the key issue is that the interlanguage in many instances is too fossilized, too idiosyncratic, and does not move reliably through better and better approximations towards target language norms.

Conclusion

To sum up, second language proficiency as a concept has not yet found a completely satisfactory expression. We have to recognize that it has been interpreted in several different ways which can be summarized as follows:

A. Levels of proficiency

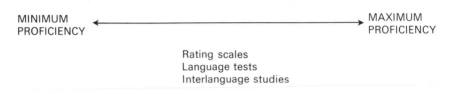

MINIMUM PROFICIENCY ←——————————————————→ MAXIMUM PROFICIENCY

Rating scales
Language tests
Interlanguage studies

B. Components of proficiency

relatively
abstract

relatively
concrete

←——————————————————————————————————→

Single concept	Twofold concept	Threefold concept	Fourfold concept	Multiple categories
Example	Example	Example	Example	Example
Expectancy grammar (Oller)	Linguistic competence Communi- cative competence	Grammatical competence Sociolinguistic competence Strategic competence (Canale and Swain)	Listening Speaking Reading Writing*	Specification according to: Roles Settings Topics Functions Notions (Council of Europe)
Linguistic competence (Interlanguage studies/error analyses)	CALP BICS (Cummins)		Formal mastery Semantic mastery Communi- cative capacity Creativity (Stern)	Phonology/ Orthography Lexicon Grammar in relation to Listening Speaking Reading Writing (Carroll)*

*(Rating scales, language tests)

Figure 16.6   Interpretations of language proficiency: a summary

One set of options relates to the *levels of proficiency* (Figure 16.6A), the different degrees of actual or required mastery of the second language, or the progression from a basic to a near-native level. This is what rating scales postulate, tests measure, and interlanguage studies (or error analyses) empirically investigate.

The second set of options lies in the categories we choose to define the essential characteristics or *components of proficiency* (Figure 16.6B) which can be expressed in relatively general or abstract terms or itemized in increasingly concrete ways. Thus, Oller (1976) has opted for a single-concept expression of proficiency: expectancy grammar. Most error analyses and interlanguage studies, too, appear to assume a single underlying linguistic competence which manifests itself through characteristic features of phonology, morphology, syntax, or discourse. Cummins (1979) has recognized a twofold division between a more academic and a more communicative component. In a similar way, those who acknowledge a distinction between linguistic and communicative competence also interpret proficiency as composed of at least two components. Canale and Swain's (1980) division of proficiency into linguistic, sociolinguistic, and strategic competence is threefold. The eleven propositions we put forward (see pp. 342–6) were condensed into four aspects of mastery. A fourfold interpretation is also implicit in the traditional division of proficiency into listening, speaking, reading, and writing. The Council of Europe inventories represent a multiple interpretation of proficiency combining roles, settings, topics, functions, and notions, while Carroll's analysis of proficiency (1968) relates four behavioural to three or more linguistic categories. Most language tests and rating scales imply a fourfold or multiple conceptualization of proficiency.

Given the complexity of language it would seem more reasonable to assume that proficiency in a language is multifaceted and can best be grasped by identifying two or more components rather than to expect it to be expressed in a single concept.

In future studies on proficiency the four approaches that have been outlined in this chapter—theoretical conceptions, rating scales, formal proficiency tests, and interlanguage research—could no doubt complement each other and serve jointly to develop progressive approximations of a more definitive formulation of proficiency of second language learners. The conceptual schemes can provide hypotheses of alternative descriptions of possible outcomes. Rating scales offer impressionistic global accounts of different stages of proficiency. Tests are useful in academic learning contexts although they may assess only limited aspects of second language proficiency. Interlanguage studies could be made so as to obtain concrete data on the development of proficiency. If these different approaches are related to each other a clearer picture of the nature of proficiency is likely to emerge.

Notes

1 An example would be the 'optimal age' issue. This is undoubtedly very important for the decision when to introduce a second language into an educational system. The fact that this question has not yet been answered in a fully satisfactory way has created difficulties for educational administrators. However, the limits of our knowledge on this question make for more responsible decision-making than spurious assertions of what one 'believes' is the optimal age. See on this issue Chapter 17:361–7.

2 Examples of such models include one by Gardner (1975,1979), Schumann (1976), Swain (1977), Bialystok (1978), Naiman *et al.* (1978). For the Bialystok model see Chapter 18:408.

3 Nevertheless, the concepts of 'habit' and 'skill' can still be usefully employed in describing certain aspects of language learning.

4 See Chapter 11, particularly Figures 11.1–11.4, for an analysis of speech acts which conceptualizes and describes this aspect of proficiency.

5 It should be noted that some authorities (for example, Canale and Swain 1980) look upon communicative competence as comprising linguistic and sociolinguistic competence whereas others have contrasted linguistic and sociolinguistic competence and have used the term 'communicative' competence only for what others have called sociolinguistic competence.

6 Clark and Clark 1977:447 offer these examples of lexical creativity: 'The mountain is jeepable.' 'The player had to be stretchered off the field.' 'The rocket faulted at lift-off.' 'Margaret 747'd to San Francisco.' 'Ned houdini'd his way out of the closet.' 'This music is very Beethoveny.'

7 The concept of 'interlanguage' ('approximative systems', etc.) captures the dynamic nature of the learner's language. See pp. 354–5 for a fuller discussion of 'interlanguage'. See also Chapter 15:330 and Note 15.

8 Two German investigators, Sang and Vollmer, have studied general language proficiency and have warned against simplified views of this concept. See Sang and Vollmer 1978; Vollmer 1979; Vollmer and Sang 1980, Vollmer and Sang, n.d. For explanations of the view of J. Cummins on proficiency see Cummins (1979, 1980, 1980a, and 1981).

9 For further explanations of the FSI proficiency levels, see Wilds (1975). Besides the American and Council of Europe proficiency levels, other examples, based on British experience, are illustrated by Carroll (1980). The difficulties in establishing sound rating scales have been perceptively analysed by Maréschal (1977), on the basis of considerable experience with establishing language norms in the

Canadian public service. Maréschal points out that some rating scales of proficiency indiscriminately mix descriptions in terms of social functions (for example, 'can meet and guide visitors') with linguistic criteria (for example, 'has a good command of the tense system').

10 A problem with rating scales to which Trim (1978) has drawn attention arises exactly from the double duty such scales frequently perform: as descriptions of performance levels and as proficiency objectives to be aimed at. Thus the levels of pronunciation on a five-point proficiency rating scale can legitimately be expressed as a set of descriptors of typical learners' pronunciation in the following manner:

Level 1   often unintelligible
Level 2   usually foreign but rarely unintelligible
Level 3/4 sometimes foreign but always intelligible
Level 5   native

However, such a scale would hardly serve as a definition of objectives in teaching pronunciation. At Level 1, for example, a teacher would not set out to make his students' pronunciation 'often unintelligible'. For an expression of expected outcomes or objectives the proficiency levels must be expressed in positive terms of what one would wish the learner to be able to do.

11 For recent attempts to widen the scope of language test so as to include a communicative component, see references in Chapter 12, Note 23.

12 For other references to interlanguage see Note 7 above.

13 The systematic and developmental nature of interlanguage accords well with features (6), (8), (9), and (10), described in our characterization of proficiency (see pp. 344–6 above).

17 Learner factors

Turning to the learner factors at the top of the diagram (box 2 in Figure 16.1), it may be a truism but it is nonetheless necessary to state that the language learner is or should be the central figure in any language teaching theory. From what has been said in Chapters 14 and 15 it is also clear that psychology and psycholinguistics have a key role to play in interpreting the concept of 'language learner'. Yet, in spite of the prolonged contact between psychology and language teaching theory, the psychological treatment of learner factors has not been easy to accommodate in language pedagogy. In certain respects the approach to the language learner has remained curiously 'unpsychological '. By and large, language teachers have looked upon language learners with fixed assumptions about how a learner should react to a given curriculum or a particular teaching approach, only to be surprised again and again, and often to be quite shocked, by the variety of reactions on the part of learners. These differences were somehow not allowed for in language teaching methods and textbooks in spite of the fact that educational psychology had for decades recognized, emphasized, and investigated the concept of individual learner differences.[1]

In other respects, however, certain learner factors have exercised language teaching theory for a long time. The questions most frequently debated have been those which have bearing on the organization of language teaching and on the selection or placement of students at different levels of instruction: What is the *optimal age* for language learning? Can a specific *language learning aptitude* be identified? If so, how can it be described and assessed? Are there differences in *learning style* or *cognitive style* which should be taken into account in pedagogy? What role do *motivation* and *attitude* play in language learning? Are there particular qualities of *personality* that favour or hinder progress in a second language? Practitioners and administrators have been very receptive to the idea of organizing language teaching in keeping with the answers to these questions. For example, they would like to start foreign languages in school systems at the psychologically right age, or they would be quite prepared to make allowance for learner aptitude or personality factors in the planning of language classes or in teaching methodology. In fact, they have tended to approach psychology with the expectation of receiving clear-cut directions on these complex issues.

As we shall see in this chapter, definitive answers to the major questions of learner psychology still elude us; therefore, in formulating a language teaching theory our conceptualizations of learner factors must, for the present, remain somewhat tentative. With these cautions in mind we will now look at a few crucial learner factors—(1) the age question, (2) language learning aptitude and other cognitive characteristics, and (3) affective and personality factors—and observe how answers to these much debated questions are only slowly beginning to emerge.

The optimal age question

Among the learner factors, the question of age in relation to second language learning has been one of the most debated issues in language teaching theory.[2] Whatever answer is given to it has far-reaching implications for the organization of language education in school systems. In this debate anecdotal opinion, practical experience, theoretical arguments, and research are mixed up; and even after more than thirty years of serious discussion and some research on this question the issue of the relationship between age and second language learning has been far from resolved.

Brief history of the argument

Anecdotally, it has been observed for centuries that young children seem to learn a second language 'more easily' than adults; and for this reason several educators of past centuries, for example, Erasmus, Montaigne, or Locke, were in favour of an early start in second language learning.[3] Educational practice in recent centuries was equivocal. The learning of languages was determined by expediency or social rather than pedagogical or psychological considerations. Early education in the public educational systems of the West, since the nineteenth century, has tended to lay stress on the mother tongue. Second language teaching was assigned to an advanced secondary education; foreign languages therefore appeared in the secondary school curriculum at whatever age such schooling began, that is somewhere between the ages of ten and fourteen. The relative lack of success of this late start in schooling prompted demands for language teaching at an earlier stage in the curriculum (Stern 1967).

In many parts of the world, however, educational necessities dictated the introduction of a second language in the early school years, either because the language was needed as a medium of instruction or because a majority of children in a society where second language skills were important did not attend school beyond their pre-teen years. Paradoxically, in certain educational systems an early start in a foreign language, for example, in the prestigious English 'preparatory' and 'public' schools, was customary. These experiences in early language learning were not considered to provide overwhelming proof of the great advantage of an early start. On the contrary, they led to a vigorous demand, around 1950, for early education in the mother tongue (UNESCO 1953).

On the question of an optimal age for second language learning, several views became current from about the same time. One of these is based on the opinion that young children, exposed to another language, seem to acquire this language rapidly and without much effort. This belief in an 'optimal', even 'critical' period of language learning in the early years gained widespread recognition during the fifties and sixties. As was mentioned in Chapter 15 (p. 323), the writings of the neurophysiologist Penfield were influential in spreading this view.[4] Penfield's argument that the early years of life before puberty were crucial for learning was derived from his observations on the effect of brain damage on speech in children and adults. It was not based on direct evidence of the greater effectiveness of early language learning. Briefly, Penfield found that children before puberty who suffer brain damage in the speech area of the cerebral cortex through accidents, brain tumours, and surgical intervention recover speech better than adolescents or adults. From this capacity of the young brain to compensate for the loss of the speech function Penfield inferred that the brain of a young child is much more receptive for the development of speech mechanisms than the adult's. This conviction led him to the view that the massive exposure of young children to different languages would be in accordance with the biological timetable and, at the same time, would bestow great social benefits. In the Montreal environment in which he lived, he had become keenly aware of the contrast between his own inability as an adult to learn French and the ease with which his children learnt other languages in the nursery.

Further theoretical support for early language learning could be derived from another theory, the 'nativist' view of first language acquisition which was strongly advocated since the sixties through the writings of Chomsky, Lenneberg, McNeill, and others.[5] Like Penfield, Lenneberg (1967), for example, regarded the years before puberty as a *biologically* active period of language development. The explanation advanced for the receptiveness to language development was that, up to adolescence, the two hemispheres of the cerebral cortex have not yet acquired the lateralization or specialization of function that characterizes the adult brain. Second language learning before puberty was thus given a kind of neurological sanction.

In subsequent years, this neurological explanation of better language learning before puberty was called into question because there is evidence that the cortical lateralization occurs much earlier, i.e., before the age of five (Krashen 1973) and that lateralization does not necessarily imply loss of any abilities (Krashen 1975,1981). If that is so, the distinction between the presumed ease of language learning before adolescence and subsequent difficulties in language learning could not be accounted for on grounds of neurological changes.

It was to find a more plausible explanation for differences between language learning before and after puberty that Schumann (1975) advanced an *affective theory* which attributes to the early years of life a greater social and emotional permeability to language influences than is available in adolescence or adulthood (see also p. 381). A more *cognitive explanation* was offered by other investigators (Rosansky 1975; Krashen 1981) in terms of Piagetian stages of intellectual growth. According to this view, the critical period of language development is the period of concrete operations, i.e., after 'the sensorimotor stage' of the earliest years, and before 'the period of formal operations' at adolescence.

All these theoretical arguments are based on the assumption that children are in effect better language learners than adolescents or adults. They do not constitute proof that this is so nor do they provide concrete evidence of the specific characteristics of such early second language learning and of the differences in the learning process between earlier and later learning.

Against the various claims that early childhood has special advantages for second language learning, others have advanced an opposing viewpoint: they have argued that greater cognitive maturity and greater learning experience on the part of the older language learners are assets. In a theoretical comparison of adults and children as language learners, Ausubel (1964) made a strong case in favour of language learning by adults and concluded:

> 'Objective research evidence regarding the relative learning ability of children and adults is sparse but offers little comfort to those who maintain the child superiority thesis. Although children are probably superior to adults in acquiring an acceptable accent in a new language, E. L. Thorndike found many years ago that they make less rapid progress than adults in other aspects of foreign language learning when learning time is held constant for the two age groups' (Ausubel 1964:421).

Empirical findings
In the first decade or two after World War II the introduction of foreign languages in the elementary school (FLES) in the U.S.A., of primary school French in Britain, and similar developments in other countries were part of a widespread search for ways of improving the effectiveness of language education by taking into account the timetable of language development in childhood. Several early language teaching experiments were undertaken during that period. But little was done to ensure that

these experiments were systematically planned and carefully evaluated. Two UNESCO-sponsored international meetings, held in Hamburg in 1962 and 1966, were intended to promote research on early language teaching and on the effectiveness of an early start (Stern 1967, 1969; Stern and Weinrib 1977). These meetings brought to light encouraging observations and reports of experiences in early language teaching. They demonstrated the feasibility of an early start in school systems and showed that young children responded to second language teaching in a positive way, but the *superiority* of an early start over a later start was not proved. In more recent years, the advantages of an early start have received further support from the successful Canadian experimental programmes in 'early immersion' (Lambert and Tucker 1972; Stern 1978a; Swain 1978). These experiments suggested that under certain circumstances the early start can be advantageous: young children appear to be remarkably responsive to language education in a 'natural' setting of language use of the kind offered by language 'immersion'.

But even here the evidence is not absolutely conclusive in favour of the younger learner. More recently, comparisons of 'early' and 'late' immersion (Genesee 1981; Swain 1981, 1981a) found that late immersion groups of children who had had only a two-year immersion at grades 7 and 8 in Canadian schools reached levels of achievement in their second language which at the grade 9 level were comparable to grade 9 early immersion children, that is children who had been 'immersed' for eight or nine years, i.e., since kindergarten.[6]

The British project on Primary French, undertaken between 1964 and 1974 (Burstall *et al.* 1974; see Chapter 4:56) constituted in effect a major longitudinal study on the question of earlier versus later second language learning. Its goal was to find out whether a start in a second language at the age of eight was practically feasible in the British school setting and whether it offered any special advantages over a start at the age of eleven, the customary age for transition to secondary education. In this ten-year enquiry, undertaken by the National Foundation for Educational Research (NFER), the progress of three cohorts of eight-year-olds, approximately 17,000 children, was systematically assessed at regular intervals over a period of five to eight years. These experimental groups were compared with two types of control groups: one was composed of children who at the time of testing were of the same age as the experimental children, but who had started French at the usual age of eleven, that is three years later; and the other control group was composed of students who were older than the experimental children at the time of testing, but who had had an equivalent period of years of exposure to French.

The results of this enquiry, first of all, showed that a foreign language in the primary school was feasible and was not detrimental to achievement in other school subjects. But, secondly, on the question of whether it offered any special advantages the results were less clear. The comparison with those children who had started a language later did not, on most measures, show that the early starters were overwhelmingly better. The early starters maintained, after two years, a certain but diminishing superiority in speaking and listening and, after four years, only for listening. Those who had started later and therefore had less time to learn were equal or superior on other measures, especially in reading and writing tests. The authors of this study saw in these results evidence that the theory of the advantages of an early start was a 'myth'. If there is any advantage at all for the early start, they argued, it is only that it allows more time for second language learning. On the age issue, they claimed, if anything, older learners are more efficient learners, because they bring to the learning task more learning experience and greater cognitive maturity. These findings and, above all, the interpretations that have been put upon them by the investigators have been questioned (for example, Buckby 1976; Nuffield Foundation 1977; Spicer 1980), and the debate on the relative advantages of early or late second language learning has gone on unabated (Stern and Weinrib 1977; Stern 1982).

Corroborating evidence for greater emphasis on adequate time for language learning rather than on the age issue *per se* was offered in the IEA eight-country study of learning French as a second language (Carroll 1975; see also Chapter 4:56–7). This enquiry made it possible to compare the effect of different patterns of language instruction including different starting ages. The results of this investigation with regard to the age issue were interpreted as follows:

> 'The data of the present study suggests that the primary factor in attainment of proficiency in French (and presumably, any foreign language) is the amount of instructional time provided. The study provides no clear evidence that there is any special advantage in starting the study of a foreign language very early other than the fact that this may provide the student more time to attain a desired performance level at a given age. In fact, the data suggest that students who start the study of a foreign language at relatively older ages make somewhat faster progress than those who start early. The recommendation that emerges is that the start of foreign language instruction be placed only so early as to permit students to have the amount of instructional time they need to achieve whatever level of competence is regarded as desirable by a given stage of their education. If necessary, the start of instruction can be delayed more than normally if more intensive instruction is given.'
> (Carroll 1975:276–7)

More recently, a few investigators have tried to study much more directly age differences in second language learning or to examine critically and review in detail whatever scientific evidence is available on the age issue. For example, in a study undertaken in the Netherlands Snow and Hoefnagel-Höhle (1978) observed the language learning of English native speakers all of whom had recently come to the Netherlands and were learning Dutch. Comparing adults and children these two investigators found (1) that all age levels improve, (2) that older learners are better than younger learners on morphology and syntax, (3) that older learners are also better than younger learners in their vocabulary progress, teenagers making the greatest progress in this area, and (4) that there are only small differences between different age groups on phonological mastery.

A summary and review of a large number of research studies on the age question by Krashen *et al.* (1979) shows how puzzlingly complex this question still is. The quintessence of this review is perhaps the statement that

> 'adults and older children in general initially acquire the second language faster than young children (older-is-better for rate of acquisition) but child second language acquirers will usually be superior in terms of ultimate attainment (younger-is-better in the long run).' (op. cit.:574)

Conclusion on the age issue
The discussion on the role of age in second language learning has been largely confined to the question of the optimal age, in other words, to the question of the relationship between age and learning outcome. What studies—with a few exceptions (for example, Ervin-Tripp 1974, Snow and Hoefnagel-Höhle 1978)—have hitherto failed to do is to attempt to identify the features that characterize second language learning processes at different maturity levels.

Yet, the optimal age question is one of interpretation which should only be asked *after* the age-specific characteristics of language learning have previously been established. The trouble with the discussion of the age issue has been that for practical reasons the optimal age question has been asked too soon, namely before the developmental characteristics of different stages of second language learning had been properly investigated. Consequently, there has been much fruitless debate, superficial comparison between adult and child, and a good deal of indecision in educational systems at what stage in the school curriculum to begin second language instruction.

Until we have more conclusive evidence from research, the following propositions may serve as a summary of the meagre state of knowledge on the age question:

1 Language learning may occur at different maturity levels from the early years into adult life. No age or stage stands out as optimal or critical for all aspects of second language learning.

2 In some respects, all age levels face second language learning in similar ways; consequently adults and children are likely to have certain strategies in common and to go through similar stages of language learning. These stages have much in common with first language acquisition.

3 Language learning—like proficiency (see Chapter 16:357)—is not monolithic (Snow and Hoefnagel-Höhle 1978:333). There are age differences in the acquisition of different aspects of language (phonology, vocabulary, syntax, etc.)

4 In certain respects pre-school children, young school children, older child learners, adolescents, and adults differ psychologically in their approach to second language learning. What these differences in developmental stages are is at present not fully understood. But it appears that young children respond more readily and intuitively to language 'acquisition' in social and communicative situations, while older learners can learn languages more readily by means of cognitive and academic approaches.[7]

5 Each stage of development may have certain advantages and certain disadvantages for second language learning.

6 It is by observation, experiment, and by educational trial-and-error and careful evaluation of such experiments at different age levels that the particular characteristics of different age levels of language learning will gradually be revealed.

7 For decisions on the best age for language learning a strictly developmental balance sheet, based on psychological studies, cannot be the only consideration. On educational, political, and philosophical grounds it may be desirable to introduce younger children to second languages even though it is not necessarily psychologically optimal. A guiding principle arrived at after a review of much of the available evidence (Stern and Weinrib 1977:20; 1978:167) has been 'to recognize that a language can be taught from any age upwards. Once this has been accepted, the decision at what stage in the educational process to introduce a foreign language can be governed by three criteria: (a) the estimated time necessary to reach a desired level of language proficiency by a specified stage in the school career of the majority of learners; (b) the educational value attributed to learning foreign languages at a given stage of the curriculum; and (c) the human and material resources required to develop and maintain an educationally sound and successful foreign language programme.'

Language aptitude and other cognitive factors

The concept of an aptitude[8] for languages is derived from everyday experience that some language learners appear to have a 'gift for languages' which others lack. It has obvious implications for planning language teaching. Should languages be taught to everybody or only to those who have sufficient aptitude? Should students with different aptitudes be placed into separate 'streams'? Can aptitude be developed by training? Can teaching be adapted to aptitude differences?

Second language learning, which is only one among several learning activities involving language aptitude, has much in common with language learning activities in the native language, the acquisition of 'special languages', codes, and other symbol systems in mathematics and in other areas of the curriculum.[9] Therefore, those psychological qualities that come into play in formal schooling generally, particularly in the learning of verbal material, are likely also to bear upon second language learning. It is to be expected that measurements of verbal characteristics through tests of verbal intelligence, verbal reasoning, word knowledge, or verbal fluency in the first language are positively correlated with measurements of second language achievement. This has indeed been confirmed by a number of studies (for example, Vernon 1960:179; Genesee 1976).[10] Intelligence tests and achievement tests in the native language have accordingly been used as predictors of second language aptitude. But the correspondence is far from perfect. Intelligence tests are in certain respects poor predictors of second language learning because they include some characteristics which have little to do with second language learning and omit others which come into play in the second language class. *The concept of second or foreign language aptitude can thus be used to focus on specific cognitive learner qualities needed in second language learning.*

Educational psychology, as we saw in Chapter 14:309, has taken up the common-sense notion of special gifts or talents, over and above a general academic or reasoning ability ('intelligence', IQ), by studying, for example, musical aptitude, manual dexterity, mathematical ability, and so on. The idea of a foreign or second language aptitude is, from one point of view, simply a refinement of the ordinary person's view of a gift for languages, and from another, an application of the psychological concept of special abilities. Such abilities have been described and assessed with the help of techniques of measurement which have been employed in educational and industrial psychology since the twenties. But the isolation of a language aptitude has been difficult and even today has not been entirely resolved, although there has been much progress over the last few decades (Carroll 1981; Wesche 1981a).

The definition of second language aptitude and its measurement depend upon underlying language teaching theories and interpretations of learner characteristics and of the language learning process. Thus, an early language aptitude test, developed in 1930, the *Symonds Foreign Language Prognosis Test*, (see also Chapter 15, Note 3), reflects approaches to language teaching of that period by stressing the capacity to handle grammatical concepts and to translate. More recent aptitude tests, such as Carroll and Sapon's *Modern Language Aptitude Test* (1959 MLAT; see Chapter 4, Note 4) and their *Elementary Modern Language Aptitude Test* (1967 EMLAT), or Pimsleur's *Language Aptitude Battery* (1966 PLAB) represent not only a more advanced approach to test construction; they also reflect the audiolingual principles of the fifties and sixties. These tests assess, for example, the discrimination of speech sounds, the capacity to relate sounds to a given set of symbols, rote memory in a language learning task, sensitivity for sentence structure, and an inductive language learning capacity—all characteristics of the audiolingual theory.

Like most psychometric devices, such as IQ tests, language aptitude tests have been developed as practical instruments of 'prognosis' and 'diagnosis'. They are intended to sort out individuals before undergoing language training. Their value lies in their capacity to make such predictions with as much accuracy as possible. The test results lend themselves to being used cautiously to arrange students in roughly homogeneous groups assuming that these groups are taught according to the principles implicit in the test. They can also be used to make a provisional selection of more promising from less promising students. They can further be employed diagnostically in order to identify strengths and weaknesses in the learner for the task of language learning. It is indeed in these ways—as well as for purposes of research on language learning—that tests of this kind have been employed (for example, Carroll 1975a and 1981; Wesche 1981a).

In addition to their *practical* value such tests contribute to a better *theoretical* understanding of the nature of language aptitude as a learner variable, and it is this aspect that interests us here. It is not claimed by those who have developed these tests that language aptitude is innate.[11] However, in whatever manner acquired, it is regarded as a group of characteristics which are relatively stable, and should be considered as a given—as a learner factor to count with. It is not yet clear whether positive aptitude characteristics could be developed by specific training or even simply by exposure to language learning—but it seems likely that they can be improved to some extent.[12]

Another aspect of the current view on aptitude is that it is not something that a person either has or has not ('I'm good at languages.' 'I'm no good at languages.') The view of language aptitude, reflected in these tests, is that aptitude is not a single entity, but a *composite of different characteristics* which come into play in second language learning. This view harmonizes with the theory that proficiency is a composite and that language learning is 'not monolithic' (see p. 367). Language aptitude then consists of several constituents which learners possess *to varying degrees*. Arguable questions are (a) whether the components of the major second language aptitude batteries identify the constituents of this composite and (b) whether this list of constituents is exhaustive.

The components of the two major second language aptitude tests, MLAT/EMLAT and PLAB are summarized in the accompanying tabulation (Figure 17.1).

The two batteries have some features in common, but differ in other respects. The MLAT/EMLAT series confines itself to a few characteristics which its authors, Carroll and Sapon, regard as significant components of second language aptitude. The PLAB, developed by Pimsleur, tries to provide a convenient package of measures which appear to be useful for a prognosis even if they cannot be regarded as constituting, strictly speaking, a 'pure' combination of second language aptitude measures. Thus, PLAB contains (a) an assessment of interest in second languages which therefore introduces a motivational component, (b) an assessment of first language vocabulary, and (c) an assessment of general school achievement. The assessment of an interest or affective component in an aptitude battery appears legitimate if we adopt the view that the affective state provides the essential impetus for the cognitive skills to become operative (Schumann 1976). Word knowledge in the first language and general academic abilities are not specific to language learning, but they are useful attributes for learning a second language in a language class.[13]

If we now focus on those characteristics which both batteries regard as specific to language learning, MLAT/EMLAT and PLAB both identify three features: (1) the ability to pay attention to, and discriminate, the speech sounds of languages, i.e., 'a phonetic coding ability'; (2) the ability to relate speech sounds to some form of graphemic representation, in other words, the ability to establish sound-symbol relationships; and (3) the ability to pay attention to the formal characteristics of a language: grammatical sensitivity. The MLAT/EMLAT series includes a fourth characteristic, lacking in PLAB, verbal rote memory. To comment on each of these:

1 *The auditory capacity*, speech sound discrimination, and memory of significant speech sounds is an ability to which, commonly, much attention is paid. It is obviously important, a *sine qua non* of audiolingual language training.

2 *Sound-symbol relations*. Second language learning in a classroom usually also involves relating speech sounds to some form of script, for example, in note taking, reading aloud, and dictation. From practical experience it is known that some students can process auditory information without the support of written symbols, whereas others have a distinct preference for visual presentation in written

	MLAT/EMLAT		PLAB	
		Ability assessed		
Test task descriptions	*Names of tests*	*Names of tests*	*Test task descriptions*	
Learn words for numbers in an artificial language.	*Number learning*	*Sound discrimination*	Learn phonetic distinctions and recognize them in different contexts.	
Listen to sounds and learn phonetic symbols for them.	*Phonetic script*	*Sound-symbol association*	Associate sounds with written symbols.	
Decipher phonetically spelt English words and identify words with similar meanings.	*Spelling clues*	*Rhymes*	List as many words as possible that rhyme with four given words.	

The ability to discriminate, remember, interpret, and produce the phonic substance of another language. Auditory alertness. The ability to relate the phonology to forms of graphemic representation.

Recognize the syntactic functions of words and phrases in sentences.	*Words in sentences*	*Language analysis*	Make judgements with the help of translations about the meanings and rules of use of an unknown language.

The ability to pay attention to morphological, syntactic, and semantic features of a language, to relate linguistic forms to each other, and to develop patterns, regularities, and rules from linguistic materials: linguistic (grammatical-semantic) sensitivity and an inductive learning ability.

Learn and recall words in an artificial language.	*Number learning* *Paired associates*		

Memory ability: the capacity to memorize and recall words in a new language. Rote memory. MLAT/EMLAT only. Not tapped by PLAB.

		Vocabulary	Identify the meaning of different words.

Word knowledge, i.e., lexical competence in the first language tested in PLAB only.

		Grade-point average in academic areas	Information gathered by tester.
		Interest in learning a foreign language	Short questionnaire.

PLAB contains a general school achievement and motivational component, not considered in MLAT/EMLAT as part of the concept of aptitude.

Figure 17.1   Constituents of second language aptitude

form. The aptitude batteries do not explore these distinctions between sensory preferences. They assume that the learner must (a) be able to process speech sounds, and (b) be able to relate them to written symbols.

3 *Grammatical abilities.* The third major characteristic of both tests is that they regard as an essential ability the capacity to isolate linguistic forms; in other words, to possess 'grammatical sensitivity' and to infer language rules from linguistic data. This quality does not imply a knowledge of grammatical terminology, or a metalanguage about language. It refers to the intuitive capacity to interpret grammatical relationships and, in a more general way, to isolate linguistic forms from their particular context.[14]

4 *Verbal memory.* The MLAT/EMLAT has also recognized as important the memory ability of the learner, a capacity to memorize and recall new verbal material in a second language by rote or simple association. PLAB does not include this memory factor.

Critics of language aptitude batteries (for example, Neufeld 1973, 1975) have questioned the theoretical justification for the constituents of language aptitude in the language aptitude tests.[15] Some of the language learning models we have referred to in Chapter 16, are based on the assumption that the processes involved in second language learning are general cognitive skills; such models therefore implicitly deny the validity of a specific language aptitude concept. Moreover, in some recent discussions on language learning the capacity to acquire languages and codes has been treated as a universal human cognitive characteristic. If this view is adopted, one could be led to question the value of the concept of a special language aptitude. However, this argument does not invalidate the aptitude concept altogether. Just as individuals, in spite of their common biological characteristic to acquire speech, differ in verbal facility in their first language, it is reasonable to suppose that there are differences in the capacity to accommodate to, and develop other phonological, lexical, grammatical, and semantic systems and to switch codes. If adaptation to new language systems and code switching are the essential and specific characteristics of second language aptitude the concept of a special aptitude seems justified. According to this interpretation, it is reasonable to suppose that second language learning involves (a) *general* cognitive and learning skills as well as (b) some *special* skills of the kind identified in the language aptitude test batteries.

It is, however, worth remembering that language aptitude tests like MLAT/EMLAT or PLAB probe only the cognitive, academic, or analytical aspects of language learning and do not capture the intuitive and non-analytical aspects nor the communicative and social features of language learning which we identified in Chapter 16:341 ff. as characteristic of language proficiency and which also play a part in second language learning (see also Chapter 18:400 ff.).

Searching for cognitive style
Side by side with the interest in discovering second language aptitude, a few attempts have been made to identify general cognitive and learning characteristics which can be assumed to be particularly relevant to second language learning: the individual's 'cognitive style'.[16]

Cognitive style has been defined as a 'characteristic self-consistent mode of functioning which individuals show in their perceptual and intellectual activities' (Witkin *et al.* 1971:3). Several cognitive style features which may have bearing on second language learning have been identified.

One such characteristic is *field dependence/independence*. In a test of field dependence, a subject must break up an organized visual field in order to isolate a part of it. In a typical test task the subject has to pick out a hidden figure from a design. The 'field-independent' person can undertake this task more successfully than a 'field-dependent' person. In language learning it is often necessary to understand language items in their context, and at the same time to classify the item out of that context to understand it paradigmatically. For example, the learner should understand an embedded phrase, a clause, or sound sequence in the context or 'field' in which it occurs; yet, it is equally necessary to be able to isolate the linguistic item from its field and to use it in other contexts. When faced with ambiguous sentences, a field-independent individual can recognize the multiple meanings, while a field-dependent person would be less able to do so. Presumably, field dependence/independence is the general cognitive ability that in the aptitude tests is assessed as grammatical sensitivity.

Another problem for the second language learner is how to inhibit the overwhelming influence of the firmly established first language habits where these are inappropriate. In other words, the learner must be able to resist irrelevant or conflicting perceptual stimuli. Some individuals appear to be more interference-prone (IP) than others. The Stroop Colour-Word Test illustrates the phenomenon on which the observation of this characteristic is based. The subject is shown a card on which a colour term, say, 'green', is written in red ink. There is a conflict between what the word designates (green) and the colour in which it is printed (red). Low IP subjects can disambiguate these conflicting stimuli; high IP subjects have difficulties in keeping conflicting and intrusive ambiguities apart. This characteristic is probably assessed in the MLAT battery by the Spelling Clue test in which the meaning of words must be inferred in spite of unusual and distracting spellings; for example:

kataklzm = (1) mountain lion
        (2) disaster
        (3) sheep
        (4) chemical reagent
        (5) population

A third cognitive-style probe distinguishes *broad* and *narrow categorizers*. The tendency to apply a limited language rule, such as the imperfect-tense marker in French (-ais), to all verb forms is an indication of too broad categorization. Such overgeneralizations often occur in second language learning. Narrow categorizing is the tendency to limit a rule to a specific context in which it was encountered. This intellectual quality has been assessed by Pettigrew's Category-Width Scale in which subjects have to make judgements which risk being either too narrow or too wide. Both operations are needed under different circumstances in language learning: the good language learner is probably a 'middle-of-the-roader' (Naiman *et al.* 1978:31), reasonably precise in the application of rules and yet prepared to take risks in order to test the limits of a rule. If we view language learning as one of hypothesis making, hypothesis testing, feedback, and revision, the language learner is constantly involved in the kind of rule-making and rule-changing behaviour that demands judgement about the application of categories explored by such tests as Pettigrew's Category-Width Scale.

Concluding remarks

If we review the interpretations of the cognitive qualities that an individual must bring to bear upon language learning, we recognize that the researchers have set out from the identification of a few basic characteristics of school learning, such as word knowledge, verbal intelligence, reasoning, and school achievement. They have then focused on those cognitive qualities needed to function in a particular type of introductory second language class, such as (a) the ability to cope with a sound system and its written representation, (b) the ability to absorb its grammatical rule system, and (c) verbal memory skills. More recent research has attempted, although quite tentatively, to identify basic cognitive characteristics underlying learning strategies such as field dependence/independence, transfer/interference, broad and narrow categorizing.

All these analyses have a certain face validity. They make sense in relation to our common-sense experience of language teaching and learning. However, they have all a common weakness: they set out from no theoretical conception or solid empirical basis of what cognitive processes second language learning actually involves, and why these and not other skills have been singled out as indicative of qualities needed for language learning. In order to understand better whether our interpretations of aptitude and other cognitive factors are sound, we need a more deliberate analysis of the language learning process itself. Before coming to grips with this problem (Chapter 18), we want first to review the other direction that research on learner factors has taken, the analysis of the affective component.

Affective and personality factors

In interpretations of the learner and learning, the cognitive skills that the learner brings to the learning task have received main emphasis. Affective and personality factors have received much less attention. But any language teacher—and for that matter, any learner—can testify that language learning often involves strong positive or negative emotions. Moreover, learners declare their feelings and intentions 'with their feet' when they opt for, or turn away from, language classes. Nothing has brought about greater concern about learner motivation than the decline in enrolments in language classes and the 'drop-out' from language programmes. Language teachers often treat the importance of motivation as self-evident.

Studies of attitudes and motivation

A more systematic investigation of affective and personality factors in language learning has interested researchers since the early fifties.[17] The most consistent research over a period of twenty-five years has been undertaken in Canada by Gardner and Lambert at McGill University (Gardner and Lambert 1972) and later by Gardner and his colleagues at the University of Western Ontario in London, Ontario (for example, Gardner 1979; Gardner and Smythe 1981). These studies have focused on learners' social attitudes, values, and the motivation of learners in relation to other learner factors and the learning outcome. The Gardner and Lambert research has been made in the framework of social psychology; it has largely been derived from post-war studies on prejudice and social attitudes to ethnic, religious, and language groups. The studies were first undertaken in the cosmopolitan but basically French-English bilingual setting of Montreal. They were later extended to studies on language groups in the U.S.A., in particular French-American groups in Maine and Louisiana, and to language problems in the Philippines. In more recent work of Gardner's Language Research Group these analyses have been applied to the attitudes and motivations of English-speaking high school students learning French as a second language in anglophone settings in Canada.

Other prominent studies on attitudes to the language learning of children in schools have been made by the research team of the National

Foundation for Educational Research (NFER) in Britain under Burstall's direction (Burstall *et al.* 1974).[18] While Gardner and Lambert have been mainly concerned with the attitudes with which students approach the language class, Burstall and the NFER team have, in addition, investigated (a) the attitudes of teachers and headmasters to language learning, and (b) the longitudinal development of attitudes over a period of several years of language learning.

The methods of investigation in both groups of studies have been similar. The instruments used consist principally of attitude tests containing such items as,

I like learning French
Learning French is a waste of time.
I think English is the best language.

to which the respondents were asked to express their agreement or disagreement.

Other methods have included open-ended expressions of view. For example, the NFER study asked subjects to answer this question:

Presumably at some stage in your school career you had to decide whether or not to drop French. What made you decide to carry on learning French?
(Burstall *et al.* 1974:256)

Another technique used has been the 'semantic differential'. Subjects were asked, for example, in one of Gardner's studies, to indicate their impressions about 'French people from France' and 'my French teacher' on scales which, among others, include items such as the following:

1	Interesting	$-:-:-:-:-:-:-$	Boring
2	Prejudiced	$-:-:-:-:-:-:-$	Unprejudiced
3	Brave	$-:-:-:-:-:-:-$	Cowardly
4	Handsome	$-:-:-:-:-:-:-$	Ugly
5	Colourful	$-:-:-:-:-:-:-$	Colourless
6	Friendly	$-:-:-:-:-:-:-$	Unfriendly
7	Honest	$-:-:-:-:-:-:-$	Dishonest
8	Smart	$-:-:-:-:-:-:-$	Stupid
9	Kind	$-:-:-:-:-:-:-$	Cruel
10	Pleasant	$-:-:-:-:-:-:-$	Unpleasant[19]

The main attitudes and motives investigated in both groups of researches have been similar:

(a) attitudes towards the community and people who speak the target language, or 'group specific attitudes'—to use Gardner's term, for example,

I would like to go to France.
I would like to get to know some French people.
The French way of life seems crude when compared to ours.

(b) attitudes towards learning the language concerned, for example,

Learning French is a waste of time.
The more I get to know French people, the more I would like to learn their language.

(c) attitudes towards languages and language learning in general, for example,

I would like to speak many languages.
I am not interested in learning foreign languages.

Both groups of enquiries have also studied the principal motives that prompt learners. Gardner has laid particular stress on a distinction between an 'instrumental' motive reflecting the practical advantage of learning a language, and the 'integrative' motive 'reflecting a sincere and personal interest in the people and culture' (Gardner and Lambert 1972:132). The difference between these two main motives is expressed, for example, in these test items:

I am studying French because
(a) I think it will someday be useful in getting a job *(instrumental)*
(b) I think it will better help me to understand French people and their way of life *(integrative)*

The studies have investigated not only the attitudes and motivation that prompted learning *prior to* language study, but also the attitudes that the learning process had engendered and the degree of motivation maintained *during* the progress of a language course. The following items illustrate such 'course related attitudes':

I find studying French
(a) very interesting
(b) no more interesting than most subjects
(c) not interesting at all
(op. cit.:154)

Now finish off these two sentences:
What I like about learning French is ...
What I don't like about learning French is ...
(Burstall *et al.* 1974:255)

The results of the Gardner–Lambert studies and the Burstall studies harmonize in many respects. Both recognize that there is a positive association between measured learning outcomes and attitudes towards the target group and the language. Gardner originally thought that, with some exceptions, an integrative motivation was needed for successful language learning. However, the empirical studies showed that in some settings successful learning was associated with the instrumental orientation. In order to resolve this apparent inconsistency, Gardner has developed a model in which the social context is assumed to determine learners' attitudes.

In attempting to link the social milieu with learners' motivational orientations, Gardner (1979) suggests that 'additive' language learning situations, where members of high status language groups add a second language to their repertoire of skills at no cost to first language proficiency (Lambert 1975), may give rise to an integrative orientation towards learning; on the other hand, instrumental orientations are more likely in 'subtractive' situations where minority language groups tend to replace the first language by a more prestigious second language.

Gardner rightly looks to the social context to account, to a certain extent, for the attitudes and motivations of individual learners. But, as he himself has pointed out (for example, Gardner 1979), the relationship between social context and attitudes are often more complex than is suggested by the distinction between additive and subtractive language situations. The social status of the second language in relation to the first language, ethnolinguistic group relations, economic or political factors, are likely to influence motivation to learn a second language (see Chapter 13). Thus, when the sociolinguistic status of a group is lower than that of the target language group (i.e., when the target language group is dominant) instrumental motivation is likely to be strongly in evidence because acquisition of the target language is likely to be a prerequisite for economic advancement. But other motivational forces may also be involved. For example, the learner may also be integratively motivated and wish to assimilate with the dominant group. However, this is not always so. The instrumental motives for learning the target language may be accompanied by a negative motivational orientation in the form of 'fear of assimilation' (Clément 1979; Taylor *et al.* 1977). Under these circumstances the individual is likely to emphasize 'psychological distinctiveness' (Giles *et al.* 1977), and second language acquisition will progress only to the point where instrumental needs can be fulfilled. In short, individual learner factors are influenced by the social context in subtle ways which have to be borne in mind in interpreting learner behaviour.

On somewhat different grounds Burstall *et al.* (1974:45) have also called into question the distinction between integrative and instrumental motivation. Burstall and her associates at the NFER found it impossible to make a distinction between these two kinds of motivation. Another way in which the NFER findings have differed from the North American studies is in the interpretation of causal relationships. Gardner sees in attitudes and motivation a principal cause of more or less successful learning. On the basis of her longitudinal studies, on the other hand, Burstall has come to the conclusion that successful early learning experiences promote not only successful later learning but also more positive attitudes.

Although there is little doubt that the affective aspect of language learning is important, the assessment by means of attitude tests and some of the conceptualizations underlying them have been questioned by some researchers (for example, Oller 1981). Further evidence that— in spite of the advances that have been made—there still remain some serious questions in the study of the 'affective domain' comes from an enquiry on the effect of bilingual exchange programmes between students in French-speaking Quebec and English-speaking Ontario. In this study students were given attitude questionnaires similar to those developed by Gardner and his colleagues before and after the exchange, and they were interviewed after the exchange. While the attitude measures show a slight change of attitude in a positive direction, the interviews suggest that the participants do not spontaneously produce the stereotypes of the kind included in attitude tests, but express an affective response to their immediate experience, and expressly refuse to generalize about the characteristics of anglophones and francophones (Hanna *et al.* 1980).

Personality factors
Studies on personality, prejudice, and child training suggest that the attitudes to countries, ethnic groups and languages, and the motives for and against language learning should be considered against the background of more deep-seated generalized attitudes or personality factors than as mere responses to immediate experiences alone. Classroom observation would lend support to the view that there are certain personality characteristics which are helpful or detrimental to successful language learning. It is sometimes said that outgoing students with histrionic talents are more successful language learners than more inhibited or introverted students. Such observations may be only stereotypes and at best half-truths, but they provide the stimulus for more systematic investigations.[20]

Following the seminal studies of the fifties on the authoritarian personality, ethnocentrism, and dogmatism (for example, Adorno *et al.* 1950; Rokeach 1960; see also Chapter 11:237), the Gardner-Lambert research has included in the test battery assessments of authoritarianism, prejudice, stereotypes, and other measures of generalized social attitudes such as 'anomie' and Machiavellianism. Ethnocentrism is the tendency to view one's own community as superior and other groups as inferior. The authoritarian personality is ethnocentric, uncritical of authority figures, conforming, traditionalist, and prejudice-prone. Machiavellian-ism is the individual's tendency to manipulate others. 'Anomie', a concept which goes back to Durkheim's analysis of the place of the individual in society (see Chapter 10:192–3) refers to the loss of an unconscious acceptance of society as it is, a concept which has been widened to express the feeling of dissatisfaction with one's role in society. All these qualities—except anomie—have been found in the studies by Gardner and Lambert to be negatively correlated with the integrative motive and successful language learning. The 'anomic' individual, because of his critical attitude to his own society, is open to the demands of a different language and culture; therefore anomie is a positive predictor of language achievement. In other words, learning a new language demands flexibility and openness to new language norms and norms of social behaviour. The work of Gardner and his colleagues suggests that certain basic social attitudes provide a positive or negative predisposition towards second language learning.

Language learning requires other qualities of personality. Recent studies have attempted to identify them and to interpret them in the light of clinical or personality psychology. An obvious problem for all learners is the size of the language learning task, and the length of time and intensity of effort required to reach a satisfactory level of proficiency. Good language learners are not necessarily those to whom a language comes very easily; but they have persevered, have overcome frustrations, and have, after many trials and errors, achieved a satisfactory level of achievement (Naiman *et al.* 1978). One group of personality variables that distinguishes successful from unsuccessful learners is likely to be such characteristics as positive task orientation, ego-involvement, need achievement, high level of aspiration, goal orientation, and perseverance.

Another group of personality characteristics relates to the social and communicative nature of language. As a second language learner moves into a new linguistic, cultural, and social environment, certain social and emotional predispositions can either help or hinder him in coping with this aspect of language learning and in meeting the affective demands that a new language imposes on a language learner.

The distinction between *introversion* and *extraversion*, which was introduced by Jung and has been measured by Eysenck (1970), refers, on the one hand, to the tendency to withdraw from social interaction and be preoccupied with inner thoughts and feelings (introversion) and, on the other, to the tendency to be outgoing and interested in people and things in the environment (extraversion). If we emphasize the interper-sonal aspect of language learning, extraversion would be an asset, but introversion might well be regarded as advantageous to the systematic study of a language. To be sociable and outgoing is not only a popular stereotype of the good language learner; it has some support from a few studies (for example, Pritchard 1952; Pimsleur *et al.* 1966). To be outgoing and uninhibited is often also recommended as an appropriate strategy to be adopted by learners, particularly in the development of communicative skills (for example, Rubin 1975; Stern 1975; Naiman *et al.* 1978).

The concept of 'empathy'—the willingness and capacity to identify with others—which has been used in clinical and personality psychology has been applied to the ability of the second language learner to identify with the communicative behaviour of users of the target language. In one series of studies (Guiora 1972; Guiora *et al.* 1972) an attempt was made to relate empathy to the capacity to pronounce the language in a native-like manner. But the empathic capacity, it has been pointed out, is best regarded as 'an essential factor in the overall ability to acquire a second language rather than simply in the ability to acquire an authentic pronunciation' (Schumann 1975:226). Empathy as a personality variable is allied to the integrative orientation and, negatively, to the concept of ethnocentrism and authoritarianism referred to above. It would be difficult to imagine an empathic individual who is strongly ethnocentric (Naiman *et al.* 1978).

To explain the application to second language learning of the concept of empathy Guiora has suggested that the psychoanalytic interpretation of ego development can be applied to language development. The concept of 'language ego' compares language learning to the acquisition of other aspects of personality, such as body image, ego boundaries, and ego flexibility. Just as a child acquires a 'body image', the individual acquires a language ego. In the early years the language ego is fluid and its boundaries are not rigid. This would be a psychoanalytic explanation for the expectation that a young child adopts a new language, a new accent, and a new dialect more readily than an older person. As the individual grows, the language ego becomes less malleable and loses its permeability. Nevertheless, it is possible to imagine that there are personality differences in adults: some individuals retain a more permeable language ego than others, in the same way as some are more suggestible than others, can be more readily hypnotized, or are more open to the influences of the social environment in which they live. Thus, the willingness and the refusal to learn a language are accounted for in terms derived from such general psychological characteristics.

Several interpretations have attempted to conceptualize and explain the affective demands that language learning makes upon the individual. It is universally acknowledged that language learning presents 'a massive learning problem' (Stern 1975:307). One interpretation (Larson and Smalley 1972) lays emphasis on the disorientation of the language learner who experiences in the foreign country the trauma of 'culture shock' and 'culture stress'. Culture shock is the state of anxiety to which the learner is exposed upon entering a new and totally unfamiliar culture. Culture stress is the more prolonged discomfort resulting from discrepancies between the self-image and the expectations of the new culture. To meet these traumatic experiences, Larson and Smalley recommend that the learner should seek a sympathetic 'family' and become a 'child' in that family and with their help seek entry into the new language and in this way familiarize himself with the new culture: 'he needs a new family to help him grow up' (Larson and Smalley 1972:46).

Other interpretations have also laid emphasis on the sense of disorientation of the language learner and his loss of status. The learner is completely dependent on others, the teacher in the language class and a friend in the second language setting. This 'infantilization' or loss of adult status that the learner has to accept can be likened to a phase of personality development. The American psychologist Ausubel (for example, Ausubel, Sullivan, and Ives 1980), has described the child's condition as one of satellization, others have spoken of affiliation. In personality growth, a gradual emancipation of the individual or 'de-satellization' is to be expected. Equally, the language learner will strive gradually to acquire his own internal language standards and sufficient competence to be relatively independent. But to reach this goal the learner must in the first place accept the infantile status, and must be prepared 'to make a fool of himself' without fear of rejection. Consequently, the mature and mentally healthy individual who is detached, self-critical, and has a sense of humour, can cope with this demand of language learning better than a rigid or status-conscious individual who lacks self-awareness or humour and who suffers a sense of deprivation in the early stages of second language learning.

In another characterization of this state of disorientation the second language learner has been described as someone who is regularly in situations which are ambigious or even incomprehensible and confusing. Consequently, *tolerance of ambiguity* has also been considered a useful characteristic of a good language learner. The learner who is capable of accepting with tolerance and patience the frustrations of ambiguity that second language learning inevitably involves is emotionally in a better position to cope with them in a problem-solving frame of mind than a student who feels frustrated or angry in ambiguous situations. In studies on tolerance of ambiguity (Budner 1962) ambiguous situations were identified as characterized by novelty, complexity, or insolubility; and tolerance of ambiguity was defined as the tendency to perceive such situations as acceptable. Intolerance of ambiguity appears in association with a high level of dogmatism and authoritarianism. In investigations of second language learning that we undertook in the seventies, tolerance of ambiguity was found to be a good predictor of success (Naiman *et al.* 1978:100).

Conclusions on affect and personality

What, then, is the current picture of the affective aspect? Research has operated with three major concepts to describe it: attitude, motivation, and personality. Gardner (1975:58) has summarized most of the components we have discussed in a model of motivational characteristics (Figure 17.2). Although this model has been developed with reference to French as a second language, its categories are not restricted to a particular language; they apply generally to learners of a second language in a school setting. Gardner distinguishes four main categories:

1 group specific attitudes,
2 course related characteristics,
3 motivational indices,
4 generalized attitudes.

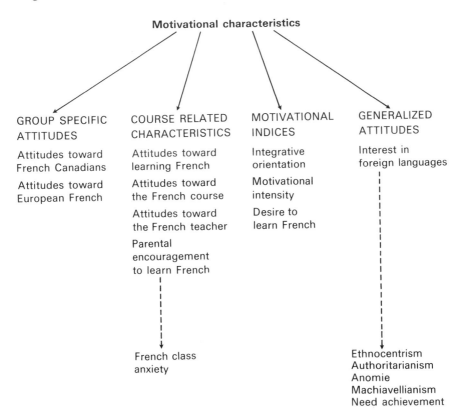

Figure 17.2   Gardner's representation of aspects of the motivation to learn French

The first component consists of *attitudes towards the community and people* who speak the target language.

The second component comprises *attitudes towards the learning situation itself*: how the individual feels about learning this language in a particular course and from a particular teacher and how he interprets his parents' feelings about learning the language. It also includes an assessment of the feelings of anxiety in the language class; the more relaxed and confident students are assumed to be more proficient than those who become anxious in the language class. While the learner entertains the attitudes in the first category *before* being placed into a learning situation, the second category refers to attitudes that develop *during* the learning process.

The third category refers to the *learner's motives for learning the language*, the goals pursued by the learner, and the intensity of effort put into the language. It will be noted that in this model Gardner has dropped the instrumental orientation, because it is the integrative motive that, in his view, is the more crucial. This category includes, then, both pre-learning factors and factors that only become evident in the course of learning.

The fourth group of variables in Gardner's scheme, *generalized attitudes*, includes a general interest in foreign languages and certain personality characteristics: ethnocentrism, authoritarianism, anomie, Machiavellianism, and need for achievement.

Gardner's scheme, in short, comprises general personality characteristics which can be said to have positive or negative bearing on second language learning; attitudes related to the second language and the second language group with which the learner approaches language learning; attitudes that develop in the course of the experience of learning the second language in the classroom setting; and goal perceptions or motives for learning the second language. This analysis reflects interpretations derived from the experience of language teaching and from research trends in social psychology, particularly research on prejudice. While it lays out a number of affective components, it does not conceptually distinguish affective elements which determine and precede the approach to learning from those that accompany or result from the learning experience, nor does it clearly distinguish the more enduring personality characteristics from the more immediate emotional responses to language learning.

Gardner's model clearly expresses the view that just as aptitude cannot be treated as a unitary characteristic of the language learner, the affective aspect is also 'something more than merely wanting to learn that language' (Gardner 1975:71). It involves a variety of different components which together make up 'a total attitudinal orientation not only towards the French speaking community but also the French class and quite possibly out groups in general' (loc. cit.).

Summing up the analysis of the affective aspect, the following distinctions can be made:

1 *basic predispositions* in the individual and relatively pervasive personality characteristics which are likely to have bearing on language learning (for example, tolerance of ambiguity, need for achievement).
2 *more specific attitudes* related to second language learning, such as attitudes to language, language learning, and to ethnolinguistic communities in general, and attitudes to particular languages and language-speaking groups such as language learners' attitudes to the French language and France and to other francophone communities, or to the English language and British, American, and other anglophone communities, and so forth.
3 *the motivation of learners* that initiates and maintains the learning process, or that leads to the avoidance or rejection of learning; the stated reasons and perceived goals as well as the subconscious drives and needs that prompt and sustain the learning effort or lead to its inhibition or rejection.

What the analyses have hitherto largely overlooked are the affective concomitants of language learning itself and of language use, that is, the learner's emotional reactions to the language as a whole, or to specific language items, both in the first and the second language, as well as those emotional concomitants that are aroused by using the language as a foreigner and those that are prompted by communicating with non-native speakers.

Further distinctions that should be made but which, in the literature, are often not made clearly enough are the following:

(a) the affective conditions which *precede* the learner's approach to second language learning.
(b) the affective conditions that are *engendered* by the learning experience, and
(c) finally, the affective conditions that ultimately *result* from the learning experience and the learning outcome.

For example, much of the work of Gardner's Language Research Group has been concerned with initial affect. Observations in the NFER study of primary French (Burstall *et al.* 1974), on the other hand, report children's reactions to the learning experience itself. Some of the theoretical concepts discussed on previous pages, such as the trauma produced by language learning, the 'infantilization', 'de-satellization' of the learner, as well as Gardner's category of 'course related attitudes' refer to affective changes that occur during the learning process. The interest in affect during learning is also reflected in some recent experimental teaching approaches which attempt to reduce the learner's negative affect and inhibitions *vis-à-vis* the new language.[21] Finally, little has been said by researchers on affective learning as an objective or result of language learning. The affective outcome should not be overlooked in defining language teaching objectives. See Chapter 22.

The question that has principally interested research is the relationship between the affective state with which the learner approaches language learning and the proficiency levels reached. Here studies seem to be unequivocal: positive attitudes related to the language and the ethnolinguistic community are closely associated with higher levels of language proficiency. Learners who have positive attitudes learn more, but also learners who learn well acquire positive attitudes. Moreover, recent studies suggest that the kind of attitudinal factors that have so far been investigated may be more influential in the early stages of language learning than later. Among the affective variables that have been studied, relationships between language learning and the more fundamental personality variables have been much more difficult to establish than relationships with those variables that are more directly connected with the language and the learning experience itself.

Research on the affective aspect has been largely prompted by the conviction that cognitive factors are not the only ones that matter in second language learning. Whatever specific findings may emerge as generalizations it may be stated that *the affective component contributes at least as much as and often more to language learning than the cognitive skills* represented by aptitude assessment. Schumann goes so far as to claim that the affective and personality states provide the essential motor of the cognitive skills that come into play. According to this view, empathy, language ego flexibility, and permeability are factors needed to engage language aptitude and other cognitive skills.

Many of the concepts used in research on the affective aspect are a somewhat speculative mixture of common-sense observations, psychological theorizing, and empirical findings. Little has so far been done to observe and record the emotional and motivational states of language learners in the course of learning. However, the theory, research, and experimentation of recent years have led to the increasing conviction of the importance of the affective component in language learning.

Conclusion

Although learner factors are not yet well understood, our selective review of some of these factors has shown that there has been in recent years an increasing awareness of specific psychological characteristics which have bearing on approaches to language learning and which can ultimately influence the learning outcome. In a cautious way we can attempt to adapt educational treatment to the diagnosis of individual differences, provided we resist the temptation of stereotyping learners for selection or teaching purposes. Our knowledge of learning styles or personality factors is simply neither comprehensive nor refined enough nor sufficiently secure to base clear-cut administrative decisions on it. Nevertheless, the awareness of learner characteristics and individual differences among language learners can sensitize teachers to possible variations in learner reactions to teaching and to differences in learning strategies. The concepts of learner characteristics should therefore have a place in our language teaching theory and both cognitive and affective factors should be included. Educational background, previous language learning experience, as well as the components of aptitude assessments and learning styles can provide an indication of the way in which the learner is likely to respond to the cognitive demands of the more academic side of language learning. An analysis of affective and personality characteristics can indicate how the individual is likely to respond to emotional, motivational, and interpersonal demands of language learning.

We will now turn to the conditions under which learning occurs and finally consider the learning process itself.

Notes

1 Individualization in foreign language teaching, which was launched as a deliberate movement in America in the early seventies (Altman and Politzer 1971) can be regarded as a systematic attempt to allow for individual differences in language learning. While this movement had rightly responded to a weakness in language pedagogy, it lost its impetus after a few years, like many other language teaching innovations, probably because its advocates had underestimated the magnitude of the task they had set themselves in trying to match individual learner characteristics with appropriate teaching techniques. For later reassessments see a symposium in the *Modern Language Journal* (Individualizing, etc. 1975) and a special issue of *System* (Altman 1977). See also Rodgers (1978). The recognition of individual learner differences that led American language teachers to explore individualization gave rise in Britain to a debate on the relative merits of streaming or mixed ability classes (for example, CILT 1972). For a discussion of these parallels see Stern (1979). For further references see also Chapter 19, Note 10.

2 For reviews and discussions of the optimal age issue, with references to many studies, see, among others, Stern (1967, 1969), Smythe, Stennet, and Gardner (1975), Stern and Weinrib (1977), McLaughlin (1978: Chapter 3), Stern, Wesche, and Harley (1978), Chun (1979), Krashen, Long, and Scarcella (1979), Brown (1980: Chapter 3), Stern and Cummins (1981). For a review of the literature on early language teaching between 1975 and 1981 see Stern (1982).

3 For example, Montaigne in his treatise on the education of children writes approvingly about his own language education: 'In my infancy, and before I began to speak, he (Montaigne's father) committed me to the care of a German ... totally ignorant of our language but very well versed in Latin. This man, whom my father had sent for and paid a large salary, had me continually with him. (Montaigne describes that his father had insisted that everybody around him also spoke to him in Latin.) I had learnt to speak as pure Latin as my master himself without art, book, grammar or precept, whipping or a single tear' (Montaigne 1580–1588/1899:77–78).

4 For references to Penfield's work see Chapter 15, Note 6.

5 See Chapter 14:293–4 and Note 20 on the discussion of nativism versus environmentalism in the interpretation of language acquisition.

6 It should be pointed out that the 'early-immersion' children at later stages of schooling, i.e., after two or three years of full immersion, normally continue in bilingual programmes, that is, a form of schooling in which only a certain proportion of the school-day, approximately 40 per cent, is spent in the target language environment. See Chapter 4, Note 13, for general references to research on immersion.

7 In Ausubel's terms (see p. 382 and also Chapter 18:398–9), young children are 'satellizers', that is, they are cognitively, emotionally, and socially dependent on parent figures, hence they may also be more responsive to the social and language norms offered by their environment than adults are likely to be. This tendency may make children more amenable to social learning ('acquisition') of second languages in natural settings than adults; in other words, as Schumann (see p. 363) has suggested, children have a more permeable language ego. Older learners have more general school experience and as a result may be more efficient than children as learners in academic settings and on cognitive language learning tasks. That is why where a language is learnt as a school subject older learners are likely, on the whole, to be better than younger ones. On similar grounds Cummins (see Stern and Cummins 1981) has suggested that the interpersonal communicative skills ('BICS') are more likely to develop in early childhood whereas, in the later years, the cognitive and academic skills ('CALP') are more readily developed. While adopting a similar point of view Krashen (1981) maintains that 'the ability to "acquire" language does not disappear at puberty ...' (op. cit.:77).

8 For recent discussions of aptitude and other cognitive factors in second language learning see Carroll (1981). Stern, Wesche, and Harley (1978) and Stern and Cummins (1981) include short overviews. Wesche (1981a) analyses aptitude in detail and illustrates the successful application of aptitude testing in a concrete adult

teaching situation. For a comprehensive critical review see Vollmer and Sang (1980). For a criticism of aptitude as spelled out in language aptitude tests see Neufeld (1973).

9 In Britain a great deal of emphasis has been laid in recent years on the principle of 'language across the curriculum' as, for example, in the Bullock Report (1975). It should however be pointed out that in spite of this emphasis the Bullock Report has not included second language activities. It has concerned itself entirely with the language component of English as a subject and English in other subject areas.

10 As we have already seen above (Chapter 16:352), in recent discussions Cummins (1980) has also pointed out that classroom language learning involves general cognitive and academic abilities. For earlier views on these relationships see also Chapter 14:294. In one study, Carroll (1975a:16) has expressed himself sceptical about the prediction of language aptitude from general verbal intelligence: 'I have concluded that tests of verbal ability are of limited significance in predicting aptitude and rates of learning for a broader range of individuals'.

11 The question of innateness is discussed by Carroll (1975a) and by Neufeld (1975) in the same volume.

12 In an interesting study Politzer and Weiss (1969) devised a training programme in the skills underlying the aptitude tests: auditory discrimination, sound-symbol relations, grammatical sensitivity, and inductive language learning. They gave this training to an experimental group and compared the results with those of a control group which did not have the training. It produced unexpected results. In the first stage the control group ended up with a higher aptitude gain score than the experimental group and at no time was the experimental group clearly superior in achievement or aptitude. Politzer and Weiss suggest three possible explanations: (1) that the training was not powerful or intensive enough; (2) that the aptitude training was perceived by the students as an additional burden unrelated to the language course and was therefore resisted; and (3) that, in fact, aptitude could only be influenced to a limited degree. In spite of the failure of this experiment, there are indications that the skill of how to learn a language can be improved (Naiman *et al.* 1978).

13 While MLAT does not specifically include word knowledge in the first language as a separate test component for the reasons stated by Carroll (1975a) (see Note 10), one of the subtests, Spelling Clues, presupposes varying degrees of familiarity with English vocabulary.

14 Carroll (1975a) distinguishes 'inductive learning ability' from 'grammatical sensitivity'. In our view, 'grammatical sensitivity'

requires 'inductive learning ability'. This ability coincides with the capacity to make linguistic forms explicit and to abstract them from a context (see Chapter 18:411 on this point). This feature of aptitude is similar to the cognitive style feature referred to below as 'field dependence/independence' (see pp. 373–4).

15 Neufeld (1973) takes both test batteries apart and concludes that they may be useful in predicting success in conventional language classes, but that they are quite deficient in 'defining and measuring language aptitude' (op. cit.:152).

16 For a more detailed discussion of cognitive styles and their relevance to language learners see Naiman *et al.* (1978:29–31) where references to the various cognitive style tests can be found. See also Brown (1980:Chapter 5) or McDonough (1981:130–33).

17 The work of Gardner and Lambert on attitude and motivation (1972) represents the classical research on affective aspects. For another approach to attitudes see Burstall (1975a) and Burstall *et al.* (1974). Oller (1981) reviews and takes a critical look at attitude research. A different and earlier approach to affective factors can be found in Brachfeld's (1936) and Stengel's (1939) papers referred to in Chapter 15:321–2. This tradition was taken up in the seventies by Lawson and Smalley (1972), and more specifically by Brown (1973) and Schumann (1975). Krashen (1981a:101–102), following Dulay and Burt, advances an 'Affective Filter' hypothesis. See also Brown (1980:Chapter 6, 1981) Stern and Cummins (1981), and McDonough (1981:Chapters 9 and 10).

18 The investigation of attitudes towards learning French formed part of the large enquiry in Britain on French in primary schools, briefly described in the section on the age question (see pp. 364–5 above). See also Chapters 4:56 and 6:106, 111.

19 The semantic differential technique, developed originally by Osgood, Suci, and Tannenbaum (1957) for measuring concepts, has been widely used to assess attitudes. The examples are taken from Gardner and Lambert (1972:157).

20 For beginnings of studies on this largely unexplored area see Naiman *et al.* (1978), Brown (1980:Chapter 6) and McDonough (1981:Chapter 9).

21 For example, Curran's Community Language Learning is an attempt to respond to changing affective states in the learning process. See Curran (1976) or Brown (1980:116–120) who gives further references.

18 Conditions of learning and the learning process

Conditions of learning: two settings

In the model of second language learning, outlined in Chapter 16 (Figure 16.1), it was suggested that the learning process is determined by learner characteristics (Chapter 17), the social context (Chapter 13) and by the conditions of learning. The two main conditions to be considered are language learning either inside the target language environment or away from it, and that means mostly in the language classroom (box 3 in Figure 16.1). Until about 1970 it was assumed in language teaching theory that the kind of learning with which theory is or should be mainly concerned was classroom learning. However, language learning research in the seventies began on a wave of reaction against research on educational treatment and against the acrimonious debate on the merits of different language teaching methods. Turning away from these frustrating arguments about classroom teaching, researchers believed that the condition which they should study in the first place was that of language learning in the target language environment and outside the classroom, that is, language learning under 'natural' conditions, 'uncontaminated' by formal teaching: 'informal', 'free', 'undirected', or 'naturalistic' language learning.[1]

Why should the distinction between these two conditions of learning be so important? Here the two technical terms, introduced by Krashen, language 'acquisition' and language 'learning' are helpful (see Chapter 15:331 and Note 17; also pp. 403–4 below). Within the target language environment there are opportunities for constant and varied language use, situations in which the learner must cope day-by-day with the new language as a living means of communication offering opportunities for absorbing or 'acquiring' the language not unlike the acquisition of the first language in infancy. In the classroom, as a rule, the second language is treated more deliberately and more analytically, and therefore it is the place for language 'learning' in Krashen's restricted sense, i.e., through systematic study and deliberate practice guided by teaching.[2]

It should be added though that educational treatment may offer opportunities *mainly* for learning, and the supportive target language setting opportunities *mainly* for acquisition. Nonetheless, learning may also take place in the target language setting, and acquisition in the classroom (Figure 18.1).

	Classroom	Target language environment
'Learning'	More likely	Less likely
'Acquisition'	Less likely	More likely

Figure 18.1   The learning/acquisition distinction relative to conditions of learning

The language environment (language context or setting) in which a learner finds himself is psychologically, i.e., from the learner's perspective, not an absolute. The Spanish and Italian *Gastarbeiter*, studied by the Heidelberg Research Project on Pidgin German (Heidelberger Forschungsprojekt 'Pidgin Deutsch' 1979), *objectively* learnt German in a target language supportive environment, because these *Gastarbeiter* worked in German-speaking industries in German-speaking cities. Equally, the five Spanish-speaking children learning English in an American school setting whose language development was studied by Lily Wong Fillmore (1979) over a period of several months were immersed in their target-language environment. Nevertheless, migrant workers or children of immigrants do not all experience the same language environment in identical ways nor do they respond to it in the same manner. Some immigrants live and work in ethnic ghettoes or in social contexts where they have, or choose to have, minimal contact with the target language. Whether the language setting is supportive or non-supportive for this or that individual learner depends partly on the specific social context and partly on the way the individual responds to that context.

Nor should we assume that learning in the 'natural' target language setting is always completely 'natural' or 'undirected'. Many countries, for example, Britain, the U.S.A., Australia or Canada for English, France and Quebec in Canada for French, East and West Germany or Austria for German, and Sweden for Swedish, provide formal instruction in English, French, German, or Swedish, for immigrants or migrant workers inside the target language environment. In other words, the language class can give added input for learning (in Krashen's sense) even within an acquisition context. And if there is no *formal* instruction in the target language environment the learner may still be more or less exposed to *informal* teaching by relatives, friends, or co-workers, or he may seek out study help from books and other specific learning aids. In the 'educative society' teaching is not confined to formal school settings. *Educational treatment can be looked upon as any deliberate creation of language learning conditions.* It may be simple and informal as when a friend helps the language learner through casual teaching. Or it may be systematic and elaborate as in a language class and involve the entire apparatus of a prepared curriculum.[3]

The distinction, therefore, between learning from exposure to the second language in the target language environment and learning from a teacher (i.e., educational treatment) is not rigid. The two conditions can be visualized as a continuum. At one extreme we may find learners learning without external help and direction purely from exposure to the second language through living in the target language environment, and at the other we find learners learning the second language exclusively in a language teaching setting. In the main, however, we are likely to find that second language learners receive input to varying degrees both from exposure and from educational treatment. Simultaneously, we must always bear in mind that the 'input' from either condition of learning is not perceived and processed by different learners in an identical manner.[4]

Making the distinction between these two main conditions of language learning, our language teaching theory must avoid *a priori* a bias in favour of one or the other.[5] Ideally, of course, the natural language setting and the educational treatment should complement each other. In practice, however, the conditions are often far from ideal. Immigrants into a new country often find no one to help them educationally; there is no opportunity for learning, and conversely, many learners of a foreign language are too far away from the target language environment to have any chance of using the new language outside the classroom and therefore have little opportunity for acquisition processes to come into operation.

What is important for the interpretation of the language learning process is that the specific conditions under which language learning occurs are factors to take into consideration. Of the various determinants impinging on language learning—social context, learner characteristics, language setting, and educational treatment— it is the educational treatment that can most readily be modified and adjusted to different social and language environments and to individual learner factors. This gives educational treatment its special importance. It will be considered in the final part of our study (Part 6).

Interpreting language learning

It is an anomaly of language teaching theory that the language learning process itself, which, after all, is crucial to the success of the enterprise, was, until recently, almost entirely neglected by research. A theory of language teaching which does not, implicitly or explicitly, include an interpretation of learning itself is hardly imaginable. Accordingly, in the model of language learning the learning process has been placed symbolically into the centre of the diagram (see box 4 in Figure 16.1). Teaching methods, as we shall see below (pp. 400–5) and in Chapter 20, make more or less clearly formulated assumptions about the learning process.

As was seen in the foregoing chapters, the application of psychology and psycholinguistics brought with it many attempts to explain this process in psychological terms. These attempts have sometimes been criticized for oversimplifying it (for example, Rivers 1964; Carroll 1966). At other times writers have attempted to iron out inconsistencies between different viewpoints (for example, Anisfeld 1966). Then again certain writers have tried to refine our understanding of the learning process, a task that Carroll and Rivers have repeatedly undertaken over the last two decades (for example, Rivers 1964, 1968/ 1981, 1972/1976; and Carroll 1966, 1971, 1974, 1981a). The learning process has also been interpreted in terms of Gagné's multiple learning model (for example, by Ingram 1975). In short, there are speculations about language learning in the light of theories, observations, and experiments derived from general psychology. If we want second language learning to be conceptually related to other forms of learning, as it should be, this is indeed a necessary part of theory development. But it cannot remain the only one. From about 1970 it has been widely acknowledged that second language learning must be studied *directly*, and not simply by extrapolation from general learning theory or from first language acquisition.

The historical development of this research in the seventies has already been described in Chapter 15. In the present chapter we will interpret the language learning process itself, as it is suggested by the theoretical and empirical research of the last ten years. We will first look at the developmental nature of the language learning process; next we will examine three persistent issues which have proved to be central to a study of language learning; thirdly we will discuss the concept of language learning strategy, and finally we will conclude this discussion by a brief sketch of the essential features of our own view of language learning.

Language learning as a developmental process

The practical problem

As a developmental process second language learning has been viewed in an idealized way as a progression from zero proficiency to one hundred per cent, full, or native-like proficiency, and it has been thought of as divided into progressive stages. The problems that have arisen in the real world are that the ideal end point is almost never reached, that the progression is hardly ever a regular one, that the learner's progress is often arrested at a point well below the ideal end point, that learners not infrequently regress, and that stages of language learning are not clearly defined.

Any language curriculum implicitly makes assumptions about the entire second language developmental process. For example, when Mackey (1965) and Halliday, McIntosh, and Strevens (1964) insisted on grading and sequencing the language input, the assumption was that such an arrangement of the language in carefully graded incremental steps would correspond to natural learning sequences. A recent conception of the learner's language development, offered by Trim as a justification of the Council of Europe Unit/Credit Scheme of a curriculum for adult learners (1978), is diametrically opposed to this view of language development. Trim writes:

'The idea of language development as a straight-line process does not stand up to closer inspection. We are not all marching at different speeds along the same road towards a common goal.' (1978:7)

'We abandon the aim of leading the learner step-by-step along a path from the beginning to the end of the subject. Instead, we set out to identify a number of coherent but restricted goals relevant to the communicative needs of the learner.' (op. cit.:9)

The question, of course, is whether learners in fact fit this very challenging non-linear interpretation of the progression in a new language any better than the linear progression Trim so roundly condemns. Research on the developmental sequence does not yet have definitive answers to this question. But the issue has begun to be investigated.

Research questions
The study of the order, sequence, and regularity of the language learning process has crystallized around a few questions. The first question that has interested investigators has been whether the learning of a second language supports the contrastive analysis hypothesis which was so confidently adopted after Lado's book *Linguistics Across Cultures* (1957): to what extent does the learning of a second language provide evidence for a transfer or interference from the first language and other previous language experiences? Alternatively, does language learning follow universal laws regardless of the learner's first language and other languages previously known? Following from these alternative hypotheses a further major question that has been predominant in the

investigations has been the question of similarities or differences between phases of second language learning and phases of first language acquisition. The hypothesis that these studies have tried to verify has been that second language learning, like first language learning, follows a lawful sequence, or 'built-in syllabus' of language acquisition (Corder 1967), and that, by and large, identical sequences are applicable to first and second language learning. These questions have been formulated as two theories (T3s in terms of Chapter 2). One is that a second language learner develops his second language by a process of restructuring his first language (the Restructuring Hypothesis); the other theory is that the second language growth is independent of a particular first language and develops rather in the manner in which a child 'creates' his first language (the Creative Construction Hypothesis).

The main research approach to the issue has been to study learners' linguistic products, their error patterns, or, more comprehensively, their linguistic output or interlanguage and to infer from the characteristics of the corpus over a period of time and from comparisons with studies of first language acquisition regularities in the second language learning process. Both observational case studies and experimental studies have been made. Some deal with younger children acquiring two languages simultaneously, while other studies have examined the process of adding a second language after the first language has already been established. Both younger and older learners, including adults, have been observed. Much of the evidence consists of examples of the development of particular phonological, morphological, syntactic, or discourse features.[6]

The results of these studies are conflicting. Instances can be cited for likenesses as well as differences between first and second language development. Equally, there are instances of transfer and interference as well as examples of inherent lawfulness of second language development.

The current state of knowledge, based on a review of investigations on interlanguage syntax, has been assessed by Hatch (1978a) in a study already referred to in Chapter 16:355. Her questions and answers on the sequence of development can be summarized as follows:

If there is a sequence is it the same regardless of the learner's native language? (op. cit.:35)	The answer to this question is not clear: there are differences of opinion about transfer or interference from the native language. (op. cit.:61).
'Is the sequence the same for child and adult learners?' (op. cit.:35)	Yes, the same systematicity and variability are observed in child and adult learners. (op cit.:61)

'If there is a sequence in second language acquisition, is it the same as that described for first language acquisition?' (op. cit.:35)	No clear answer emerges. Claims and counterclaims have been made. 'Similarities are there, but differences have also been shown' and explained on grounds of greater cognitive maturity and the influence of the first on the second language. (op. cit.:61)
'If there is a sequence, and if that sequence appears to be similar across learners, how can we explain it?' (op. cit.:35)	Many variables—interaction with others, personal factors, instruction, etc.—are important. But we know too little to offer definitive explanations. (op. cit.:62–66)

On the basis of her review, then, Hatch finds no clear evidence which would conclusively support either the Restructuring Hypothesis or the Creative Construction Hypothesis.[7] This line of research has on the whole been disappointing. It has not yet fulfilled all the expectations of a clearer understanding of second language learning as a developmental process.

A sketch of second language learning development

Standing back from the details of the empirical and theoretical debates one can perhaps interpret the psychological development of second language learning as a cognitive, affective, and social process in the following manner.

The beginnings of the learning process

At the beginning of learning a new language the learner's competence has none or hardly any of the characteristics previously described as the competence or proficiency of the first language user. Competence in the second language is at zero in all respects, or nearly so. The second language learner is, however, not in the same situation as an infant learning the first language. It has been pointed out that a second language learner knows language but not *a* language (Cook 1977:2): 'The learner already knows the potential of language and can go straight in to discovering how that potential is realized in the second language.'[8] This situation of the second language learner has affective, cognitive and social consequences.

Affectively, the second language learner has to come to terms with the frustrations of non-communication. The lack of language contact and of means of expression and the absence of a safe reference system give the learner an initial intellectual and emotional shock which has been noted, as we have seen, by some theorists. Schumann (1975), following Larson and Smalley (1972), distinguished between culture shock, language shock, and culture stress. It is, in our view, legitimate to recognize and distinguish both language and culture *shock* and both language and culture *stress*. The shock is experienced in the early stages of exposure to the language, especially when the learner is suddenly immersed into the second language environment. It is likely to be mitigated if the learner is in a language class or in some other transitional environment. Age, aptitude, past language learning experience, personality, and other learner factors may influence the learner's reactions. Language and culture stress are concomitants of the on-going learning experience.

Cognitively, the learner at the start faces disorientation with regard to all linguistic, semantic, and sociolinguistic aspects of the second language. While first language competence is experienced as compelling and completely self-evident— a secure and familiar frame of reference— the second language system appears, to begin with, as indistinct, arbitrary, puzzling, almost entirely meaningless, and often as artificial, even 'wrong', sometimes absurd, and, on many occasions, disconcertingly confusing.

The task for the learner is, first of all, to overcome the disorientation and constraints that characterize the early stage of contact with the new language, and to build up, cognitively and affectively, a new reference system and a system of meanings, to develop a feeling for right and wrong in language use, a sense of familiarity and order, and eventually to acquire the capacity to use the language 'creatively', that is, to be able to respond to communicative situations appropriately and spontaneously and to be able to think in the second language. This process has often been described—as in first language acquisition—as 'internalization', 'interiorization', or 'incorporation'. Such terms suggest that the process can be viewed as analogous not only to first language acquisition but also to social learning or conscience formation in child development.

In social terms, the child is emotionally dependent on parent figures who provide the social norms which the child unconsciously makes his own. In a similar way, the second language learner is, as far as the norms of the second language are concerned, dependent on the model given to him by the teacher, the native informant, or the second language milieu which he must also make his own. This in the second language learner is a more deliberate social strategy of following a model or of imitation than in the acquisition of the first language. The teacher or the learner's friend is at first the learner's external linguistic 'conscience' or competence, in other words, a parent figure; and an important part of the learning task consists of internalizing the language norm, i.e., achieving independence from the teacher or parent figure and acquiring an internal, intuitive standard of right and wrong. Schumann (1975), once more following Larson and Smalley (1972), has drawn attention to the infantile status of the second language learner, that is, his dependence on a supportive 'parent' figure, teacher, or friend. This linguistic and sociolinguistic dependence is a necessary early phase, a 'satellization' phase of language acquisition.[9]

Progressive patterns of language learning
The advance from zero competence to whatever level the learner wishes to attain in the second language goes through several stages. The intermediate competence levels which have been referred to as 'transitional competence' (Corder 1967) or 'interlanguage' (Selinker 1972) ideally become progressive approximations (Nemser 1971) to the second language norm set by the native speaker or teacher. Each of the interlanguages represents a competence level composed of correct and incorrect elements relative to the second language norm. It is the learner's best interpretation of the second language. It is not surprising to find that attempts have been made to relate the second language learner's progression to a child's developing levels of competence in his first language. Unlike the child, the second language learner does not reach the native-like norm in an unfailing manner. The problem for language teaching is how to help the language learner to reach a level of proficiency which, in the learner's estimation, is serviceable, and how not to become arrested at an unserviceable lower level.

In Chapter 16, language competence or proficiency was characterized by four features: formal mastery, semantic mastery, communicative capacity, and creativity. The assumption is often made that these four characteristics provide a kind of natural syllabus or sequence of second language learning: first the form of the second language is learnt, then meaning becomes attached to the form, then the communicative capacity can be developed, and finally the learner becomes sufficiently liberated in the second language to use it creatively. For example, in the early seventies, Rivers (1972) proposed a division of the language teaching operation into two broad phases of 'skill-getting' and 'skill-using'. Valette and Disick (1972) divided language teaching objectives into four phases corresponding roughly to the acquisition of form (for example, phonological, morphological and syntactical practice), followed by the acquisition of meaning, then making these consciously acquired systems automatic, and, finally, putting them to use in real life situations. Neither Rivers nor Valette and Disick imagined these stages as rigidly divided.

In our view, the four characteristics of language proficiency are best assumed to develop simultaneously from the start, and to complement each other throughout the learning process. At the beginning they are extremely rudimentary. As the learner advances they become more and more differentiated. They can however not be completely pulled apart in the way this is often done in some language teaching programmes.

Since the language learning process lasts a long time, the learner (and correspondingly the teaching curriculum) may choose to enter into a new language through an emphasis on any one or more than one of the four aspects of language proficiency, and in the course of time the emphasis may shift. To that extent it does make sense to distinguish, for example, a mainly skill-getting from a mainly skill-using phase. In accordance with this distinction it is useful to view the pattern of progression in the second language as consisting of two broad stages.

During the first stage, the learner is preoccupied with the language as a system (form and meaning). Communication at this stage is arduous and strictly limited. The learner is dependent on help, both in learning the system and in using it for communication. This *dependent* or satellization phase ends as soon as the learner feels confident enough to use the language, however defectively, for his own purposes—whether as a listener, speaker, reader, or writer.

Once this stage, experienced subjectively as a stage of greater freedom of communication, has been reached, the learner enters the de-satellization phase. Successful learners retrospectively sometimes recall a feeling of 'breakthrough', when true communication became a much more practical possibility. The learner now develops his own inner standards of correctness, and is less dependent on the external linguistic conscience of the teacher or native speaker. Before this 'threshold level' or 'turning point' has been reached, the feeling of language stress is very marked. Beyond it, it is much reduced.[10]

The foregoing account of the progressive pattern of language is, it must be remembered, a working theory (a T2) and as such speculative. Although it is based on an interpretation of several sources, it is not the result of documented empirical investigation. It could form the basis for making empirical studies. But until our knowledge of the developmental process is more secure, language teaching theory must operate with such plausible hypotheses of language development to be confirmed, modified, or rejected by systematic empirical investigations and the observation of second language learning in action.

Three central issues of language learning

The difficulties of second language learning are a common-sense fact which is universally recognized. Error analysis and interlanguage studies have been used to identify the characteristics of some of these difficulties. There are also a few valuable introspective studies of sophisticated language learners which illustrate well the enormous problems of language learning.

An insightful analysis of the experiences and difficulties in learning Danish in the target language environment was made by Terence Moore (1977), an English psychologist, who had been appointed to the Chair of Clinical Psychology at the University of Aarhus in Denmark. He illustrates the frustrations resulting from feeling restricted in communication in such events as listening to lectures in Danish, participating in small group meetings, in face-to-face conversations, and in taking part in casual talk in the second language with academic colleagues. As a clinical psychologist his experiences led him to empathize with patients who suffer from language handicaps.

Wilga Rivers (1979), the well-known specialist in language pedagogy, once kept a diary of learning Spanish while on a trip to Latin America. In spite of her unrivalled theoretical knowledge of language teaching and learning, she suffered the same frustrations that less sophisticated learners also have to put up with. She reported, for example, that in her effort to use Spanish, other languages previously studied in which she was by no means very proficient intruded into her attempts to speak Spanish, for example,

> 'When I begin to say a Spanish sentence I tend to think in German ("*ich ... aber*") that is, in my fourth, less fluent language ...' (op. cit.:69)

> 'I find myself saying *Buon giorno* instead of *Buenos días*. Why the Italian now?' (op. cit.:73)

> 'German pops still into my mind and in the morning I have to concentrate on what language I'm to use ... does using my weakest language make me feel I am "talking foreign" and therefore seem appropriate?' (op. cit.:75)

Any language teaching theory is bound to be confronted with the question of how to cope with language learners' most persistent difficulties. The speculations and controversies about language teaching reflect the key problems encountered by most learners; and different pedagogical approaches, curricula, and teaching strategies represent attempts to overcome them. The concepts of language learning research are in many instances psychological reformulations of issues that have been long-standing interpretations entertained by experienced language teachers.

Language pedagogy between 1900 and 1980 and language learning research between 1950 and 1980 have tried to come to grips with three major language learning problems which regularly arise in the overall development we have just described: (1) The first is that of the disparity between the inevitable dominance in the mind of the learner of the first language and other languages previously learnt, and the inadequacy of the learner's knowledge of the new language. Let us label this issue the *L1-L2 connection*. (2) The second is the choice between deliberate, conscious, or relatively cognitive ways of learning a second language and more subconscious, automatic, or more intuitive ways of learning it. We might call these alternatives *the explicit-implicit option*. (3) The third issue is the learner's problem of how to cope with the dilemma that is presented by the fact that it is hard, if not impossible, for an individual to pay attention to linguistic forms, the language as a code, and simultaneously to communicate in that code. This issue can perhaps be described as *the code-communication dilemma*.

Because these are three key issues in the language learning process, it can be argued that language teaching methodology, controversies about language learning, and, lately, empirical research have focussed on them. It would follow that a language teaching theory which aims at being realistic about the learning process must also take them into account. The point is not that we are looking for some patent answers to each of them. It is much more a question of understanding them as inherent problems presented by second language learning.

The L1-L2 connection

The century-old debate in foreign language pedagogy between the 'traditional' or 'grammar-translation' method and the 'direct' method centres around the discrepancy between the learner's knowledge of his first language and the target language. Should the learner be encouraged to exploit his first language knowledge and learn the new language 'crosslingually', that is, through his first language, or should he keep his second language learning completely separate and learn the target language entirely within and through the second language, that is, 'intralingually'? As a psycholinguistic theory of second language learning this conflict reappeared in Ervin and Osgood's differentiation (1954) between co-ordinate (intralingual) and compound (crosslingual) bilingualism. Around 1960, contrastive analysis was a reaffirmation of the importance of the first language in the learning of a second language. The rejection by some researchers of the contrastive hypothesis (for example, Dulay and Burt 1974) from around 1970 represents a shift towards accounting for second language learning in intralingual rather than crosslingual terms. On the other hand, Schumann's acculturation theory (1978) in the same decade was concerned again with the learner's attempt at resolving the problem of moving from his first language as an existing reference system to the target language as a new reference system.

Selinker's concept of interlanguage (1972) or other similar concepts that recognized the systematic nature of the learner's language assumed that the learner to a certain extent develops his own second language system on the basis of his first language. What remained controversial was, as was noted above, whether the interlanguage is *predominantly* a reconstruction of the second language on a first language basis, the Restructuring Hypothesis, or whether the interlanguage is 'created' by the learner independently of first language influences, as is claimed by the adherents of the Creative Construction Hypothesis. The advocates of the Creative Construction Hypothesis looked for inherent principles of second language development and for parallelism between first language learning in early childhood and second language learning. Thus, the Restructuring Hypothesis assumes the learner's first language as a basis for second language proficiency; it is in that sense a crosslingual theory of second language learning. The Creative Construction theory, by contrast, offers an intralingual interpretation. When Corder makes a case for an interlanguage continuum 'intermediate between the restructuring and the recreation hypothesis' (1978:90), this view of the language learning process parallels a pedagogic compromise between an intralingual (for example, direct method) and a crosslingual (for example, translation) teaching strategy. Neither in second language learning research (as Hatch's review had already indicated) nor in foreign language pedagogy has this issue so far been resolved, and it demands further exploration.

The explicit-implicit option

A second issue in most language learning is whether the learner should treat the language task intellectually and systematically as a mental problem, or whether he should avoid thinking about the language and absorb the language more intuitively. As a choice of teaching methodologies it crystallized between 1965 and 1970 (for example, Carroll 1966) in the debate on the relative merits of the cognitive or the audiolingual approach. It was the subject of numerous studies and discussions. Rivers (1964:115–30) dealt with it at length in her critical discussion of one of the assumptions of audiolingual teaching: 'Analogy provides a better foundation for foreign language learning than analysis' (see Chapter 15:326). A series of investigations by a group of Swedish researchers, the GUME Project (for example, Levin 1969), focused specifically on the implicit-explicit option. Around the same time Carton (1971) advocated the concept of *inferencing*: 'A language pedagogy that utilizes inferencing removes language study from the domain of mere skills to a domain that is more closely akin to the regions of complex intellectual processes' (op. cit.:57). In short, Carton opted for an explicit rather than implicit strategy of teaching.

In recent research on language learning this question reappeared as Krashen's Monitor theory, (see pp. 391–3 above; for references see Chapter 15, Note 17). Krashen's distinction between language learning (explicit) and language acquisition (implicit), treats language *learning* as a conscious process, *acquisition* as more subconscious. To learn a language (consciously) the learner must know the rules of the language. Given these conditions he can 'monitor' his linguistic output. Developing the construct of a 'Monitor', Krashen has argued that the Monitor acts as a kind of editor. It comes into play particularly in reading and writing in the second language because under these conditions there is time to go over and check the linguistic output. In spoken communication the Monitor would tend to interfere with fluency. Some language learners overuse the Monitor and become inhibited, others are overconfident and underuse it. For the development of second language proficiency, the acquisition process, in Krashen's view, is more important than learning. In other words, proficiency develops more through unselfconscious use in communication than through conscious study and the slow control of the language by the Monitor.[11]

In our view the discussion on learning versus acquisition has been inadequately related to the psychology of learning where, as we saw in Chapter 14:311, conscious and deliberate learning has for decades been contrasted with such concepts as social learning, latent learning, and blind learning, without considering these distinctions as dichotomous. Drawing attention to the same distinction between learning with or without understanding, the eminent psychologist Hilgard wrote long ago in *Theories of Learning* (1948):

'What is the place of understanding and insight? Some things are learned more readily if we know what we are about. We are better off as travelers if we can understand a timetable or a road-map. We are helpless with differential equations unless we understand the symbols and the rules for their manipulation. But we can form vowels satisfactorily without knowing how we place our tongues, and we can read without being aware of our eye movements. Some things we appear to acquire blindly and automatically; some things we struggle hard to understand, and can finally master only as we understand them.' (op. cit.:8)

Hilgard avoids a rigid choice between learning and acquisition when he writes: 'Because all learning is to some extent cognitively controlled, the distinction between blind learning and learning with understanding becomes one of degree' (op. cit.:343).

How to relate deliberate and less conscious (automatic) learning to each other in second language learning has remained another unresolved issue in second language pedagogy as much as in language learning research. That it should be investigated in association with research in general psychology has recently been advocated by Carroll (1981a). As we shall see below (p. 407) some experimental studies, for example, by Bialystok (1979, 1980) are attempts to explore the role of monitoring and inferencing in second language learning.

The code-communication dilemma

The third issue, the code-communication dilemma, has become a major focus of interest in recent years. Classroom language teaching is mainly concerned with code, and is therefore 'formal', or analytical. That is, the language is an object of academic study and practice. Language use in the natural language environment is 'communicative'. That is, it is non-analytical or 'experiential'. The learner is a participant in real communication. Both the formal and communicative teaching and learning strategies have in fact always been known, but in the past it was taken for granted that a language is learnt in the classroom through study and practice. The use of communication as a deliberate teaching strategy is a relatively recent development (see, for example, Allwright 1976; Stern 1981). Certain teaching experiments such as the Canadian immersion programme (Stern 1978) or the Welsh Bilingual Project (Beaudoin *et al.* 1981) have demonstrated that even in a quasi-foreign language situation, a communicative strategy can be an effective means of language teaching. It creates in a school setting the 'field' conditions of language learning through communication.[12]

The interplay between formal learning of the language as a code and the learning of the language through use in communication has aroused widespread attention in the late seventies, but the relative contribution of formal and communicative strategies to effective language learning is another question that has remained largely unresolved.

Studies of learning strategies

Attempts have been made by a few investigators to find out how learners cope with the difficulties that are presented by language learning. They have made efforts to study the *strategies* and *techniques* of second language learners. The term learning strategy which has come into use in dealing with this question has not been employed in the same way by all researchers. In our view strategy is best reserved for general tendencies or overall characteristics of the approach employed by the language learner, leaving learning techniques as the term to refer to particular forms of observable learning behaviour, more or less consciously employed by the learner. The study habits or detailed procedures in dealing with specific aspects of language learning, such as looking up words in a dictionary, illustrate learning techniques.

Various investigations have produced different inventories of learning strategies (for example, Rubin 1975; Stern 1975; Fröhlich 1976; Naiman *et al.* 1978). But their lists comprise more or less similar categories divided up in somewhat different ways. Thus, in the early seventies Rubin (1975), the well-known American sociolinguist, began to pursue the idea of investigating language learning by studying the strategies of successful language learners. She observed language classes directly or on videotape, listened to tapes of students discussing their own strategies, observed herself in language learning situations, and elicited observations from second language teachers. On this basis she established a provisional list of seven learning strategies.[13] She defined strategies as techniques or devices which a learner may use to acquire second language knowledge.

The OISE Modern Language Centre in Toronto, Canada, also undertook studies of language learning strategies and processes. The first attempts, similar to Rubin's, tried to examine the strategies of good language learners based on a list of ten strategies developed by the present author (Stern 1975).[14]

In one of the enquiries in the Good Language Learner Project of the OISE Modern Language Centre the investigators (Fröhlich 1976; Naiman *et al.* 1978) probed the learning strategies of some thirty outstanding adult language learners through intensive retrospective interviews. The successful learners who were asked to recall the ups and downs of their language learning careers expressed a consensus among some of the strategies to be employed: a combination of formal self-instruction with the attempt to immerse themselves in a communicative setting. This study found that '... good language learners take advantage of potentially useful learning situations, and if necessary create them. They develop learning techniques and strategies appropriate to their individual needs' (op. cit.:25).[15]

A classroom observation study at high-school level in the same project, on the other hand, did not reveal anything of value about learning strategies, probably because the highly structured setting of the conventional classroom did not offer students opportunities for displaying observable strategies. But interviews with the same high-school students were more revealing: the great variety of opinions about classroom language learning suggested that the students had distinct likes and dislikes about different classroom activities, and the study gave support to the idea of individualization. The criticisms of students, according to this enquiry, 'could be more constructively used if students were induced to reflect about their learning situation so as to identify reasons for their negative or positive reactions towards specific learning tasks and activities' (op. cit.:81).

A productive approach to the study of language learning in progress is a research method developed by Hosenfeld (1975). Briefly, this investigator invites students individually to perform typical language learning exercises in textbooks and simultaneously to think aloud as they complete the exercise. Through these introspections, Hosenfeld has been able to discover in concrete and vivid detail how students tackle learning tasks. Thus, one of these studies (Hosenfeld 1979) is a useful check on a well-known sequential classification of exercises as mechanical, meaningful, and communicative (Paulston and Selekman 1976). In this study Hosenfeld was able to show that a pupil in an individualized course, bypassing all the drills offered by the text, immediately applied the fairly advanced grammatical explanations to examples drawn from her own life experience. In other words, she moved straight from a grammatical explanation to an imagined communicative situation. This observation would lend support to the view of language learning, outlined on p. 399, which suggested that different facets of language proficiency (form, meaning, communicative capacity, and creativity) do not appear as rigidly divided into successive stages but operate more or less simultaneously. Hosenfeld's simple interview method of enquiry revealed a student's learning strategy and showed that the assumptions that teachers or textbook writers had made about the learning process did not necessarily agree with the procedures actually employed by the learner.[16]

A third approach that has been tried during the past few years in order to come to grips with understanding the second language learning process is one developed by Bialystok which consists of specific experimental tasks within a theoretical framework. Bialystok (1978) developed a model of second language learning which was broadly based on the language learning models referred to in Chapter 16; it incorporated aspects of Krashen's Monitor, and made the distinction between formal and communicative strategies, as well as the distinction between explicit and implicit ways of learning referred to above. The Bialystok model has the merit that it is designed to allow for all language output, comprehension as well as production, and it relates to learning in a formal (classroom) as well as to an informal or natural setting.

This model is on three levels, labelled input, knowledge, and output. At the input level we are outside the learner and take note of the conditions of learning: language exposure or classroom. At the knowledge level we are, so to speak, inside the 'black box' where Bialystok postulates three stores: the first, 'other knowledge', consists of the learner's first language and all the information he has gathered about languages and the world in general. The second and the third store are those that contain the target language knowledge. Some of this knowledge which is consciously held consists of grammar rules, vocabulary knowledge, and so on: the 'explicit second language knowledge store'. The 'implicit knowledge store' contains intuitively known items in the new language. The system comes into action through processes which activate all three knowledge stores. A small number of strategies which the learner may or may not employ link the input, knowledge, and output levels with one another: formal or functional (communicative) practice, monitoring, and inferencing. The output of this system is of two types: Type I is immediate and spontaneous, for

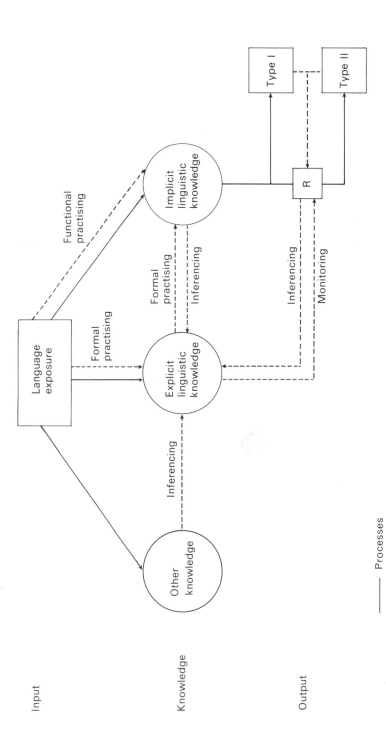

Figure 18.2 Bialystok's model of second language learning

example, talking to people or listening to a radio broadcast. The Type II output is slower and more deliberate, for example, doing a written classroom exercise with an emphasis on rules, a written test, or reading a text—all tasks which make it possible to go over one's performance and check and correct it. It is in Type II output that the Monitor can come into play.

With this framework Bialystok has devised a number of ingenious experiments in which the input is deliberately modified, and the use of different strategies is then studied. Thus, in one set of experiments Bialystok (1980) studied the inferencing strategy by examining the effect of different cues on the comprehension of a reading passage in a foreign language: what difference does it make if we provide a picture, a summary of the gist of the passage, or a glossary of words used in the passage (dictionary), or if instead of these aids, we give a short lesson on how to inference? The results of this study suggested that the deliberate provision of different kinds of contextual help (pictures, dictionary, and lesson) help learners in different ways: a thematic picture aids in global understanding, a glossary provides both global assistance and assists the reader at the detailed word level. A lesson in inferencing in this instance proved less effective than the more specific aids of a picture or dictionary.

In another experiment (Bialystok 1979) grades 10–12 high-school students and a group of adults learning French had to listen to correct and incorrect sentences in French, for example,

Maman a donné un petit pain à Paul et il a mangé le.
Il s'est dépêché mais l'autobus était déjà parti.

In one of the experiments the subjects had only to listen to each sentence and indicate if it was correct or contained a grammatical error. In a second experiment subjects had to determine which part of speech was in error. In the third experiment they were given a list of nine rules (for example, 'The object pronoun comes directly before the verb.') and they had to identify the rule that was broken. This study was undertaken to examine the distinction between implicit intuitive knowledge and the more explicit knowledge of the language. As a result of this study Bialystok was led to the pedagogical conclusion that 'the learner's intuition (his implicit knowledge store) must be developed and encouraged, and efficient strategies for consulting explicit knowledge must be trained ... Concentration on only the formal aspect of the language and rule formation not only precludes important aspects of the language but ignores as well the learner's great intuitive source' (op. cit.:101). Once more we find support there for the theory advanced on pp. 399–400, namely that the different aspects of proficiency develop concurrently.

Conclusion: a view of language learning

A conception of language learning is an essential component of a language teaching theory. Language teachers are in a good position to observe patterns of language learning and to appreciate intuitively the characteristics of poor and good learners and to surmise why some students progress and others run into difficulties. Empirical research and theorizing have helped us to develop concepts about language learning and to recognize possible relationships between learning outcomes, the learning process, learner characteristics, the conditions of learning, and the social and linguistic context in which learning occurs.

Our knowledge about language learning is still very incomplete. A better understanding is likely to result from continued investigations combining various approaches: inferences from linguistic product, i.e., interlanguage analysis; behavioural observations of learners; subjective reports of learners' experiences; and psycholinguistic experimentation.

In the meantime, in spite of the incompleteness of our knowledge, certain questions have become clearer and directions for interpreting the language learning process begin to emerge. First of all, language learning is a developmental process which cannot be fully controlled by feeding the language to the learner in slow incremental steps. A useful assumption supported by some research is that in successful learners the different components of proficiency, formal and semantic knowledge, communicative capacity, and creativity, develop concurrently. The stages in the developmental process are as yet not fully understood. It is not clear why many learners become arrested at certain interlanguage levels and why there should be a fossilization of error patterns. Is the learning process at later and more advanced levels of proficiency different from earlier and more elementary levels? Is the concept of a turning point or threshold level viable? Can it be said that after the click of the turning point, or once over the threshold, the second language forms a more serviceable and efficient configuration? Is the learner after reaching the turning point more emancipated and less dependent on the help of a native speaker or teacher?

Besides questions about the nature and stages of language development, the language learning process presents three main problems which we labelled as (1) the L1-L2 connection, (2) the explicit-implicit option, and (3) the code-communication dilemma. We have argued that these are three issues with which all language learners and language teachers must come to terms. In doing so the learning process is best understood as threefold involving the learner (a) intellectually/cognitively, (b) socially, and (c) affectively.

From all these considerations and from our review of the learning research we can derive four basic sets of strategies which we hypothesize good learners are likely to employ while less efficient learners employ them only weakly, fail to maintain them concurrently, or fail to develop them altogether.

1 Good learning involves first of all an *active planning strategy*. In view of the sheer magnitude of the language learning task the good language learner will select goals and subgoals, recognize stages and developmental sequences, and actively participate in the learning process.

2 The good language learner employs, secondly, an *'academic' (explicit) learning strategy*. Language learning is, to some extent, a perceptual and cognitive task, and good learners are prepared to study and practise. That is, they face up to the language as a formal system with rules and regular relationships between language forms and meanings. They pay attention to these features and, either independently or by comparison with the first language, develop the second language as a consciously perceived system which they constantly revise until the learning process is completed. They analyse the language and develop the necessary techniques of practice and memorization. They monitor their own performance and revise it in order to progress towards an improved second language command. They learn to exclude the first language more and more until they acquire internal standards of grammaticality and appropriateness. They are capable of treating the language as knowledge and as a skill to be acquired. Those features that language aptitude research has identified undoubtedly come into play in the application of this strategy.

3 Good language learners are likely to employ a *social learning strategy*. They recognize the inevitably dependent status in early learning and accept the infantilization and satellization involved. As they progress, they strive towards emancipation and desatellization. Good learners seek communicative contact with target language users and the target language community either in person or vicariously through writings, media, role playing, or immersion. In spite of their limitations, good learners will tend to develop and use 'communication strategies', i.e., techniques of coping with difficulties in communicating in an imperfectly known second language. Good learners become actively involved as participants in authentic language use. Neither aptitude nor proficiency tests appear as yet to have tapped the features underlying these social skills that also contribute to the development of proficiency.

4 Finally good language learners use an *affective strategy*. That is, they cope effectively with the emotional and motivational problems of language learning. Classroom learning as well as immersion in the

target language environment each entail specific affective problems which have been characterized as language shock and stress, and as culture shock and stress. In spite of these difficulties, good language learners approach the task in a positive frame of mind, develop the necessary energy to overcome frustrations, and persist in their efforts. They cultivate positive attitudes towards the self as language learner, towards language and language learning in general, and towards the target language and its society and culture. It stands to reason that certain personality characteristics and attitudes can predispose learners towards the use of appropriate affective strategies.

These, then, are in our view the basic sets of strategies required for effective language learning. Needless to say that all learners do not employ all four strategies equally and at all times. Learners of different languages, educational and cultural background, and of different age and maturity levels are likely to learn languages with different emphases on one or the other strategy and with different degrees of skill in applying these strategies. For intelligent and intellectual adults, strategies (1) and (2) may be more important, while for young children an emphasis on (3) and (4) and a minimal approach to (1) and (2) can be expected. It is plausible to assume that failure to learn can be attributed to failure to employ one or the other strategy at a time when its use would have been critical.

The aim of further learning research remains to improve our understanding of second language learning in different social contexts, under different language learning conditions, at different age and maturity levels, and at different levels of proficiency. For such research the interpretations offered in this chapter could offer a provisional theory as a T2 and T3 in the sense of Chapter 2.

For our language teaching theory here and now, however, we cannot wait for research to provide us with definitive answers. We must be prepared to make certain assumptions about language learning. At the same time we must also be prepared to modify these in the light of new evidence from our own practice or from research.

Notes

1 As was pointed out in Chapter 1, second language (SL) learning in the more restricted sense refers to the learning of a second language in the environment in which the language in question is used as the regular medium of communication.

2 As we already noted in Chapter 14:311, the psychology of learning has always made similar distinctions between different kinds of learning but, contrary to Krashen's use of the term, has not restricted the concept of learning to deliberate and conscious learning.

The learning-acquisition distinction is not common outside educational linguistics. See pp. 403–4 below and also Chapter 1:19–20.

3 For a definition of 'teaching' in this wider sense refer back to Chapter 1. A more systematic analysis of educational treatment is made in Part 6: Concepts of Language Teaching.

4 This is why several authors have insisted on a distinction between the 'input' the learner receives and the learner's 'intake': 'What elements are, in fact, processed from the data that is available is determined by what the current state of the learner's interlanguage grammar permits him to *take in* at that moment' (Corder 1978: 81–2).

5 It is interesting to observe that the main theoretical concepts which were introduced by research since the mid-seventies by implication expressed a bias *against* the contribution of language teaching and a bias *in favour* of naturalistic language learning. According to Schumann (1978), for example, 'Language learning is not a matter of method, but is a matter of acculturation, and where acculturation cannot take place ... we cannot expect to achieve much more than we are now in our foreign language programs' (op. cit.:47). With reference to Krashen's Monitor Model it has been said that 'many of the activities traditionally used in the classroom are directly involved with language learning (as distinct from language acquisition) and the Monitor Model claims that proficiency in speaking the second language cannot be obtained by explicit language learning' (Gingras 1978a:90). A consequence of the lack of interest of the prevailing language learning research in language teaching has been that language pedagogy in the seventies, with a few exceptions, continued to change and develop without research. This fact has prompted some observers (for example, Bausch and Kasper 1979; Stern and Cummins 1981) to demand specific research on language teaching and language learning in classroom settings to match the numerous studies of the seventies on free language learning.

6 Excellent reviews of these studies are presented by McLaughlin (1978) and Hatch (1978). See also Cook (1978) for a concise and comprehensive overview and bibliography. The classical investigations of learning two languages in childhood are those by Leopold (1939–1949). See also Brown (1980:Chapter 3).

7 The two hypotheses are perceptively discussed by Corder (1978:74–8) who favours 'a hypothesis intermediate between the two extremes' (op. cit.:78).

8 Corder discussing the second language learner's starting point makes a similar point: 'It is somehow counter-intuitive to suggest that the second language learner starts from scratch, that he is in effect learning language all over again. Does the fact that he already possesses language and is a language user count for nothing?' Hence,

Corder argues, the second language learner does not start from a linguistic zero (Corder 1978:76).

9 As was already suggested in Chapter 17, it is useful to relate these social aspects of second language learning to Ausubel's stages of ego development which he describes as satellization and desatellization (see Chapter 17:382). For an explanation of these concepts in personality development, see Ausubel, Sullivan, and Ives (1980).

10 The notion of a 'turning point' in the language learning process was suggested by Brachfeld (1936) in a paper referred to in Chapter 15:321–2.

11 McLaughlin (1978a) has questioned the Monitor theory and particularly the distinction between conscious 'learning' and sub-conscious 'acquisition': 'I believe that a more successful model is one that avoids recourse to conscious or subconscious experience and that ties into human information processing generally and the literature on language development' (op. cit.:330).

12 See on this issue our earlier discussion on communicative language teaching in Chapter 12, particularly pp. 258–62 and Figures 12.2 and 12.3. Dodson (1978) makes a similar distinction between 'medium-oriented', and 'message-oriented' language learning. For a further discussion of this issue see also d'Anglejan 1978 and Stern 1981, 1981a.

13 Rubin, who is also widely known for her work on language planning (see Chapter 11), defined strategies as techniques or devices which a learner may use to acquire second language knowledge. She suggests that the good language learner is (1) a willing and accurate guesser, (2) has a strong drive to communicate, (3) is often uninhibited about his weaknesses in the second language and ready to risk making mistakes, (4) is willing to attend to form, (5) practises, (6) monitors his speech and compares it to the native standard, and (7) attends to meaning in its social context.

14 The ten strategies identified by Stern (1975) are:

1 Planning strategy: a personal learning style or positive learning strategy.

2 Active strategy: an active approach to the learning task.

3 Empathic strategy: a tolerant and outgoing approach to the target language and its speakers.

4 Formal strategy: technical know-how of how to tackle a language.

5 Experimental strategy: a methodical but flexible approach, developing the new language into an ordered system and constantly revising it.

6 Semantic strategy: constant searching for meaning.

7 Practice strategy: willingness to practise.

8 Communication strategy: willingness to use the language in real communication.

9 Monitoring strategy: self-monitoring and critical sensitivity to language use.

10 Internalization strategy: developing second language more and more as a separate reference system and learning to think in it.

15 In another study (Wesche 1979) Canadian civil servants learning French were videotaped in their classes and the videotapes were later analysed for behavioural clues characterizing successful language learning. The subjects were also interviewed. The observational data suggested that 'realistic, communicative use of the second language, talking about the language (perhaps reflecting both an analytical and interest component), the number of different kinds of learning activities pursued, and an element of persistence are characteristic of those students who most rapidly improve their second language fluency in this intensive training situation' (op. cit.:422). The interviews brought to light a diversity of practice activities, insight, interest in ways of learning and remembering, and personal involvement.

16 Cohen and Hosenfeld (1981) who have strongly recommended the use of 'introspection' and 'retrospection' as important techniques for the study of language learning (see Chapter 14, Note 1) have rightly pointed out that introspection is of value not only to research but to students themselves and as an aid in teacher training.

PART SIX

Concepts of language teaching

19 The study of education and its relevance to language teaching

Among the disciplines we have considered the study of education (educational science, educational theory) is perhaps the closest to language pedagogy. Yet, it is probably the least recognized and the most neglected. Language teaching in its most widespread forms occurs in *educational* settings: school, university, college, adult class, and so on. Usually it forms part of a curriculum of studies and is meant to make an educational contribution to this curriculum. Concepts of education are applied as a matter of course in language teaching just as much as in other subjects of the curriculum. The language teacher almost inevitably operates with some notion of what teaching involves and how language teaching fits into the educational enterprises of which it customarily forms a part. It is therefore all the more surprising to note how little thought has been given to the relationship between language teaching and the study of education.

Because of lack of thought and probably also some academic snobbery, education may not have received the same consideration in language teaching theory as has been given to the other disciplines. There is hardly anything in the way of a 'history' of the relationship between the study of education and language pedagogy to report. Yet, since the *study* of education has the totality of the *practice* of education as its object, it has as much importance for language pedagogy as have linguistics, social science, psychology, or any of the other disciplines we have looked at.

As a professional field of study, education—like medicine or law—draws on a number of other studies, such as philosophy, psychology, or sociology, as source disciplines. For language teaching theory, however, education itself can be regarded as a multidisciplinary source discipline. By treating it as such, educational assumptions in language teaching can be brought to light, and language teaching can be viewed more clearly in relation to other educational activities.

Education as a discipline is commonly divided into several sub-disciplines: (1) philosophy of education, (2) history of education, (3) educational psychology, (4) educational sociology, (5) economics of education, (6) educational administration and organization, (7) educational planning, (8) comparative education, (9) curriculum, and (10) educational technology.

In considering the role of education in this final part of the book we must proceed in a somewhat different manner from the way we have treated the other disciplines in earlier parts. Once more we will look at the discipline 'in its own right', but this time we will immediately discuss the possible relevance of the different sub-disciplines for language teaching. In the present chapter we first briefly examine the majority of the sub-disciplines listed above (1–8) and then, secondly take a closer look at the last two (9 and 10) because of their special importance for language teaching. After this overview we will ask ourselves, in Chapters 20 and 21, how the concept of teaching has in fact evolved in language pedagogy and, finally, in Chapter 22 work out our own interpretation.

1 Philosophy of education

The most general and comprehensive view of education is offered by educational philosophy; but philosophers of education have interpreted their contribution in different ways. Traditionally, they have regarded it as their function to provide intellectual guidance on the great issues that education raises. More recently, this view has been emphatically rejected; some philosophers have regarded their task as one of logical analysis and conceptual clarification (O'Connor 1957:4). Others have seen their role as one of critics and questioners of common beliefs and assumptions. A more tolerant view today is that the philosopher should not reject any of these roles, but that he should not perform them as a bystander, observer, and commentator; instead, he is urged to bring his whole philosophical repertoire much more directly to bear upon actual issues of education and take part in their solution (for example, Beck 1974). According to this point of view, educational philosophy is or should be concerned with:

'(1) analysis of educational issues,
(2) clarification (or "intellectual therapy"),
(3) tackling abstract educational questions,
(4) seeking general perspectives on education,
(5) developing and employing strategies of cogitation suited to educational inquiry,
(6) dealing with "higher order" problems in education,
(7) solving "intellectual puzzles" that arise in educational inquiry,
(8) investigating the nature of conceptual thought relevant to education,
(9) studying educational language,

(10) analyzing and criticizing what is going on in other educational subdisciplines,

(11) facilitating the work of other educational subdisciplines.' (Beck 1974:16)

Educational philosophy, widely interpreted in this way, has bearing on any and every aspect of the study and practice of education, and language pedagogy is no exception.[1]

Since language teaching is concerned with a task which, although complex, can be relatively clearly specified and therefore has better defined criteria of success or failure than many other educational activities, language teachers have perhaps been less inclined than other educators to consider their activities with philosophical questions in mind or from a broader educational point of view. Yet, there is probably no aspect of language pedagogy which could not gain by being viewed from a philosophical perspective. Of particular importance for language pedagogy is the analysis of concepts and the discussion of values.

Conceptual analysis

If one approach to the philosophy of education is conceptual analysis and the clarification of terms, this is exactly a task that we have set ourselves in this book; what we have attempted to do is therefore in line with this view of educational philosophy. Language teaching theory shares with other educational activities the use of such terms as 'theory', 'practice', 'education', 'training', 'drill', 'instruction', 'curriculum', 'ends and means', and many others. As we have seen in earlier chapters in the case of some of these terms, their unexamined use can be confusing and misleading, and their analysis is as necessary for language teaching theory as it is for any other educational activity.[2]

Language pedagogy has operated, more or less consciously, with the notion of a defined curriculum (syllabus, programme, or method) and has, in recent years, attempted to distinguish between purposes of language teaching (goals, aims, or objectives) and the procedures needed (approaches, methods, or strategies) to achieve these purposes. Thus language teaching theory has become committed to an ends/means approach, and this view of the curriculum is often treated as a self-evident truth, and not as a model which has its uses but which may also have certain limitations. It is therefore valuable to recognize that the ends/means model has been questioned by some educational philosophers. Peters, for example, believes that there are 'principles implicit in different manners of proceeding or producing' (1963:87), but that they cannot really be divided into *ends* which are distinct from educational activities as *means*.[3] While Beck accepts the common-sense validity of an ends/means model he questions this model on other grounds: it implies the power of the educator to define, provide, plan, and assess the end product, educational achievement, with little or no participation on the part of the learner. In recent years the relationship between language teacher and language learner, implicit in this model, has also been seriously called into question. Educational philosophy can thus help in clarifying unstated assumptions. In similar ways, it can throw light on such key concepts which are often used far too lightly as discovery learning, individualization, interest, motivation, teaching, skill, and evaluation.

Questions of value
How important is it to learn other languages? This question involves language pedagogy in discussions of a second area of educational philosophy, questions of educational *values*. Each of the disciplines that we have considered in this book makes its own philosophical assumptions. Linguistics, for example, is conceived as an objective and 'value-free' study of language. Nevertheless, it implies value judgements such as the positive value of language itself, the value of objective linguistic enquiry, and the recognition of the study of language as worthwhile or good. These judgements, underlying linguistics, give no direction to the decision of what languages to study, nor do they tell us what the study of a particular language can contribute to the education of an individual student. But judgements of this kind are needed when the importance of language learning as a curriculum activity has to be weighed in any educational scheme. Studies on educational values have therefore direct bearing on the discussions on the value of language learning.

Moreover, the act of language learning, i.e., moving from first language to second language, may—as we saw in the discussion of social contexts—lead the learner to a comparison of *cultural values* in two different societies. The way in which members of the second language community are perceived or approached is an expression of ethnic value judgements. Even the desired degree of bilingual competence to be achieved by the student is ultimately a value question. For example, fluency in a second language is worth having if the second language is viewed as a means to communicate; and communication with another ethnolinguistic group is a value to be assessed against other values cultivated by the curriculum.

The teacher's treatment of the language learner and of the learning process also indicates philosophical values. Are learners participants in the teaching-learning process, or are they treated as passive recipients of pre-arranged mechanical activities? Educators looking at language teaching and learning rightly ask themselves, just as they ask of any other curriculum activity: What is the underlying educational philosophy of second language learning, and how does this philosophy relate to the philosophy underlying other educational activities?

These indications are sufficient to suggest the merit of a philosophical perspective for language pedagogy. See also pp. 436–7 below.

2 History of education

The importance of an historical approach to language teaching theory has already been emphasized in Chapters 5 and 6 and therefore need not be elaborated here any further. What is necessary to add in the present context is a reminder that the history of language pedagogy forms part of the *history of education* which provides the wider context, and while language teaching has been subjected to influences which in some ways set it apart from the general historical development of education, in most respects the history of language teaching can be better understood in the framework of educational history.[4] Language pedagogy as part of, and apart from, educational history can be illustrated by a few examples.

The growing importance of 'modern' languages, towards the end of the nineteenth and the early part of the twentieth century, and the gradual decline of the classics form part of a broad historical trend of extending, modernizing, and diversifying the school curriculum. In the second half of the nineteenth century modern languages took their place besides other 'modern' subjects such as history and the natural sciences. Similarly, throughout the first half of the twentieth century languages were thought of as belonging to the curriculum of *secondary* education because the curriculum conventions dictated that primary education was vernacular schooling in which foreign languages had no place. It was only during the last thirty years that the primary curriculum has become sufficiently flexible to tolerate or welcome second language learning. Language teaching also has in many respects been subject to the same influences of educational thought that have affected other curriculum subjects and indeed the entire curriculum: psychology, testing, educational research, and educational reform movements. By recognizing these broad trends which influence education the language teaching theorist can appreciate better common educational assumptions.

In other respects, however, languages went their own way. First, language teaching was exposed to the influence of phonetics and linguistics which had no exact parallel in other curriculum subjects (see Chapter 5). Second, the intellectual demands of 'content' subjects, such as history, geography, or the sciences, were viewed differently from the achievement of mastery in a modern language.[5] Third, language teachers as persons were often a group apart from teachers of other subjects, because they included native speakers of the foreign language who brought with them other pedagogical traditions and other cultural presuppositions; they did not always fit into the cultural context in which they taught their native language, nor did they necessarily conform to the ethos of the schools in which they taught.

In the sixties, at a time when educational thought emphasized creativeness, training in critical thinking, and individual differences among learners, and vehemently rejected mechanical and authoritarian modes of teaching, language pedagogy—following its own linguistic and psychological theories—stressed the need for drill, habituation, conditioning, and automatic responses. The language class of the sixties demanded a much more rigid and authoritarian environment than was regarded as educationally valid in most other curriculum areas.

The history of language pedagogy is best viewed as the result of an interplay between general educational history and influences specific to language teaching alone. Hence the problem for the historian of language pedagogy is to account for common elements and divergencies from the general trends, and it is all the more important not to view the development of language teaching theory without reference to the general history of education.[6]

3 Educational psychology

Among the disciplines making up the study of education, educational psychology is perhaps the most developed. Since it covers every aspect of education from a psychological angle, educational psychology is central to educational theory. Relevant aspects for language teaching have already been discussed in Chapters 14–18 and we therefore refer the reader to these chapters.

4 Educational sociology

As a branch of sociology, educational sociology places education as an activity and institution into a social context. It recognizes schools and other educational institutions as agencies within a society. Schools may be viewed as part of a society, reflecting the existing social structure. Thus, one of the social purposes of schooling is the maintenance of an existing social order. Welcomed in this role by some, it is criticized by others as an instrument for perpetuating social divisions and social injustice. Writings in educational sociology have demonstrated how in many societies the composition of school populations inevitably reflects the divisions in society, and to what extent school systems are openly divided according to the major social strata in that society. Languages have played their part in this class division of education. Until recently, learning foreign languages was regarded as a mark of an 'elitist' education; and in some school settings languages are taught not so much for their intrinsic merit but mainly because they give social prestige to the learner.

Educational sociology also recognizes that schools have been created as agencies of social change through which the society may deliberately strive to modify its internal social structure. Education has been used in some societies as a means of breaking down class barriers, and thus creating equality of opportunity and increasing social mobility. Languages have sometimes been introduced into primary schools and into non-academic secondary schools as a move towards more democratic education, and to counteract the privileged position of second languages characterized in the previous paragraph.

At the same time educational sociologists have shown how difficult it is for a society to modify its own internal social structure by educational intervention. The work of Bernstein in Britain, described in Chapter 10, for example, has indicated that there appears to be a close link between social class and dominant language use in the family, impeding social mobility through schooling. Likewise, in African countries the power of social forces is so great that it has not been possible to halt the trend towards urbanization merely by introducing agricultural training into schools. Social change, then, through education is likely to be effective only if it forms part of a wider social movement reaching beyond the confines of the school.[7]

The success of attempts to modify the linguistic characteristics of a society by education also depends on the backing these attempts receive from the larger society. The sociological analysis of the school in relation to society is of value to language teaching theory because it provides the concepts for interpreting the social framework within which to view the role of languages taught in a school system. Looked at sociologically, teaching a language is an intervention by which the linguistic repertoire of a population is modified. Schools can be said to have been relatively successful in making populations 'bicodal', i.e., capable of reading and writing. The attempts to teach second languages through school systems are attempts to make a population 'bilingual'.[8]

Why, one may ask, have the effects to establish literacy through schooling been so successful, whereas second language teaching has been far less so? One reason may be that in the case of literacy the efforts of the schools—because of the importance attributed to literacy in society—have usually been sustained over many years. Another is that many social transactions in our daily lives demand reading and writing. The skills once acquired are constantly in use inside and outside the school setting. Second language learning, on the other hand, has generally been provided at a slower pace and usually without the intensity and urgency of a literacy campaign. Moreover, a second language taught in school is frequently not used outside the language lesson. Where a second language is taught because it has to become the language of instruction or because it is the language of the environment, as for example French or English have been in some countries, the second language has tended to be learnt more successfully. The social use that is likely to be made of a second language has bearing on language learning. Therefore, in order to understand why language learning is *not* successful in school, it is equally important to look outside school and to ask: what importance does society attribute to the second language? The answer to that question lies less in a declaration of the value of second language learning than in the uses to which the second language is put. Efforts to create bilingualism by means of bilingual schooling—as, for example, in the immersion programme in Canada—are likely to be more successful than conventional language teaching as a subject because the language is treated in school as a medium rather than as a subject.[9] But even in these cases the success is likely to be shortlived if it is not backed by bilingual contacts and exchanges in the community at large. Thus, the success of language teaching is dependent upon major forces in society, such as the role, or perception, of languages in that society.

Besides these macro-sociological factors, education also offers opportunities for 'micro-sociological' studies. We can take a closer look at the school or classroom and its members, the teachers, students, and other participants, and observe the interactions among them. By viewing the school or class as a micro-society educational processes are brought into relationship with the study of social groups, and in this way common elements as well as special characteristics can be identified. A school class constitutes a 'formal' group, and in recent years educators have experimented with different ways of grouping on the grounds that the size, composition, and internal organization of the group can influence learning. Traditionally, the school class consists of a teacher and a conventionally established number of pupils. Modern thought on the social framework of education has led to experiments with smaller groups and individualized patterns of teaching and learning. The teacher's role in the educational setting is therefore not absolutely fixed. In the past the teacher's role as the unquestioned director of all activities at all times and a class following the teacher's directions in a uniform way was accepted as the right and normal pattern of teacher-student relations. Today teachers are frequently encouraged to cultivate a more fluid and more flexible classroom organization and not to view themselves exclusively in the role of class instructor. As we noted in the section on the history of education (see pp. 423–4 above), language teachers have been slow in applying these changes in social organization to the language class, probably because of a conviction that the nature of language learning did not permit a shift towards a more unstructured, more democratic, and more flexible group organization. However, there is today a greater awareness of the social structure and the 'social climate' of the language class. Experiments in individualization and in modification of the class composition indicate that a more flexible approach to the structure of language learning groups can be helpful in language teaching. In short, the questions of class composition, size, social climates, and group activities, which constitute the micro-sociology of educational groups and form part of educational sociology, have implications for our interpretation of the language class.[10]

5 Economics of education

This relatively new branch of educational studies applies economics to education from two points of view. Its first major concern is to establish the economic benefits of education. This approach has been of particular importance to developing countries in deciding on the distribution of limited resources. A difficult question to answer is: What economic benefits can be derived from establishing or extending an educational system? Even more difficult to answer would be the question: What economic benefits can result from instituting in a school system the teaching of a particular subject, such as a foreign language?

The second approach provides the necessary cost accountancy of educational choices and decisions by making an assessment of costs and benefits of specific educational measures in comparison with other measures. Such assessments cannot be based entirely on economic principles. They demand substantive knowledge and an assessment of the merits of an educational activity. Factors to be taken into account in calculating the costs of teaching a second language include: (a) the cost of training and supply of language teachers, (b) the cost of supervisors and non-professional aides (native assistants, language laboratory technicians, etc.), (c) the cost of materials, (d) the time for class instruction, (e) the size of the language class, and (f) the space and installations needed, for example, the cost of a special language classroom and its equipment. Thus, the extension of language classes in a school system from twenty to forty minutes may involve the doubling of the teaching force with a consequent rise of cost per student. The reduction of class size would have a similar effect. Expensive fixed installations with heavy initial capital outlay and high maintenance costs, such as a language laboratory, must be considered in relation to benefits that students can derive from such a specialized room and the saving in teaching time. Could the same educational benefits be gained in some other way at lower costs? Is it more economical to start a language in the early stages of primary education, or more intensively at a later stage of schooling? The economics of education have not been sufficiently developed to offer ready-made techniques to answer such questions easily. But as this growing sub-discipline perfects its approach, language teaching will no doubt also be considered more clearly from this perspective.[11]

6 Educational administration and organization

Since language teaching takes place within the framework of educational systems, it shares with other educational activities its dependence on the structure of the system and within the system upon the structure of the particular institution, for example, the structure of a school, college, or university. The tasks of administration are varied: administrators ensure the proper functioning of the entire system and of each institution. They are responsible for the application of the laws on which ultimately the functioning of any educational institution depends. Administration further includes the management of finances, of school buildings and services, the enrolment of students, the staffing of schools, the supervision or development of a curriculum, the organization of examinations, the assessment of student achievement, and the certification of teachers. The administrator has to gather statistical and other information, maintain records, negotiate, interview, resolve conflicts, initiate change, suggest goals, organize, decide, supervise, and evaluate.[12]

Most educational systems have a three-tier administrative structure: (1) central (national, state, or provincial), for example, Ministry of Education, Department of Education and Science (U.K.); (2) regional or local, for example, local education authority (U.K.), school board, board of education (North America); (3) institutional, for example, school or college.

Education is normally controlled by democratically elected bodies at local and regional levels; hence the administration of education is usually answerable to such elected bodies (school board, board of school trustees, or education committee). Centrally, the entire educational system, administered by the Ministry (or Department) of Education, is answerable to a national or regional parliament.

In different systems of education the powers and responsibilities are distributed in different ways between the three levels of administration. While in the earlier developments of educational systems there had been a tendency towards rigid control of schooling by a central authority, the advancement of education in recent years has tended to bring with it a wider distribution of responsibilities and greater autonomy at the local and school level.

Within each educational institution powers and responsibilities are varyingly distributed among students, staff (teachers, instructors, professors), and the principal (director, head, president, vice-chancellor, etc.). In some systems the community at large or organizations of teachers or parents have a part to play in decisions at the school or local level; in other systems teachers and parents are offered little or no opportunity to influence the conduct of the schools.

Most educational systems are organized in three broad stages: (1) primary, i.e., education for children from the beginning of mandatory schooling to early adolescence; (2) secondary, i.e., full-time education in the teens to the end of mandatory schooling and beyond; (3) tertiary or post-secondary education, i.e., further and vocational education, university education, and adult education (teacher education belongs to this tertiary level). Primary education is often preceded by pre-primary (nursery) education.

In some systems variations on these divisions lead to different arrangements across the three main stages. The basic principle, however, is universally one of schooling organized according to approximate ages and stages of growth. Customarily each of these broad stages is subdivided into yearly progressions referred to as 'form', 'class', 'standard', or 'grade'. In the past the advancement from grade to grade was handled rigidly. Students advanced year by year from one grade to the next, provided they reached certain minimum levels of achievement. If a student did not meet the requirement he had to 'repeat a grade'. In Britain a system of 'streaming' became widely accepted before World War II according to which students were allocated to one of several classes at the same age level each representing a certain level of achievement. In recent years, however, social and psychological considerations have led to greater flexibility in the progress of students and their placement according to grades or streams. In North America schools have become increasingly 'ungraded' and in Britain 'unstreamed'. At the secondary level, over the last two or three decades, schools have changed in an attempt to expand secondary education, while at the same time allowing for diversification of programmes.

The different branches and levels of school administration and the organization of school systems constitute the framework within which languages have their place as educational activities. As such languages usually present no special administrative or organizational problems. But a language teacher working within a particular system should of course be broadly familiar with the structure and operation of that system.

However, in countries in which languages are politically, educationally, or socially sensitive issues, particularly in bilingual and multilingual countries, special problems do arise. For example, there may be public pressure to strengthen the language provision; on the other hand such an increase in language teaching may be resisted for financial or educational reasons. Changes in language provision may be demanded on political grounds but on the same grounds they may arouse political opposition, and administrators sometimes find themselves in a politically charged conflict. From earlier chapters we know how much languages are bound up with external and internal community relations in which national or group stereotypes and prejudices may affect judgements and decisions. Under these circumstances ethnic and language questions can play a crucial role in administration. This may not come as a great surprise or shock to many administrators because educational administration is viewed today very largely as a social process involving the management of human relations (Getzels *et al.* 1968).

Decisions about language provision sometimes demand changes in the administrative or organizational structure. For example, as was pointed out previously, second language teaching in the past conventionally occurred only in the secondary school. The postwar trend to introduce a major second language in the primary school was therefore a departure from the accepted curricular distribution between primary and secondary education. Even more drastic are the changes needed to establish an 'immersion' or 'bilingual' programme in which the second language becomes a language of instruction. Here the second language provision affects the composition of the school staff, the organization of the entire school programme, the curriculum, and may even have legal implications, if the educational legislation had previously provided for a uniform language of instruction. A further example of special organizational arrangements for language learning is the teaching of the language of wider communication to immigrants and other language minorities and the teaching of minority languages in ethnically mixed societies. The wider recognition of ethnolinguistic minorities has been reflected in many countries in greater language diversity in schools.

In summary, languages can be expected always to contribute to the total scheme of education. In order to be effective the teaching of languages must have a clearly defined place within the educational system which constitutes the wider setting. Without understanding the system as a whole and its institutions language teachers are not in a position to play their role constructively. This does not mean that language teachers always have to adapt themselves to an existing system; the demands of language education may require that the system of education has to be modified to accommodate the language provision.[13]

7 Educational planning

As was seen in the previous section, an educational system is a large and complex organization which involves the co-ordination of many components: personnel, students, parents, curriculum, learning materials, buildings, equipment, finance, and so on, directed to a common purpose. It operates on several levels: a central or national and/or regional level, the local level, and the institutional level. None of the factors involved in the system is static. The size of the child population to be educated may grow or shrink. Ideas on educational goals or curriculum change. The finances available for education may increase or decrease. Buildings become obsolete. The distribution of responsibility between central, regional, and school levels is subject to political and ideological shifts. New technology introduces unforeseen possibilities of educational development. Because of the size and complexity of an educational system and the many changes to which it is exposed, the concept of planning—derived from economic and social planning—can be applied to education. An obvious case in point is the planning of educational provision, school places, and teacher supply in accordance with forecasts of the size of the school population. But demographic projections provide only one component in the planning process. What is needed is the development of a co-ordinated central educational plan which is regularly revised, as new factors appear. It is recognized today that in advanced educational systems planning makes possible rational and economical development of education.

Planning does not mean an inflexible central control. The planning process itself includes constant renewal and revision. Planning is also compatible with distribution of responsibility so that part of the plan is central, another part regional, and certain aspects—particularly curricular planning—may be done at the school level.[14]

In language pedagogy the concepts of language planning and educational planning are combined. Language teaching in educational systems depends on long-term organization. The basic linguistic or sociolinguistic research, the preparation of curricula and pedagogical materials, the education of language teachers—all of these cannot be done at short notice. Consequently a combination of language planning and educational planning can very properly be applied to language pedagogy.[15]

8 Comparative education

For language teachers the study of education from an international and comparative point of view, as it is undertaken by comparative education, is of particular importance because of the international nature of language education. It is quite common for language teachers to work abroad, sometimes as students when it is part of their own professional education and sometimes, after the completion of their training, to widen their experience. Knowing how to approach a different educational system is therefore invaluable for their work as language teachers. Moreover, because teaching a foreign language is necessarily concerned with life and culture of another country it is invariably also concerned with education in that country. A last and perhaps the most important reason from the point of view of language teaching theory is that thought about language pedagogy is profoundly influenced by beliefs about language teaching and learning abroad. Although these beliefs in many instances are not based on accurate information and may in fact be quite misleading, they affect theory development and language teaching policy. Thus, the expansion of foreign language education in the U.S.A. through the provisions of the National Defense Education Act 1958, after the Sputnik crisis in 1957, was prompted by the view that the technological advance of the Soviet Union was made possible by a superiority of Soviet education in foreign languages. This interpretation of the influence of Soviet language teaching was probably exaggerated and may even have been quite false but it profoundly influenced language teaching in the U.S.A. The more information about language learning in other countries is accurate and realistic, the better it is for language pedagogy everywhere.

Comparative education studies educational institutions and processes from two points of view. First, it studies education in a country or region in the context of that country's or region's culture, society, and economy. These 'area studies' (Bereday 1964) employ the methods of political science, sociology, anthropology, and history with a focus on education. Second, it undertakes cross-cultural comparisons, 'comparative studies' (op. cit.), of particular educational phenomena across different countries such as the curriculum, school examinations, the relations between home and school, the role of the teacher, central or local educational administration.

The value of comparative education as an approach to educational studies has been recognized for many years. Almost since the beginning of formal schooling in the Western world, educators have been tempted to look across national boundaries and to compare educational institutions. Government commissions on education have frequently included the experience of other countries in their deliberations.[16]

As a specialized field of studies comparative education has developed since the early part of the century. In the twenties it was strengthened by the setting up of the International Bureau of Education. Since World War II the establishment of the United Nations Educational, Scientific, and Cultural Organization (UNESCO) has included international and comparative educational studies. The UNESCO Institute for Education in Hamburg, established in 1954, is almost entirely devoted to a comparative approach to major educational issues and problems. Universities have also begun to include comparative education as a specialist study, and the educational literature has been greatly enriched by studies from a comparative point of view.[17] Very few studies have so far been undertaken which look at *language teaching* internationally and comparatively.[18]

Comparative educational studies have been criticized for being too subjective and impressionistic. In order to infuse into comparative education some of the empirical rigour of educational research a large project of comparative studies was initiated in the early sixties by an international group of educational researchers who formed for that purpose a council which later became the International Association for the Evaluation of Educational Achievement (IEA). The argument of the IEA group was that in curriculum studies it is difficult to 'experiment' but the differences in curriculum and educational provision in various countries constitute an unexplored 'laboratory' of educational enquiry.

During the period from 1961 to 1973 this group first investigated the teaching of mathematics in twelve countries (Husén 1967). In the mid-sixties the mathematics study was followed by international comparative studies in other curriculum areas, social studies, reading, the teaching of literature, natural science, and civic education (Walker 1976; Purves and Levine 1975). At the same time, too, a comparative IEA study on the teaching of English as a foreign language in ten countries and of French as a foreign language in eight countries was launched. Each of these studies followed the same pattern. Achievement in the various subject areas of the curriculum was measured across countries by means of especially constructed international achievement tests suitable for predetermined stages of schooling. Four age levels for testing were envisaged, although in a particular study not all of these levels were necessarily examined: Population I were ten-year-olds, representing the later stages of primary education; Population II were fourteen-year-olds representing the earlier or middle phases of secondary education; Population III consisted of approximately sixteen-year-old school leavers. Finally, the most advanced set of tests was intended for students about to enter university (Population IV). In addition to tests, information was collected with the help of questionnaires on educational systems, schools, teachers, and students. The tests and questionnaires were constructed by an international panel consisting of representatives of the participating countries. In each of the countries a nationally recognized educational research institute, in Britain, for example, the National Foundation for Educational Research in England and Wales or the Scottish Council for Research in Education, was responsible for data gathering at the national level. The task of drawing together internationally all the information collected at the national level was in the hands of international committees, one for each subject area. Finally, an international expert or a team of experts in the subject in question had the task of writing the final report on the international study.

The two studies, which investigated English and French as a foreign language, gathered information on language learning in fifteen countries (Carroll 1975; Lewis and Massad 1975).

English	**French**
Belgium	Chile
Chile	England
Federal Republic of Germany	New Zealand
Finland	Netherlands
Hungary	Rumania
Israel	Scotland
Italy	Sweden
Netherlands	U.S.A.
Sweden	
Thailand	

Both these studies have shown how difficult and, at the same time, how rewarding it is to make such cross-national enquiries because of the likenesses and differences between language teaching in different countries which only come to light by making comparative studies of this kind. The object of such studies is emphatically not to conduct an 'olympiad of language teaching', but to use the different experiences in various educational systems to establish what factors are of importance in the national development of second language proficiency. These studies therefore attempt, first, to establish the levels of achievement in English and French among carefully selected samples of students in various parts of the world. Second, the investigations are designed to relate the differences in proficiency to a great variety of factors in the different educational systems which might explain the differences. The findings of these monumental investigations were published in 1975 and constitute a valuable international data base for language teaching. As such they were used more recently in studies on French in Nigeria and on English in India, Zambia, and Ivory Coast.[19]

As was said on p. 420 above, two of the educational sub-disciplines need to be looked at more closely because of their special relevance to language teaching: curriculum and educational technology.

9   Curriculum

Curriculum as a field of educational studies is fairly new.[20] As we shall see below in this chapter and in Chapter 22, it is of particular importance to language teaching theory. The term 'curriculum' is commonly used in two related senses. It refers, first, to the substance of a programme of studies of an educational institution or system. Thus, we can speak of the school curriculum, the university curriculum, the curriculum of French schools, or the curriculum of Soviet education. In a more restricted sense it refers to the course of study or content in a particular subject, such as the mathematics curriculum or the history curriculum. It is, therefore, used as a synonym of what in British universities and schools is sometimes referred to as the 'syllabus' for a given subject or course of studies. In recent years, however, the term 'curriculum' has come to refer not only to the subject matter or content, but also to the entire instructional process including materials, equipment, examinations, and the training of teachers, in short all pedagogical measures related to schooling or to the substance of a course of studies. In other words, curriculum is concerned with 'what can and should be taught to whom, when, and how' (Eisner and Vallance 1974:2).[21]

In the recent history of education questions of curriculum have been raised repeatedly, even before curriculum had been recognized as a distinct area of educational studies. In Great Britain several influential government commissions have periodically examined the educational offerings of the school system. Their reports—particularly those concerned with secondary education, for example the Hadow Report (1926), the Spens Report (1938), and the Norwood Report (1943)— have been milestones in British secondary schooling. In Canada, the Hall-Dennis Report, *Living and Learning* (1968), is a prime example in recent decades of a proposal for school curriculum reform.

In the U.S.A. the school curriculum has been under review since the early fifties and much of the modern emphasis on curriculum change and development throughout the world has been influenced by American curriculum enquiries in the fifties and sixties. The questioning of educational content and methods brought about government action as well as initiatives from private foundations, for example the Ford Foundation. A large number of curriculum projects in the fifties and sixties led to reports, the rewriting of textbooks, and the production of new curriculum materials in mathematics, the natural and social sciences, and the humanities.[22] Regional 'laboratories' were set up as centres of curriculum reform. New approaches to foreign language teaching were prompted by similar considerations. For example, the A-LM materials, produced under a grant from the National Defense Education Act (1958), provided in the early sixties new types of course materials which acted as a model for language programmes for several years to come.[23]

In Great Britain during the same period, the lead was taken by the Nuffield Foundation in conjunction with the Ministry of Education (later the Department of Education and Science). Here, too, curriculum reform focused on the revision of textbooks and the preparation of new materials by teams of curriculum workers. The Department of Education and Science, which, traditionally in Britain, has had little direct influence on the school curriculum, was instrumental in the setting up in 1965 of the Schools Council for Curriculum and Examination. This body has led the curriculum reform movement in Britain in recent times.[24] Curriculum reform, therefore, provided the background for new approaches to language teaching and for the development of new language teaching materials in Britain of which the Nuffield/Schools Council's sets of courses in French, Spanish, Russian, German, and Latin, produced from about 1965, were outstanding examples.[25]

Curriculum theory
This twenty-five year period of curriculum reform has gradually given rise to a systematic approach to curriculum development and change as well as to the formulation of basic principles of curriculum; in short, it has led to 'curriculum theory'.[26]

Curriculum theory is concerned with (1) the underlying ideological and philosophical assumptions of curriculum (curriculum philosophy); (2) the conceptualization of three main components of curriculum: (a) purposes and content, (b) instruction, and (c) evaluation; and (3) curriculum processes: (a) systematic curriculum development, (b) the implementation of curriculum in educational institutions, and (c) curriculum evaluation.

(1) *Curriculum philosophies.* Discussions on the school curriculum reveal different philosophical orientations which affect the goals, content, methods, and materials of education. For example, Eisner and Vallance (1974) have distinguished five major orientations:

The first is that the school curriculum should develop *cognitive processes.* The principal function of the school is not to transmit a predetermined content but to train children in skills of enquiry, to develop their cognitive functioning, to help them to learn how to learn. If we adopt this conception, we might regard it as the main object of language teaching not to acquire a second language to perfection but to provide a training of the mind or learning how to learn languages.[27]

A second orientation is described as *self-actualization* or *curriculum as consummatory experience.* According to this point of view schooling should offer something to the child here and now and through the curriculum school 'should enter fully into the child's life' (op. cit.:9). The curriculum should be meaningful at the given stage of the child's growth rather than provide him with experiences which are useful to him only when he is adult. If this principle is applied to second language learning, the place of languages in the curriculum can be called into question in many instances. Where a language is learnt as a foreign language in a school it has often mainly future reference. It is not so much a question of what a child can do with a language here and now than what he might do with it later. In certain situations of second language learning, for example, in teaching a language to immigrants, however, its immediate relevance is as obvious as learning to read. Where languages lack this immediate relevance language teachers have given thought to the problem that arises with this curriculum orientation in mind. They have attempted to include in their classwork activities and experiences which are immediately relevant during the educational process, such as project work, school journeys, or student exchanges.

This orientation has direct bearing upon the optimal age issue in language teaching. While it appears to be impossible to prove that language learning at any particular age is more effective than at any other (see Chapter 17), the introduction of a language to young children can provide what many educators would regard as a worthwhile experience *at that stage* in a child's life. For, so this argument runs, at no stage in education should pupils be encouraged to believe that their native language is the only valid language. To counteract this tendency second languages should be part of education at all stages, and regardless of the economic advantages of second language learning this would be the educational justification for early language learning.

A third orientation, *social reconstruction/relevance*, lays emphasis on the needs of the society which are to be met by education and curriculum. This position can be illustrated by the 'immersion programme', offered in Canada to English-speaking children with the intention of making these children bilingual.[28] Bilingualism, in this situation, although also of personal value to the individual, is mainly introduced as a social good to be developed through schooling because of its importance as a binding force in the society across its linguistic divisions.

The fourth orientation, identified by Eisner and Vallance, *academic rationalism*, emphasizes the heritage of classical scholarship and a 'common literacy' as the main core and content of the curriculum. This tradition is familiar to many language teachers, because languages have been justified since the nineteenth century on the grounds that they provide a gateway to the great literatures of other nations.[29]

The fifth orientation is described as *curriculum as technology*. In this approach values are not questioned or consciously established. Instead, the emphasis is on the efficient identification of goals and means. It is a 'technological' approach. But because it takes values as given and claims to be 'value-neutral' Eisner and Vallance criticize the failure of this orientation to recognize the value judgements underlying its own procedures. While there has been much enthusiasm for technology in the sixties, in recent years a technical approach to curriculum and, as we shall see later, the whole technology of education has been the subject of much criticism (see p. 445 below). Nevertheless, if it is recognized that after value decisions have been made, 'curriculum as technology' can indeed be useful, there is no reason to condemn this instrumental approach to curriculum.

These five orientations, which, according to Eisner and Vallance, each represent a particular philosophical position can be useful in clarifying major curriculum decisions. They are of course not mutually exclusive. Eisner and Vallance show that the exclusive reliance on certain orientations can produce three 'curriculum fallacies': the emphasis on learning how to learn may detract from the importance of what is being learnt, while the exclusive attention to content, as, for example, in the orientation of academic rationalism, can be equally one-sided. A third fallacy is the belief that there is a universally right curriculum which can be established without taking note of the historical, political, or social circumstances to which it relates.[30]

(2) *Essential components of curriculum.* Although the terms used to talk about curriculum are not uniform, the basic concepts are broadly agreed upon. Three major distinctions are commonly made; all of them are of direct importance to language pedagogy.

(a) *Purposes and content.* The first group of concepts refers to the 'aims' (goals or objectives) and the 'content' (substance or subject matter). Usually it comprises both sets of concepts. Curriculum understood this way answers the questions: What is to be learnt? What is the curriculum planned to achieve? Accordingly, one definition states that curriculum is a 'structured series of intended learning outcomes' (Johnson 1967:130). Whether or not the term curriculum includes more than this there is no question that modern curriculum theory has laid a great deal of emphasis on (a) the definition of goals, and (b) the clarification of content.

Typical of this trend has been an impressive co-operative venture, initiated in the fifties by the American educationist Bloom, to establish an ordered classification or 'taxonomy' of educational objectives. The impact of Bloom's taxonomies of objectives can still be felt today. The impetus for this venture originally came from a demand to co-ordinate the development of educational tests more closely with the purposes of education. It was an attempt to clarify concepts which, although important for curriculum and test development, had always remained vague and unsatisfactory. The work on these taxonomies and the subsequent studies on curriculum evaluation were initiated at a meeting of college examiners attending a convention of the American Psychological Association in 1948. It led to several meetings among these American examiners and culminated in two famous handbooks on taxonomies of educational objectives. A departure from conventional practice was that in these two books and subsequent writings educational objectives were not defined for different subject areas; instead they were expressed in three major psychological categories: cognition, affect, and psychomotor skills. But only the first two were formulated in a detailed taxonomy of objectives, one on the cognitive domain (Bloom 1956), and the other on the affective domain (Krathwohl *et al.* 1964).

In order to make educational objectives more precise some educational theorists in the sixties demanded that objectives be defined with an even greater degree of concreteness in operational or behavioural terms so that the desired outcome of a teaching programme would be exactly specified: What should the learner be able to do that he could not do at the beginning of the course? Objectives, expressed as concrete acts or items of knowledge, are referred to as 'behavioural', 'performance', or 'instructional' objectives. During this period the definition or 'writing' of performance objectives received prominent attention in education, particularly in North America. It should be added that several educators immediately questioned the value of this concern with explicit and detailed definitions of objectives and even more so the listing of minute behavioural objectives. The implication that education must always lead to a fixed predictable product was not accepted by them. Nevertheless, the attempts to specify educational objectives were a significant contribution to curriculum theory in the sixties. Language teachers, too, have been influenced by them.[31]

(b) *Instruction.* The second major group of concepts centres around the process of teaching and learning to reach these objectives. Consequently, the *how* of education—teaching methods, the time allocation, the selection and arrangement of content, the modes of presentation, the classroom, the media used, and so on—can also be considered part of curriculum.[32] The narrower definition of curriculum refers only to the aspects under (a) as 'curriculum' and subsumes aspects under (b) under the term 'instruction', while the wider definition comprises (a) and (b). But there is no major theoretical difference between these two definitions of curriculum, because both make a conceptual separation of ends from means. It will be recalled (p. 421 above) that some philosophers have questioned the ends/means distinction in education. No doubt their point of view can be more easily accommodated if curriculum includes instruction than if curriculum and instruction are treated as conceptually separate topics.

An important aspect of curriculum of a much older vintage, to be considered under this heading, is the arrangement of subject matter in a rational sequence. The discussion of principles governing such arrangements had originally given rise to the concept of 'curriculum' as a course or run. The systematic organization of content goes back to the work of the German educator Herbart; most school systems and most curriculum subjects have deeply ingrained habits of ordering subject matter which have been hallowed by tradition. But the subject divisions and the conventional ordering of material in a sequence have repeatedly been criticized. Increasingly it has been recognized that the developmental stages of child growth and the individual differences among learners make it impossible to impose a single and 'correct' sequence on all curricula. See also Chapter 18:394–5 and 399–400.

In present-day education a great variety of curriculum patterns are envisaged. They range from the traditional fixed course of study, via schemes of flexible instruction, to the idea of completely free and independent learning without schooling ('deschooling'). Programmed instruction, computer-aided instruction, individualized (or personalized) learning, or mastery strategies reflect a variety of different principles guiding the organization of the curriculum.

As we will see later, in language teaching, too, accepted curriculum patterns and conventional ways of presenting a language have been challenged.

(c) *Evaluation.* The third aspect of curriculum, evaluation, refers to the assessment of whether teaching achieves its object. This concept expresses the idea that it is not good enough in any educational scheme to be clear about one's intentions and to organize learning experiences in a planned way. The educator must also ensure that the objectives he has set himself are in fact attained. Evaluation serves to make judgements about the progress and performance of individual students exposed to the curriculum in question. It comprises informal assessments, such as the nod of the head and expressions of right or wrong, as well as the intuitive self-assessment a student might make of his own work. At the more formal end of the spectrum of evaluative measures it includes teacher-made classroom tests, standardized tests, and internal or external examinations, or whatever other devices are used (for example, interviews and observation) to assess outcomes. As we have already seen in earlier chapters (for example, in Chapter 16), in language teaching, too, the question of evaluation is a very important issue.

(3) *Curriculum processes.* The development of a new curriculum, its implementation in a school system and its periodic evaluation have been recognized as activities that must be carefully planned and orchestrated. Otherwise costly efforts may be vitiated or distorted in their application. Curriculum theory has developed these 'curriculum processes' into a specialization which can usefully be applied to second language curricula.

(a) *Curriculum development.* Taking the components of the curriculum as given, the question is what steps should be taken to develop new curricula and carry them into effect. Answers to this question are concerned with efficiency of curriculum construction and its implementation in a school system. As we have already noted, a great deal of experience has been gathered over the last thirty years in devising steps for curriculum making and in planning the development of teaching materials. It is in this systematic approach to planning, design, implementation, and operation that the curriculum in terms of goals, content, instruction, and evaluation has come into its own.

The development of a new curriculum and its implementation affect the classroom teacher most directly but go beyond the classroom itself. They are matters for a whole school or an entire school system. Where does the initiative for curriculum development and curriculum change come from? It can originate at various levels. In many educational systems of the past the central government, the Ministry of Education, alone took responsibility for curriculum and through school inspection attempted to ensure that its directions were carried out. But as education has become more decentralized and more democratic, curriculum development has originated in a more flexible way from different sources, the schools, teachers' and parents' organizations, the universities, from industry or the trade unions, specially appointed commissions, or from examination boards. In recent years many countries have found it necessary to create curriculum centres in which curriculum specialists, subject matter specialists, administrators, and teacher s jointly work in the preparation of a curriculum and often even design teaching materials to go with a new curriculum.

(b) *Implementation and the management of curriculum change.* When a curriculum has been developed and assuming that the right kind of teaching materials have been created, there is still a problem of *implementing the new curriculum*. The finest and most up-to-date curriculum ideas can be vitiated if they are imposed upon the teachers concerned without having made sure that the changes the new curriculum demands are understood by them. The willing participation of teachers in implementing curriculum changes is recognized as an essential aspect of introducing a new curriculum. This also implies that the underlying principles are incorporated into the training of new teachers, and that experienced practitioners are offered the opportunity to become familiar with the new directions through various forms of in-service training.

(c) *Curriculum evaluation. Curriculum* evaluation is conceptually distinct from *student* evaluation which has already been briefly described on pp. 439–40. It is a quality control of the curriculum in answer to two main questions: first, has the curriculum selected goals and a content which are sound and educationally justifiable? The answer to this question requires a philosophical interpretation of the goals and the subject matter; it is an assessment of validity and of the value of the curriculum. Second, given a certain curriculum with its own objectives and presuppositions, is the instruction of a kind that will lead to success among the students to whom the curriculum is directed? Evaluation in this sense is, therefore, an attempt to assess the extent to which a curriculum meets its own objectives. The application of carefully designed tests to selected groups, classroom observations, and interviews with teachers, parents and students play a role in such assessments.[33]

A distinction, introduced by Scriven (1967), between *formative* and *summative evaluation* has been found useful. Scriven distinguishes between evaluation of a curriculum which is in the process of development and which is assessed during the stages of preparation (formative evaluation) and an assessment of the completed curriculum (summative evaluation).

It should be added that Bloom and his associates (Bloom, Hastings, and Madaus 1971) have applied this distinction to *student evaluation*. They refer to formative evaluation as the assessment of progress during the learning process. Summative student evaluation is the assessment of student achievement at the end of a course of teaching, in answer to the question whether the student has reached a certain mastery level envisaged by the curriculum.

Relevance to second language of curriculum theory
As we shall see later (see Chapter 22), these concepts of curriculum have become highly relevant to language pedagogy. It is, however, only very recently that language teachers have begun to take note of ideas in

curriculum theory. Previously the language curriculum went very much its own way (see Chapter 21). There are certain parallels between the development of general curriculum theory and the development of a curriculum theory in language teaching, but very little movement of thought across these two trends has taken place. In language pedagogy most aspects of curriculum—the selection of content, its arrangement into a sequence, and instructional procedures—have been the subject of theoretical formulations, some questioning, and some experimentation. The schemes elaborated by Mackey (1965) and Halliday *et al.* (1964) were probably the most elaborate attempts at designing a language curriculum. As will be seen subsequently (see Chapter 21), Mackey's scheme formalizes and refines established traditions of language courses.

Under the impact of the language sciences rather than in response to educational thinking about curriculum the common grammatical ordering of language courses has been called into question. It is no longer regarded as the only or even the best principle of arrangement. Since the late sixties other criteria for ordering the presentation of a language—situational, semantic, or sociolinguistic—have been considered as possible alternatives. Even more radical are schemes which abandon all formal ordering and simply confront the learner with the experience of language use on the assumption that a language can only be learnt in the context of meaningful communication.[34] Whatever the merits of these proposals, the discussions on the language curriculum have gone on without much reference to curriculum theory.

Changes in thought on language and language learning and changes in educational policy constantly impinge on language pedagogy, and curriculum change frequently occurs. Unfortunately, language pedagogy has not yet made much use of the available collective wisdom in curriculum theory to cope with curriculum decisions in an economical and effective way.[35]

10 Educational technology

As a distinct field of educational studies educational technology today has resulted from the coalescence of two major trends: (1) the application of technological devices, in other words, of 'gadgets' in education; (2) the development of a 'technology' of instruction.

Gadgets

The use of 'audiovisual aids' or 'media' is familiar enough to language teachers. The tape recorder, filmstrip projector, and language laboratory have played a key role in the transformation of language teaching during the past twenty-five years. Nowhere has there been more intense debate about the pedagogical merits of technological devices than among language teachers. In the fifties, with the industrial production of tape recorders, the beginnings of a language laboratory industry, and the first audiovisual and audiolingual courses, technology appeared to usher in a new and hopeful era of language teaching. The technological revolution of the language classroom reached a peak around 1960. Whether or not to invest funds in a language laboratory had to be faced by many schools and universities all over the world. Associations were formed to promote the use of audiovisual aids in language teaching and new journals appeared, especially devoted to media in language teaching.[36] The language laboratory and the new 'audiolingual' or 'audiovisual' methods of teaching seemed to complement each other perfectly. But within a few years, as questions were raised about the theories underlying the new methods of teaching, doubts also began to be expressed about the merits of the language laboratory. Two American studies, in particular, the Keating Report (1963) and the Pennsylvania Study (Smith 1970), which questioned the efficacy of the language laboratory as an aid to language learning, gave rise to heated arguments among supporters and opponents of the 'New Key' methods. The seventies—less confident about technological developments and more conscious of educational costs than the sixties—hardly strengthened the unquestioned belief in the value of technological aids to language teaching.[37]

Nevertheless, it would be facile to dismiss language teaching technology as a passing fashion. Many aspects of technology have become an integral part of the language teacher's equipment; and the changing position and the major functions of media deserve to be investigated. In the context of the present chapter it is important to stress that the technology of language teaching is part of a much wider trend in education: the development of educational technology. The technological revolution that has made such an impact on language teaching has simultaneously in a more general way also affected other areas of education.

A more comprehensive view of educational technology links modern media with devices of the past which are examples of an earlier technology. The invention of writing systems, the development of the printing press, or the use of slate, paper, steel nib, ink, or pencil are reminders of the fact that schooling is always dependent on the state of technology. What distinguishes the modern era from earlier stages of educational history is not the influence of technology as such, but the scope and scale of media available for educational use. One list 'boasts ninety-one major categories from "Aquarium and Terrarium" to "Workbook" with 138 additional subsections! (Gillette 1973:34). Because of this bewildering variety educators have attempted to systematize the use of media and to incorporate audiovisual media into a broader conception of a technology of instruction.

The development of a technology of instruction
Educational technology is not viewed today simply as the application of mechanical or electronic aids in education. Media and other gadgets are of course recognized as an important part of educational technology. But 'educational technology' is generally interpreted more widely. In Britain, the National Council for Educational Technology defines it as 'the development, application, and evaluation of systems, techniques and aids to improve the process of human learning' (quoted from Leedham 1973:7). Elsewhere it has been described even more broadly as 'a systematic way of designing, applying and evaluating the total process of teaching and learning' (Gillett 1973:2). Equally broad is the description of educational technology as 'modern organization theory approach to the achievement of educational objectives through the application of optimal strategies incorporating both teaching and learning resources' (Davies and Hartley 1972:11). The emphasis has thus shifted from the uses of different media such as the language laboratory and the audiovisual apparatus to a scientific interpretation of the entire process of teaching and learning,

The principal influences that have shaped this modern conception of educational technology are psychology of learning, programmed instruction, and the 'systems approach'. Its psychological basis is not any particular theory of learning, but the work of Skinner and Gagné has been particularly influential. The principles of programmed instruction have provided notions and techniques to specify objectives and to select empirically the procedures to reach these objectives. The systems approach, derived from engineering and industry, considers the teacher, the learner, the materials, and media as constituent parts of a purposeful whole or 'system'.

Thus, educational technology has two major areas of research and practice: (a) its broadest aim is to establish teaching-learning systems in industry, the armed forces, the civil service, or in schools; (b) its second function is the development of media and other devices and their application to the process of teaching.

The following is the list of the most frequently used media on which, over the last two decades, experience has been gathered and research has been carried out: films, filmstrips; radio, television, closed circuit television; teaching machines and programmed instruction; overhead projector; tape recorder; computer aided instruction (CAI); simulation and games.

Research concerns itself with the learning that is stimulated by the use of a particular device. Thus a film or filmstrip provides a visual stimulus, a tape recorder an auditory one. The visual one can be a word or picture. Which is more effective: the word or the picture? How does an audio presentation compare with a visual one, or how does either compare with an audiovisual presentation? Questions of this kind which have implications for language teaching can be investigated by research on media.[38]

Through the way in which educational technology has become defined over the last two decades, it has introduced into educational thought and practice an element of the organizational skill, efficiency, regularity, and economy of industrial production and distribution. This has clear advantages: for if education is to be provided on a large scale it cannot be handled by hit-or-miss methods. A systems approach offers a certain guarantee of reliable development. Equally, the use of media would find its place on a rational basis of efficacy in the overall instructional design. But there are also clear dangers in educational technology which are today recognized. Because of its emphasis on formal steps of organization and the efficient and economical use of media, educational technology focuses on means rather than the substance or ends. The contents and goals have of course to be identified by the educational technologist. But his function is not to question them. Therefore the emphasis on technology, systems, and on the apparatus it creates tends to favour a conventional and traditional approach. The sophistication of the techniques is not necessarily matched by the sophistication in content or objectives. In the U.S.A. where educational technology in its broadest sense has found the most widespread application it has also been subjected to the most severe criticism:

'The kind of education directed toward the development of what has been termed here the autonomous individual would surely have to be entirely different from that which is being developed by the federally sponsored new technology of education. Indeed, the new technology of education appears to be directed in the opposite direction. It is an extension of the machine's control over man that is evident in every factory.'
(Travers 1973a:990)

It is clear from the recent literature on educational technology that besides the recognition of the advantages of a scientific approach to the educational process and of the use of engineering aids, there is a constant stream of criticism and warnings against the excesses of mechanization (for example, Travers 1973a), while others attempt to 'demystify' the question (Gillett 1973) and to see technology in perspective (Richmond 1970).

The conclusion of this review of educational technology is that the experience, research, theory, and discussion on educational technology outside the field of language pedagogy are prerequisites to an understanding of the application of technology to language teaching.[39]

Conclusion

The overview of the field of educational studies has shown that there is little justification for the neglect of education as a discipline in language pedagogy. Education is a diverse and complex field of enquiry which has direct bearing on many facets of language teaching. Several points of contact exist and are beginning to be developed. Educational theory provides a broad framework and essential concepts for language pedagogy. The different sub-disciplines constitute useful resources. Without the educational component language teaching theory would be isolated from other kindred educational activities and would be liable to become the victim of unexamined educational beliefs entertained without much understanding. Deliberate attempts should be made to keep educational thought under regular review and to consider its implications for language pedagogy, and in this way develop the same kind of two-way bond that should characterize the relationship between language teaching theory and all its source disciplines. As we shall see in the next two chapters, language pedagogy has had considerable trouble in developing its concept of teaching. An educational perspective can perhaps be helpful in overcoming some of these difficulties.

Notes

1 Among present-day writers, Peters, Professor of Philosophy of Education at the University of London Institute of Education, has been foremost in the philosophical analysis of educational concepts, for example, Peters (1973), a work which includes a useful annotated bibliography on the philosophy of education (pp. 271–3). See also Reid (1962), Schofield (1972), Beck (1974), or Wilson (1977).

2 For example, the treatment of the concept of 'theory' in Chapter 2 can be regarded as an attempt to clarify by discussion one such concept, i.e., theory.

3 Peters' views on the ends/means issue have been critically and perceptively discussed by Beck (1974:34–37).

4 For example, Watson's study (1909), referred to in Chapter 5:86, considered the role of French and other languages in the context of the development of a modern school curriculum.

5 That is, in the nineteenth century modern languages were often regarded as intellectually modest achievements in comparison to the rigour of the studies of the classical languages. They were frequently associated with a dilettante education suitable for young ladies of leisure. Modern language teachers struggled against this image. In the mid-twentieth century the view of languages being different and intellectually inferior was revived but on quite different grounds. The treatment of language learning as primarily a matter of drill,

conditioning, and automatization gave those who were opposed to language teaching an argument for saying that language teachers themselves had little to offer for an *intellectual* education. Thus in a university the drill approach to languages advocated by audiolingualists led to the accusation that languages cannot be truly academic subjects suitable for a university education.

6 In order to obtain an overview of the history of education, the reader is advised to consult a classic, such as Boyd's *History of Western Education* which appeared first in 1921 and has been brought up to date by King (Boyd and King 1972). Other handy and readable introductions include, among others, Thut (1957) or Lawrence (1970). For historical research consult Brickman (1973).

7 Useful introductions to sociology of education are Banks (1976) and Musgrave (1979), both against a British background, and Boocock (1980), based on American experience and including a crosscultural chapter. Readings in educational sociology should be linked with the study of Part 3, Concepts of Society.

8 The importance of social context in language education has repeatedly been emphasized in previous chapters. See particularly Chapter 13 which deals with the social context of language learning and teaching, and Chapters 16 to 18 which, from the point of view of the psychology of the learner, have drawn attention to the effect of the role of language in society on the learner and the learning process.

9 For references see Chapter 4, Note 13.

10 See, for example, Yates (1966) on the question of grouping in education. For the social interaction in classrooms, see Amidon and Hough (1967). Individualization and small group activities have been advocated in language teaching since the early seventies. See, for example, Altman and Politzer (1971), Altman (1972), Salter (1972), Disick (1975). See also Chapter 17, Note 1, for a brief comment on individualization in language pedagogy. Streaming and grading in schools in general have been widely discussed, for example, by Barker-Lunn (1970), Davies (1975), Jackson (1964), Kelly (1975), and Rosenbaum (1976), and in language classes by CILT (1972), Fearing (1969), MLA (1977), Partington (1969), Wesche (1981a) and Terwilger (1970). On the class size issue see Ryan and Greenfield (1975).

11 Very few systematic studies of the economics of language teaching have been published. Among general works dealing with the economics of education consult Vaizey (1962), Blaug (1970), or Benson (1978).

12 This list of administrative activities is partially based on headings of the *Educational Administration Abstracts*.

13 In order to get to know a school system one has to visit schools, talk

to teachers, parents and pupils. Books can help but by themselves are hardly sufficient. It is possible to obtain descriptive or historical accounts of the school systems of most countries, for example, Dent (1977), or Bell and Grant (1977) for England and Wales. A more technical approach to questions of school organization and administration are discussed in works such as Baron and Taylor (1969), Baron, Cooper and Walker (1969), Lewis and Loveridge (1965), or Newell (1978). The importance of taking note of the educational context was already emphasized in Chapter 13.

14 The idea of a planning approach to education in different parts of the world has found an institutional expression in the International Institute for Educational Planning (IIEP) in Paris which functions under the aegis of UNESCO. For introductory readings see UNESCO (1970), which provides a useful historical perspective, Birley (1972), an introductory text from a British perspective, Green (1971), a series of helpful papers, or from a more recent point of view Weiler (1980).

15 For examples of language planning applied to second language teaching see Chapter 13.

16 For example, Matthew Arnold who has been described as 'the pioneer of comparative education' (Hans 1958:2) visited the Continent for the Newcastle Commission in 1859, for the Taunton Commission in 1865, and in 1886 for the Cross Commission. See on this point also Bereday (1964:8).

17 For introductions to comparative education, the reader should consult, among others, the works by King (1973), Mallinson (1975), or Tretheway (1976). Since 1979 UNESCO has revived the useful *International Yearbook of Education* which had ceased publication in 1969 with Vol. 31. In 1979, Holmes, of the London Institute of Education, opened the new series with an international guide to national systems of education (Holmes 1979). The new series of the *International Yearbook* began in 1980 with Vol. 32 (Holmes 1980). In the seventies OECD also published a useful classification and brief descriptions of educational systems in nine slim volumes, one for each member state of OECD and one summary volume (OECD (Organization for Economic Co-operation and Development) 1972–75).

18 Among exceptions are a study of foreign language teaching in the Soviet Union (Lewis 1962), two international studies of languages for younger children (Stern 1967, 1969), and a survey of language teaching in schools in Europe (Halls 1970).

19 Students of the present writer have written doctoral theses on language education in these different countries and have made use of IEA tests and questionnaires in order to collect data on the countries concerned and in order to establish comparisons with the IEA

studies: Seshadri (1978), Africa (1980), and Ituen (1980). See also Chapter 11, Note 16.

20 It is difficult for the novice in curriculum studies to find his way through the sizeable literature on curriculum that is available. A lucid and balanced introduction and overview with helpful references to the entire field is a small book by Taylor and Richards (1979). The great classic of curriculum on basic principles of curriculum and instruction, which has influenced curriculum studies for decades, is a slim volume by Tyler (1949).

21 Various definitions of curriculum have been discussed by Richmond (1970a) and Beauchamp (1975:6–8) who distinguishes 'a curriculum' as 'a plan of studies', 'a curriculum system' as 'the organized framework within which curriculum decisions are made', and 'curriculum' as a field of study. See also Taylor and Richards (1979:11) on 'What is the curriculum?'

22 Goodlad *et al.* (1966) have summarized the major American curriculum projects of the sixties.

23 See the entry on the Glastonbury materials in the historical overview Chapter 6:106.

24 Owen (1973) has considered the self-conscious study of curriculum questions in the context of British education.

25 For an account of the work of the Nuffield Language Project in the sixties, see Spicer (1969).

26 See Chapter 8 on curriculum theory and research in Taylor and Richards (1979).

27 As will be seen in Chapter 22, our view of the second language curriculum will take this orientation into account, although it will be considered only as one component among others.

28 For references see Chapter 4, Note 13.

29 This element of common literacy which was fostered by classical scholarship plays an important part in native language literary education. The shared knowledge of the great books of a nation belongs to a nation's culture. The second language curriculum which introduces the language in a cultural context may well include the great books of the target language community. In the past, following the classical tradition, this was often considered the main or only justification for foreign language study.

30 Taylor and Richards (1979) also lay emphasis on the philosophical orientation of curricula in a chapter on conceptions and ideologies.

31 Among language teaching theorists Valette has been foremost, in several of her writings since the late sixties, to apply the Bloom taxonomies to language teaching, for example, Valette (1969, 1971). The Council of Europe's Threshold Level Project is also an attempt to specify language learning objectives in precise operational terms, for example, van Ek (1975). In 1980 the Ontario

Ministry of Education (Canada) published a 'core programme' for French which expressed the French curriculum through a carefully designed list of objectives and sub-objectives, each of which was illustrated by sample activities (Ontario 1980).

32 Taylor and Richards (1979) refer to this as 'the curriculum in operation': 'It is in the school and the classroom that students of the curriculum must look to see what the curriculum is, and in doing so to begin to appreciate just how complex is the task of giving reality to the aims and objectives (and conceptions of education) which it was developed to convey' (1979:17).

33 For a general introduction to current thought and work on curriculum development and evaluation see Lewy (1977). Different approaches to curriculum evaluation are also discussed by Taylor and Richards (1979).

34 Beginnings of these alternative principles of curriculum development can be observed from about 1970, for example, Newmark (1971), Reibel (1971), Council of Europe (1971), Stern (1973).

35 An instructive illustration of the interaction between the different phases of curriculum change in language teaching, without any marked reference to curriculum theory, is offered by the experience of *français fondamental* in the fifties and sixties. (See also Chapter 8:161–2). In the early fifties when the Commission for Elementary French (later known as CREDIF) in its centre at St Cloud near Paris undertook its basic research this group of scholars was concerned entirely with the selection of lexical and grammatical items as a resource for elementary French language courses. But the word list and the list of grammar rules as such which this centre had established failed to make much impact upon textbooks and textbook writers. Not until around 1960, when the St Cloud centre demonstrated the use of its own research findings for the creation of new materials by developing its own courses, for example, *Voix et Images de France*, or *Bonjour, Line!* did *français fondamental* gain its well deserved recognition as a data base for programme development. But *Voix et Images de France* and *Bonjour, Line!* were not just a set of materials. Their application in the classroom demanded from the teacher new techniques of instruction. The St Cloud centre insisted that only teachers who had been specially trained in the approved 'method' should be permitted to use this programme. This stipulation today appears unnecessarily rigid. Yet, the example of the CREDIF research and development illustrates well the problematic nature of the interaction in curriculum development between research on content, materials development, and implementation. In other words, the curriculum problems in language teaching call for a curriculum theory.

36 *The Audio-Visual Language Journal (Journal of Applied Linguistics*

and Language Teaching Technology) appeared since the early sixties as *The Journal of the Audio-Visual Language Association*. The journal was renamed in the seventies *British Journal of Language Teaching* and the association the British Association for Language Teaching. Another journal devoted to the technology of language teaching in both senses of the term is *System* (since 1980 published by Pergamon Press).

37 There is a vast literature on language teaching technology. Readers might familiarize themselves in the first instance with the scope of this field by reading papers on the language laboratory, programmed instruction and audio-visual materials in Vol. 3 of the *Edinburgh Course in Applied Linguistics* (Allen and Corder 1974). The history of the language laboratory has been described by Léon (1962). See also Note 39 below.

38 The experiments on language learning by Bialystok, described in Chapter 18:407–9, illustrate a possible paradigm for research which might be used for investigating techniques of this kind in language teaching. See also the research questions raised by Carroll in the fifties (Chapter 15:323).

39 Richmond (1970) with ample and skilfully chosen quotations provides an excellent basis for a discussion of the concept of educational technology. A simple introduction to educational technology (in the media sense) is offered by Leedham (1973) who describes broadcasting, closed-circuit television, film, programmed learning, and multi-media systems, as well as buildings and resource systems. Readings, providing some of the classical papers, for example, by Skinner, Gagné, Pressey, Mager, as well as criticisms of technology, can be found in books by Davies and Hartley (1972) and Pula and Goff (1972). Saettler (1968) has written a detailed and well documented history of instructional technology (mainly from an American perspective). Gillett's attempt to demystify educational technology represents a 'humanist's approach' to gadgets (Gillett 1973). For research on media the article by Levie and Dickie (1973) in the *Second Handbook of Research on Teaching* (Travers 1973) should be consulted. With reference to language teaching, in addition to the suggestions in Note 37, consult also for programmed instruction, Howatt (1969) and for the language laboratory, Dakin (1973) or Green (1975), and for visual aids, Wright (1976). For a discussion of computers and other recent developments in language teaching technology, see, for example, Olsen (1980), Fitzpatrick (1981), Hill (1981), and Holmes and Kidd (1982).

20 Language teaching theories as theories of teaching method

The conceptualization of language teaching has a long, fascinating, but rather tortuous history. For over a century, language educators have attempted to solve the problems of language teaching by focusing attention almost exclusively on teaching *method*. Although the question of how to teach languages has been debated even longer than that—for over twenty-five centuries, to use Kelly's expression (1969)—theory development as a debate on teaching methods has evolved particularly over the last hundred years. This debate has provided the main basis for recent interpretations of language teaching. The names of many of the methods are familiar enough; yet the methods themselves are not easy to grasp, because their names have not been applied in a consistent and unambiguous way. What constitutes a particular method is not always clear. A teacher may say that he employs, for example, 'the direct method' or 'the audiovisual method'. Does his conception of the direct method or the audiovisual method correspond to clearly specified characteristics? Does the direct method teacher conduct his classes in the same way as another teacher who also claims to use the same method? Would an impartial observer be able to recognize the method as the one the teacher says he uses? Even the generic term 'method' is not unequivocal.[1]

Yet, in spite of these uncertainties the fact remains that language teaching theory over the decades since the end of the last century has advanced mainly by conceptualizing teaching in terms of teaching *methods*. The method debate has brought into focus important issues of language teaching and learning,[2] and in recent years the debate has led to the demand for theoretical clarification as well as for empirical research. Therefore, any present-day theory of language teaching must at least attempt to understand what the methods stand for and what they have contributed to current thought on teaching. The designations of methods, for example, grammar-translation, direct, audiolingual—as names of theories frequently do—point to an outstanding characteristic; but much more is included under the name 'method' than the feature that has given it its name. A method, however ill-defined it may be, is more than a single strategy or a particular technique; it is a 'theory' of language teaching in the T2 sense (see Chapter 2) which has resulted from practical and theoretical discussions in a given historical context. It usually implies and sometimes overtly expresses certain objectives, and a particular view of language; it makes assumptions about the language learner; and underlying it are certain beliefs about the nature of the language learning process. It also expresses a view of language teaching by emphasizing certain aspects of teaching as crucial to successful learning.

The following brief sketches in more or less historical sequence of a few of the labelled methods will indicate (1) outstanding features, (2) main sources, (3) history of the method, (4) objectives, (5) teaching techniques, (6) theoretical assumptions, and (7) an assessment of the method in question. These sketches are necessarily tentative; as will be seen again and again, methods are not well documented.[3]

Grammar-translation or traditional method

Principal features
As its name suggests, this method emphasizes the teaching of the second language grammar; its principal practice technique is translation from and into the target language.

Sources and history
No full and carefully documented history of grammar-translation exists. There is evidence that the teaching of grammar and translation has occurred in language instruction through the ages (Escher 1928; Kelly 1969); but the regular combination of grammar rules with translation into the target language as the principal practice technique became popular only in the late eighteenth century. One of the best known of such teaching grammars was Meidinger's *Praktische Französische Grammatik* (1783). The combination of brief presentations of grammar points and massive translation practice as a distinct teaching strategy was also applied in Ollendorff's language courses which came into popular use around 1840. The sequential arrangement used by Ollendorff in his lessons 'became standard: a statement of the rule, followed by a vocabulary list and translation exercises. At the end of the course translation of connected prose passages was attempted' (Kelly 1969:52). Ollendorff's method was praised by contemporaries as an active, simple, and effective method, because as soon as a rule had been presented it was applied in short translation-practice sentences. Other textbook writers, for example, Seidenstücker and Ahn, in each course-book, chapter, or 'lesson', combined rules, vocabulary, text, and sentences to be translated as the typical pattern of the grammar-translation method. In the mid-nineteenth century, Ploetz in Germany adapted Seidenstücker's French textbook for use in schools and thus

grammar-translation became the principal method of teaching modern languages in schools. In his elementary grammar (1848) Ploetz laid emphasis on the practice of verb paradigms, while in the more advanced *Schulgrammatik der französischen Sprache* (1849) systematic grammar was the central theme of the course. In the final decades of the nineteenth century grammar-translation was attacked as a cold and lifeless approach to language teaching, and it was blamed for the failure of foreign language teaching. The majority of language teaching reforms in the late nineteenth century and throughout the first half of the twentieth developed in opposition to grammar-translation.

In spite of many attacks, grammar-translation is still widely employed today, if only as a contributory strategy in conjunction with other strategies. A glance at many currently used textbooks, particularly in the less commonly taught languages, confirms the strong hold of grammar-translation.[4] In language programmes in the universities in English-speaking countries translation of texts from and into the foreign language has remained a standard procedure. In the early sixties Dodson (1967) reaffirmed teaching techniques based on a grammar-translation strategy under the name of 'bilingual method'. The cognitive code-learning theory to be discussed later in this chapter (see pp. 461 ff.) has taken up again some of the features of the grammar-translation method.

Objectives

In the nineteenth century grammar-translation was considered by practitioners as a necessary preliminary to the study of literary works, and even if that goal was not reached grammar-translation was regarded as an educationally valid mental discipline in its own right. Grammar-translation lays little or no emphasis on the speaking of the second language or listening to second language speech; it is a mainly book-oriented method of working out and learning the grammatical system of the language. Nevertheless, it must be recognized that Ploetz, for example, defined the objective of his *Schulgrammatik* as the 'thorough control of the language without one-sided attention to theory (i.e., grammatical theory, HHS), leading to fluent comprehension of French writings as well as to the independent use of the language in speech and writing'.[5]

Teaching techniques

The language is presented in short grammatical chapters or lessons each containing a few grammar points or rules which are set out and illustrated by examples. The grammatical features that are focused upon in the coursebook and by the teacher in his lesson are not disguised or hidden. A technical grammatical terminology is not avoided. The learner is expected to study and memorize a particular rule and examples, for instance, a verb paradigm or a list of prepositions. No systematic approach is usually made to vocabulary or any other aspect of the second language. Exercises consist of words, phrases, and sentences in the first language which the learner, with the help of a bilingual vocabulary list, translates into the target language in order to practise the particular item or group of items. One of the features of grammar-translation introduced by Meidinger was to increase the complexity of the learning task by constructing practice sentences illustrating a number of rules simultaneously. This approach tended to make language learning appear as a matter of problem- or puzzle-solving (see Chapter 5:91). Other exercises are designed to practise translation into the first language. As the learner progresses, he may advance from translating isolated sentences to translating coherent second language texts into the first language or first language texts into the second language.

Theoretical assumptions
The target language is primarily interpreted as a system of rules to be observed in texts and sentences and to be related to first language rules and meanings. Language learning is implicitly viewed as an intellectual activity involving rule learning, the memorization of rules and facts related to first language meanings by means of massive translation practice. The first language is maintained as the reference system in the acquisition of the second language. Basing itself on a faculty psychology, this method for learning modern languages was justified—like Latin and Greek had been—as a mental training.

Assessment
In spite of the virulent attacks that reformers made, the grammar-translation or traditional method has maintained itself remarkably well.[6] As we have already noted in our study of language learning (Chapter 18:402) the first language as a reference system is indeed very important for the second language learner. Therefore translation in one form or another or other crosslingual techniques can play a certain part in language learning. Moreover, some learners endeavour to understand the grammatical system of the second language. Hence grammar teaching, too, may have some importance for them. Furthermore, thinking about formal features of the second language and translation as a practice technique put the learner into an active problem-solving situation. In the terms of the basic strategies already set out (Chapter 18:411) it forms part of the 'academic' (explicit) learning strategy. Finally, grammar-translation appears didactically relatively easy to apply. The major defect of grammar-translation lies in the overemphasis on the language as a mass of rules (and exceptions) and in the limitations of practice techniques which never emancipate the learner from the

dominance of the first language. In addition, the sheer size of the task of memorization and the lack of coherence with which the language facts have been presented to the learner invalidate the claim, made in the nineteenth century, that this method provides a safe, easy, and practical entry into a second language.

The direct method

Principal feature
The direct method is characterized, above all, by the use of the target language as a means of instruction and communication in the language classroom, and by the avoidance of the use of the first language and of translation as a technique.

Sources
The lack of comprehensive documentation of this important development in language pedagogy has already been noted. Again, Kelly (1969) is the most accessible source for a historical interpretation, although his treatment of the direct method is scattered over the different chapters of his work. A systematic attempt to trace the origins and development of the direct method in Germany has been made by Rülcker (1969).[7]

History
Historically, the language teaching reforms from 1850 to 1900, particularly in Europe, attempted to make language teaching more effective by a radical change from grammar-translation. Various methods were developed during this period attesting to the general discontent with the prevailing theory and practice. Gouin's *L'art d'enseigner les langues* (1880) is a good example of fundamental reform in theory. The preface and introduction to Sweet's *The Practical Study of Languages* illustrates the criticisms and radicalism of the contemporary reform movements:

> '... it is significant to observe that though there is great conservatism in scholastic circles—as shown in the retention of antiquated text-books, in the prejudice against phonetics, and so on—there are, on the other hand, many signs of dissatisfaction with these methods.

> This dissatisfaction is strikingly shown by the way in which new "methods" are run after—especially the more sensational ones, and such as have the good fortune to be taken up by the editor of some popular periodical.

> But none of these methods retain their popularity long—the interest in them soon dies out. There is a constant succession of them; Ollendorff, Ahn, Prendergast, Gouin—to mention only a few—have

all had their day. They have all failed to keep a permanent hold on the public mind because they have all failed to perform what they promised: after promising impossibilities they have all turned out to be on the whole no better than the older methods.'
(Sweet 1899/1964:2–3)

The proposed reforms went under a variety of names: 'reform method', 'natural method', 'psychological method', 'phonetic method', etc., but the most persistent term to describe the various features of new approaches in language teaching was the term 'direct method'. A clear statement of moderate directions of the direct method is contained in the six articles of the International Phonetic Association, discussed in Chapter 5.

The impetus to the direct method can be partly attributed to practical unconventional teaching reformers who responded to the need for better language learning in a new world of industry and international trade and travel, such as Berlitz and Gouin. It was partly also stimulated by linguistic scholarship, linguistic theory, philology, and phonetics. Historically, the development of the direct method is closely linked with the introduction of phonetics into language pedagogy. Both phonetics and the direct method emphasized the use of the spoken language. Conceptually, however, they are not necessarily linked.

As we saw in Chapter 6:98 the advocacy of the direct method aroused much controversy among language teachers around the turn of the century; but in several countries (for example, Prussia and France) the reforms gained recognition in ministerial guidelines and are clearly evident in the contemporary textbooks.

Although in subsequent decades the direct method was not integrally applied, its influence on theory and practice was profound and widespread. For example, in the U.S.A. de Sauzé (1929; see Chapter 6:100) as Director of Foreign Languages in Cleveland, Ohio, introduced the 'Cleveland Plan' into Cleveland public schools in 1919. This plan consisted principally of a carefully devised scheme of graded instruction of French and other languages over a period of years in elementary and high schools. An essential feature of the plan was the use of the second language as a medium of instruction in the language class and the avoidance of translation as a technique of teaching. The Cleveland Plan can be regarded as a consistent twentieth century application of the direct method. According to de Sauzé, the Cleveland Plan was successful in arousing the students' interest and in raising the standard of second language learning in Cleveland schools. But de Sauzé's direct method policy was exceptional in America.

In Britain, too, the direct method left its mark as a challenge to teachers; but the policy that was recommended in the interwar years was a compromise, i.e., to adopt from the direct method its emphasis on the spoken language and many of its techniques, but not to taboo translation or grammatical explanation in the first language (for example, IAAM 1929). The direct method—with or without a 'phonetic introduction'—had its main influence in Europe on the early stages of learning French or English, while advanced language teaching continued to rely mainly on the traditional approach. The mixture was referred to in Britain as the 'compromise method' or as the 'oral method'. Collins, the author of one of the most widely used French courses of the interwar years, and influential as an H.M.I., advocated this approach; he coined the slogan to teach French 'as Frenchly as possible' (Collins 1934). This compromise was in fact often closer to grammar-translation than to the direct method.

Although the integral direct method and its companion, the phonetic method, had virtually disappeared from the language classes in the schools in the interwar period, certain techniques remained: above all, the use of second language narratives, question-and-answer techniques, and other direct method exercises. In several European educational systems the translation of texts was totally replaced by direct study of oral and printed texts, renarration, and writing of compositions based on pictures and episodes told by the teacher. Above all, as a result of the influence of the direct method many teachers down to the present have regarded as an ideal in language pedagogy, although unattainable in practice, the total avoidance of translation as a practice technique and the total avoidance of the use of the first language as a means of explanation and communication in the foreign language classroom. The direct method debate has thus introduced into the conceptualization of language teaching a rift between what teachers actually do in the language class and what they believe they ought to do.

In recent years, some American language educators (for example, Hester 1970; Diller 1975, 1978) have reaffirmed the direct method as a valid approach to language teaching. In their interpretation it is a 'cognitive' or rationalist method which emphasizes second language use without translation in the language classroom. This new version of the direct method does not avoid grammatical explanation and formal practice, but it lays greater emphasis on language use in genuine acts of communication (see Note 14 below) than on language drill as it occurs in the audiolingual method (see below).

Objectives
The direct method represents a shift from literary language to the spoken everyday language as the object of early instruction, a goal that was totally lacking in grammar-translation. The mind training objective of grammar-translation is not central to the direct method. For the rest, the direct method represents more a change in means than in the ends of

language teaching, and it can be said that the direct method did not convey a fundamentally different view of the main goals of language instruction from that of its predecessors.

Techniques

The standard procedure involves the classroom presentation of a 'text' by the teacher. The text is usually a short specially constructed foreign language narrative in the textbook. Difficult expressions are explained in the target language with the help of paraphrases, synonyms, demonstration, or context. To elucidate further the meaning of the text the teacher asks questions about it, and the students read the text aloud for practice. Grammatical observations are derived from the text read and students are encouraged to discover for themselves the grammatical principle involved. Much time is spent on questions and answers on the text or on talk about wall pictures. Exercises involve transpositions, substitutions, dictation, narrative, and free composition. Since the direct method class involves much use of the spoken language, stress is also laid on the acquisition of a good pronunciation. This is why in the early stages of the history of the direct method phonetics—especially phonetic transcription—was regarded as an important part of this method.

Theoretical assumptions

Linguistically, language teaching was to be based on phonetics and on a scientifically established coherent grammar (Viëtor 1882). The learning of languages was viewed as analogous to first language acquisition, and the learning processes involved were often interpreted in terms of an associationist psychology. Hence the emphasis on sounds and simple sentences and direct association of language with objects and persons of the immediate environment, for example, the classroom, the home, the garden, and the street (Rülcker 1969:19–20).

Assessment

The direct method was the first of the methods in which the impetus came both from the inventiveness of a few practitioners and from the critical and theoretical thought about the nature of language and language learning of a few linguistic scholars such as Sweet and Viëtor. The direct method was also a first attempt to make the language *learning* situation one of language *use* and to train the learner to abandon the first language as the frame of reference. It demanded inventiveness on the part of teachers and led to the development of new non-translational techniques of language instruction. The use of a text as a basis of language learning, demonstrations of pictures and objects, the emphasis on question and answer, spoken narratives, dictation, imitation, and a host of new types of grammatical exercises have resulted from the direct method. Language pedagogy in the present century, for example, Palmer in the twenties and the audiolingual and audiovisual methods in the fifties and sixties, adopted many of the techniques first developed by direct method teachers. On the L1-L2 issue, the direct method constitutes a radical attempt to exclude L1 in L2 learning.

Two major problems have persistently troubled direct method teaching. One has been how to convey meaning without translating, and how to safeguard against misunderstanding without reference to the first language. Another has been how to apply the direct method beyond elementary stages of language learning. The direct method—like other new methods—has extended the repertoire of language instruction in the early stages of teaching, but has added relatively little to the teaching of advanced learners. In a way, particularly because of the insistence on the use of the second language in classroom communication, the direct method can legitimately be looked upon as a precedessor of present-day 'immersion' techniques.

The reading method

Principal feature
This method deliberately restricts the goal of language teaching to training in reading comprehension.

Source
Some of the writings of West (for example, 1926a), Bond (1953) and Coleman's volume in the Modern Foreign Language Study (Coleman 1929) provided contemporary arguments for this approach. However, no documented study of this method has come to our notice.

History
As a creation of the twenties this theory was advocated by some British and American educators. West (1926), teaching English in India, argued that learning to read fluently was more important for Indians learning English than speaking. West recommended an emphasis on reading not only because he regarded it as the most useful skill to acquire in a foreign language but also because it was the easiest, a skill with the greatest surrender value for the student in the early stages of language learning. Basing himself on Thorndike's *Teacher's Word Book* (1921) he constructed readers with a controlled vocabulary and regular repetition of new words. On similar grounds, Coleman (1929) drew the conclusion from the Modern Foreign Language Study that the only practical form of language teaching in American high schools would be to concentrate on reading skills. Equally, Bond developed a reading

method approach to college language courses at Chicago University between 1920 and 1940. In describing the evolution of the reading method at the University of Chicago Bond (1953) wrote about the beginnings in 1920–21:

> '...one already discerns the separation of the active and passive phases of language learning, the analytical approach to grammar for reading comprehension purposes, the emphasis on an increased reading experience of both intensive and extensive types, the postponement of speech and writing training, the continuous attention to the spoken word, and the concern for the individual learner that were to become the hallmark of the Reading Method.'
> (op. cit.:29–30)

The student was given detailed instructions on reading strategies (for example, op. cit.:130–131). The course of study that was developed over a period of decades provided graded reading materials and a systematic approach to learning to read. The spoken language was not entirely neglected, but it was the reading objective that received the main emphasis.

The reading method was much criticized both at the time it was advocated in America and retrospectively during World War II when *speaking* languages became a national priority in the U.S.A. However, since the war there has been a renewed interest in the teaching of languages for specific purposes such as reading of scientific literature.

Objectives
The reading method was a theory of language teaching which deliberately restricted the goal of language instruction to one of practical attainable utility.

Techniques
The techniques were not radically different from those developed under previous methods. As under grammar-translation, the use of the first language was not banned in language instruction. The introduction of the second language was oral as in the direct method because facility in pronunciation and 'inner speech' were regarded as an important aid in reading comprehension. Several techniques were adopted from native language reading instruction. Above all, vocabulary control in reading texts was regarded as of prime importance, and so was the distinction between intensive reading for detailed study and extensive rapid reading of graded 'readers' for general comprehension.

Theoretical assumptions
This method had a strongly pragmatic basis. Its educational assumptions were similar to those current in the American school curriculum of

the twenties, namely to gear educational activities to specified ultimate practical uses.

Assessment

The reading method grew out of practical educational considerations, not from a shift in linguistic or psychological theory. It was in keeping with American educational theory of the twenties. It introduced into language teaching some important new elements: (a) the possibility of devising techniques of language learning geared to specific purposes, in this case the reading objective; (b) the application of vocabulary control to second language texts, as a means of better grading of texts; (c) the creation of graded 'readers'; and (d) thanks to vocabulary control, the introduction of techniques of rapid reading to the foreign language classroom.

The audiolingual method

Principal features

This method of the sixties has several distinctive characteristics: (1) separation of the skills—listening, speaking, reading, and writing—and the primacy of the audiolingual over the graphic skills; (2) the use of dialogues as the chief means of presenting the language; (3) emphasis on certain practice techniques, mimicry, memorization, and pattern drills; (4) the use of the language laboratory; (5) establishing a linguistic and psychological theory as a basis for the teaching method.

Sources

The audiolingual method has been described in some influential books which appeared from about 1960, such as Brooks (1960/1964), Stack (1960/1966/1971), Lado (1964), Rivers (1964, 1968), Chastain (1971, 1976). The early development of its linguistic principles have been traced by Moulton (1961/1963). But again, as in the methods already reviewed, detailed analytical and critical studies, from a present-day perspective, of the origins, development and impact of audiolingualism are lacking.

History

While the principal methods of the first half of the century, the grammar-translation and direct methods, had largely developed in the European school systems, audiolingualism is in origin mainly American. But it has had a considerable influence on language education in most parts of the world, even where it has been critically and sceptically received from the outset, as for example in Britain or Germany.

A distinct audiolingual method can hardly be identified until the late fifties. It appeared under various names. In the fifties it was most frequently referred to as the aural-oral method. The term 'audiolingual' was proposed by Brooks as a more pronounceable alternative (Brooks 1964:263). Brooks himself also popularized another term which referred to the same method as 'New Key', a term derived from a work by Langer, *Philosophy in a New Key*.[8] Carroll (1966) called the method the 'audiolingual habit theory', while the Pennsylvania Study (Smith 1970) referred to it as the 'functional skills strategy'.

Whatever it was called, its period of clearest definition as a distinct language teaching theory and of greatest influence was quite brief; it lasted from about 1959 to 1966. From the beginning of this period, but increasingly so since 1964, audiolingualism was challenged. Eventually, by 1970, it was severely criticized on theoretical and pragmatic grounds; and demands for a new orientation became more and more vocal.

As most observers have noted, the origins of audiolingualism are to be found in the 'Army Method' of American wartime language programmes in World War II (see Chapter 6:102). The growth of the theory and practice of the Army Method, described by Moulton (1961/1963), was expressed in the five slogans, listed by Moulton, already referred to in Chapter 8:158. Bloomfield's seminal (1942) pamphlet, the writings and teachings of Fries and Lado at the English Language Institute of the University of Michigan, the development of contrastive linguistics, the new technology of the language laboratory, and the generous financial support for language research and development in the U.S.A., resulting from the National Defense Education Act (NDEA 1957), were factors contributing to the development of audiolingualism. The audiolingual theory was probably the first language teaching theory that openly claimed to be derived from linguistics and psychology. But audiolingualists did not only assert to have placed language teaching on a scientific basis; they endeavoured to show that the principles derived from the scientific disciplines could be applied in concrete and usable form in language teaching materials and day-to-day practice.

The greater effectiveness of audiolingualism was challenged almost as soon as the claims for it were advanced. The study by Scherer and Wertheimer (1964; see Chapters 4:56 and 6:106) constituted a first attempt to seek empirical proof. The subsequent studies by Chastain and Woerdehoff (1968), the Pennsylvania Project (Smith 1970), and the GUME Project in Sweden (Levin 1972) continued the search for concrete evidence of the merits of audiolingualism. The theoretical bases of audiolingualism were questioned by Carroll, Rivers, Saporta, and Anisfeld as early as 1964 (Valdman 1966; Rivers 1964; see Chapter 15:327–9). The famous address by Chomsky (1966) to the Northeast Conference (see Chapters 6:108 and 15:327), shook the theoretical bases of audiolingualism and led to a prolonged and heated debate on the audiolingual method between 1966 and 1972. Meanwhile teaching materials and teaching practice had only just caught up with the audiolingual thought and classroom innovations. The discrepancy between the rapid changes in theoretical positions and the slower development of practice led to the sense of confusion and disorientation in the early seventies which was described in previous chapters.

Objectives

In the audiolingual method the dominant emphasis is placed on 'the fundamental skills', i.e., listening and speaking. While reading and writing are not neglected, listening and speaking are given priority and in the teaching sequence precede reading and writing. Like the direct method, audiolingualism tries to develop target language skills without reference to the mother tongue. Brooks (1960/1964), for example, regards a co-ordinate command of the second language as the ideal outcome of language learning. While audiolingualists were not impervious to the cultural aspects of second language instruction, language learning, in the first instance, was viewed as the acquisition of a practical set of communicative skills.

Techniques

In what way do the techniques of the audiolingual method differ from those of grammar-translation or the direct method? Audiolingualism does not *emphasize* a presentation of grammatical knowledge or information as grammar-translation does but it does not taboo it completely. It does reject the intellectual, problem-solving approach of grammar-translation and does not favour the isolation of paradigmatic features such as lists of pronouns or verb forms. The use of the first language in the language class or in learning materials is not as severely restricted in the audiolingual method as it was in the direct method. The direct method was criticized by audiolingualists for its lack of a linguistic basis and its failure to grade language data with sufficient scientific care.

The learning process is viewed in the audiolingual method as one of habituation and conditioning without the intervention of any intellectual analysis. In other words, on the explicit-implicit issue, it favours an implicit rather than an explicit learning strategy. Emphasis is laid on active and simple practice. The intention is to make language learning less of a mental burden and more a matter of relatively effortless and frequent repetition and imitation. The audiolingual method has introduced memorization of dialogues and imitative repetition (mimicry) as specific learning techniques. In addition, it has developed pattern drills (also called structural drills or pattern practice). Such drills were not unknown before, for example in the work of Palmer. But they became essential features of audiolingualism and as such were diversified and refined as a technique of language learning beyond anything previously known. Audiolingual techniques, therefore, appeared to offer the possibility of language learning without requiring a strong academic background and inclination. The simplicity and directness of approach that was advocated seemed to bring language learning within the scope of the ordinary learner. Moreover, speaking, which in language learning had hitherto been more of an addition to book learning, was now brought right into the centre of the stage, and the teaching techniques with tape recordings and language laboratory drill offered practice in speaking and listening which, without being actual conversations, rehearsed the verbal exchanges of ordinary talk in the stylized form of stimulus and response.

Theoretical assumptions
Audiolingualism reflects the descriptive, structural, and contrastive linguistics of the fifties and sixties. Its psychology is avowedly be-haviouristic. Mainly following Skinner, but also influenced by neo-behaviourists such as Osgood, its psychology is an interpretation of language learning in terms of stimulus and response, operant conditioning, and reinforcement with an emphasis on successful error-free learning in small well-prepared steps and stages. The lack of sophistication and of consistency in its application of psychological and linguistic theory has repeatedly been criticized, for example, by Rivers (1964), Carroll (1966), and Chomsky (1966).

Assessment
In the early sixties audiolingualism had raised hopes of ushering in a golden age of language learning. By the end of the decade it became the whipping boy for all that was wrong with language teaching. Its theoretical basis was found to be weak. But also in practical terms its hopes had not been fulfilled. Empirical research did not conclusively establish its superiority, and teachers, using audiolingual materials and applying the audiolingual method conscientiously, complained about the lack of effectiveness of the techniques in the long run and the boredom they engendered among students.

In view of these criticisms it is necessary to remind oneself of the major contributions of audiolingualism to language teaching. First, it was among the first theories to recommend the development of a language teaching theory on declared linguistic and psychological principles. Second, it attempted to make language learning accessible to large groups of ordinary learners. In other words, this theory proposed that language teaching should be organized in such a way as not to demand great intellectual feats of abstract reasoning to learn a language. Third, it stressed syntactical progression, while previously methods had tended to be preoccupied with vocabulary and morphology. Fourth, it led to the development of simple techniques, without translation, of varied, graded, and intensive practice of specific features of the language. Last, it developed the separation of the language skills into a pedagogical device. The audiolingual method introduced specifically designed techniques of auditory and oral practice, while previously oral practice had been simply textbook exercises read aloud, and the sequencing of different language skills had not been treated consistently as pedagogically relevant.

The audiovisual method

Principal feature
A visually presented scenario provides the chief means of involving the learner in meaningful utterances and contexts.

Sources
The method is described in the introduction to the programme with which it was first put into effect, *Voix et Images de France* (CREDIF 1961). More recent developments of this method are reflected in Renard and Heinle (1969), CREDIF (1971), and *Voix et Visages de la France* (Heinle *et al.* 1974).

History
This method was developed in the fifties in France at the Centre de Recherche et d'Etude pour la Diffusion du Français (CREDIF) by a team directed by Guberina and Rivenc. The principles underlying this method were applied in a small number of programmes prepared and published by the CREDIF team, *Voix et Images de France*, a French course intended for adult beginners, *Bonjour Line*, an equivalent programme for young children, and a revised version of *Voix et Images de France*, entitled *De vive voix*. Adaptations of some of these programmes were produced in America (Renard and Heinle 1969) and in the U.K. (Gross and Mason 1965); and a newer programme based on the same principles was produced in Canada under the title of *Dialogue Canada* (Commission de la fonction publique 1974–77), prepared for the use of Canadian government language schools. The CREDIF methods as well as the programmes were made widely known through teachers' courses in which originally a rigid training in the principles of the audiovisual method and its application was given. In recent years, a more flexible view of teaching techniques and sequences has been advocated by the CREDIF team.

Objectives

Language learning is visualized as falling into several stages: a first stage to which the audiovisual method is particularly applicable in which the learner becomes familiar with everyday language as defined in *français fondamental*; a second stage involving the capacity to talk more consecutively on general topics and to read non-specialized fiction and the newspaper; and a third stage involving the use of more specialized discourse of professional and other interests. The audiovisual method is intended particularly for the first stage.

Techniques

Audiovisual teaching, as developed in the CREDIF method, consists of a carefully thought-out but rigid order of events. The lesson begins with the filmstrip and tape *presentation*. The sound recordings provide a stylized dialogue and narrative commentary. A filmstrip frame corresponds to an utterance. In other words, the visual image and spoken utterance complement each other and constitute jointly a semantic unit. In the second phase of the teaching sequence the meaning of sense groups is explained ('*explication*') by the teacher through pointing, demonstrating, selective listening, question and answer. In the third phase, the dialogue is repeated several times and memorized by frequent replays of the tape-recordings and the filmstrip, or by language laboratory practice. In the next stage of the teaching sequence, the *development phase* ('*exploitation*' or '*transposition*'), students are gradually emancipated from the tape-and-filmstrip presentation: for example, the filmstrip is now shown without the tape recording, and the students are asked to recall the commentary or make up their own; or the subject matter of the scenario is modified and applied to the student himself, his family or friends, by means of question and answer or role playing. Besides this thorough treatment of the dialogue situation, each lesson contains a portion for grammatical drill which practises a pattern or a group of patterns which has previously occurred in the context of the tape and filmstrip dialogue presentation. Grammatical as well as phonological features are practised. No importance is attributed to linguistic explanations. Writing and reading, as in the audiolingual method, are delayed, but in due course are nonetheless given emphasis.

Theoretical assumptions

The audiovisual method seeks a basis in linguistics. It derives its grammatical and lexical content from descriptive linguistic studies such as *français fondamental*. But in contrast to the antecedents of the audiolingual method, the audiovisual method stresses the social nature and situational embeddedness of language:

'... le langage est avant tout un moyen de communication entre les êtres ou les groupes sociaux ...'
(CREDIF 1961:viii)

The visual presentation is, therefore, not an added gimmick. It is intended to simulate the social context in which language is used.

The assumed learning process of this method has an affinity with Gestalt psychology. It proceeds from a total view of the situation to particular segments of language. By its insistence on a non-analytical learning approach and its well defined teaching sequence the method makes definite assumptions about optimal ways of language learning. The learner is encouraged to absorb in a global fashion the utterances he hears on the tape in the context he sees on the screen, in other words, not to analyse. Equally, in teaching French phonology or grammar, the authors insist that intonation, rhythmic patterns, and semantic units should not be broken down. But the practice sequences, based on the global presentation, are not fundamentally different from those of the audiolingual method. However, the stimuli in the exercises are pictorial and the attempt is made to practise all features to be learnt in a meaningful context. Pure pattern practice without attention to meaning and outside a context is avoided.[9]

Assessment

The audiovisual approach, developed by CREDIF, represents a distinctive modern attempt to come to grips with the problems of language learning. It has defined three different levels of language instruction.[10] It has attempted to place language learning into a simplified social context and to teach language from the outset as meaningful spoken communication. The replacement of the printed text of the direct method by a scenario, presented visually by filmstrip and aurally by corresponding tape recordings, has provided a fresh alternative in language pedagogy, and was—at the time when it was devised in the fifties—a responsive and, at the same time, responsible way of exploiting technology for the benefit of language learning. Like the audiolingual method, it bases itself on declared linguistic and psychological principles.

The audiovisual method is open to two major criticisms. Like the direct method, from which much of its pedagogy derives, it has difficulties in conveying meaning; the visual filmstrip image is no guarantee that the meaning of an utterance is not misinterpreted by the learner. The equivalence between utterances and visual images is often theoretically questionable, and presents practical difficulties. The other criticism that can be made is that the rigid teaching sequences imposed by this method are based on an entirely unproved assumption about learning sequences.

Cognitive theory

Principal features
This theory or method has been interpreted by some as a 'modified, up-to-date grammar-translation theory' (Carroll 1966:102) and by others as a modified, up-to-date direct method approach (Hester 1970; Diller 1971, 1975, 1978). In its recent forms, as expressed by Diller (1971, 1978) or Chastain (1976), it lays emphasis on the conscious acquisition of language as a meaningful system and it seeks a basis in cognitive psychology and in transformational grammar.

Sources
No single theorist can be identified as the main proponent of a cognitive approach. Carroll (1966) was the first to characterize a cognitive theory of language teaching. Chastain (1969, 1976) gives a helpful interpretation of cognitive theory and teaching. Diller (1971, 1975, 1978) has contrasted the cognitive and audiolingual methods. As a fully-fledged language teaching theory the cognitive method has not as yet been critically examined. In the early eighties its contribution has been overshadowed by the increasing shift of interest to communicative approaches.[11]

History
As an alternative to the audiolingual method the cognitive theory developed from the mid-sixties in response to the criticisms levelled against the audiolingual method. The rediscovery of grammar-translation or the direct method was no mere turning back of the clock. It was an attempt to bring to language pedagogy the new insights of psychology, psycholinguistics, and modern developments in linguistics. Several language programmes have been published since the early seventies which claim to be based on cognitive theory. But the practice techniques that this method has yielded have hardly introduced much that is new. The main effects of the cognitive theory seem to have been that it has loosened the tight hold that the audiolingual method had exercised on materials and practice and that it removed the stigma that had been placed on grammar-translation and direct method practices.

Objectives
Broadly speaking, the goal of cognitive teaching is the same as that proposed by audiolingual theorists (Chastain 1976:146–7), but certain differences in immediate objectives are apparent. Cognitive theory is less concerned with the primacy of the audiolingual skills. Instead it emphasizes the control of the language in all its manifestations as a coherent and meaningful system, a kind of consciously acquired

'competence' which the learner can then put to use in real-life situations. Carroll defines the objective in these terms:

> 'The theory attaches more importance to the learner's understanding of the structure of the foreign language than to the facility in using that structure, since it is believed that provided the student has a proper degree of cognitive control over the structures of the language, facility will develop automatically with use of the language in meaningful situations.'[12]
> (Carroll 1966:102)

Techniques
The techniques are characterized by Carroll as follows:

> '... learning a language is a process of acquiring conscious control of the phonological, grammatical, and lexical patterns of the second language, largely through study and analysis of these patterns as a body of knowledge.'
> (loc. cit.)

In other words, the cognitive approach does not reject, disguise or de-emphasize the conscious teaching of grammar or of language rules. It does not avoid the presentation of reading and writing in association with listening and speaking. Instead of expecting automatic command of the language and habit-formation from intensive drill, it seeks the intellectual understanding by the learner of the language as a system; and practice of meaningful material is regarded as being of greater merit than the drive towards automatic control. The behaviouristic view of learning in terms of conditioning, shaping, reinforcement, habit-forma-tion, and overlearning, has been replaced by an emphasis on rule learning, meaningful practice, and creativity.

Theoretical assumptions
Like the audiolingual method, cognitive theory looks for a rationale in linguistics and psychology. Rejecting behaviourism and structural linguistics, it seeks in transformational grammar and cognitive psychol-ogy a basis for second language teaching. Cognitive theory reflects the theoretical reorientation in linguistics and psycholinguistics that was initiated by Chomsky in the sixties. Diller (1978) has formulated four principles of cognitivism which contrast with the five principles by which Moulton (1961/1963) had characterized audiolingualism.

1 '*A living language is characterized by rule-governed creativity*' (Diller 1978:23). This principle clearly based on two concepts derived from Chomsky—language is rule-governed and creative—implies the teaching of a language as a consciously learnt system.

2 *'The rules of grammar are psychologically real'* (op. cit.:26). The user of a given language gives evidence of knowing the rules of the language by applying them automatically. The fact that the rules are applied automatically, however, does not mean that they must be learnt automatically. A new language, like the rules of a game of chess, 'are best learned in conjunction with demonstration and practice of the action' (op. cit.:29). That is to say, the learning of a skill can be deliberate (i.e., explicit in the terms of Chapter 18); it becomes automatic through use.

3 *'Man is specially equipped to learn languages'* (op. cit.:29). Learning language is a human characteristic. It is biologically founded in man. But it is not confined to childhood. The capacities of children have been overrated, those of adults underrated. Language learning can occur at any time in life in 'a situation of meaningful use' (op. cit.:30). It is an activity of the learner, not something that is 'just impressed upon us from the outside' (op. cit.:34).

4 *'A living language is a language in which we can think'* (op. cit.:34). Language is bound up with meaning and thinking. Learning a language 'involves learning to think in that language. *Meaningful practice* rather than drill is the only way this can come about' (op. cit.:37).

Assessment

Cognitive theory is principally a critique of audiolingualism in the light of changes in linguistic and psycholinguistic theory. It has pinpointed theoretical and practical weaknesses of the earlier theory and has drawn attention to important facets of language and language learning which the audiolingual theory had disregarded or underemphasized, such as creativity and meaning. It has also re-discovered valuable features in grammar-translation and in the direct method. On the implicit-explicit issue of language learning cognitive theory is avowedly explicit. However, by overlooking the merits of audiolingualism cognitive theorists have sharpened the battle of the dogmas without providing convincing evidence of doing any more than redressing the balance in certain respects.

Conclusion: methods as language teaching theories

The method arguments have not been confined to the six methods we have analysed, nor have new methods ceased to be proposed, with the development of cognitivism in the early seventies.[13] But these six sketches will be sufficient to show that the labelled methods have originated mainly in three ways.

(a) Partly they have been responses to changing demands on language education resulting from social, economic, political, or educational circumstances. The grammar-translation method matched educational beliefs affecting schooling in the nineteenth century. The direct method, evolved in a period of European political and commercial expansion and of increasing trade and travel through the development of railways. The reading method was a reflection of views on the curriculum in the twenties. The audiolingual and audiovisual methods developed in the period of rising nation states in the Third World and in a time of new international awareness in the Western world that followed World War II.

(b) The methods have, secondly, resulted from changes in language theories and in new psychological perspectives on language learning. For example, the direct method has antecedents in associationist psychology and in the language sciences of the nineteenth century. The audiolingual, audiovisual, and cognitive theories—more than language teaching theories ever before—have sought to find a basis in linguistics and psychology.

(c) Lastly, most of the methods reflect that experience, intuitions, and opinions of practising teachers. It is the dissatisfactions and failures of teachers and pupils with a particular method that have contributed to the constant critique of methods and the demand for reform and new emphases.

Each of the different methods has contributed new insights and has attempted to deal with one or the other of the three issues of language learning which we pinpointed in Chapter 18. Thus, the grammar-translation and cognitive theories have recognized a language as an orderly system of rules which a learner, to a certain extent at least, can consciously acquire by study methods (the explicit option). Both grammar-translation and audiolingualism—each in different ways—have treated the transfer/interference phenomenon from the first language as important for language learning (the L1-L2 connection). Grammar-translation has based its entire teaching strategy on the use of the first language as a reference system. Audiolingualism, through contrastive linguistic analysis, has made a brave, although not very successful, attempt to overcome interference by systematically laying emphasis on differences between the first and the second language. The direct method and the audiolingual method have recognized the value for the learner to immerse himself into the second language, the direct method by the refusal to translate, and the audiolingual method by the insistence on intensive practice and habituation. The reading method and the audiolingual method have provided experience in isolating particular language skills, reading in the one case or listening and speaking in the other, in contrast to a more global approach practised by other methods. All methods have emphasized the need for systematic practice. But while the grammar-translation and the cognitive approach have presented the language as an intellectual learning problem, the audiolingual and audiovisual method have advocated a relatively unthinking drill and training approach (the explicit-implicit option). The problem of meaning in a second language, which for the learner plays a central role, was overcome by the grammar-translation method by the simple translation device. Among the newer methods, the direct method advocates were aware of the problem of meaning and recommended a number of techniques to cope with it, for example, demonstration, visual aids, explanation in the second language, or context; but only the audiovisual method has given consistent attention to meaning by insisting on systematic visual support.

All the methods examined in this chapter can be characterized as analytical. That is to say none of them have explored the possibility of non-analytical, participatory, or experiential ways of language learning as a deliberate teaching strategy. In the terms of the three issues discussed in Chapter 18 they have resolved the code-communication dilemma by emphasizing the learning of 'code' rather than learning the language through becoming involved in communicative activities.[14] A communicative strategy in this sense has only emerged during the last few years and has hardly attained (and hopefully will never attain) the fixity of a teaching 'method'. Nevertheless, the communicative approach has so profoundly influenced current thought and practice on language teaching strategies that it is hardly possible today to imagine a language pedagogy which does not make some allowance at all levels of teaching for a non-analytical (experiential or participatory), communicative component.

All the methods we have sketched have in common two major weaknesses. One is that they represent a relatively fixed combination of language teaching beliefs, and another is that they are characterized by the over-emphasis on single aspects as the central issue of language teaching and learning. This characteristic has made historical sense and has contributed new insights but eventually has formed an inadequate basis for conceptualizing language teaching. Moreover, all the methods make assumptions, and often quite elaborate and detailed ones about the learner and ways of learning. While these assumptions appear plausible in principle, they have not been tested critically and systematically against the realities of actual learning.

Methods, thus, have constituted theories of language teaching derived partly from practical experience, intuition, and inventiveness, partly from social, political, and educational needs, and partly from theoretical considerations; but they have neither been systematically stated as coherent theories of language teaching and learning nor have they been critically verified by empirical evidence, except in a few recent instances.[15]

It is because of the fundamental weakness of the method concept that, over a period of about two decades, the conviction has gradually spread that language teaching cannot be satisfactorily conceptualized in terms of teaching method alone. These changes in the concept of teaching are the subject of the next chapter.

Notes

1 Several years ago, Anthony (1963/1965; see also Anthony and Norris 1969) observed 'the undergrowth of overlapping terminology that surrounds this field' (1965:93) and proposed a distinction between 'approach', 'method', and 'technique'. *Approach* constitutes the axiomatic or theoretical bases of language teaching. *Method* is procedural and is interpreted in Mackey's terms (see Chapter 21) as 'the selection of materials to be taught, the gradation of those materials, their presentation, and pedagogical implementation to induce learning' (Anthony and Norris 1969:2). Within one approach there can be more than one method; but each method must be based upon the selected approach. *Technique* 'is implementational' (1965:96). It describes a 'particular trick, stratagem, or contrivance' (ibid.) used in the classroom. It must harmonize with a method and consequently also with the underlying approach. Anthony and Norris conclude that 'method must be based on axioms, and it must be implemented through techniques selected to lead the student to the desired language behavior, as defined by those axioms' (1969:6). While these definitions were helpful in sorting out the distinction between theoretical assumptions ('approach'), teaching strategies ('methods'), and specific classroom activities ('technique'), they did not reflect the broad and ill-defined way in which the term 'method' was actually used until recently and is even still used today.

2 The scope of three of these major language learning problems has already been identified in Chapter 18:400–405.

3 Readers might find it useful to relate the accounts in this chapter to the historical survey in Chapter 6.

4 See, for example, the widely popular *Teach Yourself* series of language books.

5 'gründliche Erlernung der Sprache ohne einseitige Richtung auf das Studium der Theorie, nicht nur bis sum geläufigen Verstehen der Schriftwerke der Franzosen, sondern auch bis zum selbständigen mündlichen und schriftlichen Gebrauche des Idioms' (quoted in a short article by Sachs in 1893, on the ever new editions of the popular Ploetz teaching grammars). For bibliographical details on teaching grammars by Meidinger, Ollendorff, Ahn, Ploetz, and others see Kelly (1969).

6 To my knowledge no systematic studies have ever been made to find out to what extent grammar teaching and translation techniques are actually still employed today in the teaching of different languages and at different levels of instruction.

7 An unpublished Chicago thesis by Escher (1928) traces the historical development. See also our discussion of the IPA articles in Chapter 5.

8 Brooks (1964:6) was influenced by Langer in the distinction she made in *Philosophy in a New Key* between sign and symbol. He thus attempted to give his theory of language teaching a basis in linguistic philosophy. I must confess I have never understood in what way Langer's distinction between sign and symbol was of consequence to Brooks' language teaching theory. It is noteworthy that the words 'sign' or 'symbol', after being discussed at length in Chapter 1, are no longer mentioned in the subsequent pages of Brooks' work.

9 For an account of the audiovisual method see the Introduction to *Voix et Images de France* (CREDIF 1961). See also the account by Guberina (1964) who can be considered the theoretician of the audiovisual methodology.

10 That is, a first level of elementary everyday conversation (*niveau un*), an intermediate level involving more advanced conversation and reading of newspapers, magazines, and other non-specialized literature (*niveau deux*), and a third level of more differentiated language use according to professional interests and specializations.

11 In our examination of language learning issues (see Chapter 18:403–4) the cognitive approach in contrast to the audiolingual habit theory appeared as the 'explicit' teaching response under the heading of 'Explicit-Implicit Option'.

12 It is worth noting that the assumption of the cognitive theory that this facility would develop *automatically* in meaningful situations has not been confirmed by subsequent experience and has ultimately led in turn to the questioning of this theory.

13 As we noted in Chapter 6 (see especially Figure 6.1), several new methods have emerged in the seventies and have aroused interest among teachers and the general public, for example, the Silent Way (Gattegno 1972, 1976), Community Language Learning (Curran 1976), Suggestopedia (Lozanov 1979; Scovel 1979), the Dartmouth Method, (Rassias 1971), and the Natural Method (Terrell 1977). For discussions of some of these see Benseler and Schulz (1979), Diller (1975, 1978) and Stevick (1976, 1980). For a concise, comprehensive, and up-to-date review of different teaching methods with useful references, see Rivers (1981: Chapter 2). See also Brown (1980).

14 Diller (1975, 1978) has attributed to the direct method the non-analytical participatory experiential characteristic of communicative language teaching. It should however be noted that communicative

teaching is not always understood as being non-analytical. Another interpretation of this concept is learning a language with attention to sociolinguistic and discourse features. Such an approach can be very analytical, but it takes more features into account than phonology and syntax. See on this point Chapter 12:258–62. Different interpretations of communicative language teaching are discussed by Stern (1981, 1981a).

15 The comparisons of teaching methods in the research studies of the sixties referred to above, illustrate attempts to examine language learning empirically, for example, Scherer-Wertheimer (1964), the Pennsylvania Project (Smith 1970), Chastain and Woerdehoff (1968) and the GUME Project (Levin 1972).

21   The break with the method concept

During the sixties and seventies several developments indicate a shift in language pedagogy away from the single method concept as the main approach to language teaching. These developments deserve our attention because they indicate a valuable new direction of thought in language pedagogy: to overcome the narrowness, rigidities, and imbalances which have resulted from conceptualizing language teaching purely or mainly through the concept of method. The scope of the developments to consider is varied. Nevertheless, together they point to a wider and more differentiated interpretation of teaching.

We will examine, first, attempts to place methods into a more comprehensive framework. This was done by several widely known teachers' guides. We will, secondly, turn to a remarkable effort in the sixties to reinterpret the method concept in a more constructive way through 'method analysis' and 'methodics'. We will, then, look at two smaller studies which are important because they explored the possibility of uncovering fundamental principles underlying different methods of teaching. Finally we will consider the contribution of empirical approaches to the study of teaching.

Teachers' guides

The first approach, then, to be considered has been one which has incorporated methods into more comprehensive statements about language teaching. This has been done very effectively in several widely known and very influential teachers' guides, such as those already referred to in Chapter 2 as examples of theories of language teaching: Brooks (1960/1964), Lado (1964), Rivers (1968/1981), Grittner (1969/1977), and Chastain (1971, 1976).

The contents of these guides indicate how in the view of modern theorists-practitioners language teaching can be conceptualized. Figure 21.1 presents an analysis of seven language teaching guides by chapter content. The method issue undoubtedly plays a central part in their conception of language teaching; but it appears in a wider context. As can be seen from Figure 21.1 the guides usually offer an historical orientation to social, political, and educational factors in language teaching (3),[1] and they analyse the reasons for the place of languages in the curriculum (4). They define teaching aims and objectives (4). Since Gouin, Sweet, and Palmer it has become customary in language teaching guides to justify language teaching practice on the basis of a linguistic interpretation of the nature of language and a psychological or, more recently, a psycholinguistic view of language learning (1 and 2). Their main concern, however, is the pedagogical treatment of different aspects of language instruction (6). Since the sixties, this has been done in terms of skills—listening, speaking, reading, and writing (7), or in terms of language content—phonology, grammar, vocabulary, literature, and culture (5); at times also in terms of stages of instruction—beginners, intermediate, and advanced (8). Under these headings the guides usually contain prescriptions, examples, and justifications of techniques of instruction; they also present a view of language testing (10). Frequently, special chapters deal with materials, equipment, and technical aids such as the language laboratory or the use of visual and audiovisual media (9). The treatment is frequently rounded off with a discussion of the role of the teacher and other professional issues (11, 12).

These guides commonly reflect the writers' experience as teachers or teacher trainers, their interpretations of the contemporary literature of linguistics, applied linguistics, and psycholinguistics, and their personal views on the method question. For example, Brooks (1960, 1964), Lado (1964) and Rivers (1968) adopted the audiolingual method while Chastain (1971, 1976) made a case for combining audiolingualism with a cognitive approach. Rivers in the 1981 edition of her guide recommends an eclectic approach because teachers 'faced with the daily task of helping students to learn a new language cannot afford the luxury of complete dedication to each new method or approach that comes into vogue' (op. cit.:54). In her view, eclecticists try 'to absorb the best techniques of all the well-known language-teaching methods into their classroom procedures, using them for the purposes for which they are most appropriate' (op. cit.:55). Such an eclectic approach seems to be in keeping with the intuitions of many language teachers.

In terms of our model in Chapter 3, the guides form a valuable link between the 'theoretic' at level 1 and the 'practical' at level 3. Looked at critically as a class, the guides frequently fail to make a clear distinction between firmly attested knowledge, research evidence, widely held opinion, personal views of the writer, and hypotheses or speculations to be tested. These books, therefore, are best treated as the personal language teaching theories of experienced and sophisticated theorists and practitioners. From the point of view of this chapter, their value lies in the fact that they attempt to offer a comprehensive and coherent interpretation of all aspects that the writer of a guide regards as important in language teaching. They are the most clearly defined global interpretations of language teaching at our disposal.

Figure 21.1 Distribution of main topics in seven major language teaching guides. Sections within chapters are indicated by brackets. (The listing of these topics is not an exhaustive analysis of all major topics in the guides. For a more detailed analysis of the content the guides themselves should be consulted.)

Analysis of topics	Brooks (1964)	Chastain (1976)	Finocchiaro and Bonomo (1973)	Grittner (1977)	Hornsey (1975)	Lado (1964)	Rivers (1981)
1 *Nature of language. Linguistics.*	Theory of language. Language and talk.	First language learning.	Teaching and learning a foreign language: (What is language?)	What is language? The new linguistics.		Language and linguistics.	Theories of language and language learning.
2 *Psychology of language learning. The learner.*	Mother tongue and second language. Language learning.	Research. First language learning. Audiolingual theory and teaching. Cognitive theory and teaching. The student. Meeting student needs.	Teaching and learning a foreign language: (Language learning).	How well can Americans learn a second language? Psychology and language learning: motivation and method.		A modern theory of language learning.	Theories of language and language learning. And what else? (Learning languages early or late.)
3 *Historical, sociopolitical and educational context.*	Language teaching: (American school) (Problems facing the teacher.)	Perspectives.		The historical roots of foreign language teaching in America.		Principles of language teaching.	
4 *Reasons, aims, objectives.*	Objectives of the language course. Language learning.	Why a second language?	Developing a curriculum: (Some basic premises).	Why should Americans study a foreign language? Goals of foreign language instruction: minimum essentials.			Objectives of language teaching. And what else? (LSP.)
5 *Content (a) Phonology.*			Teaching the features of the language. (Teaching the sound system.)	The pattern drill. Learning the four skills in a cultural context: (Introducing the sounds ...)	Pronunciation.	Phonemics across languages. Intonation and rhythm.	Teaching sounds.

(continued)

	Brooks (1964)	Chastain (1976)	Finocchiaro and Bonomo (1973)	Grittner (1977)	Hornsey (1975)	Lado (1964)	Rivers (1981)
Analysis of topics							
(b) Grammar.	Pattern practice.		(Teaching the grammar system.)	The pattern drill.	Grammar. Limited aims—the single structure.	Pattern practice. From sentences to patterns.	Theories of language and language learning. Structured practice.
(c) Vocabulary.	Vocabulary.		(Teaching the vocabulary system.)			Live words and their meanings.	And what else? (Vocabulary learning.)
(d) Literature.	Language and literature.			The study of literature.		Cultural content and literature.	
(e) Culture.	Language and culture.	Teaching culture.	Providing cultural insights.	(Culture, ethnicity, and human relations.)		Language and culture.	Cultural understanding.
6 Teaching methods/ strategies/ techniques.	Methods and materials. Pattern practice.	Audiolingual theory and teaching. Cognitive theory and teaching. General guidelines for teaching a second language.	Making effective use of materials and techniques. What if ...? Some do's and don'ts.	The pattern drill. Psychology and language learning: motivation and method. Individualized instruction.	Drills and exercises.	Pattern practice. Principles of language teaching.	Language teaching methods. Structured practice.
7 Skills *(a) Listening comprehension.*		Listening comprehension.	Developing the communication skills: (Listening-speaking).	Learning the four skills.		Phonemes across languages.	Listening comprehension.
(b) Speaking.		Speaking.	(Listening-speaking.)	(Speaking ability.)		Intonation and rhythm. The consonant and vowel network.	Speaking skill: learning the fundamentals. Speaking skill: expressing personal meaning.
(c) Reading comprehension.	Reading and writing.	Reading.	(Reading.)	(Reading ability.)	Exploiting a text. Reading.	Reading.	Reading skill.

(continued)

Analysis of topics	Brooks (1964)	Chastain (1976)	Finocchiaro and Bonomo (1973)	Grittner (1977)	Hornsey (1975)	Lado (1964)	Rivers (1981)
(d) *Writing*.	Reading and writing.	Writing.	(Writing.)	(Writing ability.)	Writing.	Pattern practice. Writing.	Writing skill.
8 *Curriculum design. Teaching beginners. Teaching intermediate. Teaching advanced.*	Continuity for the learner.	Lesson planning. Classroom activities. Diversifying instruction. The first day of class (Appendix 1.)	Developing a curriculum. Planning a balanced programme.		Sixth form work. Grammar: (Grading and selecting).	Establishing a linguistic beachhead.	And what else? (Planning the language lesson) (Classroom management.)
9 *Equipment, materials, and technological aids.*	The language laboratory. Methods and materials.	The language laboratory (Appendix 4). Selecting a basic text (Appendix 2).	Making effective use of materials and techniques of instruction.	The language laboratory and other electronic media.	Drills and exercises: (French drills in the language laboratory) (Critique of an elementary lab-drill) Visuals.	Technological aids. The language laboratory. Visual aids. Teaching machines and programmed learning.	Technology and language learning centres. And what else? (The textbook.)
10 *Testing and evaluation.*	Tests and measurements.	Evaluation.	Testing and evaluation.	Evaluation of the foreign language programme.		Language testing.	Testing: principles and techniques.
11 *The teacher.*	Building a profession.	Sources of new ideas (Appendix 3). Professional organizations and journals (Appendix 5).		Evaluation of the foreign language programme.			And what else? (Keeping abreast professsionally.)
12 *Other topics.*					Using documentary data.		

In some ways, however, the guides have perpetuated the concept of teaching method as a distinct entity and as the central concept in language teaching. Most of them operate within the framework of a particular method or combination of methods. While they sometimes adopt a critical and detached position towards the method of their choice, the centrality of the method issue, as it had become expressed in the labelled methods, has not been called into question by most of the guides.

Method analysis and methodics

In Chapter 20 the different methods of language teaching were described as if they were complete and separate entities; and as we saw in the foregoing pages, some teachers argue that 'there is some good in all of them' and have adopted a point of view of eclecticism which recently gained support in the second edition of Rivers' guide (1981). But such eclecticism is still based on the notion of a conceptual distinctiveness of the different methods. However, it is the distinctiveness of the methods as complete entities that can be called into question. There is no agreement as to what the different methods precisely stand for nor how they could be satisfactorily combined. The inadequacy of methods as theories of language teaching has again and again been pointed out:

> 'Such terms as "the Direct Method", "the Simplification Method", "the Situation Method", "the Natural Method", "the Film Method", "the Conversational Method", "the Oral Method", "the Linguistic Method", can only be vague and inadequate because they limit themselves to a single aspect of a complex subject, inferring that that aspect alone is all that matters.'
> (Mackey 1965:156)[2]

Since the sixties a number of attempts have been made to develop a broad conceptual framework for language teaching and thereby to break away from the narrowness and partisanship implicit in the method notion.

The most influential of these frameworks evolved from studies by Mackey and other linguists whose ideas on this question were first formulated during the fifties in London. The concepts were developed systematically ten years later and can be found in two seminal books, already mentioned in a different context (Chapter 8), *Language Teaching Analysis* (Mackey 1965) and *The Linguistic Sciences and Language Teaching* (Halliday, McIntosh, and Strevens 1964).[3]

Starting from the profusion and confusion of language teaching methods, Mackey asks: 'What must a method include? Surely it includes what all teaching includes, whether it be the teaching of arithmetic or astronomy, of music or mathematics' (op. cit.:156). Language teaching, according to Mackey, demands a matching of materials, teacher, and learner. As we saw in Chapter 3: 39–41 (see also Figure 3.5), Mackey places these factors in a wider social and political context. However, his principal focus was the analysis of textual teaching materials, 'method analysis' in a specific and technical sense. Halliday, McIntosh, and Strevens (1964), whose ideas are akin to Mackey's, do not restrict themselves to an analysis of teaching materials. Their concepts are intended to be applicable to the entire language teaching process. Mackey's 'method analysis' and the 'methodics' of Halliday, McIntosh, and Strevens are theoretical models of the processes of bringing the second language to learners and of helping them to learn the second language.

The basic concepts of Mackey's method are *selection, gradation, presentation,* and *repetition.* Starting out from the language as it is used by native speakers, a language 'method' first demands a *selection* of content. Mackey sees the choice to be made as primarily one of selecting linguistic items according to the purpose, length, and level of a projected language course. As we saw in Chapter 8 (see Figure 8.1), Halliday, McIntosh, and Strevens correspondingly refer to *limitation* as the initial concept subsuming under it the *restriction* to a particular dialect or register, and within it the *selection* of the language items to be taught.

Selection and limitation, therefore, describe the important task of linguistic choices to be made by the curriculum developer in preparation for actual teaching. Both schemes analyse what kinds of choices are needed, and what criteria to use in making these choices. For example, Mackey emphasizes that frequency of linguistic items is not the only criterion to apply; range, availability, coverage, and learnability should also be considered. The outcome of selection is an inventory of phonological, grammatical, lexical, and semantic items for a syllabus, course, or textbook.

The language items selected must be arranged in some order. Mackey as well as Halliday, McIntosh, and Strevens attribute importance to this *gradation* or *grading* phase. Mackey distinguishes *grouping,* i.e., the fitting together of items that go together, and *sequence,* the order in which items follow each other; the gradation phase is for him a linguistic or psycholinguistic ordering of the language items. Halliday, McIntosh, and Strevens make a similar distinction between *staging* and *sequencing.* But for them it is a task of arranging the language items in line with the requirements of particular courses.

Once the language items have been assembled and ordered they must be communicated to the learner. This phase is referred to in both schemes as *presentation.* At this point the analyses diverge. Mackey distinguishes between the presentation in the textual materials, which is studied by *method analysis* in the specific sense, from the presentation by the teacher, which is taken care of by *teaching analysis.* Method analysis asks: 'What does the learner see when he opens his textbook? How much of the language does it teach him? How are the forms and meanings of the language taught?' (Mackey 1965:228). Halliday, McIntosh, and Strevens mean by presentation 'the kernel of the teaching process, the confrontation of the pupil with the items being taught' (1964:213). This includes classroom teaching, instruction by television or in language laboratories, and audiovisual courses. Halliday, McIntosh, and Strevens make the distinction between *initial presentation* or 'first-time teaching' and *repeated teaching*, i.e., the opportunities provided for practice, reinforcement, and remedial teaching. In a similar vein, Mackey distinguishes *repetition*, i.e., practice, from *presentation*. In his view it is through repetition that correct language habits are established before language can be used independently by the learner.[4]

Presentation and repetition, then, are that part of the teaching process which was the main concern of the method debate. But neither scheme takes sides on the method issues. Instead, Mackey distinguishes a number of procedures for presenting meaning: 'differential' procedures in which the first language is used, obviously derived from grammar-translation; 'ostensive', 'pictorial', and 'contextual' procedures, derived from the direct method or the audiovisual method. But what in the method debate was viewed almost as articles of faith is placed into perspective and treated by Mackey as a number of options in the teaching process. The repetition phase is analysed by Mackey in terms of audiolingual-habit training, but with equal emphasis on the four skills. The training in reading incorporates some of the activities of the reading method.

The Halliday-McIntosh-Strevens scheme is less specific on teaching procedures; it favours modern technological developments and appears to adopt a position nearer to the audiovisual than the audiolingual method. But both schemes place language teaching procedures into a wider framework.

The final phase in the scheme of Halliday, McIntosh, and Strevens is *testing*:

'(the teacher) must . . . know how far his teaching is effective: that is to say, to what extent learning is taking place among his pupils.' (1964:214)

Mackey's method analysis does not directly include a testing stage, because its main focus is the analysis of materials. The *measurement* phase which completes it provides guidelines for a quantitative analysis of the four phases — selection, gradation, presentation, and repetition. The purpose of measurement is, therefore, an evaluation of materials.

But method analysis is followed by *teaching analysis*. In the teaching analysis, the method (in Mackey's sense, i.e., the textbook) is assessed for suitability in relation to the syllabus, the learner, and the characteristics of the teachers as well as the conditions under which teaching occurs. Teaching involves pre-teaching activities, classroom activities (lessons), and testing. At a pre-teaching phase, the teacher must adapt the course or textbook to particular pupils and plan the presentation and practice. The classroom activities are conceptualized in terms similar to those in the preceding method analysis. Many of the procedures referred to are familiar from the audiolingual and audiovisual methods. The use of media is included in the teaching analysis. Finally, the teaching process is completed by the measurement of language learning, in other words, testing.

The following tabulation (21.2) summarizes the two interpretations of language teaching.

Method and teaching analysis (Mackey 1965)		Methodics (Halliday, McIntosh, and Strevens 1964)	
(Method analysis:)			
1. Selection		1. Limitation	restriction selection
2. Gradation	grouping sequencing	2. Grading	staging sequencing
3a. Presentation	3c. (Teaching analysis:)	3. Presentation	initial teaching repeated teaching
3b. Repetition	Syllabus Learner and teacher Planning Techniques	reinforcement	remedial teaching
4a. Measurement of method	4b. Measurement of learning: testing	4. Testing	

Figure 21.2   A comparison of method analysis and methodics

Comment

The two schemes represent a break with the preoccupation with single aspects of the method debate and clearly conceptualize different phases of language teaching. Without being deliberately related to curriculum theory, they include in fact concepts of curriculum development (selection and gradation) as well as concepts of curriculum implementation (presentation, repetition, and testing), and concepts of curriculum evaluation (Mackey's method measurement). These schemes are first attempts to provide the framework for comprehensive approaches to language teaching and for an interpretation of language teaching *as it is* and not only as it should be. They also clearly distinguish concepts of teaching from concepts of learning. When both schemes were published, they had not been empirically verified. In other words, it was not clear whether these frameworks offered a helpful set of concepts for planning, for the analysis of language programmes, or for research on language teaching. The two systems and the terminology introduced by both schemes were widely employed in subsequent years but neither scheme was tested in a very systematic way, and the potential of these schemes as theories of language teaching has not been appreciated as fully as it might have been. Nor have any attempts been made to relate either scheme to the curriculum studies in educational theory that were in the process of development around the same time.[5]

Conceptual analyses of methods

Bosco and Di Pietro

A few other attempts have been made to overcome the divisiveness of the methods by analysing methods systematically. One of these was made by Bosco and Di Pietro (1970). Setting out from the analogy of distinctive-feature analysis in phonology which characterizes speech sounds by the absence or presence of a limited number of features, Bosco and Di Pietro identified among the most common instructional 'strategies' eleven distinctive features, divided into eight psychological and three linguistic ones.

The psychological features are:

1 *functional* versus *non-functional*: is the goal communication or understanding of linguistic structure?
2 *central* versus *non-central*: is the method psychologically directed to 'central' cognitive processes or to 'peripheral' sensorimotor conditioning?
3 *affective* versus *non-affective*: does the method stress the affective domain or not?
4 *nomothetic* versus *non-nomothetic*: are language rules explicitly brought into focus or not?
5 *idiographic* versus *non-idiographic*: does the method encourage the learner to develop his unique style of personal expression?
6 *molar* versus *non-molar* (or *molecular*): does the method encourage a synthesis or integrated view of the language and its expression, or is the language presented predominantly as an inventory of separate 'molecules'?
7 *cyclic* versus *non-cyclic*: does the method periodically return to points of learning or does it proceed from point to point in a linear fashion?

8 *divergent* versus *non-divergent*: does the method encourage the acquisition of discrete specific skills, for example, phonetic discrimination, listening comprehension, oral expression, etc. or does it treat the language skills in an undifferentiated manner?

The three linguistic features are:

1 *general* versus *non-general*: does the method analyse the second language as an example of universal features, or does it treat each language as unique, particular, or specific?
2 *systematic* versus *non-systematic*: does the method suggest an ordered system of linguistic analysis, or does it deal with linguistic features without any order?
3 *unified* versus *non-unified*: does the method attempt to build up a total structure of the language, or does it deal with each rule in isolation?

With the help of this inventory of eleven features, Bosco and Di Pietro defined different methods by the features they have in common and features that are specific. Thus, the grammar-translation (GT), direct (DM), and audiolingual methods (AL) are interpreted by Bosco and Di Pietro as displaying the following features (Figure 21.3):

As can be seen from this tabulation, the grammar-translation method is characterized by the presence of these features: central (cognitive), nomothetic (emphasis on rules), and general (based on linguistic

| | | Strategies | |
Psychological features	GT	DM	AL
1. Functional	–	+	+
2. Central	+	–	–
3. Affective	–	+	–
4. Nomothetic	+	–	+
5. Idiographic	–	–	–
6. Molar	–	+	–
7. Cyclic	–	–	–
8. Divergent	–	–	+
Linguistic features			
1. General	+	–	–
2. Systematic	–	–	+
3. Unified	–	–	–

Key: GT Grammar-translation
DM Direct Method
AL Audiolingual
\+ indicates the presence of the feature
\– indicates its absence

Figure 21.3   Bosco and Di Pietro's feature analysis of language teaching methods

universals). The direct method is interpreted as functional, affective, and molar, and the audiolingual method as functional, nomothetic, divergent, and systematic. None of the methods are explicitly idiographic (i.e., encouraging personal expression), or explicitly cyclic. Nor do any of them aim at building up the language into a unified structure.

This scheme constitutes a distinct step forward in the interpretation of language teaching, because it isolates a limited number of criteria with which to describe and analyse any language teaching method. In this way it identifies common features and differences among the methods. At the same time, the inventory gives rise to questions and criticisms. Some of the features overlap. For example, the psychological feature 6 (molar versus non-molar) overlaps with the linguistic feature 2 (systematic versus non-systematic) and 3 (unified versus non-unified). Second, the features are presented as if they were all equal. In effect the scope and direction of the analysis of different pairs of features are very disparate. For example, some pairs refer to teaching techniques, for example, features 2, 4, 6, or 8, while others refer to goals, for example, features 1, 3, or 5, and others again to course design, for example, feature 7. Further, it is not clear on what grounds the features could be attributed to a method except by a process of intuitive interpretation. For example, why would the direct method, but not the audiolingual method, be described as affective? Lastly, once more the assumption is made that methods constitute unambiguous distinct entities which can thus be subjected to a feature analysis.

What is of great value in this scheme is (a) that it clarifies some of the options that are open to the language teaching theorist, and (b) that it establishes common elements transcending different methods. Bosco and Di Pietro conclude that an optimal instructional strategy can be based on all or any of the features in the grid. 'An ideal strategy expressed in these terms by no means imposes upon teachers a restricted set of practices. The variations in instructional style are endless as are the ways in which each of these features may be interpreted in textual materials' (1970:52). Thus, this scheme represents a major attempt to overcome the separateness and restrictiveness of methods and to discover essential features underlying all language pedagogy.

Krashen and Seliger

Another feature analysis of teaching methods was made by Krashen and Seliger (1975). It identified eight features some of which overlap with Bosco and Di Pietro's list:

1 +*Discrete point.*[6] Taken from language testing terminology, this feature refers to the treatment of the grammar rules and lexical items. Are features of the language treated as isolated items or is the

language treated globally? The global element was emphasized in the audiovisual method, whereas the early examples of grammar-translation and audiolingual programmes consider each item very much on its own. This feature is similar to Bosco and Di Pietro's distinction between 'molar' and 'molecular', 'divergent' and 'non-divergent', 'unified' and 'non-unified'.

2 +*Deductive* refers to the presentation of rules before practice versus the inference of rules from practice (*inductive*). The +*Deductive* is often attributed to the grammar-translation while the direct method and audiolingualism are said to be inductive. This feature is not specifically identified by Bosco and Di Pietro; the nearest feature in their list is the pair (4), nomothetic versus non-nomothetic.

3 +*Explicit.* While a deductive approach is necessarily explicit, the inductive approach may either end up with an explicit formulation of a rule or it may be designed so as to leave the rule implicit. The grammar-translation and cognitive methods are +*Explicit,* while the direct and audiolingual methods largely, but not entirely, rely on an implicit approach (−*Explicit).* This feature, then, refers to the explicit/implicit option described in Chapter 18 or to the nomothetic/non-nomothetic set of Bosco and Di Pietro.

4 *Sequence* refers to the arrangement of the language content. Are the language items based on contrastive principles, on increasing complexity, on utility, on frequency, or on a 'natural' order of acquisition? To use Mackey's term, on what principle of *gradation* is the language curriculum based? In the older methods, grammar-translation and direct, gradation was treated as a matter of pedagogical common sense and was not a question at issue. The grading of vocabulary first appeared as an important aspect of the reading method and then became central to the audiovisual courses. CREDIF's analyses and programmes constitute pioneer efforts in systematic gradation. Audiolingual programmes express a strong awareness of the importance of carefully designed progressions. Audiolingualists criticized the direct method for its casual handling of gradation. Gradation or grading—it will be remembered—was also an essential feature of Mackey's Method Analysis and of Halliday, McIntosh, and Strevens' Methodics. In the seventies some language training programmes reacted against the principle of strict gradation, mainly because it was theoretically difficult, on linguistic grounds, to justify any sequential arrangement which is not to a certain extent arbitrary. While Bosco and Di Pietro do not treat sequence as such, psychological feature 7 (cyclic versus non-cyclic) and their linguistic feature 2 (systematic versus non-systematic) refer to related issues of curriculum design.

5 *Performance channel* refers to the separation and combination of listening, speaking, reading, and writing, specific to a method. A

method may demand 'single channel' or a 'multiple channel' approach. For example, the audiolingual and audiovisual methods gave priority to listening and speaking. Mackey as well as Halliday, McIntosh, and Strevens have borne this in mind in the concept of staging which particularly refers to distinct stages of audiolingual and graphic emphases in teaching a second language. This feature coincides with Bosco and Di Pietro's feature 8: divergent versus non-divergent, i.e., the separation or non-separation of language skills.

6 *Exercise type: 'focus on'* versus *'focus away'* refers to a feature in the design of language drills. A drill may be designed in such a way as to focus the learner's attention on the point to be practised, as is commonly done in grammar-translation or cognitive practice: 'focus on'. Alternatively, exercises may be designed so as to lead the learner's attention away from the point to be practised. According to Lado (1964), for example, it is an essential characteristic of audiolingual pattern practice to be designed in such a way as 'to force the student to use the problem pattern while thinking of something else, e.g., the message' (op. cit.:106). He defines pattern practice as 'rapid oral drill on problem patterns with attention on something other than the problem itself' (op. cit.:105). Bosco and Di Pietro's feature 2 (central versus non-central) is related to this feature.

7 *Extent of control* is the degree to which the programme is designed so as to avoid the possibility of learner errors. Audiolingualism, following Skinnerian principles of programmed instruction, favoured an organization of language courses which ideally made it impossible to make many errors. Subsequent studies on error analysis and interlanguage led to a more positive outlook on the role of errors in language learning on the assumption that, without the chance of errors, the learner cannot develop his own internalized standards of correctness. Cognitivists who favour this point of view, therefore, prefer language practice which is less strictly controlled by the teacher or the programme and offers more freedom for creative use of the language by the learner, inviting of course correspondingly an increased opportunity for errors. This aspect is not covered in Bosco and Di Pietro's scheme.

8 The final feature, identified by Krashen and Seliger, *feedback*, relates to the degree to which the teacher corrects errors: 'errors corrected versus errors ignored' (Krashen and Seliger 1975:180). This option has not appeared as a distinguishing feature of different methods: 'in all forms of formal instruction, the student is made aware, at least some of the time, when he or she has made an error' (loc. cit.). But teachers no doubt differ in the regularity, speed, or detail of error correction. Halliday, McIntosh, and Strevens' concept of 'remedial teaching' refers to the same element in the teaching process. It is only

in recent communicative approaches to language teaching that the withholding of explanation and feedback as a phase in the process of instruction was deliberately cultivated in order to give learners a chance for developing their own 'communication strategy'.

The analysis of features of language teaching by Krashen and Seliger was largely prompted by points at issue during the early seventies on audiolingual and cognitive theories, and is therefore less comprehensive than that of Bosco and Di Pietro. Neither scheme in its entirety is systematic enough to offer a coherent and comprehensive statement of language teaching. However, both analyses throw into relief common and divergent aspects in language teaching theories and practices and contribute useful analytical categories to a conceptual clarification of language teaching.

Empirical approaches to the study of teaching

While the studies we have considered so far have endeavoured, each in their own way, to create as comprehensive and systematic a framework as possible for the analysis of teaching, other attempts have simultaneously been made to find out more about teaching through empirical investigations.

Experimental studies
An important empirical approach to resolving the problems and controversies of language teaching methods has been to undertake experimental comparisons. As we saw previously (Chapter 4:54 ff.), such studies go back over many years. From the point of view we are discussing in the present chapter these studies constitute a major advance in the analysis of teaching, although they have by no means gone undisputed. Instead of simply arguing about the merits and demerits of different methods of teaching, they have attempted to put the methods to an empirical test, and thus a welcome element of objective enquiry has been introduced in an area in which speculation and opinion had been dominant (see Chapter 4:63).

In the sixties a few groups of well-known studies, to which reference has already been made on several occasions, attempted to resolve the question of whether the audiolingual approach is more effective than the grammar-translation (or cognitive) approach.[7] This type of investigation demonstrated clearly the wish to put changes in teaching method to the empirical test in real-life situations. The Scherer-Wertheimer experiment (1964) was carried out in the context of teaching German at the University of Colorado and involved the co-operation of a practitioner (Scherer) with a psychologist (Wertheimer). The Pennsylvania Project

(Smith 1970) was a large-scale research project directly involving the participation of many classes and teachers in the high schools throughout the State of Pennsylvania. The studies by Chastain and colleagues were also carried out in a college and high-school setting. The Swedish GUME Project took place in the setting of language classes in high schools and in adult education. Some studies were made to gauge the effectiveness of the language laboratory (for example, Keating 1963; Smith 1970; Green 1975). A further example of empirical research in school settings is provided by the Canadian studies on 'bilingual education' or 'immersion' carried out in primary and secondary schools in Montreal, Ottawa, Toronto and some other centres. These studies compared immersion with traditional forms of second language learning.[8]

Important and valuable as these investigations have been, in many of them a serious weakness has appeared precisely in the area with which this chapter is concerned: the unsatisfactory nature of the method concept. Most of the studies have operated with teaching method as the main category of comparison. Neither from a theoretical nor a practical point of view are such contrasting pairs of concepts as audiolingual versus grammar-translation, language laboratory versus non-laboratory, immersion versus non-immersion, as clearly distinct from each other as the labels suggest. In experimental research it is not sufficient to accept these labels at their face value. For an investigation on teaching methods to be convincing, it is crucial that the theoretical distinctions between the methods are clearly defined, and can be empirically backed by classroom observation or by some other technique of documenting the instructional variables. It is in this respect that several investigations of the last two decades have left much to be desired.

On the positive side, what has experimental research contributed to the interpretation of language teaching? On the whole it has yielded a much more realistic understanding of language teaching and learning. The research has in fact demonstrated that the options are not as clearcut as the terminological divisions suggested. It has also provided a sobering check on some of the claims, often extravagant ones, that innovators and advocators of different methods have been prone to make. Thanks to studies of this kind language teachers and administrators today, at least in some countries, are more inclined than previously to take into account the findings of empirical research before introducing new methods of language teaching.

Research on teaching through classroom observation
In the last few years, a few research studies have begun to focus more closely on the conditions of teaching and treatment factors so as to overcome the weaknesses of the broad and ill-defined 'method' categories. We can only briefly illustrate here what directions this research is taking.

It is easy to say that we must know 'what goes on in the classroom' in order to understand better what language teaching is really like. A great many events take place in any classroom. The observer cannot, nor does he want to, observe them all. He pays attention only to those events that are significant from the point of view that he has decided to adopt. The choice of certain aspects as significant and the omission of others implies a conceptual framework. In educational research, classroom observation has an established tradition. Literally hundreds of observation systems have been developed.[9] But each of the different schemes has been designed for its own purposes and with its own assumptions about what events in the classroom to pay attention to. Few of these have been specifically prepared for language classrooms. Most of those that have been used for observations on language teaching have been derived from the Flanders System of Interaction Analysis. This observation scheme, developed by Flanders in the fifties (Flanders 1970), is an offshoot of studies which tried to assess the social climate of classrooms and other educational groups. The underlying philosophy of the Flanders system was the belief that a 'democratic' classroom management is preferable to an 'authoritarian' one, and observations were directed to this belief.[10] Interaction analysis had originally been applied to classes in which general school subjects, for example, social studies or science, were taught. A question which fails to have been properly considered is to what extent the categories of observations in the Flanders system respond to the critical issues of second language teaching. Several adaptations of Flanders to second language teaching have been developed. The investigators have of course realized that modifications and additions were needed if justice was to be done to the events of language classes; but the more basic question whether the strategies of interaction which a Flanders system categorizes are the most significant in language teaching and learning has hardly been asked, let alone answered.

One of the best known of these adaptations, FLINT, the Foreign Language Interaction Analysis System, includes all the categories of the Flanders system and adds a number of other items, particularly whether the first language or the second language is used in class.[11] Moskowitz, the originator of FLINT, has used this system in teacher education. She has found that it provides useful feedback to student teachers and that it can sensitize them to classroom interactions, to teacher talk, and student talk respectively (Moskowitz 1967, 1968, 1970, 1971, 1976).[12]

A comprehensive scheme for foreign language classes was developed by Fanselow (1977) called FOCUS: 'Foci for Observing Communication Used in Settings'. It is Fanselow's intention to describe and conceptualize what 'teachers actually do'. He recognizes the need for a scheme which can describe and analyse the events of the language class without using ill-defined descriptors such as *'drill, reinforcement, mechanical, communicate, pace, audiolingual . . .* ' (1977:19). Fanselow's scheme distinguishes five characteristics of communication in the language class: (1) *source*: who communicates? (2) for what pedagogical *purpose*? (3) in what *medium*? (4) *how* is that medium *used*? and (5) what *content* is communicated? For each of these questions Fanselow offers certain subcategories under which to classify the answers to the question. Fanselow's claim is that this scheme can overcome the vagueness and confusion of talk about the language class by applying systematically a set of technically defined categories. Another approach has been to apply to language classes a scheme of linguistic analysis, developed in Britain by Sinclair and Coulthard (1975) which analyses a lesson in terms of discourse functions and moves.[13] Whether schemes like this actually identify and distinguish different ways of language teaching with validity and reliability, is still an open question. But undoubtedly in order to understand language teaching better categories of analysis and empirical verification are needed.

What these and other investigators, for example, Allwright (1975), Chaudron (1977) and Naiman *et al.* (1978), have been looking for but have not yet discovered are comprehensive and theoretically sound models for investigating language instruction which would be helpful in the description and analysis of all possible kinds of second language teaching. As Naiman *et al.* (1978) noted: '. . . the absence of an empirical scheme analysing language teaching was felt to be a disadvantage and led to ad hoc inquiries on relevant aspects of teaching. Research should therefore be conducted into the identification and classification of teaching techniques and into the effectiveness of alternative techniques for different kinds of students' (op. cit.:101).

The observation schemes that have so far been developed appear to lack criteria by which to capture the essential and specific characteristics of second language teaching and learning. These could perhaps be discovered if the analysis of second language teaching were more deliberately related to the process of second language learning and to the kinds of issues characterized in our discussion of second language learning (Chapter 18). What these studies on language teaching have however again made clear is that the methods illustrated in Chapter 20 are inadequate for conceptualizing and interpreting language teaching.

Conclusion

The net effect of the different approaches to teaching which we have sketched in this chapter has been that language teaching is now no longer conceptualized in terms of a single undifferentiated methodological prescription. Language teaching theorists at the present time shun the simple formula. The various efforts described in this chapter[14] suggest a more differentiated and more empirically sustained view of language teaching which can be consistently and comprehensively applied to the great variety of situations in which second language teaching occurs.

Notes

1 The numbers in brackets refer to the analysis of topics in Figure 21.1.
2 Hawkins (1981: Appendix D) illustrates the same point by reproducing Jespersen's and Mackey's list of methods and adding his own which makes up an inventory of some forty-odd labelled methods. Hawkins concludes: 'Our brief review of the history of language teaching made it clear that we should resist the temptation to grasp at any more panaceas' (op. cit.:228).
3 According to Mackey (1965a:150) the 'development of method analysis goes back to the 1940s when a series of proposals were made in London for a descriptive rather than prescriptive approach to language teaching. These later came out as a group of articles in the 1950s'. These articles dealt with the concept of method (Mackey 1950), selection (Mackey 1953), grading (Mackey 1954) and presentation (Mackey 1955). In the same year in which Mackey's book appeared (1965) he also presented his complete scheme in a compact version at the Georgetown Round Table (Mackey 1965a).
4 Mackey's theory, therefore, adopts in this respect the principles of audiolingualism.
5 Several of Mackey's students and collaborators did, however, pursue certain directions suggested by Mackey in his *Language Teaching Analysis,* for example, studies on selection (Laforge 1972), on vocabulary (for example, Savard 1970; Mackey, Savard, and Ardouin 1971).
6 The plus (+) sign indicates presence and the minus (−) sign absence of a feature.
7 See Chapter 6 for references to some investigations in their historical sequence and Chapter 20:463 where they are mentioned in the context of the development of audiolingualism. In Chapter 4 the question of empirical research has been discussed in relation to language teaching theory and practice in general.
8 For references on immersion research see Chapter 4, Note 13. The IEA studies (Carroll 1975; Lewis and Massad 1975), referred to in Chapter 19:432–3, are further illustrations of empirical approaches to questions of language pedagogy.
9 For a brief history of the observation schemes and their relevance to language teaching, see Naiman *et al.* (1978). For a more recent comprehensive review of classroom research in language teaching see Long (1980).

10 The Flanders system has its roots in studies on social climates by Lewin, Lippitt, and White (1939) and by Anderson (1939). Both papers are reproduced in Amidon and Hough (1967), referred to in Chapter 19, Note 10.

11 Besides Moskowitz' FLINT other second language classroom observation schemes include one by Jarvis (1968) and another by Wragg (1970).

12 In an Alberta study on teaching French by an audiovisual programme, an investigator (McEwen 1976), developed a classroom observation scheme, the Second Language Category System. McEwen recognized that the events of the language class, even in very simple structured programmes, are not uni-dimensional. McEwen's scheme allowed for three dimensions and demanded a threefold analysis in terms of content, thought processes, and verbal functions. In applying this system McEwen recorded as many as twenty-seven events per minute. Other investigators have tried to focus on particular aspects in the language class. For example, Allwright (1975) and Chaudron (1977) investigating error correction have noted the frequent misunderstandings between teacher and students that occur when teachers correct errors.

13 Inspired by Fanselow's and Sinclair and Coulthard's schemes of classroom observation and analysis an (unpublished) observational study, undertaken in the OISE Modern Language Centre, analysed the differences between learning French in a conventional second language class and an immersion class. For a short excerpt from this unpublished report see Stern and Cummins (1981:227). See also Sinclair and Brazil (1982).

14 There are of course other developments in the same direction which we have not considered in this chapter. Thus, it might be pointed out that the new approaches to the language curriculum which have been such a dominant feature of the seventies (Chapter 6:109–10) were implicitly a critique of the method concept. They contributed to the shift away from the preoccupation with teaching method by focusing on the *content* and the *objectives* of teaching.

22 An educational interpretation of language teaching

It is clear from the discussion of methods, teachers' guides, experimental studies, and various conceptual schemes we have considered in the two foregoing chapters that, among the basic concepts we have analysed in this book, the concept of teaching itself is as yet the least clearly formulated. In our search we did not find a particular model or interpretation that one could recommend as a fully satisfactory expression to be confidently adopted for decision making or in research.

The 'methods' have successively pointed to important features of language teaching, but in some respects they were too broad and ill-defined and in others not comprehensive enough. The teachers' guides have provided comprehensive overviews and analyses of teaching in pedagogical terms, but they have been developed from a personal perspective with specific situations in mind, such as language teaching in American high schools, and they have in the main been addressed to a specific class of readers, i.e., student teachers, and they have not sufficiently distinguished between personal viewpoints, controversial issues, and established knowledge. The experimental investigations of language teaching methods have introduced an element of empirical enquiry which had hitherto been lacking, and classroom observation studies have further contributed to this trend, but they have so far tended to focus on isolated classroom events such as error correction. Method analysis and methodics and the feature analyses developed by Bosco and Di Pietro (1970/71) and by Krashen and Seliger (1975), represent attempts to develop conceptual frameworks or inventories for a dispassionate study of language teaching. All of these efforts jointly can be considered as steps towards clarification of the concept of teaching.

Drawing to some extent on all these approaches, we attempt in this chapter to develop an alternative conception which introduces the educational component that had largely been lacking in the interpretations we have examined in Chapters 20 and 21. If we try to express the concept of teaching more deliberately in terms of educational theory and research, it is of course not suggested that language teaching theory should slavishly follow educational theory. The specific characteristics of language teaching, namely that it is concerned with language and language learning, imposes its own specifications. Nevertheless, language teaching as an educational activity should at least take into consideration what educational theory has to offer and what language teaching has in common with other educational activities.

Accordingly, we will apply to the analysis of teaching concepts of curriculum which we have referred to in Chapter 19:435–41. These concepts can conveniently be placed into a model for the general study of teaching which has been developed by two educational researchers, Dunkin and Biddle (1974).

The advantage of employing this model in conjunction with concepts of curriculum is that it can be applied individually for the kind of self-examination that can lead to personal theory development. At the same time, as Dunkin and Biddle have shown, the scheme offers a useful map for research on teaching.

In this chapter we confine ourselves to an outline of this model and indicate the main categories of teaching so as to complete our discussion of the chief concepts at the interlevel in Figure 3.7 (see Chapter 3). A more detailed study of teaching which would take us to the practice level in the diagram 3.7 is beyond the scope of this book and is the subject of a further study in preparation.

A model of teaching

The model developed by Dunkin and Biddle (1974:38) for the study of classroom teaching distinguishes four main categories of variables: *presage, context, process* and *product*.[1] *Presage* variables are the characteristics which teachers as individuals or as a group bring to teaching, their own formative experiences, their training, and their personal qualities. The *context* consists of the conditions within which the teacher must operate, the community, the school, its environment, and the pupils themselves. The central focus of the scheme is the *classroom*: what teachers do and what pupils do in the classroom, teacher classroom behaviour and pupil classroom behaviour collectively described as *process variables*. Lastly, the *product variables* refer to the outcome of the teaching-learning process: 'those changes that come about in pupils as a result of their involvement in classroom activities with teachers and other pupils' (Dunkin and Biddle 1974:46). Here a distinction is made between immediate effects of teaching, which can often be measured by tests, and the less accessible long-term effects. In short, this scheme summarizes various relationships that can be and have been investigated in research on teaching: context-process, pre-sage-process, process-process (i.e., the relationship among processes in the classroom), and process-product relationships. The scheme provides a well defined framework to view particular investigations in a context of theory and research. In their book *The Study of Teaching* Dunkin and

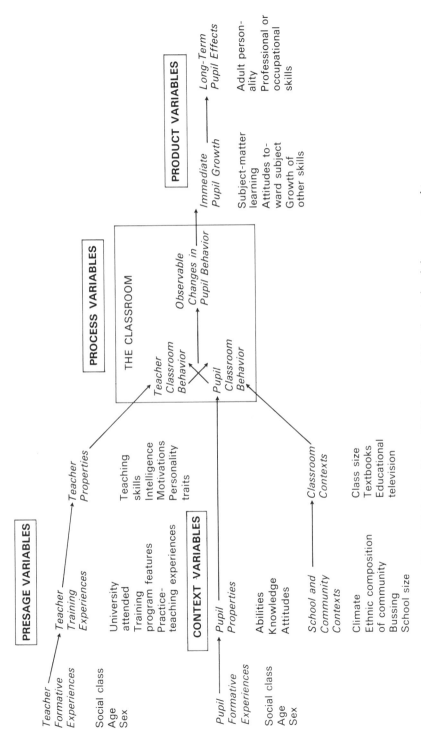

Figure 22.1   Dunkin and Biddle's model for the study of classroom teaching

Biddle critically examine the whole field of research of classroom teaching in terms of these few essential relationships. They also recognize that underlying the different studies on classroom teaching are conceptualizations and philosophical positions ('commitments') which have to be critically examined.

As can easily be seen, the model in Figure 22.1 is very similar to the one that we have applied to the interpretation of language learning in Figure 16.1. If teacher characteristics are incorporated in the learning model and due consideration is given to educational treatment, the learning model accords well with the interpretation of teaching suggested by Dunkin and Biddle (1974) so that we have a model that can be used to study simultaneously or in parallel language *teaching* as well as *learning*.

The model we propose (Figure 22.2) identifies two principal actors in the scheme, *the language teacher* and *the language learner*. Learner characteristics have already been considered (Chapter 17). The teacher, like the learner, brings to language teaching certain characteristics which may have bearing on educational treatment: age, sex, previous education, and personal qualities. Above all, the language teacher brings to it a language background and experience, professional training as a linguist and teacher, previous language teaching experience, and more or less formulated theoretical presuppositions about language, language learning and teaching.

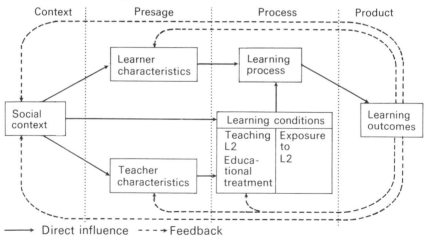

*Figure 22.2   A teaching-learning model
(combining features of Fig. 22.1 and Fig. 16.1)*

The *social context* (see Chapter 13) which influences the learner and which has bearing on the degree of supportiveness supplied by the language environment affects the teacher as much as the learner and indirectly influences the educational treatment.

Teaching in curriculum terms

Different from the presentation in the Dunkin and Biddle diagram, we have separated what the teacher does, i.e., educational treatment, from what the learner does, the learning process. Again, different from Dunkin and Biddle, teaching is not expressed simply as 'teacher classroom behaviour'. In our conception 'educational treatment' includes observable classroom activities, and indeed it is necessary to pay close attention to such observable behaviour rather than talking about teaching in generalities. The language classroom studies, mentioned in Chapter 21, contribute an important component to our understanding of language teaching. But classroom episodes in isolation are like snippets of conversation out of context. The intention of an episode or even a lesson becomes clear only if it is placed into a sequence or context. Outward behaviour does not mean much to us if we do not include in our observations what teachers say and do about their plans and their intentions and if they do not show us their work schemes, curricula, syllabuses, or courses of study.

The whole point of educational treatment is that it is provided as a 'course' or 'curriculum', i.e., a given subject matter is taught over time which, in our case a language, unfolds a certain structure or 'syllabus', has coherence and, stage by stage, aims to develop proficiency and other learning outcomes. Classroom teaching episodes are therefore viewed in the context of a curriculum and of activities which reach beyond the particular classroom setting. The teacher as curriculum developer plans the activities, prepares or selects materials, adapts materials to particular uses, divides the total set of materials and the classroom activities into steps and stages. As a classroom practitioner he may organize both in-class and out-of-class events. Beyond the classroom itself, there may be private reading, homework assignments, projects, papers and other practice activities related to classroom language learning. In an 'open school' the classroom may not be the principal location for learning. Teachers also arrange student exchanges, invite target language visitors, and plan student travel and other contact experiences with speakers of the second language in its natural environment. In short, teaching, interpreted in terms of curriculum, is represented as planned action with certain *ends*[2] in view and *means* to reach them. As we pointed out in Chapter 19:421, a means-ends view of teaching is unavoidable in language pedagogy.

Ends

Both *objectives* and *content* should be identified and distinguished in the analysis of teaching. As we have already seen the 'method' debate has always implied tacit divergencies in objectives among the different methods. But the lack of awareness of a shift in objectives has contributed to the confusions that have surrounded this debate.[3] The concept of 'selection' or 'limitation', introduced as a principle by method analysis and methodics, implied a deliberate choice of language content to meet certain ends and to reach a level of language skill in a certain time. The feature analysis of Bosco and Di Pietro also points to differences in goals although this was not specifically stated in their scheme.[4] The emphasis on a language needs analysis that was advocated in the late seventies (for example, Richterich and Chancerel 1978/1980 and Munby 1978) as well as the concept of language for special purposes (Strevens 1977a) are efforts in the same direction: they aim to specify the objectives and the content of the language curriculum.

	BEHAVIOURS																
	Cognitive and psychomotor skills										*Affective domain*						
	Knowledge and perception				*Manipu-lation*		*Understanding and production*				*Participation*						
	Knowledge of elements	*Ability to differentiate and discriminate among elements*	*Knowledge of rules and patterns*	*Ability to differentiate and dis-criminate among rules and patterns*	*Ability to reproduce elements and patterns*	*Ability to manipulate elements and patterns*	*Ability to grasp explicit (surface) meaning of utterances or patterns G.1 paraphrase G.2 English equivalents*	*Ability to produce utterances or patterns conveying the desired explicit meaning*	*Ability to analyse utterances or patterns in terms of implicit (deep) meaning*	*Ability to analyse utterances or patterns conveying the desired implicit meaning*	*Greater awareness of the phenomenon*	*Increased tolerance of differences*	*Demonstrated interest in the phenomenon*	*Satisfaction derived from achievement*	*Continuing desire to improve competence and increase understanding*	*Active promotion of cross-cultural understanding*	
CONTENT	*A*	*B*	*C*	*D*	*E*	*F*	*G*	*H*	*I*	*J*	*K*	*L*	*M*	*N*	*O*	*P*	
1.0 Spoken language 1.1 Vocabulary 1.2 Grammar 1.3 Phonology																empty	*Language*
2.0 Written language 2.1 Vocabulary 2.2 Grammar 2.3 Spelling																empty	*Language*
3.0 Kinesics (or body language)									improbable	improbable						empty	*Language*
4.0 Way-of-life culture 4.1 Society 4.2 Culture									improbable	improbable							*Culture*
5.0 Civilization		empty			empty	empty	improbable	empty	improbable	empty						empty	*Culture*
6.0 Arts		improbable		improbable	empty	empty	improbable	empty	improbable	empty						empty	*Culture*
7.0 Literature		empty		empty	empty	empty		empty		empty						empty	*Literature*
8.0 Communication 8.1 Face-to-face 8.2 Telephone 8.3 Message	empty	empty	empty	empty	empty	empty					empty	empty	empty	empty	empty	empty	*Communi-cation*

■ empty cells □ improbable cells

Figure 22.3 An example of Valette's tables of specifications for behaviour and content in second language teaching

From this point of view the schemes developed by Valette around 1970 to apply to language teaching the Bloom taxonomies of educational objectives (see Chapter 19:438) are outstanding pioneering efforts in the development of an educational approach to the analysis of language teaching. Through cross-tabulations which listed horizontally Bloom-type behaviour categories and vertically content categories, Valette (1971; see Figure 22.3) gave the expressions of content and objectives a concise and precise form, and was able to show in the paper that went with the table of specifications (Valette 1971) how test items could explore in concrete ways the different cells in this scheme. The original Bloom taxonomies were not prepared with language teaching in mind, and Valette herself has made several modifications and adaptations.[5]

The present writer and his associates have for some time used similar cross-tabulations of objectives and content areas, employing wider categories than appear in Valette's scheme. One tabulation of this kind which was developed in 1980–81 recognizes four categories of behavioural objectives and four content categories (see Figure 22.4)

The four categories of objectives are, once again, inspired by the Bloom taxonomy but deviate from it in that no attempt is made to apply Bloom's concepts as directly as Valette's scheme in Figure 22.3 does. It recognizes *proficiency* in the second language as a first and major objective (see also Chapter 16, especially Figure 16.3). The second one is *knowledge* which comprises an explicit knowledge about the second

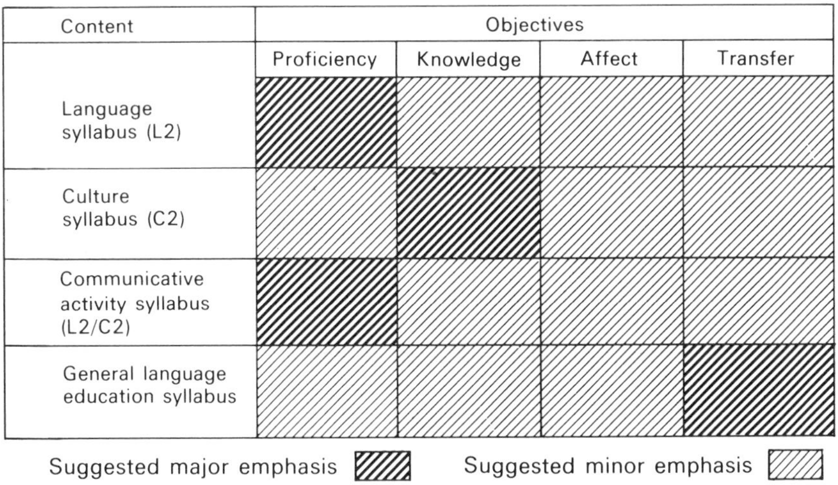

Content	Objectives			
	Proficiency	Knowledge	Affect	Transfer
Language syllabus (L2)				
Culture syllabus (C2)				
Communicative activity syllabus (L2/C2)				
General language education syllabus				

Suggested major emphasis ▨   Suggested minor emphasis ▨

Figure 22.4   A curriculum model for language teaching adapted from Stern (1980) and Ullmann (1982)

language (L2) and knowledge about the corresponding culture (C2). The third objective expresses the belief that the cultivation of *affective objectives* forms an integral part of the scheme. This objective includes values and attitudes related to the language and culture. A final behavioural category, which is described as *transfer*, acknowledges as an objective the possibility of learning a particular language with the purpose of generalizing beyond the language in question. This objective repeats the three L2-specific objectives on a more general plane and specifies the aim to learn a second language in such a way as to learn about language learning in general, in terms of (a) proficiency, i.e., skill in language learning , (b) conceptual knowledge, as well as (c) more generalized values and attitudes.

The content categories are broadly conceived as language, culture, communication, and general language education. *Language* implies the particular L2 or varieties of the L2, *culture*, the target culture (C2) or several target cultures (C2s) (for example, the culture of France and/or French-speaking Africa and/or French-speaking Canada; the culture of Britain and/or English-speaking North America or Australia, etc.). *Communication* refers to activities in the language or suggests content other than the language itself which engages the learner as a participant in communication with speakers of the second language either directly or vicariously. Finally, *general language education* is that content beyond the particular second language and target culture which will enable the learner to go 'beyond the language given'.[6] Without elaborating these broad categories any further, it is clear that the concepts of language, culture, society, and the learner, developed in the previous parts of this book, enter into the construction of a curriculum that applies these categories.[7]

The cross-tabulation makes clear that content categories and objectives interact so that certain cells represent the principal matching of content and objectives, whereas other cells represent a more subsidiary content and purpose. The table .merely provides a map or ordered presentation of the categories. The actual circumstances of teaching require the interpretation of these categories in order to decide which objectives and content categories to give priority to. Factors which would determine these decisions are the overall purpose of the language instruction, and the age or maturity and previous experience in schooling and language learning on the part of the students. Thus, language learning in secondary education or at the university level is likely to be relatively evenly spread over the different categories. On the other hand, a second language in early childhood education or language teaching in professional education for adults is likely to emphasize communication and proficiency rather than general language education and transfer.

The identification of objectives and content as an important component in interpreting language teaching (see Chapter 6:109 and Chapter

21, Note 14) has become, since the seventies, a major focus in language teaching theory and practice. It cannot be its only focus but this emphasis has counterbalanced the overconcern with teaching interpreted as teaching *method* that had been so prevalent in the sixties.

Means

In curriculum theory, as we saw in Chapter 19:438, a second aspect is the notion of instruction, i.e., teaching in the specific sense: what the teacher does to induce learning, and here, as was pointed out at the beginning of the book (Chapter 1:20) we adopt a wide definition: language teaching comprises all and any procedures which are intended to bring about language learning.

Making a conceptual distinction between ends (content and objectives) and means (instruction) is particularly important in language teaching because the confusion between them has been another constant source of trouble in the debate on teaching methods.[8] The teacher sets up conditions for learning such as grouping or timing; he employs materials and other equipment, and the procedures he selects lead to specific classroom activities.

Instruction, in the specific sense of curriculum theory, brings us to the areas of most intense controversy in the method debate. It is appropriate therefore to follow in the direction initiated by methodics, method analysis, and the feature analyses, and abandon the notion of the fixed 'method', i.e., an unalterable combination of techniques, the 'package deal', supposedly clearly distinguishable from other methods which a teacher or researcher has to operate with in its entirety. Instead, it is analytically more effective, and pedagogically more flexible to operate with the broader concept of *teaching strategy* under which can be subsumed a large number of specified *teaching techniques*. These two concepts correspond to 'learning strategy' and 'learning technique' introduced in our discussion on language learning (see Chapter 18:405; 411).[9] Moreover, curriculum theory has also employed the strategy concept. As in the case of the learning strategies, it is not possible to propose a definitive and exhaustive list of teaching strategies, but we can begin by identifying those which can be derived from the three crucial issues in language learning which we have labelled the L1-L2 connection, the code-communication dilemma, and the explicit-implicit option (Figure 22.5). These three issues present us with six major strategies, expressed in pairs as three parameters:

(a) The *intralingual-crosslingual (intracultural-crosscultural) dimensions* concern the use or non-use of L1 in L2 learning. Techniques which remain entirely within the second language are called *intralingual* or *intracultural*. Techniques which use the first language and native culture as a frame of reference are called *crosslingual* or *crosscultural*. No *a priori* judgement is made condemning or commending either

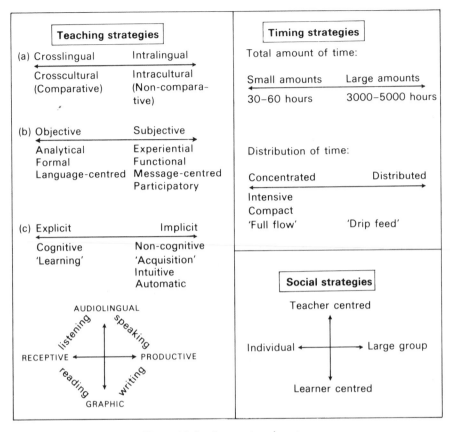

Figure 22.5   Instructional options

intralingual/intracultural or crosslingual/crosscultural techniques, because on theoretical grounds a case can be made for movement along this language and culture dimension.[10]

(b) The *objective-subjective* (analytical-experiential) *dimension* results from the code-communication dilemma. It refers to the possibility of treating the target language and culture as codes and as such as *objects* of study and mastery or as something to experience *subjectively* through participation in personal contact and communicative acts. Language learning in the classroom tends to be mainly objective and analytical whereas language learning 'in the street' (Macnamara 1973) is subjective, participatory, and non-analytical. The assumption is made that an objective and a subjective strategy are legitimate and both are needed in varying measures depending on learners, opportunities for learning, stages of the learning process, and learners' goals.[11]

(c) The *explicit-implicit dimension* relates to techniques which encourage the learner either to adopt vis-à-vis the new language a cognitive or reasoning approach, that is, in Krashen's terms, to bring the

Monitor into play, or, alternatively, to employ techniques which encourage more intuitive absorption and automaticity, in Krashen's terms, to develop 'acquisition' processes. We can hypothesize that explicit-implicit techniques are not irreconcilable. But presumably their applicability varies according to learner characteristics, stages of the learning process, and conditions of learning.[12]

Strategies can be ordered along other dimensions which have become more clearly identified during the last two decades. Particularly *the four skills* can be deliberately separated as listening, speaking, reading, and writing or combined along at least two dimensions as receptive and productive or audiolingual and graphic.[13] Other choices of broad strategies of which recently there has been a greater awareness relate to the *time element of instruction*: the total amount of time available and the distribution of time either concentrated or distributed,[14] and to *social and interpersonal arrangements*: the size and composition of classes, individualized, small group or large group instruction, teacher-centred or student-centred ways of teaching, and in this connection arises also the question of interpersonal relations in the language class. In this context concepts of satellization/infantilization and desatellization/emancipation developed in our interpretation of language learning (see Chapter 18:399–400) may be useful as hypotheses in studying the human relationships in language learning.[15]

These broad strategy options which have been only briefly sketched here have not yet been well described nor have their uses and relative effectiveness been studied in any systematic way. Carefully designed research and experimentation on these different aspects of language instruction are likely to lead to a better understanding of second language teaching and learning.

Stages and sequences.
The principle of arranging the content of language teaching as a course or sequence is deeply ingrained in language teaching practice and is implicit in the notion of curriculum. What is less certain is what criteria should guide the division into stages and the sequencing of content. Past experience and thought has ranged from the abandonment of any deliberate ordering of content (the 'non-syllabus') to very tight sequencing, from broad two-stage schemes to well defined series of mastery levels.[16] No single scheme or simple formula of ordering content can be expected or proposed. Nevertheless, since a language cannot be mastered in a single stride a pedagogical progression and the division into stages which meet specified learning conditions are inevitable. We assume that such a progression would be based on several content criteria (for example, linguistic, cultural, or communicative). It would take into account what is known about language learning as a developmental process (see Chapter 18). It would lead to the definition

of mastery levels and an ordered arrangement which would be justified on grounds of principles derived from the subject matter, learning objectives, and our knowledge about learners and learning. In the final analysis it would be empirically tested and modified in accordance with such empirical findings.

Learning outcome

The 'product' variable in Dunkin and Biddle's model appears in our study of teaching and learning primarily as the actual, language proficiency attained by learners. Since we have already considered in detail the concept of objectives and content in this chapter and of proficiency as the result of language learning in Chapter 16 we need not elaborate this outcome here. Besides proficiency, there are of course other cognitive and affective learning outcomes to bear in mind.[17] Following Dunkin and Biddle, immediate and long-term outcomes should be distinguished. The immediate outcomes are important for feedback to further teaching and learning. Their assessment is diagnostic and 'formative' and can influence continued teaching and learning. The sequence teaching—learning—outcome—evaluation—further teaching form a cycle which can be repeated until the end of a course has been reached. This cycle may be a benign or a vicious circle. The fact that in many cases language teaching has been relatively unproductive is the continuing challenge to teaching and research.

Long-term, the outcome can be considered from the point of view of the individual learner, the point of view of the teacher, and from the point of view of society. For the individual learner the outcome should be a more or less permanent acquisition of a second language. Where the language has been forgotten through disuse such a more permanent outcome would be indicated by greater ease of relearning at a later stage and the ability to tackle new languages. Long-term learning outcomes would also include the more or less permanent attitudes the learner has acquired through language learning.

For the individual teacher, the evaluation of his own teaching and of the learning of his pupils provides feedback for further teaching. It is a necessary part of the teaching-learning cycle. In the long term, the teaching—learning—outcome—feedback cycle also changes the teacher's teaching capabilities hopefully making him a more experienced and more competent teacher. But we must also take note of possible negative effects on teachers; for example, language teachers are often subjectively aware of the fact that the constant interchange with second language learners negatively affects their own proficiency as speakers of the language.

More intangibly, but nonetheless important, are the lasting effects of language learning on society: language-learning is expected to infuse into society a second language or bilingual element. For example, language learning in European countries can be seen as a means of facilitating communication among different language communities, thus welding the European society more closely together. Equally, in North America, bilingual education or foreign language teaching is not only viewed as influenced by society, but if it is truly effective, as influencing the society in the direction of greater acceptance of bilingualism, multilingualism, improved community relations, or an international outlook. Therefore, language teaching can potentially contribute to sociopolitical changes. Whether it has these long-term effects cannot be assumed *a priori*. Evidence would have to be gathered in particular instances to find out to what extent language learning has any recognizable long-term social effects and what kind. Language teaching can also inject into society rational or irrational views about language and languages, about culture and cultures and can contribute to an international or interethnic literacy.

For research no less than for teaching the interpretation of learning outcomes is a constant challenge. To what extent can particular outcomes, for example, a higher level of proficiency of one student and a low level of proficiency of another, or positive attitudes in one group of students and negative attitudes in another group, be convincingly attributed to any one of the antecedent factors or a combination of factors, the educational treatment, the learning process, teacher or learner factors, or contextual variables? In the search for answers the combination of theoretical sophistication, the combination of different research approaches, and practical insights are likely to lead in the direction of greater discrimination in interpretations and greater effectiveness of language teaching. The important consideration is that, in the long run, the language learning outcome may influence and modify the sociocultural and sociolinguistic context which forms the background against which the processes of teaching and learning are initiated.

As Dunkin and Biddle had pointed out, research on teaching has investigated relations between these different groups of variables: presage (teacher/learner)-process, context-process, process-process, and process-product. Language teaching research has only recently begun to study these different relationships, and has tended to focus on a few aspects in isolation without adequate consideration of a broader framework for individual studies. The teaching-learning model which has been outlined is intended to enable us to view different aspects of language teaching in relation to one another and in this way to obtain a more balanced view of the teaching component for the threefold purpose of theory development, practical decision making, and for research.

Conclusion

We have in the present chapter made the attempt to express language teaching in educational terms and have applied to language teaching categories of curriculum theory and a research model, developed for the study of teaching. Our contention is that this educational approach is useful because in this way we are able to relate the final basic concept of our study, teaching, to the discipline to which it is most closely allied, education. Moreover, this approach makes it possible to analyse language teaching comprehensively and to relate it to other basic concepts and, beyond language teaching, to other areas of educational activity.

We do not claim that the model we have outlined here is the only one by which to analyse the concept of teaching within a language teaching theory. Indeed we can envisage other approaches to represent language teaching which have different purposes and would therefore operate with different categorizations.[18] As with the other basic concepts in earlier parts, our main object in this part of the book has been to suggest some categories enabling us to think systematically about the concept of language teaching itself.

Notes

1 Dunkin and Biddle's model follows a terminology proposed by Mitzel (1960) in the *Encyclopedia of Educational Research*; Mitzel, however, only distinguishes three variables: presage, process, and product.

2 In educational discussions and in language teaching, a hierarchical distinction is sometimes made between 'goals' as a very broad and ultimate category, 'aims' as a more specific set of purposes, and 'objectives' as the most precisely defined ends in view which can often be described in terms of behavioural outcomes. Such a hierarchical differentiation may have its uses, provided it is recognized that these distinctions cannot always be clearly applied to expressed learning outcomes. We have not adopted this distinction in our discussion.

3 The direct method and the audiolingual method, for example, did not only propose new techniques of teaching and learning, but implied also a new emphasis on speaking and listening as learning goals.

4 For example, feature 1, 'functional versus non-functional', poses the question whether the goal is communication, as in the direct, the audiolingual, or the reading methods, or whether it is the understanding of linguistic structure, a goal attributed by Bosco and Di Pietro to the grammar-translation and the cognitive methods.

Feature 3, 'affective versus non-affective', raises the question of whether the method includes an affective goal. A few curricula which lay emphasis on 'humanistic techniques' and interpersonal relations are beginning to make this objective explicit. Feature 5, 'idiographic versus non-idiographic', relates to another goal, not specifically covered by any of the recognized methods, but not unknown to teachers, and, in a way, expressed already by Gouin: the goal of helping the learner to develop his unique style of personal expression and to relate language learning to his own purposes. Feature 8, 'divergent versus non-divergent', refers to language learning directed to specific skills, for example reading, as in the reading method, or listening and speaking as in the audiolingual method, or an overall global proficiency or competence, as in the direct method or the grammar-translation method.

5 Valette's first attempts to apply the Bloom taxonomies to language teaching appeared in 1969 and 1971. Valette soon recognized that the Bloom scheme had to be modified if it was to express the objectives of language teaching. See, for example, Valette and Disick (1972) and Valette (1981).

6 Hawkins (1981) has elaborated this aspect of second language learning at the school level in a work on modern languages in the curriculum. Bosco and Di Pietro's linguistic feature 'general/non-general' may have been prompted by similar considerations.

7 For a rationale of three of these four categories see also Chapter 12:261–2, especially Figure 12.3. In Figure 12.3 the 'structural' and 'functional' aspects correspond to the 'Language syllabus' in Figure 22.4, the 'sociocultural aspect' in 12.3 to the 'Culture syllabus' in 22.4, and the 'experiential aspect' in 12.3 is equivalent to the 'Communicative activity syllabus' in 22.4. The 'General language education syllabus' in Figure 22.4 has not arisen in the discussion in Chapter 12 and is therefore not represented in Figure 12.3. For earlier discussions of this curriculum scheme see Stern (1976) and Stern *et al.* (1980). The present version has been the result of collaboration between the author and Rebecca Ullmann, one of his co-workers. It has been reported in papers by Stern (1980) and Ullmann (1982). The four-syllabus scheme has also been adopted as an expression of a multidimensional curriculum in a statement on curriculum priorities for the eighties, proposed by the American Council on the Teaching of Foreign Languages (1980:28).

8 The failure to make this distinction is a weakness of the Bosco and Di Pietro analysis. The Krashen and Seliger scheme *in toto* is much more a conceptualization of instruction than of content and objectives; therefore the question of making this distinction does not arise there.

9 This is in effect what is advocated by those who describe themselves

as eclecticists (for example, Rivers 1981). However, in my view, eclecticism does not recognize the fundamental weaknesses in the method concept as such nor does it offer any guidance on what basis and by what principles aspects of different methods can be selected and combined.

10 This dimension is not mentioned in the two feature analyses.

11 This dimension is discussed in greater detail in Stern (1981a). The same aspect appears in Bosco and Di Pietro in feature 1, 'functional/non-functional'. It is not covered by Krashen and Seliger.

12 This dimension is central to the preoccupations of the two feature analyses. In Bosco and Di Pietro feature 2 (central/non-central) and feature 4 (nomothetic/non-nomothetic) and in Krashen and Seliger ± Deductive, ± Explicit and Focus on/Focus away are concerned with the same parameter.

13 The reading method and the audiolingual method have explored the separation of skills as a teaching strategy. More recently proponents of the 'natural method', reviving earlier recommendations of a similar nature, have advocated a delay in productive skills and a greater insistence on allowing receptive skills to develop first (for example, Terrell 1977). Bosco and Di Pietro's feature 8 (divergent/non-divergent) and Krashen and Seliger's 'performance channel' deal with this aspect. In his book on language teaching as communication Widdowson (1978) has introduced a further refinement by distinguishing the practice of the skills in the abstract from their practice in a communicative situation. In other words he has combined the four skills dimension with the objective-subjective parameter.

14 The question of total time and to a lesser extent the distribution of time have been looked into by several researchers (for example, Carroll 1975, Burstall *et al.* 1974, Stern *et al.* 1976, Swain 1981, 1981a). For interesting administrative measures resulting from this in Ontario language education, see Stern 1979. Intensive and compact courses are described by Hawkins and Perren (1978), and by Benseler and Schulz (1979a), Freudenstein (in press) and Stern (in press). See also Stern (1982).

15 The social and interpersonal aspects of language learning and teaching have been referred to in previous chapters, first in the historical review of the recent decades (Chapter 6:110–11), then in the chapter on language learning under the heading of social learning and affective strategies (Chapter 18:411–12) and, finally, in Chapter 19 in the discussion of the sociology of the classroom (p. 426). As an important development in language teaching they have been recognized by Brown (1980) and Stevick (1980). The schemes by Bosco and Di Pietro and Krashen and Seliger do not clearly identify the social component. Marginally, Krashen and

Seliger's two final features 'control' and 'feedback' imply observations about interaction between teacher and class. The observation schemes, such as Fanselow's FOCUS, on the other hand, focus on the interaction component but mainly quantitatively; they seem to lack an underlying rationale about teacher-student interaction in a language learning setting. The concept of self-directed learning or 'learner autonomy' (Holec 1980,1981), endorsed by the Council of Europe Modern Languages Project, illustrates a shift from teacher-centred to more student-centred teaching: 'We must . . . aim to produce a learner who is increasingly aware, self-reliant, better able to learn directly from experience, gradually outgrowing the need for a teacher' (Trim 1981:xiv). A similar point of view is expressed by Stern (1980a) in a discussion of language learning 'on the spot'.

16 See Chapter 16 (pp. 352–3) on rating scales and Chapter 18 (pp. 399–400) on developmental stages of language learning. The concept of stage and sequence appears as a central principle in methodics (Halliday, McIntosh, and Strevens 1964) and method analysis (Mackey 1965, 1965a; see Chapter 21:483). Some of the features in the feature analyses, i.e., cyclic/non-cyclic (Bosco and Di Pietro) and sequence (Krashen and Seliger) identify this issue. A well developed scheme of stages by Valette and Disick (1972), referred to in Note 5 above, is briefly explained by Valette (1981). Recent British experience in graded tests illustrates a belief in stages as an important principle of organizing instruction (Harding, Page, and Rowell 1980; and Buckby *et al.* 1981). Scepticism about ordering a language in curriculum terms has been expressed by Newmark (1966) and Macnamara (1973). Principles of curriculum organization are discussed by Shaw (1977) and Stern *et al.* (1980).

17 Bosco and Di Pietro no doubt had these in mind in their psychological feature 3(affective/non-affective) and feature 5 (idiographic/non-idiographic: does the method encourage the learner to develop his unique style of expression?)

18 For example, one can envisage a decision-making model in which language teaching is viewed from the language teacher's perspective who, analogous to a psychotherapist, arranges teaching, in accordance with phases of the learning process, around the gradual emancipation of the learner from support by the teacher. For other recent views on language teaching, see, for example, Altman (1981) and Politzer (1981).

Conclusion

Language teachers—probably more than other professionals—find that they are constantly bombarded from all sides with a surfeit of information, prescriptions, directions, advice, suggestions, innovations, research results, and what purports to be scientific evidence. As was pointed out in the Introduction, it is difficult to find one's way through this maze, and this book was written to help teachers to do just that so that they can develop their own judgement and define their own theoretical position.

Our object was not to offer another formula or prescription. Instead, we have attempted to present a 'map' which can provide orientation, a synoptic view, and perspective. Our hope has been that practitioners can use this book to arrive at a coherent view of language teaching by reflecting as systematically as possible on a few fundamental questions, and by bringing to bear on their thoughts some of the collective knowledge that is available in the vast literature on language pedagogy as well as in the theories and the research of a number of disciplines. From the point of view of language teaching, these disciplines make up the applied discipline we have referred to as educational linguistics.

To begin with, in Part 1 we laid emphasis on the complementary nature of practice, theory, and research. The central focus of the book has been the development of ideas about language teaching ('theory') rather than language teaching practice in many of its concrete manifestations and detail.[1] But the practical experience of teaching and learning languages was never far from our mind, and readers were urged in chapter after chapter to relate the topics under discussion to their own experience as teachers or learners, thus to look at that experience more reflectively with more consciously formulated concepts, making use of the available interpretations and theories, and, in this way, to recognize the theoretical issues underlying practice.

This is also the reason why a *research outlook* is important to complement practice and theorizing. In Chapter 4, where the role of research was developed, we urged readers to adopt a positive but not subservient attitude to research. The substantive parts of the book gave examples of various research studies that had been undertaken, and we discussed in what way they have helped in advancing our knowledge. We have also indicated research that has not yet been done but needs doing. Reviewing the research contribution has revealed the unevenness of research activity. Certain research themes have been taken up vigorously, whereas others, which can claim to be no less important, have been neglected or have even been completely ignored. The sudden efflorescence of empirical research on second language learning (see Part 5) has been a welcome development which has begun to fill a serious gap in our knowledge, although much remains to be done even in that area. However, the importance of research on learning is no reason to neglect research on teaching, descriptive language research, studies of cultures, historical research, or critical investigations on current innovations.

Our study centred around a few simple but basic questions we asked about four key concepts:[2]

What do we mean by *language*?
How do we understand *language learning*?
To what extent does *social context* impinge upon our understanding of language and language learning?
And, finally, how do we interpret the concept of *language teaching*?

Although we have attempted to give answers to these questions in the text, it has never been suggested anywhere in these pages that they could be answered once and for all with any sense of finality. Rather, they are the kinds of questions one has to ask again and again if as a profession we wish to deal with issues in fresh and appropriate ways and want to avoid stagnation or professional decline.

Four main parts of the book (Parts 3-6), each dealing with one of the key concepts—language, society, language learning, and language teaching—and the corresponding disciplines, combined with an historical perspective (Part 2), jointly constitute the case for the *multifactor and multidisciplinary interpretation of language teaching* that was advanced tentatively in Chapter 3. The history of language teaching has shown that language teaching theory again and again has fallen into the trap of oversimplifying the issues. It has tended to adopt a single-factor and single-discipline approach, often unwittingly so. As we saw in Part 6 (Chapter 20), teaching methods overemphasized isolated strategies and paid attention to teaching procedures at the expense of objectives and content. The recent infusion of a scientific, discipline-oriented approach in a certain way had a similar effect: it led to a preoccupation with a single discipline at the expense of other disciplines which are no less important, first linguistics, then psychology, and more recently, sociolinguistics. As was pointed out in Chapter 3:47, we cannot rely on linguistics alone, nor only on psychology or sociolinguistics, nor for that matter on educational theory. These different fields jointly perform essential and mutually supporting functions in establishing a scholarly basis for language pedagogy. If any conclusion stands out from this study it is the multifactor, multidisciplinary, and multilevel character of language teaching theory.

We have identified the history of language pedagogy, the language sciences, the social sciences, psychology, and educational theory as the five fields of study which are essential to the development of a satisfactory theory of language teaching.

1 An *historical approach* is needed if language teaching is not to fall victim to a succession of passing fashions. The usefulness of a historical perspective became evident not only in the chapters on history and through the historical sketch (Chapters 5, 6) but also in the accounts of the different disciplines in relation to language teaching. Looked at historically, the developments we examined in linguistics, social science, psychology, and education fell into place. But the lack of historical documentation was found to be a disadvantage.

2 *Language* is obviously a key concept, and therefore linguistic and sociolinguistic studies on the nature of language are indispensable. The models of language (Figures 7.2 and 9.3) and the discussion of proficiency in Chapter 16 have indicated linguistic categories needed to define language for the purposes of language education, and these definitions in turn bear upon the scope and treatment of language in the curriculum (see Chapter 22, Figure 22.4).[3]

3 If a language is to be presented in a *sociolinguistic and sociocultural context*, sociology, anthropology, and sociolinguistics are necessary for a language teaching theory. This means that, parallel to a pedagogical grammar, a *sociolinguistic and sociocultural guide* is needed as a resource for a curriculum that is intended to be 'context-sensitive' and not only linguistic in a narrow sense. Here the data base is even less satisfactory than for the linguistic component. We lack sociolinguistic and cultural 'grammars' for the languages we teach (see Figure 12.1).

4 Of all the key concepts *learning* is the one that understandably has received the lion's share of speculation, theorizing, controversy, and research. Some research has been going on since the fifties, but in the seventies there was a veritable 'explosion' of studies. In spite of this prolonged research effort we do not yet have a clear picture of how second language learning operates and why it is often arrested or fails altogether. Thus the likenesses and differences of adults and children as second language learners have not been accounted for satisfactorily, nor have the stages of second language learning been adequately

described and empirically verified. Nevertheless, productive new concepts (for example, 'interlanguage', 'acquisition', 'acculturation'), sophisticated hypotheses and comprehensive schemes of analysis (for example, Figures 16.1 and 18.2) have given us better insight into language learning, enabling us to formulate theories and explanations, to design research studies, and to diagnose individual patterns of language learning.

5 In spite of the prolonged debate on teaching method, the *concept of teaching* as such has remained the least developed. It is only gradually emancipating itself from the method debate through conceptual schemes, empirical studies, and classroom observation. In our view a more deliberate interpretation of language teaching in curriculum terms and, more broadly, in terms of educational theory is needed if we want to arrive at a more balanced and more comprehensive view of teaching. An educational interpretation of language teaching is clearly interdisciplinary (as is the study of education itself, see Chapter 19): in the analysis of teaching we used concepts of objectives which are psychological and concepts of content which derive from linguistics, sociolinguistics, cultural studies and educational theory (see Figure 22.4). The teaching strategies which we identified (see Figure 22.5) have an equally multidisciplinary origin. They are partly derived from the history of language teaching itself and partly from key issues in the psychology of language learning and other psychological or sociological studies.

Although the five fields of study we examined are all needed equally for a language teaching theory it was surprising to note how diverse the *patterns of relationships between language teaching and each of the disciplines* has been.[4] For example, linguistics has moved from a period of confident application in the fifties and early sixties through a period of disorientation as a result of new linguistic theories in the years 1965 to 1970 to a reassessment of the role of linguistics in the early seventies, ending in the late seventies with the emergence of a more confident applied discipline of educational linguistics.

Psychology and psycholinguistics have also interacted with language teaching in a consistent manner over a long period of time, but the interaction has in many ways been different from that of linguistics. Language teaching has always operated with certain psychological assumptions and, since the fifties, has used psychology as a resource, and since the sixties, psycholinguistics. Until 1970 there was a tendency to extrapolate from general psychology to the psychology of second language learning. It is only in the seventies that an independent empirically-based psychology of second language learning began to develop which, to a certain extent, parallels and contributes to the 'emancipation' of educational linguistics.

By contrast, sociological and anthropological research has as yet provided little direction to the study of society and culture in language teaching. Language teaching theorists have not so far taken the kind of positive action in the area of culture and society that parallels the initiative in linguistics and language learning research.

As we saw in Part 6, the relationship between language teaching theory and education as a field of study is perhaps among all of the disciplines the one that has as yet been least systematically explored. It may be that it was taken for granted by language teaching theorists that the concepts of education are applicable. But the application of educational thoughts, values, and practices has been sporadic and sometimes not very discriminating.[5] The particular characteristics of second language learning have often not been sufficiently borne in mind and at the same time highly relevant developments in general educational theory have been completely overlooked by language pedagogy.

Finally, the history of language pedagogy itself cannot be said to have exercised a significant influence on the development of language teaching theory. Apart from such rare exceptions as Kelly's *25 Centuries of Language Teaching* very little has been done to treat the history of language teaching systematically as a source of current theory development. In our present study, of course, we have attempted in a limited way to remedy this deficiency and to establish a sense of historical continuity in theory development; but that is no substitute for systematic historical research.

Although our study has confirmed us in our conviction that these fields of study are vital for language education, the developments that we have described suggest that none of the disciplines is such that it can be 'applied' to language teaching practice in a simple and direct way. The ups and downs of the relationship between linguistics and language teaching and between language teaching and psychology have been particularly instructive in this respect (see Chapter 9 and Chapter 15). What all the disciplines need is a 'filter', 'buffer', or 'mixer' between the practice of language teaching and the fundamental fields of study. Hence a mediating stage or Interlevel between the Foundations at Level 1 and Practice at Level 3 was postulated in the model described in Figure 3.7.[6] The integration of the five different approaches which we have considered in Parts 2–6 of this book can be regarded as the task of educational linguistics. It is understood that an integrated viewpoint can come about only gradually.

In this study we have turned our main attention in one direction (see Figure C.1, overleaf), that is, to the relationship between the key concepts in our model at Level 2 and the human sciences at Level 1. In other words, *educational linguistics*, the subject of this book, *is the scholarship that relates language education to the language-related disciplines.* On this discipline-oriented basis the next step would be to turn to the study of

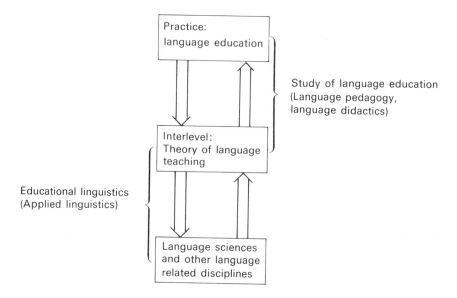

*Figure C.1   The relationship of educational linguistics
to the study of language education*

the practice of language education which, in the diagram (Figure C.1; see also Figure 3.7) relates Level 2 to the practice at Level 3: 'the study of language education' (also referred to as 'language pedagogy' or 'language didactics'). While educational linguistics is mainly 'discipline-oriented' the study of language education is 'practice- and problem-oriented'. On the basis of educational linguistics, the study of language education will examine the methodology of language teaching and its institutional organization. We are here at the threshold of another enquiry. Ultimately, the interaction between these two approaches—educational linguistics and the study of language education—is needed to develop a comprehensive theory of language teaching and learning. It is a challenging task for all those who believe in a consistent and professional development of second language education.

Notes

1 As was pointed out previously (Chapter 22:498), a study of practice, Level 3 in the conceptual framework, is in preparation.
2 The questions are discussed in full in Chapter 3:47–49.
3 The scope and treatment of language have been left open. In actual curriculum studies it would of course be necessary to describe the language syllabus as an inventory and sequence.
4 For a more detailed discussion of the relations between the disciplines and language teaching practice see Stern, Wesche, and Harley (1978).

This article indicates four different models of interaction: the Separation or 'Hands-Off' Model (i.e., language teaching and the disciplines have nothing to do with each other), the Application Model (i.e., the disciplines can be applied directly); the Resource Model (i.e., language teachers should feel free to use the disciplines as available resources and draw on them as they see fit); the Common Ground or Convergent Model (i.e., the disciplines and language teaching have much in common and should interact on a basis of equality and mutuality). The 'ideal' relationship is represented by the Common Ground or Convergent Model. These models are also briefly explained in Stern (1978b).

5 Examples of application are programmed instruction, taxonomies of objectives, individualization of instruction, interaction analysis.

6 The institutional mechanisms that have been developed to represent the interlevel have been discussed by Stern, Wesche, and Harley (1978). Language centres which have been established since the late fifties have often fulfilled this function. For a discussion of language centres from this point of view see Stern (1969b, 1974).

Bibliography and citation index

'Actes du premier colloque international de linguistique appliquée,' organized by the Faculty of Letters and Human Sciences of the University of Nancy, France: 26–31 October 1964. *Annales de l'Est*, Mémoire no. 31, 1966, with a foreword by Bernard Pottier and Guy Bourquin. Nancy: Faculté des Lettres et des Sciences humaines de l'Université de Nancy. [107]

Adam, R.S. 1959. 'Social Factors in Second Language Learning, with Special Reference to the Fiji Islands.' Unpublished Ph.D. thesis, University of London. [267(n 18)]

Adorno, T.W., Frenkel-Brunswick, E. Levinson, D.J. and **Sanford, R.N.** 1950. *The Authoritarian Personality.* New York: Harper and Row. [214(n 9), 237,379]

Africa, H. 1980. 'Language in Education in a Multilingual State: A Case Study of the Role of English in the Educational System of Zambia.' Unpublished Ph.D thesis, University of Toronto. [244(n 16), 449(n 19)]

Agard, F.B. and **Dunkel, H.B.** 1948. *An Investigation of Second-Language Teaching.* Boston: Ginn. [54]

Akmajian, A., Demers, R.A. and **Harnish, R.M.** 1979. *Linguistics: An Introduction to Language and Communication.* Cambridge, Mass.: M.I.T. Press. [151(n 22)]

Alatis, J.E. (ed.) 1968. *Contrastive Linguistics and its Pedagogical Implications.* Report of the 19th Round Table on Linguistics and Language Studies. Washington, D.C.: Georgetown University Press. [168,171(n 11), Di Pietro 1968]

Alatis, J.E. (ed.) 1970. *Linguistics and the Teaching of Standard English to Speakers of Other Languages or Dialects.* Report of the 20th Round Table on Linguistics and Language Studies. Washington, D.C.: Georgetown University Press. [Spolsky 1970]

Alatis, J.E. (ed.) 1978. *International Dimensions of Bilingual Education.* Georgetown University Round Table. Washington D.C.: Georgetown University Press. [Stern 1978, Swain 1978]

Alatis, J.E. (ed.) 1980. *Current Issues in Bilingual Education.* Georgetown University Round Table on Languages and Linguistics, 1980. Washington, D.C.: Georgetown University Press. [69(n 7), Cummins 1980a]

Alatis, J.E., Altman, H.B. and **Alatis, P.M.** (eds.) 1981. *The Second Language Classroom: Directions for the 1980's.* Essays in honour of Mary Finocchiaro. New York and Oxford: Oxford University Press. [116(n 15), 268(n22), Altman 1981, Brown 1981, Krashen 1981a Politzer 1981, Stern 1981, Valette 1981, Widdowson and Brumfit 1981]

Alatis, J.E. and **Twaddell, K.** (eds.) 1976. *English as a Second Language in Bilingual Education.* Washington D.C.: TESOL, 1976. [Paulston 1975]

Albright, R.W. 1958. *The International Phonetic Alphabet: its Background and Development.* Monograph of the *International Journal of American Linguistics*, 24: Part III (Publication VII of the Indiana University Research Center in Anthropology, Folklore and Linguistics). [90,96(n 13)]

Allen, E.D. and **Valette, R.M.** (1977). *Classroom Techniques: Foreign Languages and English as a Second Language.* Second edition. (First edition, 1972: *Modern Language Classroom Techniques: A Handbook*) New York, etc.: Harcourt Brace Jovanovich. [5(n 3)]

Allen, H.B. (ed.) 1965. *Teaching English as a Second Language*. New York: McGraw-Hill. [Anthony 1963]

Allen, J.P.B. 1973. 'Applied grammatical models in a remedial English syllabus' in Corder and Roulet, 1973:91–106. [174]

Allen, J.P.B. 1980. 'A Three-Level Curriculum Model for Second Language Education.' Keynote address at the Annual Conference of the Ontario Modern Language Teachers' Association, Toronto, April 1980. mimeo. [261–2]

Allen, J.P.B. and **Corder, S.P.** (eds.) 1973–77. *The Edinburgh Course in Applied Linguistics*. Vol 1. *Readings for Applied Linguistics*, 1973; Vol 2. *Papers in Applied Linguistics*, 1975; Vol 3. *Techniques in Applied Linguistics*, 1974; Vol 4. *Testing and Experimental Methods*, (edited by Allen J.P.B. and Davies, A.) 1977. London and Oxford: Oxford University Press. [105] (See also separate entries below)

Allen, J.P.B. and **Corder, S.P.** (eds.) 1973. *Readings for Applied Linguistics*. Edinburgh Course in Applied Linguistics, Vol 1. London: Oxford University Press. [Jakobson, 1960]

Allen, J.P.B. and **Corder S.P.** (eds.) 1974. *Techniques in Applied Linguistics*. Edinburgh Course in Applied Linguistics, Vol 3. London: Oxford University Press. [451(n 37)]

Allen, J.P.B. and **Corder, S.P.** (eds.) 1975. *Papers in Applied Linguistics*. Edinburgh Course in Applied Linguistics, Vol 2. London: Oxford University Press. [150(n 22) Allen and Widdowson 1975, Brown 1975, Corder 1975, Criper and Widdowson 1975, Ingram 1975, van Buren 1975]

Allen, J.P.B. and **Davies, A.** (eds.) 1977. *Testing and Experimental Methods*. Vol 4 of Edinburgh Course in Applied Linguistics. London: Oxford University Press. [70(n 16)]

Allen, J.P.B. and **van Buren, P.** (eds.) 1971. *Chomsky: Selected Readings*. London: Oxford University Press. [150(n20), Chomsky 1959, 1966]

Allen, J.P.B. and **Widdowson, H.G.** 1974. 'Teaching the communicative use of English.' *IRAL*, 12:1–21. [178]

Allen, J.P.B. and **Widdowson, H.G.** 1975. 'Grammar and language teaching' in Allen and Corder 1975:45–97. [131,149–50(n13,19)]

Allwright, R.L. 1975. 'Problems in the study of the language teacher's treatment of learner error' in Burt and Dulay 1975:96–109. [494,496(n 12)]

Allwright, R.L. 1976. 'Language learning through communication practice.' *ELT Documents* 3:2–14. [405]

Altman, H.B. (ed.) 1972. *Individualizing the Foreign Language Classroom: Perspectives for Teachers*. Rowley, Mass.: Newbury House. [447(n 10)]

Altman, H.B. (Guest editor) 1977. Special issue: 'Individualized instruction'. *System* 5/2. [387(n 1)]

Altman, H.B. 1981. 'What is second language teaching?' in Alatis, Altman and Alatis 1981: 5–19. [513(n 18)]

Altman, H.B. and **Politzer, R.L.** (eds.) 1971. *Individualizing Foreign Language Instruction: Proceedings of the Stanford Conference, May 6–8, 1971*. Rowley, Mass.: Newbury House. [111,387(n 1), 447(n 10)]

AMA. See Assistant Masters Association.

American Council on the Teaching of Foreign Languages, 1980. *Proceedings of the National Conference on Professional Priorities*. Boston, Mass., November 1980. Hastings-on-Hudson: ACTFL Materials Center. [511(n7), Stern 1980]

Amidon, E.J. and **Hough, J.B.** (eds.) 1967. *Interaction Analysis: Theory, Research, and Application*. Reading, Mass.: Addison-Wesley. [447(n 10), 495(n 10) Anderson 1939, Lewin *et al.* 1939]

Andersen, R.W. (ed.) 1981. *New Dimensions in Second Language Acquisition Research*. Rowley, Mass.: Newbury House. [Oller 1981]

Anderson, D. 1969. 'Harold E. Palmer: A biographical essay' in Palmer and Redman 1969:133–66. [95(n 11), 100]

Anderson, H.H. 1939. 'The measurement of domination and socially integrative behaviour in teachers' contacts with children'. *Child Development* 10:73–89; also in Amidon and Hough 1967:4–23. [495(n 10)]

Andersson, T. 1953. *The Teaching of Foreign Languages in the Elementary School.* Boston: Heath. [105]

Andersson, T. 1969. *Foreign Languages in the Elementary School: A Struggle against Mediocrity.* Austin: University of Texas Press. [87]

Andersson, T. and Boyer, M. 1970. *Bilingual Schooling in the United States.* Washington, D.C.: U.S. Government Printing Office. [Mackey 1970]

Angiolillo, P.F. 1947. *Armed Forces' Foreign Language Teaching: Critical Evaluation and Implications.* New York: Vanni. [87,104]

Anisfeld, M. 1966. 'Psycholinguistic perspectives on language learning' in Valdman 1966:107–19. [145,167,168,327,394]

Annan, N. (Lord Annan) (Chairman) 1962. *The Teaching of Russian* (The Annan Report). London: H.M.S.O. [282]

Anthony, E.M. 1963. 'Approach, method and technique.' *English Language Teaching* 17:63–7; reprinted in Allen 1965:93–7. [474(n 1)]

Anthony, E.M. and Norris, W.E. 1969. *Method in Language Teaching.* ERIC Focus Reports on the Teaching of Foreign Languages, No.8. New York: MLA/ERIC Clearinghouse on the Teaching of Foreign Languages and ACTFL. [32(n 3), 474(n 1)]

Antier, M. 1965. 'Panorama de l'enseignement des langues vivantes en France.' *Le français dans le monde* 35:15–21. [96(n 17)]

Apelt, W. 1967. *Die kulturkundliche Bewegung im Unterricht der neueren Sprachen in Deutschland in den Jahren 1886–1945.* Berlin: Volkseigener Verlag. [87,97]

Applied Linguistics (journal) Oxford: Oxford University Press. [112,335(n14)]

Applied Psycholinguistics (journal). Cambridge: Cambridge University Press. [112,335(n14)]

Archambault, R.D. (ed.) 1965. *Philosophical Analysis and Education.* London: Routledge and Kegan Paul. [25–6]

Archer, R.L. 1941. 'Educational psychology American and British: some points of comparison'. *British Journal of Educational Psychology* 11:128–34. [320,322]

Ardener, E. (ed.) 1971. *Social Anthropology and Language.* London: Tavistock Publications. [215(n 17), Robins 1971]

Assistant Masters Association 1979. *Teaching Modern Languages in Secondary Schools: A Book for and by Language Teachers in the Classroom.* London, etc.: Hodder and Stoughton. [5(n 3), 101,264(n 9)]

Atkins, H.G. and Hutton, H.L. 1920. *The Teaching of Modern Foreign Languages in School and University.* London: Arnold. [247]

Austin, J.L. 1962. *How to Do Things with Words.* Oxford: Clarendon Press; Cambridge, Mass.: Harvard University Press. [222,242(n 3)]

Ausubel, D.P. 1964. 'Adults versus children in second-language learning: psychological considerations.' *Modern Language Journal* 48:420–4. [363–4]

Ausubel, D.P. 1967. *Learning Theory and Classroom Practice.* Bulletin, No. 1. Toronto: Ontario Institute for Studies in Education. [307–9]

Ausubel, D.P., Novak, J.D. and Hanesian, H. 1978. *Educational Psychology: A Cognitive View.* New York: Holt, Rinehart and Winston. Second edition. [315(n 27)]

Ausubel, D.P., Sullivan, E.V. and Ives, S.W. 1980. *Theory and Problems of Child Development.* Third edition. New York: Gruner and Stratton. [382,388(n 7), 414(n 9)]

Axtell, J.L. 1968. *The Educational Writings of John Locke.* A critical edition with introduction and notes. Cambridge: Cambridge University Press. (Most relevant paragraphs are on pp 266–89). [77–8]

Bagster-Collins, E.W. 1930. 'History of modern language teaching in the United States' in Modern Foreign Language Study and Canadian Committee on Modern Languages 1930:3–96. [87]

Baldegger, M., Müller, M. and Schneider, G. 1980. *Kontaktschwelle Deutsch als Fremdsprache*. Strasbourg: Council of Europe. [110,179]

Banathy, B.H. and Sawyer, J.O. 1969. 'The primacy of speech: an historical sketch.' *Modern Language Journal* 53:537–44. [87]

Banks, O. 1976. *The Sociology of Education*. Third revised edition. New York: Schocken Books. [447(n 7)]

Barker-Lunn, J.C. 1970. *Streaming in the Primary School*. Slough: National Foundation for Educational Research. [447(n 10)]

Baron, G., Cooper, D.H. and Walker, W.G. 1969. *Educational Administration: International Perspectives*. Chicago: Rand McNally. [447(n 13)]

Baron, G. and Taylor, W. (eds.) 1969. *Educational Administration and the Social Sciences*. London: Athlone Press. [447(n 13)]

Bausch, K.R. 1979. 'Die Erstellung von didaktischen Grammatiken als Exempel für das Verhältnis von Angewandter Linguistik, Fremdsprachendidaktik und Sprachlehrforschung' in Bausch 1979a:2–24. [176]

Bausch, K.R. (ed.) 1979a. *Beiträge zur Didaktischen Grammatik: Probleme, Konzepte, Beispiele*. Königstein/Ts: Scriptor. [Bausch 1979]

Bausch, K.R. and Kasper, G. 1979. 'Der Zweitsprachenerwerb: Möglichkeiten und Grenzen der "grossen" Hypothesen.' *Linguistische Berichte* 64:3–35. [335(n 15, n 16), 413(n 5)]

Bazan, B.M. 1964. 'The danger of assumption without proof'. *Modern Language Journal* 48:337–46. [30]

Bearne, C.G. and James, C.V. (eds.) 1976. *Modern Languages for the 1980s*. London: CILT. [115(n 12)]

Beauchamp, G.A. 1975. *Curriculum Theory*. Third edition. Wilmette, Ill.: Kagg Press. [449(n 21)]

Beaudoin, M., Cummins, C., Dunlop, H., Genesee, F. and Obadia, A. 1981. 'Bilingual education: a comparison of Welsh and Canadian experiences.' *Canadian Modern Language Review* 37:498–509. [405]

Beck, C. 1974. *Educational Philosophy and Theory: An Introduction*. Boston: Little, Brown and Co. [420,446(n 1, 3)]

Bell, D.W. 1960. 'Problems in modern language teaching.' *Educational Research* 2:112–22. [68(n 6)]

Bell, R. and Grant, N. 1977. *Patterns of Education in the British Isles*. London: Allen and Unwin. [447(n 13)]

Bellack, A.A. and Kliebard, H.M. (eds.) 1977. *Curriculum and Evaluation*. Berkeley, Cal.: McCutchan. [Scriven 1967]

Bender, M.L., Bowen, J.D., Cooper, R.L. and Ferguson, C.A. (eds.) 1976. *Language in Ethiopia*. London: Oxford University Press. [244(n 16)]

Benedict, R. 1934. *Patterns of Culture*. New York: Houghton Mifflin. [198, 214(n 7,8), 248]

Benedict, R. 1946. *The Chrysanthemum and the Sword: Patterns of Japanese Culture*. Boston: Houghton Mifflin. [214(n 9)]

Bennett, W.C. 1951. *Area Studies in American Universities*. New York: Social Science Research Council. [265(n 10)]

Benseler, D.P. and Schulz, R.A. 1979. 'Methodological trends in college foreign language instruction: a report' in U.S.A. 1979a:59–70. [116(n 15), 475(n13)]

Benseler, D.P. and Schulz, R.A. 1979a. *Intensive Foreign Language Courses*. Language in Education series, no. 18. Washington, D.C.: Center for Applied Linguistics/ERIC. [512(n14)]

Benson, C.S. 1978. *The Economics of Public Education.* Boston: Houghton Mifflin. [447(n 11)]

Bereday, G.Z. 1964. *Comparative Method in Education.* New York: Holt, Rinehart and Winston. [432,448(n 16)]

Bernstein, B.B. 1964. 'Aspects of language and learning in the genesis of the social process' in Hymes, 1964:251–63. [212]

Bernstein, B.B. 1971. *Class, Codes and Control.* Vol 1: *Theoretical Studies Towards a Sociology of Language.* London: Routledge and Kegan Paul. [211, 216–17(n 25,26), 232,257]

Bernstein, B.B. (ed.) 1973. *Class, Codes, and Control.* Vol 2: *Applied Studies Towards a Sociology of Language.* London: Routledge and Kegan Paul. [217(n 26)]

Besse, H. 1979. 'Contribution à l'histoire du français fondamental.' *Le français dans le monde,* 19/148:23–30. [94(n 2)]

Bialystok, E. 1978. 'A theoretical model of second language learning.' *Language Learning* 28:69–83. [358(n 2), 407–9]

Bialystok, E. 1979. 'Explicit and implicit judgements of L2 grammaticality.' *Language Learning* 29:81–103. [404,409]

Bialystok, E. 1980. 'Inferencing: testing the hypothesis-testing hypothesis.' Unpublished manuscript; to appear in Seliger and Long, in press. [404, 409]

Bibeau G. 1982. *L'éducation bilingue en Amérique du Nord.* Montreal: Guérin. [69(n 13)]

Bierstedt, R. 1966. *Emile Durkheim: A Biography interwoven with the Writings of the French Sociologist and Philosopher.* The Laurel Great Lives and Thought Series. New York: Dell Publishing Co. [213(n 2)]

Bierwisch, M. 1970. 'Semantics' in Lyons, 1970:166–184. [132,150(n 16)]

Biggs, P. and Dalwood, M. 1976. *Les Orléanais ont la parole.* London: Longman. [267(n 20)]

Birkmaier, E.M. 1960. 'Modern languages' in Harris 1960:861–88. [95(n 10)]

Birkmaier, E.M. (ed.) 1968. *Britannica Review of Foreign Language Education,* Vol 1. Chicago: Encyclopedia Britannica. [Seelye 1968]

Birley, D. 1972. *Planning and Education.* London: Routledge and Kegan Paul. [448(n 14)]

Bishop, G.R. (ed.) 1960. *Culture in Language Learning.* Northeast Conference on the Teaching of Foreign Languages, 1960. Reports of the Working Committees. New Brunswick, N.J.: Rutgers, The State University. [251,266(n 11)]

Blanc, M. and Biggs, P. 1971. 'L'enquête socio-linguistique sur le français parlé à Orléans.' *Le français dans le monde* 85:16–25. [258,267(n 20)]

Blaug, M. 1970. *An Introduction to the Economics of Education.* London: Alan Lane; The Penguin Press. [447(n 11)]

Bloch, B. 1949. 'Leonard Bloomfield.' *Language,* 25:87–98. [136]

Bloch, B. and Trager, G.L. 1942. *Outline of Linguistic Analysis.* Special Publication of the Linguistic Society of America. Baltimore: Linguistic Society of America. [104,157]

Bloom, B.S. (ed.) 1956. *Taxonomy of Educational Objectives: The Classification of Educational Goals.* Handbook 1: *Cognitive Domain.* New York: McKay. [438]

Bloom, B., Hastings, J.Y. and Madaus, G. (eds.) 1971. *Handbook of Formative and Summative Evaluation of Student Learning.* New York: McGraw-Hill. [441, Valette 1971]

Bloomfield, L. 1914. *Introduction to the Study of Language.* New York: Holt. [136]

Bloomfield, L. 1933. *Language.* New York: Holt. London: Allen and Unwin, 1935. [102,136–7,150(n 18), 171(n 7), 243(n 10)]

Bloomfield, L. 1942. *Outline Guide for the Practical Study of Foreign Languages.* Special Publications of the Linguistic Society of America. Baltimore: Linguistic Society of America. [88,99,104,123,127,157,171(n 13), 433,463]

Boas, F. (ed.) 1911/1922. *Handbook of American Indian Languages*. Part I: 1911, Part II: 1922. Bulletin 40, Bureau of American Ethnology, Smithsonian Institution. Washington, D.C.: Government Printing Office; reprinted Osterhont N.B., The Netherlands: Anthropological Publications, 1969. [201]

Boas, F. *et al.* (eds.) 1938. *General Anthropology*. Boston: Heath. [195]

Boas, F. 1964. 'On grammatical categories' in Hymes 1964:121–23. [202]

Bolinger, D. 1968. 'The theorist and the language teacher.' *Foreign Language Annals* 2:30–41. [173]

Bolinger, D. and **Spears**, D.A. 1981 *Aspects of Language*. Third Edition. New York: Harcourt Brace Jovanovich. [151(n 22)]

Bond, O.F. 1953. *The Reading Method: An Experiment in College French*. Chicago: University of Chicago Press. [460–61]

Bongers, H. 1947. *The History and Principles of Vocabulary Control*. Woerden (Holland): Wocopi. [170(n 5)]

Boocock, S.S. 1980. *Sociology of Education: An Introduction*. Second edition. Boston: Houghton Mifflin. [447(n 7)]

Booth, C.J. 1889/1891. *Life and Labour of the People*. Vol I: 1889; Vol II: 1891. First edition. London and Edinburgh: Williams and Norgate. [193]

Boring, E.G. 1929. *A History of Experimental Psychology*. New York: Appleton–Century-Croft. [313(n 5)]

Bosco, F.J. and **Di Pietro**, R.J. 1970. 'Instructional strategies: their psychological and linguistic bases.' *IRAL* 8:1–19; also in Lugton and Heinle 1971:31–52. [486–91, 497, 511(n 8,), 512(n 11,12,13,15), 513(n 16,17)]

Bottomore, T.B. 1971. *Sociology: A Guide to Problems and Literature*. London: Allen and Unwin. Second edition. First edition 1962. [192,200–201,213(n 1), 253]

Boyd, W. and **King**, E.J. 1972. *The History of Western Education*. Tenth edition. First edition by W. Boyd 1921. London: A. and C. Black. [447(n 6)]

Brachfeld, O. 1936. 'Individual Psychology in the learning of languages.' *International Journal of Individual Psychology* 2:77–83. [321–2,390(n 17), 414(n 10)]

Breen, M.P. and **Candlin**, C.N. 1980. 'The essentials of a communicative curriculum in language teaching.' *Applied Linguistics* 1:89–112. [115(n 14)]

Breen, M.P. and **Candlin**, C.N. forthcoming. *The Communicative Curriculum in Language Teaching*. London: Longman.

Breul, K. 1898. *The Teaching of Modern Foreign Languages and the Training of Teachers*. Cambridge: Cambridge University Press. [154]

Breymann, H. and **Steinmüller**, C. 1895–1909. *Die neusprachliche Reformliteratur von 1876 bis 1909: eine bibliographisch-kritische Übersicht*. Leipzig. [93]

Brickman, W.W. 1949/1973. *Research in Educational History*. Norwood, Pa: Norwood Editions. [447(n 6)]

Bright, W. (ed.) 1966. *Sociolinguistics: Proceedings of the UCLA Sociolinguistics Conference, 1964*. The Hague: Mouton. (Reprinted 1971). [218, Ferguson 1966, Haugen 1966a]

British Journal of Educational Psychology (journal). Issued by the British Psychological Society. Edinburgh: Scottish Academic Press. [319]

British Journal of Language Teaching (formerly, *Audio-Visual Language Journal*) issued by the British Association of Language Teaching. [450–51(n 36)]

Brooks, N. 1960/1964. *Language and Language Learning*. Second Edition. (First edition 1960) New York, etc.: Harcourt, Brace and World. [30,106,168,171(n 12), 250–2, 266(n 11), 298,333(n 2), 462,475(n 8), 477,478,479(Fig 21.1)]

Brooks, N. 1966. 'Language teaching: the new approach.' *Phi Delta Kappan* 47:357–9. [30]

Brown, G. 1975. 'Phonological theory and language teaching' in Allen and Corder, 1975: 98–121. [130,149(n 12)]

Brown, H.D. 1973. 'Affective variables in second language acquisition.' *Language Learning* 23:231–44. [390(n17)]

Brown, H.D. (ed.) 1976. 'Papers in second language acquisition.' Proceedings of the Sixth Annual Conference on Applied Linguistics, University of Michigan, Jan 30–Feb 1, 1975. *Language Learning* Special Issue, No 4. [111,330, Dulay and Burt 1976, Kennedy and Holmes 1976, Schumann 1976, Tarone *et al.* 1976]

Brown, H.D. 1980. *Principles of Language Learning and Teaching.* Englewood Cliffs, N.J.: Prentice-Hall. [244(n17), 334(n4), 336(n19), 387(n2), 390(n16,17,20,21), 413(n6), 475(n13), 512(n15)]

Brown, H.D. 1981. 'Affective factors in second language learning' in Alatis, Altman, and Alatis 1981:111–129. [390(n17)]

Brown, E.K. and Miller, J.E. 1980. *Syntax: A Linguistic Introduction to Sentence Structure.* London, etc.: Hutchinson. [149(n13)]

Brumfit, C.J. 1980. 'From defining to designing: communicative specifications versus communicative methodology in foreign language teaching' in Müller 1980:1–9. [268(n24)]

Brumfit, C.J. and Johnson, K. (eds.) 1979. *The Communicative Approach to Language Teaching.* Oxford: Oxford University Press. [179,258,268(n22) Morrow 1979]

Bruner, J.S. 1960/1977. *The Process of Education.* Reissued in 1977 with a new preface. Cambridge, Mass.: Harvard University Press. [308]

Bruner, J.S. 1966. *Toward a Theory of Instruction.* Cambridge, Mass.: Harvard University Press. [308]

Buchanan, M.A. 1927. *A Graded Spanish Word Book.* Toronto: University of Toronto Press. [101]

Buchanan, M.A. and MacPhee, E.D. 1928. *Modern Language Instruction in Canada.* Toronto: University of Toronto Press. [87]

Buckby, M. 1976. 'Is primary French in the balance?' *Modern Language Journal* 56:340–6. [365]

Buckby, M., Bull, P., Fletcher, R., Green, P., Page, B., and Roger, D. 1981. *Graded Objectives and Tests for Modern Languages: An Evaluation.* London: Schools Council. [513(n16)]

Budner, S. 1962. 'Intolerance of ambiguity as a personality variable.' *Journal of Personality* 39:29–50. [382]

Bühler, K. 1934. *Sprachtheorie.* Jena: Fischer. [223–4]

Bullock Report 1975. *A Language for Life.* Report of a Committee of Inquiry appointed by the Secretary of State for Education and Science under the chairmanship of Lord Bullock. London: H.M.S.O. [389(n9)]

Burstall, C. 1975. 'French in the primary school: the British experiment.' *Canadian Modern Language Review* 31:388–402. [277–8]

Burstall, C. 1975a. 'Factors affecting foreign-language learning: a consideration of some recent research findings.' *Language Teaching and Linguistics: Abstracts* 8:5–25; also in Kinsella 1978:1–21. [390(n17)]

Burstall, C., Jamieson, M., Cohen, S. and Hargreaves, M. 1974. *Primary French in the Balance.* Windsor: NFER Publishing Company. [56,59,65,69(n12), 111,270,275, 277,279,364,376,377,378,385,390(n17), 512(n14)]

Burt, M.K. and Dulay, H.C. (eds.) 1975. *New Directions in Second Language Learning, Teaching and Bilingual Education.* Selected papers from the Ninth Annual TESOL Convention, Los Angeles, March 1975. Washington, D.C.: TESOL. [330, Allwright 1975, Dulay and Burt 1976]

Burt, M.K., Dulay, H.C. and Finocchiaro M. (eds.) 1977. *Viewpoints on English as a Second Language.* New York: Regents. [Dulay and Burt 1977]

Butler, C.S. 1979. 'Recent developments in systemic linguistics.' *Language Teaching and Linguistics: Abstracts* 12:71–89. [150(n19)]

Cameron, N. 1947. *The Psychology of Behavior Disorders: A Biosocial Interpretation.*
Boston: Houghton Mifflin. [216(n 21), 294]

Campbell, R.N. 1980. Statement in a symposium on 'Toward a redefinition of applied
linguistics' in Kaplan 1980:7. [36–38]

Canada. 1967–70. *Report of the Royal Commission on Bilingualism and Biculturalism.*
6 vols. Ottawa: Queen's Printer. [244(n 16), 275,282]

Canadian Modern Language Review/Revue canadienne des langues vivantes. Until 1982,
The Journal of the Ontario Modern Language Teachers Association. Since 1982,
published independently at Welland, Ontario, Canada: 4, Oakmount Road. [69(n13)]

Canale, M. and Swain, M. 1980. 'Theoretical bases of communicative approaches to
second language teaching and testing.' *Applied Linguistics* 1:1–47. [116(n 15), 242–
3(n 6,7), 258,268(n 22), 347,349,357,358(n 5)]

Candlin, C.N. 1973. 'The status of pedagogical grammars' in Corder and Roulet
1973:55–64. [175]

Candlin, C.N., Bruton, C.J. and Leather, J.L. 1976. 'Doctors in casualty: applying
communicative competence to components of specialist course design.' *IRAL* 14:245–
72. [178,229]

Carmichael, L. (ed.) 1946. *Manual of Child Psychology.* Second edition. New York:
Wiley; London: Chapman. [MacCarthy 1946]

Carroll, B.J. 1980. *Testing Communicative Performance: An Interim Study.* Oxford:
Pergamon Press. [268(n 23), 358(n 9)]

Carroll, J.B. 1953. *The Study of Language: A Survey of Linguistics and Related
Disciplines in America.* Cambridge, Mass.: Harvard University Press.
[54,209,299,322–3]

Carroll, J.B. 1956. 'Introduction' to Whorf 1956:1–34. [215(n14)]

Carroll, J.B. 1960 'Wanted: a research basis for educational policy on foreign language
teaching.' *Harvard Educational Review* 30:128–40. [54]

Carroll, J.B. 1961/63 *Research on Teaching Foreign Languages.* Publications of the
Language Laboratory; Series Preprints and reprints: Vol III B. Ann Arbor, Mich.:
University of Michigan; also in Gage 1963:1060–100. [68(n 2,4)]

Carroll, J.B. 1964. *Language and Thought.* Englewood Cliffs, N.J.: Prentice-Hall.
[324,334(n 8)]

Carroll, J.B. 1966. 'The contributions of psychological theory and educational research
to the teaching of foreign languages' in Valdman 1966:93–106; also in Müller
1965:365–81 and *Modern Language Journal* 1965 49:273–81. [25,107,324,
394,403,463,465,469]

Carroll, J.B. 1966a. 'Research in foreign language teaching: the last five years' in Mead
1966:12–42. [68(n 4)]

Carroll, J.B. 1967. 'Research problems concerning the teaching of foreign or second
languages to younger children' in Stern 1967:94–109. [68(n 4), 269]

Carroll, J.B. 1968. 'Language testing' in Davies 1968:46–69. [349,350–1
(Figs 16.4,16.5), 357]

Carroll, J.B. 1969. 'Psychological and educational research into second language
teaching to young children' in Stern 1969:56–68. [53,269]

Carroll, J.B. 1969a. 'Modern languages' in Ebel 1969. [269(n 4)]

Carroll, J.B. 1969b. 'Guide for the collection of data pertaining to the study of foreign or
second languages by younger children' in Stern 1969:201–50 and appendixes.
[269(n 4), 70(n 16)]

Carroll, J.B. 1971. 'Current issues in psycholinguistics and second language teaching.'
TESOL Quarterly 5:101–14. [25,32(n 4), 169,329, 335(n 13), 394]

Carroll, J.B. 1974. 'Learning theory for the classroom teacher' in Jarvis 1974a:113–49.
[336(n 19), 394]

Carroll, J.B. 1975. *The Teaching of French as a Foreign Language in Eight Countries.*
[56,112,276–7,353,365–6,432–4,495(n 8), 512(n 14)]

Carroll, J.B. 1975a. 'Aptitude in second language learning' in Taggart 1975:8–23. [369,389(n 10,11,13,14)]

Carroll, J.B. 1981. 'Twenty-five years of research on foreign language aptitude' in Diller 1981:83–118. [68(n 4), 368–9,388(n 8)]

Carroll, J.B. 1981a. 'Conscious and automatic processes in language learning.' *Canadian Modern Language Review* 37:462–74. [394,404]

Carroll, J.B. and Sapon, S.M. 1959. *Modern Language Aptitude Test* (MLAT). New York: Psychological Corporation. [68(n 4), 323,369–73]

Carroll, J.B. and Sapon S. 1967. *Modern Language Aptitude Test—Elementary.* (EMLAT) New York: Psychological Corporation. [369–73]

Carton, A.S. 1971. 'Inferencing: a process in using and learning language' in Pimsleur and Quinn 1971:45–58. [403]

Catford, J.C. 1959. 'The teaching of English as a foreign language' in Quirk and Smith 1964:137–59. [22(n 1)]

Center for Applied Linguistics. 1961. *Second Language Learning as a Factor in National Development in Asia, Africa, and Latin America.* Summary statement and recommendations of an international meeting of specialists held in London, December 1960. Washington, D.C. Center for Applied Linguistics. [284(n 2)]

Centre for Contemporary European Studies, University of Sussex. 1972. *French Studies in the Secondary School.* Report of a Conference held at Brighton, 1972. Brighton: University of Sussex. [265(n 10)]

Chambers, J.K. and Trudgill, P. 1980. *Dialectology.* Cambridge: Cambridge University Press. [149(n 7)]

Chastain, K. 1969. 'The audio-lingual habit theory versus the cognitive code-learning theory: some theoretical considerations.' *IRAL* 7:97–106. [56,469]

Chastain K. 1971. *The Development of Modern Language Skills: Theory to Practice.* Philadelphia: Center for Curriculum Development. (See also Chastain 1976.) [56,169,462,477–81]

Chastain, K. 1976. *Developing Second-Language Skills: Theory to Practice.* Chicago: Rand McNally. (Second edition of Chastain, 1971) [5(n 3), 169,250,266(n 11,13), 462,469,477–479(Fig 21.1)]

Chastain, K.D. and Woerdehoff, F.J. 1968. 'A methodological study comparing the audio-lingual habit theory and the cognitive code-learning theory.' *Modern Language Journal* 52:268–79. [56,69(n 10), 463,476(n 15), 491–2]

Chaudron, C. 1977. 'A descriptive model of discourse in the corrective treatment of learners' errors.' *Language of Learning* 27:29–46. [494,496(n 12)]

Cheydleur, F.D. 1929. *French Idiom List, Based on a Running Count of 1,183,000 Words.* New York: Macmillan. [101]

Chomsky, N. 1957. *Syntactic Structures.* The Hague: Mouton. [105,141–144]

Chomsky, N. 1959. Review of *Verbal Behavior* by B.F. Skinner (New York: Appleton-Century-Crofts, 1957). *Language* 35:26–58. Reprinted with a further comment by Chomsky in Jakobovits and Miron 1967:142–71. Excerpts of the review also reprinted in Allen and van Buren 1971:136–9, 147–8. [141,298–300,307,314(n 13)]

Chomsky, N. 1965. *Aspects of the Theory of Syntax.* Cambridge, Mass.: M.I.T. Press. [129,141–3,146,218,315(n 20), 342]

Chomsky, N. 1966. 'Linguistic theory' in Mead 1966:43–9. Reprinted also in Allen and van Buren 1971:152–9 with an explanatory introduction by the editors. [108,144–6,167,173,300,327,335(n 11),463–4,465]

Chomsky, N. 1968. *Language and Mind.* New York: Harcourt Brace and World. [295,300]

Christophersen, P. 1973. *Second-Language Learning: Myth and Reality.* Harmondsworth, Middlesex: Penguin Books. [16]

Chun, J. 1979. 'A survey of research in second language acquisition' in Croft 1980:181–98. [387(n 2)]

CILT (Centre for Information on Language Teaching and Research) 1970. *Report on the Survey of Research into Spoken Language, 1968*. London: CILT. [171(n 15)]

CILT Reports and Papers No 8. 1972. *Teaching Modern Languages Across the Ability Range*. London: Centre for Information on Language Teaching and Research. [387(n 1), 447(n 10)]

Clark, H.H. and Clark, E.V. 1977. *Psychology and Language: An Introduction to Psycholinguistics*. New York: Harcourt Brace Jovanovich. [301,314(n 10,11), 315(n 20,21),342,358(n 6)]

Clark, J.L.D. 1971. *Leadership in Foreign-Language Education: The Foreign Language Teacher and Research*. New York: ERIC Clearinghouse on Languages and Linguistics/ Modern Language Association. [53,70(n 16)]

Clément, R. 1979. 'Ethnicity, Contact and Communicative Competence in a Second Language.' Paper presented at an international conference on social psychology and language at the University of Bristol. [378]

Clifford, G.J. 1978. 'Words for schools: the applications in education of the vocabulary researches of Edward L. Thorndike' in Suppes 1978:107–98. [100]

Closset, F. 1949. *Didactique des langues vivantes*. Brussels: Didier. [77,94(n 3,5), 95(n 6), 156,171(n 6)]

Cohen, A. 1975. 'Successful immersion education in North America.' *Working Papers on Bilingualism* 5:39–46. [34(n 13)]

Cohen, A. and Hosenfeld, C. 1981. 'Some uses of mentalistic data in second-language research.' *Language Learning* 31: 285–313. [313(n 1), 415(n 16)]

Coleman, A. 1929. *The Teaching of Modern Foreign Languages in the United States*. New York: Macmillan. [101,264(n 7), 460]

Coleman, A. (compiler) 1933. *An Analytical Bibliography of Modern Language Teaching, 1927–1932*. Chicago: Chicago University Press. [Fife 1933]

Collins, H.F. 1934. 'England and Wales: Modern Languages' in Percy 1934:417–28. [458]

Comenius see Keatinge 1910.

Commager, H.S. 1970. *Meet the U.S.A.: Including a Practical Guide for Academic Visitors to the United States*. Fifth edition; first edition 1945. New York: Institute of International Education. [266(n 15)]

Commission de la fonction publique du Canada. 1974–77. *Dialogue Canada*. Ottawa: Ministre des approvisionnements et services Canada. [466]

Conant, J.B. 1947. *On Understanding Science: An Historical Approach*. New Haven: Yale University Press. [33(n 6)]

Cook, V.J. 1969. 'The analogy between first- and second-language learning.' *IRAL* 7:207–16. [328]

Cook, V.J. 1977. 'Cognitive processes in second language learning.' *IRAL* 15:1–20. [397]

Cook, V.J. 1978. 'Second-language learning: a psycholinguistic perspective.' *Language Teaching and Linguistics: Abstracts* 11:73–89. [413(n 6)]

Cooke, D.A. 1974. 'The Role of Explanation in Foreign Language Instruction.' Unpublished Ph.D. thesis, University of Essex. [95(n 5)]

Cooper, R.L. 1970. 'What do we learn when we learn a language?' *TESOL Quarterly* 4:312–20. [328]

Cooper, R.L. 1980. 'Sociolinguistic surveys: the state of the art.' *Applied Linguistics* 1:113–28. [244(n 16)]

Corder, S.P. 1967. 'The significance of learners' errors.' *IRAL* 5:161–70; also in Richards 1974:19–30. [335(n 15), 336(n 16), 395–6,399]

Corder, S.P. 1973. *Introducing Applied Linguistics*. Harmondsworth, Middlesex: Penguin Books. [176(Fig 9.1)]

Corder, S.P. 1973a. 'Linguistic theory and applied linguistics' in Corder and Roulet 1973:11–19. [173–5]

Corder, S.P. 1975. 'Applied linguistics and language teaching' in Allen and Corder 1975:1–15. [50(n 1)]

Corder, S.P. 1978. 'Language-learner language' in Richards 1978:71–93. [403,413 (n 4,7,8)]

Corder, S.P. 1981. *Error Analysis and Interlanguage.* Oxford: Oxford University Press. [64,125,332,336(n 15), 354]

Corder, S.P. and Roulet, E. (eds.) 1973. *Theoretical Linguistic Models in Applied Linguistics.* 3rd AIMAV Seminar, Neuchâtel May 1972. Brussels: AIMAV, Paris: Didier. [Allen 1973, Candlin 1973, Corder 1973a, Widdowson 1979a]

Coste, D. *et al.* 1976. *Un niveau seuil.* Strasbourg: Council of Europe. [110,112,179,226,349]

Coulthard, M. 1975. 'Discourse analysis in English: a short review of the literature.' *Language Teaching and Linguistics: Abstracts* 8:73–89 also in Kinsella 1978:22–38. [149(n 17)]

Coulthard, M. 1977. *An Introduction to Discourse Analysis.* London: Longman. [149(n 17)]

Council for Cultural Co-operation of the Council of Europe. (ed.) 1963. *New Trends in Linguistic Research.* Strasbourg: Council of Europe. [Strevens 1963]

Council of Europe 1971. *Modern Language Learning in Adult Education: Linguistic Content, Means of Evaluation and their Interaction in the Teaching of and Learning of Modern Languages in Adult Education* (Rüschlikon Symposium). CCC/EES (71) 135. Strasbourg: Council of Europe. [450(n 34)]

Council of Europe 1973. *Systems Development in Adult Language Learning: A European Unit/Credit System for Modern Language Learning by Adults.* Strasbourg: Council for Cultural Cooperation of the Council of Europe. Reissued in 1980; see Trim *et al.* [Richterich 1973]

Council of Europe 1981. *Modern Languages (1971–1981).* Report presented by CDCC Project Group 4 with a résumé by J.L.M. Trim, Project Adviser. Strasbourg: Council for Cultural Co-operation of the Council of Europe. [285(n 11), Fitzpatrick 1981, Holec 1981, Trim 1981]

Cowie, A.P. (ed.) 1981. *Lexicography and its Pedagogic Applications.* Thematic issue of *Applied Linguistics* 2/3. [150(n 15)]

CREDIF: Centre de Recherche et d'Etude pour la Diffusion du Français 1961/1971. *Voix et Images de France: cours audio-visuel de français, premier degré.* First edition 1961. Première partie: livre du maître. Paris: Didier, 1971. [466,475(n 9)]

Criper, C. and Widdowson, H.G. 1975. 'Sociolinguistics and language teaching' in Allen and Corder 1975:155–217. [284(n 1)]

Croft, K. (ed.) 1980. *Readings on English as a Second Language: For Teachers and Teacher Trainees.* Second edition. Cambridge, Mass.: Winthrop. [Chun 1979, Schumann 1975, Stern 1975]

Cronbach, L.J. 1977. *Educational Psychology.* Third edition. New York: Harcourt Brace Jovanovich. [311,315(n 27)]

Crystal, D. 1971. *Linguistics.* Harmondsworth: Penguin Books. [149(n 13), 151 (n 22)]

Cummins, J. 1979. 'Cognitive/academic language proficiency, linguistic interdependence, the optimal age question and some other matters.' *Working Papers on Bilingualism* 19:197–205. [352–3, 356–7,358(n 8)]

Cummins, J. 1980. 'The cross-lingual dimensions of language proficiency: implications for bilingual education and the optimal age issue.' *TESOL Quarterly* 14:175–187. [352–3,358(n 8), 389(n 10)]

Cummins, J. 1980a. 'The construct of language proficiency in bilingual education' in Alatis 1980:81–103. [345–6(Fig 16.2),358(n 8), 389(n 10)]

Cummins, J. 1981. *Bilingualism and Minority Language Children.* Language and Literacy Series. Toronto: OISE Press. [358(n 8), 389(n 10)]

Curran, C.A. 1976. *Counseling-Learning in Second Languages*. Apple River, Ill.: Apple River Press. [109,390(n 21), 475(n 13)]

d'Anglejan, A. 1978. 'Language learning in and out of classrooms' in Richards 1978:218–37. [405,414(n 12)]

d'Anglejan, A. and Tucker, G.R. 1973. 'Sociolinguistic correlates of speech style in Quebec' in Shuy and Fasold, 1973:1–27. [237–8,284(n 5)]

Dakin, J. 1973. *The Language Laboratory and Language Learning*. London: Longman. [451(n 39)]

Darian, S.G. 1969. 'Background of modern language teaching: Sweet, Jespersen and Palmer.' *Modern Language Journal* 53:545–50. [95(n 11)]

Darian, S.G. 1972. *English as a Foreign Language: History, Development and Methods of Teaching*. Norman: University of Oklahoma Press. [94(n 3), 95(n 6)]

Darwin, C. 1877. 'A biographical sketch of an infant.' *Mind* 2:285–94. [313(n 6)]

Das Gupta, J. 1970. *Language Conflict and National Development: Group Politics and National Language Policy in India*. Berkeley: University of California Press. [236–7,244(n 15)]

Dato, D.P. (ed.) 1975. *Developmental Psycholinguistics: Theory and Applications*. Georgetown University Round Table on Languages and Linguistics. Washington, D.C.: Georgetown University Press. [Dulay and Burt 1975, Krashen 1975]

Davies, A. (ed.) 1968. *Language. Testing Symposium: A Psycholinguistic Approach* London: Oxford University Press. [Carroll 1968]

Davies, I.K. and Hartley, J. (eds.) 1972. *Contributions to an Educational Technology*. London: Butterworth. [444,451(n 39)]

Davies, R.P. 1975. *Mixed Ability Grouping: Possibilities and Experiences in the Secondary School*. London: Temple Smith. [447(n 10)]

De Francis, J. (ed.) 1951. *Report on the Second Annual Round Table on Linguistics and Language Teaching*. Monograph Series on Languages and Linguistics, No 1 (Sep. 1951) Washington, D.C.: Georgetown University Press. [68(n 7)]

Dent, H.C. 1977. *Education in England and Wales*. London: Hodder and Stoughton. [447(n 13)]

de Sauzé, E.B. 1929. *The Cleveland Plan for the Teaching of Modern Languages, with Special Reference to French*. Fifth edition 1959. Philadelphia: Winston. [100,457]

Dicks, H.V. 1950. 'Personality traits and national-socialist ideology.' *Human Relations* 3:111–54. [214(n 9)]

Diebold, A.R. Jr. 1965. 'A survey of psycholinguistic research, 1954–1964' in Osgood and Sebeok 1965:205–91. [314(n 14)]

Diller, K.C. 1970. 'Linguistic theories of language acquisition' in Hester 1970:1–32. [169]

Diller, K.C. 1971. *Generative Grammar, Structural Linguistics, and Language Teaching*. Rowley, Mass.: Newbury House. [169,469]

Diller, K.C. 1975. 'Some new trends for applied linguistics and foreign language teaching in the United States.' *TESOL Quarterly* 9:65–73. [116(n 15), 458,469,475(n 13,14)]

Diller, K.C. 1978. *The Language Teaching Controversy*. Rowley, Mass.: Newbury House. (Revised edition of Diller, 1971) [77,95(n 6), 100,146,169,458,469–71, 475(n 13), 476(n 15)]

Diller, K.C. (ed.) 1981. *Individual Differences and Universals in Language Learning Aptitude*. Rowley, Mass.: Newbury House. [Carroll 1981, Wesche 1981a]

Dinneen, F.P. 1967. *An Introduction to General Linguistics*. New York, etc.: Holt, Rinehart and Winston. [148(n 1,3), 150(n 18,20,22)]

Di Pietro, R.J. 1968. 'Contrastive analysis and the notions of deep and surface grammar' in Alatis 1968:65–80. [168]

Di Pietro, R.J. 1971. *Language Structures in Contrast*. Rowley, Mass. Newbury House. [168]

Disick, R.S. 1975. *Individualizing Language Instruction: Strategies and Methods*. New York: Harcourt Brace Jovanovich. [447(n 10)]

Dittmar, N. 1976. *Sociolinguistics: A Critical Survey of Theory and Application*. London: Arnold. [242(n 1)]

Dodge, J.W. (ed.) 1972. *Other Words, Other Worlds: Language-in-Culture*. Northeast Conference on the Teaching of Foreign Languages. Reports of the Working Committees. New York: MLA Materials Center. [266(n 15)]

Dodson, C.J. 1967. *Language Teaching and the Bilingual Method*. London: Pitman. [454]

Dodson, C.J. 1978. 'The independent evaluator's report' in Schools Council Committee for Wales 1978:47–53. [414(n 12)]

Dollard, J. and Miller, N.E. 1950. *Personality and Psychotherapy: An Analysis in Terms of Learning, Thinking and Culture*. New York: McGraw-Hill. [216(n 21)]

Dreitzel, H.P. (ed.) 1970. *Toward a Theory of Communication*. Recent Sociology, No. 2. London: Macmillan. [194]

Dulay, H.C. and Burt, M.K. 1974. 'You can't learn without goofing: an analysis of children's second language learning strategies' in Richards 1974:95–123. [336(n 16), 354,402]

Dulay, H.C and Burt, M.K. 1975. 'A new approach to discovering universals of child second language acquisition' in Dato 1975: 209–33. [336(n 16)]

Dulay, H.C. and Burt, M.K. 1976. 'Creative construction in second language learning and teaching' in Brown 1976:65–79; also in Burt and Dulay 1975:21–32. [336(n 16)]

Dulay, H.C. and Burt, M.K. 1977. 'Remarks on creativity in second language learning' in Burt, Dulay and Finocchiaro 1977:95–126. [330–1,336(n 16)]

Dunkel, H.B. 1948. *Second-Language Learning*. Boston: Ginn. [54]

Dunkin, M.J. and Biddle, B.J. 1974. *The Study of Teaching*. New York: Holt, Rinehart and Winston. [51(n 4), 498–500(Fig 22.1), 508]

Duwes, G.C. 1534. *An Introductorie for to learne to rede, to pronounce, and to speke Frenche trewly, compyled for the right high excellent and most vertuous Lady Mary of Englande, daughter to our most gracious soveraign Lorde Kyng Henry the Eight*. (taken from Lambley 1920:86) [77,85–6]

Ebel, R.L. (ed.) 1969. *Encyclopedia of Educational Research*. 4th edition. New York: Macmillan. [Carroll 1969a]

Educational Administration Abstracts. (journal) Issued jointly by the University Council for Educational Administration and the Department of Educational Administration, Texas A and M University. [447(n12)]

Eisner, E.W. and Vallance, E. (eds.) 1974. *Conflicting Conceptions of Curriculum*. Berkeley, Cal.: McCutchan. [434,436–7]

Ellegard, A. and Lindell, E. (eds.) 1970. *Direkt eller insikt?* Lund: Gleerups. [70(n 14)]

Ellison, F.P. 1969. 'The teaching of Portuguese in the past fifty years' in Walsh, 1969: 235–49. [87]

Emmans, K., Hawkins, E. and Westoby, A. 1974. *Foreign Languages in the Private Sector of Industry and Commerce*. York: Language Teaching Centre, University of York. [283]

English Language Teaching Journal (journal) Oxford: Oxford University Press [104,115(n9)]

Entwistle, N.J. 1973. *The Nature of Educational Research*. Bletchley, Bucks: Open University Press. [59,63]

Ervin, S.M. and Osgood, C.E. 1954/1965. 'Second language learning and bilingualism' in Osgood and Sebeok 1965:139–46. [298,333(n 2), 402]

Ervin-Tripp, S. 1974. 'Is second language learning like the first?' *TESOL Quarterly* 8:137–44. [366]

Ervin-Tripp, S.M. 1971. 'Sociolinguistics' in Fishman, 1971:15–91. [227]

Escher, E. 1928. 'The Direct Method of Studying Foreign Languages: A Contribution to the History of its Sources and Development.' Unpublished Ph.D. thesis, University of Chicago. [453]

Ewing, N.R. 1949–50. 'Trends in modern language teaching.' *Educational Review* 1:147–57; 2:31–42,133–44.

Eysenck, H.J. (ed.) 1970 *Readings in Extraversion-Introversion: I. Theoretical and Methodological Issues*. London: Staples Press. [380]

Fanselow, J.F. 1977. 'Beyond Rashomon: conceptualizing and describing the teaching act.' *TESOL Quarterly* 11:17–39. [493,513(n 15)]

Fearing, P. 1969. 'Non-graded foreign language classes.' *Foreign Language Annals* 2:343–7; also published as Focus Report No. 4. ERIC Focus Reports on Foreign Language Teaching. New York: MLA/ERIC Clearinghouse on the Teaching of Foreign Languages, 1969. [447(n 10)]

Ferguson, C.A. 1959. 'Diglossia.' *Word* 15:325–40. Also in Ferguson, 1971:1–26. [232,234,243(n 11)]

Ferguson, C.A. 1962. 'Background to second language problems' in Rice, 1962:1–7. [19,232]

Ferguson, C.A. 1966. 'National sociolinguistic profile formulas' in Bright 1966:309–24. [244(n 16)]

Ferguson, C.A. 1971. *Language Structure and Language Use: Essays by Charles A. Ferguson*. Selected and introduced by A.S. Dil. Stanford, Cal.: Stanford University Press. [Ferguson 1959]

Ferguson, C.A. 1975. 'Toward a characterization of English foreigner talk.' *Anthropological Linguistics* 17:1–14. [125]

Fife, R.H. (compiler) 1931. *A Summary of Reports on the Modern Foreign Languages with an Index to the Reports*. Publications of the American and Canadian Committees on Modern Languages, vol. 18. New York: Macmillan. [115(n 5), 249,264(n 7)]

Fife, R.H. 1933. 'Publications of the American and Canadian Committees on Modern Languages: a brief summary of the publications' in Coleman 1933:2–13. [115(n 5)]

Fillmore, C.J., Kempler, D. and Wang, W.S.Y. (eds.) 1979. *Individual Differences in Language Ability and Language Behavior*. New York: Academic Press. [Fillmore 1979]

Fillmore, L.W. 1979. 'Individual differences in second language acquisition' in Fillmore et al. 1979:203–28. [392]

Findlay, J.J. 1932. 'The psychology of modern language learning.' *British Journal of Educational Psychology* 2:319–31. [319–20,333(n 2)]

Finocchiaro, M. and Bonomo, M. 1973. *The Foreign Language Learner: A Guide for Teachers* New York: Regents Publishing Co. [5(n 3), 479(Fig 21.1)]

Firth, Sir Charles 1929. *Modern Languages at Oxford, 1729–1929*. London: Oxford University Press. [87]

Firth, J.R. 1957. *Papers in Linguistics: 1934–1951*. London: Oxford University Press. [209].

Fishman, J.A. 1966. 'The implications of bilingualism for language teaching and language learning' in Valdman 1966:121–32. [15]

Fishman, J.A. (ed.) 1968. *Readings in the Sociology of Language*. The Hague: Mouton. [218, Stewart 1968]

Fishman, J.A. (ed.) 1971. *Advances in the Sociology of Language* vol 1. The Hague: Mouton. [218–9, Ervin-Tripp 1971, Labov 1971]

Fishman, J.A. 1972. *The Sociology of Language: An Interdisciplinary Social Science Approach to Language in Society.* Rowley, Mass.: Newbury House. [204,206,230,235,236,238,242(n 1)]

Fishman, J.A. *et al.* 1966. *Language Loyalty in the United States.* The Hague: Mouton. [236]

Fishman, J.A., Ferguson, C.A. and Das Gupta, J. (eds.) 1968. *Language Problems of Developing Nations.* New York: Wiley. [237,244(n21), Rubin 1968]

Fisiak, J. (ed.) 1981. *Contrastive linguistics and language teaching.* Oxford: Pergamon Press. [168]

Fitzpatrick, A. 1981. 'The use of media and the construction of multimedia systems for communicative language learning.' *Council of Europe* 1981:50–55. [451(n39)]

Flanders, N.A. 1970. *Analyzing Teaching Behavior.* Reading, Mass.: Addison-Wesley. [493,495(n 10)]

Flechsig, K.H. (compiler). 1965. *Neusprachlicher Unterricht I.* Weinheim/B: Beltz. [263(n3), 264(n8), Schön 1925]

Flugel, J.C. and West, D.J. 1964. *A Hundred Years of Psychology: 1833–1933.* First edition 1933. Third edition with Part V: 1933–1963, revised by D.J. West. London: Duckworth. [313(n 5)]

Fodor, J. and Katz, J.J. (eds.) 1964. *The Structure of Language.* Englewood Cliffs, N.J.: Prentice Hall. [Harris 1952]

Foreign Language Annals (journal) Issued by the American Council on the Teaching of Foreign Languages. Hastings-on-Hudson: ACTFL. [70(n14)]

Forrester, D.L. 1975. 'Other research into the effectiveness of language laboratories' in Green 1975:5–33. [69(n 11)]

Fraenkel, G. 1969. 'A chapter in the history of language study.' *Linguistics* 53:10–29. [87,114]

France: Ministère de l'Education Nationale, 1954. *Le Français élémentaire.* Paris: Centre National de Documentation Pédagogique. See also France, 1959. [105]

France: Ministère de l'Education Nationale, 1959. *Le Français fondamental (1er degré).* New edition of *Français élémentaire.* Paris: Institut Pédagogique National. [105 (see France, 1954)]

Freud, S. 1904. *Zur Psychopathologie des Alltagslebens.* Vienna: Internationaler Psychoanalytischer Verlag. Translated into English as *Psychopathology of Everyday Life,* published in 1914. Reissued as a Pelican Book in 1938. Harmondsworth: Penguin Books. See also Strachey: 1955–64. [292,313(n8)]

Freud, S. See Strachey.

Freudenstein, R. (ed.) in press. *Multilingual Education through Compact Courses.* Oxford and Munich: Pergamon Press/Hueber Verlag. [512(n14), Stern in press]

Fries, C.C. 1945. *Teaching and Learning English as a Foreign Language.* Ann Arbor: University of Michigan Press. [158–9]

Fries, C.C. 1949. 'The Chicago Investigation.' *Language Learning* 2:89–99. [159]

Fries, C.C. 1952. *The Structure of English: An Introduction to the Construction of English Sentences.* New York: Harcourt, Brace & Co. [142,159]

Fries, C.C. 1961. 'The Bloomfield School' in Mohrmann, C., Sommerfelt, A. and Whatmough, J., 1961:196–224. [137,150(n 18)]

Frink, O. 1967. *Intensive Language Training.* Occasional Papers in Language, Literature and Linguistics Series A, 4. Athens, Ohio. [87]

Fröhlich, M. 1976. 'Case Studies of Second Language Learning.' Unpublished M.A. thesis, University of Toronto. [405–6,412]

Fucilla, J.G. 1967. *The Teaching of Italian in the United States: A Documentary History.* New Brunswick, N.J.: American Association of Teachers of Italian. [87]

Fudge, E.C. 1970. 'Phonology' in Lyons, 1970:76–95. [149(n 12)]

Fudge, E.C. 1973. *Phonology.* Harmondsworth: Penguin. [149(n 12)]

Gage, N.L. (ed.) 1963. *Handbook of Research on Teaching*. Chicago: Rand McNally. [308, Carroll 1961/1963)]

Gage, N.L. and **Berliner, D.C.** 1979. *Educational Psychology*. Second edition. Chicago: Rand McNally. [315(n 27)]

Gagné, R.M. 1975. *Essentials of Learning for Instruction*. Expanded edition. New York: Holt, Rinehart and Winston. [315(n 22)]

Gagné, R.M. 1977. *The Conditions of Learning*. Third edition. New York: Holt, Rinehart and Winston. [309,315(n 22), Ingram 1975]

Galton, F. 1883. *Inquiries into Human Faculty and its Development*. London: Macmillan. [292,313(n 7)]

Gardner, R.C. 1975. 'Motivational variables in second language learning' in Taggart 1975:45–73. [358(n 2), 383–4]

Gardner, R.C. 1979. 'Social psychological aspects of second language acquisition' in Giles and St. Clair 1979:193–220. [237,358(n 2), 375,378]

Gardner, R.C. and **Lambert, W.E.** 1972. *Attitudes and Motivation in Second Language Learning*. Rowley, Mass.: Newbury House. [375–7,390(n 17,19)]

Gardner, R.C. and **Smythe, P.C.** 1981. 'On the development of the attitude/motivation test battery.' *Canadian Modern Language Review* 37:510–25. [375]

Garfinkel, H. 1967. *Studies in Ethnomethodology*. Englewood Cliffs, N.J.: Prentice-Hall. [194,221,228]

Gattegno, C. 1972. *Teaching Foreign Languages in Schools: The Silent Way*. New York: Educational Solutions. [109,475(n 13)]

Gattegno, C. 1976. *The Common Sense of Teaching Foreign Languages*. New York: Educational Solutions. [475(n 13)]

Geissler, H. 1959. *Comenius und die Sprache*. Pädagogische Forschungen, no. 10. Heidelberg: Quelle und Meyer. [95(n 11)]

Genesee, F. 1976. 'The role of intelligence in second language learning.' *Language Learning* 26:267–80. [368]

Genesee, F. 1981. 'A comparison of early and late immersion programs.' *Canadian Journal of Behavioral Sciences* 13:115–28. [364]

Getzels, J.W., **Lipham, J.M.** and **Campbell, R.F.** 1968. *Educational Administration as a Social Process: Theory, Research, Practice*. New York: Harper and Row. [429]

Gilbert, M. 1953/1954/1955. 'The origins of the reform movement in modern language teaching in England.' *Durham Research Review* 4:1–9 (Part I); 5:9–18 (Part II); 6:1–10 (Part III). [86,98,114(n 1)]

Giles, H. (ed.) 1977. *Language, Ethnicity and Intergroup Relations*. London: Academic Press. [244(n 17), Giles *et al*. 1977, Taylor *et al*. 1977]

Giles, H., **Bourhis, R.Y.** and **Taylor, D.M.** 1977. 'Towards a theory of language in ethnic group relations' in Giles 1977:307–48. [378]

Giles, H. and **St. Clair, R.N.** (eds.) 1979. *Language and Social Psychology*. Oxford: Blackwell. [244(n 17), Gardner 1979]

Gillett, M. 1973. *Educational Technology—Toward Demystification*. Scarborough, Ont.: Prentice-Hall of Canada. [444,445,451(n 39)]

Gingras, R.C. (ed.) 1978. *Second-Language Acquisition and Foreign Language Teaching*. Arlington, Va.: Center for Applied Linguistics. [19–20, 332 Gingras 1978a, Krashen 1978, Schumann 1978]

Gingras, R.C. 1978a. 'Second-language acquisition and foreign language teaching' in Gingras 1978:88–97. [415(n 5)]

Godel, R. 1957. *Les sources manuscrites du Cours de Linguistique Générale de F. de Saussure*. Geneva and Paris: Droz and Minard. [148(n 3)]

Godel, R. 1966. 'F. de Saussure's theory of language' in Sebeok 1966: Appendix I. 479–93. [148(n 2,3)]

Goldschmidt, W. (ed.) 1959. *The Anthropology of Franz Boas*. Memoir 89, American Anthropological Association. [214(n 7)]

Goodlad, J.I., **von Stoephasius, R.** and **Klein, M.F.** 1966. *The Changing School Curriculum*. New York: Fund for the Advancement of Education. [449(n 22)]

Gorer, G. 1948. *The Americans: A Study in National Character*. London: Cresset Press. [214(n 9)]

Gorer, G. and **Rickman, J.** 1949. *The People of Great Russia: A Psychological Study*. London: Cresset Press. Also New York: Norton, 1962. [214(n 9)]

Gorman, T.P. (ed.) 1970. *Language in Education in Eastern Africa*. Nairobi, etc.: Oxford University Press. [111,244(n 16)]

Gougenheim, G., Michéa, R., Rivenc, P. and **Sauvageot, A.** 1964. *L'élaboration du français fondamental (1er degré): Etude sur l'établissement d'un vocabulaire et d'une grammaire de base*. New edition. (First edition 1956 entitled *L'élaboration du Français Elémentaire*.) Paris: Didier. [55,104,115(n 6), 171(n·14)]

Gouin, F. 1880. *L'art d'enseigner et d'étudier les langues*. Paris. Translated by Swan, H. and Betis, V. as *The Art of Teaching and Studying Languages*. London: George Philip, 1892. [78,98,152–3,170(n 1), 333(n 1), 456]

Green, P.S. (ed.) 1975. *The Language Laboratory in School: Performance and Prediction—An Account of the York Study*. Edinburgh and New York: Oliver and Boyd. [451(n 39), 492, Forrester 1975]

Green, T. (ed.) 1971. *Educational Planning in Perspective* Guildford: Futures—IPC Science and Technology Press. [448(n 14)]

Greenberg, J.H. 1968. 'Anthropology: I. The field' in Sills 1968: vol 1. 304–13. [195]

Greene, J. 1972. *Psycholinguistics: Chomsky and Psychology*. Harmondsworth: Penguin Books. [150(n 20), 301,314(n 16)]

Greene, J. 1975. *Thinking and Language*. London: Methuen. [295,313(n 3)]

Gregory, M. 1980. 'Language as a social semiotic'. The recent work of M.A.K. Halliday. Applied Linguistics 1:74–81. [150]

Grittner, F.M. 1977. *Teaching Foreign Languages*. Second edition. (First edition, 1969) New York: Harper and Row. [9(n 3), 77,95(n 10), 115(n 14), 477,479(Fig21.1)]

Gross and **Mason.** 1965. See *CREDIF* 1971.

Guberina, P. 1964. 'The audio-visual global and structural method' in Libbish 1964: 1–17. [475(n 9)]

Guiora, A.Z. 1972. 'Construct validity and transpositional research: toward an empirical study of psychoanalytic concepts.' *Comprehensive Psychiatry* 13:139–50. [381]

Guiora, A.Z., Beit-Hallahani, Brannon, R.C.L., Dull, C.Y. and **Scovel, T.** 1972. 'The effects of experimentally induced changes in ego states on pronunciation ability in a second language: an exploratory study.' *Comprehensive Psychiatry* 13:421–8. [381]

Gumperz, J.J. 1968/1977. 'The speech community' in Sills 1968: vol 9. 381–6. [214(n 5), 232]

Gumperz, J.J. and **Hymes, D.** (eds.) 1972. *Directions in Sociolinguistics: The Ethnography of Communication*. New York: Holt, Rinehart and Winston. [Hymes 1972a, Schegloff 1968]

Guntermann, G. and **Phillips, J.K.** 1981. 'Communicative course design: developing functional ability in all four skills.' *Canadian Modern Language Review* 37:329–43. [268(n 24)]

Hadow Report. 1926. *The Education of the Adolescent*, prepared by a Consultative Committee of the Board of Education. London: H.M.S.O. [435]

Hall, C.S. and **Lindzey, G.** 1970. *Theories of Personality*. Second edition. (First edition 1957) New York: John Wiley. [33(n 8), 34(n 10)]

Hall, M. and **Dennis, L.A.** (Co-chairmen) 1968. *Living and Learning: The Report of the Provincial Committee on Aims and Objectives of Education in the Schools of Ontario*. Toronto: Newton. [435]

Hall, R.B. 1947. *Area Studies: With Special Reference to their Implications for Research in the Social Sciences*. New York: Social Science Research Council. (Pamphlet No.3). [263(n 2), 265(n 10)]

Halliday, M.A.K. 1973. *Explorations in the Functions of Language.* London: Edward Arnold. [223–8]

Halliday, M.A.K., McIntosh, A. and Strevens, P. 1964. *The Linguistic Sciences and Language Teaching.* London: Longman. [22(n 1), 33(n 5), 35,107,125,138–40,164–5,167,172(n 19), 185,395,482–6,489–90,513(n 16)]

Halls, W.D. 1970. *Foreign Languages and Education in Western Europe.* London: Harrap. [115(n 7), 265(n 9), 448(n 18)]

Hamp, E. 1961. 'General linguistics—The United States in the fifties' in Mohrmann *et al.* 1961:165–95. [138]

Handschin, C.H.H. 1923. *Methods of Teaching Modern Languages.* Yonkers-on-Hudson, N.Y.: World Book Co. [155]

Hanna, G., Smith, A.H., McLean, L.D., and Stern, H.H. 1980. *Contact and Communication: An Evaluation of Bilingual Student Exchange Programs.* Toronto: OISE Press. [70(n 18), 379]

Hannerz, U. 1973. 'The second language: an anthropological view.' *TESOL Quarterly* 7:235–48. [213(n 5)]

Hans, N. 1958. *Comparative Education: A Study of Educational Factors and Traditions.* Third edition. First edition 1950. London: Routledge and Kegan Paul. [448(n 16)]

Harding, A., Page B., and Rowell, S. 1980. *Graded Objectives in Modern Languages.* London: CILT. [513(n 16)]

Harley B. (Guest editor) 1976. 'Alternative programs for teaching French as a second language in the schools of Carleton and Ottawa School Boards.' *Canadian Modern Language Review* 33: entire issue no. 2. [69(n 13)]

Harris, C.W. (ed.) 1960. *Encyclopedia of Educational Research.* Third edition. New York: Macmillan. [Birkmaier 1960, Mitzel 1960]

Harris, M. 1968. *The Rise of Anthropological Theory: A History of Theories of Culture.* New York: Crowell. [214(n 6,7)]

Harris, Z.S. 1947. *Methods in Structural Linguistics.* Chicago: Chicago University Press. Published in 1951 as *Structural Linguistics.* Chicago: Chicago University Press. [137]

Harris, Z.S. 1952. 'Discourse analysis.' *Language* 28:1–30; also in Fodor and Katz 1964:355–83. [133]

Harrison, W., Prator, C. and Tucker, G.R. 1975. *English Language Policy Survey: A Case Study in Language Planning.* Arlington, Va: Center for Applied Linguistics. [16]

Hartmann, R.R.K. and Stork, F.C. 1972. *Dictionary of Language and Linguistics.* New York: John Wiley. [1:16]

Hatch, E.M. (ed.) 1978. *Second Language Acquisition: A Book of Readings.* Rowley, Mass.: Newbury House. [332,335(n 15), 413(n6), Snow and Hoefnagel-Höhle 1978]

Hatch, E. 1978a. 'Acquisition of syntax in a second language' in Richards 1978:34–70. [355,396–7,403]

Hatch, E. and Farhady, H. 1982. *Research Design and Statistics for Applied Linguistics.* Rowley, Mass.: Newbury House.

Haugen, E. 1953. *The Norwegian Language in America: A Study in Bilingual Behaviour.* 2 vols. Philadelphia: University of Pennsylvania Press; second edition, Bloomington: Indiana University Press, 1969. [211,232]

Haugen, E. 1956. *Bilingualism in the Americas: A Bibliography and Research Guide.* Publication of the American Dialect Society, No. 26. University, Alabama: University of Alabama Press. [216(n 24)]

Haugen, E. 1966. *Language Conflict and Language Planning: The Case of Modern Norwegian.* Cambridge, Mass.: Harvard University Press. [216(n 24), 244(n 20,21)]

Haugen, E. 1966a. 'Linguistics and language planning' in Bright 1966:50–66. [239] 244(n 21)

Haugen, E. 1972. *The Ecology of Language: Essays by Einar Haugen.* Selected and introduced by A.S. Dil. Stanford, Cal.: Stanford University Press. [211]

Hawkins, E. 1981. *Modern Languages in the Curriculum.* Cambridge: Cambridge University Press. [5(n 2), 70(n 14), 148(n 4), 495(n 2), 511(n 6)]

Hawkins, E. and Perren, G.E. (eds.) 1978. *Intensive Language Teaching in Schools.* London: Centre for Information on Language Teaching and Research. [512(n14)]

Hayter, W. (Chairman) 1961. *Report of a Sub-Committee of the University Grants Committee on Oriental, Slavonic, East European and African Studies.* (The Hayter Report) London: H.M.S.O. [282]

Heidelberger Forschungsprojekt 'Pidgin-Deutsch' 1979. 'The acquisition of German syntax by foreign migrant workers' in Sankoff 1979:1–22. [340,392]

Heinle, C.H., Coulombe, R. and Smith, F.S. (Project Development Staff) 1974. *Voix et Visages de la France.* Chicago: Rand McNally. 35–53. [466]

Henderson, E.J.A. 1971. 'Phonology' in Minnis 1971. [149(n12)]

Henmon, V.A.C. 1929. *Achievement Tests in the Modern Foreign Languages.* Prepared for the Modern Foreign Language Study and the Canadian Committee on Modern Languages. New York: Macmillan. [101,333(n3)]

Henning, C.A. (ed.) 1977. *Proceedings of the Los Angeles Second Language Acquisition Forum* ESL Section. Los Angeles, Cal.: University of California at Los Angeles. [Swain 1977]

Hester, R. (ed.) 1970. *Teaching a Living Language.* New York: Harper and Row. [458,469, Diller 1970]

Hilgard, E.R. 1948. *Theories of Learning.* New York: Appleton-Century-Crofts. [404]

Hilgard, E.R. and Bower, G.H. 1975. *Theories of Learning.* Englewood Cliffs, N.J.: Prentice Hall. [315(n22,24)]

Hill, A.A. 1958. *Introduction to Linguistic Structures: From Sound to Sentence in English.* New York: Harcourt Brace. [137]

Hill, B. 1981. 'Some applications of media technology to the teaching and learning of languages.' *Language Teaching and Linguistics: Abstracts* 14:147–61. [451(n39)]

Hill, W.F. 1977. *Learning: A Survey of Psychological Interpretations.* Third edition (First and second editions: 1963, 1971). New York: Crowell. [315(n22)]

Hirst, P.H. 1966. 'Philosophy and educational theory' in Scheffler 1966:78–95. [26]

Hirst, P.H. and Peters, R.S. 1970. *The Logic of Education.* London: Routledge and Kegan Paul. [22]

H.M.I. Series 1977. *Modern Languages in Comprehensive Schools.* Matters for discussion, no. 3. London: H.M.S.O. [116(n15)]

Hoijer, H. 1964. 'Cultural implications of some Navaho linguistic categories' in Hymes, 1964: 142–60. [206,215(n15)]

Holec, H. 1980. *Autonomy and Foreign Language Learning.* Strasbourg: Council of Europe; also Oxford: Pergamon Press, 1981. [513(n15)]

Holec, H. 1981. 'Learner autonomy and language learning' in Council of Europe 1981:66–74. [513(n15)]

Holland, J.G. and Skinner, B.F. 1961. *The Analysis of Behavior.* New York: McGraw-Hill. [305]

Holmes, B. 1979. *International Guide to Education Systems.* Paris: UNESCO. [448(n17)]

Holmes B. 1980. *International Yearbook of Education.* Vol. 32. Paris: UNESCO. [448(n17)]

Holmes, G. and Kidd, M.E. 1982. 'Second-language learning and computers.' *Canadian Modern Language Review* 38:503–16. [451(n39)]

Hörmann, H. 1979. *Psycholinguistics: An Introduction to Research and Theory.* New York: Springer Verlag. Second edition of translation by H.H. Stern and P. Lepmann. [314(n12), 315(n21)]

Hornby, A.S. (with the assistance of A.P. Cowie and J.W. Lewis) 1974. *Oxford Advanced Learner's Dictionary of Current English.* London: Oxford University Press. [149(n15)]

Hornsey, A.W. (ed.) 1975. *Handbook for Modern Language Teachers.* London: Methuen. [5(n3), 479(Fig21.1.)]

Hosenfeld, C. 1975. 'The new student role: individual differences and implications for instruction' in Jarvis 1975:129–67. [406]

Hosenfeld, C. 1979. 'Cora's view of learning grammar.' *Canadian Modern Language Review* 35:602–7. [65, 406]

Howatt, A.P.R. 1969. *Programmed Learning and the Language Teacher*. London: Longman. [451(n 39)]

Hsu, F.L.K. 1969. *The Study of Literate Civilizations*. In series (edited by G. and L. Spindler) 'Studies in Anthropological Method'. New York: Holt, Rinehart and Winston. [266(n 15)]

Hübner, W. 1925. 'Kulturkunde im neusprachlichen Unterricht.' *Die Neueren Sprachen* 33:161–75. [263(n 5)]

Hudson, R.A. 1980. *Sociolinguistics*. Cambridge: Cambridge University Press. [148(n 6), 217(n 26), 238, 242(n 1,2), 243(n 10), 244(n 17), 284(n 4)]

Huse, H.R. 1931. *The Psychology of Foreign Language Study*. Chapel Hill: University of North Carolina Press. [319,322]

Husén, T. 1967. *International Study of Achievement in Mathematics: A Comparison of Twelve Countries*. Vols. I and II. Stockholm: Almqvist and Wiksell; and New York: Wiley. [432]

Hymes, D. (ed.) 1964. *Language in Culture and Society: A Reader in Linguistics and Anthropology*. New York: Harper and Row. [202,215(n12,13,15), 218, Bernstein 1964, Boas 1964, Hoijer 1964]

Hymes, D. 1972. 'On communicative competence' in Pride and Holmes 1972:269–93. [111,146,221,229]

Hymes, D. 1972a. 'Models of the interaction of language and social life' in Gumperz and Hymes 1972:35–71. [221–8]

IAAM see Incorporated Association of Assistant Masters, etc.

Illich, I. 1971. *Deschooling Society*. New York: Harper and Row. (Also Harmondsworth, Middlesex: Penguin Books, 1973.) [21]

Incorporated Association of Assistant Masters in Secondary Schools, 1929. *Memorandum on the Teaching of Modern Languages*. London: University of London Press. [99,101,155,170(n 3), 248–9,264–5(n 9), 458]

Incorporated Association of Assistant Masters in Secondary Schools, 1949. *The Teaching of Modern Languages*. London: University of London Press. [101,170(n 3), 264–5(n 9)]

Incorporated Association of Assistant Masters in Secondary Schools, 1956. *The Teaching of Modern Languages*. Revised edition. London: University of London Press. [101,170(n 3), 264–5(n 9)]

Incorporated Association of Assistant Masters in Secondary Schools, 1967. *The Teaching of Modern Languages*. Fourth edition. London: University of London Press. [101,264–5(n 9)]

Individualizing instruction in foreign languages. 1975. A series of articles based on a conference symposium. *Modern Language Journal* 59:323–66. [387(n 1)]

Ingram, D.E. 1980. 'Applied linguistics: a search for insight' in Kaplan 1980:37–56. [38,41]

Ingram, E. 1975. 'Psychology and language learning' in Allen and Corder 1975:218–90. [70(n 14), 315(n 26), 336(n 19), 394]

Ingram, S.R. and Mace, J.C. 1959. 'An audio-visual French course.' *Modern Languages* 40:139–43. [106]

Inkeles, A and Levinson, D.J. 1969. 'National character: the study of modal personality and sociocultural systems' in Lindzey and Aronson, 4:418–506. [214(n 10)]

Interlanguage Studies Bulletin (journal). Utrecht: University of Utrecht [335(n14)]

Ituen, S. 1980. 'Societal Needs and Expectations for the Teaching of International

Languages: A Case Study of French in Nigeria and English in Ivory Coast.' Unpublished Ph.D. thesis, University of Toronto. [244(n 16), 448(n 19)]

Jackson, B. 1964. *Streaming: An Educational System in Miniature*. London: Routledge and Kegan Paul. [447(n 10)]

Jakobovits, L.A. 1968. 'Implications of recent psycholinguistic developments for the teaching of a second language.' *Language Learning* 18:89–109; also in Jakobovits 1970: Chapter 1. [328,336(n 19)]

Jakobovits, L.A. 1970. *Foreign Language Learning: A Psycholinguistic Analysis of the Issues*. Rowley, Mass.: Newbury House. [38,328,335(n 12), Mackey 1970]

Jakobovits, L.A. and Miron, M.S. (eds.) 1967. *Readings in the Psychology of Language*. Englewood Cliffs, N.J.: Prentice-Hall. [314(n 13), Chomsky 1959]

Jakobson, R. 1960. 'Closing statement: linguistics and poetics' in Sebeok, 1960:353–7. Extracts also in Allen and Corder, 1973:53–7. [221,223–8]

James, C. 1980. *Contrastive Analysis*. London: Longman. [168]

James, C.V. and Rouve, S. 1973. *Survey of Curricula and Performance in Modern Languages 1971–72*. London: Centre for Information on Language Teaching and Research. [283]

Jarvis, G.A. 1968. 'A behavioral observation system for classroom foreign language skill acquisition activities.' *Modern Language Journal* 52:335–41. [496(n 11)]

Jarvis, G.A. (ed.) 1974. *Responding to New Realities*. The ACTFL Review of Foreign Language Education, No. 5. Skokie, Ill.: National Textbook Company and American Council on the Teaching of Foreign Languages. [252, Nostrand 1974]

Jarvis, G.A. (ed.) 1974a. *The Challenge of Communication*. ACTFL Review of Foreign Language Education, No. 6. Skokie, Ill.: National Textbook Company. [Carroll 1974]

Jarvis, G.A. (ed.) 1975. *Perspective: A New Freedom*. ACTFL Review of Foreign Language Education, No. 7. Skokie, Ill.: National Textbook Company. [406, Hosenfeld 1975]

Jernudd, B.H. 1973. 'Language planning as a type of language treatment' in Rubin and Shuy 1973:11–23. [245(n 21)]

Jernudd, B.H. and Das Gupta, J. 1971. 'Towards a theory of language planning' in Rubin and Jernudd, 1971:195–215. [238]

Jespersen, O. 1904. *How to Teach a Foreign Language*. London: Allen and Unwin. Translated from the Danish original *Sprogundervisning* by S. Yhlen-Olsen Bertelsen. [51(n 6), 88,91,99]

Johnson, F.C. 1969. 'The failure of the discipline of linguistics in language teaching.' *Language Learning* 19:235–44. [173]

Johnson, K. 1977. 'The adoption of functional syllabuses for general language teaching courses.' *Canadian Modern Language Review* 33:667–80. [260,268(n 24)]

Johnson, M. Jr. 1967. 'Definitions and models in curriculum theory.' *Educational Theory* 17:127–40. [438]

Jones, R.L. and Spolsky, B. (eds.) 1975. *Testing Language Proficiency*. Arlington, Va.: Center for Applied Linguistics. [Wilds 1975]

Joos, M. 1961. *The Five Clocks: A Linguistic Excursion in the Five Styles of English Usage*. New York: Harcourt, Brace and World. [125]

Journal of Multilingual and Multicultural Development. (journal) Clevedon, U.K.: Tieto. [112,335(n14)]

Jump, J.R. 1961. 'Two hundred years of Spanish grammars.' *Modern Languages* 42:24–6. [87]

Jung, C.G. 1918. *Studies in Word-Association*. Translated by M.D. Eder. London: Heinemann. Re-issued in 1969 by Routledge and Kegan Paul, London. Also in Vol. 2 of *The Collected Works of C.G. Jung*, edited by H. Read *et al.*, 1973, London: Routledge and Kegan Paul. [292]

Kaplan, R.B. (ed.) 1980. *On the Scope of Applied Linguistics.* Rowley, Mass.: Newbury House. [36, Campbell 1980, Ingram 1980, Spolsky 1980]

Kari, J. and **Spolsky, B.** 1973. *Trends in the Study of Athapaskan Language Maintenance and Bilingualism.* Navaho Reading Study Progress Report, No. 21. Albuquerque: University of New Mexico. [243(n 13)]

Katz, J.J. 1966. *The Philosophy of Language.* New York: Harper and Row. [315 (n 20)]

Keating, R.F. 1963. *A Study of the Effectiveness of Language Laboratories.* (The Keating Report) New York: Columbia University Teachers College, Institute of Administrative Research. [69(n 11), 106,443,492]

Keatinge, M.W. (translator) 1910. *The Great Didactic of John Amos Comenius.* Translated into English and edited with biographical, historical and critical introductions. Second edition. First edition 1896. Reissued from the 1910 edition. New York: Russell and Russell. [94(n5)]

Kelly, A.V. (ed.) 1975. *Case Studies in Mixed Ability Teaching.* London: Harper and Row. [447(n 10)]

Kelly, L.G. 1969. *25 Centuries of Language Teaching.* Rowley, Mass.: Newbury House. [1,80–3,98,452–3]

Kelly, L.G. 1971. 'English as a second language: an historical sketch.' *English Language Teaching* 25:120–32. [87]

Kennedy, G. and **Holmes, J.** 1976. Discussion of 'Creative construction in second language learning and teaching' in Brown 1976:81–92. (See also Dulay and Burt 1976.) [336(n 16)]

King, E.J. 1973. *Other Schools and Ours.* Fourth edition. London: Holt, Rinehart and Winston. [448(n 17)]

Kinsella, V. (ed.) 1978. *Language Teaching and Linguistics: Surveys.* London, etc.: Cambridge University Press. [Burstall 1975a, Coulthard 1975, Le Page 1975, Stern and Weinrib 1977, Strevens 1977a]

Kloss, H. 1966. 'Types of multilingual communities: a discussion of ten variables.' *Sociological Inquiry* 36:135–45. [266]

Kneller, G.F. 1971. *Introduction to the Philosophy of Education.* Second edition. (First edition, 1964) New York: Wiley.

Koordinierungsgremium im DFG—Schwerpunkt 'Sprachlehrforschung' (ed.) 1977. *Sprachlehr- und Sprachlernforschung.* Kronberg, Ts: Scriptor. 4:[70(n 16)]

Krashen, S.D. 1973. 'Lateralization, language learning, and the critical period: some new evidence.' *Language Learning* 23:63–74. [362]

Krashen, S.D. 1975. 'The development of cerebral dominance and language learning: more new evidence' in Dato 1975:179–92. [362]

Krashen, S.D. 1978. 'The monitor model for second language acquisition' in Gingras 1978:1–26. [311, 336(n 17)]

Krashen, S.D. 1981. *Second Language Acquisition and Second Language Learning.* Oxford, etc.: Pergamon. [331,336(n 17), 362, 363, 388(n 7), 391(n 7), 404,412(n 2)]

Krashen, S.D. 1981a. 'Effective second language acquisition: insights from research' in Alatis, Altman, and Alatis 1981:95–109. [390(n17)]

Krashen, S.D., Long, M.A. and **Scarcella, R.C.** 1979. 'Age, rate and eventual attainment in second language acquisition.' *TESOL Quarterly* 13:573–82. [366,387(n 2)]

Krashen, S.D. and **Seliger, H.** 1975. 'The essential contribution of formal instruction in adult second language learning.' *TESOL Quarterly* 9:173–83. [336(n 17), 488– 90, 497, 511(n 8), 512(n 11,12,13,15), 513(n 16)]

Krathwohl, D.R., Bloom, B.S. and **Masia, B.B.** 1964. *Taxonomy of Educational Objectives: The Classsification of Educational Goals.* Handbook 2: *Affective Domain.* New York: McKay. [438]

Kreidler, C.W. (ed.) 1965. *Report of the Sixteenth Annual Round Table Meeting on Linguistics and Language Studies.* Georgetown University Monograph Series on

Languages and Linguistics, No. 18. Washington, D.C.: Georgetown University Press. [Mackey 1965a]

Kress, G. (ed.) 1976. *Halliday: System and Function in Language.* Selected papers. London: Oxford University Press. [140,150(n 19)]

Kroeber, A.L. and Kluckhohn, C. 1952. *Culture: A Critical Review of Concepts and Definitions.* Papers of the Peabody Museum of American Archaeology and Ethnology, 47/1. Cambridge Mass.: Harvard University. Reissued in Vintage Books. New York: Random House, 1963. [214(n 10), 247,263(n 3)]

Labov, W. 1971. 'The study of language in its social context' in Fishman 1971:152–216. [219]

Labov, W. 1972. *Sociolinguistic Patterns.* Philadelphia: University of Pennsylvania Press, Oxford: Blackwell. [219]

Labov, W. and Fanshel, D. 1977. *Therapeutic Discourse: Psychotherapy as Conversation.* New York, San Francisco and London: Academic Press. [179,229]

Ladefoged, P., Glick, R. and Criper, C. 1972. *Language in Uganda.* London: Oxford University Press. [244(n16)]

Lado, R. 1957. *Linguistics Across Cultures: Applied Linguistics for Language Teachers.* Ann Arbor: University of Michigan Press. [105,159,168,266(n 11), 395]

Lado, R. 1961. *Language Testing: The Construction and Use of Foreign Language Tests.* London: Longman; also New York: McGraw-Hill, 1964. [163,316(n 30)]

Lado, R. 1964. *Language Teaching: A Scientific Approach.* New York: McGraw-Hill. [77,168,171(n 12), 266(n 11), 462, 477, 478, 479(Fig 21.1), 490(n 60)]

Lafayette, R.C. 1978. *Teaching Culture: Strategies and Techniques.* Washington, D.C.:ERIC Clearinghouse on Languages and Linguistics, Center for Applied Linguistics. [263(n 2)]

Laforge, L. 1972. *La sélection en didactique analytique.* Québec: Les Presses de l'Université Laval. [495(n 5)]

Lambert, W.E. 1963. 'Psychological approaches to the study of language. Part I: On learning, thinking and human abilities.' *Modern Language Journal* 47:51–62. [324,334(n 7,8)]

Lambert, W.E. 1963a. 'Psychological approaches to the study of language. Part II: On second language learning and bilingualism.' *Modern Language Journal* 47:114–21. [324,334(n 7,8)]

Lambert, W.E. 1975. 'Culture and language as factors in learning and education' in Wolfgang 1975:55–83. [378]

Lambert, W.E. and Tucker, G.R. 1972. *Bilingual Education of Children: The St. Lambert Experiment.* Rowley, Mass.: Newbury House. [69(n 13), 107,111,364]

Lambley, K. 1920. *The Teaching and Cultivation of the French Language in England during Tudor and Stuart Times.* With an introductory chapter on the preceding period. Manchester: Manchester University Press; London: Longman. [84,95(n 9)]

Lamendella, J.T. 1969. 'On the irrelevance of transformational grammar to second language pedagogy.' *Language Learning* 19:255–70. [173]

Langacker, R.W. 1972. *Fundamentals of Linguistic Analysis.* New York, etc.: Harcourt Brace Jovanovich. [126,149(n 8)]

Langacker, R.W. 1973. *Language and its Structure: Some Fundamental Linguistic Concepts.* Second edition. New York: Harcourt Brace Jovanovich. [151(n 22)]

Language and Language Behavior Abstracts (journal) San Diego, Cal.: Sociological Abstracts, Inc. [71(n 24)]

Language Learning: A Journal of Applied Linguistics. Ann Arbor, Michigan: University of Michigan. [104,115(n 10), 159,330]

Language Planning Newsletter. Honolulu, Hawaii: East-West Culture Learning Institute, East-West Center. [244(n 19)]

Language Problems and Language Planning (journal) Austin Texas: University of Texas Press. [244(n 19)]

Language Teaching: The International Abstracting Journal for Language Teachers and Applied Linguistics. (formerly, *Language Teaching and Linguistics: Abstracts*.) Issued by the Centre for Information on Language Teaching and Research, London. Cambridge: Cambridge University Press. [71(n 24)]

Larson, D.N. and **Smalley, W.A.** 1972. *Becoming Bilingual: A Guide to Language Learning*. New Canaan, Conn.: Practical Anthropology. [382,390(n 17), 398,399]

Lawrence, E. 1970. *The Origins and Growth of Modern Education*. Harmondsworth: Penguin. [447(n 6)]

Lawton, D. 1968. *Social Class, Language, and Education*. London: Routledge and Kegan Paul. [217(n 26)]

Leavitt, S.E. 1969. 'A history of the teaching of Spanish in the United States' in Walsh 1969:222–34. [87]

Lee, V. 1973. *Social Relationships and Language: Some Aspects of the Work of Basil Bernstein*. Walton Hall, Bletchley: Open University Press. [217(n 26)]

Lee, W.R. 1971. 'Ten years of the teaching of English as a foreign language.' *English Language Teaching* 26:3–13. [87]

Leech, G. 1974. *Semantics*. Harmondsworth: Penguin Books. [150(n 16), 150(n 21).

Leedham, J. 1973. *Educational Technology: A First Look*. Bath: Pitman. [444,451(n 39)]

Legge, D. 1975. *An Introduction to Psychological Science: Basic Processes in the Analysis of Behaviour*. London: Methuen. [313(n 3)]

Le Maître Phonétique (journal) Published by the International Phonetic Association from 1886–1970. Since 1971: *Journal of the International Phonetic Association* [99,114(n 3)]

Lenneberg, E.H. 1967. *Biological Foundations of Language*. New York: Wiley. [302,314(n 10), 362]

Léon, P.R. 1962. *Laboratoire de Langues et Correction Phonétique: essai methodologique*. Publication du Centre de Linguistique Appliquée de Besançon. Paris: Didier. [87,450(n 37)]

Leopold, W.F. 1939–49. *Speech Development of a Bilingual Child: A Linguist's Record*. Vol. 1. *Vocabulary Growth in the First Two Years*. 1939; Vol. 2 *Sound Learning in the First Two Years*. 1947; Vol. 3 *Grammar and General Problems in the First Two Years*. 1949; Vol. 4 *Diary From Age Two*. 1949a. Evanstown, Ill.: Northwestern University Press. [314(n 19), 413(n 6)]

Le Page, R.B. 1975. 'Sociolinguistics and the problem of competence.' *Language Teaching and Linguistics: Abstracts* 8:137–56. Also in Kinsella 1978:39–59. [242(n 1)]

Lester, M. (ed.) 1970. *Readings in Applied Transformational Grammar*. New York: Holt, Rinehart and Winston. [Newmark 1966]

Levenston, E.A. 1973 Teaching indirect object structures in English: a case study in applied linguistics. (mimeo) [174]

Levenston, E.A. 1975. 'Aspects of testing oral proficiency of adult immigrants to Canada' in Palmer and Spolsky 1975:66–74. [260]

Levenston, E.A. 1979. 'Second language lexical acquisition: issues and problems.' *Interlanguage Studies Bulletin* 4:147–60. [150(n 14)]

Levie, W.H. and **Dickie, K.E.** 1973. 'The analysis and application of media' in Travers 1973:858–82. [451(n 39)]

Levin, L. 1969. *Implicit and Explicit: A Synopsis of Three Parallel Experiments in Applied Psycholinguistics*. Gothenburg (Sweden): Department of Educational Research, Gothenburg School of Education, University of Gothenburg. Research Bulletin No. 1. [403]

Levin, L. 1972. *Comparative Studies in Foreign Language Teaching*: The GUME *Project*. Stockholm: Almqvist and Wiksell. [56,69(n 10), 463,476(n 15)]

Lewin, K., Lippitt, R. and White, R. 1939. 'Patterns of aggressive behaviour in experimentally created "social climates".' *Journal of Social Psychology* 1939:271–99; also in Amidon and Hough 1967:24–46. [496(n 10)]

Lewis, E.G. 1962. *Foreign and Second Language Teaching in the USSR*. London: ETIC/ The British Council. [448(n 18)]

Lewis, E.G. and Massad, C.E. 1975. *The Teaching of English as a Foreign Language in Ten Countries*. New York: Wiley. [56,112,280,353,433–4,495(n 8)]

Lewis, L.J. and Loveridge, A.J. 1965. *The Management of Education*: A Guide for *Teachers to the Problems of New and Developing Systems*. New York: Praeger. [447(n 13)]

Lewis, M.M. 1936. *Infant Speech: A Study of the Beginnings of Language*. Second edition 1951. London: Routledge and Kegan Paul. [302]

Lewis, M.M. 1947. *Language in Society*. London: Nelson. [210,216(n 22)]

Lewy, A. (ed.) 1977. *Handbook of Curriculum Evaluation*. Paris: UNESCO; and New York: Longman. [450(n 33)]

Libbish, B. (ed.) 1964. *Advances in the Teaching of Modern Languages*. Vol. 1. Oxford: Pergamon Press. [Guberina 1964, Stack 1964]

Lind, M. 1948. 'Modern language learning: the intensive course as sponsored by the United States Army and implications for the undergraduate course of study.' *Genetic Psychology Monographs* 38:3–82. [87,104]

Lindzey, G. and Aronson, E. (eds.) 1969. *The Handbook of Social Psychology*. 5 vols. Second edition. Reading, Mass.: Addison-Wesley. [Inkeles and Levinson 1969]

Lindzey, G., Hall, C. and Thompson, R.F. 1975. *Psychology*. New York: Worth Publishers. [313(n 3,4)]

Linguistic Reporter (journal) Washington D.C.: Center for Applied Linguistics. [68(n7), 106]

Littlewood, W. 1981. *Communicative Language Teaching: An Introduction*. Cambridge: Cambridge University Press. [179,268(n 22)]

Locke, J. 1693. *Some Thoughts Concerning Education*. London. Available in: (1) edition by Quick, R.H. 1880. London: Cambridge University Press. Second edition, 1889. (2) abridged and edited by Garforth, F.W. 1964. London: Heinemann (for language pedagogy see pp 194–208). (3) Axtell 1968. [78]

Long, M.H. 1980. 'Inside the "black box": methodological issues in classroom research on language learning.' *Language Learning* 30:1–42. [495(n9)]

Lozanov, G. 1979. *Suggestology and Outlines of Suggestopedy*. New York: Gordon and Breach, Science Publishers. [475(n 13)]

Lugton, R.C. and Heinle, C.H. (eds.) 1971. *Toward a Cognitive Approach to Second-Language Acquisition*. Language and the Teacher: A Series in Applied Linguistics, No.17. Philadelphia, Pa: Center for Curriculum Development. [Bosco and Di Pietro 1970]

Luria, M.A. and Orleans, J.S. 1928. *Luria-Orleans Modern Language Prognosis Test*. Yonkers, N.Y.: World Book Company. [333(n 3)]

Lynd, R.S. and Lynd, H.M. 1929. *Middletown: A Study in American Culture*. New York: Harcourt Brace. Also New York: Harcourt, Brace and World, 1956. [193,213(n 3)]

Lynd, R.S. and Lynd, H.M. 1937. *Middletown in Transition: A Study in Cultural Conflicts*. New York: Harcourt Brace. [193]

Lyons, J. 1968. *Introduction to Theoretical Linguistics*. Cambridge: Cambridge University Press. [123,126,151(n 22)]

Lyons, J. (ed.) 1970. *New Horizons in Linguistics*. Harmondsworth: Penguin Books. [Bierwisch 1970, Fudge 1970, Matthews 1970, 124]

Lyons, J. 1971. 'Structural organization of language 2: grammar' in Minnis 1971:55–74. [131,149(n 13)]

Lyons, J. 1977. *Semantics*. London and New York: Cambridge University Press. [132]

Lyons, J. 1977a. *Chomsky*. Fontana Modern Masters Series. London: Fontana/Collins. First edition 1970. [140,150(n 20)]

Lyons, J. 1981. *Language and Linguistics: An Introduction*. Cambridge: Cambridge University Press. [149(n 7,12,13), 150(n 16), 151(n 22)]

Lyons, J. and Wales, R.J. (eds.) 1966. *Psycholinguistics Papers: The Proceedings of the 1966 Edinburgh Conference*. Edinburgh: Edinburgh University Press. [McNeill 1966a, 315(n 20)]

McCarthy, D. 1946. 'Language development in children' in Carmichael 1946:492–630. [293]

McDonough, S.H. 1981. *Psychology in Foreign Language Teaching*. London: Allen and Unwin. [390(n 16,17,20), 336(n 19)]

McEwen, N.Z. 1976. 'An Exploratory Study of the Multidimensional Nature of Teacher-Student Verbal Interaction in Second Language Classroom.' Unpublished Ph.D. thesis. University of Alberta. [496(n 12)]

Mackey, W.F. 1950. 'The meaning of method.' *English Language Teaching* 5:4–10, 495(n 3).

Mackey, W.F. 1953. 'What to look for in a method: selection.' *English Language Teaching* 7:77–85. [495(n 3)]

Mackey, W.F. 1954. 'What to look for in a method: grading.' *English Language Teaching* 8:45–58. [495(n 3)]

Mackey, W.F. 1955. 'What to look for in a method: presentation.' *English Language Teaching* 9:41–56. [495(n 3)]

Mackey, W.F. 1965. *Language Teaching Analysis*. London: Longman. [33(n 5), 35,68(n 6), 78–80,107,164–6,167,185,395,441–2,482–5,490,495(n 3), 513(n 16)]

Mackey, W.F. 1965a. 'Method Analysis: a survey of its development, principles and techniques' in Kreidler 1965:149–62. [495(n 3), 513(n 16)]

Mackey, W.F. 1970. 'A typology of bilingual education.' *Foreign Language Annals* 3:596–608. Also in Andersson and Boyer 1970:63–82; Mackey 1972, Appendix D:149–71; see also Mackey 1976: Chapters 6 and 7. [271–5]

Mackey, W.F. 1970a. Foreword to Jakobovits 1970:vii–xiii. [39]

Mackey, W.F. 1972. *Bilingual Education and a Binational School*. Rowley, Mass.: Newbury House. [Mackey 1970]

Mackey, W.F. 1976. *Bilinguisme et contact des langues*. Paris: Editions Klincksieck. [Mackey 1970]

Mackey, W.F. 1978. 'Organizing research on bilingualism: the IRCB story.' *McGill Journal of Education* 13:116–27. [69(n 9)]

Mackey, W.F., Savard, J.G. and Ardouin, P. 1971. *Le vocabulaire disponible du français*. Paris: Didier. [495(n 5)]

McLaughlin, B. 1978. *Second-Language Acquisition in Childhood*. Hillsdale, N.J.: Lawrence Erlbaum Associates, and New York: Wiley. [298,303,315(n 20), 332,387(n 2), 413(n6)]

McLaughlin, B. 1978a. 'The Monitor Model: some methodological considerations.' *Language Learning* 28:309–32. [414(n 11)]

Maclay, H. 1971. 'Linguistics: overview' in Steinberg and Jakobovits 1971:157–82. [150(n 21)]

Macnamara, J. 1966. *Bilingualism and Primary Education: A Study of Irish Experience*. Edinburgh: Edinburgh University Press. [14]

Macnamara, J. 1967. 'The bilingual's linguistic performance: a psychological overview.' *Journal of Social Issues* 23:58–77. [298]

Macnamara, J. 1973. 'Nurseries, streets and classrooms: some comparisons and deductions.' *Modern Language Journal* 57:250–4. [506,513(n 16)]

McNeill, D. 1966a. 'The creation of language by children' (with prepared comments by C. Fraser and M. Donaldson) in Lyons and Wales 1966:99–132. [315(n 20)]

McNeill, D. 1966. 'Developmental psycholinguistics' in Smith and Miller 1966:15–84. [315(n20)]

Malinowski, B. 1923. 'The problem of meaning in primitive languages' in Ogden and Richards 1923:451–510 (or 1946:296–336). [207–9,216(n 22), 223]

Malinowski, B. 1935. *Coral Gardens and their Magic.* London: Allen and Unwin. [138]

Mallinson, V. 1953. *Teaching a Modern Language.* London: Heinemann. [77,94(n 3,5)]

Mallinson, V. 1975. *An Introduction to the Study of Comparative Education.* Fourth edition. First edition 1957. London: Heinemann. [448(n 17)]

Marckwardt, A.H. 1963. 'English as a second language or English as a foreign language.' *PMLA* 78:25–8. [16]

Marckwardt, A.H. 1967. 'Teaching English as a foreign language: a survey of the past decade.' *Linguistic Reporter* 9/5: Supplement 19. [87]

Maréchal, R. 1972. *Histoire de l'enseignement et de la méthodologie des langues vivantes en Belgique des origines au début du 20e siècle.* Paris: Didier. [84,87,97]

Mareschal, R. 1977. 'Normes linguistiques: détermination, description, contenu, utilité.' *Canadian Modern Language Review* 33:620–31. [358(n 9)]

Martin-Gamero, S. 1961. *La Enseñanza del Inglés en España* (desde la edad media hasta el siglo XIX). Madrid: Editorial Gredos. [87]

Mason, E.J. and Bramble, W.J. 1978. *Understanding and Conducting Research*: *Applications in Education and the Behavioral Sciences.* New York: McGraw-Hill. [63]

Matthews, P.H. 1970. 'Recent developments in morphology' in Lyons 1970:96–114. [149(n 13)]

Mead, G.H. 1934. *Mind, Self and Society: From the Standpoint of a Social Behaviorist.* Chicago: University of Chicago Press. [209]

Mead, M. 1928. *Coming of Age in Samoa.* New York: Morrow. [198]

Mead, M. 1930. *Growing Up in New Guinea.* New York: Blue Ribbon. [198]

Mead, M. 1935. *Sex and Temperament in Three Primitive Societies.* New York: Morrow. [198]

Mead, R.G., Jr. (ed.) 1966. *Language Teaching: Broader Contexts. Northeast Conference on the Teaching of Foreign Languages: Reports of the Working Committees.* New York: MLA Materials Center. [108,335(n 11), Carroll 1966a, Chomsky 1966]

Meidinger, J.V. 1783. *Praktische französische Grammatik.* Liège. [453]

Merkley, D. 1977. *French Vocabulary: A Curriculum Aid.* Aurora, Ontario, Canada: York County Board of Education. [61]

Miller, G.A. and Buckhout, R. 1973. *Psychology: The Science of Mental Life.* New York: Harper and Row. [313,(n 4)]

Miller, G.A., Galanter, E. and Pribram, K.H. 1960. *Plans and the Structure of Behavior.* New York: Holt. [314(n 15)]

Mills, C.W. 1959. *The Sociological Imagination.* New York: Oxford University Press. Also Harmondsworth: Penguin, 1970. [194]

Minnis, N. (ed.) 1971. *Linguistics at Large.* The fourteen linguistic lectures presented by the Institute of Contemporary Arts, London, 1969–70. London: Gollancz. New edition 1973: St. Albans: Paladin. [Henderson 1971, Lyons 1971, Ullmann 1971]

Mitchell, G.D. 1968. *A Hundred Years of Sociology.* Chicago: Aldine. [194,213(n 1)]

Mitzel, H.E. 1960. 'Teacher effectiveness' in Harris 1960:1481–6. [510(n 1)]

Modern Foreign Language Study and Canadian Committee on Modern Languages. 1930. *Studies in Modern Language Teaching.* American and Canadian Committees on Modern Languages, Vol. 17. New York: Macmillan. [Bagster-Collins 1930]

Modern Language Association of America. 1901. *Report of the Committee of Twelve of the Modern Language Association of America.* Boston: D.C. Heath. [99]

MLA: Modern Language Association of Great Britain. 1977. *Mixed Ability Teaching in*

Modern Languages. A questionnaire enquiry. London: Modern Language Association. [447(n 10)]

Modern Language Journal Published for the National Federation of Modern Language Teachers Associations by the University of Wisconsin Press, Madison, Wisconsin. [70(n 14)]

Modern Studies 1918. The report of the Committee (appointed by the Prime Minister) on the position of Modern Languages in the educational system of Great Britain (The Leathes Committee report). London: H.M.S.O. [99–100,247,282]

Mohrmann, C., Sommerfelt, A. and **Whatmough, J.** (eds.) 1961. *Trends in European and American Linguistics: 1930–1960*. Utrecht: Spectrum. [Fries 1961, Hamp 1961, Moulton 1961]

Montaigne, M. de. 1580–1588. *Essais*. Edited by Villey, P. and Saulnier, V.L. Paris: Alcan 1965. [Montaigne 1899]

Montaigne, M. de 1550–88/1899. *Essays. The Education of Children*. Edited by L.E. Rector, 1899. New York: Appleton. [388(n 3)]

Moore, T. 1977. 'An experimental language handicap (personal account).' *Bulletin of the British Psychological Society* 30:107–10. [313(n 1), 401]

Morgan, B.Q. 1928. *German Frequency Word Book*. New York: Macmillan. [101]

Morgan, L.H. 1877. *Ancient Society*. New York: Holt. New edition edited by E. Leacock in Meridian Books. New York: World Publishing Company, 1963. [196]

Morris, I. 1957. 'The persistence of the classical tradition in foreign-language teaching.' *English Language Teaching* 11:113–19. [87]

Morrow, K. 1979. 'Communicative language testing' in Brumfit and Johnson 1979:143–57. [268]

Moskowitz, G. 1967. 'The FLINT system' in Simon and Boyer 1967–70: 1, Section 2, No. 15; 3, No. 15. [493]

Moskowitz, G. 1968. 'The effects of training foreign language teachers in Interaction Analysis.' *Foreign Language Annals* 1:218–35. [493]

Moskowitz, G. 1970. *The Foreign Language Teacher Interacts*. Revised edition. Minneapolis, Minn.: Association for Productive Teaching. [493]

Moskowitz, G. 1971. 'Interaction Analysis: a new modern language for supervisors.' *Foreign Language Annals* 5:211–21. [493]

Moskowitz, G. 1976. 'The classroom interaction of outstanding foreign language teachers.' *Foreign Language Annals* 9:135–57. [493]

Moulton, W.G. 1961/1963. 'Linguistics and language teaching in the United States: 1940–1960' in Mohrmann, Sommerfelt, and Whatmough, 1961:82–109. Also *IRAL* 1, 1963:21–41. [86,115(n 7), 151,157–8,171(n 8,9), 462–3]

Müller, G. (compiler) 1965. *International Conference: Modern Foreign Language Teaching—Report*. (Report on a meeting held in Berlin, August 1964) Berlin: Pädagogisches Zentrum and Cornelsen. [55,107,334(n 9), Carroll 1966, Stern 1965]

Müller, K.E. (ed.) 1980. *The Foreign Language Syllabus and Communicative Approaches to Teaching: Proceedings of a European–American Seminar*. Special issue of *Studies in Second Language Acquisition* 3/1. [268(n 22), Brumfit 1980]

Munby, J. 1978. *Communicative Syllabus Design: A Sociolinguistic Model for Defining the Content of Purpose-Specific Language Programmes*. Cambridge: Cambridge University Press. [259,502]

Murdock, G.P. *et al.* 1964. *Outline of Cultural Materials*. Fourth revised edition. (First edition 1961). New Haven: Human Relations Area Files. [200,214–5(n 11), 252]

Musgrave, P.W. 1979. *The Sociology of Education*. Third edition. London: Methuen. [447]

Nagel, E. 1961. *The Structure of Science: Problems in the Logic of Scientific Explanation*. London: Routledge and Kegan Paul; New York: Harcourt, Brace and World. [32,33(n 6), 34(n15)]

Naiman, N., Fröhlich, M., Stern, H.H. and Todesco, A. 1978. *The Good Language Learner*. Research in Education Series, no. 7. Toronto: Ontario Institute for Studies in Education. [111, 313(n 1), 332,334(n 4), 353, 358(n 2), 374, 380, 381, 383, 389(n 12), 390(n 16,20), 405,406,412,494,495(n 9)]

Nemser, W. 1971. 'Approximative systems of foreign language learners.' *IRAL* 9:115–23; also in Richards 1974:55–63. [399]

Neufeld, G.G. 1973. 'Foreign language aptitude: an enduring problem' in Rondeau 1973:146–62. [372,389(n 8), 390(n 15)]

Neufeld, G.G. 1975. 'A theoretical perspective on the nature of linguistic aptitude' in Taggart 1975:74–90. [372,389(n 11)]

Newell, C.A. 1978. *Human Behavior in Educational Administration*. Englewood Cliffs: Prentice-Hall. [448(n 13)]

Newmark, L. 1966. 'How not to interfere with language learning.' *International Journal of American Linguistics* 32:77–83; also in Lester 1970:219–27. [513(n 16)]

Newmark, L. 1971. 'A minimal language-teaching program' in Pimsleur and Quinn 1971:11–18. [450(n 34)]

Nickel, G. (ed.) 1971. *Papers in Contrastive Linguistics*. Cambridge: Cambridge University Press. [168]

Nida, E.A. 1957. 'Some psychological problems in second language learning.' *Language Learning* 8:7–15. [334(n 4)]

Noblitt, J.S. 1972. 'Pedagogical grammar: towards a theory of foreign language materials preparation.' *IRAL* 10:313–31. [175–6]

Norris, W.E. 1971. *TESOL at the Beginning of the '70's: Trends, Topics and Research Needs*. Pittsburgh: Department of General Linguistics and University Center for International Studies. [115(n 7)]

Norwood Report 1943. *Curriculum and Examinations in Secondary Schools*, prepared by the Secondary School Examinations Council. London: H.M.S.O. [435]

Nostrand, H.L. 1966. 'Describing and teaching the sociocultural context of a foreign language and literature' in Valdman 1966:1–25. [251,252,266(n 11,12)]

Nostrand, H.L. 1973. 'French culture's concern for relationships: relationism?' *Foreign Language Annals* 6:469–80. [266(n 11)]

Nostrand, H.L. 1974. 'Empathy for a second culture: motivations and techniques' in Jarvis 1974:263–327. [251,252–3,266(n 11)]

Nuffield Foundation 1977. *The Early Teaching of Modern Languages: A Report on the Place of Language Teaching in Primary Schools*. London: Nuffield Foundation. [365]

O'Connor, D.J. 1957. *An Introduction to the Philosophy of Education*. London: Routledge and Kegan Paul. [26,420]

O'Connor, J.D. 1973. *Phonetics*. Harmondsworth: Penguin Books. [149(n 12)]

OECD: Organization for Economic Co-operation and Development 1972–75. *Classification of Educational Systems in OECD Member Countries*. 9 vols, one for each country plus one summary volume. Paris: OECD. [448(n 17)]

Ogden, C.K. 1930. *Basic English: A General Introduction with Rules and Grammar*. First edition. London: Kegan Paul, Trench, Trubner and Co. [101,102,161,170(n 5)]

Ogden, C.K. and Richards, I.A. 1923. *The Meaning of Meaning: A Study of the Influence of Language upon Thought and of the Science of Symbolism*. With supplementary essays by B. Malinowski and F.G. Crookshank. London: Trubner and Co.; Kegan Paul, Trench, Trubner. Eighth edition New York: Harcourt, Brace and World, 1946. [207–9, Malinowski 1923]

Ohannessian, S., Ferguson, C.A. and Polomé, E.C. (eds.) 1975. *Language Surveys in Developing Nations: Papers and Reports on Sociolinguistic Surveys*. Arlington, Va.: Center for Applied Linguistics. [244(n 16)]

Oller, J.W. Jr. 1970. 'Transformational theory and pragmatics.' *Modern Language Journal* 54:504–7. [177–8]

Oller, J.W. Jr. 1976. 'Evidence for a general proficiency factor: an expectancy grammar.' *Die Neueren Sprachen* 2:165–74. [349,352,356(Fig. 16.6),357]

Oller, J.W. Jr. 1979. *Language Tests at School: A Pragmatic Approach*. London: Longman. [187(n 6), 268(n 23), 314(n 18), 316(n 30)]

Oller, J.W. Jr. 1981. 'Research on the measurement of affective variables: some remaining questions' in Andersen 1981:14–27. [379,390(n 17)]

Oller, J.W. Jr. and Richards, J.C. (eds.) 1973. *Focus on the Learner: Pragmatic Perspectives for the Language Teacher*. Rowley, Mass.: Newbury House. [187(n 6), 331,336(n 19)]

Olmsted, D.L. 1950. *Ethnolinguistics So Far*. Studies in Linguistics: Occasional Papers, No. 2. Norman, Oklahoma: Battenburg Press. [215(n 12)]

Olsen, S. 1980. 'Foreign language departments and computer-assisted instruction.' *Modern Language Journal* 64:341–349. [451(n39)]

Ontario Ministry of Education 1974. *Report of the Ministerial Committee on the Teaching of French* (Gillin Report). Toronto: Ontario Ministry of Education. [285 (n 11)]

Ontario Ministry of Education 1980. *French, Core Programs 1980: Curriculum Guidelines for the Primary, Junior, Intermediate, and Senior Divisions*. Toronto: Ontario Ministry of Education. [450(n 31)]

Orléans Archive 1974. *Etude sociolinguistique sur Orléans: Catalogue des enregistrements*. Colchester: Department of Languages and Linguistics, University of Essex. [268(n 20)]

Osgood, C.E. and Sebeok, T.A. (eds.) 1954. 'Psycholinguistics: a survey of theory and research problems.' *Journal of Abnormal and Social Psychology* 49: Supplement. Reprinted as *Psycholinguistics: A Survey of Theory and Research Problems* with *A Survey of Psycholinguistic Research, 1954–1964* by A.R. Diebold. Bloomington: Indiana University Press, 1965. [103,105,128,295–8,304,305,314(n 14), Diebold 1965, Ervin and Osgood 1954/1965]

Osgood, C.E., Suci, G.J. and Tannenbaum, P.H. 1957. *The Measurement of Meaning*. Urbana, Ill.: University of Illinois Press. [390(n 19)]

Oskarsson, M. 1978. *Approaches to Self-Assessment in Foreign Language Learning*. Strasbourg: Council of Europe. [353]

Otter, H.S. 1968. *A Functional Language Examination*. Series Language and Language Learning. London: Oxford University Press. [96(n 17)]

Owen, J.G. 1973. *The Management of Curriculum Development*. Cambridge: Cambridge University Press. [448(n 25)]

Palmer, F.R. 1971. *Grammar*. Harmondsworth: Penguin Books. [141,149(n 13), 150(n 20)]

Palmer, F.R. 1981. *Semantics: A New Outline*. Cambridge: Cambridge University Press. First edition, 1976. [150(n 16,21)]

Palmer, H.E. 1917. *The Scientific Study and Teaching of Languages*. London: Harrap. Re-issued in a new edition by Harper H. in the Series Language and Language Learning. London: Oxford University Press, 1968. [88,100,155–6,317–19]

Palmer, H.E. 1921. *The Oral Method of Teaching Languages*. Cambridge: Heffer. [100,156,170(n 4),318]

Palmer, H.E. 1922. *The Principles of Language-Study*. London: Harrap. Reissued 1964 in the Series Language and Language Learning. London: Oxford University Press. [100,156(n 4), 170,318]

Palmer, H.E. and **Redman H.V.** 1969. *This Language Learning Business*. First edition: London: Harrap, 1932. Re-issued in Series Language and Language Learning. London: Oxford University Press. [319, Anderson 1969]

Palmer, L. and **Spolsky, B.** (eds.) 1975. *Papers on Language Testing: 1967–1974*. Washington, D.C.: TESOL. [Levenston 1975]

Palsgrave, J. 1530. *L'Esclarcissement de la langue françoyse*. London. Edited by F. Genin, Paris, 1852. [86]

Parry, A. 1967. *America Learns Russian: A History of the Teaching of the Russian Language in the United States*. Syracuse, N.Y.: Syracuse University Press. [87]

Partington, J.A. 1969. 'Streams, sets, and mixed-ability groups.' *Modern Languages* 50:117–20. [447(n 10)]

Passy, P. 1899. *De la méthode directe dans l'enseignement des langues vivantes*. Bourg-la-Reine: IPA. [99]

Passy, J. and **Rambeau, A.** (eds.) 1897. *Chrestomathie française: morceaux choisis de prose et de poésie avec prononciation figurée à l'usage des étrangers (précédés d'une introduction sur la méthode phonétique)*. Fifth edition, London: Harrap (1926). [96(n 13)]

Paulston, C.B. 1974. *Implications of Language Learning Theory for Language Planning: Concerns in Bilingual Education*. Papers in Applied Linguistics: Bilingual Education Series 1. Arlington Va: Center for Applied Linguistics. [16]

Paulston, C.B. 1975. 'Ethnic relations and bilingual education: accounting for contradictory data.' *Working Papers on Bilingualism* 6:1–44. Also in Alatis and Twaddell 1976:235–62. [34(n 13), 243(n 14), 271]

Paulston, C.B. and **Bruder, M.N.** 1976. *Teaching English as a Second Language: Techniques and Procedures*. Rowley, Mass.: Newbury House. [5(n 3)]

Paulston, C.B. and **Selekman, H.R.** 1976. 'Interaction activities in the foreign classroom, or how to grow a tulip-rose.' *FL Annals* 9:248–54. [407]

Peal, E. and **Lambert, W.E.** 1962. 'The relation of bilingualism to intelligence.' *Psychological Monographs* 76/546:1–23. [295]

Peers, E.A. 1945 *'New' Tongues, or Modern Language Teaching of the Future*. London: Pitman. [285(n 9)]

Penfield, W.G. 1953. 'A consideration of neurophysiological mechanisms of speech and some educational consequences.' *Proceedings of the American Academy of Arts and Sciences* 82:199–214. [334(n 6)]

Penfield, W.G. and **Roberts, L.** 1959. *Speech and Brain-Mechanisms*. Princeton: Princeton University Press; London: Oxford University Press. [334(n 6)]

Penfield, W.G. 1965. 'Conditioning the uncommitted cortex for language learning.' *Brain* 88:787–98. [334(n 6)]

Percy, Lord E. (ed.) 1934. *The Yearbook of Education*. London: Evans. [Collins 1934]

Perren, G.E. (ed.) 1979. *Foreign Languages in Education*. National Congress on Languages in Education. Papers and Reports, no. 1 (1978). London: CILT. [69(n 8), 116(n 15), 285(n 9,10)]

Perren, G.E. (ed.) 1979a. *The Mother Tongue and Other Languages in Education*. National Congress on Languages in Education. Papers and Reports, no. 2 (1978). London: CILT. [69(n 8), 116(n 15), 285(n 9,10)]

Peters, R.S. 1963. *Authority, Responsibility and Education*. Second edition. London: Allen and Unwin. [421]

Peters, R.S. (ed.) 1973. *The Philosophy of Education*. Oxford Readings in Philosophy. London: Oxford University Press. [446(n 1)]

Peters, R.S. and **White, J.P.** 1973. 'The philosopher's contribution to educational research' in Taylor 1973:93–112. [70(n 17)]

Phillips, J.K. (ed.) 1981. *Action for the '80s: A Political, Professional, and Public Program for Foreign Language Education*. Skokie, Ill.: National Textbook Company. [Stern and Cummins 1981]

Piaget, J. 1923. *Le langage et la pensée chez l'enfant.* First edition 1923, second 1930, eighth 1968. Neuchâtel: Delachaux et Nestlé. [294,314(n 19)]

Pike, K.L. 1945. *The Intonation of American English.* Ann Arbor: University of Michigan Press. [171(n 10)]

Pike, K.L. 1960. *Language in Relation to a Unified Theory of the Structure of Human Behavior.* Santa Anna: Summer Institute of Linguistics. Second revised edition, 1967, entitled: *Language in Relation to a Unified Theory of Human Behavior.* The Hague: Mouton. [137]

Pimsleur, P. 1960. Report of the Conference on Psychological Experiments related to Second-Language Learning. (Mimeographed report of a conference held at the University of California in Los Angeles, Dec. 1959–Jan. 1960.) [334(n 7)]

Pimsleur, P. 1966. *Pimsleur Language Aptitude Battery.* (PLAB) New York: Harcourt Brace Jovanovich. [369,370–3]

Pimsleur, P. and **Quinn, T.** (eds.) 1971. *The Psychology of Second Language Learning.* Papers from the Second International Congress of Applied Linguistics, Cambridge, September, 1969. Cambridge: Cambridge University Press. [Carton 1971, Newmark 1971, Reibel 1971, 336(n 19)]

Pimsleur, P., Sundland, D.M. and **McIntyre, R.D.** 1966. *Underachievement in Foreign Language Learning.* New York: MLA Materials Center. [381]

Pinloche, A. 1913. *La nouvelle pédagogie des langues vivantes: observations et réflexions critiques.* Paris: Didier. [77]

Politzer, R.L. 1981. 'Effective language teaching: insights from research' in Alatis, Altman and Alatis 1981:21–35. [513(n 18)]

Politzer, R.L. and **Weiss, L.** 1969. *Improving Achievement in Foreign Language.* Philadelphia: Center for Curriculum Development. [389(n 12)]

Polomé, E. and **Hill, C.P.** 1981. *Language in Tanzania,* Ford Foundation Survey of Language Use and Language Teaching in East Africa. Oxford: Oxford University Press. [244(n 16)]

Preyer, W. 1882. *Die Seele des Kindes.* Leipzig: Griebens Verlag. Fourth edition 1895. Fifth to ninth edition prepared by K. Schaefer. Ninth edition 1923. [313(n 6)]

Pride, J.B. and **Holmes, J.** (eds.) 1972. *Sociolinguistics: Selected Readings.* Harmondsworth: Penguin Books. [Hymes 1972]

Pritchard, D.F. 1952. 'An investigation into the relationship of personality traits and ability in modern language.' *British Journal of Educational Psychology* 22:157–8. [381]

Pula, F.J. and **Goff, R.J.** 1972. *Technology in Education: Challenge and Change.* Ohio: Charles A. Jones Publishing Co. [451(n 39)]

Purves, A. and **Levine, D.** (eds.) 1975. *Educational Policy and International Assessment.* Berkeley, Cal.: McCutchan. [432–3]

Quirk, R., Greenbaum, S., Leech, G. and **Svartvik, J.** 1972. *A Grammar of Contemporary English.* London: Longman. [16,71(n 25), 143,187(n 3)]

Quirk R. and **Smith, A.H.** (eds.) 1964. *The Teaching of English.* London: Oxford University Press. (First published in 1959 by Martin, Secker and Warburg.) [Catford 1959]

Qvistgard, J., Schwarz, H. and **Spang-Hanssen, H.** (eds.) 1974. *Applied Linguistics: Problems and Solutions.* Vol. 3 of the Proceedings of the AILA Third Congress, Copenhagen, 1972. Heidelberg: Julius Groos Verlag. [Stern 1974]

Radcliffe-Brown, A.R. 1952. *Structure and Function in Primitive Society: Essays and Addresses.* London: Cohen and West. [195,198–9,206,215(n 18)]

Rassias, J.A. 1971. 'New dimensions in language training: the Dartmouth College experiment.' *ADFL* 3:23–7. [475(n 13)]

Redman, H.V. 1967. 'Harold E. Palmer—Pioneer teacher of modern languages.' *English Language Teaching* 22:10–16. [95(n 11)]

Reibel, D.A. 1971. 'Language learning strategies for the adult' in Pimsleur and Quinn 1971:87–96. [450]

Reid, L.A. 1962. *Philosophy and Education: An Introduction.* London: Heinemann. [446(n 1)]

Reid, L.A. 1965. 'Philosophy and the theory and practice of education' in Archambault 1965:17–37. [26]

Renard, C. and Heinle, C.H. 1969. *Implementing Voix et Images de France, Part I in American Schools and Colleges.* Center for Curriculum Development in Audio-Visual Language Teaching. Philadelphia and New York: Educational Division. [466]

Rice, F.A. (ed.) 1962. *Study of the Role of Second Languages in Asia, Africa, and Latin America.* Washington, D.C.: Center for Applied Linguistics. [232–4,284(n 2), Ferguson 1962, Samarin 1962, Stewart 1962]

Richards. J.C. (ed.) 1974. *Error Analysis: Perspectives on Second Language Acquisition.* London: Longman. [64, Corder 1967, Dulay and Burt 1974, Nemser 1971, Selinker 1972, 332,335(n 15), 336(n 19)]

Richards, J.C. (ed.) 1978. *Understanding Second and Foreign Language Learning: Issues and Approaches.* Rowley, Mass.: Newbury House. [332,335(n 15), Corder 1978, d'Anglejan 1978, Hatch 1978a, Richards 1978a, Rodgers 1978, 336(n 19)]

Richards, J.C. 1978a. 'Models of language use and language learning' in Richards 1978:94–116. [347]

Richmond, W.K. (ed.) 1970. *The Concept of Educational Technology: A Dialogue with Yourself.* London: Weidenfeld and Nicholson. [451(n 39)]

Richmond, W.K. 1970a. *The School Curriculum.* London: Methuen. [449(n 21)]

Richterich, R. 1973. 'Definition of language needs and types of adults' in Council of Europe 1973:31–88, also in Trim *et al.* 1980. [259]

Richterich, R. 1978. 'The analysis of language needs: illusion—pretext—necessity' in *A European Unit/Credit System for Modern Language Learning by Adults.* Strasbourg: Council of Europe: 4–6. [53]

Richterich, R. 1980. 'Definition of language needs and types of adults' in Trim *et al.* 1980:29–88. (First published in Council of Europe 1973:29–62.) [259]

Richterich, R. and Chancerel, J.L. 1978/1980. *Identifying the Needs of Adults Learning a Foreign Language.* Strasbourg: Council of Europe. Also Oxford: Pergamon Press. 1980. [110,259,502]

Rivenc, P. 1979. 'Le français fondamental vingt-cinq ans après.' *Le français dans le monde* 19/148:15–22. [94(n 2)]

Rivers, W.M. 1964. *The Psychologist and the Foreign Language Teacher.* Chicago and London: University of Chicago Press. [76,107,266(n 11), 324–27,336(n 19), 394,403,462,463,465]

Rivers, W.M. 1968. See Rivers 1968/1981.

Rivers, W.M. 1972. 'The foreign language teacher and cognitive psychology, or Where do we go from here?' in Rivers 1976:109–30. [108,169,329,394,399]

Rivers, W.M. 1975. *A Practical Guide to the Teaching of French.* New York: Oxford University Press. [5(n 3),187(n 3)]

Rivers, W.M. 1976. *Speaking in Many Tongues: Essays in Foreign Language Teaching.* Expanded second edition. (First edition with preface by H.H. Stern 1972.) Rowley, Mass.: Newbury House. [329,394,399, Rivers 1972]

Rivers, W.M. 1979. 'Learning a sixth language: an adult learner's daily diary.' *Canadian Modern Language Review* 36:67–82; also in Rivers 1981:500–15 (Appendix B). [313(n 1), 401]

Rivers, W.M. 1968/1981. *Teaching Foreign-Language Skills*. Second edition. (First edition, 1968.) Chicago and London: University of Chicago Press. [5(n 3), 94,(n 1), 108,115(n 14), 169,251,263(n 2), 266(n 11), 326, 335(n 10), 394,475(n 13), 462,477,478,479(fig.21.1), 482,512(n 9)]

Rivers, W.M., Azevedo, M.M., Heflin, W.H. Jr. and Hyman-Opler, R. 1976. *A Practical Guide to the Teaching of Spanish*. New York: Oxford University Press. [5(n 3)]

Rivers, W.M., Dell'Orto, K.M. and Dell'Orto, V.J. 1975. *A Practical Guide to the Teaching of German*. New York: Oxford University Press. [5(n 3), 187(n 3)]

Rivers, W.M. and Temperley, M.S. 1978. *A Practical Guide to the Teaching of English as a Second or Foreign Language*. New York: Oxford University Press. [5(n 3)]

Roberts, P. 1964. *English Syntax*. New York: Harcourt Brace. [167]

Robins, R.H. 1951. *Ancient and Mediaeval Grammatical Theory in Europe with Particular Reference to Modern Linguistic Doctrine*. London: Bell. [148(n 1)]

Robins, R.H. 1961. 'John Rupert Firth.' *Language* 37:191–200. [138]

Robins, R.H. 1971. 'Malinowski, Firth, and the "Context of situation"' in Ardener 1971:33–46. [216(n 20)]

Robins, R.H. 1979. *A Short History of Linguistics* London: Longman. First edition 1967. [148(n 1)]

Robins, R.H. 1980. *General Linguistics: An Introductory Survey*. London: Longman. Third edition. First edition, 1964. [151(n 22)]

Robinson, W.P. 1972. *Language and Social Behaviour*. Harmondsworth: Penguin Books. [217(n 26), 221,223–7,242(n 4)]

Rodgers, T. 1978. 'Strategies for individualized language learning and teaching' in Richards 1978:251–73. [387(n 1)]

Rokeach, M. 1960. *The Open and Closed Mind: Investigations into the Nature of Belief Systems and Personality Systems*. New York: Basic Books. [379]

Rondeau, G. (ed.) 1973. *Some Aspects of Canadian Applied Linguistics*. Montreal: Centre Educatif et Culturel. [Neufeld 1973, Stern 1973]

Rosansky, E.J. 1975. 'The critical period for the acquisition of language: some cognitive developmental considerations.' *Working Papers on Bilingualism* 6:92–102. [363]

Rosenbaum, J.E. 1976. *Making Inequality: The Hidden Curriculum of High School Tracking*. New York: Wiley. [447(n 10)]

Ross, J. 1974. 'Enquête sociolinguistique et description syntaxique' in Verdoodt; 1974:137–54. [267(n 20)]

Rothwell, W. 1968. 'Teaching French: old wine in new bottles.' *Bulletin of the John Rylands Library* 51:184–99. [87]

Roulet, E. 1972. *Théories grammaticales, descriptions et enseignement des langues*. Paris: Fernand Nathan; Bruxelles: Labor. [187(n 4)]

Roulet, E. 1980. *Langue maternelle et langues secondes: vers une pédagogie intégrée*. Paris: Hatier-Crédif. [5(n 2)]

Rowntree, B.S. 1901. *Poverty: A Study of Town Life*. London: [193]

Rowntree, B.S. 1941. *Poverty and Progress: A Second Social Survey of York*. London: Longmans, Green. [193]

Rubin, J. 1968. 'Language and education in Paraguay' in Fishman, Ferguson and Das Gupta, 1968:477–88. [235]

Rubin, J. 1971. 'Evaluation and language planning' in Rubin and Jernudd 1971:217–52. [240,245(n 21)]

Rubin, J. 1973. Introduction to Rubin and Shuy 1973:v–x. [240,245(n 21)]

Rubin, J. 1973a. 'Language planning: discussion of some current issues' in Rubin and Shuy 1973:1–10. [245(n 21)]

Rubin, J. 1975. 'What the "good language learner" can teach us.' *TESOL Quarterly* 9:41–51. [381,405–6,414(n 13)]

Rubin, J. 1979. 'Concerning language planning in 1979.' *AILA Bulletin* 1:1–8. [244(n 19)]

Rubin, J. and Jernudd, B.H. *Can Language Be Planned? Sociolinguistic Theory and Practice for Developing Nations.* An East-West Center Book. Honolulu, Hawaii: University of Hawaii Press. [244(n 19, 21), Jernudd and Das Gupta 1971, Rubin 1971]

Rubin, J. and Jernudd, B.H. (with the assistance of M. Stetser and C. Bonamalay) (compilers) 1979. *References for Students of Language Planning.* Honolulu, Hawaii: East-West Center. [244(n 19, 21]

Rubin, J. and Shuy, R.W. (eds.) 1973. *Language Planning: Current Issues and Research.* Washington, D.C.: Georgetown University Press. [244(n 19,21), Jernudd 1973, Rubin 1973, 1973a]

Rülcker, T. 1969. *Der Neusprachenunterricht an höheren Schulen: zur Geschichte und Kritik seiner Didaktik.* Frankfurt, etc.: Diesterweg. [87,97,114(n 1), 263(n 3), 456,459]

Rutherford, W.E. 1968. *Modern English: A Textbook for Foreign Students.* New York: Harcourt, Brace and World. [168]

Ryan, D.T. and Greenfield, T.B. 1975. *The Class Size Question: Development of Research Studies Related to the Effects of Class Size, Pupil/Adult, and Pupil/Teacher Ratios.* Toronto: Ontario Ministry of Education. [447(n 10)]

Sachs, K. 1893. 'Die Neubearbeitungen der Ploetzschen Lehrbücher.' *Archiv für das Studium der neueren Sprachen und Literaturen* 91:327–9. [454,474(n 5)]

Saettler, P. 1968. *A History of Instructional Technology.* New York: McGraw-Hill. [451(n 39)]

Salter, M. 1972. 'Introduction.' *Group Work in Modern Languages.* York: Materials Development Unit, Language Teaching Centre, University of York. [447(n 10)]

Samarin, W.J. 1962. 'Lingua francas, with special reference to Africa' in Rice 1962:54–64. [234]

Sang, F. and Vollmer, H.J. 1978. *Allgemeine Sprachfähigkeit und Fremdsprachenerwerb: Zur Struktur von Leistungsdimensionen und linguistischer Kompetenz des Fremdsprachenlerners.* Berlin: Max-Planck-Institut für Bildungsforschung. [358(n 8)]

Sankoff, D. (ed.) 1979. *Linguistic Variation: Models and Methods.* New York: Academic Press. [Heidelberger, etc. 1979]

Sapir, E. 1921. *Language.* New York: Harcourt Brace. [195,202]

Sapir, E. 1934. 'The emergence of the concept of personality in a study of cultures.' *Journal of Social Psychology* 5:408–15; also in Sapir 1970:194–207. [197–8]

Sapir, E. 1970. *Culture, Language and Personality: Selected Essays.* Edited by D.G. Mandelbaum. Berkeley, Cal.: University of California Press. (Chosen from larger collection of *Selected Writings of Edward Sapir in Language, Culture and Personality.* Edited by D.G. Mandelbaum, 1949.) [202, Sapir 1934]

Saporta, S. (ed.) 1961. *Psycholinguistics: A Book of Readings.* New York: Holt, Rinehart and Winston. [314(n 14)]

Saporta, S. 1966. 'Applied linguistics and generative grammar' in Valdman 1966:81–92. [144,161,167,171(n 16)]

Saussure, F.de 1916. *Cours de linguistique générale.* Edited by Bally, C., Sechehaye, A. and Riedlinger, A. Paris: Payot. Third edition: 1965. [121,126]

Savard, J.G. 1970. *La valence lexicale.* Paris: Didier. [495(n 5)]

Savard, J.G. 1977. 'Besoins langagiers et fonctions langagières.' *Canadian Modern Language Review* 33:632–46. [259]

Savard, J.G. and Laforge, L. (presenters). 1981. *Proceedings of the 5th Congress of L'Association Internationale de Linguistique Appliquée (AILA).* Montreal 1978. Publication of the International Centre for Research on Bilingualism. Quebec: Les Presses de l'Université Laval. [Stern 1981a]

Savignon, S.J. 1972. *Communicative Competence: An Experiment in Foreign Language Teaching.* Philadelphia: Center for Curriculum Development. [111]

Saville-Troike, M. (ed.) 1977. *Linguistics and Anthropology.* Georgetown University Round Table on Languages and Linguistics, 1977. Washington, D.C.: Georgetown University Press. [242(n 1), Sherzer 1977]

Scheffler, I. (ed.) 1966. *Philosophy and Education*. Second edition. Boston: Allyn and Bacon. [Hirst 1966]

Schegloff, E.A. 1968. 'Sequencing in conversational openings.' *American Anthropologist* 70:1075–95. Also in Gumperz and Hymes 1972:346–80. [228]

Scherer, G.A.C. and Wertheimer, M. 1964. *A Psycholinguistic Experiment in Foreign-Language Teaching*. New York, etc.: McGraw-Hill. [56,61,69(n 10), 106,334(n 7), 463,476(n 15), 491]

Schofield, H. 1972. *The Philosophy of Education: An Introduction*. London: Allen and Unwin. [446(n 1)]

Schön, E. 1925. 'Probleme der französischen Kulturkunde in der höheren Schule.' *Neue Jahrbücher für Wissenschaft und Jugenbildung* 1925:245–58. (Reprinted in Flechsig, 1965.) [248,263(n 6)]

Schools Council Committee for Wales. 1978. *Bilingual Education in Wales, 5–11*. London: Evans/Methuen. [Dodson 1978]

Schröder, K. 1959. *Die Entwicklung des Englischunterrichts an den deutschsprachigen Universitäten bis zum Jahre 1850*. Ratingen: Henn. [87]

Schultz, D. 1975. *A History of Modern Psychology*. Second edition. New York: Academic Press. [313(n 5)]

Schumann, J.H. 1975. 'Affective factors and the problem of age in second language acquisition.' *Language Learning* 25:209–35; also in Croft 1980:222–47. [336(n 18), 363,381,388(n 7), 390(n 17), 398,399]

Schumann, J.H. 1976. 'Second language acquisition research: getting a more global look at the learner' in Brown 1976:15–28. [336(n 18), 358(n 2), 370]

Schumann, J.H. 1976a. 'Social distance as a factor in second language acquisition.' *Language Learning* 26:135–43. [336(n 18)]

Schumann, J.H. 1978. 'The acculturation model for second language acquisition' in Gingras 1978:27–50. [238,244,(n 17),270, 331,336(n 18), 402,413(n 5)]

Scovel, T. 1979. Review of Lozanov, G., *Suggestology and Suggestopedy*. *TESOL Quarterly* 13:255–66. [475(n 13)]

Scriven, M. 1967. 'The methodology of evaluation' in Tyler, Gagné and Scriven 1967:39–83; also in Bellack and Kliebard 1977:334–71. [441]

Searle, J.R. 1969. *Speech Acts: An Essay in the Philosophy of Language*. Cambridge: Cambridge University Press. [223–6]

Searle, J.R. 1976. 'A classification of illocutionary acts.' *Language in Society* 5:1–23. [226]

Sebeok, T.A. (ed.) 1960. *Style in Language*. Cambridge, Mass.: M.I.T. Press. [221, Jakobson 1960]

Sebeok, T.A. (ed.) 1966. *Current Trends in Linguistics*. Vol. 3: *Theoretical Foundations*. The Hague, Paris: Mouton. [Godel 1966]

Sebeok, T.A. (ed.) 1972. *Current Trends in Linguistics* 9/1. The Hague, Paris: Mouton. [Strevens 1972]

Seelye, H.N. 1968. 'Analysis and teaching of the cross-cultural context' in Birkmaier 1968:37–81. [251,252,266(n 11)]

Seelye, H.N. 1974. *Teaching Culture: Strategies for Foreign Language Educators*. Skokie, Ill.: National Textbook Company and American Council on the Teaching of Foreign Languages. [251,252,263(n 2), 266(n 11,14,15)]

Seliger, H.W. 1979. 'On the nature and function of language rules in language teaching.' *TESOL Quarterly* 13:359–69. [32(n 3)]

Seliger, H.W. and Long, M. (eds.) in press. *Classroom Oriented Research in Language Learning*. Rowley, Mass.: Newbury House. [Bialystok 1980]

Selinker, L. 1972. 'Interlanguage.' *IRAL* 10:219–31. Also in Richards 1974:31–54. [125,335(n 15),355,399,402]

Selinker, L., Swain, M. and Dumas, G. 1975. 'The interlanguage hypothesis extended to children.' *Language Learning* 25:139–52. [335(n 15), 354]

Seshadri, C. 1978. 'Second-Language Planning for a Multilingual Country: English Language Instruction in India.' Unpublished Ph.D. thesis, University of Toronto. [244(n 16), 448(n 19)]

Sexton, V.S. and Misiak, H. (eds.) 1976. *Psychology Around the World*. Monterey, Cal.: Brooks/Cole. [313(n 2)]

Shannon, C.E. and Weaver, W. 1949. *The Mathematical Theory of Communication*. Urbana, Ill.: University of Illinois Press. [296]

Shaw, A.M. 1977. 'Foreign-language syllabus development: some recent approaches.' *Language Teaching and Linguistics: Abstracts* 10:217–33. [259,513(n 16)]

Sherzer, J. 1977. 'The ethnography of speaking: a critical appraisal' in Saville-Troike 1977:43–57. [220]

Shuy, R.W. (ed.) 1973. *Sociolinguistics: Current Trends and Prospects*. 23rd Annual Round Table on Languages and Linguistics. Washington, D.C.: Georgetown University Press. [Whiteley 1973]

Shuy, R.W. and Fasold, R.W. (eds.) 1973. *Language Attitudes: Current Trends and Prospects*. Washington, D.C.: Georgetown University Press. [d'Anglejan and Tucker 1973]

Sills, D.L. (ed.) 1968. *International Encyclopedia of the Social Sciences*. 17 vols. New York: Free Press. [Greenberg 1968, Gumperz 1968]

Simmins, C.A. 1930. 'The mental processes involved in learning a foreign language.' *Modern Languages* 12:37–43. [321]

Simon, A. and Boyer, E.G. (eds.) 1967–70. *Mirrors for Behavior: An Anthology of Classroom Observation Instruments*. Vols. 1–14. Philadelphia: Research for Better Schools. [493, Moskowitz, 1967]

Simpson, J.M.Y. 1979. *A First Course in Linguistics*. Edinburgh: Edinburgh University Press. [148(n 1), 149(n 12,13), 150(n 16,20), 151(n 22)]

Sinclair, J.McH. (ed.) 1980. *Applied Discourse Analysis*. Thematic Issue of *Applied Linguistics* 1/3. [150(n 17)]

Sinclair, J.McH. and Brazil, D. 1982. *Teacher Talk*. Oxford: Oxford University Press. [496(n 13)]

Sinclair, J.McH. and Coulthard, R.M. 1975. *Towards an Analysis of Discourse*. London: Oxford University Press. [179,229,494]

Skinner, B.F. 1954. 'The science of learning and the art of teaching.' *Harvard Educational Review* 24:86–97; also in Smith and Moore 1962:18–33. [305]

Skinner, B.F. 1957. *Verbal Behavior*. New York: Appleton-Century-Crofts. [105,129,141,298–9,307]

Skinner, B.F. 1958. 'Teaching machines.' *Science* 128:969–77. [305]

Skinner, B.F. 1961. 'Teaching machines' *Scientific American* (November issue: 1–13) Reprint: San Francisco: Freeman. [305–6]

Reprint: San Francisco: Freeman. [306–7]

Skutnabb-Kangas, T. and Tukoomaa, P. 1976. *Teaching Migrant Children's Mother-tongue and Learning the Language of the Host Country in the Context of the Sociocultural Situation of the Migrant Family*. Helsinki: Finnish National Commission for UNESCO. [243(n 14)]

Slagter, P.J. 1979. *Un nivel umbral*. Strasbourg: Council of Europe. [110,179]

SLANT: Second Language Acquisition Notes and Topics (journal) San Francisco, Cal.: San Francisco State University. [335(n 14)]

Slobin, D.J. 1979. *Psycholinguistics*. Glenview, Ill.: Scott, Foresman. Second edition. First edition 1971. [315(n 21)]

Smith, F. and Miller, G.A. (eds.) 1966. *The Genesis of Language: In Children and Animals*. Cambridge, Mass.: M.I.T. Press. [315(n 20), McNeill 1966]

Smith, L.E. (ed.) 1981. *English for Cross-Cultural Communication*. London: Macmillan. [17,285(n 7)]

Smith, P.D. Jr. 1970. *A Comparison of the Cognitive and Audiolingual Approaches to*

Foreign Language Instruction: The Pennsylvania Foreign Language Project. Philadelphia, Penn.: Center for Curriculum Development. [56,61,70(n 14), 108,443,463, 476(n 15), 491–2]

Smith, W.I. and Moore, J.W. (eds.) 1962. *Programmed Learning: Theory and Research. An Enduring Problem.* Selected readings. Princetown, N.J.: Van Nostrand. [Skinner 1954]

Smythe, P.C., Stennet, R.G. and Gardner, R.C. 1975. 'The best age for foreign language training: issues options and facts.' *Canadian Modern Language Review* 32:10–23. [387(n 2)]

Snow, C.E. and Hoefnagel-Höhle, M. 1978. 'Age differences in second language acquisition' in Hatch 1978:333–44. [366,367]

Snow, R.E. 1973. 'Theory construction for research on teaching' in Travers 1973:77–112. [33(n 6, 8)]

Spens Report 1938, *Secondary Education with Special Reference to Grammar Schools and Technical High Schools,* prepared by a Consultative Committee of the Board of Education. London: H.M.S.O. [435]

Spicer, A. 1969. 'The Nuffield foreign languages teaching materials project' in Stern 1969:148–61. [60,449(n 25)]

Spicer, A. 1980. 'The early teaching of modern languages: the British experience.' *Canadian Modern Language Review* 36:408–21. [365]

Spolsky, B. 1970. 'Linguistics and language pedagogy: applications or implications?' in Alatis 1970:143–55. [51(n 2), 145,174,182,185]

Spolsky, B. (ed.) 1972. *The Language Education of Minority Children: Selected Readings.* Rowley, Mass.: Newbury House. [243(n 14)]

Spolsky, B. (ed.) 1973. *Current Trends in Educational Linguistics.* Hague: Mouton. [51(n 2)]

Spolsky, B. 1973a. 'The field of educational linguistics' in Spolsky 1973. [51(n 2)]

Spolsky, B. 1978. *Educational Linguistics: An Introduction.* Rowley, Mass.: Newbury House. [51(n 2), 237,243(n 13,14), 244(n 18)]

Spolsky, B. 1980. 'The scope of educational linguistics' in Kaplan 1980:67–73. [36]

Spolsky, B., Green, J.B. and Read, J. 1974. *A Model for the Description, Analysis, and Perhaps Evaluation of Bilingual Education.* Navajo Reading Study Progress Report No. 23. Albuquerque, N.M.: University of New Mexico. [271,273(Fig.13.2)]

Stack, E.M. 1960. *The Language Laboratory and Modern Language Teaching.* New York: Oxford University Press. Second edition, 1966; third edition, 1971. [106,462]

Stack, E.M. 1964. 'Advances in language teaching in the United States' in Libbish 1964:66–90. [160]

Steinberg, D.D. and Jakobovits, L.A. (eds.) 1971. *Semantics: An Interdisciplinary Reader in Philosophy, Linguistics and Psychology.* Cambridge: Cambridge University Press. [Maclay 1971, 150(n 21)]

Stengel, E. 1939. 'On learning a new language.' *International Journal of Psychoanalysis* 2:471–9. [322,390(n 17)]

Stern, C. and Stern, W. 1907. *Die Kindersprache: Eine psychologische und sprach-theoretische Untersuchung.* Leipzig: Barth. Fourth edition 1928.

Stern, H.H. 1964. 'Modern languages in the universities: achievements and present trends.' *Modern Languages* 45:87–97. [87]

Stern, H.H. 1965. 'Final report on the work of groups and committees' (Summing up of 1964 Berlin Conference) in Müller 1965:43–60. [162]

Stern, H.H. 1966. 'Recent developments in foreign language teaching in Great Britain.' *Neusprachliche Mitteilungen aus Wissenschaft und Praxis* 1966:16–27. [106,115(n 7)]

Stern, H.H. 1967. *Foreign Languages in Primary Education.* (Revised version of a report originally published in 1963 as one of the International Studies in Education of the

Unesco Institute for Education, Hamburg) London: Oxford University Press. [56,69(n 12), 106,323,361,364,387(n 2), 448(n 18), Carroll 1967]

Stern, H.H. 1968–69. 'Foreign language learning and the new view of first-language acquisition.' *Child Study* 30:25–36; also in Stern 1970:57–66 under the title 'First and second language acquisition.' [315(n 20), 328]

Stern, H.H. (ed.) 1969. *Languages and the Young School Child.* London: Oxford University Press. [56,69(n 12), 108,364,387(n 2), Carroll 1969, 1969b, Spicer 1969, Stern 1969a]

Stern, H.H. 1969a. 'Languages for young children: an introductory survey of current practices and problems' in Stern 1969:9–35 (see esp. Table 1, p 10). [16]

Stern, H.H. 1969b. 'Language centers today and a new modern language center at OISE' *Canadian Modern Language Review* 25:9–21, also in Stern 1970:13–24. [521(n 6)]

Stern, H.H. 1970. *Perspectives on Second Language Teaching.* Toronto: Ontario Institute for Studies in Education. [68(n 6), 69(n 9), 328,335(n 11), Stern 1968–69, 1969b]

Stern, H.H. 1971. 'A general model for second language teaching theory and research.' Unpublished paper. [51(n 5)]

Stern, H.H. 1972. Preface to Rivers 1972:vii–xi; see Rivers 1976. [329]

Stern, H.H. 1973. 'Language teaching materials: the next phase' in Rondeau 1973:261–72. [450(n 34)]

Stern, H.H. 1974. 'Directions in language teaching theory and research' in Qvistgard *et al.* 1974:61–108. [51(n 5), 115(n 11)]

Stern, H.H. 1974a. 'Retreat from dogmatism: toward a better theory of language teaching.' *Canadian Modern Language Review* 30:244–54. [51(n 5), 169]

Stern, H.H. 1975. 'What can we learn from the good language learner?' *Canadian Modern Language Review* 31:304–18; also in Croft 1980:54–71. [381,406, 405–6,414(n 14)]

Stern, H.H. 1976. 'Mammoths or modules.' *Times Educational Supplement* 8 October 1976. Special Inset on modern language teaching, p 44. [511(n 7)]

Stern, H.H. 1978. 'Bilingual schooling and foreign language education: some implications of Canadian experiments in French immersion' in Alatis 1978:165–88. [70(n 13), 405]

Stern, H.H. 1978a. 'French immersion in Canada: achievements and directions.' *Canadian Modern Language Review* 34:836–54. [70(n 13), 364]

Stern, H.H. 1978b. 'Language research and the classroom practitioner.' *Canadian Modern Language Review* 34:680–7. [70(n 16), 521(n 4)]

Stern, H.H. 1979. 'Of honeymoons, hangovers and bootstraps in foreign language teaching.' The Modern Language Association Twentyman Lecture 1978. *Modern Languages* 60:1–19. [116(n 15), 387(n 1), 512(n 14)]

Stern, H.H. 1980. 'Directions in foreign language curriculum development' in American Council on the Teaching of Foreign Languages 1980:12–17. [503(Fig 22.4), 504,511(n 7)]

Stern, H.H. 1980a. 'Language learning on the spot: some thoughts on the language aspect of student exchange programs.' *Canadian Modern Language Review* 36:659–69. [513(n 15)]

Stern, H.H. 1981. 'Communicative language teaching and learning: toward a synthesis' in Alatis, Altman and Alatis 1981:131–48. [405,414(n 12), 476(n 14)]

Stern, H.H. 1981a. 'The formal-functional distinction in language pedagogy: a conceptual clarification' in Savard and Laforge, 1981:425–55. [405,414(n 12), 476(n 14), 512(n 11)]

Stern, H.H. 1982. *Issues in Early Core French: A Selective and Preliminary Review of the Literature, 1975–1981.* Toronto: City of Toronto Board of Education. [70(n 14),365,387(n 2), 512(n 14)]

Stern, H.H. in press. 'The time factor and other aspects in compact course development' in Freudenstein in press. [512(n 14)]

Stern, H.H. and **Cummins J.** 1981. 'Language teaching/learning research: a Canadian perspective on status and directions' in Phillips 1981:195–248. [4,284(n 6), 336(n 19), 387(n2), 388(n 7,8), 390(n 17), 413(n 5), 496(n 13)]

Stern, H.H., **Swain, M.** and **McLean, L.D.** 1976. *French Programs: Some Major Issues.* Toronto: Ontario Ministry of Education. [72(n 28), 512(n 14)]

Stern, H.H., Swain, M., McLean, L.D., **Friedman, R.J., Harley, B.** and **Lapkin, S.** 1976a. *Three Approaches to Teaching French: Evaluation and Overview of Studies Related to the Federally-Funded Extensions of the Second Language Learning (French) Programs in the Carleton and Ottawa School Boards.* Toronto: Ontario Ministry of Education. [66,72(n26), 111(n 28)]

Stern, H.H., **Ullmann, R., Balchunas, M., Hanna, G., Schneidermann, E.** and **Argue, V.** 1980. *Module Making: A Study in the Development and Evaluation of Learning Materials for French as a Second Language.* Toronto: Ontario Ministry of Education. [60,315(n 28), 511(n 7), 513(n 16)]

Stern, H.H. and **Weinrib, A.** 1977. 'Foreign languages for younger children: trends and assessment.' *Language Teaching and Linguistics: Abstracts* 10:5–26. Also in Kinsella 1978:152–72. [69–70(n 12,14), 364,365,367,387(n 2)]

Stern, H.H., **Wesche, M.B.** and **Harley, B.** 1978. 'The impact of the language sciences on second-language education' in Suppes 1981:397–475. [4,70(n 16), 72(n29), 387(n 2), 388(n 8), 520(n4), 521(n6)]

Stevick, E.W. 1976. *Memory, Meaning and Method.* Rowley, Mass.: Newbury House. [475(n 13)]

Stevick, E.W. 1980. *Teaching Languages: A Way and Ways.* Rowley, Mass.: Newbury House. [475(n 13), 512(n 15)]

Steward, J.H. 1950. *Area Research: Theory and Practice.* New York: Social Science Research Council (Bulletin 63). [265(n 10)]

Stewart, E.C. 1971. *American Cultural Patterns: A Cross-Cultural Perspective.* Pittsburgh: University of Pittsburgh Regional Council for International Education. [266(n 15)]

Stewart, W.A. 1962. 'An outline of linguistic typology for describing multilingualism' in Rice 1962:15–25. [22(n 4), 232–4,243(n 12), 237,270]

Stewart, W.A. 1968. 'A sociolinguistic typology for describing national multi-lingualism' in Fishman 1968:531–45. (Revised version of Stewart, 1962.) [17,22(n 4), 232–3,237,270]

Stieglitz, G.J. 1955. 'The Berlitz Method.' *Modern Language Journal* 39:300–10. [98]

Stott, D.H. 1946. *Language Teaching in the New Education.* London: University of London Press. [322]

Strachey, J. (ed.) 1955–64. *The Standard Edition of the Complete Psychological Works of Sigmund Freud.* London: Hogarth Press and Institute of Psycho-Analysis. Vol. 6: *The Psychopathology of Everyday Life* 1960. Vol. 13: *Totem and Taboo and Other Works* 1955. Vol. 21: *The Future of an Illusion, Civilization and its Discontents, and Other Works* 1961. Vol. 23: *Moses and Monotheism, An Outline of Psycho-Analysis and Other Works* 1964. [197,292]

Strevens, P.D. 1963. 'Linguistic research and language teaching' in Council for Cultural Co-operation 1963:81–105. [68(n 6)]

Strevens, P.D. 1963a. *The Study of the Present-Day English Language: A Triple Bond between Disciplines.* Leeds: Leeds University Press. [161]

Strevens, P.D. 1972. 'Language teaching' in Sebeok 1972:702–32. [96(n 16), 99,102,115(n 7), 160]

Strevens, P.D. 1976. 'A theoretical model of the language learning/teaching process.' *Working Papers on Bilingualism* 11:129–52. [41–2, also Fig 3.6, 51(n 3,4)]

Strevens, P.D. 1977. *New Orientations in the Teaching of English.* Oxford: Oxford University Press. [41,51(n3)]

Strevens, P.D. 1977a. 'Special-purpose language learning: a perspective.' *Language Teaching and Linguistics: Abstracts.* 10:145–63; also in Kinsella 1978:185–203. [110,126,502]

Strevens, P.D. (ed.) 1978. *In Honour of A.S. Hornby.* Oxford: Oxford University Press. [149(n 15)]

Studies in Second Language Acquisition (journal) Bloomington, U.S.A.: Indiana University. [335(n 14)]

Suppes, P. (ed.) 1978. *Impact of Research on Education: Some Case Studies.* Washington, D.C.: National Academy of Education. [Clifford 1978, Stern, Wesche and Harley 1978]

Swain, M. 1977. 'Future directions of second language research' in Henning 1977:15–28. [358(n 2)]

Swain, M. 1978. 'Bilingual education for the English-speaking Canadian' in Alatis 1978:141–54. [70(n 13), 364]

Swain, M. 1981. 'Time and timing in bilingual education.' *Language Learning* 31:1–15. [364,512[n 14]]

Swain, M. 1981a. 'Linguistic expectations: core, extended and immersion programs.' *Canadian Modern Language Review* 37:486–97. [364,512(n 14)]

Swain, M. and Harley, B. 1979. 'Editorial.' *Working Papers on Bilingualism* 19:i–ii. [330]

Swain, M. and Lapkin, S. 1981. *Bilingual Education: A Decade of Research.* Toronto: Ontario Ministry of Education. [70(n 13), 72(n 28), 107]

Swain, M and Lapkin, S. 1982. *Evaluating Bilingual Education: A Canadian Case Study.* Clevedon, Avon: Multilingual Matters (First published 1981 as *Bilingual Education: A Decade of Research.* Toronto: Ontario Ministry of Education.)

Sweet, H. 1899. *The Practical Study of Languages: A Guide for Teachers and Learners.* London: Dent. Also published in the Series Language and Language Learning, edited by R. Mackin. London: Oxford University Press, 1964. [88,96(n 15), 170(n 2), 263(n 1), 317–8,333(n 1), 456–7]

Symonds, P.M. 1930. *Foreign Language Prognosis Test* (Form A and B) New York: Columbia University Teachers College. [333(n 3), 368–9]

System: The International Journal of Educational Technology and Language Learning Systems. Oxford: Pergamon Press. [450]

Taggart, G. (ed.) 1975. *Attitude and Aptitude in Second Language Learning.* Proceedings of the 5th Symposium of the Canadian Association of Applied Linguistics, Toronto, May 1974. [Carrol 1975a, Gardner 1975, Neufeld 1975]

Tarone, E. 1979. 'Interlanguage as chameleon.' *Language Learning* 29:181–91. [335(n 15)]

Tarone, E., Frauenfelder, U. and Selinker, L. 1976. 'Systematicity/variability and stability/instability in interlanguage systems' in Brown 1976:93–134. [335(n 15)]

Tarone, E., Swain, M. and Fathman, A. 1976. 'Some limitations to the classroom applications of current second language acquisition research.' *TESOL Quarterly* 10:19–32. [70(n 16)]

Taylor, D.M., Maynard, R. and Rheult, E. 1977. 'Threat to ethnic identity and second-language learning' in Giles 1977:99–118. [378]

Taylor, I. 1976. *Introduction to Psycholinguistics.* New York: Holt, Rinehart and Winston. [315(n 21)]

Taylor, P.H. and Richards, C. 1979. *An Introduction to Curriculum Studies.* Windsor: NFER Publishing Co. [449(n 20,21,26,30), 450(n 33)]

Taylor, W. (ed.) 1973. *Research Perspectives in Education.* London: Routledge and Kegan Paul. [Peters and White 1973]

Terrell, T.D. 1977. 'A natural approach to second language learning and acquisition.' *Modern Language Journal* 61:325–37. [475(n 13), 512(n 13)]

Terwilger, R.I. 1970. 'Multigrade proficiency grouping for foreign language instruction.' *Modern Language Journal* 54:331–33. [447(n 10)]

TESOL Quarterly: A Journal for Teachers of English to Speakers of Other Languages Washington, D.C.: School of Languages and Linguistics, Georgetown University. [330]

Thomas, W.I. and Znaniecki, F. 1918–21. *The Polish Peasant in Europe and America.* 5 vols. Boston: R.G. Badger, Gorham Press. Second edition New York: Knopf 1927. [193]

Thomson, R. 1968. *The Pelican History of Psychology.* Harmondsworth: Penguin Books. [313(n 5)]

Thorndike, E.L. 1921. *The Teacher's Word Book.* New York: Teachers College. [100,155,460]

Thouless, R.H. 1969. *Map of Educational Research: A Survey of Salient Research for those Engaged in the Practice of Education.* Slough: National Foundation for Educational Research in England and Wales. [68(n 3)]

Thrasher, F.M. 1927. *The Gang: A Study of 1313 Gangs in Chicago.* Revised edition 1937. Chicago: University of Chicago Press. [193]

Thut, I.N. 1957. *The Story of Education: Philosophical and Historical Foundations.* New York: McGraw-Hill. [447(n 6)]

Titone, R. 1968. *Teaching Foreign Languages: An Historical Sketch.* Washington, D.C.: Georgetown University Press. [79,94(n 3), 95(n5,6,7,11), 98]

Titone, R. 1974. *Methodology of Research in Language Teaching: An Elementary Introduction.* Bergamo, etc.: Minerva Italica. [70(n 16)]

Tomb, J.W. 1925. 'On the intuitive capacity of children to understand spoken language.' *British Journal of Psychology* 6:53–55. [323]

Travers, R.M.W. (ed.) 1973. *Second Handbook of Research on Teaching.* Chicago: Rand McNally. [33(n 6), Levie and Dickie 1973, Snow 1973, Travers 1973a]

Travers, R.M.W. 1973a. 'Educational technology and related research viewed as a political force' in Travers 1973:979–96. [445]

Travers, R.M.W. 1978. *An Introduction to Educational Research.* Fourth edition. New York: Macmillan. [63]

Travers, J.F. 1979. *Educational Psychology.* New York: Harper and Row. [315(n 27)]

Tretheway, A.R. 1976. *Introducing Comparative Education.* New York: Pergamon Press. [448(n 17)]

Trim, J.L.M. 1978. *Some Possible Lines of Development of an Overall Structure for a European Unit/Credit Scheme for Foreign Language Learning by Adults.* Strasbourg: Council of Europe. [353,359(n 10), 395]

Trim, J.L.M. 1980. *Developing a Unit/Credit Scheme of Adult Language Learning.* Prepared for the Council of Europe. First edition 1978. Oxford: Pergamon Press. [110,285(n 11)]

Trim, J.L.M. 1981. 'Résumé' in Council of Europe 1981:ix–xxvi. [513(n 15)]

Trim, J.L.M., Richterich, R., Van Ek, J.A. and Wilkins, D.A. 1980. *Systems Development in Adult Language Learning: A European Unit/Credit System for Modern Language Learning by Adults.* Prepared for the Council of Europe. Oxford, etc.: Pergamon. First published 1973 by Council of Europe, Strasbourg. [116(n 15), 285(n11), 412(n11), Richterich 1973, Wilkins 1973]

Trudgill, P. 1974. *Sociolinguistics: An Introduction.* Harmondsworth: Penguin Books. [242(n 1)]

Tyler, R.W. 1949. *Basic Principles of Curriculum and Instruction.* Chicago: University of Chicago Press. [449(n 20)]

Tyler, R.W., Gagné, R.M. and Scriven, M. (eds.) 1967. *Perspectives of Curriculum Evaluation.* AERA Monograph Series on Curriculum Evaluation No. 1. Chicago: Rand McNally. [Scriven 1967]

Ullmann, R. 1982. 'A broadened curriculum framework for second languages.' *ELT Journal* 36:255–62. [503(Fig 22.4), 511(n 7)]

Ullmann, S. 1971. 'Semantics' in Minnis 1971:75–87. [132,149(n 16)]

UNESCO 1953. *The Use of Vernacular Languages in Education.* Monographs on Fundamental Education, VIII. Paris: UNESCO. [362]

UNESCO 1955. *The Teaching of Modern Languages.* A volume of studies deriving from the International Seminar organized by the Secretariat of UNESCO at Nuwara Eliya, Ceylon, in August, 1953. Series Problems in Education, Vol. 10. Paris: UNESCO. [104]

UNESCO 1970. *La planification de l'éducation: Bilan, problèmes et perspectives.* Paris: UNESCO. [448(n 14)]

U.S.A. 1979. *Strength through Wisdom: A Critique of U.S. Capability.* The President's Commission on Foreign Language and International Studies. Nov. 1979. Washington, D.C.: U.S. Government Printing Office. [112, 265(n 10), 285(n 11)]

U.S.A. 1979a. *Background Papers and Studies.* The President's Commission on Foreign Language and International Studies. Washington, D.C.: U.S. Government Printing Office. [116(n 15), Benseler and Schulz 1979, Warriner 1979]

Vaizey, J. 1962. *The Economics of Education.* London: Faber and Faber. [447 (n 11)]

Valdman, A. (ed.) 1966. *Trends in Language Teaching.* New York, etc.: McGraw-Hill. [463, Anisfield 1966, Carroll 1966, Fishman 1966, Nostrand 1966, Saporta 1966, Valdman 1966a]

Valdman, A. 1966a. 'Introduction' in Valdman 1966:xv–xxii. [145,171(n 17), 174]

Valdman, A. (ed.) 1977. *Pidgin and Creole Linguistics.* Bloomington: Indiana University Press. [124,284(n 4)]

Valette, R.M. 1969. *Directions in Foreign Language Testing.* New York: ERIC Clearinghouse on the Teaching of Foreign Languages and of English in Higher Education, and Modern Language Association. [450(n 31), 511(n 5)]

Valette, R.M. 1971. 'Evaluation of learning in a second language' in Bloom, Hastings, and Madaus 1971:817–53. [315(n 28), 450(n 31), 502–3,511(n 5)]

Valette, R.M. 1981. 'The evaluation of second language learning' in Alatis, Altman and Alatis 1981:159–74. [511(n 5), 513(n 16)]

Valette, R.M. and Disick, R.S. 1972. *Modern Language Performance Objectives and Individualization: A Handbook.* New York: Harcourt Brace Jovanovich. [399,511(n 5), 513(n 16)]

van Buren, P. 1975. 'Semantics and Language teaching' in Allen and Corder 1975:122–54. [150(n 16)]

Vander Beke, C.E. 1929. *French Word Book.* New York: Macmillan. [101,162]

van Ek, J.A. 1975. *The Threshold Level in a European Unit/Credit System for Modern Language Learning by Adults.* Systems Development in Adult Language Learning. Strasbourg: Council of Europe. [110,112,178–9,226,349,449(n 31)]

van Gennep, A. 1910. 'Un ethnographe oublié du XVIIIe siècle: J.N. Demeunier.' *Revue des idées* 7:18–28. [214(n 6)]

Verdoodt, A. (ed.) 1974. *Applied Sociolinguistics.* Proceedings, Vol. II of the Third Congress of the Association Internationale de Linguistique Appliquée, Copenhagen, 1972. Heidelberg: Julius Groos. [Wilkins 1974, Ross 1974]

Vernon, P.E. 1960. *Intelligence and Attainment Tests.* London: University of London Press. [368]

Viëtor, W. (pseudonym: Quousque tandem) 1882. *Der Sprachunterricht muss umkehren! Ein Beitrag zur Überbürdungsfrage.* Heilbronn. Second edition 1886. [91, 98,459]

Vollmer, H.J. 1979. 'Why are we interested in "general language proficiency"?' *Lingua et Signa* 1 (in press). [358(n 8)]

Vollmer, H.J. and Sang, F. 1980. Competing Hypotheses about Second Language Ability: A Plea for Caution. mimeo. [358(n 8), 389(n 8)]

Vollmer, H.J. and Sang, F. no date. Zum psycholinguistischen Konstrukt einer internalisierten Erwartungsgrammatik. mimeo. [358(n 8)]

Walker, D.A. 1976. *The IEA Six Subject Survey: An Empirical Study of Education in Twenty-One Countries.* Stockholm: Almqvist and Wiksell; and New York: Wiley. [433]

Walsh, D.D. (ed.) 1969. *A Handbook for Teachers of Spanish and Portuguese.* Lexington, Mass.: Heath. [Ellison 1969, Leavitt 1969]

Wardhaugh, R. 1969. 'TESOL: Current problems and classroom practices.' *TESOL Quarterly* 3:105–16. [1,34(n 9)]

Wardhaugh, R. 1969a. *Teaching English to Speakers of Other Languages: The State of the Art.* Washington, D.C.: ERIC Clearinghouse for Linguistics. [108,115(n 7)]

Wardhaugh, R. 1977. *Introduction to Linguistics.* Second edition. First edition 1972. New York: McGraw-Hill. [151(n 22)]

Warriner, H.P. 1979. 'Foreign language teaching in the schools—1979—Focus on methodology' in U.S.A. 1979a:49–58. [116(n 15)]

Watson, F. 1909. *The Beginnings of the Teaching of Modern Subjects in England.* London: Pitman. [86,446(n 4)]

Watson, J.B. 1913. 'Psychology as the Behaviorist views it.' *Psychological Review* 20:158–77. [313(n 9)]

Watson, J.B. 1914. *Behavior: An Introduction to Comparative Psychology.* New York: Holt. [313(n 9)]

Watson, J.B. 1919. *Psychology from the Standpoint of a Behaviorist.* Philadelphia: Lippincott. [293,313(n 9)]

Watts, G.B. 1963. 'The teaching of French in the United States: a history.' *The French Review* 37/1: Part 2 (whole issue). [87]

Weiler, H.N. 1980. *Educational Planning and Social Change: Report on an IEEP Seminar.* Paris: UNESCO and International Institute for Educational Planning. [448(n 14)]

Weinreich, U. 1953. *Languages in Contact: Findings and Problems.* Originally published as No. 1 in the series 'Publications of the Linguistic Circle of New York' (New York). The Hague: Mouton, 1963. [210,216(n 23), 232]

Weinstock, R. 1980. 'A Functional Study of Discourse Structure in Conversational English.' Unpublished Ph.D. thesis, University of Toronto. [229]

Wesche, M.B. 1979. 'Learning behaviours of successful adult students on intensive language training.' *Canadian Modern Language Review* 35:415–30. [414(n 15)]

Wesche, M.B. 1981. 'Communicative testing in a second language.' *Canadian Modern Language Review* 37:551–71. [268(n 23)]

Wesche, M.B. 1981a. 'Language aptitude measures in streaming, matching students with methods, and diagnosis of learning problems' in Diller 1981:119–54. [368,388(n 8)]

West, M. 1926. *Bilingualism (with Special Reference to Bengal).* Bureau of Education, India. Occasional Reports No. 13. Calcutta: Government of India Central Publications Branch. [101,460]

West, M.P. 1926a. *Learning to Read a Foreign Language: An Experimental Study.* New York, etc.: Longmans, Green and Co. [101,460]

Whiteley, W.H. 1973. 'Sociolinguistic surveys at the national level' in Shuy 1973: 167–80. [244(n 16)]

Whiteley, W.H. (ed.) 1974. *Language in Kenya.* Nairobi: Oxford University Press. [244(n 16)]

Whiting, J. and Child, I. 1953. *Child Training and Personality: A Cross-Cultural Study.* New Haven: Yale University Press. [198]

Whitney, W.D. 1875. *The Life and Growth of Language*: An Outline of Linguistic *Science*. New York: Appleton. [148(n 2)]

Whorf, B.L. 1956. *Language, Thought, and Reality*: Selected Writings of Benjamin Lee *Whorf*. Edited and introduced by J.B. Carroll. Cambridge, Mass. M.I.T. Press. [205,215(n 14)]

Widdowson, H.G. 1978. *Teaching Language as Communication*. Oxford: Oxford University Press. [116(n 15), 178–9,259,268(n 22), 512(n 13)]

Widdowson, H.G. 1979. *Explorations in Applied Linguistics*. Oxford: Oxford University Press. [29,79,268(n 22)]

Widdowson, H.G. 1979a. 'Directions in the teaching of discourse' in Widdowson 1979:89–100. First published in Corder and Roulet 1973:65–76. [179]

Widdowson, H.G. 1979b. 'Two types of communication exercise' in Widdowson 1979:65–74. First published in the AILA/BAAL Seminar Proceedings on The Communicative Teaching of English, University of Lancaster, March 1973. [266(n 16)]

Widdowson, H.G. and Brumfit, C.J. 1981. 'Issues in second language syllabus design' in Alatis, Altman and Alatis 1981:199–210. [266(n 24)]

Wilds, C.P. 1975. 'The oral interview test' in Jones and Spolsky 1975:29–44. [358(n 9)]

Wilkins, D.A. 1972. *Linguistics in Language Teaching*. London: Arnold. [149(n 12,13), 150(n 15), 151(n 22), 187(n 1,5)]

Wilkins, D.A. 1973. 'The linguistic and situational content of the common core in a unit/ credit system' in Trim *et al.* 1980:129–46. [187(n 7), 494]

Wilkins, D.A. 1974. 'Grammatical, situational, and notional syllabuses' in Verdoodt 1974:254–65. [187(n 8), 494]

Wilkins, D.A. 1976. *Notional Syllabuses*. London: Oxford University Press. [110,113,132,178,179,223–6,494]

Wilson, J. 1977. *Philosophy and Practical Education*. London: Routledge and Kegan Paul. [446]

Witkin, H.A., Oltman, P.K., Raskin, E. and Karp, S.A. 1971. *A Manual for the Embedded Figures Test*. Palo Alto, Cal.: Consulting Psychologists Press. [373]

Wolfgang, A. (ed.) 1975. *Education of Immigrant Students*. Toronto: Ontario Institute for Studies in Education. [Lambert 1975]

Worsley, P. *et al.* 1970. *Introducing Sociology*. Harmondsworth: Penguin Books. Second edition, 1977. [195,200,213(n 1)]

Working Papers on Bilingualism (journal) Toronto: OISE Modern Language Centre. [330]

Workpapers in TESL. (journal) Los Angeles, Cal.: University of California. [335(n 14)]

Wragg, E.C. 1970. 'Interaction analysis in the foreign language classroom.' *Modern Language Journal* 54:116–20. [496(n 11)]

Wright, A. 1976. *Visual Materials for the Language Teacher*. London: Longman 1976. [451(n 39)]

Wundt, W. 1877–1905. *Völkerpsychologie*. Vol. I: *Die Sprache*. Leipzig: Wilhelm Engelmann Verlag. [292]

Yalden, J. 1976. 'Information resources in second language teaching and learning: a guide for teachers, researchers, and educators. *Canadian Modern Language Review* 32:316–48. [69(n 9)]

Yalden, J. 1981. *Communicative Language Teaching*: Principles and Practice. Language and Literacy Series. Toronto: OISE Press. [268(n 22)]

Yates, A. 1966. *Grouping in Education*: A Report Sponsored by the Unesco Institute for *Education, Hamburg*. New York: Wiley. [447(n 10)]

Zeydel, E.H. 1964. 'The teaching of German in the United States from colonial times to the present.' *German Quarterly* 37:315–92. [87]

Index